CHILDREN'S ILLUSTRATED

BIBLE

CHILDREN'S ILLUSTRATED
BIBLE

Retold by
VICTORIA PARKER

Consultant
JANET DYSON

HERMES
HOUSE

CONTENTS

THE GREAT KINGS......128

EXILE AND RETURN......186

A CHILD IS BORN......244

THE MAN OF MIRACLES......302

DEATH AND RESURRECTION......360

SPREADING THE WORD......418

The World's Best-selling Book

If you enjoy reading books, you'll enjoy reading the Bible. It doesn't matter whether you are a Christian, Muslim, Jew, Buddhist, or have no religious beliefs at all. After all, the Bible is a whole library of different types of books with exciting tales and heroic adventures. Most people enjoy reading the stories of the Bible best of all. However, there are also beautiful poems and songs, many of which have been set to music and are sung in places of worship today. There are fascinating letters and diaries that give us a glimpse of how people thought and lived long ago, and many hundreds of wise proverbs and laws that are as relevant to the people of today as they were in Old Testament times –

"Without wood, a fire goes out; without gossip, quarrelling stops" is just one example.

For many people, the Bible is a vital way of getting to know God. Others read it simply because they enjoy the wonderful pieces of writing or because it is a valuable record of centuries of history. Either way, the Bible is a book that tells us of the lessons of the past, inspires us with hope for the future, and helps us to find a way forward in our own lives.

NOAH'S ARK
This story tells us that God brought a great flood, which covered the Earth. This medieval wall-painting shows Noah's Ark, in which humans and animals survived the flood to repopulate the Earth again.

The Old Testament

Over the centuries, many editions of the Bible have been published in different languages, and have been updated or adapted to suit people at different times. Most editions begin with a section called the Old Testament, which is usually made up of 39 individual books. Modern Jewish bibles, however, consist

A FEW OF GOD'S CREATIONS
The Book of Genesis, the first book in the Bible, tells how God created the Earth and all the animals that live there. The camel and wild goat were among the animals that the peoples of the Old Testament domesticated (bred for human use). The camel and ass carried heavy loads for long distances. Goats provided hair that could be spun and woven into clothes and blankets.

of only this section, and often the 39 books are condensed into as few as 22. Roman Catholic, Greek Orthodox, and some Protestant bibles have more than 39 books in the Old Testament. This is because some additional writings called the Apocrypha (meaning 'hidden away') are included. These are considered by some faiths as less important accounts than the Old Testament Scriptures (sacred writings).

SACRED SCROLLS
The first five books of the Bible are sacred to the Jewish people, who call them the Torah. The books are written as scrolls (lengths of paper wound on wooden rollers). The words of the Torah are written in Hebrew, the language of the Jewish people, as seen in the photograph on the left. The alphabet used to write the Torah is the Hebrew alphabet, not the Roman alphabet in which the words in this book are written.

The stories of the Old Testament span thousands of years before the birth of Jesus Christ. Most of them are set in the time of the world's first civilizations in Mesopotamia, Assyria, Babylonia and Egypt. However, the books of the Old Testament are the sacred writings of the Jews, and tell the story of the Jewish people from the very beginning of the world, almost to the days of the Roman Empire.

The New Testament

At least three or four centuries elapsed between the final events recorded by the Old Testament and the time of Jesus of Nazareth (Jesus Christ). The stories of Jesus's life and the establishment of the Christian Church following His death are told by 27 books which make up the New Testament. This section of the Bible covers a time span of only 60 or 70 years. The books were written by people who either knew Jesus personally or were in close contact with people who had known Jesus well. Four of Jesus's followers, Matthew, Mark, Luke and John, wrote individual accounts of

SLAIN ENEMIES
The Israelite hero David kills his Philistine enemies and shows the bodies to Saul, his king.

FALLEN IDOL
The Philistines stole the Israelites' holiest object, the Ark of the Covenant. When the Ark was put beside the statue of Dagon, the Philistines' god, the statue broke.

His life. Their books have come to be known as Gospels, which means 'good news'.

A Search for Happiness

The terms 'Old Testament' and 'New Testament' were first used after all 66 books of the Bible were gathered together. The word 'testament' means 'covenant' or 'promise'. Its use in this context comes from the prophet Jeremiah, who lived at a time of great suffering for the Jews. The neighbouring Babylonians had conquered Israel and exiled the Jewish people from the country that they believed was their Promised Land given to them by God. Jeremiah prophesied (foretold) that their suffering would one day be replaced by unending happiness, for God was going to make a 'new covenant' with the Jewish people.

Besides Jeremiah, many other Old Testament prophets prophesied a glorious future for Israel. They promised the coming of a Jewish Messiah (Saviour) who, through pain and suffering, would establish the mightiest of all kingdoms. Christians believe that Jesus Christ was this Messiah promised by the Scriptures, while the Jews do not. The New Testament books, therefore, are not accepted as part of the Bible by the Jewish people. For Christians, however, they record the life and teachings of an extraordinary religous leader and the founder of their faith. For them, the New Testament follows on from the promises made in the Old Testament writings and show how the life and teachings of Jesus Christ fulfil them.

BAPTISM
Water from a font such as this is used to baptize people when they join the Christian Church.

FRIENDS
All sorts of people followed Jesus, including people such as Mary Magdalene, who had been a public outcast.

CHILD PRODIGY
Jesus was obviously special, even as a boy, when He was able to talk learnedly with Jewish elders.

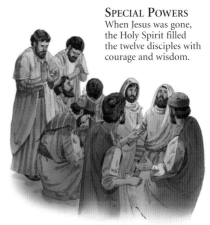

SPECIAL POWERS
When Jesus was gone, the Holy Spirit filled the twelve disciples with courage and wisdom.

A Written Record

The books of the Bible were written by many different authors over about a thousand years. Many of the Old Testament books lived in people's memories and were handed down by word of mouth long before scribes actually wrote them down. Then they were carefully copied, word for word, on to parchment, a type of paper made from animal skin. They were written entirely in Hebrew (the original Jewish language) except for a very few passages, which were written in another ancient language from Syria, called Aramaic.

HOLY GRAIL
The chalice used in Christian Church services symbolizes the Holy Grail, the cup from which Jesus drank wine at the Last Supper.

The New Testament authors wrote in Greek, the most common language of the Roman Empire. People have struggled to keep all these precious writings safe through the centuries. The oldest complete copy of the New Testament that still exists today is a papyrus version which dates from AD400. However, a manuscript fragment of John's writing that dates back to around AD200 has also been found.

DANGEROUS JOB
The first followers of Christ were often at risk of being imprisoned by both the Jewish and Roman authorities.

A STORY FOR EVERY MOOD

This volume contains over two hundred stories which lead you through the entire Bible from the beginning to the end. You will find heroes and villains (*David and Goliath, The Good Samaritan*), bad kings and beautiful queens (*Ahab, Esther*), great warrior leaders (*Joshua*) and poor old beggars (*Bartimaeus*). There are tales of love (*Isaac and Rebekah*), of brutality (*Samson and Delilah*), and of betrayal (*Judas Plots Betrayal*), as well as heart-rending tragedies (*Jephthah*). Uplifting stories of courage and triumph (*Daniel and the Lions*), or miracles and mystery (*Crossing the Red Sea, Jesus the Healer*) can be read alongside spine-tingling adventures such as *Jonah and the Whale*. Finally, in the *Revelation to John*, there is a vision of good triumphing over evil.

THE CHOSEN PEOPLE

*A journey that begins with God's creation of the
world, and Adam and Eve in the Garden of Eden.
The stories include the dramatic adventure of Noah's
Ark and trace the foundation of the Jewish race.
The baby Moses, found in the bulrushes, is destined
to lead the Jewish people, who prepare to travel to a
new land that has been promised to them by God.*

Introduction

THE Bible is a collection of 66 books which were written over a period of nearly 1,600 years, starting from around 1400BC. Many of the stories in the Bible had been passed down from one generation to another by word of mouth and were well known for a long time before they were written down. Different books were written by different authors, and as time went by they were gradually all put together into one bigger book. This big book became the Bible. The word "Bible" comes from the Greek word "biblia", which simply means "books". The stories are all linked, together they form the story of God's relationship with his people.

As well as forming the first part of the Christian Bible, the Old Testament is also the sacred book of the Jewish people. The 39 books of the Old Testament, that tell the story of the people of ancient Israel over many centuries, appear in both the Jewish and the Christian holy texts, but in a slightly different order.

This section covers the first part of the Bible, from God's creation of the world, to the Israelites' crossing of the Red Sea. It includes the first stories of the Bible, from the Creation to the story of Adam and Eve's temptation in the Garden of Eden. This is a very important story in the Bible as it tells of the first sin in the world. It shows how Adam and Eve, even while they were still living in the Garden of Eden, disobeyed God, and were cast out of Paradise into the world.

Their two sons, Cain and Abel, were the first people born into the world, and the first people born after Adam and Eve left Eden. Cain commits a sin when he kills his younger brother Abel, and his punishment is worse than God's punishment of Adam. Cain is told he must wander the world for the rest of his life, and that the ground will no longer grow crops for him. God also puts a mark on him, to remind him of his sin, and warn other people to leave him alone. After Cain and Abel we find the story of Noah and the mighty flood, which happens because the descendants of Adam and Eve have abandoned God,

Jewish *Torah*
The book shown above is the Torah. It contains the first five books of the Old Testament that make up the Jewish religious laws. There is also a prayer shawl, and a *dreidel*, used in games played at the Hanukkah festival, the only time that the Jews can play games of chance.

and no longer live a good life. So for the only time in history God decides to wipe all life from the face of the planet. He spares only Noah and his family, who have maintained their belief in God and tried to live their lives as God wished. He seals them away, along with pairs of all the animals of the world, in the Ark that God instructed Noah to build, and He saved them from the flood.

The story called 'God's Promise to Abram' marks the start of the most important part of the Old Testament. After the flood, Noah's descendants, just like the descendants of Adam before him, have abandoned and neglected God. Rather than destroy the world, God chooses Abraham and his descendants to become His own people, His special race on earth. The story tells how God makes an agreement, or covenant, with Abraham. If Abraham follows God's instructions, and continues to have faith in Him, Abraham's descendants will become a great people and will one day inherit the land of Canaan, called the promised land. Abraham has faith in the promise of God, and packs up his family to move to Canaan, where he settles with his family.

God's covenant with Abraham is re-established with his descendants, we see the birth of his son, Isaac, and his grandson, Jacob, and we see how God speaks to these men when they grow up, and reminds them of the promise He made to Abraham. God promised Abraham that his descendants would become a great nation, as many people as there are stars in the sky, and with Jacob we see this start to come true. Jacob fathers twelve sons who eventually become the forefathers of the twelve tribes of Israel. One son, Joseph, is sold by his brothers and taken to Egypt. The Israelites' 400 years of exile, as God told Abraham would happen, begin with Joseph's arrival in Egypt. Jacob and his family follow Joseph there to escape a terrible famine, and while they are living there, firstly as free people but later as slaves, their numbers multiply.

God said to Abraham that his descendants would live in Egypt for 400 years, and would be led to freedom and to the promised land, and we see this come miraculously true when the great leader, prophet and law-giver Moses leads the great nation to freedom across the Red Sea.

Many of the stories illustrate God testing the faith of His people. Some pass the test, like Abraham who is prepared to sacrifice his own son if it is God's will. Others, such as Cain, are weaker. But, here and throughout the whole of the Old Testament, God continues to forgive His people for their sins. He realises that the people that He created are not perfect, and is willing to accept wrong-doing from them if they remain faithful to Him and are truly sorry for their sins. Then, through His chosen leaders, He guides them to the promised land.

❧ THE CHOSEN PEOPLE ☙

This section covers the first stories in the Old Testament, from the creation of the world to Moses leading the Israelites from Egypt.

CREATION
Genesis, Ch. 1 & 2.
MAN'S FALL FROM GRACE
Genesis, Ch. 3.
NOAH
Genesis, Ch. 6 to 9.
ABRAHAM
Genesis, Ch. 12 to 23.
ISAAC
Genesis, Ch. 24.
JACOB
Genesis, Ch. 25 to 35.
JOSEPH
Genesis, Ch. 37 to 47.
MOSES
Exodus, Ch. 1 to 14.

Wadi-Musa, Jordan
This town, on a hillside in what is now the country of Jordan, is Wadi-Musa. It lies directly on the route that the Israelites would probably have taken on their exodus from Egypt, heading north towards the promised land.

Illuminated letter
Bibles have always been regarded as very important books that contain the words of God to His people, so great care used to be taken in making the Bible look very ornate. The letter above would have taken someone a very long time to do.

Land of the Patriarchs

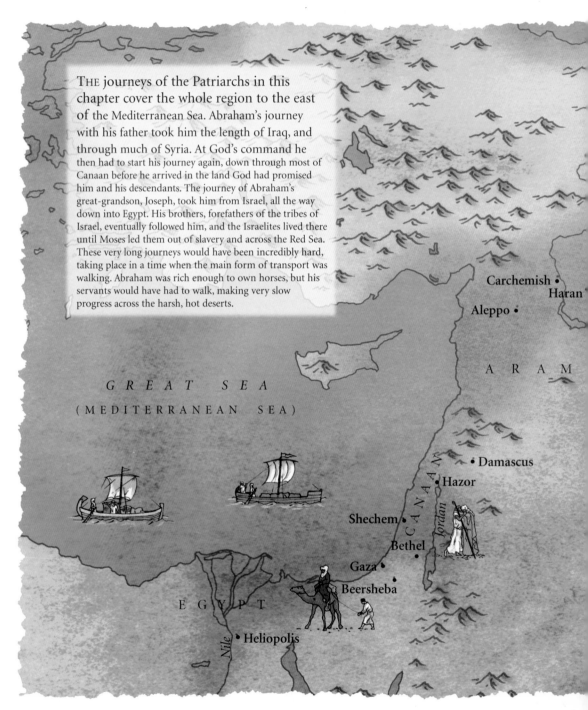

THE journeys of the Patriarchs in this chapter cover the whole region to the east of the Mediterranean Sea. Abraham's journey with his father took him the length of Iraq, and through much of Syria. At God's command he then had to start his journey again, down through most of Canaan before he arrived in the land God had promised him and his descendants. The journey of Abraham's great-grandson, Joseph, took him from Israel, all the way down into Egypt. His brothers, forefathers of the tribes of Israel, eventually followed him, and the Israelites lived there until Moses led them out of slavery and across the Red Sea. These very long journeys would have been incredibly hard, taking place in a time when the main form of transport was walking. Abraham was rich enough to own horses, but his servants would have had to walk, making very slow progress across the harsh, hot deserts.

Carchemish •

Haran

Aleppo •

A R A M

GREAT SEA

(MEDITERRANEAN SEA)

• Damascus

• Hazor

Shechem •

C A N A A N

Jordan

Bethel •

Gaza •

E G Y P T

Beersheba •

Nile

• Heliopolis

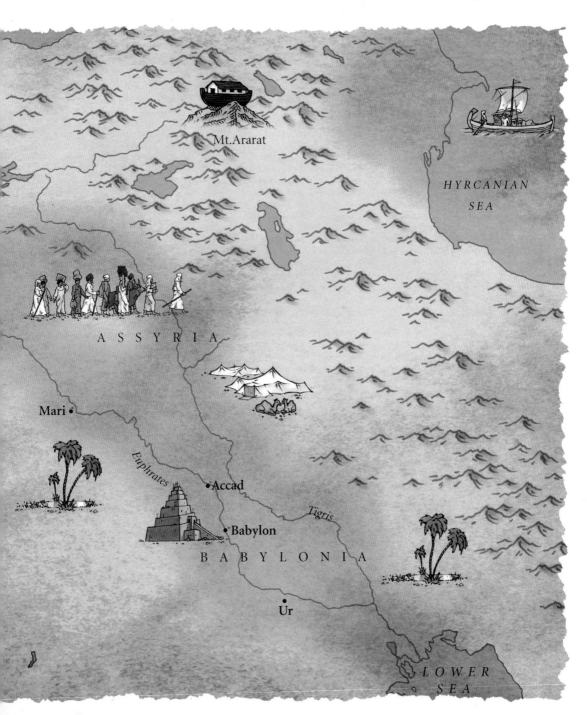

Mt.Ararat

HYRCANIAN
SEA

A S S Y R I A

Mari •

Euphrates

• Accad

Tigris

• Babylon

B A B Y L O N I A

Ur

LOWER
SEA

The Creation

IN the beginning, nothing existed except God's Spirit, hovering over a darkness and never-ending water. Then God spoke. "Let there be light," He said, and suddenly there was brightness all around. God thought that the light was good, and He separated it from the darkness. He called the light Day and the dark Night. God looked on as evening drew in and watched as morning arrived. He had formed the very first day.

On the second day, God said, "Let there be skies to divide the watery wastes. Some waters will float above the skies and some will lie below." It all happened just so, and God called the skies Heaven.

Next God said, "Let all the waters under heaven be gathered into one place, so that dry land may appear. I name the waters Sea, and the dry land Earth." God looked at His work and was pleased. He commanded things to grow and at once tiny green shoots began to sprout all over the earth. As plants of all kinds took root, leafy tendrils uncurled and stretched, stems burst into bushes and trees sprang upwards. Then evening came once again and morning, making the third day.

"Let there be lights in the skies to shine on the Earth," said God. "They will mark out the passing days, months, seasons and years." He made the burning sun to rule over the day and the cooler moon to govern over the night, together with the stars. Then He set them all moving in the heavens. God was again happy with what He had done, and the fourth day came to an end.

The stars
God created the stars, along with the sun and the moon, to mark out the passing days. People have since learned how to tell the time from the sun, and mark the seasons by the movement of the stars. In the Bible, the word 'star' is used to describe any light in the sky, other than the sun and moon.

What is a day?
In the Bible, the word 'day' can mean a period of 24 hours, or an indefinite period of time. In the Creation story, everything happens in six days. Some people think this is using 'day' in its sense of 'period of time'. Others believe it is just a way of expressing God's creative energy. Finally, others believe that Creation took place in literally six days.

"Let living creatures swim in the seas and birds fly through the skies," said God, on the fifth day. Instantly, coral covered the sea beds, crabs burrowed into sand and limpets clung to rocks, shoals of fish darted through rivers and beneath waves, and sea monsters lurked in the deep. Above the Earth, flocks of birds spread their wings for the first time and began to flap and flutter, soar and swoop. And God thought it was all good work. He blessed every single creature and told them to fill the waters and the skies He had given them for their homes.

On the sixth day, God said, "Now for the living creatures of the Earth – from tiny creeping things to the largest wild beasts." He made creatures with fur, scales and hair; beasts that grunted, growled and snorted; animals

> " *And God saw everything that He had made, and behold, it was very good.* "

with claws, paws, hooves, and tails; living things that galloped and slithered. God made animals of every kind and sent them out to live in the land that He had made. He watched them and thought He had done well.

Last of all, God made people - men and women - that looked just like Him. "You shall rule over the fish of the sea and the birds of the air and the animals of the land," He told them. "You own the Earth," He said, and He blessed them. "Go and fill the whole world. I am giving the plants to you and all the living creatures for food."

As the sixth day drew to a close, God looked all around at everything He had done, and He was very pleased. The heavens and the Earth were finished, and everything had happened just as He had wished. The seventh day came and God was tired. He rested, and blessed the seventh day of the week as a holy time of rest for all people.

The animals
When God had made the land and the sea, He made the animals which lived there. The only animals named in this story are whales. Otherwise, animals are listed in very general terms. From the air come birds, from the water all the fish and animals of the seas, and from the land come cattle, beasts and creeping things. These descriptions are supposed to cover all animals, from the tiniest to the most enormous, from ants to elephants.

❧ ABOUT THE STORY ❧

The Creation story tells of how the world began. In simple language, it describes the wonder of the universe, and God's power in creating it.

There is a great deal of repetition of key phrases, which mirrors the orderly way in which God created the world. The Creation story can only be understood by believing in God, not by science. The world was created by God and depends on Him for its continued existence.

The Garden of Eden

AFTER God had gathered the waters together into the sea and commanded the Earth to appear on the third day of Creation, He had been pleased with His work. But when He had looked all around Him, God had seen that the land was dry and brown. He had not yet brought rain to water the land, so nothing could grow. And besides, God had not yet created people to plough the earth, to sow crops and to care for flowers and trees.

As God thought of all these things, He sent a fine mist up from the ground. Gradually, drops of wetness drifted down and covered the face of the Earth. Then God scooped up some of the damp dust and began to shape it. Very carefully He formed a figure, until He was happy with the way it looked. Then God breathed into the figure's nostrils a deep, long breath - the breath of life. The figure blinked awake and the first Man became a living being. God looked at him with love and called him Adam.

Next, God created a special garden in a place called Eden. He ordered water to spring from the ground, and at once a river appeared. It flowed right through the garden to the edge of Eden, before bursting over the boundary and becoming four smaller rivers. The river Pishon flowed around the land of Havilah. The second river, the Gihon, circled the land of Cush. The Tigris wound its way east of Assyria. The fourth river was the mighty Euphrates.

God set about planting trees of many different kinds. All were rich with fruit, but none was more beautiful than the trees at the centre of the garden: the Tree of Eternal Life and the Tree of the Knowledge of Good and Evil.

❧ ABOUT THE STORY ❧

This is a continuation of the Creation story, dealing with God's creation of man and woman. First God creates man, then, as a companion for him, He creates woman. He gives them the Garden of Eden to live in. They can take fruit from any tree, including the Tree of Life, which will give them eternal life. The only restriction God puts upon them is to forbid them to eat from the Tree of the Knowledge of Good and Evil.

THIS SECOND DESCRIPTION OF CREATION IS WRITTEN FROM A DIFFERENT POINT OF VIEW, THIS TIME FOCUSING ON MAN. IT TALKS OF GOD SPECIFICALLY IN RELATION TO THE PEOPLE HE CREATED.❧

Adam naming the animals
God brought all the animals to Adam so he could give them names. It is possible that this was so that Adam could get to know all the different animals over which God had made him master. Adam could learn which would work for him, like horses and sheep, cows and pigs, and which would run free, like lions and tigers.

God took the man He had made and placed him in Eden. "You may eat all the fruit you wish from any of my trees except the Tree of the Knowledge of Good and Evil," God warned him. "If you taste a mouthful of the fruit from that tree, you will become mortal and will one day die." Then He gave Adam His beautiful garden to care for.

God created all the animals of the earth, and all the birds that fly in the skies. He brought them to Adam to see what he would call them. One by one Adam gave them all names: the lion and the lioness, the bull and the cow, the peacock and the peahen, giraffes, zebras and antelopes . . . God ordered that from that day onwards, and ever after, every living creature on the earth should be called just as Adam had said that day.

> **"** *Out of the ground God made to grow every tree that is good for food.* **"**

God looked at each pair of animals and birds and saw that they were content together. But Adam stood alone and God realized that he was lonely. "It is not good for the man to be on his own," He thought to Himself. He sent Adam into a deep sleep, took out one of his ribs, and mended the wound. Then God tenderly shaped the rib until He was pleased with the figure He had created - the very first Woman. Then God woke Adam from his dreams and gave him his companion. Adam was delighted. "At last!" he cried. "I have something just like myself!" And Adam and Eve lived happily in God's garden of paradise.

The rivers of Eden
Of the four rivers named in this story, only the Tigris and the Euphrates are known today. There have been many attempts to identify the others as, for example, the Nile and the Indus. However no one knows for certain. The picture here shows part of the Euphrates, the largest river in western Asia.

God makes Adam
This picture shows a statue of God imagining Adam. Although it looks like Adam is looking from behind God's head, this is the sculptor's way of trying to show the picture of Adam that existed in God's mind before Adam was made, and shows how God made Adam in His own image. He formed his body from dust, just like a potter is able to make jugs from clay.

Serpent in the Garden

OF all the hundreds of creatures God had made, the snake was by far the most wily. One day he saw that Eve was going for a walk through the Garden of Eden without Adam, and he seized the chance to talk to her. "Did God tell you not to eat anything in the garden?" he asked Eve.

"We're allowed to eat any fruit except from the tree in the middle," Eve said. "God says that if we do, we will die."

"Of course you won't die!" the snake mocked. "God has told you not to eat it because it has the power to make you just like Him. You already know goodness, but when you eat from the Tree of Knowledge, you will know evil too."

Eve went to see the Tree of the Knowledge of Good and Evil for herself. How beautiful it was! Its branches were heavy with fruits. "What could be so wrong about wanting to be wiser?" she wondered. Eve reached out and plucked a plump globe. It looked and smelled so good, surely it must be delicious to eat! She took a bite, and it was the most wonderful thing she had ever tasted! Soon there was nothing left but the seeds and stalk. "I must take some to Adam," she thought, and they both ate until they were full.

Straight away, Adam and Eve realized that they had made the most dreadful mistake. Now they knew what it meant to disobey God. They suddenly felt ashamed of their nakedness and covered themselves up with fig leaves.

When Adam and Eve heard the Lord approaching they ran off. How could they face God after the terrible thing they had done? "Where are you?" the Lord asked.

Adam knew he had to tell the truth. "I heard you coming," he replied, "and I was afraid because I was naked."

Tree of Knowledge
This picture shows the Tree of the Knowledge of Good and Evil, also called the Tree of Wisdom. There are many different views as to what 'the knowledge of good and evil' might mean. One view is that it means the knowledge of right and wrong. Another is that it means the knowledge of everything in the universe. Yet another view is that the tree was just an ordinary tree, chosen by God to provide a test of man's obedience to Him.

Which fruit?
The fruit growing on the Tree of the Knowledge of Good and Evil is not named in the Bible. Most people represent it as an apple, but it is more likely to be a pomegranate, like in the picture.

God roared like thunder. "Who told you that you were naked?" He demanded. "Have you eaten the forbidden fruit?"

"It was Eve who gave it to me!" Adam protested.

God turned to Eve and, with great sadness, said, "Tell me what you have done."

Eve hung her head in misery. "The snake tricked me into eating it," she cried.

Adam and Eve knew that they had filled the Lord with unhappiness and they stood before Him in utter despair.

First, God punished the snake. "You will be the most cursed of all creatures," He said. "You will crawl on your belly and eat dirt all your life."

Next God told Eve, "Childbirth will be painful, yet you will long to be with your husband and master."

> 66 *Cursed is the ground because of you, in toil you shall eat of it all your life.* 99

To Adam He said, "Because you listened to your wife rather than listening to my commands, the very ground itself will be cursed. You will work hard to grow crops, and you will need to fight weeds. After a life of hard work, you will die and return to the dust from which I made you."

Finally, God made clothes for Adam and Eve. "Now you know both good and evil, I cannot let you stay here," He explained. "If you also ate fruit from the Tree of Eternal Life, you would have to live with the pain of your shame for ever." Then God drove Adam and Eve out of Eden, and set angels with flaming swords to guard the entrance.

A DAM AND EVE HAVE SINNED AGAINST GOD, AND THEY SUFFER BECAUSE OF THIS. THE PUNISHMENT FOR THEIR SIN IS SEPARATION FROM GOD AND EXPULSION FROM THE GARDEN, OUT INTO THE WILDERNESS.

The Fall of Man

Adam and Eve's disobedience to God and their expulsion from the Garden of Eden is often called The Fall, or The Fall of Man, which represents all mankind's later sins. This picture shows Adam and Eve fleeing from the garden. Above them, an angel whirls a flaming sword and nearby stands a skeleton, symbolizing death.

⋄ ABOUT THE STORY ⋄

God gave Adam and Eve everything they needed to live happily together. However, they destroy the peace and innocence of the Garden of Eden by giving in to temptation and doing the one thing God has forbidden. God punishes them for their disobedience. Instead of having the eternal life God originally promised, Adam will be turned back into the dust from which he came, which means that he will eventually die.

Cain and Abel

After the Lord had thrown Adam and Eve out of paradise, in time Eve gave birth to a son. Cain was the very first baby to be born into the world, and Eve was delighted and amazed. "With the help of the Lord, I have created a new life!" she cried. Imagine her happiness later on when she had another baby – a brother for Cain, called Abel.

The two boys grew up together into strong young men. Cain chose to be a farmer and looked after the land, while Abel preferred the life of a shepherd and cared for his flock. The day came when they had to choose the best of their efforts to offer to God. Cain picked the fattest ears of corn and vegetables he had grown, while Abel took some of the first lambs that had been born in his flock. Both the men were satisfied with the fruits of their labours.

First, the Lord examined Abel's gifts and was pleased with them. But to Cain's horror, He didn't accept the older brother's presents. Cain's face fell and his heart filled with rage. What made Abel's offerings any better than his own?

The Lord said to him, "What has made you so angry? Why do you look so gloomy? You know that if you do good, I will be pleased. If you don't, sin is there waiting for you. You must always be ready to fight off evil, or it will leap at you and eat you up."

Cain should have crushed his hurt pride and made up his mind to be a better person. Instead, he found it easier to wallow in self-pity, blaming God for being unfair. Because Cain hadn't listened to the Lord's words, he didn't notice that the warning was coming true. Gradually, he

Farmers and wanderers
Cain was a farmer who works the land to grow crops. To punish him for killing Abel, God decreed that the land would no longer produce any crops for Cain, and ordered him to leave his home. This was even worse than the punishment God had imposed upon Adam, which had been to work land that was choked with weeds and thistles. Instead of living the settled existence of a farmer, Cain was condemned to a lonely life of wandering through the desert, without a home to shelter him, or a family to support him. 'Nod', the name of the faraway place Cain was banished to, means 'wandering' in Hebrew. Today, there are still tribes of wandering people, called nomads, living in desert areas of the Middle East.

Abel's sacrifice
Here, Abel has built an altar to burn his offerings to God. Later in the Bible, it becomes an offence against God if anyone other than a priest builds an altar.

grew more and more jealous of his younger brother until wickedness swallowed him, and he began to dream up plots to get Abel out of the way. One day, Cain asked his brother to go out into the fields with him. Cain found himself alone with Abel, and seizing the opportunity, he attacked his brother by surprise and killed him.

Cain was sure that no one had seen what he had done, but he was wrong. God sees everything that happens everywhere. God called to him and asked, "Cain, where is your brother, Abel?"

Cain's reply was sullen and sarcastic. "I don't know," he lied, brazenly, "I'm not my brother's keeper!"

Then the Lord accused him of his crime. "Cain! What have you done?" God was furious. "I can hear your brother's blood crying out to me from the soil where you spilled it! The very earth itself is condemning you for this terrible deed, and it will no longer grow things for you. Instead of farming your land, you must now be homeless. Go away, out of my sight, and spend the rest of your life wandering from place to place!"

Cain was devastated. "Lord! This is more than I can bear," he wept. "You, my God, are cursing me and no longer want anything to do with me. I am being sent away from the land I know and cast out among strangers. I might well die!"

"If anyone kills you," commanded the Lord, "they shall face an even more terrible punishment." He put a mark on Cain's forehead so that anyone he came across would recognize him and know to leave him alone. Then Cain was banished eastwards to a faraway place called Nod, which lay at the very edge of the world.

“ *And when they were in the field Cain rose up against his brother Abel, and killed him.* **”**

❖ ABOUT THE STORY ❖

This story contains the first mention of sin. Cain is given a chance to lead a good life, but he lets jealousy get the better of him. Instead of behaving as a loving brother should, he commits a terrible crime. When God punishes him, he protests and is unrepentant. God sends him away, having first put a mark upon him. The mark serves both to protect Cain from enemies, and to remind him always of his sin.

Why did God reject Cain's offering?
In this story, no explanation is given as to why God accepts Abel's offering and rejects Cain's. However, elsewhere in the Bible, God tells Moses that all first-born animals must be sacrificed to Him (Exodus 13:2) and that the first fruits of a harvest must be offered to Him (Leviticus 23:10). The events in this story suggest that Abel was careful to make the correct offering but that Cain was not.

Noah and the Flood

IN the early days of the world, people lived much longer than they do now. Adam reached the age of 930 years old! He and Eve had many hundreds of children between them, all of whom lived for 800 years or more and who had many hundreds of children of their own. Over the centuries, each family grew. . . and grew. . . and grew. . . until men and women were everywhere throughout the world. But wickedness spread with them all over the Earth.

God watched as, one by one, people forgot about Him. He saw that they went about their own business, with no thought for anyone else, and that they carried only evil in their hearts. How it pained Him to look on the beautiful

world He had made and see that it had turned so bad! God regretted having given people life. They had spoiled everything He had so lovingly created. Very sadly, God came to a fearful decision. "I will wipe out the human race and get rid of all living creatures from the face of the Earth," He thought, " – except for Noah."

> ❝ *The Lord saw that the wickedness of man was great in the Earth.* ❞

Out of all the millions of men and women, Noah was the very last good man on the Earth – the only person who tried to live his life as God wished. Because of this, the Lord loved Noah and wanted to spare him and his family. "The world is full of evil and I am going to destroy all the people and creatures in it," God told Noah. "I am going to drown every living thing apart from you, your wife, your three sons Shem, Ham and Japheth, and their wives. Do as I tell you and you will be saved. I want you to build a huge ship out of gopher wood, 300 cubits long, 50 cubits wide and 30 cubits high and make it watertight. Shape it into an ark by covering it with a roof, put a door in the side, and give it three decks with lots of separate compartments. When the time comes, load up a male and female of every animal and bird, take plenty of food for yourselves and all the creatures, and I will shut the door."

Noah did exactly as God had told him, ignoring the people who laughed at such a seemingly ridiculous task. Then the Lord locked them all safely away. For a week they

---

❧ ABOUT THE STORY ❧

As time goes by, people begin to forget about God. They are no longer grateful to Him for the beautiful world He has created for them. God decides He has to destroy them all, except for Noah. Noah is the only man who lives a good life and respects God, so he is spared. God separates Noah and his family from the rest of the people by shutting them safely inside an ark. Everyone outside perishes in the flood.

Flood stories
There are stories of great floods in many cultures all over the world. In a Babylonian tale called *The Epic of Gilgamesh* the gods are angry because noisy people are keeping them awake, so they plan a great flood. They instruct Gilgamesh's ancestor to build a boat and take his family and animals on board. Like Noah, only those inside the ark survive. This 8th century Assyrian carving shows Gilgamesh with a lion.

Ship building
Noah and his sons would have built the ark using three layers of logs laid over each other, all coated with a sticky liquid called bitumen to make it watertight.

watched black storm clouds gather, blotting out the skies and sending dark shadows which covered the Earth. And after the seventh day, it began to rain.

> ❝ *All the fountains of the great deep burst forth, and the windows of the heavens were opened.* ❞

It was as if fountains had burst up from the depths of the sea, while at the same time waterfalls poured down from heaven. Ponds at once became lakes; trickling streams gushed into raging torrents; swollen rivers burst their banks, swamping towns then submerging cities – and still the rain came down. People, animals and birds all fled together, higher and higher into the hills, desperately trying to find dry land on which to rest. But the waters caught them, waves tossed them, and swirling currents sucked them down. As the oceans rose, giant tidal waves crashed across whole countries, sweeping away every living thing until the Earth became a silent, underwater world. And still the rain came down. Day after day it fell, thundering down on top of the Ark. Day after long day all that Noah and his family could hear was the rain. All that they ever saw were the dark clouds and the steadily rising waters. Eventually, only the mountain tops were visible, and soon even they were hidden in the deeps.

Then there was nothing to be seen from the windows of the ark except water in every direction, stretching away as far as the eye could see, until it met the sky.

THE EPIC OF GILGAMESH MYTH IS VERY SIMILAR TO THE STORY OF NOAH. AS BOTH COULD BE DRAWN FROM MEMORIES OF AN ACTUAL EVENT IN THE SAME GENERAL AREA, THIS IS NOT AT ALL SURPRISING. ◁

Noah's ark
The word 'ark' means 'box' or 'chest' in Hebrew. It is used here to represent a safe place provided by God. This detail from a wall painting in Saint-Savin Abbey in France shows the different decks of the ark. Noah's family and the animals are safe inside.

Wood from the trees
The Bible says that the ark is made out of gopher wood. It is not known exactly from which tree this came. This is because people studying the original texts cannot agree on how the wood named in the Bible should be translated, but it is believed it could be the cypress tree, like this one. Whichever wood was used, a huge amount was needed to make a boat the size of Noah's ark.

God's Covenant to Noah

FOR 40 days and 40 nights, it kept raining. But just when Noah and his family thought it would go on forever, it stopped. Trapped inside the ark, the people and animals fell silent and listened. The constant hammering of rain on the roof had died away.

The ark drifted helplessly on the ocean. Then they heard the noise of a great wind blowing up. It howled and wailed, gusting around the ark as God began to dry up the waters. For five months the seas very slowly sank back, until one day everyone inside the ark felt a jolt. The bottom of the ship had scraped against dry land. The ark finally grated to a halt. "At last!" thought Noah, and he peeped excitedly out of the window. But still there was nothing to see except water all around. It was many more days before he saw land. Suddenly Noah realized that the craggy points were mountains! And the ark had come to settle at the top of the very highest, Mount Ararat. But he didn't dare to open the door.

Weeks went by and everyone grew more and more impatient to leave the ark. But was it safe yet? Exactly how much land was out there? He took one of the ravens they had brought with them and released it. It flew up into the clear sky, enjoying its new freedom, but it did not return, and Noah feared it had not found land.

Noah waited until everyone could bear it no longer, and then he sent out a dove. Later the same day, it came flying wearily back to the ark. Their faces fell. The dove had not found anywhere to settle. Noah reached out his hand and gently drew the bird back into the safety of the ark.

THE DOVE HAS BECOME A SYMBOL OF PEACE THROUGHOUT THE WORLD. THIS IS WHY PEOPLE RELEASE DOVES INTO THE AIR AT INTERNATIONAL EVENTS, SUCH AS THE START OF THE OLYMPIC GAMES. ~

Forty days and nights
This picture shows the return of the dove. The Bible says the rains lasted 40 days and nights. Some take this literally, but some now feel that the writer just meant 'a long time.'

~ ABOUT THE STORY ~

By sending the flood, God took the world back to the state of chaos it was in before the Creation. When the water subsides, there is a new beginning. Noah gives thanks to God and sacrifices some of the animals to Him. God blesses Noah and promises that He will never again destroy people in another such flood. This promise is often called God's Covenant to Noah.

Another seven days passed with everyone in the ark. Then Noah again released the dove. All day long they watched the skies. As evening drew in, they caught sight of a tiny speck approaching. Closer and closer flapped the bird, until everyone could see it carried a green olive leaf in its beak. How they celebrated!

But Noah still did not let anyone go outside. He waited for another week and then set the dove free once more. This time the bird did not come back. Noah opened the door and peered into the distance. Dry ground lay wherever he looked and he heard God calling. "Noah, it's time for you and your family to leave the ark. Let all the animals go and leave them to run free across the earth."

Noah did just as he was told. After all the days of darkness on the water, everyone was so glad to feel solid ground under their feet. He built an altar and offered thanks to God. And in turn God blessed Noah, his sons and their wives, telling them to live happily together.

> 66 *'I establish my covenant with you, that never again shall all flesh be cut off by a flood.'* 99

"I shall never again wreak such a terrible destruction on my people and creatures - no matter how wicked the world becomes," said the Lord. "To show I will keep my word, I will set a sign in the sky. Whenever you see a band of bright colours break through the clouds, you will know that I remain true to what I have said." And God put the rainbow in the sky, to remind everyone of His promise.

Mount Ararat

This map shows one of the possible locations of Mount Ararat, near the Black Sea in what is today the country of Armenia. No one can be sure exactly where Mount Ararat is. The Bible says that 'the ark came to rest on the mountains of Ararat'. We do not know whether the Bible means on Mount Ararat itself, or in that area. People have been looking for the remains of the ark for a long time. It caused great excitement when an archaeologist claimed to have found wooden remains in Lake Kop, actually on Mount Ararat, but no one has yet been able to prove whether this is Noah's ark or not.

BLACK SEA

CASPIAN SEA

Mt. Ararat

Nineveh

MESOPOTAMIA

Tower of Babel

NOAH died at the age of 950 years old, 350 years after the flood. He lived long enough to see the birth of several generations of his family and watch them spread out into different countries all over the world.

Over time, some of Noah's thousands of descendants travelled far to the east and settled on a plain in the land of Shinar. After the families had travelled for so long, facing many hardships and dangers on the way, they were anxious to establish a proper home for themselves. They were fed up with tents and moving from place to place. Individual houses would not do; they were too easy for enemies to attack. Now that they had come so far, they weren't about to risk the chance of having to flee from their homes. Instead, the men and women decided to build a whole city where they would be protected. They could then live, work and bring up their children in comfort and safety. "And besides," they said to each other, "if we build our own city, we won't just have a wonderful home, everyone will think we're really important, too." "Yes, people are sure to come from all around to see it," they gossiped, "and won't they be jealous!"

Everyone set about the massive task of making enough bricks to build, not only the city walls, but also all the houses, shops and streets. Day after day, month after month, they baked mud into hard blocks and used tar to cement them together. Gradually, the city took shape.

Because it was all going so well, the men and women began to get carried away with their achievements. They grew proud and suggested ever grander schemes.

> **Let us build ourselves a city, and a tower with its top in the heavens.**

Finally one day, they hit upon the boldest plan of all. "Let's build a tower!" someone cried. "What a brilliant idea! Let's put it right in the middle of the city!" one man shouted. "We'll make it so tall that it reaches heaven," yelled another, "then we'll be nearer to God!" The people cheered and began to build.

Building the Tower of Babel
This picture shows a 17th century artist's view of how the tower would have looked in Biblical times. It shows what it would have been like building the tower in the 17th century. Here the tower is being built out of stone, when at the time the story takes place it would actually have been made of mud bricks.

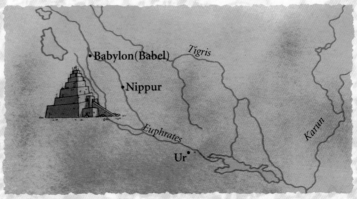

The Tower of Babel
The Tower of Babel is most likely to have been a ziggurat, constructed by people in this area and also in South America as religious buildings. Remains of ziggurats have been found not only at Babel, but also Ur, Nippur, and several other places in this area.

Brick by brick, higher and higher, upwards and ever upwards, the tower rose towards the sky. Several times, the workers thought they had built it tall enough and came down to admire it. But as they stood back, craning their necks in an effort to see the top, they were always dissatisfied. "We can build higher than that," one would scoff. "Yes, I bet we could make it a little taller still," another would encourage. "I suppose the higher it is, the more everyone will admire us," another would sigh. And they'd start work all over again.

When God looked down and saw what the people were doing, He was very worried. "They are becoming so vain!" He said to Himself. "They are accomplishing a great deal, but they don't know when to stop. Soon there will be no limit to what they want. I have to do something to halt them. They could get themselves and others into terrible trouble with their foolish desires."

With one stroke, God shattered the people's over-confidence. He changed the words coming out of their mouths so that no one could communicate. Everyone found themselves listening to their friends speaking nonsense, while they each spoke a gibberish that no one else could understand. To add to everyone's annoyance, no building could be done. It was impossible for the architects to give instructions, the builders couldn't call to their workmates, and they were forced to down tools.

Eventually, the people gave up trying to talk to each other in frustration. They drifted away from the unfinished city and went off on their own to new places. And from that time onwards, people in different parts of the world have spoken different languages.

❧ ABOUT THE STORY ❧

This story shows that pride comes before a fall – God is not happy with the way the people are acting, so he changes the words they speak. This is how the Bible explains why people in different places speak different languages. This is linked to the word 'babble' which means to talk in a way that is hard to understand. We can see the link because, after God changed their words, the people could not understand each other.

Medieval scene
This detail from a medieval painting shows the building of the Tower of Babel. The men on the right are passing stones to the masons who are standing on the top of the tower, gradually adding the layers of bricks to build the tower as high as they can.

God's Promise to Abram

ONE of the descendants of Noah's son Shem was a man called Abram. Abram had grown up in Ur in Mesopotamia and married a woman called Sarai, before moving to the city of Haran with his elderly father, Terah, and his nephew, Lot. Not long after they had set up home Terah died, leaving Abram and Lot to build their lives alone.

The men worked hard, raising large numbers of sheep and cattle, and they became wealthy. Their houses were filled with beautiful possessions. They had servants to wait on them and friends for company. But Abram and Sarai did not have the one thing they wanted most – a child.

> 66 *Go to the land that I will show you and I will make you a great nation.* 99

Nevertheless, Abram and Lot were settled, and had no plans to move elsewhere. But one day, God spoke to Abram. "Abram, I want you to leave this place and everyone you know. Take your family, your servants, and all you own, and go where I tell you. Do as I say and you will be blessed. I will make you known as a great man, and your family will become a great people." So Abram instructed his household to pack up everything, told Lot to do the same, and they all wandered into the wilderness.

For many months the people lived in tents, moving their animals wherever the grazing seemed good. God guided them just as He had said, and brought them eventually to the country of Canaan. "Look at this land," the Lord commanded Abram. "One

day, all this will belong to your descendants." Abram built an altar and gave thanks to God. How relieved everyone was to stop travelling! The tents went up and the animals were put out to grass. At last God had shown them the place that was to be their new home.

But it wasn't long before trouble arose. Abram and Lot had so many animals that their herdsmen found the grazing areas were overcrowded. They started to quarrel over the pasture. No matter how Abram and Lot tried to solve things, there just didn't seem to be enough nearby pasture. "There's nothing for it. We'll have to split up," decided Abram. "There's ample land here for us both if we spread out. But which way will you go?"

Lot looked around him. His eyes fell on the Jordan valley, looking like the Garden of Eden. "I'll go east," he said.

It was strange after Lot and his household had gone. In the quietness, Abram again heard God calling him. "Lift up your eyes, Abram, and look all around you in every direction. All the land you see will be owned by your family forever, and you will have as many descendants as there are specks of dust on the face of the Earth. Go out and explore the countryside. I am giving it all to you."

In the days that followed, Abram grew more and more bothered about what the Lord had said. He and Sarai were still childless, and rapidly getting too old to start a family. How could God's words come true? The Lord told Abram to look up at the sky. "Do you see how many stars there are?" He asked. "Too many to count - just as it will be with your descendants. Bring me some animals and birds for sacrifice and I will show you that I mean what I say."

The following day, Abram killed some creatures for sacrifice. He cut the animals into two and placed the halves opposite each other, together with the birds, as was the custom. Then he kept watch over the offering and waited to see what would happen. As the Sun set, Abram fell into a deep sleep. He dreamt he was alone and he was terrified. Then he heard the voice of God, saying, "For 400 years your descendants will be slaves in a strange land. But

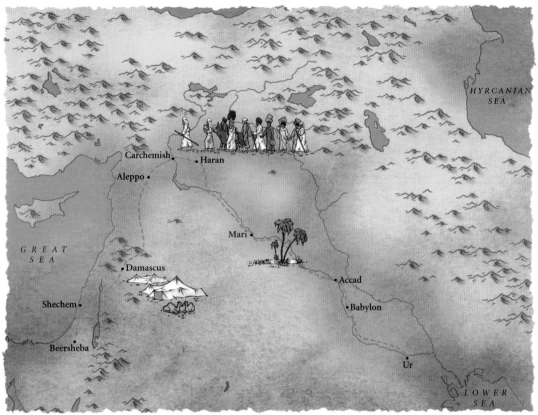

I will punish their captors and they will escape, returning to your promised land. You yourself will live for many years and will die in peace." In the pitch black of the night, Abram saw a blazing torch and a flaming fire pot pass between the sacrificed animals, and he knew that God had made a promise with him that could not be broken.

The Journey of Abram

Abram's journey started in Ur with his father, Terah. Their whole family moved to Haran, hundreds of miles to the north. Then God told Abram to move, so he set out from Haran without knowing where he was going to stop. God guided Abram to Beersheba, in Canaan. Here Abram settled, in the land that the Israelites would return to claim centuries later.

Sacrifices

The picture here shows a procession of people carrying animals to be sacrificed. In ancient times, the practice of sacrificing animals to God was commonplace. Sometimes this was done to honour God, or give thanks. At other times, it was to make amends for some wrong-doing.

❖ ABOUT THE STORY ❖

God tells Abram that his descendants will become a great people and that the land of Canaan will belong to them. Abram is unsure as he has no children, but he sees a sign from God, he hears God's voice and no longer has any doubts.

Promise of a Son

AFTER God had made His covenant with Abram, he and his wife couldn't wait for the time when they would have a child. But the days passed into months, the months turned into years, the years stretched into decades, and there was no sign that Sarai would have a baby. As the couple grew older, their hope turned into impatience and frustration. "Take my maid Hagar as a second wife," Sarai told Abram, at her wits' end. "God might let her have children for you."

As soon as Hagar realized that she was pregnant, she began to put on airs and graces and look down on Sarai. "I have succeeded where you failed," she told her former mistress, "so I must be better than you." She started to order Sarai about, becoming more and more rude to her, until one day Sarai had had enough. She punished Hagar so severely that she ran into the desert.

An angel found Hagar weeping by a spring. "What are you doing here?" he asked. "God wants you to return to your mistress and behave yourself better. You will soon give birth to Abram's son and he will grow up to be a mighty ruler. The Lord wants you to call him Ishmael." And Hagar did just as the angel told her.

Years went by and Abram turned 99 years old. Just as he and Sarai had given up hope of ever having children together, the Lord spoke to him once more. "I am God Almighty and I will keep my covenant to you. I tell you again, your descendants will be kings who will rule over Canaan. I want you to change your name to Abraham, and I want Sarai to become Sarah."

> **"** *'Behold, you are with child, and shall bear a son; you shall call his name Ishmael.'* **"**

"How can a child be born to a man who is nearly 100 years old and a woman who is 90?" the cowering Abraham protested. "And what about my son, Ishmael?"

❧ ABOUT THE STORY ❧

Because of his faith, Abraham is prepared to wait patiently until God gives him the child He promised. Sarah, on the other hand, grows more desperate the older she gets. Unable to wait any longer and doubtful as to whether God will ever fulfil His promise, she suggests that Abraham has a child with Hagar. But Ishmael is not the son God promised to Abraham, and Sarah is not happy until she has a son of her own.

Old oak tree
People used to like sitting under oak trees because of the shade of its leaves. Big oak trees standing alone were also often used as landmarks for travellers.

Annunciation
When the angel appeared to Hagar in the desert, this was an annunciation. The word 'annunciation' means proclamation, or announcement.

God thundered, "Ishmael will be the leader of a great nation. But this time next year, Sarah will have a son of her own, whom you must call Isaac."

Some weeks later, Abraham was sitting and wondering about the Lord's words, when he saw three strangers approaching. Abraham knew they were messengers from God and he rushed to his nearby tent for food and drink while the men cooled off under a broad oak tree.

"God will visit you next spring and Sarah will have a son," the men told Abraham, as they refreshed themselves. Abraham didn't realize that Sarah was listening at the tent door and could hear everything. "How can we have a baby now?" she scoffed out loud. "We're both far too old!"

"Nothing is too difficult for the Lord," the strangers insisted, and they went on their way, leaving the couple quite bewildered.

At last the time came when God fulfilled His vow. On a beautiful spring day Sarah gave birth to a son whom they called Isaac – all just as the Lord had said.

"God has made me so happy!" sang Sarah. "No one who hears of this can fail to be happy too!"

But despite the celebrations, Abraham was saddened. Now Sarah had had a child of her own, she wanted to get rid of Ishmael and his mother. Abraham loved each of the boys and hated the thought of losing Ishmael. God reassured him. "Don't worry, do as Sarah says," He told Abraham. "I will make both of your sons the founders of great peoples."

The next morning, before anyone else was awake, Abraham said a last and sad goodbye to Hagar and Ishmael and sent them off into the desert. They walked

and walked through the heat and the dust until they were exhausted, and the supplies of food and water that they had brought with them were all gone. There was no sign of life in any direction and Hagar knew that they were going to die. She couldn't bear to watch Ishmael suffer, so she laid him down under a shady bush and wandered a little way off before collapsing with grief. But God heard Hagar weeping and He sent an angel to comfort her. "Have no fear," said the angel. "Ishmael will not die. God has promised that he will grow to be a great man. Now go and take care of him." Summoning all her remaining strength, Hagar picked herself up. To her surprise, she saw a spring a little way off and she dashed to get water to revive her son. Hagar and her son lived together in the wilderness for a long time and Ishmael grew up to be a brave warrior, the father of all the Arab peoples.

Living in tents
Today, some people live a nomadic lifestyle in the deserts of the Middle East, as Abraham did. They keep herds of animals and follow them around wherever there is good grazing. Abraham, though, was used to living in one place, so would not have been as used to this life as these Bedouin people.

Banished!
This shows Abraham banishing Hagar and Ishmael. Abraham does not want to lose Ishmael, and wishes that God would recognize both his sons. Abraham always accepts God's will, but his love for Ishmael causes him to question God on this occasion.

Arabs
Abraham's first son, Ishmael, grew up to be a great warrior. While Isaac was the father of the Israelite nation, Ishmael grew up to become the ancestor of all the Arab people.

Abraham and Isaac

AFTER the many years of waiting, Abraham and Sarah's happiness was complete. Isaac grew to be a lively, strong little boy. As his parents watched him run errands and play in the fields with the other children, it was hard for them to believe that their son was a part of the Lord's great plan.

Then one day, Abraham heard God calling him once again. "Abraham! Take your only son, Isaac – who I know you love dearly – and go to a mountain I will show you. There, I want you to offer him to me as a sacrifice."

Abraham was truly horrified. How could God be asking him to kill his own son? The Lord knew how long

Abraham and Sarah had been desperate for children, and how precious their son Isaac was! What could Abraham say to Sarah? And how on earth could he tell Isaac?

Abraham mentioned nothing to his family of God's terrible request. The next morning, he rose early and took his son and two servants to cut firewood, which they loaded on to a donkey. The awful secret Abraham carried was far heavier. They set off across the countryside, Abraham hanging his head in misery. After three days, Abraham knew they had reached God's chosen place.

❧ ABOUT THE STORY ❧

Although Abraham is horrified at the idea of killing his son, he puts his faith in God and obeys Him. He follows God's instructions until the point where he is about to make the sacrifice. When God is certain that Abraham's faith is strong, He spares the boy and repeats His promise, that Abraham's descendants will become a great people. By proving that he puts God above all, Abraham has passed the test God set for him.

Climbing the mountain
God would not usually ask anyone to make a child sacrifice. It seems clear, though, that God never actually intended Abraham to sacrifice his son.

Dome of the Rock
The Bible describes the sacrifice as taking place on a mountain in the land of Moriah. This is believed to be the hill in Jerusalem where King Solomon later built his magnificent temple. Later still, in the 7th century AD, the Muslims conquered Jerusalem and built a mosque where the temple had stood. This mosque, called the Dome of the Rock, still stands today.

"Stay here with the donkey and wait for us," he told the servants. "Isaac and I are going to go and make an offering to God." Then Abraham and Isaac began to climb the steep hillside.

After a while, Isaac grew a little puzzled. "Father," he asked. "I'm carrying the wood, you have a knife and some fire, but where is the lamb we're going to offer?"

Abraham tried hard to keep his voice steady. "My son," he replied with great anguish, "God will provide Himself with a lamb."

Side by side, the two went on until they reached the spot for the sacrifice. They gathered stones and built an altar. Then, Abraham arranged the firewood. The time had come. Tenderly, Abraham bound Isaac and lifted him on to the sacrificial pile. He stretched out his hand for the knife. Overcome by grief, Abraham steeled himself to obey God. He raised the blade up over the terrified boy.

All at once he heard someone calling his name. "Abraham! Abraham!"

Abraham stopped still. Slowly, he lowered the knife and listened. Then he fell to his knees. It was the voice of the Angel of the Lord.

"Here I am," Abraham replied.

"Abraham!" called the Angel of the Lord. "Do not harm the boy! Since you would have given God your only son, He knows now that you are true to Him."

Abraham could hardly believe his ears. Slowly, he raised his eyes to look at the trembling, terrified boy tied to the altar. His son had been spared! There was some movement in a thicket and Abraham caught sight of a ram, snared in the brambles and struggling to break free. Weeping with

> ❝ *Because you have not withheld your son I will multiply your descendants* ❞

joy, Abraham lifted Isaac down from the firewood. He took the animal and offered it in Isaac's place, giving great thanks to God. And the Angel of the Lord called to Abraham for a second time from Heaven. "Abraham, the Lord says that because you have obeyed Him, both you and your son shall be blessed. You will have as many descendants as there are stars in the sky, as many descendants as there are grains of sand on the seashore, and they shall become a great people."

Abraham and Isaac
God knew where he planned to put Abraham's faith to the test, but it was not near Abraham's house. It took Abraham and Isaac three days to make the journey from their home in Beersheba to Mount Moriah, at the other end of the Salt Sea. It must have been a terrible journey for Abraham, giving him a long time to reflect on what he knew God had asked him to do. Even after this gruelling journey, Abraham was still faithful to God, and would have sacrificed his only son had God demanded it.

Isaac and Rebekah

THE years passed and Abraham outlived Sarah, reaching an extremely old age, just as God had told him he would. The most important thing to the elderly man was seeing their son, Isaac, settled with a wife before he died. Abraham had to be sure that Isaac would carry on the family, so God's promise that his descendants would become a great nation could be fulfilled. He called his most trusted servant to him and said, "Go back to my country of Mesopotamia, where I grew up all those years ago. Find Isaac a good woman from my own family to be his wife." Honoured to be entrusted with such an important task, the servant loaded up ten camels with lots of expensive gifts of jewellery, perfume and silks and set off on the difficult trek across the desert.

Abraham's servant was tired and dusty when he eventually reached the city of Nahor and he made straight for the waterhole. Dusk was falling and the women were coming to draw their water for the night. "Maybe I'll find one among them fit to be Isaac's wife," the servant thought to himself. "Oh God," he prayed silently, "please help me pick the right girl. Show me which one I should choose and give me a sign so that I can be sure. I'll ask the girl to give me a drink from her water jug, and if she says yes and offers to fetch me some water for the camels too, I'll know she's the one Isaac should marry."

> **Before he had done speaking, behold Rebekah came out with her water jar upon her shoulder.**

While Abraham's servant was still deep in prayer, a beautiful young girl made her way up to the well. She lowered her jug down into the depths and drew it up again, heavy with water. There was something about the girl that caught the servant's attention. "But surely the very first young woman couldn't be the one?" he wondered. Hurrying up to her, he asked, "May I have a little of your water to drink?"

"Of course," she answered with a smile, and poured him some straight away. She watched as the servant refreshed himself and then laughed, "Your camels look as if they could do with a drink, too." She went off to water the thirsty animals. Abraham's servant was so surprised that he nearly forgot why he was there. Luckily, he remembered in time and rushed to offer her some of the gold jewellery he had brought as presents.

He asked the girl who she was, and could hardly believe it when the girl replied, "I am Rebekah, daughter of Bethuel." Bethuel was Abraham's nephew! He thanked God for guiding him straight to his master's relatives.

The servant accompanied Rebekah back home and her brother, Laban, hurried to make his guest welcome, stabling the camels and setting out a feast. But the servant couldn't bring himself to eat anything until he knew whether or not Rebekah would agree to be Isaac's wife. After he'd explained everything, Laban and Bethuel, Rebekah's father, agreed it could only be God's work. "We must do as He wishes," they told Abraham's servant, "Rebekah shall go with you to marry Isaac." Before the celebrations began, the servant shared out Abraham's presents: more gold and silver jewellery for Rebekah, together with richly embroidered materials; valuable trinkets and ornaments for the rest of the family. They feasted until late into the night and the following morning, Rebekah left for the long trip to her new home.

It was late one evening when Isaac looked up and saw the tiny shapes of camels approaching in the distance. Suddenly nervous and not knowing quite what to expect, he slowly began to walk out to meet them.

"Who's that?" Rebekah asked the servant, as she caught sight of the broad-shouldered young man walking hesitantly towards them.

"He's your husband," came the reply, to Rebekah's delight. Abraham's servant explained to Isaac everything that had happened, how God had made sure that Isaac and Rebekah would be together, and Isaac welcomed Rebekah as his wife with love in his heart.

The Tribes of Israel

Isaac's grandsons were to become the fathers of the twelve tribes of Israel. When the Israelites reached the promised land, each tribe was promised an area that they could call their own, but they could only claim the areas that were allotted to them once they had defeated the people that were already there. The Israelite tribe of Dan, in the north, originally lived around the city of Beth-dagon, but they could not defeat the Philistines and force them to leave, so they had to move to a new area.

Abraham's gifts

The gift a bridegroom gives to his bride's family is called a dowry, given as compensation for the loss of a daughter. It might include jewellery like this, necklaces, rings, earrings and nose rings.

Water carrier

Rebekah may have been carrying a water pot like this when she met Abraham's servant.

⸎ ABOUT THE STORY ⸎

It is important that Isaac marries, so he can have children and fulfil God's promise. Abraham's servant prays to God to help him find the right girl. Rebekah appears, as if in answer to his prayer. Rebekah's family agree to the wedding, knowing it to be God's will.

Jacob and Esau

GOD blessed Isaac and Rebekah with twins. But when the babies were born, it was strange to see that they looked nothing like each other. Esau, the elder, was covered with red hair, and Jacob, the younger, was smooth-skinned. The parents loved both children, but as time went by and the boys grew up, each secretly grew to have a favourite. Isaac became particularly fond of Esau, because he proved to be good at hunting and Isaac's favourite meal was venison. Rebekah, though, grew to love Jacob best,

because he didn't like running about outdoors and preferred to stay quietly at home with her.

Because of their different characters, Esau and Jacob were often to be found arguing - especially over Esau's birthright. Even though Esau was only minutes older than Jacob, as the first-born, he was the heir to all Isaac's riches and would become head of the family when their aging father died. But one day, Jacob saw an opportunity to seize the precious birthright for himself. He was cooking some lentil soup when Esau returned home from a long hunting trip, faint with hunger. "Give me some of that, I'm famished!" his brother demanded.

Jacob was angry at his rudeness. "I'll swap you some soup for your birthright," he bargained.

Esau didn't even think about what he was doing. "All right. It won't be any good to me if I've died of starvation," he snapped, tormented by the good smell.

"Swear you mean it," said Jacob solemnly, holding the steaming bowl just out of Esau's reach.

"I swear on my life that I give you my birthright!" yelled Esau. "Now hand me the soup before I collapse!" In a few gulps, it was all gone.

Years went by and Isaac became old and blind. He knew that he didn't have long to live and he called Esau to him. "My best son," he said, tenderly. "Go and hunt a deer so I may taste the venison you cook for me just one more time. Hurry, so I can give you my blessing before I die."

But Rebekah had overheard. She was well aware that if a man on his deathbed blessed or cursed someone, it sealed their future either good or bad. She was determined that Isaac should bless Jacob instead of Esau, and dashed off to

> ❝ *Then Jacob gave Esau bread and pottage of lentils and he ate and drank. Thus Esau despised his birthright.* ❞

Wild goats

Esau would have hunted animals such as the ibex, a type of wild goat. Ibexes are still found in rocky areas of the Middle East today. He would have used weapons similar to those that some hunters use today such as traps and nets, as well as a bow and arrows.

Old age

Isaac was already over a hundred when he blessed the wrong one of his sons, but he lived on until the age of 180. Many people in the Bible lived to extraordinary ages, for example Abraham lived to 175, Adam to 930 and Noah to 950. The oldest man in the Bible is Noah's grandfather, Methuselah, who lived until he was 969. Old people were held in great respect for their experience and wisdom.

The birthright

A father's special blessing to his oldest son, normally just before he died, was called the birthright. It gave the son leadership over his brothers, but it also placed on him the responsibility of taking care of the family after his father's death. While it most often went to the eldest son, a father could choose to give it to a younger son, or to someone else. A birthright could be sold, or given away before it was passed on by the blessing, but once the special blessing had been given, it could not be taken back. This is why fathers usually waited until they thought they were soon to die before passing on the birthright.

Esau would have known how important the birthright was, and the fact that he gave it away so easily shows that he did not deserve to receive his father's blessing.

clothes, covered his hands, face and neck with the hairy goat skins, and sent him in to see Isaac.

"Father, it's me, Esau," lied Jacob.

Isaac was surprised. "That was quick!" he said.

"God helped me in my hunting," Jacob replied. Isaac was suspicious, but feeling Jacob's hairy skin reassured him. He ate the food, kissed his son, and blessed him with every good wish. "God will make you rich and prosperous, a ruler of great men, and master over this family. May God reward everyone who blesses you and curse everyone who wishes you bad luck!"

Scarcely minutes after Jacob had left, Esau arrived. "Here we are, father," he said. "Enjoy the delicious meal I have brought you and then you can bless me."

Isaac began to tremble. "Who are you?" he asked.

"Don't you recognize your first-born son?" Esau laughed. "It's me, Esau."

Isaac was pierced with anguish. "But I've already blessed somebody else and I can't take it back!"

Esau was devastated. "Father, bless me too!" he begged.

"I can't, my son," the grief-stricken Isaac told him. "I've blessed your brother with everything. He will become rich, a ruler of men and master of the family."

The tears streamed down Esau's face and Isaac blessed him as best he could. "Your life will be difficult, but you will become a great warrior and a great leader, and you will break away from your brother's control."

From that day on, Esau hated Jacob bitterly and plotted how he might kill him. But just in time, Rebekah sent Jacob away to live with her brother in Haran, so he would be safe from harm.

find him. "Be quick," she instructed Jacob. "Go and get two young goats so I can cook them up into a tasty meal for you to take to your father. He'll think you're Esau and will give you his final blessing."

"But Esau is much more hairy than me," Jacob objected. "If father realizes that I'm trying to trick him, he will probably curse me instead of blessing me."

"Leave that to me," Rebekah replied, so Jacob did what he was told. Then his mother dressed him in Esau's best

❖ ABOUT THE STORY ❖

Part of the birthright Isaac will pass down to his son is God's promise to Abraham, that his descendants will be a great people and that the land of Canaan will one day be theirs.

Although Jacob deceives his father in order to receive the birthright, the blessing is still valid. Rebekah suffers for her role in the deception because her favourite son is forced to run away from home.

The Journey of Jacob
Jacob's journey from Beersheba to his mother's family in Haran is a long one. On the way to meet Laban, Jacob saw his vision of the angels travelling up and down a stairway to heaven. He renamed the place at which he saw this vision Bethel, which means 'house of God'. When he returns after 20 years away, he meets his brother Esau by the river Jabbok, at a place called Penuel.

Haran

GREAT SEA

Penuel

Bethel (Luz)

Beersheba

Jacob's Ladder

JACOB's path to safety lay across the desert. The journey was so tough that at times he'd wonder if it wouldn't have been better to stay and face Esau's anger. By day he'd roast as the sun baked down, while at night he'd shiver out in the open under the stars. At least he didn't find it difficult to sleep – even though he had only rocks for pillows. At the end of each day, he'd gratefully collapse with exhaustion and fall asleep at once.

> " *He dreamed that there was a ladder and the top of it reached to heaven.* "

One night Jacob had a vivid dream that there was a huge staircase stretching all the way from the earth to heaven. Angels were going up and down between the two, and at the very top of the stairs stood God Himself. The Lord spoke to Jacob and repeated the promise He had made to Abraham. "Your descendants will become a great people," He said. "No matter where you go, I will keep you safe and bring you back home to this land."

As soon as Jacob woke, he took the large, flat stone that had been under his head and stood it upright in the ground to mark where he had been lying. He anointed it with oil in a sacred ritual and named the spot Bethel, or God's house. Then he prayed that God would keep His word and be with him on his journey, before continuing on his way.

Angels
The word 'angel' means messenger. In the Bible, angels are the messengers of God. They appear in front of people to tell them God's commands, or to inform them of something God wants them to know. The phrase 'the angel of the Lord' is used to describe how God came to people in human form, to give them a special message.

❧ ABOUT THE STORY ❧
While Jacob is dreaming, God appears to him, standing at the top of a huge staircase often called 'Jacob's ladder'. God repeats the promise He made to Abraham, which He renewed with Jacob's father Isaac – that Jacob's descendants will become a great people and will inherit the land of Canaan.
Jacob asks God to protect him on his journey across the desert and promises to serve Him if he does so.

Jacob and Rachel

As Jacob drew near to Haran, he came to a field where shepherds were watering their flocks at a well. He spoke to them, hoping they could give him directions, "My brothers, where do you come from?"

They said, "We are from Haran." Jacob knew that this was very close to where Laban lived.

"Do you know Laban of Nahor?" Jacob asked them.

"Yes, we know him well," they replied. One of the men pointed across the pasture at a shepherdess approaching with her sheep. "That's his daughter, Rachel," he said

Jacob waited patiently until his cousin had driven her flock up to the well. He watched as she began trying to roll away the heavy stone that covered the well mouth and leaped up to help. "I'm Jacob," he told her, to her great surprise. "I'm your Aunt Rebekah's son." And he greeted her properly with a kiss. With great excitement, Rachel ran off to tell her father that his nephew was here.

> ❝ *Then Jacob kissed Rachel and wept aloud. And Jacob told Rachel that he was her father's kinsman.* ❞

Just as Laban had rushed to welcome Abraham's servant so many years before, he now hurried out to meet Abraham's grandson. Laban greeted Jacob as if he were his long-lost son and took him home, where Jacob explained everything to him.

AS ABRAHAM'S SERVANT HAD FOUND HIS MASTER'S FAMILY, SO JACOB IMMEDIATELY FINDS HIS MOTHER'S FAMILY AND HIS FUTURE WIFE. GOD IS ALWAYS PRESENT, MAKING SURE THAT EVERYTHING HAPPENS ACCORDING TO THE WAY THAT GOD HAS PLANNED IT. ❧

❧ ABOUT THE STORY ❧

This story tells of the beginning of Jacob's love for Rachel, one of the Bible's outstanding examples of human love. Rachel is described as a woman of great beauty and Jacob falls in love with her as soon as he lays eyes upon her. His love remains strong until the day Rachel dies. Rachel is important as her sons are the ancestors of three of the tribes of Israel: Benjamin, Ephraim and Manasseh.

Women in the Bible
Women in ancient times played an important part in daily life. Probably their most significant role was that of mother. A mother was honoured, feared and obeyed in her household. She was responsible for naming her children, and for their early education. They went to worship at religious gatherings and brought offerings for sacrifice. If there were no male heirs, a woman could inherit land and property from her parents.

The Wedding of Jacob

LABAN welcomed Jacob to live with him and the grateful young man tried to show his thanks by working in his uncle's fields, shepherding his flocks. After four weeks had gone by, Laban called Jacob to him. "It isn't fair that you should work for me for nothing," he said, generously. "What can I give you as payment?" Jacob didn't need to think about it. Over the past month he had fallen deeply in love with Rachel and wanted to marry her. Rachel was young and full of life, and her beauty made her elder sister, Leah, seem plain and dull in comparison.

> 66 *'I will serve you seven years for your younger daughter Rachel.'* 99

"I will work for you for nothing for seven years if you promise to let me marry Rachel," Jacob told his uncle. "I'd rather give her to you than anyone else," the delighted Laban replied. So Jacob remained working for his uncle and the seven years flew past as if they were only seven days. At last the wedding day arrived and Laban threw a great feast. He invited all his friends and neighbours from miles around and they celebrated well into the evening. Then Laban covered his daughter's face with her wedding veil and sent her to Jacob's tent.

Next morning, Jacob was horrified to find that it was Leah, not Rachel, who was lying by his side. He woke Laban in a fury. "You've tricked me into marrying the

MOSES WOULD LATER FORBID A MAN FROM MARRYING HIS WIFE'S SISTER DURING HIS WIFE'S LIFETIME. THE TENSION BETWEEN JACOB AND HIS WIVES SHOWS THE WISDOM OF THE LAWS GOD GAVE TO MOSES ❦

Wearing a veil
Jacob could not tell which sister he was marrying because Leah's face was hidden by her veil. The tradition of brides wearing veils continues in many cultures today, though often the face is only partly covered. In some Middle Eastern countries the women wear veils all the time, not just at their weddings.

Powerful plant
In ancient times, people believed that the root of the mandrake plant had the power to increase wealth and overcome infertility. Women who were unable to have children used to go in search of mandrakes. Although Jacob loved Rachel, it was Leah and the maids who gave him the children he wanted first.

wrong sister!" he yelled at the top of his voice. "I didn't work for you for seven years to have Leah for my wife!"

Quite calmly, his uncle replied, "In this country, it's not the done thing for the younger daughter to take a husband if her older sister is still single. Now that Leah is a married woman, I'm more than happy to give you Rachel too – in return for another seven years' work, of course. Also, you must wait until the week of Leah's wedding festivities is over before marrying her."

There was nothing Jacob could do and because he loved Rachel so much, he agreed to his uncle's demands. At the end of the week, he and Rachel were finally allowed to be together, and Jacob began seven years more work.

As soon as Jacob and Rachel were married, poor Leah found herself left out and ignored. God saw how rejected and miserable she felt and He took pity on her, blessing her with a baby boy. Leah went on to have three more of Jacob's sons while Rachel remained childless. "Jacob, I shall die if we can't have a baby!" she wept one day.

Her husband was just as frustrated. "What can I do about it? It's all up to God," Jacob yelled back.

"Then marry my maid, Bilhah," Rachel cried. "If she has children, they'll count as mine."

Bilhah gave birth to two sons. But, no matter how hard she tried, Rachel couldn't stop hoping for children of her own. God kept her waiting a long time before He granted her wish. Even after Leah's maid, Zilpah, bore Jacob two sons, and Leah herself had a further two boys and a daughter, Rachel remained childless. Finally, God took pity on her, and He sent Rachel a little boy. She was overjoyed and treasured her son, calling him Joseph.

Wine sets
At Jacob's wedding feast, wine would have been served with the food. Wealthy people had bronze wine sets made up of three pieces: a juglet to scoop the wine out of a storage jar, a strainer to filter out any impurities, and a shallow bowl to drink from.

❧ ABOUT THE STORY ❧

Jacob deceived his brother, Esau, out of his birthright. Now it is his turn to be deceived by his uncle. Although Jacob has already worked for Laban for seven years before the wedding, he is tricked into marrying the wrong sister, and forced to work another seven years in order to marry Rachel. Jacob has God's blessing, though, and he fathers twelve sons, who go on to be the forefathers of the twelve tribes of Israel.

Jacob's Return

JACOB endured the further seven years' work he had agreed to do for Laban in return for Rachel's hand in marriage. But he planned to leave his cheating uncle as soon as the time was up. When that day arrived, Laban was horrified. "You're the only reason I've become so wealthy," he told Jacob. "God must truly be with you, because everything you turn your hand to is a success. What can I do to make you change your mind?" Jacob saw the chance to start building a flock of his own and told his uncle that he would only stay if Laban would let him have any sheep or goats that had spotted or black coats. Laban readily agreed, secretly thinking he would trick Jacob once again. He told his sons to sort out all the non-white animals and hide them in pastures far away. But God helped Jacob outwit his uncle. He blessed the remaining flocks so that some lambs and kids were born with spotted and black coats. Slowly, Jacob separated out a flock, and at the end of six years, he was a rich man.

As Laban and his sons grew more and more jealous at how well Jacob had done for himself, living with his uncle became increasingly unpleasant for Jacob. He prayed to God for guidance and decided that it would be best to return home. Jacob knew that Laban would be very angry at losing not only his daughters but also his best shepherd and would make it extremely difficult for him to leave. So he didn't tell his uncle he was going. He waited until sheep-shearing time, when Laban and his sons had to stay away in the fields, then he fled with his wives, children, servants, flocks and possessions.

When Laban found out, he dashed off in pursuit. After a week's hard riding, he caught up with Jacob and the two men had a bitter argument. Laban accused Jacob of stealing his daughters and his animals, while Jacob reminded Laban that he had deliberately deceived him more than once. No doubt things would have come to blows, but God had warned Laban in a dream not to harm Jacob in any way. Eventually, when neither man would apologize, they agreed to make up for the sake of Jacob's children, and they went their separate ways in peace.

Now Jacob's main worry was his brother. While he hoped that Esau had had a change of heart during the 20 years they had been separated, Jacob feared the worst. He remembered the deep hatred there had been between them, and Jacob suspected that Esau was still determined to kill him. In an effort to patch things up, Jacob sent messengers on ahead with gifts. But just in case his brother wasn't prepared to forgive him, Jacob split his household up into two groups. Then if Esau attacked the family group, Jacob could be sure that at least some of them stood a good chance of escaping.

Meeting place
When Jacob and Esau met again after 20 years the meeting took place where the river Jabbok flows into the river Jordan, above, to the north of the Dead Sea. Today, the Jabbok is known as the river Zerqa.

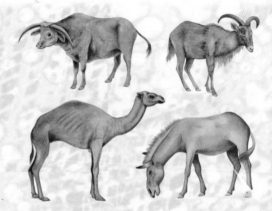

Sending gifts
It was common practice for two people to send gifts to each other before meeting. The gifts were usually related to the people's occupations, so Jacob, as a herdsman, sent livestock like sheep, goats and camels to Esau.

As they drew close to their journey's end Jacob became more and more troubled. One evening he took himself off to find a quiet place where he could think. Though Jacob was sure he was alone, a stranger appeared from out of the darkness and challenged him to wrestle. They struggled all night long, equally matched in strength and will, and neither grew any nearer to winning. When dawn began to break the two men broke apart, worn out. "What's your name?" asked the stranger.

"Jacob," came the weary reply.

"From now on you will be known as Israel," the stranger commanded, vanishing as suddenly as he had appeared. Jacob was left on his knees in awe. His new name meant 'he who has grappled with the Lord', and he realized he had been fighting with God Himself. After having cheated to become Isaac's heir and having been sent away from the land the Lord had especially chosen for Abraham, Jacob had proved his

> **❝ So Jacob called the place Penuel, saying 'For I have seen God face to face.' ❞**

worth and God had blessed him with a new beginning.

Then Jacob went down to meet Esau, who had come with 400 men at the ready. Telling his family to stay back, Jacob nervously walked to his brother. Jacob left God to decide his fate and bowed down before his brother. To his complete amazement, Esau ran to meet him. "Welcome home!" he cried, throwing his arms around Jacob, and the brothers both wept with happiness.

Dreams from God
Dreams are used in the Bible as a means by which God can send messages to the sleeper. God's warning to Laban is an example of such a dream.

Jacob's prayer
Jacob prays to God that Esau will not harm him or his family, and trusts in God to keep them all safe.

❖ ABOUT THE STORY ❖

When Jacob is near Canaan, just before he is reunited with his brother, he wrestles with a stranger, who turns out to be God Himself. This is the culmination of a lifetime's struggle for Jacob. He is unlike Abraham and Isaac, in that his faith did not come easily to him. In the end, though, he has proved his worth and God blesses him with a new name and a new beginning.

Joseph and his Brothers

JACOB settled in the land of Canaan with his large family: his four wives had had many children between them. Just like his father, Isaac, Jacob had a favourite child – Joseph, the son of his beloved wife Rachel. When the boy reached 17 years old, Jacob gave him a special present: a beautiful long-sleeved coat, elaborately woven in many different colours and patterns. His 11 brothers knew that the expensive gift showed Jacob thought of Joseph as his heir – despite the fact that he wasn't the eldest – and they were extremely jealous. Their resentment and hatred grew when Joseph described two dreams he had had. "First I saw us all working in the fields, tying up sheaves of corn," he told them. "But all of a sudden, your sheaves turned to mine and bowed to it! And my second dream was even more peculiar. This time it was the Sun, the Moon and 11 stars that all bowed down to me!"

His brothers were immensely annoyed. "So are you saying that you're going to rule over us?" they mocked, sarcastically. Even his father was irritated.

"Do you really want us and your mother to come and grovel at your feet?" Jacob snapped. But all the same, he couldn't put his son's words out of his mind.

It was usual for the brothers to ignore Joseph as far as they could and they often sneaked off together, taking their flocks over the fields without him. Jacob would send Joseph after them to report back on what they were up to – which only made the brothers dislike him even more. One day the 11 boys had travelled to the very furthest pastures, thinking they had left Joseph behind as usual, when they noticed a bright-coated figure in the distance, heading their way. "It's the dreamer," groaned one.

"Coming to spy on us again," sneered another.

"Wait a minute," interrupted a third. "This could be the chance we've been waiting for. We're a long way from home and there's no one around. Why don't we do away with him?" The others soon took up the idea.

"We could kill him and hide the body where no one will find it," said one. "And we could tell Father that a wild animal attacked him," suggested another. They were enjoying laying their plans but Reuben, the eldest, was shocked. Thinking quickly, he

> **They said, 'Here comes this dreamer. Come now, let us kill him.'**

came up with a way to stop them. "I say we don't kill Joseph," he urged. "Do any of you really want to be responsible for his death? Why don't we dump him in a pit?" The brothers reluctantly agreed. Little did they know that Reuben intended to come back and rescue Joseph.

When the boy reached his brothers they suddenly turned on him and attacked him, kicking him to the ground. Enraged by the sight of the coat, they ripped it off and stamped on it in the dirt, before throwing their bruised and bleeding brother into a disused well. All except Reuben were well satisfied with their work and while the upset Reuben wandered off, out of earshot of Joseph's cries for help, the others sat down to eat.

Halfway through the meal the brothers were startled to hear people approaching. Nervously, they looked up and saw a band of Ishmaelite traders coming towards them, their camels loaded down with exotic spices. Judah's eyes lit up. "Here's a way to make ourselves some money and solve the problem of what to do with Joseph at the same time," he told his brothers, cunningly. "These merchants are on their way to Egypt. I'm sure they'd be glad to have a slave to sell when they get there." And the boys took 20 pieces of silver in exchange for their brother.

When Reuben returned, he was totally horrified to find the pit empty. "What have you done!" he screamed. "Whatever am I going to do now?" He wept bitterly while his brothers got on with the business of making up an excuse for their father. They killed a young kid, took the

remaining tatters of Joseph's coat and smeared them with blood, then went to give Jacob the evidence that his favourite son had been killed by wild animals.

At the sight of the savaged coat, Jacob wept uncontrollably, beside himself with grief. He mourned Joseph day after day, and no one could comfort him.

Joseph sold into slavery

Joseph leaves his home in Hebron to go and join his brothers in the normal pastures at Shechem, but they are trying to avoid their brother so they have moved on to other meadows. Someone tells Joseph where they have gone, so he follows them to Dothan. When he is sold he is taken hundreds of miles away, down into Egypt where he works for Potiphar.

Slave traders

This illustration shows Joseph's brothers selling him to the Ishmaelite traders, also called Midianites. They are the same group of people that Gideon, one of the Judges, fought against in the Old Testament Book of Judges.

Sold!

These coins are shekels, and they are the sort of coins that Joseph's brothers were given when they sold him.

❖ ABOUT THE STORY ❖

Joseph's brothers are irritated by his strange dreams, and jealous of Jacob's favouritism. They plan to kill him, but God is on Joseph's side and his life is spared. Instead, he is sold and taken to Egypt, where the meaning of his dreams will eventually become clear.

Joseph in Egypt

JOSEPH had been betrayed by his brothers and felt lost and terrified. He spent every minute of his uncomfortable journey wondering what would become of him and worrying about what his brothers would have told their father. When they reached Egypt, Joseph realized it was unlikely he'd ever see home again. The Ishmaelites sold Joseph as a slave to Potiphar, the captain of the Egyptian royal guard, and he found himself working in the house of Pharaoh.

Even though it felt to Joseph as though he'd been abandoned, God watched over him, keeping him safe and blessing everything he did. People soon noticed that Joseph seemed to be unusually lucky; even Potiphar realized that everything worked out well when Joseph was around, so he put him in charge of his household.

But Joseph also attracted unwelcome attention. Potiphar's wife began to fancy the young man she saw taking control of everything so well. She took great pleasure in spending her day tracking Joseph down and finding new ways to flirt with him. Joseph didn't want to have anything to do with her. "My master has been good to me. There's no way I'd go behind his back," Joseph would tell the woman firmly. "Anyway, loving another man's wife is a sin against God." But Potiphar's wife wouldn't give up. Each time Joseph said no to her, it simply made her more determined. "If sweet talk isn't working, I'll have to try something a bit more obvious," she thought to herself in the end. She waited for a quiet moment and then flung herself at Joseph, grabbing him and pulling him close to her. Struggling frantically, Joseph

wriggled free, leaving Potiphar's wife grasping a torn handful of tunic. "No one rejects me like this and gets away with it," she thought to herself in a rage. She waited until her husband came home and then began to create a terrible fuss. "Your slave broke into my room and tried to attack me," she wailed. "It was so frightening! I screamed as loud as I could and he ran off, catching his tunic on the door." Potiphar was angry and hurt. Without giving Joseph a chance to explain, he had him flung into prison.

Even locked up inside a deep, dark dungeon, God didn't desert Joseph. The prison warden knew how successful Joseph had been as Pharaoh's housekeeper, and he made

Pyramids
Ancient Egypt is probably most famous for its pyramids. These massive constructions took around 20 years to complete. Each one housed the tomb of a pharaoh, buried deep inside. The sphinx is a lion's body with a human head. This one was carved about 4000 years ago for the Pharaoh Khafre.

Royal signature
The kings of Egypt are referred to in the Bible as the Pharaohs. 'Pharaoh' originally meant the royal palace, and was only later used to mean the ruler himself. The picture signs, or hieroglyphs, shown here are the Egyptians' writing, and spell out the name of Rameses II on a tablet called a cartouche.

him responsible for taking care of the prison, giving him special rights and privileges. Two of the prisoners in Joseph's charge were also members of Pharaoh's household: his baker and his butler. One morning, Joseph found them both deep in thought, looking very puzzled. "We've each had a strange dream," they told him, "and we haven't a clue what they mean."

"Dreams come from God," Joseph said. "Tell me about them and I'll see if I can interpret them for you."

The butler went first. "I dreamt that I was looking at three bunches of grapes on a vine and I pressed them into wine for Pharaoh."

> " *But the Lord was with Joseph, and gave him steadfast love.* "

"Your dream means that in three days' time you will be released and will go back to your job," Joseph assured the delighted man. "I beg you, don't forget me. If it's possible for you to ask Pharaoh to pardon me, I'd be so grateful."

Then it was the baker's turn. "I dreamt that I was carrying three baskets of cakes on my head, but birds flew down and pecked away every crumb."

Joseph was troubled. "I fear your dream means that in three days Pharaoh will hang you," he said, and for three days, the men waited in agony to see what would happen.

Everything that Joseph had predicted came true. The baker was put to death, but Pharaoh restored the butler to his former job. The butler was so overjoyed that he tried to wipe all memories of the dungeon from his mind. He threw himself back into his old job and forgot about Joseph, who continued to spend his days locked up in Pharaoh's dark and damp prison.

❧ ABOUT THE STORY ❧

Throughout Joseph's time in Egypt, God watches over him and he soon does well. He rejects the love of Potiphar's wife, for he knows that it is a sin to love another man's wife. The woman's lies cause him to be thrown into prison but, even there, God stays with him and Joseph is well treated. Using the gift given to him by God, Joseph interprets the dreams of the butler and the baker, and his predictions come true.

Cupbearers
Not all slaves were forced to work as builders or farmers - some were given an important role in the household, and were greatly trusted by their masters. Joseph soon rose to such a position of responsibility. We do not know what his title was, but one of the highest officials was the cupbearer. His duty was to taste food and drink before serving it to the royal family, to ensure it did not contain poison. This painting shows a cupbearer serving an Egyptian prince and princess.

Pharaoh's Dream

Two years after the butler had been released from prison, Pharaoh was troubled by vivid dreams that he couldn't understand. All of his wise men offered opinions on what they meant, but Pharaoh knew they were only guessing. There seemed to be no one in the whole of his kingdom who could interpret them correctly.

It was only then that the butler remembered Joseph, and Pharaoh rushed to have him brought up from the dungeon. "I was standing by the River Nile," Pharaoh told him, "and seven fat cows came to graze at the grassy riverbank. As I watched, seven thin cows came and ate them – but the thin cows didn't get any bigger. In my second dream, I saw seven plump ears of corn being swallowed up by seven thin, shrivelled ears of corn."

The whole court waited anxiously to hear what Joseph would say. "God is warning you that there will be excellent harvests throughout Egypt for seven years, followed by seven years of devastating famine," he announced. "You should put someone in charge of stockpiling grain over the next seven seasons, otherwise your people will starve." Pharaoh knew exactly who he wanted for such a responsible task – the man before him. So Joseph went from being a captive in Pharaoh's prison to his right-hand man, dressed in the finest robes and wearing Pharaoh's ring, and he went through the country, making sure the peoples' stores were filling with grain.

After seven years, just as Joseph had predicted, the crops suddenly failed – not just in Egypt but in the lands beyond, too. Families found themselves and their animals without food and unable to grow anything in the dry ground. Joseph opened the storehouses and starving people came from far and wide for corn. Imagine Joseph's shock when one day, among the desperate people, he recognized ten of his own brothers. His only sadness was that his favourite brother, Benjamin, wasn't with them.

> ❝ *And Pharaoh said to Joseph, 'Behold, I have set you over all the land of Egypt.'* ❞

Storing grain
Joseph was responsible for storing-up grain for the famine. Severe famines have been recorded in Egypt at this time, caused by the Nile's annual floodwaters either being too low, or flooding too high. Either situation was very bad for farming.

Signet rings
This ancient Egyptian signet ring is probably like the one Pharaoh gave Joseph. Handing over the ring was a sign that Pharaoh was giving Joseph great power. Signet rings were also used to sign documents. By pressing it into clay or wax, the writing made a signature.

❧ ABOUT THE STORY ❧

Joseph is the only person who can interpret Pharaoh's dreams. So Pharaoh appoints him to a position of authority. Joseph's predictions come true and it is only because of his gift of interpretation that the Egyptians survive the famine. Joseph is reunited with his brothers, but the roles have been reversed. Joseph forgives them for the past and treats them with love, and Jacob is reunited with his favourite son.

In the 20 years since the men had sold their brother into slavery, Joseph had changed a great deal and they had no idea who he really was. Joseph resisted the urge to hug them and instead treated the foreigners severely. He spoke to them in Egyptian, using an interpreter. "You are spies come to search out our storehouses," he accused the famished, exhausted men.

"No, we're from a starving family in Canaan," they explained. "Our youngest brother is at home with our father." Joseph pretended not to believe them and threw them in prison. After three nights, he saw them again.

"Prove that you are telling the truth," demanded Joseph. "You can go back with your corn, but one of you must stay until you bring me this youngest brother of yours."

"This is our punishment for killing Joseph," whispered Reuben, not realizing that Joseph could understand. When he saw the guilt on his brothers' faces he turned away and wept. Then he gave orders for Simeon to be bound and had every sack filled with corn, replacing their money, too.

The brothers were deeply shaken when they arrived home and found that their silver had mysteriously appeared back in their sacks. Their father was even more upset. "I lost Joseph and now I've lost Simeon," Jacob wept. "I won't let you take Benjamin or he might not come back either." But the famine lasted longer than the corn, and the family soon faced starvation again. Jacob was still determined not to let his sons return to Egypt, but when Judah promised to guard Benjamin with his life, Jacob reluctantly changed his mind. He loaded them up with gifts of exotic spices, making sure they had enough money to pay back the silver they owed.

When Joseph saw Benjamin, he wept with joy. He left the room and sent in the finest food and drink to the men. Also Joseph told his steward to fill the sacks and replace their money again, this time hiding his own silver drinking goblet in Benjamin's sack.

The brothers hadn't got very far on their return journey when Joseph sent his steward chasing after them, on the pretence of looking for the precious goblet. They were bewildered and horrified when it was found in Benjamin's sack. Back at Joseph's house they threw themselves at his mercy. "You're all free to leave," Joseph told them, "except the man in whose sack the goblet was found."

 I am your brother Joseph, who you sold into Egypt. "

Judah knew this would break Jacob's heart. "Please let Benjamin go, or my father will die of grief," he pleaded. "Allow me to stay here in his place."

Joseph could bear it no longer. "I am your brother, Joseph, who you sold into slavery in Egypt," he told the astonished men, "and I forgive you for everything. It was all God's work. Spend the remaining years of the famine here, where I can look after everyone."

Jacob wouldn't believe that Joseph was not only alive, but lord of all Egypt under Pharaoh. But when the two men met and Jacob looked into Joseph's eyes, he knew that God had given back the son he thought was dead. "Now that I've seen you again, I can die happy," he said, thanking God. And Jacob lived out the rest of his days in Egypt.

Joseph and his brothers
When Joseph meets his brothers again for the first time in 20 years they have no idea that the grand Egyptian official in front of them is the boy they sold as a slave, and Joseph does not immediately reveal his true identity to them. The picture on the right, from a 6th-century manuscript, shows the brothers filling their sacks with grain. Joseph wears a long cloak, while his brothers are dressed in short tunics. These are not, in fact, the clothes that would have been worn in Egypt at the time of Joseph, but it is common for artists to show people wearing the clothes of the artist's time.

Moses in the Bulrushes

WHEN Joseph reached the age of 110 years old, he realized he was going to die. He called his brothers to him and promised them that God would one day return their families to Canaan - the land that the Lord had given to Abraham's descendants. But for now, the descendants of Joseph and his brothers would remain in Egypt.

Over hundreds of years their families grew and spread through the country, and they became a strong, successful people. There came a time when the Pharaoh grew worried about the huge number of powerful Israelites living in Egypt. 'Surely there are now more of these Hebrew foreigners living in our country than there are Egyptians!' he thought to himself.

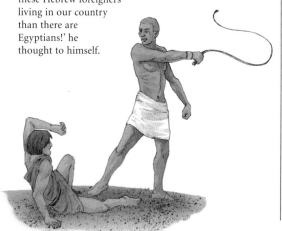

'What happens if there is a war? They might join with the enemy against us and try to take Egypt for themselves.' Pharaoh came to the conclusion that the only way to protect his people was to crush the Israelites completely. He commanded that they should all be taken as slaves and set to hard labour. It was no use anyone trying to resist Pharaoh's soldiers. Soon, groups of Israelites were to be seen digging dusty roads, ploughing up rocky fields, and being flogged when they collapsed in the baking sun. But Pharaoh wasn't satisfied. Even though he could control the Israelites' activities, he couldn't control their spirit. The more harshly they were treated, the more bitter and defiant they became. And worst of all, the number of Israelites in Egypt continued to grow! Pharaoh decided to be totally ruthless and wipe them out. He gave the order that all newborn Israelite boys should be put to death.

> 66 *Pharaoh commanded, 'Every son born to the Hebrews you shall cast into the Nile.'* 99

The terrified Israelites did everything they could to save their newborn sons. Anguished parents all over Egypt tried to hide their baby boys away or smuggle them out of the country to relatives or friends. They'd do anything to save their sons from the swords of Pharaoh's soldiers. One woman from the tribe of Levi managed to hide her baby boy in her house for three months. Every minute, she was afraid that an Egyptian would hear him crying. But as the baby grew bigger, she knew it would be impossible to keep

Finding Moses
This illustration shows Pharaoh's daughter standing on the riverbank, surrounded by her maids. In the story, the basket is covered, but here it is shown to be open, with the baby clearly visible. When illustrating a story, artists will often change details like this, to make their pictures more interesting or dramatic.

Adoption
Adoption is not common in the Old Testament. Families had other ways of dealing with the problem if parents could not have children, for example by the practice of polygamy, where a man has more than one wife. When an adoption did take place, it was more likely to be within the family.

him safe at home forever. She wove a basket out of bulrushes from the river Nile and made it watertight. Then the grief-stricken mother laid her baby in it, covered it over, and set the cradle floating among the reeds at the river's edge. The poor woman couldn't bear to leave her son without knowing what happened to him, yet she knew she was in danger if she was found nearby. So she told her daughter to stay close and watch what happened.

It wasn't long before the little girl saw a young woman coming down to the river to bathe, accompanied by many maids. "It's Pharaoh's daughter herself!" the girl realized, and watched, trembling, as the princess caught sight of the basket. Pharaoh's daughter sent a maid to fetch it, and the women all crowded round, excited to see what was inside. Gingerly, the princess began to remove the cover. Whatever could it be? Maybe someone had hidden precious jewellery, or rich spices? She was amazed to lift out of the basket a wriggling baby boy! As the baby looked up at her and began to cry, the princess's heart melted. 'This must be a Hebrew child,' she thought.

As soon as the baby's sister saw that the princess had taken pity on the baby, she plucked up her courage and approached the royal party. The little girl curtseyed and took a deep breath. "Maybe I could find an Israelite nurse to help you look after him?" she suggested. The princess thought it was an excellent idea.

The woman couldn't believe it when Pharaoh's daughter employed her to look after her own child. "I am calling him Moses," the princess said, "because it means 'to draw out' and I drew him out of the water." The princess loved Moses as if he were her own child.

❖ ABOUT THE STORY ❖

Pharaoh is troubled by the growing number of Israelites in Egypt, fearing they will rebel against him. He forces them all into slavery, and even gives an order that all Israelite baby boys must be killed. However, it is God's will that the Israelites will return to Canaan and will inherit the land He promised them, so Moses is spared. He is brought up in the royal household, as the son of Pharaoh's daughter.

The name of the plant
Although it is said that Moses was found among the rushes, these are more likely to have been papyrus plants, which grew in abundance beside the Nile. 'Rushes' was a word that was used as a general word for plants that grew in water.

Farming in Egypt
Most Israelites in Egypt were farmers. They depended on the river Nile, which flooded every year and spilt fertile soil over its banks and watered the ground.

The Burning Bush

EVEN though Moses grew up in the heart of the Egyptian royal family, he could never forget that he was an Israelite. It pained him to see that while he lived a life of luxury, all around his people suffered terribly at the hands of the Egyptians. It had become so usual to see Egyptians beating Israelite slaves that nobody took any notice. But once, Moses came across an Israelite being kicked to the ground, and suddenly he found himself rushing at the Egyptian attacker. He hit him until he was dead. Nobody was about, so Moses took the body and buried it. But next day, as he tried to split up an argument between two Israelites, one of them angrily said, "Who gave you the right to judge us? Are you going to kill us like you killed the Egyptian?" Somehow, Moses had been found out. He knew he would be in trouble if Pharaoh heard of his crime, so he fled Egypt to the land of Midian.

Moses would have been homeless if he hadn't stopped to help seven sisters trying to water their sheep. In return for his kindness, their father, Jethro, invited Moses to stay with them and also gave him work as a shepherd. Moses lived happily with Jethro's family, eventually falling in love and marrying one of Jethro's daughters, Zipporah.

Shepherding was a quiet life in comparison to the Egyptian royal household. Moses would take his flock out onto the mountain pastures with nothing but the sun and the animals for company. One day, he was deep in thought when a nearby thornbush suddenly burst into flames. After recovering from the shock, Moses went to have a closer look. He was amazed to see that although the bush was on fire, it wasn't burning up. He was even more amazed when a voice called from the flames.

> ❝ *'I will send you to Pharaoh, that you may bring forth my people out of Egypt.'* ❞

"Moses! Moses!" Moses was terrified. "You are standing on holy ground," came the voice, "and I am the God of Abraham, Isaac and Jacob. I have seen how my people suffer in Egypt and I have heard their cries for help. I want you to go to Pharaoh

The fire of God
Usually when a bush or plant burns, the flames spread over the field, as here, and the grass catches fire, burns up and is destroyed. However, the bush Moses saw was burning in a different way. Although it was on fire, the flames did not destroy it. Moses was amazed by this unusual sight. God's presence is often symbolized by fire, which serves as a reminder of his power and holiness.

Moses's sandals
In ancient times, most poor people went barefoot, as sandals were a luxury. They were mainly worn when travelling long distances. Moses would probably have worn sandals woven from papyrus, palm leaves and grass, like the Egyptian ones here.

and rescue them. Then take them to the land I promised would be given to Abraham's descendants."

"Who am I, to be able to do all that?" he said, anxiously.

"I will be with you," replied God.

"But the people will ask me who you are," said Moses. "What shall I say?"

"I am who I am," thundered the voice. "Tell them that the God of their fathers has sent you."

"What if they don't believe me?" Moses protested.

"Throw your shepherd's crook to the ground," the voice commanded. Moses did as he was told and watched as the crook became a hissing snake. "Take hold of the snake's tail," the voice ordered. Moses forced himself to reach out his hand and the snake became his crook again.

"Now put your hand inside your shirt," it instructed. Once again, Moses did as he was told. When he pulled his hand out, he was horrified to see that his skin was covered with sores. Quickly, he thrust his hand back inside his shirt, and on drawing it out found the skin healed.

While Moses was still marvelling at these miracles, the voice spoke again. "If the people don't believe these signs, take some water from the river Nile and sprinkle it on the ground. The drops will turn into blood."

Yet Moses still had one worry – he hated speaking in public. "Take Aaron, your brother," He commanded. "He can act as your spokesperson while you show the people the signs I have sent you. Now go, and remember that I will be with you."

With a heart full of fear, Moses came down from the mountain to prepare himself for the seemingly impossible task that lay ahead.

Holy ground

This detail from a mosaic in San Vitale Church in Italy, shows Moses removing his sandals. God asked him to do so as a sign of respect, because he was walking on holy ground. In the Middle East at this time it was customary to perform religious ceremonies barefoot. This helped to keep holy places free from dirt. Moses's meeting with God took place on Mount Sinai, also called Mount Horeb. This is believed to be the mountain known today as Jebel Musa, which means Mountain of Moses.

⋆ ABOUT THE STORY ⋆

Although Moses was brought up at the Egyptian court, he is concerned about his people, the Israelites. He kills an Egyptian man when he sees him attacking an Israelite slave. Because of this, he has to flee from Egypt. After living as a shepherd, Moses is visited by God, who calls upon him to go to Pharaoh and rescue the Israelites from slavery. At first, Moses hesitates, but he is persuaded by God's miracles.

Moses Warns Pharaoh

WHEN Moses told his father-in-law what God had instructed him to do, Jethro gave him his blessing, saying that he shouldn't delay in doing the Lord's work but leave at once. So Moses, his wife Zipporah and their sons packed up all their belongings, said goodbye to the comfort and safety of their home, and headed off towards the possible dangers lying in wait in Egypt.

God had already tried to reassure Moses by telling him that the Egyptians who wanted to kill him were now dead. But Moses was still very anxious about God's command. He grew more nervous when the Lord again appeared to him during the journey. He warned Moses that even if he performed all the miracles, Pharaoh still might not believe that he was sent by God. "Tell Pharaoh that the people of Israel are as dear to me as a first-born child," He commanded Moses. "You must warn Pharaoh that if he doesn't free my people, I will wreak a terrible vengeance."

God had told Moses' brother, Aaron, to meet Moses along the way, and the two men carefully discussed every detail of all they had to say and do. How important it was that they convinced Pharaoh! The freedom of the whole Hebrew race was resting on their shoulders, and if they failed, the Egyptian people would suffer too.

The first thing they did on reaching Egypt was to gather together the leaders of all the Israelite communities. Aaron gave a rousing speech, inspiring them with great hope and courage. And when they saw that Moses had the power to perform miracles they gasped and fell on their knees, praising God. The people realized that the Lord was truly

> ❝ *But Pharaoh said 'Who is the Lord that I should heed his voice and let Israel go?'* ❞

The slaves suffer
Moses and Aaron had hoped to improve the lives of the Israelite slaves. However, Pharaoh was so angry at their request for freedom that he ordered the slave-masters to treat the slaves even more harshly than before. He did not care that it was the will of God that they be freed.

SEVERAL TIMES GOD IS SAID TO HAVE HARDENED PHARAOH'S HEART AND MADE HIM OBSTINATE, BUT THIS WAS NOT DONE AGAINST PHARAOH'S WILL. GOD JUST LET PHARAOH HAVE WHAT HE WANTED. ∾

Symbol of life
This Egyptian symbol of life is called the *ankh*. Only kings, queens and gods were allowed to carry it. It was believed that whoever was holding the ankh had the power to give life, or take it away from others. This ankh is decorated with a dog-headed sceptre, which symbolizes power.

with them; He had answered their prayers and sent Moses to deliver them out of the cruel hands of the Egyptians. They were eager to follow him and do whatever he said.

After this success, Moses and Aaron felt more confident. But the most difficult task was yet to come. They had to get an audience with Pharaoh, and then tell the king of Egypt that what he was doing to the Israelites was wrong.

As they had expected, Pharaoh was outraged when the two Hebrew men dared to criticize him. "Who is this God of yours that you say has sent you?" he roared. "And even if he exists, why should I listen to him?"

"Our God has commanded all the Israelite people to travel into the desert and make a sacrifice of thanks to Him," Moses and Aaron protested. "If we don't obey, He'll strike out at everyone with His anger."

"I know nothing about your God," spat Pharaoh in a rage, "and I certainly will not set the Israelites free!" He turned to his royal guard. "Get these two out of here," he yelled. "Since they put these ridiculous ideas into the Israelites' heads, it's all the slaves can think about. Their work is getting slower and slower." As the soldiers dragged Moses and Aaron away, Pharaoh furiously commanded, "Tell all the slave-masters to stop giving the Hebrews straw to make their bricks. They'll have to go out into the fields and find straw for themselves. And if they make any fewer bricks than before, there'll be serious trouble!"

Of course, it was impossible for the Israelites to find their own straw and still make as many bricks as before. When Moses and Aaron saw how savagely the Egyptians beat them for failing at their work, they felt as if it was all their fault. "Why ever did you send me, Lord?" Moses cried. "Ever since we spoke to Pharaoh, the people have suffered more, not less."

"Reassure the people that their God has not forgotten them," the Lord told Moses. "If I have to, I will force Pharaoh to let them go. Try once more to talk to him, and if he still refuses to obey me, wait and see what I will do. In the end, Pharaoh will be glad to see them go!"

Moses and Aaron did as God commanded. "I've told you before, I don't believe a word you say," Pharaoh scoffed. "If a god really had sent you, you'd be able to perform miracles." At this, Moses threw his crook on the ground and it became a snake. But Pharaoh wasn't impressed. He had many magicians in his court and they too threw down staffs which turned into snakes. Even though Moses' snake swallowed all the magicians' snakes, Pharaoh simply sneered. Moses was just as far away from rescuing the Israelites as ever.

A meeting with Pharaoh
This engraving shows Moses changing his staff to a snake. But Pharaoh has seen magicians do this, so he is not impressed, and has no faith in God.

⊷ **ABOUT THE STORY** ⊷

Moses is very aware that God has made him, and his brother Aaron, responsible for the freedom of the Israelite people. Pharaoh, though, remains arrogant and refuses to believe in God. Instead of freeing the Israelites as is God's will, he makes them suffer even more. The Israelites too suffer from a lack of faith, and turn against Moses. But God reassures Moses, and he approaches Pharaoh again, but to no avail.

Plagues of Egypt

GOD saw that even a miracle wouldn't convince Pharaoh to let the Israelites go, and He knew that Pharaoh's heart was as hard as stone. The Lord told Moses and Aaron to go to the river Nile the following morning and wait for Pharaoh. As soon as Pharaoh was near, Moses drew himself up. "We were sent to you by God and you have failed to recognize Him!" Aaron thundered. "You have disobeyed His commands and refused to let the Hebrew people go. Now prepare to see how powerful the God of the Israelites really is." Moses lashed his crook down on the waters. Instantly, the river began to run red with blood. Each drop of water in every pool, lake, canal, stream and river throughout Egypt turned to blood. As the fish choked and died, the stench of rotting was everywhere, and for seven days there was no fresh water.

But Pharaoh remained unmoved. His magicians showed him that they could make water turn red through trickery, and Pharaoh ignored what Moses and Aaron had done. So God commanded the two men to strike the Nile with the sacred crook again. Straight away the bloody waters began to bubble as frogs started to hop out onto the banks. First there were hundreds, then thousands. Soon every Egyptian house was filled with leaping, croaking creatures. The Egyptians couldn't cook, eat or sleep without frogs jumping on them. Even the royal palace was overrun with the slimy creatures. Pharaoh called Moses and Aaron to him. "Tell your God to take away the frogs and I will let the Israelites go." The rejoicing men prayed to the Lord and the frogs immediately began to die. But the cheating Pharaoh told Moses that he had changed his mind, and the Israelites had to stay where they were.

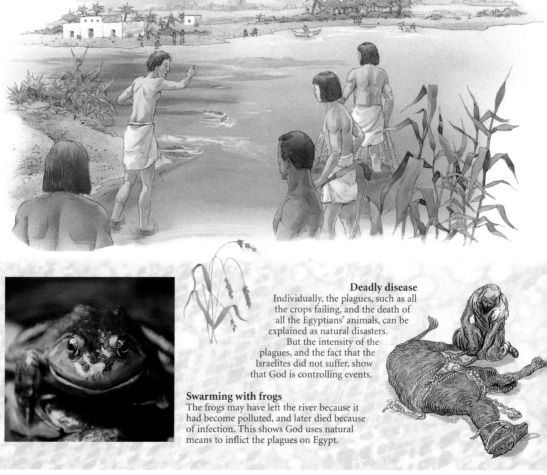

Deadly disease
Individually, the plagues, such as all the crops failing, and the death of all the Egyptians' animals, can be explained as natural disasters. But the intensity of the plagues, and the fact that the Israelites did not suffer, show that God is controlling events.

Swarming with frogs
The frogs may have left the river because it had become polluted, and later died because of infection. This shows God uses natural means to inflict the plagues on Egypt.

At this, God commanded the two men to hit the earth with Moses' crook. Each tiny speck of dust turned into a squirming maggot – it looked as if the whole of the ground was moving! Maggots wriggled over every man, woman and animal, and as fast as they brushed them off, they found more crawling over their skin.

Then God sent a plague of flies. "But you'll see that there will be no insects where the Israelites live," they told Pharaoh. Almost before they had finished speaking, huge humming clouds of flies came swarming through the air, settling in their millions on the Egyptian households without going anywhere near a single Israelite.

The very next day, the Egyptian farmers found all their animals struck down with a mysterious disease. They could do nothing but watch as every cow, sheep and camel died, while the animals belonging to the Israelites remained healthy. But this only infuriated Pharaoh, and made him determined not to give in to the Israelites.

God told Moses to take two handfuls of soot and scatter it into the wind. The breeze carried it far and wide, and people found their skin breaking out into hideous sores. Then the two men sent a hailstorm so fierce that anything caught outside would die. The Lord hurled down bolts of thunder and flashes of lightning, and pelted the Egyptians with piercing hailstones. Pharaoh said that the Israelites could leave, and the sun broke through the clouds.

But the sunshine did not last long. Pharaoh told Moses and Aaron that he had once more lied to them, and the skies darkened again the very same day. A strange rustling noise blew towards Egypt on the wind, and the people realized that it was the wings of swarms of locusts. Millions of the insects fell on the earth like a black carpet, stripping the soil bare by devouring every remaining leaf and shoot. Utter destruction faced the whole country and Pharaoh once again tried to compromise with Moses and Aaron. He promised to let all the male Israelites go free - but it wasn't enough. Moses raised his hand and Egypt

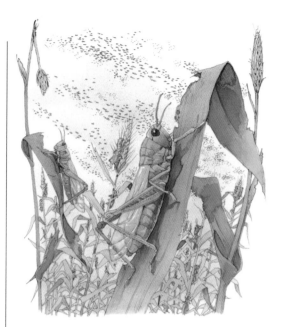

66 *And the locusts came up over the whole land of Egypt.* **99**

suddenly found itself in darkness. God had blotted out the Sun, leaving the Egyptians in inky blackness.

After three days, Pharaoh could take it no longer. "Go!" he ordered Moses and Aaron. "And take every last Israelite with you! But I say this on one condition – they have to leave all their flocks and herds behind."

"You know we cannot agree to that," Moses answered.

Pharaoh gripped the arms of his throne so hard that his knuckles turned white. "Then the Israelites will remain as slaves in Egypt forever," he hissed, "and if you ever dare to enter my presence again, you will be put to death."

❧ ABOUT THE STORY ❧

God brings about the plagues to show His supreme power. The Egyptians worshipped many gods of their own. By destroying the symbols of the Egyptian gods, God shows He is more powerful. However, despite the plagues, Pharaoh refuses to obey God's will.

In the dark
Some people say that the darkness was caused by an eclipse, but this could not last three days. It is more likely that earth washed down by the storms dried into dust. This was whirled up into a dust-storm by a strong wind that stopped the sun getting through.

The Passover

How arrogant Pharaoh was! The Egyptians traditionally believed that their Pharaoh was a god, and he expected to be treated as one. He certainly wasn't used to people telling him his laws were wrong and defying his orders. No matter how much suffering was inflicted on his people, Pharaoh couldn't bring himself to acknowledge the existence of the Hebrew God - let alone admit that the Lord was far mightier than he was. Moses and Aaron had correctly predicted plagues nine times, and even Pharaoh's counsellors had been convinced. "Don't you understand that Egypt is ruined?" they had pleaded in frustration with Pharaoh. "You must let the Israelites go to worship their God!" But Pharaoh shut himself away in his palace, closing his eyes to his people's wretchedness and blocking his ears to their cries.

After Pharaoh's final threat, God again spoke to Moses. "I will bring one last plague upon Pharaoh and his country. It will be so terrible that he will end up begging the Israelites to leave Egypt. Tonight, all first-born children will die – from the family of Pharaoh himself to the very poorest household. I will even kill first-born animals. Through the whole of Egypt, only the Israelites will be spared from grief. This is what you are to tell them to do. Each Hebrew household must kill a male lamb at sunset and sprinkle some of its blood around the front door. The lamb is then to be roasted and eaten with bitter herbs and flat bread, and any left overs must be burnt. The people must hurry and go to bed early. Tell them to lock themselves inside their houses and, whatever happens, not

 For I will pass through the land of Egypt and I will smite all the first born. **"**

Holy book
This is an illuminated page of a Jewish book called the Haggadah. Parts of the book are read or recited during the Passover feast. The Haggadah contains stories, poems and rituals that are significant to the Jewish religion, including sections of the Torah. The Torah is the name given to the first five books of the Old Testament in the Bible, the most important part of Jewish scriptures.

Ruling pharaoh
Rameses II is believed to have been the ruling Pharaoh at the time of the Passover. This picture shows part of a colossal statue of him on a huge temple cut into the rocks at Abu Simbel in Nubia. When the Aswan Dam was built in the 1960s, the whole temple had to be taken down and moved to a new location so it would not be flooded.

to go outside until morning. For at midnight I will pass over the whole land and slay the first-born child in every household that isn't marked with blood. This night will be known as the Passover and you must remember it each year as a holy festival." With dread and fear in his heart, Moses hastened to call the Israelite leaders together and give them God's instructions.

The next day, it wasn't the sun that woke the land of Egypt – it was the sound of screaming. As each family found their beloved first-born child lying dead in their bed, they sent up heartbroken cries that tore the air, until it seemed as if the whole of Egypt was wailing. Somebody had died in every household from the royal palace to the darkest prison – except for the homes of the Israelites.

Even before the dawn had fully broken, Moses and Aaron were summoned to see Pharaoh. They found the once-proud king completely broken by grief. His eyes were swollen with weeping, his face wrenched into haggard lines of pain, and his shoulders slumped with the heaviness of utter misery. "Leave my land," he groaned in agony, barely able to speak. "Take whatever you want and go." Moses and Aaron knew that, this time, Pharaoh's words came from the heart. Without further hesitation, they turned to go and spread the good news to the Israelites. But the thin crackle of Pharaoh's voice stopped them. "Ask the Lord to bless me, too," he whispered.

And so it was that, after 430 years of slavery, the Israelites finally left Egypt. The Egyptians hurried them away with presents of gold, silver, fine materials and other expensive gifts. And led by Moses, over six hundred thousand men, women and children set off on foot on their long journey into the wilderness.

Passover today

Today, Jewish families hold a feast to remember the Passover as God commanded. They gather together to eat specially prepared food that symbolizes the sufferings of the Israelites in Egypt. The meal begins after dark and before any food is eaten, the youngest child asks the oldest family member to retell the story of the Passover.

Hyssop

Hyssop, the name given to the leaves of the marjoram plant, was a common symbol of purity. Moses told the Israelites to use a bunch of hyssop to smear the lamb's blood around their doors on the night of the Passover.

❖ ABOUT THE STORY ❖

Although many people, even in Pharaoh's household, are convinced about the existence of God, Pharaoh remains arrogant. It is only when God sends the final plague that Pharaoh realises Moses is right. Pharaoh abandons his pride, releases the Israelites and asks for God's blessing. The Passover is so called because God 'passed over' the houses of the Israelites, meaning He spared them from the plague.

Crossing the Red Sea

THE minute the Israelites had gone, Pharaoh regretted his decision. The rate at which grand buildings and beautiful monuments were going up slowed right down as soon as the slave labour departed. Each time Pharaoh caught sight of a deserted building site he was reminded that he had lost some of his power. He imagined his former slaves travelling further out of his grasp, and he became more and more resentful. After several days of being tormented by his own thoughts, Pharaoh finally called a meeting of his counsellors. "We should never have let the Hebrews go!" he raged. "I want as many troops as possible sent after them. You must find the Israelites and bring them back!"

Meanwhile, the Israelites were making good progress through the desert, helped by God. By day a whirling column of cloud guided them and by night a blazing pillar of flame lit the way.

The Israelites were at first puzzled when they looked back and saw a cloud of dust coming towards them at top speed. Then, as they recognized the glints of golden armour in the sun, and heard the noise of thundering hooves, panic spread among them. "Did you bring us here to die!" they shrieked at Moses. "It would have been better to live in slavery under the Egyptians than die here!"

"Have faith in the Lord who brought you here," he said.

Moses fell silent, believing wholeheartedly that God would answer his prayer. He listened as the people's cries changed from terror to wonderment. The column of cloud had moved behind them, smothering the Egyptians in darkness so they could not see where they were going.

> 66 *The Lord drove the sea back and made the sea dry land and the waters were divided.* 99

Then God told Moses to stretch out his hand towards the Red Sea ahead of them. At once, a mighty gale blew up from the east. Moses commanded the Israelites to press forward. Though no one dared protest to Moses a second time, each person knew that they were heading straight for the ocean. Surely they would all be drowned! But when they drew nearer, the Israelites could hardly believe their eyes. The wind had driven back the waters, leaving a path of dry land through the waves. They walked all night long, with walls of water towering over them on either side.

In the morning, when every last Israelite had crossed safely, Moses turned and looked back. The Egyptians had tried to follow them across the ocean floor, but the wheels of their chariots had sunk into the mud, along with their horses and the soldiers. In the chaos, they had become very afraid. "Run! Run! God must truly be with the Israelites!" some of them were yelling.

Moses stretched out his hand once more. Instantly, the walls of water came roaring down on the Egyptians. When the tide at last settled, it was as if the desperate men and all their equipment had never been there.

Weeping with relief and overcome with gratitude, the Hebrew people threw themselves to the ground, giving thanks to God. Then Moses' sister Miriam took up her tambourine to sing God's praises – after over 400 years the Israelites were on their way to their Promised Land.

Crossing the Red Sea

No one knows exactly where Moses crossed the Red Sea. We know the Israelites went from Rameses to Succoth. After this, their route, in blue, may have crossed the Reed Sea. The green route shows they may have crossed the Bitter Lake. Finally, the mauve route shows a journey along the Great Sea.

Chariots

The Egyptians' horse-drawn chariots would have been very light, made mainly of wood and leather, with a few bronze or iron fittings. The chariots were mostly open at the back, and had hooks or racks on the outside to hold weapons.

❖ ABOUT THE STORY ❖

By parting the waters of the Red Sea for them, God shows the Israelites that He intends to free them from slavery. Under the watchful gaze of God's chosen leader Moses, He guides them safely out of Egypt and sets them on the long journey towards the Promised Land.

Poetry in the Old Testament

Poetry and song played an important part in people's lives at the time of the Old Testament. Poetry would have been recited aloud and would generally have been accompanied by music, so the difference between a poem and a song was not as marked as it is for us today. Songs were sung by all kinds of people, for all kinds of reasons and at many different times.

People who worked at particular occupations probably had special songs, for example, the 'Song of the Well' (Numbers 21:17–18) might have been sung by people drawing water from a well, or by people actually digging the well. Another mention of songs connected to occupations occurs in Isaiah 16:10, where there is a description of singing in the vineyards while making wine.

Songs were also used on special occasions, such as when people arrived or departed. When Jacob tries to steal away from Laban's house without his uncle's knowledge, Laban is angry that he was not given the opportunity to send his nephew away with songs and music, as was the custom (Genesis 31:27). Songs of celebration were sung at weddings, and laments were sung for the dead.

Songs were not usually heard as voices alone; they were nearly always accompanied by instruments. The main purpose of

instruments in the Old Testament appears to be to accompany songs. The Hebrew language is very rhythmic so even passages of the Old Testament which are not really poetry can sound like poems, especially if they are part of someone's speech.

The poetry in the Old Testament does not rhyme, but it does use other devices common to all poetry, such as similes (where something is likened to something else, such as 'they went down into the depths like a stone'), metaphors (where something is described as if it were something else, 'the earth swallowed them')

Miriam's song

After the Israelites have crossed the Red Sea, Moses' sister Miriam, raises a tambourine and begins to dance. All the other women join her in the dance, and Miriam sings a song of praise to God. The words of her song (on the opposite page) tell of the Israelites' escape from Egypt and the crossing of the Red Sea.

THIS SHOWS AN ILLUMINATED, OR ORNATELY DECORATED, SONG. THIS OFTEN HAPPENED WITH RELIGIOUS SONGS.

and alliteration (where several words close to each other begin with the same letter, like 'your people pass' where the 'p' is repeated).

The use of imagery (visually descriptive language) is abundant in the poetry of the Old Testament. It draws on the universe, including the stars, the Moon and the Sun, on nature, including the seasons, the weather and the sea, and on the activities of the countryside, such as shepherding, harvest time and wine making. However, the inspiration behind all the songs and poetry in the Old Testament is the love and worship of God.

❖ THE SONG OF MIRIAM ❖

I will sing to the Lord for He has triumphed gloriously;
the horse and his rider He has thrown into the sea.
The Lord is my strength and my song,
and He has become my salvation;
this is my God, and I will praise Him,
my father's God and I will exalt Him.
The Lord is a man of war;
the Lord is His name.

Pharaoh's chariots and his host He cast into the sea;
and his picked officers are sunk in the Red Sea.
The floods covered them;
they went down into the depths like a stone.
Thy right hand, O Lord, glorious in power,
thy right hand, O Lord, shatters the enemy.
In the greatness of thy majesty thou overthrowest thy adversaries;
thou sendest forth thy fury, it consumes them like stubble.
At the blast of thy nostrils the waters piled up,
the floods stood up in a heap;
the deeps congealed in the heart of the sea.
The enemy said, "I will pursue, I will overtake,
I will divide the spoil; my desire shall have its fill of them.
I will draw my sword, my hand shall destroy them."
Thou didst blow with thy wind, the sea covered them;
they sank as lead in the mighty waters.

Who is like thee, O Lord, among the gods?
Who is like thee – majestic in holiness, terrible in glorious deeds, doing wonders?
Thou didst stretch out your right hand, the earth swallowed them.

Thou hast led in thy steadfast love the people whom thou hast redeemed,
thou hast guided them by thy strength to thy holy abode.
The peoples have heard, they tremble;
pangs have seized on the inhabitants of Philistia.
The chiefs of Edom will be terrified,
the leaders of Moab will be seized with trembling,
the people of Canaan will melt away;
terror and dread will fall upon them.
By the power of your arm they will be as still as a stone,
until your people pass by, O Lord,
until the people you bought pass by.
You will bring them in and plant them
on the mountain of your inheritance,
the place, O Lord, you made for your dwelling,
the sanctuary, O Lord, your hands established.
The Lord will reign for ever and ever.

Judaism and the Old Testament

The books of the Old Testament form the Scriptures, or sacred writings, of the Jewish people. They tell the story of their ancestors, the Israelites, or Hebrews. To Jews, the most important part of the Old Testament is the first five books: Genesis, Exodus, Leviticus, Numbers and Deuteronomy. These five books are called the Torah, which means 'teaching'. The Torah contains stories, poetry, prayers and laws which teach people about God, and how they can live their lives according to His will. Of particular importance are God's covenant with Abraham, and the laws God reveals to His people through Moses.

Jewish people go to worship in the synagogue on the Sabbath, which, for them, is Saturday. Parts of the Torah are read aloud each Sabbath, by a rabbi or by another member of the congregation. After a year, the whole Torah has been read and a celebration called Simcha Torah takes place. People hold the scrolls on which the Torah is written high above their heads, and dance in a procession around the synagogue. At the next reading, the Torah is begun all over again.

Many Jewish festivals commemorate events from the Bible. For example, the Festival of the Passover, which is celebrated with a special meal, reminds Jews of how God sent a plague to kill all first-born babies, except those in the homes of the Israelites, which He 'passed over'. The festival Yom Kippur is a solemn day of fasting and prayer. In the Bible, a goat was sent into the wilderness as a sacrifice. During the festival of Succoth, also known as the Feast of Tabernacles, people camp in tents to remember the Israelites' years of wandering in the wilderness.

The Star of David
This is used as a Jewish and Israeli symbol. David was an Israelite king who captured Jerusalem and made it his capital city.

Patriarch's family tree
In the Bible, Abraham is the first great leader of the Israelites. At his death, the leadership passes to his son, Isaac, to Isaac's son, Jacob and finally to Joseph. Abraham, Isaac, Jacob and Joseph are known as the Patriarchs, meaning the male heads of a family. Jacob's other sons were also thought of as Patriarchs, and were the forefathers of the twelve tribes of Israel.

ABRAHAM   SARAH

ISAAC   REBEKAH

ESAU   JACOB   LEAH   RACHEL   ZILPAH   BILHAH

REUBEN   SIMEON   LEVI   JUDAH   ISAACHAR   ZEBULUN   DINAH   JOSEPH   BENJAMIN   GAD   ASHER   DAN   NAPHTALI

TIMELINE 2200BC TO 1400BC

Abraham, who was to become the first father of the Israelites, was born.

ANIMALS PREPARED FOR SACRIFICE

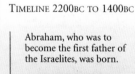

ISAAC MEETS REBEKAH

Abraham's sons, Ishmael and Isaac, are born.

Jacob, father of the twelve tribes of Israel, is born.

On his way to Haran Jacob sees a vision, sent by God, of a stairway to heaven, and God's covenant is renewed with Jacob.

Jacob gets married and his sons, including Joseph, are born.

Joseph is sold to traders and taken to Egypt, where he finds favour with Pharaoh.

Jacob and his family move to Egypt to live with Joseph.

Over the years the Israelites increase in number. Later pharaohs make them slaves to protect their power.

JACOB AND ESAU ARE REUNITED

2200BC   2100BC   2000BC   1900BC   180

The Origins of the Bible

The words of the earliest books of the Old Testament were passed down by word of mouth before they were written down in Hebrew. The first five books may have been written as early as 1400BC, and the latest books not until around 450BC. It took almost a thousand years for the whole Old Testament to be written down.

The books of the Bible were written by many different authors, but not all can be identified. Some may have had several authors, or may have been altered by other people. The first five books of the Bible are traditionally believed to have been written by Moses and are sometimes called The Five Books of Moses. There are passages which he could not have written, such as the account of his death.

The Old Testament in most Christian Bibles is divided into four sections: the Pentateuch (the first five books); the Historical Books (the following 12); Poetry and Wisdom (the next five) and Prophets (the last 17). The books in the Jewish Bible are arranged differently, putting the five books of the Pentateuch, what the Jews call the law, or Torah, first. This is followed by the books of Joshua and Judges, both books of Samuel and Kings, Isaiah, Jeremiah and Ezekiel with the minor prophets. The Jewish people call this section the Naviim. Finally come the Writings, the Kethubim, which includes the remainder of the books, including Psalms, Proverbs, and the books of Ruth and Daniel.

The Jewish Talmud
This contains the Mishnah, the oral law of the Jews.

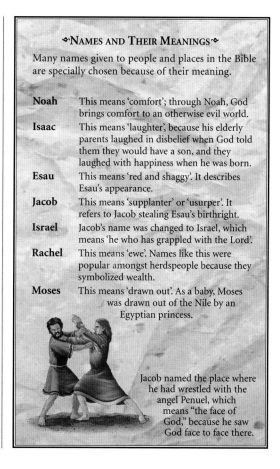

⟡ NAMES AND THEIR MEANINGS ⟡

Many names given to people and places in the Bible are specially chosen because of their meaning.

Noah	This means 'comfort'; through Noah, God brings comfort to an otherwise evil world.
Isaac	This means 'laughter', because his elderly parents laughed in disbelief when God told them they would have a son, and they laughed with happiness when he was born.
Esau	This means 'red and shaggy'. It describes Esau's appearance.
Jacob	This means 'supplanter' or 'usurper'. It refers to Jacob stealing Esau's birthright.
Israel	Jacob's name was changed to Israel, which means 'he who has grappled with the Lord'.
Rachel	This means 'ewe'. Names like this were popular amongst herdspeople because they symbolized wealth.
Moses	This means 'drawn out'. As a baby, Moses was drawn out of the Nile by an Egyptian princess.

Jacob named the place where he had wrestled with the angel Penuel, which means "the face of God," because he saw God face to face there.

THE PYRAMIDS WOULD HAVE LOOMED OVER THE ISRAELITES AS THEY WORKED FOR PHARAOH

THE EGYPTIANS MAKE LIFE VERY HARD FOR THE ISRAELITES

1700BC

1600BC

Moses is born, and is rescued from the Nile by an Egyptian princess.

Moses kills an Egyptian, and flees to exile in a distant land called Midian.

Moses sees the burning bush, and hears God's command to return to Egypt and free the Israelites.

After over 400 years as slaves, Moses leads the Israelites out of Egypt to the Promised Land.

MOSES COMMANDS THE RED SEA

1500BC

1400BC

LOOK OVER
JORDAN

*The Israelites are at first homeless wanderers in the
desert. With God's help, and under the guidance of
their leader, Moses, they overcome many setbacks
and reach their Promised Land. Their first leader,
Joshua, is strong and wise, but when he dies, and as
the people settle down, their faith in God wanes.
They are punished by having to face more
years of wandering.*

Introduction

THIS chapter covers the part of the Old Testament from halfway through Exodus to the end of Ruth. At the beginning of this section, the Israelites are a group of homeless wanderers in the desert, and by the end they have settled in the Promised Land. This section tells of their struggles along the way and charts the rises and falls of their faith in God.

The first story, "Manna from Heaven", describes the early years in the wilderness, when God provides manna and quails to feed his starving people. In "The First Battle", the Israelites experience their first victory in their campaign to take over the Promised Land. When they arrive at Mount Sinai, God tells Moses the laws by which he wants his people to live their lives, including the most important laws known as the Ten Commandments. According to God's instructions, a holy tent called a tabernacle is built. This is to be God's home on earth, a visible sign that He is living among His people. The Israelites carry it with them until they settle in Canaan and set it up permanently.

On leaving Mount Sinai, another period of wandering begins and the Israelites grow weary of the months of hardship. When they finally reach the borders of Canaan, they are too afraid to obey God's order to attack the local people. God is so angry at their disobedience, he punishes them by sentencing them to a further 40 years of wandering. As the years go by, the Israelites who had fled from Egypt grow older and die, and a new generation grows up. These young people have never known anything but the struggles of the travelling life and are better adapted than their parents were. They fight battle after battle with the local people, trying to drive them from their homes and take over their lands.

A long journey
The Exodus began in the fertile Nile valley, which must have made the hardships of the wilderness even harder to take.

Calm before the storm
Before the Israelites invaded the Promised Land, they camped here, at the Oasis of Jericho, near Gilgal, to rest.

The story "Death of Moses" tells of the great leader's last days. Although Moses does not enter the Promised Land, he climbs to the top of Mount Nebo to see with his own eyes the land his people will inherit. Before he dies, he hands over the leadership to his successor, Joshua. The following stories describe Joshua's impressive achievements as leader, from crossing the mighty River Jordan to storming the great city of Jericho. He goes on to capture the town of Ai, and he is tricked into making a treaty with the people of Gibeon. In the story "The Longest Day", he manages to overcome five of the region's kings in one long battle. At last, after many victories and much bloodshed, the Israelites finally take over the land of Canaan. The Promised Land is divided between the tribes, and the Israelites settle down to a life of farming and home-making.

After the death of Joshua, no single leader takes over. Instead, the Israelites are ruled by a succession of Judges, including Deborah, Gideon, Jephthah and Samson. Before the Judges begin to rule, there has been peace for many years. But as time goes by, people start to forget the struggles of the past and the hard-won victories. Instead of continuing to wage war on their enemies, as God had ordered, they begin to live alongside them as neighbours. Despite the Judges' warnings, they even start to worship the Canaanite gods. Time after time, God punishes his people by letting them fall into the hands of foreign rulers. After a period of suffering, they beg for forgiveness, and God appoints a Judge to save them. But as soon as the Judge dies, they slip back into their sinful ways.

Pilgrims to Jerusalem
A trip to the holy city of Jerusalem, first colonized by the Israelites at the time of Joshua, has been a goal for religious pilgrims like these for hundreds of years.

In contrast to all the discord in the stories of the Judges, the book ends with the story of Ruth – a gentle tale that deals with family life and everyday issues. Although it relates to the same period as the Judges, its subject matter is very different. The story ends with the birth of Ruth's baby, who will grow up to become the grandfather of the greatest king of Israel, David.

Throughout this section, the Israelites' faith in God ebbs and flows. After the Exodus from Egypt, their faith is strong and they look forward with excitement to reaching the Promised Land. When thirst and hunger take over, though, their faith weakens until God provides food and water. They go on to win their first victory. God is well aware of the weaknesses of His people, and accepts a great deal of wrongdoing from them. The story of the Golden Calf is another low point, when the people turn from God and start to worship an idol. Their faith is re-established with the building of the tabernacle. Once back on their travels, the Israelites become impatient again and begin to have doubts about Moses as their leader. When they disobey God's instruction to invade Canaan, their punishment is another 40 years of wandering. While a period of strong faith follows the crossing of the Jordan, it ebbs away after Joshua's death. *Look over Jordan* shows the remarkable faith and leadership of Moses, who continually defends his erring people against the wrath of God.

✦ LOOK OVER JORDAN ✦

This section covers the Israelites' time in the wilderness after the Exodus, their entry into the Promised Land and settling down in their new country.

IN THE WILDERNESS
Exodus, Ch. 16 to 18.
Numbers, Ch. 11 to 22.
THE TEN COMMANDMENTS
Exodus, Ch. 19 & 20.
THE DEATH OF MOSES
Deuteronomy, Ch. 31 to 34.
ENTERING THE PROMISED LAND
Joshua, Ch. 1 to 4.
JOSHUA IN CANAAN
Joshua, Ch. 6 to 24.
THE TIME OF THE JUDGES
Judges, Ch. 1 to 17.
RUTH
Ruth, Ch. 1 to 4.

Holy mountain
Mount Sinai, which at the time of the Bible was called Mount Horeb, was already a holy place before God gave Moses the Ten Commandments there. It was where Moses was first spoken to by God from the burning bush, when he was told he was to lead the Israelites from slavery in Egypt. He was told by God to remove his sandals, a common sign of respect still followed in many places of worship today.

Egypt to the Promised Land

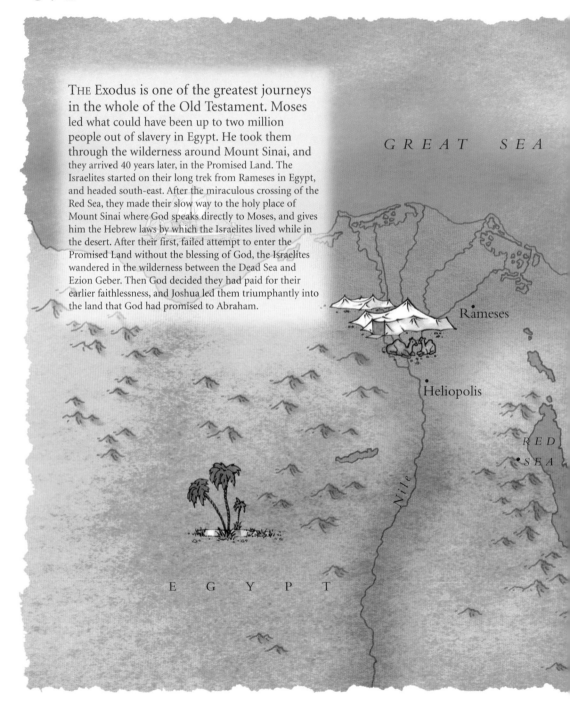

THE Exodus is one of the greatest journeys in the whole of the Old Testament. Moses led what could have been up to two million people out of slavery in Egypt. He took them through the wilderness around Mount Sinai, and they arrived 40 years later, in the Promised Land. The Israelites started on their long trek from Rameses in Egypt, and headed south-east. After the miraculous crossing of the Red Sea, they made their slow way to the holy place of Mount Sinai where God speaks directly to Moses, and gives him the Hebrew laws by which the Israelites lived while in the desert. After their first, failed attempt to enter the Promised Land without the blessing of God, the Israelites wandered in the wilderness between the Dead Sea and Ezion Geber. Then God decided they had paid for their earlier faithlessness, and Joshua led them triumphantly into the land that God had promised to Abraham.

GREAT   SEA

Rameses

Heliopolis

RED
SEA

Nile

E G Y P T

Hazor•

Shechem•

Bethel•
Jericho•

• Gaza

Beersheba

• Ezion Geber

Mt.Sinai

M I D I A N

Manna from Heaven

JUST as God had promised centuries earlier, Abraham's descendants had now become a great people – the Israelite nation. The mighty Egyptian Pharaoh had done everything in his power to crush them but had been defeated, all thanks to the work of the Lord. For the first time in over four centuries, the Israelites were free, but homeless.

Imagine how tough it must have been for the hundreds of thousands of people who found themselves wandering through the Sinai Desert, not knowing where they were going or when they might get there. Mothers nursing their babies, children wailing with tiredness and men weighed down by their family's belongings. Day after day they plodded on together with only the cold, uncomfortable nights and the occasional rest days of the Sabbath to mark out time passing. The weeks seemed to melt together into an endless nightmare of heat, dust and walking . . . heat, dust and walking, and gradually their food began to run out. "We can't keep going like this!" some people moaned.

"We'd rather be back in Egypt," agreed others, feeling terribly hungry. "At least there we weren't starving."

God heard the suffering Israelites and called to Moses. "Reassure the people that I am with them," He said. "I shall make sure they don't go hungry."

Moses and Aaron gathered the famished people in a huge crowd. Aaron lifted his voice so his words of hope could be heard over the constant sound of crying, and the glory of the Lord suddenly came blazing through the clouds. Once again, Moses heard God speaking to him. Aaron announced the message. "Know that the Lord is

with you," he thundered, as the crowd tried to shield themselves from the blinding light. "Today, He will give you meat to eat, and tomorrow, He shall bring you bread!"

In the evening, as dusk fell, flocks of quails appeared in the sky and fluttered down to land around the camp. The starving Israelites dashed eagerly back and forth catching the little birds, then settled down to a feast of roasted

> **❝** *Then the Lord said to Moses, 'Behold, I will rain bread from Heaven for you.'* **❞**

⋄ ABOUT THE STORY ⋄

After weeks of wandering in the desert, the Israelites begin to lose faith in God. God sees their suffering and sends them quails and manna to eat. Although He promises to provide enough food every day, some people doubt Him and stockpile manna. God is disappointed, but He forgives them and continues to provide for them. When the people complain of thirst, God provides water, despite their lack of faith.

The manna appeared for six days and on the morning before the Sabbath, Moses told the people to gather twice as much. "There will be no manna tomorrow," Moses explained, "so we can spend the day worshipping God and resting, as is proper." When the Sabbath dawned, they found that the manna they had kept overnight was just as delicious as before. But once again, there were some who disobeyed. They went out looking for more. When the Lord saw these groups of greedy people, He was very disappointed. "How long will the people ignore my wishes?" He said to Moses. Yet He kept sending the manna day after day, to feed the hungry Israelites.

It wasn't long, however, before the Israelites were again complaining. When they reached Rephidim, they made camp, but there was no water to be found round about.

"If we keep following Moses and Aaron through this wilderness, we'll surely die of thirst," the people gasped angrily. "Tell God to send us water – or else!" they croaked through cracked lips at Moses and Aaron.

When the Lord heard the people's challenge, He was again deeply saddened. But even so, He still didn't desert them. He instructed Moses to strike a rock with his crook. As the rock split apart with an almighty crack, a jet of icy water came gushing through, creating a waterfall from which everyone could quench their thirst.

quail meat. That night, for the first time in weeks and weeks, they slept without the nagging ache of hunger interrupting their dreams.

Next morning, the Hebrews awoke to find strange, round, white flakes covering the ground. At first, they thought it was frost. But on closer inspection, they were amazed to discover that it was a type of bread that tasted of honey. "We'll call it manna," they cried excitedly, "which means bread from the Lord!" They rushed to gather as much as they could, but a stern order from Moses stopped them. "The bread is a gift from God. Take only as much as you need for today," he warned. Some people didn't listen and secretly hoarded manna in their tents. But they soon came to regret it when next day they found that the manna had turned mouldy. They also realized that there was no need to have saved it, for once again, there was fresh manna everywhere.

A flock of quails

A quail is a small, brown, short-tailed bird, like a tiny pheasant. Quails cross the Sinai Peninsula on their migrations between Europe and Africa. They can fly quickly for short periods of time but get tired on longer journeys. When this happens, they fly very slowly and very low making them easy to catch.

Daily bread

During their 40 years in the wilderness, the Israelites relied on the manna for food. The only time it would last overnight was the day before the Sabbath, the only time that God said they should collect more than they could eat in a day. This shows how in control God was, and how reliant the Israelites were on Him.

What is manna?

The word 'manna' means 'What is it?' in Hebrew. In the Bible, manna is described as white, like coriander seeds, and tasting like wafers made with honey. It is not known exactly what this substance is. Some people believe it is a sweet, white substance produced by some desert plants, such as the hammada shrub (see right). However, the regular appearance of the manna on six days out of seven, and the amount of it, point to God carrying out His will by controlling natural events.

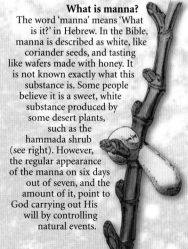

The First Battle

IN every area the Israelites travelled through, they made the local people very nervous. Imagine how intimidating it would be if you lived in a small desert community, and suddenly over 600,000 people looking for a home arrived on your doorstep – people you knew had defeated the mighty Egyptian army! The Israelites must have expected trouble to brew up sooner or later, and it first happened while they were camped at Rephidim. The leader of a local tribe, a man called Amalek, came to meet Moses, challenging the Israelites and declaring war.

Even though there were a lot of Israelites, they weren't at all ready to go out and fight. They had been travelling through the desert for many months and had little remaining strength to attack an enemy. But, unfortunately, they also had no choice. Moses searched through the people and entrusted the courageous young Joshua with the job of somehow turning the weary Israelites into fierce soldiers. "I want you to choose men for our troops and lead them in the battle against Amalek tomorrow," Moses told him. "Don't be afraid! God will be with us."

Next day, Aaron and Hur accompanied Moses to the top of a nearby hill. With beating hearts they watched as Joshua and the Israelites raced out to meet the savage Amalekites and clashed into a seething tangle of blood and determination. Praying to the Lord, Moses took his crook and lifted up his arms to Heaven. Almost straightaway, Aaron and Hur noticed that the Israelites began to have the upper hand. In the midst of all the slashing and stabbing, they could see Amalekites dropping on every side. But it wasn't to last. Moses gradually grew tired, and when he could hold his shaking arms up no longer, the tide suddenly

> ❝ *Joshua mowed down Amalek and his people with the edge of the sword.* ❞

turned. At once it seemed as if there were Amalekites everywhere, killing Israelites whichever way Aaron and Hur looked. In desperation, the two men moved a rock so Moses could sit on it and then took up position on either side, each holding up one of Moses's hands. All day, Aaron and Hur supported Moses without wavering. No matter how cold or weary their muscles became, they kept his arms aloft. And when the Sun finally set, they heard cheering. The Israelites had won their first battle!

Now rumours had already spread of how God had brought the Israelites out of slavery and defeated the Egyptian army. And when news of this most recent victory reached Jethro, Moses's father-in-law, he rushed to be with Moses and join in the celebrations. Jethro knew that his son-in-law had become a great leader, but even so, he was surprised to see how the people relied on Moses to decide everything for them. Jethro found Moses surrounded by huge crowds, each of whom wanted private guidance from God and a solution to their individual problems. The people thought nothing of waiting around all day in the hope of talking to Moses. Jethro was shocked. "This is no good!" he told his son-in-law. "You'll soon be exhausted and the people will never get anything done. The nation has grown too big for you to manage on your own. Divide the people into groups, appointing a good man at the head of each one. Choose leaders you can trust to make their own decisions on everyday matters, while you deal with the more important issues, making sure that God's will is being done." So Moses set wise judges as governors over the people and arranged the Israelites into a strong nation under his command and the leadership of the Lord.

Joshua
This story contains the first mention of Joshua, when Moses chooses him as his assistant. Joshua achieves victory in this first battle. Later, when the Israelites reach the border of Canaan, he and another man called Caleb are the only ones who trust God's judgement and are prepared to invade when God tells them to. Because of this, only Joshua and Caleb of the original Israelites actually enter Canaan. Joshua, like Moses, has patience and humility, and he goes on to succeed Moses as leader of the Israelites, and to fight many successful campaigns in Canaan.

❖ ABOUT THE STORY ❖
Joshua is given the difficult task of organizing the Israelites into an army to fight the Amalekites. During the battle, Moses raises his crook to Heaven in prayer. As long as he holds up his arms, God is on the Israelites' side, but whenever he lowers them, the Amalekites fight back. At sunset, God brings the Israelites victory. Moses then appoints judges to rule over the people. He is now free to deal with the most important matters.

The Ten Commandments

THREE months after they had left Egypt, the Israelites reached a mountain called Mount Sinai and made camp there. This peak, which thrust up towards Heaven itself and towered over the wilderness all around, was believed to be a holy place, and Moses climbed to the top to talk to the Lord alone.

"The people have seen what I did to the Egyptians for their sake, they have seen how I lifted them out of slavery and have been with them ever since, looking after them on their wanderings," said the Lord. "All the Earth is mine – and if the Israelites are true to me and my wishes, I shall make them a holy nation. Tell the people to prepare themselves," God ordered Moses, "for in three days' time, I shall come down to Mount Sinai myself to give you my sacred laws. All the people will be able to see me descend from Heaven, but you must put up barriers around the foot of the mountain so no one sets foot on this holy ground. If anyone disobeys, they will die."

> 66 *And Moses went up to God, and the Lord called to him out of the mountain.* 99

On the morning of the third day, spears of lightning suddenly started to stab through the clouds and giant drumrolls of thunder came rumbling over the people's heads, threatening to bring the heavens tumbling down on top of them. While the Israelites stood gazing upwards like fearful statues, the skies split open with a mighty blast of trumpets and flames came bursting through, consuming the peak in fire. The ground began to tremble and quake as Mount Sinai was turned into a blazing torch, and the people tried to shield themselves from the searing light and burning heat. Above them, the smoke gathered in a heavy cloud, which spread a shadow all around and darkened their faces. And when the thick fog had completely wrapped the mountain top from their view, all eyes turned to the small figures of Moses and Aaron making their way up the slopes. Closer and closer the two men drew to the dense, smouldering cloud, then – without hesitating – they walked straight into it.

God spoke to Moses on the mountain top, telling him all the laws for His people to obey, but ten were the most important:

You must not have any other God except me.

You must not make and worship statues or pictures of anything in the skies, on Earth or in the sea.

Mount Sinai
It is not known exactly where Mount Sinai is, but it is usually identified as a mountain called Jebel Musa (above). God appeared to Moses on Mount Sinai, also known as Mount Horeb, and gave him the Ten Commandments.

Forbidden idols
An idol is an image of a god used as an object of worship. Other tribes and nations commonly made images of their gods and worshipped these. God made it clear to the Israelites that He could never be represented by an object, and that they must never make idols to worship.

God's contract
The laws God gave to Moses would be carved onto two stone tablets as a contract between God and His people.

You must use the Lord's name only in a respectful way.

You must keep the Sabbath, the seventh day of the week, as a holy day of rest and worship.

You must love your father and mother.

You must not kill anyone.

You must not love anyone else's husband or wife.

You must not steal.

You must not lie.

You must not envy other people's possessions.

Meanwhile, at the foot of the mountain, the Israelites were terrified. The smoke pouring out above them was thicker than ever, lightning was whipcracking across the clouds, and above the raging of the thunderstorm could be heard the blaring of almighty trumpets. How relieved the people were when they saw Moses and Aaron coming down from the mountain, and even more amazing, they saw that they were completely unharmed! But they were no less terrified by God's power.

"Don't be so afraid," Moses told them. "God has chosen to appear to you like this so you'll never forget who He is and what He wants of you."

"We'll do everything the Lord says," everyone agreed, and that night Moses wrote down every word God had spoken in a book of laws, which the Israelites would keep, to make sure they remembered God's commands.

Early next morning, Moses set about building a huge altar at the foot of the mountain. All the people gathered in front of it, impatient to find out what God had said. Then the whole crowd listened in silence as Moses read his book of laws aloud. When he had finished, the nation solemnly swore to obey the Lord's words.

YOU SHALL HAVE NO OTHER GODS BEFORE ME.

❈

YOU SHALL NOT MAKE FOR YOURSELF A GRAVEN IMAGE, OR ANY LIKENESS OF ANYTHING THAT IS IN HEAVEN ABOVE OR THAT IS IN THE EARTH BENEATH OR THAT IS IN THE WATER UNDER THE EARTH.

❈

YOU SHALL NOT TAKE THE NAME OF THE LORD YOUR GOD IN VAIN.

❈

REMEMBER THE SABBATH DAY, TO KEEP IT HOLY.

HONOUR YOUR FATHER AND YOUR MOTHER.

❈

YOU SHALL NOT KILL.

❈

YOU SHALL NOT COMMIT ADULTERY.

❈

YOU SHALL NOT STEAL.

❈

YOU SHALL NOT BEAR FALSE WITNESS.

❈

YOU SHALL NOT COVET YOUR NEIGHBOUR'S HOUSE.

❈

❖ ABOUT THE STORY ❖

In this story, God comes down from Heaven to reveal His sacred laws. The people watch in amazement as Moses and Aaron disappear up the mountain to hear the laws. The most important laws are the Ten Commandments – the ten basic rules by which God wants His people to live their lives from now on. The Ten Commandments and the other laws form God's covenant with His people.

The Golden Calf

GOD summoned Moses again to the top of Mount Sinai, this time without Aaron. The Israelites watched nervously as Moses ventured into the darkness of the low, hovering cloud all on his own and disappeared from view. The people were eager for God to talk to them once more, and they kept a vigil at the foot of the mountain. But days passed into weeks without any sign of Moses, and the Israelites started to get impatient. "Where is Moses?" they wondered, tired with waiting. "Whatever is he doing?"

"He can't be talking to God all this time!" some said.

"He's abandoned us!" cried others, angrily.

"Tell us what to do!" the people shouted, surging forwards. "Give us a new god to follow!"

Aaron could see he had a riot on his hands and he was very worried. Thinking quickly, he ordered everyone to take off their gold jewellery and bring it to him. Soon a heap of glittering treasure was piled at his feet, and after melting it down, Aaron made the gold into the likeness of a calf. All the time Aaron was working he could hear the people growing out of control, and he hurried to build an altar too. "Here is your new god," he roared, taking the dull-eyed monster to show them. To his relief the people were delighted, and he declared a feast day to the new god.

At the top of the mountain, God looked down at the Israelite camp and was beside Himself with wrath. "I am furious with these unfaithful people," He thundered. "I will destroy them all!" But Moses begged the Lord to be merciful and managed to convince the Lord to leave punishing the people to him. Moses hurried off down the mountain, carefully carrying two stone tablets on which the Lord had written the laws by His very own hand.

Long before he reached the camp, the angry Moses could hear the wild noise of celebrating. When he finally caught sight of the Israelites he was enraged and slammed the stone tablets to the ground, where they shattered into a million pieces. He seized the idol and burnt it, before grinding it down into razor-sharp grains which he threw into the Israelites' water and made them drink.

"Don't blame me!" cried Aaron. "You know how sinful the people can be! I just collected their gold jewellery, threw it into the fire, and out came this golden calf all by itself!" he lied, daringly.

Apis the Bull
This picture shows the Egyptian god, Apis the Bull. The golden calf made by Aaron may have been modelled on Apis; as the Israelites had lived to Egypt, they knew about bull worship. In Egypt, the bull or calf was a symbol of fertility and strength.

The Levites
The Levites in the story were members of the tribe of Levi, which was Moses's own tribe. They were God's faithful followers, who helped Moses to punish the sinful Israelites. The Levites later became the assistants of the priests of the tabernacle. The picture shows the Levites slaying the Israelites.

When Moses realized that even his own brother's heart had become evil, he stood in the gateway of the camp, blocking anyone from leaving. "Who is on the side of the Lord?" he demanded of the whole nation. "If anyone remains faithful to God, come and stand by me." Straight away, members of Moses's own tribe of Levi pushed their way through to Moses. His eyes were cold, and his voice was stern and unforgiving. "Now put on your swords and slay all the unbelievers," he instructed the Levites. Moses didn't speak again until nearly 3,000 people lay dead. "You have sinned a great sin," he admonished the grief-stricken Israelites. "I will speak to the Lord, to see if I can somehow make up for it."

> *Moses's anger burned hot, and he threw down the tablets and broke them.*

Once more God forgave the Israelites their faithlessness and renewed His covenant with them. He also again wrote the laws by hand on to two stone tablets. "Now go and lead my people to the Promised Land," He told Moses. "I will send my angel to lead the way. But the people have today sinned greatly against me and I shall not forget it."

Swords
The Levites used swords to kill the unfaithful Israelites. The sword is the most frequently mentioned weapon in the Bible. The earliest swords were usually like daggers – straight, double-edged and mainly used for stabbing. By the time of this story the Philistines, the Sea People, had introduced swords with longer blades. These swords were kept in a sheath attached to a belt when they were not in use, and they became more and more popular. Swords have been found all over the Middle East, and many of the sword hilts were very richly decorated, often with symbols of strength, such as lions, to help the wearer in battle.

Gold
Some of the Israelites would have learned metalworking while in Egypt, so they could have helped Aaron make the golden calf. They could also have made the sort of gold jewellery shown here – rings, bracelets and nose-rings – that were worn by women at the time.

⚬ ABOUT THE STORY ⚬
Impatient for Moses to reappear, the Israelites begin to lose faith in God, begging Aaron to find them another god. Aaron makes the golden calf, which he presents to them as their new god. God is furious and ready to destroy them. However, Moses intervenes. Only the faithful Levites stand by Moses and carry out God's punishment. God then forgives his people and renews his covenant with them.

The Tabernacle

MOSES gathered all the people of Israel together and said, "The time is close at hand when we must leave Mount Sinai. However, before we move on to the Promised Land of Canaan, there is one very important thing God has asked of us that we must do. We must build Him a tabernacle – a holy tent where we can meet and pray – and a sacred chest called an ark to keep safe the stone tablets of His law. Anyone who would like to contribute towards these things is welcome to give materials, and any offers of help to do the building will be gratefully received."

The people went back to their tents very excited. What an honour it was to have the responsibility of making these things for the Lord Himself! Everyone began searching through their belongings, all eager to provide their most prized possessions, to make the tabernacle and ark as splendid as possible.

Soon people all over the camp were flooding towards Moses's tent to offer their treasures. They gave their jewellery, ornaments and dishes of silver and bronze; sweet-smelling acacia wood; rich materials, and the very best linen and animal skins. The leaders of the tribes offered precious gem stones and exotic spices and oils. Everyone was so happy to be able to offer things to God!

Moses soon had more treasure than could be used and had to order the Israelites to stop coming with their gifts. Then he appointed expert craftsmen to take charge of the building and the work started. Bit by bit, with great care, the Israelites constructed everything according to the design that God Himself had given Moses on Mount

Sinai. There was to be an outer enclosure with the tabernacle inside, housing the ark itself. They also needed holy robes for Aaron, whom God had chosen as the High Priest, and for his sons, the priests who would serve the Lord inside the tabernacle. Everyone did their absolute best, for each person knew that only perfection would do.

Finally, the time came when everything was ready. Moses waited until the first day of the first month, just as God had ordered, and then painstakingly assembled everything. First, Moses set up the tabernacle itself. It had wooden walls, but looked from the outside like a grand tent because it was covered over on three sides from roof to floor. On the outside was strong weatherproof leather.

┈ **ABOUT THE STORY** ┈

The word "tabernacle" comes from the Latin **tabernaculum**, *meaning "tent". The significance of the tabernacle is that it shows God coming to live with His people. He sets up His tent amongst their tents. The tabernacle is a confirmation that God has forgiven His people for their past sins. The Israelites carry it with them on their journey and are reassured to know that God is travelling with them.*

Sacred lamps
The type of seven-armed lamp-stand that Moses set up in the Holy Place is called a "menorah". It had a main stem, with three branches protruding from either side of this. The main stem supported a lampholder, and each branch ended in a flower-shaped lampholder. The whole lamp-stand was made of gold.

Trees in the desert
The ark was made from acacia wood, as the acacia was one of the few trees that would have grown in the desert. Acacia trees still grow in dry parts of the world today.

Moses set the entrance to the tabernacle at the eastern end, through a curtain hanging from five pillars. Then he prepared the inside. All around the ceiling and walls, Moses hung linen curtains in a wonderful blaze of violet, purple and scarlet. Then, just as God had instructed, Moses hung up a curtain called the Veil to divide the tabernacle into two rooms. The innermost room was called the Holy of Holies, and it was here that Moses positioned the Ark of the Covenant. Inside the sacred chest he laid the holy stone tablets on which God had written the Law. Then Moses sealed the lid. Returning back outside the Holy of Holies, Moses then set an altar in front of the Veil. He ordered the priests to keep incense burning there day and night, so that beautiful-smelling smoke would waft up, accompanying their prayers to Heaven. Then Moses set up the second room inside the tabernacle, the Holy Place, with a seven-armed lamp-stand and a table holding 12 sacred loaves, each representing one of the 12 tribes. Going outside the tabernacle, Moses positioned the priests' wash basin, and filled it with water before Aaron and his sons purified themselves with cleansing rituals. Next Moses set up the Altar of Burnt Offering and made the very first of the daily sacrifices that were to take place there. Finally, Moses put up the enclosure wall, to screen everything from view.

When Moses's work was finished, everyone saw a cloud descend over the tabernacle and a light enter the Holy of Holies – so bright that not even Moses could enter there. From that moment onwards, the Israelites only moved off on their travels when God gave the sign by lifting the cloud from the tabernacle.

" The people of Israel had done all the work and Moses blessed them. "

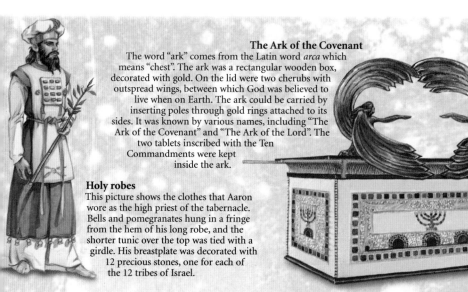

The Ark of the Covenant
The word "ark" comes from the Latin word *arca* which means "chest". The ark was a rectangular wooden box, decorated with gold. On the lid were two cherubs with outspread wings, between which God was believed to live when on Earth. The ark could be carried by inserting poles through gold rings attached to its sides. It was known by various names, including "The Ark of the Covenant" and "The Ark of the Lord". The two tablets inscribed with the Ten Commandments were kept inside the ark.

Holy robes
This picture shows the clothes that Aaron wore as the high priest of the tabernacle. Bells and pomegranates hung in a fringe from the hem of his long robe, and the shorter tunic over the top was tied with a girdle. His breastplate was decorated with 12 precious stones, one for each of the 12 tribes of Israel.

In the Wilderness

AT God's command, the Israelites left Mount Sinai and set out on the final stages of their journey towards Canaan. The Lord had sent so many signs to prove He was with them that the people should have forged ahead with confidence. But as the months of hardship went on, their faith wavered once again. Eventually, even Aaron and Miriam, Moses's own family, became discontented. "Who does Moses think he is? After all, he's not the only one God has appeared to!" The Lord was furious and summoned them to the tabernacle. "How dare you!" He roared. "I may sometimes talk to people in a dream, but Moses sees me as I am and talks to me face to face!" Miriam hung her head in shame and was horrified to see that her hands were covered with the sores of leprosy! She was cast out of the camp at once and left to suffer in the wilderness. Aaron knew that Miriam's only hope was for Moses to ask the Lord for mercy. Aaron begged Moses for help, and a week later Miriam found herself healed.

The miserable rabble eventually reached Canaan. However, several tribes were already settled in the country, people who would fight to defend their homes. So God instructed Moses to send 12 men to spy out the land. After 40 days they returned with wonderful reports of how beautiful and fertile the countryside was. But they also warned that the local tribes would be hard to conquer, and spread fear with stories of giant men and earthquakes. Only Joshua and Caleb trusted that it was the time to attack. But the scared Israelites would not follow them.

> " *The Lord said to Moses, 'How long will this people despise me?'* "

The Lord was furious. "How long will you people go on refusing to believe what I say?" He thundered in the tabernacle. "Because you have turned your backs on the country I promised you, I shall give Canaan to your children instead. You will be condemned to wander for 40 years. You will die homeless, and your bodies will rot here in this wilderness, all except Joshua and Caleb!" At this threat, the Israelites grew desperate. Many of them rushed out early next morning to begin an attack. But without God's blessing the raiders were all killed. And in the camp, all the spies that told lies about Canaan were found dead of a mysterious disease.

With hope of entering the Promised Land now gone, the Israelites felt they had nothing left to lose. They thought Moses had lured them away from their homes for nothing but an empty promise. They no longer cared for his leadership and began to rise up against him. When three ringleaders called Korah, Dathan and Abiram demanded that they and 247 other men should be allowed to be priests, Moses decided he'd had enough. "Do what you like with them, Lord!" he cried. Next day, in front of all those gathered to worship, Moses announced, "These men want to be priests. It is against God's wishes, but I am powerless to stop them." As he finished speaking, there was a resounding crack and the ground swallowed up the would-be-priests, their families and all their belongings.

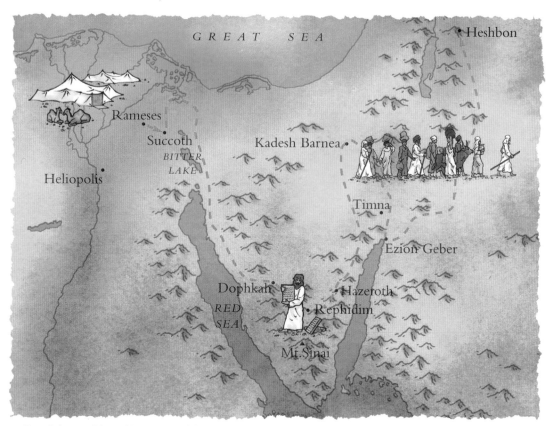

To end the people's uprisings once and for all, the Lord told Moses to instruct each tribe to bring him a rod with their leader's name written on it. When Moses put all the rods in the tabernacle, everyone was amazed to see that Aaron's blossomed with flowers and budded into almonds. Everyone was warned by this sign that Aaron was God's chosen High Priest, and Moses kept the rod as a reminder to everyone not to question God's will again.

The Exodus from Egypt
After the miraculous crossing of the Red Sea, the Israelites still had a long way to go to reach the Promised Land. They first made their way through the wilderness by the Bitter Lake. At Rephidim Moses performed the miracle of getting water from the rock for the Israelites. Then the Israelites camped at Sinai, and Moses received the Ten Commandments from God. At Kadesh Barnea Moses sent out the spies whose false report condemned the Israelites to 40 years wandering in the desert.

A great leader
Despite the Israelites' lack of faith, Moses remains loyal to his people, constantly appealing to God for mercy on their behalf. God himself pays tribute to Moses, telling Miriam and Aaron that He singles out Moses by appearing to him face to face, rather than in a dream or vision (Numbers 12: 6-8). Moses never seeks power for himself, and he is happy to spend his life carrying out God's will.

A sign from God
To try and end the problems of the Israelites, God sent a sign, a blossoming almond branch, to show them all that Aaron was His chosen priest.

> ❧ **ABOUT THE STORY** ❧
>
> *Once again, the Israelites begin to doubt Moses's word. God is furious at their contempt for Moses. When the people refuse to obey Him and invade the cities of Canaan, God's punishment is severe – He sentences them to another 40 years in the wilderness.*

Balak and Balaam

THE years of wandering continued and the Israelites who had disobeyed God began to age and die – Miriam and Aaron among them – just as the Lord had vowed they would. A new generation began to grow up to take their place: tough young people who had never known anything but the hardships of the travelling life, and who were well-trained in fighting skills. As the nation moved around the borders of Canaan, the local tribes came out to defend their homes, and though sometimes the Israelites were forced back by the sheer number of warriors facing them, on many occasions they engaged in fierce battles. With the help of the Lord they began to win victory after victory, slaying the Amorite kings, Sihon of Heshbon and Og of Bashan, and taking their lands. Then they moved on into the plains of Moab.

The Moabites had heard of the destruction of the Amorite peoples, and when they saw the Israelites heading in their own direction, they were very frightened. Balak, the son of the king, decided there was nothing for it but to ask a great prophet called Balaam for help. Hastily, he sent several courtiers off to Balaam with money and an urgent message: "These Israelites we face won their way out of slavery in Egypt. How can we take on such a mighty people and win? Please come to Moab and put a curse on them, so we'll be able to drive them out of our lands."

Balaam listened to the courtiers and told them that he would answer their request for help the following morning, once he'd given it careful consideration. But that night, God appeared to him in his dreams. "Do not grant these people what they ask," He instructed Balaam, "for I have blessed the Israelite nation." Next day, the courtiers' faces fell as Balaam told them of his decision, and their hearts were heavy as they hurried back.

When Balak heard the disappointing news he began to panic, and instantly despatched some of his most highly regarded nobles – laden down with even more riches – to Balaam. "Balak will give you whatever you want," they begged the wise man. "Only please, we beg you, return with us to Moab and put a curse on the Israelites." Balaam felt very sorry for the desperate nobles. However, he still refused to help. "Even if Balak gave me his whole treasure-house, I couldn't go against the word of God," he explained. But during the night God spoke to him once again. "I shall allow you to go with the Moabites after all," He told Balaam, "but do only what I tell you to do."

On rising next morning, the nobles were overjoyed to see Balaam saddling up his donkey. "There's no time to lose!" they cried, full of renewed hope, and hurried him

> **'The word that God puts in my mouth, that must I speak.'**

❧ ABOUT THE STORY ❧

Balaam has the power to bless or curse people. Balak wants Balaam to help the Moabites by putting a curse on the Israelites. However, the Israelites have God's blessing, and Balaam will not go against God's will. Balaam blesses the Israelites instead of cursing them.

Telling the future

Balaam was a diviner, someone who tries to tell the future by magic. Several different forms of divination are mentioned in the Bible. One of these is astrology. Astrologers use the position of the Sun, Moon, planets and some of the star constellations to predict the future. Unlike other forms of divination, astrology was not actually forbidden by Moses's law, but people did look down on it. They did not see it as a proper science in the same way that they did astronomy, which involves studying the movements of the stars and planets.

off at once on the road back to Moab. Unfortunately, before they had gone very far, Balaam's donkey started to play up. She suddenly veered off the road and charged into a field, with the prophet clinging on for dear life. After heaving on the donkey's harness with all his strength, Balaam finally managed to bring her to a halt. As soon as he'd got his breath back, the cross prophet struck the animal with his staff.

After carrying on a little way the donkey suddenly shied again, this time crushing Balaam up against a wall and bruising his leg. The prophet was amazed that his usually peaceful animal was behaving in this way, and once again dismounted to give the donkey a beating.

Imagine Balaam's dismay when, before they had got much further down the road, he felt the donkey's legs begin to buckle beneath him. He managed to jump off just in time before the animal rolled over and lay down. "That's it!" yelled Balaam in anger, and he began to hit the donkey even more savagely than before.

Unbeknown to Balaam and the others, the donkey had taken fright three times because on each occasion the Angel of the Lord had suddenly appeared in front of her, blocking the way. Now, the poor animal was startled once again to find that she could talk! "What have I done?" she brayed at Balaam. "Why are you punishing me? I've never let you down before!"

Balaam was stunned, but he still managed to stutter a reply. "You made a fool of me, you stupid animal!" As soon as the words had left his lips, God lifted the veil that had been clouding the prophet's eyes and he saw the Angel of the Lord standing in front of him, brandishing his sword of flame. Balaam at once fell on his knees before the terrifying angel and prayed to God.

"I have sinned! But I didn't know the donkey was swerving to avoid you," he cried. "Have you come to tell me that I shouldn't be going to Moab? If so, I'll turn back straight away."

"You may go and meet Balak, but be careful to say only what I tell you to say," the angel warned, sternly. Then he vanished, and the baffled men continued on their way.

Balak couldn't wait for the prophet to arrive at his palace, but rushed out to meet him instead. Wasting no time he took Balaam up into the mountains, from where they could see all the tribes of Israel camped below. Three times, on three different peaks, Balak made a sacrifice to the Lord. And each time, on each peak, Balaam heard God telling him not to curse the Israelites, but to bless them. "Israel shall crush the people of Moab," Balaam prophesied. "The descendants of Jacob shall invade your cities and destroy them!" Needless to say, Balak was furious. He banished Balaam straight back home without delay. But everything came to pass just as Balaam had foretold, and the Israelites crushed the peoples of the plains of Moab.

Throwing arrows
Another way that people like Balaam may have tried to tell the future was through the practice of rhabdomancy. To do this, they would have taken a group of sticks or arrows, like those shown here, and thrown them into the air. Depending on how they landed they believed they could tell the future. Divination was widely practised, but it was forbidden by God through Moses.

Balaam's donkey
In ancient times, donkeys were very important especially to poorer people. They were the main form of transport and could travel up to 30km a day.

Death of Moses

WHEN Moses reached the age of 120 years old, the Lord told him it was his time to die. It must have been bitterly disappointing for Moses, after all he had done to free the Israelites from slavery and guide them safely through the wilderness, that he would not live to enter the Promised Land. Yet over and above his sadness, he longed to take his place in Heaven and be with God forever.

Summoning up his dwindling strength, Moses called the nation to gather together so he could speak to them for the last time. Moses looked out over the sea of faces, all anxiously looking up at him, to hear what he had to say. "The Lord has told me that I will not be going over the River Jordan with you," Moses told them.

The massive crowd gasped with one voice. They were deeply shocked. How would they manage to invade Canaan without Moses to tell them how? And whoever would be able to replace God's right-hand man?

Moses motioned for the worried people to calm down, and, when the noise from the worried crowd had died away, he raised his voice once again. "When the time comes to enter the Promised Land, the Lord Himself will go before you, destroying the peoples in your path. He will not let you down or abandon you, but will be with you always, leading you to victory."

Then Moses summoned Joshua to come and stand beside him, where all the people could see him. "Here is your new leader," Moses announced. "God has commanded that you shall follow Joshua!" A cheer rose up from the

❧ ABOUT THE STORY ❧

Moses was already 80 years old when he left Egypt. He has spent the last 40 years of his life wandering in the wilderness. The length of time taken to reach the Promised Land was God's punishment to the Israelites for their lack of faith. Moses's faith has remained strong, despite the fact that he is not to enter the land that was promised to his ancestors. The people's mourning is a tribute to Moses's greatness.

Mourning a death
When Israelites were in mourning, they had certain rituals to perform. They might remove their sandals, leave their hair unbrushed, or cover their head with a hand. At funerals, some people would hire mourners, like the Egyptian ones shown here, to make a better show at the burial.

Burial place
No one knows exactly where Moses was buried. Some people believe that the church on Mount Nebo, shown below, was built where his grave is situated.

front of the crowd and rippled backwards through the people like a wave, and Moses turned to rest his trembling hands on the young man's broad shoulders. "Be strong and courageous, Joshua," he bade him. "For the day will come when you will lead these people triumphantly into the land that the Lord promised their fathers. Trust in God, and He will be with you in whatever you do."

> " *The Lord will be with you, He will not fail you, do not be afraid.* "

Moses was worried that, once he had gone, the people would forget everything he'd told them and turn to wickedness. So he wrote down each word of all the laws that God had given him and entrusted them to the safe keeping of the priests of the ark, so they could make sure that all the Israelites knew and understood them. Next, he went with Joshua to the tabernacle, to present the new leader of the people to the Lord. Finally, Moses called the elders of all the tribes together and gave them his blessing.

When all Moses's preparations were at last done, he went on his own to the top of Mount Pisgah.

"Look all around you," said the Lord, showing Moses the beautiful countryside of Canaan stretching away into the distance. "This is the land I promised to Abraham, Isaac and Jacob. Although you will not enter it yourself, I vow that it will belong to your descendants."

Moses died content that he had seen Canaan with his own eyes and with faith that it would indeed one day be his people's home. The whole Israelite nation had witnessed Moses's mighty power and great deeds, and they mourned his passing bitterly for 30 days.

MOSES WAS A GREAT MAN. ALTHOUGH HE WAS 120 YEARS OLD WHEN HE DIED, ACCORDING TO THE BIBLE, "HIS EYES WERE NOT DIM, NOR HIS NATURAL FORCE ABATED".

Hebrew laws
The first five books of the Old Testament contain the Hebrew laws, also known as the Law of Moses. These are God's instructions to His people as to how they must live their lives. The most important laws are the Ten Commandments, but others cover a wide range of subjects, like laws on how to keep healthy, and punishments for lots of different crimes.

Moses's punishment
Many years earlier, Moses had once disobeyed God. His punishment was that he would not enter the Promised Land but only look upon it. This view shows Canaan over the sea of Galilee as Moses may have looked on it before his death.

Rahab and the Spies

NOW Moses was gone, the responsibility of rousing the Israelites to take the Promised Land rested squarely on Joshua's shoulders. But even though this was a hugely daunting task, Joshua was not afraid. God spoke to him, inspiring him with confidence and courage. "It is time for you to lead the Israelites across the River Jordan, into the country I have promised will be yours. I never failed Moses and I will not fail you either, so be strong and brave-hearted! As long as you keep my laws, you will have nothing to fear. I will be with you always and you will have victory!" Standing tall and steadfast, Joshua commanded his officers to prepare the people for the invasion without delay.

Excitement rippled through the camp as the news spread to make ready. After 40 years, the moment that the travellers had been waiting for had finally arrived! The Israelites were about to see for themselves the wonderful countryside that their parents and grandparents had struggled for so long to reach. And God had promised them success. The Promised Land would at last be theirs! Everyone was so eager that even though there were hundreds of thousands of people to mobilize, the preparations took only three days.

Meanwhile, Joshua sent two men on a dangerous secret mission. "Go and investigate the city of Jericho," he told them. "I want you to find out as much as you can about its defences and its army." And the two spies slipped away.

Under cover, the men managed to dodge inside Jericho's gates and walk through the city, mingling with the enemy. After they had found out all they could, they went to the house of a woman called Rahab, who had promised to keep them safe for the night. But in the narrow streets of Jericho nothing went unseen. It didn't take long for neighbourhood gossip and rumours to reach the ears of the king, who immediately sent soldiers to Rahab's house. "Open up by royal command!" they yelled, battering at the door. "Open up or we'll force the door down!"

Rahab remained perfectly calm. "Whatever are you making all this fuss about?" she smiled sweetly, welcoming the soldiers into her house.

"Where are they?" the soldiers snarled, upturning tables and dragging curtains aside. "Come on. We know you've got them – you're hiding two Israelites, foreign spies and enemies in here somewhere!"

Rahab's faith
Rahab was a prostitute who lived in a house that formed part of the town wall of Jericho. She knew that the Israelites planned to capture the town, and she feared for her own life and for the lives of her family. Rahab had heard how God had helped the Israelites on their journey from Egypt, and she believed in His power. She declared her faith in God and begged the spies to save her family, in return for her helping them. When the Israelites destroyed Jericho, Rahab and her family were the only people who were spared.

Spies on a rope
The rope that Rahab used to help the spies escape could have been made of twisted hair or strips of animal skin. In Egypt, rope was also made from woven papyrus strips.

Spies
A spy is a person who secretly collects information on the activities, movements and plans of an enemy, and then reports this to someone else. This story illustrates the use of spies in Bible times, and they are still used all over the world today. Spies are also known as secret agents.

"Israelites? No!" Rahab gasped, pretending to be shocked. "You don't mean they were spies! It's true that two men came to stay with me, but I had no idea they were Israelites!" She paused, and then said, "In that case, I'm afraid you've missed them. They waited until darkness fell and then they went out somewhere." Rahab's voice grew urgent. "You'll have to hurry – it's nearly dark and the city gates are about to shut! They can't have got very far. If you go quickly, you might just catch them." The soldiers rushed out of the house in a terrible hurry and dashed off down the street.

The minute the soldiers were out of sight, Rahab rushed up to the roof, where she had hidden the Israelites under a heap of reeds that she had laid out to dry in the sun. The two men were highly relieved when they saw that the fingers uncovering them were Rahab's – not those belonging to the King of Jericho's soldiers!

 We have heard how the Lord dried up the waters of the Red Sea.

"It's too risky for you to stay here any longer," Rahab warned them in a whisper. "You must go and hide in the hills, where the soldiers can't find you. But before you go, please promise me one thing. Everyone here is terrified of your people. We know how the Red Sea turned aside and let you pass out of Egypt, and we've heard how you crushed King Sihon and King Og and took their lands. Nearly everyone believes that God is on your side and that anyone who faces you is doomed. In return for the help I have given you,

promise me that you will spare me and my family when the Israelites come marching into Jericho."

The men took her hands. "When we attack, make sure everyone is locked inside your house and tie a scarlet cord at the window. We will then spare everyone inside, for the sake of the kindness you have shown us."

Rahab's house was built into the city wall itself. Opening up a window, she peered out nervously to see if anyone was around. Then she tied a rope firmly on to the ledge and flung the other end out into the darkness, listening to it tumble down a long way below. After a moment's anxious goodbye, the two Israelites climbed silently down, quite unseen, and escaped into the night.

Tribes of Canaan

When the Israelites arrived in the land of Canaan, there were already many tribes of people living there. The Bible tells us that the Canaanites were descended from Noah's son Ham, and the Israelites were descended from one of Noah's other sons, Shem. Noah said that the descendants of Shem would one day rule over Ham's descendants, which comes true at this point in the Bible. God tells the Israelites that they have to kill all the Canaanites, and that they are not allowed to live alongside them. This is because God knows that His people might be tempted to worship the gods of Canaan, like Baal. The tribes that the Israelites do not utterly defeat, such as the Midianites and the Philistines, appear as enemies of the Israelites later in the Bible. You can see here the spies escaping out of Rahab's window in the wall of Jericho.

Crossing the Jordan

THE Israelites had faith in the Lord's promise that they would successfully storm Jericho, and when they heard the reports from Joshua's spies, they were elated. Now they knew that even their enemies believed that God was with them, and shook with fear in anticipation of their coming. However, in order to attack the great city itself, the Israelites had to first find a way to cross the flood of the mighty River Jordan.

The morning came when Joshua gave the order to advance over the river bank, and the mass of Israelites camped all over the plain prepared to march. First to move off were the priests, who carried high the Ark of the Covenant for all to see. Following behind, a safe distance from the holiness of the ark, came 40,000 soldiers, armed

> 66 *The priests who bore the ark stood on dry ground in the midst of the Jordan.* 99

~ ABOUT THE STORY ~

God tells Joshua that He is with him, just as He was with Moses before. And just as God held back the waters of the Red Sea, He now holds back the mighty Jordan so that the Israelites can cross the river and step on to the land God promised their ancestors so long ago. At last, their years of wandering in the desert are over. They build a memorial with 12 rocks from the river bed, to mark the site of the amazing miracle.

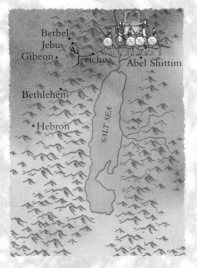

Bethel
Jebus
Gibeon
Ai
Jericho
Abel Shittim
Bethlehem
Hebron
SALT SEA

Entering the Promised Land
After 40 long years in the wilderness, and many trials and lapses of faith, the Israelites enter the Promised Land. Led by Joshua, they make their way up the east side of the Salt Sea from the wilderness around Mount Sinai. They briefly make camp at Abel Shittim, before God leads them into Canaan, and the Israelite nation witnesses the miraculous crossing of the River Jordan.

Altar by the Jordan
At Joshua's command the Israelites build an altar by the river. This is to remind the people of the miracle that God performed for them.

and ready for war. Closer and closer came the great crowd of people to the fast-flowing waters of the Jordan, with the city of Jericho looming ever larger on the opposite side. When the priests had reached the edge of the river, Joshua gave them God's command. "As soon as your feet are in the water, go no further." One by one the holy men stepped down into the Jordan, and as they stood still in the midst of the channel, with the ark raised aloft, they found that the water level began to lower. The Lord was holding back the river at a spot higher up the valley, preventing it from sweeping the Israelites away. As Joshua watched, the waters started to drain from around the priests' feet and a dry path emerged across to the far bank. He wasted no time in giving the order for the army to advance, and rank by rank the troops marched past the sacred ark across the exposed river bed.

When the very last soldier was safely on the opposite side of the Jordan, the Lord told Joshua to send a man from each Israelite tribe to fetch a rock from around the priests' feet. When this was done, the priests themselves moved off over the dried-up river bed, step by step, carefully bringing the ark into the Promised Land. The moment the priests' feet had reached the Jericho side, the Israelites heard a distant rumbling, like the sound of far-off thunder. The noise rapidly turned into a roar, then a deafening boom, and suddenly they saw the waters of the Jordan come crashing down the river bed once more, spraying over the channel and overflowing the banks, soaking the Israelites who were standing, watching in awe as immense waves plunged onwards, rushing down to the sea.

"Take these 12 rocks and build a memorial to mark the site of this miracle forever," Joshua commanded the stunned soldiers. Then the Israelites began to cheer.

The Israelites' trust in their new leader had been rewarded, and each soldier stood with awe and respect in his heart for Joshua, just as they had done for Moses. "We will follow you wherever you take us and do whatever you command," the people cried to Joshua. And they knew that God Himself was among them as they turned to face the army of the powerful city of Jericho.

A nation on the move
Some people have tried to work out how many Israelites entered Canaan. The word *lp* is used in some Bible accounts, and people do not know what it means. Some think it means a thousand people and others "armed men". Depending on which meaning they use, the number varies between two million and 500,000 people.

THE PRIESTS CARRY THE ARK OF THE COVENANT INTO THE RIVER AHEAD OF THE PEOPLE. AS GOD'S HOME ON EARTH WAS BELIEVED TO BE BETWEEN THE WINGS OF THE ANGELS ON THE LID OF THE ARK, THIS WAS A SIGN TO THE PEOPLE THAT GOD WAS LEADING THEM TO THE PROMISED LAND.

The river runs dry
In 1927, an earthquake caused mud to block the River Jordan for 21 hours. God may have used natural forces to perform the miracle described in the story.

Fall of Jericho

JOSHUA and his 40,000 soldiers stood on the plain facing the great city of Jericho. Its towering stone walls stared blankly back at them – too high to climb, too thick to batter down – and the huge, sturdy city gates had been bolted and barred. Not even the smallest mouse would have found a chink in the defences to creep in or out. There were no weak points for the Israelites to attack, and Joshua decided that there was nothing for it but to sit and wait for the citizens to run short of food and water. But God had quite a different war plan and sent a messenger to tell Joshua what to do.

Following the Lord's commands, the next day the Israelite leader gave the soldiers the order to march. "Put on your armour and pick up your weapons," Joshua told them. "I want you to parade right round the outside of the city, in full view of the enemy. The priests will go with you at the centre of the march carrying trumpets and holding high the Ark of the Covenant. Everyone is to be very careful not to utter a single word until I give the signal. I won't give the signal today, but you must all be ready for when I do. Then I want you to shout until your lungs are fit to burst." The soldiers were more than a little puzzled by this strange battle strategy, but they all had faith in their commander, so they set off round the city.

WHEN THE ISRAELITES HAD KILLED EVERYONE, THEY DESTROYED THE CITY. THE FIRST FRUITS OF THEIR CONQUEST OF CANAAN – THE CITY, WITH EVERYONE AND EVERYTHING IN IT – WERE OFFERED TO GOD ❧

Ancient Jericho
The place generally identified with Old Testament Jericho is the site of Tell es-Sultan (shown to the left). The first settlements grew up around an oasis. From about 8000BC, town after town was built and destroyed on the site. The first town had walls around it, and Jericho is the oldest walled city in the world.

Trumpet call
The trumpets used by the priests in the story were called *shophars*. They were made of rams' horns, and were used to call people to battle and also to worship. The shophar is still used by rabbis today in some Jewish religious ceremonies.

The terrified inhabitants of Jericho watched and waited, listening to the fanfare of trumpets outside their walls. The full might of the Israelite army was on display, and the icy silence of the warriors made their blood run cold. The sight of the ark filled them with dread. They knew it was the sacred chest of the all-powerful Israelite God – the God who had helped them defeat the Egyptians and the Amorites. When would the attack come on their own city?

Every morning for six days the Israelites tramped their way round the city. Each time the people of Jericho saw the army, they prepared themselves to face an invasion; and each time the Israelites withdrew, they grew more and more anxious. Whatever were the Israelites up to?

When dawn broke on the seventh day, Joshua gave the army a new command: today they were to circle the city seven times. Imagine the panic that rose among the inhabitants of Jericho when they realized something was at last about to happen. The soldiers must have been able to hear the people's frightened cries. "Why aren't they stopping? They're not going back to their camp! Any minute now, they'll turn and head straight for us . . . The ark will strike us down! The Israelites are coming!"

But the expected attack still didn't arrive. As soon as the ark had passed around the city seven times, Joshua gave the sign. The 40,000 soldiers opened their mouths and bellowed with all their strength, adding their voices to the blasts of the priests' trumpets.

The din was ear-splitting. Inside Jericho, no one could hear themselves speak. The unearthly noise circled the entire city like the howling of souls in torment, pressing in on all sides and seeming to grow louder at every second.

> ❝ *The people raised a great shout and the wall fell down flat.* ❞

Outside the city, the almighty noise echoed and re-echoed around the hills and the Israelites felt the very ground beneath their feet begin to vibrate.

As the air throbbed, the earth trembled and then quaked, until with one great shudder the massive walls of Jericho came tumbling down. Immediately the soldiers rushed on the city, scrambling their way in over the heaps of crumbled stone. Only Rahab and her family were spared, just as the spies had promised. The fame of another Israelite victory spread far and wide across Canaan, and Joshua's name was spoken with fear throughout the land.

Fighting with bronze

Joshua's invasion of Jericho took place in about 1400BC, during a period known as the Late Bronze Age. Most weapons at this time were made of bronze. These pictures show some of the weapons the Israelites might have been carrying when they stormed into the city. They include battleaxes, a spearhead, a dagger and an arrowhead.

⚜ ABOUT THE STORY ⚜

This story shows that God is with the Israelites. He tells Joshua about the unusual way in which he must take the city of Jericho. Jericho is the first Canaanite city to be taken, and the Israelites honour God by devoting it to Him. The only citizens to be spared are Rahab and her family. She helped the Israelite spies and this is God's recognition of that faithful act. After the defeat of Jericho, Joshua's fame spreads.

Battle of Ai

SPURRED on by the victory at Jericho, Joshua immediately sent scouts further into the land of Canaan to spy out the Israelites' next target, the city of Ai. The news they brought back was encouraging. They felt that an army of two or three thousand soldiers should be able to defeat the city. But the ease with which Jericho had fallen had made the scouts over-confident. They had severely under-estimated how fiercely the small population of Ai would fight to protect their city. The determined citizens forced back the warriors sent by Joshua, leaving many Israelites dead, and chasing the rest away into the desert.

Joshua was deeply shocked. "Why, Lord?" the Israelite commander cried, striding up and down his tent. "Why have you let this happen?"

"What did you expect?" came the Lord's thunderous reply. "Israel has sinned against me!"

Joshua was baffled. "How? What do you mean?"

"There is one among you who has disobeyed my commands," roared the Lord. "Until he is found and punished, the Israelite nation must stand on its own!"

Next morning, Joshua gathered all the Israelites before him. Guided by God, his eyes slowly scanned the massive crowd, and came to rest on the tribe of Judah. In a steely voice, Joshua called for the households of the tribe to pass in front of him. As soon as Joshua saw the Zerahites, something made him shout, "Stop!" As the family stood trembling, Joshua slowly lifted an accusing finger. "You!" he breathed, pointing at a man called Achan. "You're the sinner who has brought God's wrath upon us!"

Achan immediately fell on his knees in front of the enraged Israelite leader and confessed. At the conquest of Jericho, Joshua had given strict orders that all precious booty was the property of the Lord, to be placed in the treasury for safekeeping. Yet Achan had stolen a beautiful mantle, along with some gold and silver, and hidden them.

Digging for history

Most of the discoveries that have been made about this time have come from archaeologists, people who learn about the past by digging up old buildings and objects. The archaeologists in the picture have found a place where they think ancient people lived and they are trying to find objects, or artefacts, that have been left behind. For example, finding cooking pots may tell them what people ate at the time. There are specialists who only study the area around the Salt Sea, now called the Dead Sea, trying to find out about the people and places mentioned in the Bible. A lot of objects, such as things made of leather or wood, seldom survive, but enough has been found to give us a good idea of what life may have been like.

Luxury robe
This picture shows the type of robe that Achan might have stolen from Jericho. It would have been worn by a nobleman, and would have been made of expensive fabrics, richly embroidered and decorated.

The Lord told Joshua to try a second attack on the city of Ai and instructed him to set a clever trap. At night, 30,000 soldiers crept into the hills behind the city. Next day, while these troops lay in wait out of sight, the rest of the Israelite army attacked the city from the front. However, the soldiers of Ai were well-prepared and their king was delighted to find that, just as before, his fighters soon got the upper hand. Bit by bit, the Israelites were beaten back. Even when the order came for the Israelite army to retreat, the warriors of Ai didn't give up. They chased the retreating Israelites into the wilderness.

But, unbeknown to the King of Ai, everything had happened exactly according to plan. The Israelites had only pretended to be overcome in order to lure the fighters away from the city. Now the Israelite ambush rushed into Ai and began the destruction of the city.

> 66 *Joshua burned Ai and made it for ever a heap of ruins.* 99

Out in the countryside, Joshua saw smoke start to rise as Ai was set on fire, and he gave the signal for his fleeing troops to turn and face their pursuers. With utter horror, the King of Ai realized they had been trapped. The invaders were closing in on his army from the front and from the city at the rear and there was no hope of escape.

By sunset, the King of Ai's dead body hung from a tree. His army lay slain in the wilderness and his people lay dead in the streets. All the kings of the lands beyond the Jordan swore to join forces to take revenge on the Israelites.

While the miserable man begged for mercy at Joshua's feet, messengers were sent to search his tent. They quickly returned with the stolen treasures. "God punished us for your wrongdoing by taking the lives of our soldiers," Joshua coldly told Achan. "Now, you must be punished, and pay the same price that they did." And then the people stoned Achan to death.

Shekels

The Bible tells us that Achan stole "two hundred shekels of silver, and a wedge of gold of 50 shekels' weight". The shekel was not a coin, but a weight. Most of the people at this time measured amounts of silver and gold in terms of how much they weighed, rather than how much they were worth.

Achan's death

This picture shows Achan being punished for his sin. In the Bible, we are told that after the stoning, Achan was burned, together with his oxen, his sheep and goats, his tent and all that he had. He had committed a sin against God that all the Israelites had suffered for, so according to the law God gave to Moses on Mount Sinai he had to be punished.

❖ ABOUT THE STORY ❖

God brings about the Israelites' defeat at Ai because He knows Achan has disobeyed Him. He punishes all the people for one man's sin. This can be compared to the way in which Adam's sin affected the whole of humanity. Once Achan has been punished, the Israelites have God's blessing again, and their second attack is a success. This story shows that God will always find those who disobey Him, and will punish them.

Tricked by the Gibeonites

NOT far to the south-west of Ai lay the mighty city of Gibeon. The Gibeonites were a strong and powerful people, but news of how Joshua had razed the great city of Jericho to the ground and slaughtered the people of Ai had struck fear into their hearts. The Israelites weren't far off, and the Gibeonites knew that if they waited for the Israelites to arrive they might suffer the same fate as the people who were once their neighbours. Instead, the Gibeonites made a cunning plan . . .

Joshua was resting in his tent where the Israelites had camped at Gilgal when a messenger suddenly dashed in. "The scouts have reported that strangers are approaching, sir," he panted, all out of breath.

Joshua sat up, immediately alert and ready for action. "Send soldiers out to meet them and escort them to me," he commanded. He was always suspicious when anyone was seen heading for their huge army camp.

When the strangers were brought to his tent, Joshua was amazed. These weren't royal messengers sent from any Canaanite king, they were just a ragbag rabble of peasants! Joshua found himself facing a dirty, stinking group of exhausted people, whose patched clothes were in tatters and whose worn-out shoes were falling off their feet. "At last we have found you!" they cried, falling on their knees

with gratitude in front of Joshua. "We have been travelling for many weeks to get here. Even though we live far away, news of your wonderful God has reached our tribe. You are obviously a blessed people, and we would like to join you. Our elders have sent us as ambassadors to ask you to make a treaty with us."

Joshua was not convinced by the flattery. "How can I be sure that you are who you say you are?" he queried. "The tribes of Canaan know well that we have sworn never to make peace with them. You might therefore be people from the very cities we plan to attack, come in disguise to try to trick us into making peace."

Wine
There are frequent references to both drinking and making wine in the Bible as the land was well suited to growing vines.

Baking bread
The Gibeonites in the story carry bread in their packs. Bread was the most important food in this area at the time. The picture shows an Egyptian model of two servants baking bread. One is sitting down and tending the fire, while the other servant is kneading the dough. The model dates from around 1900BC.

It took the Israelite army only three days to reach the city of Gibeon, and Joshua realized his dreadful blunder at once. His first guess had been completely right – the Gibeonites were local people who had dressed up to trick him, to try and escape death at the hands of a huge army led by God Himself. Joshua was furious that he'd allowed himself to be persuaded by their story, but it was now too late. Even though the army were eager to attack and take their revenge, Joshua knew that to break his solemn vow to let them live would bring God's wrath upon them, even though they would have killed them all had they not made the peace. The Gibeonites were therefore spared, but to punish them for their lies they were taken as slaves to spend the rest of their days working for the great Israelite army and the tabernacle of their God.

66 *Now you are cursed, and you shall always be slaves for the house of my God.* 99

The dejected travellers reached inside their packs and produced hunks of stale, mouldy bread and battered, torn wineskins. "When we set off from our homes, this bread was still warm from the oven and the wineskins were brand new," they said, earnestly. "Please make our long, hard journey worthwhile. We beg you to make a peace treaty with our people."

Joshua granted the travellers their precious peace treaty, and all the Israelite elders swore to let their people live. The tattered group were eager to be off with their wonderful news, and they hurried away from the Israelite camp at once. After all, they had many weeks of travelling ahead before they would reach home.

Carved in stone
This Egyptian stone contains the first mention of the nation of Israel outside the Bible. It dates from around 1230BC, when Pharaoh Mereneptah was ruling. The inscription on the stone describes his military campaign in Canaan, and says that he defeated the Israelites.

Canaanite man
The picture on this Egyptian glazed brick shows what a nobleman from Canaan might have looked like at around the time the Israelites settled in the area.

> ◦ **ABOUT THE STORY** ◦
>
> *Joshua makes a treaty of peace with the Gibeonites, and the Israelites swear a solemn oath not to harm them. Oaths were regularly used in treaties, as a way of enforcing the terms. Once Joshua realizes that he has been tricked, it is too late. He has to honour the treaty.*

The Longest Day

KING Adonizedek of Jerusalem was among the Canaanite rulers who had sworn to join forces to drive the Israelites out of Canaan. He knew that presenting a strong, united front was their only hope against the massive Israelite army. The fall of the mighty city of Jericho had spelt out disaster for any city that tried to stand alone. Now the Gibeonites had weakened their number by betraying the Amorite kings' pact. In saving themselves from destruction, they had abandoned everyone else to a more certain doom, and Adonizedek was enraged. He immediately sent messengers to the four kings that neighboured his lands, saying, "The Gibeonites have made peace with the enemy. I say we should destroy the city of

> ❝ The Sun stood still and the Moon stayed, until the nation took vengeance. ❞

Gibeon ourselves. Send your armies straight away and together we'll take our revenge on these deserters." So King Hoham of Hebron, King Piram of Jarmuth, King Japhia of Lachish and King Debir of Eglon immediately mobilized their forces and declared war on their one-time ally.

Gibeon was soon under siege. The citizens had scarcely finished celebrating how they had tricked the fearsome Israelites, when the five savage armies of the hill kings surrounded them on all sides and the city found itself in the very position it had tried so hard to avoid! The

Defeated enemies
On the left is a decorative palette showing the first king of Egypt, King Narmer, holding a defeated enemy by the hair. On the right is a picture of an Israelite with his foot on the neck of an enemy. Both these images show typical gestures of subjection of enemies after battle. It was a sign that the enemy knew they had been defeated. In the Bible, we are told that Joshua's captains put their feet on the necks of the five defeated kings. As Joshua marched through Canaan, his army defeated many more cities along the way. These cities were called city-states, and were like small countries.

Gibeonite leaders now sent messengers to their former enemy to beg for help to get them out of trouble.

The news that the Amorite kings of the hills had gathered against Gibeon reached Joshua in the middle of the night, but he immediately gave the army the order to march. There would be no better chance to crush several important Canaanite tribes all in one go, and God reassured Joshua of victory. Without waiting for daybreak he made the army strike camp immediately, marching all night through the darkness.

The Israelite attack came as a complete surprise. While all the Amorite forces were facing Gibeon, half-asleep and half-awake, the full strength of the Israelite army fell on them from behind. The soldiers panicked. Some stayed to fight and were hacked down as the Israelites rushed upon them. Others turned and tried to flee. But even though they were out of reach of the Israelite swords, suddenly the Lord sent huge hailstones the size of rocks from above, stoning them to death as they ran.

Then Joshua gave a mighty shout. "Sun, stand still in the sky! Moon, hang where you are in the heavens! Let time itself be stopped until we have crushed these enemies completely!" To the horror of the Amorite armies, the Lord heard Joshua's plea. Hour after hour, the Israelites continued to hack down their enemies, yet, to the terrified Amorites, the day didn't get any shorter.

In the midst of the killing, a messenger came running up to Joshua excitedly. "Sir, the five kings tried to escape, but some of our troops found them," he told Joshua. "They were hiding in a cave at Makkedah, but we've now got them cornered. What shall we do with them?"

Joshua wanted to deal with the rebel kings himself, to make an example of them to any other Canaanite peoples that might dare go against the Israelites. "Block the cave mouth up with rocks," he instructed the messenger. "That will hold them fast until we've finished destroying everything they own!" And while the Amorite kings were locked up, the Israelites slaughtered their people.

At the end of the extraordinarily long day, the Israelites had crushed five of their strongest enemies. When not one Amorite soldier remained alive, Joshua gave the command for the five kings to be brought out of the cave. He threw them to the ground in front of the Israelite war leaders. "You should never be afraid, people of Israel!" Joshua cried. "For this is what the Lord has promised will happen to our enemies." In front of the Israelites, the kings were hanged, one by one, and their bodies thrown back into the cave from which they had just come.

∾ ABOUT THE STORY ∾

God reassures Joshua that He is with him and that the Israelites will win. When the battle begins, God sends hailstones which rain down on the enemy from above. Then He grants Joshua's request and makes the Sun stand still. The day does not end until the Israelites have defeated their enemies. In the Bible, we are told that there was no day like that before or after it. This is another great success for Joshua's leadership.

Light or darkness?
The Longest Day in this story is usually taken to mean that daylight lasted longer than usual. However, it could be that the story refers to an eclipse of the Sun, which would mean that the darkness of the night lasted longer than usual. There is no mention of it being daylight, so it could be that the darkness helped the Israelites win.

Dividing the Promised Land

NOT content with having slain the five Amorite kings and crushing their armies, Joshua next attacked and destroyed each of their cities, killing every person found there. News of the terrible bloodshed spread at once through Canaan and, with hearts full of dread, the Canaanite chiefs realized that no one stood a chance of being spared. Their choice was either to sit back and wait for their people to be slaughtered, or to come out and fight. So, under the leadership of King Jabin of Hazor, the rulers mobilized their armies. Hundreds of thousands of troops, horses and chariots gathered in a massive camp at Merom. The soldiers were all in full battledress, and determined to stop the Israelites from taking their homeland.

Report after report reached Joshua's ears of the vast army preparing to attack. But God reassured him. "Have no fear," He told Joshua, "for I will deliver all these troops slain into your hands. Tomorrow, you will kill their horses and burn their chariots." Joshua trusted the Lord and immediately led the Israelites into an attack. The battle was more savage and bloody than any either army had suffered before. When the ruthless killing was eventually over, the bodies littering the battlefield were Canaanite. As God had vowed, they lay next to the corpses of their horses and the smoking wrecks of their once glorious chariots. The Israelites had won their mightiest victory yet.

For several more years, Joshua was to continue waging wars against the Canaanite tribes, conquering more and more of the Promised Land until at last most of the country was theirs. Then the fighting ceased. It was time to divide the land up between the 12 Israelite tribes.

The boldest Israelite elders made haste to lay claim to the areas they wanted for their families or that they thought were rightfully theirs. One of the first to get his allocation was Caleb, Moses's courageous scout and now an old man of 85, who finally received the reward the Lord had promised him. For having faith in God's order to invade Canaan when everyone else was faint-hearted, Joshua granted him the great city of Hebron and the surrounding hill country. However, not everyone was as sure about which part of the beautiful country they wanted to live in. Seven tribes simply couldn't decide! So after sending three men from each to survey the land, Joshua divided it up into seven parts and the tribe chiefs drew lots for their new homes.

The only tribe not to be given an entire area was the Levites, whom God had long ago chosen to be His priests. They were given 48 cities in different parts of the country, so they could lead the Israelites in worship. The tabernacle itself was set up permanently in the city of Shiloh, at the heart of the Promised Land.

Finally the Lord told Joshua to appoint six cities as Cities of Refuge. In these places, people accused of crimes would be protected against those wanting to take their revenge, and they would be assured a fair trial.

With the country organized, the Israelites began to move into their allocated areas. But it wasn't always easy. Handfuls of Canaanite people still stubbornly remained in some far-flung places, and the powerful Israelite families had to either drive them off their land or force them into slavery. The Reubenites and Gadites met particular problems. Along with half the tribe of Manasseh, Joshua had given them some of the first lands the Israelites had conquered – the plains of Moab. However, these lay on the far side of the Jordan. The tribes were concerned that the river acted as a boundary dividing them from the rest of the Israelites.

As the other 10 tribes settled into their own areas, they were appalled to

hear that the Reubenites and Gadites were building a huge altar on the banks of the Jordan. Thinking that they were setting themselves up as priests or even turning to other gods, the Levite High Priest, Phineas, and the chiefs of the other tribes raced to stop them. The Reubenites and Gadites were astonished to find that such an important committee had travelled so far to see them. "Whatever are you doing?" the priest and chiefs asked the puzzled people. "Hasn't God's wrath in the past taught you a lesson? If you offend God's commands, He will strike down not only you, but all of us!"

> ❝ *Let us build an altar to be a witness between us and you.* ❞

With shock, the Reubenites and Gadites realized what the other Israelites thought they were up to. "The Lord knows we weren't building an altar to any other god!" they gasped in horror. "We are just worried because we are going over the river. We feared that your descendants might see our lands as outside Israel's borders and turn against our descendants. So we have built a copy of the Altar of the Lord, which now stands at Shiloh, to stand as proof that we follow the same God." The priests and elders were highly relieved and left the Reubenites and Gadites to settle into their lands in peace.

And so it happened that the Israelites at last took possession of the Promised Land, just as God had promised Abraham that they would.

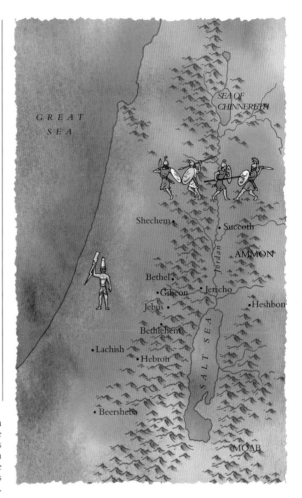

The war for Canaan
The Israelites fought a long war over all of Canaan to take possession of the land that God had given them. With God's help they quickly spread out over the country. Here you can see, in red, the area that they had conquered, including the cities of Jericho and Bethlehem, as far south as Abraham's home town of Beersheba, and north as far as Shechem.

Altars built to God
An altar is a table or flat-topped block used as the focus for a religious ritual. In the Old Testament, altars were mainly used for making sacrifices or offerings to God. The Hebrew word for altar, *mizbeah*, means "place of sacrifice". Smaller altars were used for burning incense. In later times, events taking place at an altar were supervised by a priest, but in ancient times, people built their own altars and offered sacrifices on them. Noah, Abraham, Isaac, Jacob and Moses all built altars, usually to remember an event in which they had dealings with God, such as Jacob seeing his ladder to heaven, with God waiting at the top.

❖ ABOUT THE STORY ❖

The Israelites conquer most of the Promised Land. When each tribe is given its own area, the Reubenites and Gadites are concerned that their land is separated from the rest of Israel by the Jordan. They build an altar to bind themselves to the rest of Israel through their faith.

Death of Joshua

By the time Joshua had become a very elderly man, there had been peace in Israel for many years. The Israelites' enemies were overcome, the land was fairly divided, and the 12 tribes were settled contentedly throughout the country. The mighty war leader's work was done.

At the age of 110 years and knowing death was near, Joshua summoned all the Israelites together one last time so he could address them. Joshua's tone was serious and stern, and as the Israelites listened to his stirring words, their blood tingled in their veins. "Remember where you have come from and all the great things God has done for your sake," the aged warrior urged his people. "Your fathers of old lived far off in the lands beyond the River Euphrates and they served other gods. But the Lord chose Abraham and guided him away to a new life, showing him this very country you now own. The descendants of his son, Jacob, fell into slavery in Egypt, but God sent Moses and Aaron to set our ancestors free, striking the whole of that land with terrible plagues. God Himself led our fathers out of Egypt. When the Egyptians gave pursuit with chariots and horsemen, the Lord heard our fathers' cries. He smothered the Egyptian army in darkness and drowned their troops and horses in the Red Sea, every last one of them. Then the Lord brought your families safely through the wilderness to the lands bordering the Jordan. He delivered the mighty Amorite kings into your hands and gave you their royal cities. Then He helped you across the River Jordan and crushed each Canaanite tribe for you.

"Do not forget that it is the Lord who has done all these things for you. It was He who drove your enemies out of the Promised Land; they didn't go because of your swords and bows and arrows. It was He who gave you a land you hadn't toiled to cultivate; today you enjoy eating the fruits of vineyards and olive groves that you didn't plant. And it was He who gave you cities that you hadn't sweated to build; you live in homes constructed by the sweat and work of other people's hands.

"But mind this – in order to serve the Lord, you must fear Him and follow His commands sincerely and faithfully. If you are not prepared to keep to His law, then so be it: worship other gods. But you must choose."

The Israelites listened carefully to Joshua's words and thought long and hard about the seriousness of what he was saying. Then voices began to cry out from the crowd. "We won't abandon the Lord!" they shouted. "Not after He

❝ *The people said, 'The Lord our God we will serve.'* ❞

delivered us from slavery in Egypt and worked miracles
for us and gave us the Promised Land! We will serve the
Lord truly! He is our only God!"

With trembling hands, the elderly war chief motioned
for the huge throng of Israelites to be calm. "If you do
wrong and turn to sin, you will not be forgiven," he
warned the waiting crowd. "If you forsake the Lord and
turn to worshipping idols and false gods, you will bring
the full force of His wrath down upon you."

Undeterred, the Israelites replied as if with one voice,
"We will serve the Lord our God! We will obey Him and
do whatever He tells us."

Joshua was content that the people were speaking from
their hearts and that they really meant what they were
promising. Finally, he felt that he could die in peace.
Taking the holy book of God's laws, he wrote in it that the
Israelites had renewed their covenant. Then, slowly but
steadily, the great leader took a large stone from nearby
and set it up in the sanctuary of the Lord. "This rock has
heard everything that has passed between us and God
today," he told the committed people. "If you disobey the
Lord, it will bear witness that you have broken your word,
and you will be punished for your sins."

Not long afterwards, the battle-scarred warrior passed
away. Amid great grief and mourning, the Israelites
carried his body to the part of the Promised Land where
he had made his home, the high hill country of Ephraim,
and there they laid him to rest.

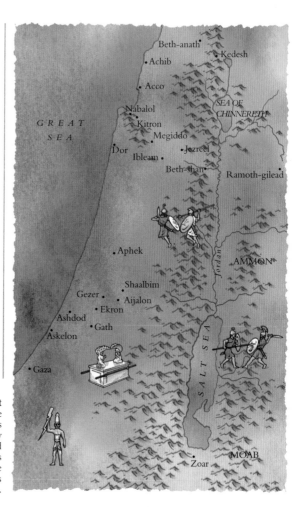

The battle still to be fought
Joshua was a great warrior and a mighty leader, but when he
died he had not conquered all Israel. This map shows the cities
he had not conquered. The Philistines were particularly
difficult to defeat, and their fortified towns, such as Gaza and
Gath, remained undefeated until the reign of King David. This
meant that all around the Israelites there were people
worshipping idolatrous gods, like Baal and Ashtoreth, and this
proved to be too much of a temptation after Joshua's death.

Ancient city
One of the cities captured by Joshua
in his long battle to gain complete
control of the Promised Land was
called Megiddo. King Solomon later
chose Megiddo as one of his main
fortified cities outside Jerusalem. The
site where ancient Megiddo stood is
believed to be Tell el-Mutesellim, in
north-west Israel. Archaeologists
who have dug there have found
evidence of a large town that, at
different times, contained stables,
storehouses, palaces, office-type
buildings and a gateway.

⟡ ABOUT THE STORY ⟡

*Joshua is soon to die, and no
single person will take over his
role as leader. He reminds the
Israelites of their history and
how God has helped them at
every step, from their escape
from Egypt to their new lives in
Israel. The Israelites choose to
renew their covenant with God.*

Israelites Disobey the Judges

FOR a long time after Joshua's death, the Israelites were careful to keep their promise to obey God's commands and live according to His laws. Without a war chief or king at the nation's head, it was up to the wise officials called Judges to bind the people together in their single faith. However, as the years went by, the brave men and women who had invaded Canaan grew old and passed away. There were no longer eyewitnesses to tell of all the wonderful things that God had done for the Israelites, so many people began to wonder whether they had ever happened at all. Perhaps the miracles of crossing the River Jordan dry-footed, and the miraculous collapse

of the walls of Jericho, and the day that the sun stood still for Joshua and his warriors, were just the stuff of legends.

One of Joshua's last orders had been to drive out all the inhabitants of Canaan. Even though the Israelite war parties continued to have great success in taking new territories, they sometimes allowed the local people to remain as slaves. Other times, the Israelites simply moved into areas and settled down among the tribes. The Judges often repeated Joshua's warning about what would happen if the Israelites mixed with the Canaanites: the temptation to follow the pagan gods would prove too much, and the Lord would turn away from them in anger, resulting in the fall of the nation. And the time indeed came when an angel came down from Heaven with a final caution that God was losing patience. "It's thanks only to the Lord that you were brought safely out of Egypt and into the land He swore to give your ancestors," the angel said, sternly. "He made a special covenant with the Israelite nation; your part of the bargain was to drive out the pagan peoples from this land and break down their altars to false gods. Now God finds you have disobeyed His commands and are living among these unbelievers. The Lord will no longer fight these tribes for you and, if you aren't careful, your neighbours will become your enemies."

At this threat the despairing Israelites wept with remorse and prayed for forgiveness. But it wasn't long before they were carrying on just as before. God's anger grew as His chosen people turned their backs on Him, and in His turn He withdrew His protection.

Without God on their side, the Israelites soon found themselves in the hands of King Eglon of Moab. The

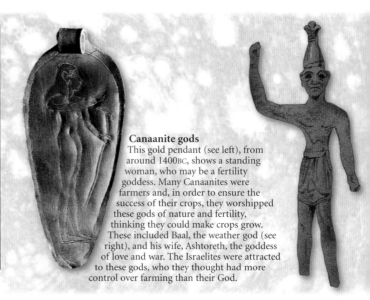

❧ ABOUT THE STORY ❧

Despite the angel's warning, the Israelites begin to forget God's laws. They live alongside the Canaanites, and start to worship their gods. The Judges try to enforce God's laws but in vain. Finally, God loses patience and removes His protection. The Israelites fall under the control of their neighbours. It is only because of the bravery of Ehud that the Israelites win back God's favour, and their freedom.

Canaanite gods
This gold pendant (see left), from around 1400BC, shows a standing woman, who may be a fertility goddess. Many Canaanites were farmers and, in order to ensure the success of their crops, they worshipped these gods of nature and fertility, thinking they could make crops grow. These included Baal, the weather god (see right), and his wife, Ashtoreth, the goddess of love and war. The Israelites were attracted to these gods, who they thought had more control over farming than their God.

> **The people of Israel did
> what was evil in the sight
> of the Lord.**

Israelites lived under Moabite control for 18 long years – plenty of time for them to think back on the ways they had offended God and to feel true repentance. Yet at last God chose to give His betrayers yet another chance and answered their cries for help.

A party of Israelites had gone one day to pay tribute at the Moabite court, and King Eglon had received their gifts and sent them on their way when he suddenly received word that one of them had returned – a man called Ehud, saying he had a secret message. Intrigued, Eglon agreed to give him another audience. However, Ehud insisted that his message was private and for the king's ears alone. Still more curious, Eglon hurried Ehud up to his roof chamber.

No sooner had Eglon closed the doors behind them than Ehud drew a two-edged sword and stabbed it into the king's stomach. In horror, as he lay dying, Eglon realized that Ehud was left-handed, and his soldiers must have checked for weapons only on the normal side of the body.

By the time King Eglon's servants had realized something was wrong, Ehud had escaped from the palace and was nearly home. The minute he reached Ephraim, he took out a trumpet and gave the signal to go to battle. The Israelites swooped down on the Moabite soldiers and slaughtered 10,000 of them. Finally, they had won back the Lord's favour and their freedom.

❀ THE JUDGES OF ISRAEL ❀

OTHNIEL *(1374-1334BC)*
*From Kiriath Sepher in Judah.
Saved the Israelites from the armies of
western Mesopotamia.*

EHUD *(1316-1236BC)*
*From Benjamin.
Saved the Israelites from the Moabites,
the Ammonites and the Amalekites.*

SHAMGAR
*Was a judge during the early rule of
Deborah. Killed six hundred Philistines.*

ABIMELECH
Ruled for three years. From Manasseh.

TOLA *(1126-1103BC)*
*A minor judge.
From Issachar.*

JAIR *(1103-1081BC)*
*A wealthy man and a minor judge.
From Gilead, in east Manasseh.*

IBZAN *(1100-1093BC)*
*A minor judge.
From Bethlehem, in Judah.*

ELON *(1093-1083BC)*
*A minor judge.
From Zebulun.*

ABDON *(1083-1077BC)*
From Ephraim. A minor judge.

SAMSON *(1103-1083BC)*
*From Dan.
Attacked the Philistines.
Was betrayed by Delilah.*

ELI *(ruled for 40 years)*
*Was the priest at the tabernacle at
Shiloh. Became Samuel's guardian.*

SAMUEL *(1059-1043BC)*
*The last judge and a prophet. Brought
the nation of Israel together. Under
him, the Philistine invasions ended.*

Deborah the Judge

THE Israelite people knew that from the very earliest times in their history, each time they had turned away from God and broken His commands, they had brought a severe punishment upon themselves. Surely the years that the Lord had allowed the ruthless Moabites to rule over them – the worst sentence yet – should have taught them a lesson they wouldn't forget? Unfortunately, this wasn't so. When Ehud died, the people quickly fell back into their old habits. Yet again the furious Lord turned his back on His people, leaving them to their own fate, and yet again they were conquered by an enemy: this time King Jabin of the Philistines. Now Jabin's army was feared far and wide – not only because it was under the command of the famous General Sisera, but also for its squadron of 900 indestructible iron chariots. The threat of his crack troops hovered over the Israelites, and King Jabin ruled the nation harshly for 20 years.

At that time, there was a prophetess called Deborah, who lived in the hill country of Ephraim. Deborah had been appointed one of Israel's judges and she was well respected by the people for her wise counsel and just decisions. Totally unexpectedly, a man called Barak received a message that Deborah wanted to see him and, although he was very puzzled, he went at once to meet her. "The Lord commands you to gather 10,000 men and go to Mount Tabor," Deborah told him. "There, God will bring General Sisera and King Jabin's army out to fight you, and you will win!" Barak was more than a little

startled; he was totally amazed! However, he agreed to do as he was told – just as long as Deborah went too. "Of course I will go with you," she assured him. "But, even though you will be victorious in the battle, the greatest glory will not be yours. Sisera himself will be defeated by a woman." Undeterred, Barak steeled himself to his task and set about finding soldiers.

The news reached General Sisera that the Israelites were gathering on the slopes of Mount Tabor, intent on rebelling, and he at once prepared his forces for war. How frightened the Israelites must have been, facing rank upon

❧ ABOUT THE STORY ❧

Once again, the Israelites have forgotten God and are worshipping the gods of the Canaanites. So, once again, God removes His protection, and the Israelites come under the rule of King Jabin. After 20 years of hardship, Deborah comes to the rescue of her people, instructing Barak to gather an army. Deborah joins him, and together they defeat Jabin's army. Jael deceives General Sisera and kills him.

Deborah the Judge
Deborah is one of the few women in the Bible to hold a position of power. She was a prophet who was also one of the Judges. Like most of the Judges, she was a military leader, but she was also a judge in the modern, legal, sense of the word. According to the Bible, she sat under "the palm tree of Deborah", and the Israelites came to consult her there when they wanted to have their disputes settled. She was well known throughout all the tribes of Israel, and highly respected. In the Bible, she is described as "a mother in Israel".

rank of chariots and row on row of accomplished, professionally trained soldiers! But Deborah urged them on and inspired them with faith. "Up and fight, Israel!" she cried, before they went into attack. "Today, the Lord will deliver this great army into your hands."

Deborah's words proved true and, quite against all the odds, Sisera's army was utterly routed. But when the fighting was finished and there was not a single Canaanite warrior left alive, the most important corpse of all was not to be found on the battlefield. Sisera had escaped.

Stumbling through the hills in a panic, the general was completely shocked by the defeat and physically drained. Yet somehow he managed to dodge all the Israelite troops combing the area, trying to hunt him down. In a clever move, he made for the tent of a woman called Jael – an unlikely hiding place since Jael was originally Israelite. However, her husband – a direct descendant from Moses's father-in-law – had changed his loyalties, having split from his tribe and made peace with King Jabin. As Sisera had hoped, Jael readily smuggled him inside her tent – which was just as well since he was utterly exhausted and could go no further. Kindly, Jael covered the slumped army chief with a rug, assuring him that he could sleep safely while she kept watch. Little did the general know that he was never to wake up. While Sisera dreamt, Jael hammered a tent peg right through his skull.

Even though Jabin's army was gone and his warlord dead, Barak and the Israelites didn't rest. The warriors carried on fighting until they had slain the Canaanite king himself and destroyed his palace at Hazor. Now surely this time the Israelites would make sure they did everything as the Lord wanted. Alas, no. Within the space of 40 years the obstinate people had again turned to wicked ways, and an enraged God left them to be conquered by the Midianites.

> " *The Lord will sell Sisera into the hands of a woman.* "

THE SONG OF DEBORAH

MOST BLESSED OF WOMEN BE JAEL,

THE WIFE OF HEBER THE KENITE,

OF TENT-DWELLING WOMEN MOST BLESSED.

HE ASKED WATER AND SHE GAVE HIM MILK,

SHE BROUGHT HIM CURDS IN A LORDLY BOWL.

SHE PUT HER HAND TO THE TENT PEG

AND HER RIGHT HAND TO THE

WORKMAN'S MALLET;

SHE STRUCK SISERA A BLOW,

AT HER FEET HE SANK, HE FELL;

WHERE HE SANK, THERE HE FELL DEAD.

The Song of Deborah
The Song of Deborah is one of the earliest passages in the Old Testament. It is a victory song – a celebration of the Israelites' victory over General Sisera. The song explains the details of the battle and Sisera's defeat.

Flooding of the river
Part of *The Song of Deborah* tells exactly how the Israelites won the battle. God sent a storm, which caused the River Kishon to flood. Sisera's chariots, which were in this area, were swept away. The Israelite soldiers were unharmed, as they were positioned on higher ground, on Mount Tabor.

Gideon and the Angel

THE Midianite tribes hated the Israelites with a passion and treated them more cruelly than any enemy before. They made life as miserable for the Israelites as possible: they attacked their homes whenever they had the chance; and they burnt their crops and killed their flocks, leaving the land wasted and the Israelites starving.

In these difficult times, the Israelites were forced to go to great lengths to try to outwit the Midianites, such as threshing any small amounts of wheat they could save in the wine press to keep it out of sight. A young farmer called Gideon was doing just this one day when a man appeared beside him out of nowhere. "You have a brave heart," the man told Gideon. "God is with you."

Gideon thought the man's words were even more odd than the weird way he had suddenly arrived. "If the Lord is indeed with us, how come we live under such terror?" he answered, bitterly. "Why doesn't God perform some amazing miracle to save us, like He did for our fathers? I tell you, the Lord has given up on us and left us to be punished by our enemies."

The stranger looked at Gideon without blinking. "You will take on the Midianites and set Israel free," he said.

"How on earth can I do that?" he scoffed. "My clan is the weakest, and I'm the youngest in my family!"

"The Lord will be with you," replied the stranger.

Still full of doubts, Gideon went off to find some food and drink to offer the uninvited guest. But when he laid down the meat and bread in front of him, the man only touched it with the tip of his staff. Instantly, the food burst into flames and the stranger disappeared. Gideon realized that he had been face to face with an angel.

Later that evening, a voice spoke to Gideon out of the darkness: it was the Lord Himself, instructing him to destroy his own father's altar to Baal and erect one to God instead. Gideon was afraid – he knew he'd be in very serious trouble. But that night, he did as he had been told. The people were furious when they saw what had been done and immediately suspected Gideon. Joash, Gideon's father, refused to punish his son as he felt sure that there must be a good reason for his son's outburst.

From that day onwards, Gideon was somehow different. But it was only when the Midianites, the Amalekites and all the other Eastern tribes crossed the Jordan and gathered ready for a battle, that Gideon showed exactly how much the Spirit of the Lord had altered him. Sounding a trumpet to call the Israelites to arms, he roused the people to strike back. A massive force

~ ABOUT THE STORY ~

Again, God rejects His people and they fall into the hands of the Midianites, under whom they suffer great hardship. Then God chooses their saviour, Gideon. Though afraid for his life, Gideon does as God asks and destroys his father's altar, building a new altar to God. Then he gathers an army and defeats the Midianites. Gideon refuses to rule over the Israelites, telling them that the Lord is their ruler.

Gideon and the angel
This picture shows Gideon talking to the angel. At first, Gideon is doubtful about the angel's message that he will save Israel. He does not think himself worthy. He asks for a sign from God, and when he sees the food burst into flames, he accepts God's will.

> ❝ *With the 300 men that lapped I will give the Midianites into your hand.* ❞

of 32,000 men quickly formed – but the Lord told him the army was too big! "If this many Israelites defeat the Midianites, they'll think that they've done it," God told Gideon, "I want them to know that the victory is my work." Gideon gave permission for all those who were afraid to return home, and soon only 10,000 soldiers remained. "They are still too many," God sighed. "Take them down to the water and watch how they drink. If anyone laps the water like a dog, take him to one side. Tell those who scoop up the water with cupped hands that they're no longer needed." Before long, Gideon's army was down to a mere 300 men, and God was satisfied that with this number in their army, they would know who to thank for their victory. So Gideon prepared his battle plan.

That night, three squads of 100 men crept from all directions up to the Midianite camp, each with a trumpet and a pitcher with a blazing torch inside. On Gideon's signal, the men blasted away and smashed their pitchers so that their torches flashed from all around in the darkness. In the confusion, the troops thought they were being attacked by a mighty army, and they ended up fighting among themselves. As panic spread, the troops began to flee, but they could not escape. Gideon sent messengers to Ephraim, where fighting men joined the chase.

The Israelites gave pursuit until the enemy were utterly defeated. The rejoicing nation begged Gideon to become their sole leader, but the young man refused. "I will not rule over you, and my son will not rule over you; the Lord will rule over you," he told the people. And Israel lived in peace for the rest of Gideon's life.

Asherah
In the Bible, God tells Gideon to destroy his father's altar to Baal, the Canaanite god, and to cut down the "asherah" beside it. Asherah is the name of a Canaanite fertility goddess associated with Baal, and an asherah pole is an image of that goddess, which would generally have been carved out of one big tree-trunk.

Canaanite goddess
This limestone relief shows a Canaanite goddess standing under an arch of flowers. It was decorated with red paint, traces of which can still be seen. Unlike the Israelites, the Canaanites made images of their gods and goddesses, and worshipped these.

Pottery jars
The picture to the left shows the type of pottery pitcher, or jar, that Gideon and his men would have taken with them on the night that they attacked and defeated the Midianites.

Jephthah

IMMEDIATELY after Gideon died, Israel's troubles began once more. One of Gideon's sons, Abimelech, couldn't get over how his father had passed up the chance to be ruler over all Israel. He was tormented by thoughts of the missed opportunity, so he tricked his kinsmen out of a lot of money and paid thugs to kill all 70 of his brothers, before setting himself up as the King of Shechem and Bethmillo. But his supporters began to argue and fight among themselves, and after things in his country got worse, Abimelech was eventually killed when a woman dropped a millstone on his head.

> *Jephthah crossed over to the Ammonites and he smote 20 cities.*

Within 50 years the Israelites faced yet more chaos. The Ammonite people declared war on the Israelites. As the Israelites had done in the past, they cried out to the Lord for help. At first the Lord hardened His heart, but just in time He decided to give them another great war leader.

The man the Lord chose as His new hero might have been considered unsuitable in many ways. Jephthah was the son of a man called Gilead, but, as he had been born illegitimate, he was despised by all the members of Gilead's lawful family. As soon as his brothers had grown old enough to gang up against him, they had driven him away from home. Left to fend for himself in the land of Tob, Jephthah had made a name for himself as a fearsome bandit. Under his leadership, a band of villains had plundered the countryside, terrorizing the local people.

Jephthah's daughter
Human sacrifice was not something God would be pleased by, so this element of the story is surprising. It has been suggested that, instead of sacrificing his daughter, Jephthah sent her away to live a life of celibacy, in service to God. Other sources argue, however, that this is incompatible with the fact that the Bible clearly states that Jephthah kept his vow.

Timbrels and cymbals
Percussion instruments, such as cymbals and timbrels, or tambourines, were used to accompany singing and dancing. During the Exodus from Egypt, Moses's sister, Miriam, played a tambourine while she and the other women sang and danced. Israelite women would often celebrate the return of victorious armies by coming out of the town, singing and dancing with their timbrels.

Spoils of battle
This picture shows a gold amulet, or charm, in the shape of a flying falcon. It is now in the Israel Museum, Jerusalem. This is the type of valuable ornament that Jephthah and his men would have plundered from the towns they conquered.

Now the Israelites faced the full force of the Ammonite army, and a ruthless warrior such as Jephthah was just the sort of commander they needed to organize their counter-attack. The elders of the tribes hurried to the land of Tob to beg the man who had been disowned by his Israelite brothers to come back and lead their troops into battle. "I will only return with you on one condition," Jephthah demanded. "That if the Lord grants us victory, you will make me your leader." The panic-stricken Israelite elders quickly agreed to his demand.

Messengers soon arrived from the King of the Ammonites, demanding the return of land the Israelites had taken when they had originally invaded Canaan. Jephthah wasted no time in sending a clear message straight back that they would not do so. "The Lord will judge this day between the people of Israel and the Ammonites!" he cried, rousing the soldiers to fight. Then Jephthah prayed to God and made a solemn vow, "Lord, if you deliver these enemies into our hands, I will sacrifice to you whatever I see first when I reach home." And so Jephthah and his army went to war and slaughtered the Ammonite forces.

News of the warlord's great victory travelled before him, and as Jephthah drew near to his house his daughter came out to celebrate his return, playing a tambourine. Jephthah couldn't believe his eyes. Instead of rushing to throw his arms round his daughter, he howled with grief, throwing himself down into the dirt and tearing at his clothes in despair. "I have vowed to the Lord that I would sacrifice the first thing I saw on my return," he wept, unable to meet her eyes. "And I cannot take back my promise," he

moaned. Jephthah's daughter bore the dreadful news with courage and faith. "It is right that you keep your bargain with God," she said quietly. "Only grant me some time to prepare myself."

After two months had passed, Jephthah paid the price for the wicked things he had done in the past, slaying his daughter by his own hand. But each year afterwards, on the anniversary of her death, the Israelite women gathered together to remember her.

The journeys of Jephthah
When Jephthah was rejected by his family, he fled north from his home to the land of Tob. Here he made a name for himself as a great leader and a fearsome bandit. When Israel was being threatened by the Ammonites, the elders of the threatened tribes thought that Jephthah was the person to help them out. So they went to see him to ask if he would rescue them. Jephthah led his armies throughout the area to the east of the Jordan, destroying and burning the Ammonite towns, such as Abel-keramim, and defeating the Ammonites at every stage. With God on his side, the Ammonites could not win. But his foolish attempt to make a deal with God proves his undoing, when on his return to Mizpah his daughter is the first person that comes out of his door to meet him, so he has to sacrifice her as he vowed.

> ∾ **ABOUT THE STORY** ∾
>
> *After more years of trouble, God chooses a new leader, Jephthah. When the Israelites ask him to lead their troops into battle against the Ammonites, he makes a bargain with them, that he remain their leader if he is successful. However, his bargain with God is not so clever. Unfortunately for Jephthah, the first thing he sees on returning from battle is his daughter. He cannot break his vow to God, so he has to kill her.*

Samson and the Philistines

FOR decades the Israelites had struggled with the war-like Philistines for control of the Promised Land. No matter how many defeats each nation suffered, they both refused to give up; and even though Barak and Deborah had previously crushed the entire Philistine army, the Philistines had slowly regained their strength. Now Israel once again fell into Philistine hands.

Yet God didn't entirely abandon the Israelites. He blessed a childless couple with a very special baby, Samson, sending an angel to tell them that one day he would stand up against the Philistines. The angel also warned the parents never to cut his hair.

Samson grew into a tall and exceptionally strong young man. But when he fell in love with a Philistine girl, his mother and father were utterly dismayed. They didn't know

that it was all part of God's plan, and begged Samson to reconsider. But the wedding plans continued.

A grand wedding feast took place with 30 Philistine guests of the bride invited. Everyone threw themselves into the celebrations and Samson decided to add to the fun by asking a riddle. He thought back to the time when he had been travelling to visit his bride-to-be and a lion had jumped out at him. The mighty Samson had killed the

Jaffa
This picture shows a view of Jaffa, on the Mediterranean coast of Israel. Today, it is part of the city of Tel Aviv but in Old Testament times, it was part of Philistia (the land of the Philistines). In the Bible, it is called Joppa.

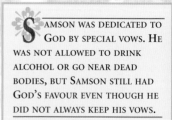

SAMSON WAS DEDICATED TO GOD BY SPECIAL VOWS. HE WAS NOT ALLOWED TO DRINK ALCOHOL OR GO NEAR DEAD BODIES, BUT SAMSON STILL HAD GOD'S FAVOUR EVEN THOUGH HE DID NOT ALWAYS KEEP HIS VOWS.

The Philistines
On the left is a Philistine warrior's coffin. The Philistines were the Israelites' greatest enemies. According to the Bible, they came from the Greek island of Crete and settled on the southern coastal plain of Canaan in the 12th century BC. The Philistines had five main cities, each with its own ruler. The country of Palestine takes its name from the Philistines.

surprised lion with his bare hands. Later, on his return, Samson had seen that a swarm of bees had made a hive in the lion's carcass, and without fear he had reached in and taken a piece of the delicious honeycomb. These events made a nicely perplexing riddle:

"Out of the eater came something to eat,
Out of the strong came something sweet."

"Solve it by the end of the week," Samson challenged the Philistines, "and I will give each of you a set of fine clothes. If you fail, you must buy me rich clothes instead."

For days the guests racked their brains, until they were almost driven mad. As the baffled Philistines ran out of ideas, they decided to cheat. They went to the bride and told her that her life depended on telling them the secret.

Samson's young bride was so scared that she plagued her husband desperately for the answer to the riddle. On the seventh day, when she broke down and wept, Samson gave in. And before the sun went down, the Philistines had their answer.

> " *The Spirit of the Lord came mightily upon him and the ropes became as flax.* "

When Samson realized that he had been tricked by his guests he was furious. He stormed over to the nearest Philistine town and killed 30 citizens. He took the clothes that they were wearing, and he gave them to the Philistine wedding guests to keep his side of the bargain. Then, broken-hearted, he returned all alone to his father's house.

The Philistines turned on his sweetheart and her father and burnt them inside their house. Samson was grief-stricken. "I swear I shall not stop until I have taken my vengeance on the whole nation," he vowed solemnly. But first he had to deal with the lynch mob who had arrived looking for him. Cunningly, he allowed the Israelites to tie his hands and lead him to his captors. There he broke free and seized a large jawbone that was lying at his feet. He attacked the Philistines in a frenzy, and by the time he stopped, he had killed 1,000 of his greatest enemies single-handed.

The Philistines didn't give up trying to catch Samson. When they found him sleeping one night, he escaped by simply lifting the city gates and walking away with them! It seemed as if it would never be possible to conquer the man with the strength of the Lord Himself.

Chosen by God
Samson was singled out by God from birth as special, so could ask God to perform a miracle and supply water to quench his thirst in the desert at Lehi.

Samson the Nazirite
Samson was a Nazirite – one who is dedicated to the service of God by special vows. Nazirites were not allowed to drink alcohol, nor to eat raisins or vinegar. They were forbidden from cutting their hair, and they had to avoid going near dead bodies. As the episode with the lion shows, Samson did not take his Nazirite vows very seriously.

∾ ABOUT THE STORY ∾

The Israelites have fallen under the rule of the Philistines. God sends a saviour in the form of a baby boy. As a young man, Samson disappoints his parents by marrying a Philistine girl, but this is part of God's plan for him, and the alliance is short-lived. Samson is furious that he has been tricked into revealing the riddle about the lion, and he takes revenge. This is the first of Samson's personal battles against the Philistines.

Samson and Delilah

NEWS of Samson's feats of strength against the hated Philistines spread like wildfire through Israel and the people's hero found himself made a Judge. This only inflamed the Philistines' hatred further, and they put Samson even higher on their 'wanted' list.

While the Philistine leaders plotted and schemed, Samson fell in love with a girl called Delilah. But Samson hadn't learnt his lesson. Like his former wife, Delilah was a Philistine. And unknown to him she was soon bribed by Philistine chieftains to use her charms to get Samson to reveal the secret of his strength. She was completely snared by the promise of enough silver to make her very rich, and she did all she could to captivate the great

Israelite Judge. Often when they were alone together Delilah would cuddle up to Samson and ask, "Why won't you tell me how someone could take away your power?" Her innocent eyes and frustrated, enquiring tone gave her a childish air, and Samson never dreamt that Delilah was a cunning woman intent on deceiving him. She nudged and nagged, coaxed and cajoled, until Samson was forced to tell her something just to keep the peace! But he decided to have a little fun, and tease her for a while.

Little did Samson know that he was playing very dangerous games indeed. "If I am tied with seven new bowstrings, I will lose all my strength," he whispered to Delilah, with no idea that Philistine soldiers were hiding in the very next room. "Let me try, just for fun," begged Delilah, and bound him as tightly as she could. Then she stood back and put Samson to the test, crying out, "The Philistines are coming!" and daring him to break free. Imagine the disappointment on Delilah's face when the laughing Samson snapped out of his bowstrings as if they were threads of cotton. "You fibbed!" she cried, stamping her foot. "Please tell me the real secret of your strength!"

"All right, all right," Samson shrugged. "If I'm bound with new, unused ropes, all my strength will leave me." Delilah clapped her hands with glee and rushed to tie him just as he had instructed. Yet once more Samson burst free, and the Philistine ambush stayed where they were.

"You're just mocking me," Delilah pouted. "Stop fooling around, now, and tell me the truth."

Samson pretended to be serious. "Take the seven braids of my hair and weave them into your loom, then you'll find my strength will fade." Very carefully, Delilah did as

Samson and Hercules

This picture shows a statue of the head of Hercules. In Greek and Roman mythology, Hercules was a hero of incredible strength and courage who performed 12 difficult tasks, or labours. After his death, he was made a god. In general, the word "Hercules" is used to mean a man of exceptional strength.

Parallels have been drawn between Samson, the strong man of the Bible, and Hercules, the strong man of Roman myth, comparing Samson's many feats of strength with Hercules' labours. However, while Hercules is a mythological character, there is strong historical evidence for Samson's existence. His birth and death are carefully documented, and the story of Samson as told in the Bible is closely connected with known historical events.

Dagon

Dagon was one of the main Philistine gods. He is often depicted as a fish god, but this is believed to be because of a confusion with the Hebrew word *dag* which means "fish". Another Hebrew word, *dagan* means "grain" and it is possible that Dagon was a vegetation or grain god. He was first worshipped in Mesopotamia from at least 2500BC onwards.

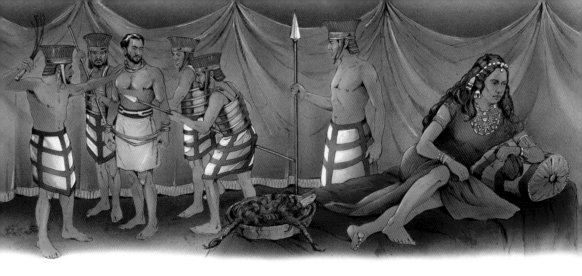

> ## If I be shaved then my strength will leave me and I shall become weak.

she was told. But when she was finished and had made the weaving secure, Samson simply broke the loom with a flick of his head, enjoying the joke more than ever.

"How can you say you love me when you tell me nothing but lies!" Delilah sobbed. She sulked for weeks, making life so awful for Samson that in the end he could bear it no longer.

"If my hair is cut, I shall be like any other man," he confided. And Delilah knew he was telling the truth.

This time Delilah planned everything down to the last detail, so nothing could go wrong. She was so confident of success that she sent messages to the chieftains to come and collect Samson – bringing her money, of course – before she'd even taken him prisoner. First, she soothed Samson to sleep in her lap. Then, when he was snoring soundly, she gave the signal for a servant to creep in and cut off his precious long braids. Finally, with a small self-satisfied smile, she breathed in his ear to wake him. "Samson! Samson!" she whispered. "The Philistines are really coming!" Without realizing that his hair was gone, Samson sprang up to face the soldiers. But the strength of the Spirit of the Lord had indeed left him, and he was soon overpowered. As Samson stood before the Philistines in chains – knowing helplessness for the first time in his life – the cruel, merciless warriors blinded him by gouging out his eyes. Then, rejoicing at the great Israelite leader's misery, they flung him into the jail at Gaza.

Betrayed by Delilah
The name Delilah means "flirt", and the word has come to mean "a temptress". Delilah's greed for money leads her to collaborate with the Philistines and to betray Samson.

⋆ ABOUT THE STORY ⋆

Samson is persuaded by Delilah's charms to reveal the secret of his strength. When Samson's hair is cut, one of his Nazirite vows is broken. Until now, this was a vow he had kept. The vow is a sign of his dedication to God. Though Samson is physically strong, he is morally weak. His weakness symbolizes the weakness of all the Israelites, who have repeatedly broken God's laws and turned to other gods.

Destruction of the Temple

IN the double darkness of the prison dungeons and his blindness, Samson was put to work grinding corn, which hurt him at every move because of the shackles round his wrists and ankles. He had no family with him, no friends, and no possessions – only God and time. And as time passed, Samson's hair began to grow again without him even realizing.

The day came when the Philistines held an important festival in praise of their god, Dagon. Every man, woman and child was out in the streets to watch the sacrifices and join in the rejoicing, and this particular year the celebrations were better than ever. The Philistines had something really special to thank Dagon for, and they were determined to throw a party to remember. For Dagon had delivered into their hands the powerful Israelite leader who had single-handedly been the cause of thousands of Philistine deaths.

The merry-making went on and on, and the worshippers grew wilder and wilder. Voices began to call for the famous prisoner to be brought up out of the jail and paraded for all the Philistines to see, so they could enjoy mocking and jeering at him to their hearts' content. Then the word went round that Samson was to be displayed in the temple itself, and the size of the crowds swelled immediately. How the Philistines longed to look down on their once dreaded enemy and sneer at him and show him in person just how much they hated him!

As soon as the first people caught sight of the wretched, blind Samson shuffling into the temple, they began to yell insults and ridicule him, and soon the noise and excitement was at fever pitch. The Philistine chieftains ordered Samson to be positioned right in the middle of the temple floor, between the two main supporting pillars, in order to give as many of their subjects as possible a good view. And the Israelite champion stood there as he

> **Strengthen me, I pray, this once that I may be avenged upon the Philistines.**

was told, quite broken and slumped, trying to block out the insults and obscenities that came hurtling through the darkness to his ears.

But as if from nowhere, a small spark of an idea suddenly began to glimmer in the blackness that now floated permanently before Samson. Slowly he bent down to the boy who was there to lead him about, and said, "Will you help me feel where the pillars are, so I can lean on them." Samson felt the lad take his hands and guide them out on to the cool rock on either side of him. Then silently Samson called out to the Lord with all the passion that was inside him. "O Lord, God, remember me, I pray," he beseeched, as he stood all on his own in the midst of his enemies. "I pray to you, O God, please give me my strength back just one more time – so I can be avenged

Samson's story
This picture of Samson dates from the 13th century. This means that it is not a realistic painting, but could tell the story of Samson to people at the time who could not read.

Grinding grain
Grinding grain would have been humiliating for Samson, as it was a job normally done by slaves. Samson, though, was probably put to work at a large mill, usually worked by oxen.

upon these people for the loss of my eyes." And Samson drew himself up and braced himself against the pillars, suddenly feeling the Spirit of the Lord flooding as strongly through his body as ever.

"Let me die with the Philistines!" he cried out, and heaved with all his might.

Not one of the Philistines had been able to hear above their own commotion what Samson had said. Yet they had seen him open his mouth and cry to Heaven, and had watched with mounting horror as the crushed, dejected prisoner had straightened

up into a broad-shouldered warrior. Now their scornful cries of derision at once changed to howls and screams of terror as the pillars began to tremble and dust came crumbling down upon them from the ceiling. Before anyone could flee, Samson broke the pillars with an almighty crack and the roof and walls of the huge temple came crashing inwards, burying the thousands of people inside under tons of rubble.

That day, the mighty Samson died along with the Philistines. But he killed more enemies by dying than he had killed during all his life.

❧ ABOUT THE STORY ❧

Samson appears to be a broken man, but his faith is still strong, and God answers his prayer. Through Samson, God finally releases the Israelites from Philistine rule. Samson's destruction of the temple is symbolic of the Israelites' defeat of the Philistines.

Samson
This map shows the area of Samson's war with the Philistines. It shows Lehi, where he killed the Philistines with the jawbone. You can also see Gaza from where he took the city gates, and Hebron where he left them. Finally, there is the Temple of Dagon at Gaza that he destroyed as he died.

The Book of Ruth

DURING the days when the Judges ruled Israel, there was once a great famine that struck the land. Many people were forced either to leave their homes and settle elsewhere, or stay and starve. One man who chose to take his family away to safety was Elimelech. With his wife, Naomi, and his two sons, he went to live in Moab, where the crops were much more plentiful. There they were very happy at first, both boys taking Moabite wives: one called Orpah and the other Ruth. But in the space of ten years, all three men died, leaving their widows sad and lonely. Naomi longed to return to Israel, and made up her mind to go back. The brave widow talked to Orpah and Ruth about her difficult decision. "I consider you both my own daughters, but I shall go back to Israel on my own," she told the two young women. "There's no need for you to come too. You both belong here with your own people." Orpah and Ruth were devastated, but Naomi was insistent. Finally, sobbing with grief, Orpah agreed to remain in

> **66** *Where you go, I will go, your people shall be my people and your God, my God.* **99**

Moab. Ruth, however, flatly refused. "Wherever you go, I will go," she told Naomi, determinedly. "Your people will be my people, and your God my God. Only death itself will keep me from your side." So the two women set out on the long journey to Naomi's home town of Bethlehem.

They arrived at Bethlehem in the middle of the harvest, so Ruth managed to find work straightaway. As was the custom, she went with the other women of the city into the fields to gather the barley that the reapers had left behind. Ruth worked hard from morning until sunset. Her efforts were noticed by a landowner called Boaz, who asked his professional reapers who the young woman was. When Boaz heard that Ruth was Moabite and discovered how faithful she had been to her mother-in-law, he summoned Ruth to see him. "Stay in my fields, under my protection," he told her. "Whenever you get thirsty, help yourself to the water drawn for my reapers."

Ruth was quite overcome with his generosity. "Thank you," she blushed, quite embarrassed by the special treatment. "But why are you being so kind to me?"

Boaz smiled and told her gently that he had heard all about her kindness to Naomi. "May God reward you well for all that you have done," he praised her.

Later on, when the harvesters stopped to eat, Boaz not only called Ruth to come and join them but also gave her more than enough food. The young woman could hardly believe her good luck and hurried back to her work.

"Where on earth have you been working?" marvelled Naomi when she saw the huge sack of grain and the large bundle of food her daughter-in-law had brought home.

❧ ABOUT THE STORY ❧

Although the Israelites have been turning away from God, this story illustrates how, for many individuals, faith in Him remains strong. It also shows that God is just as concerned with the lives of ordinary people as He is with the affairs of great leaders. Ruth discovers her new faith through her love for her mother-in-law. She goes on to produce a son who will become the grandfather of David, the first King of Israel.

Everyday life
The picture shows Ruth working in the fields. While this story relates to the same period as the stories of the Judges before it, its tone and content are very different. It deals with ordinary life, which would have been relevant to many people of the time. Most people during the period of the Judges still had to make a living from the land.

Meeting place
Business deals often took place at the town gates, like the gates of Damascus shown here, as there were plenty of people around to act as witnesses. Boaz was not Ruth's nearest male relative, so he had to meet the man who was, called a "kinsman-redeemer", and buy the right to acquire Naomi's land and marry Ruth. The kinsman-redeemer gave his sandal to Boaz as a sign of the agreement.

"The landowner's name is Boaz," she began, but could get no further before Naomi interrupted her.

"Boaz?" the widow cried, her face lighting up with excitement. "Boaz is one of my dead husband's closest relations! This has to be the Lord's work! Thanks be to God!" And the two women's hearts were filled with gladness.

When the harvest was over Ruth found herself out of work.

"We'll have to tell Boaz that we're family and maybe he will take pity on us," Naomi told her. Ruth put on her finest clothes and went off to find Boaz.

Boaz was sleeping by his grain to protect it when Ruth arrived. She silently went to the end of his sleeping mat and covered herself with the corner of Boaz's robe. When Boaz woke, he was deeply moved by Ruth's plea. "I will do everything in my power to look after you," he said.

The next day, Boaz formally took Ruth and her mother-in-law under his protection. He met Ruth's "kinsman-redeemer", Naomi's nearest living male relative, and bought the right to marry her, sealing the deal, as was customary, by receiving his sandal.

Boaz cared for Ruth and Naomi from that day onwards. He married Ruth, and in due course she gave birth to their son, Obed, who was to become the grandfather of David, the greatest of all the Israelite kings.

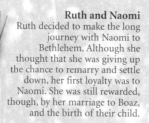

Ruth and Naomi
Ruth decided to make the long journey with Naomi to Bethlehem. Although she thought that she was giving up the chance to remarry and settle down, her first loyalty was to Naomi. She was still rewarded, though, by her marriage to Boaz, and the birth of their child.

Threshing and winnowing
After the barley had been harvested, it was beaten with a threshing board, then winnowed – tossed into the air with a fork so that the grain separated from the stalks. The light stalks blew away while the heavy grain fell straight to the floor.

Jebus (Jerusalem)

Bethlehem

Hebron

SALT SEA

MOAB

Kir-hareseth

Moses

MOSES is one of the great leaders in the Bible. His life was eventful from the very start. Desperate to save her baby son from the Pharaoh's decree that all Hebrew male babies should be killed, Moses's mother put him into a reed basket and hid him among the bulrushes that grew beside the Nile. Found by one of Pharaoh's daughters, he was brought up by her at the royal court.

As a young man, Moses felt sympathy for his fellow-Israelites, who were often ill-treated by their Egyptian masters. When he witnessed an Egyptian overseer beating an Israelite slave, he was so angry, he killed the man. The news reached Pharaoh's ears and Moses fled to safety outside Egypt's borders. During this time, he received a sign from God, in the form of a burning bush, telling him that he was to become the saviour of the Israelite people.

After battling against a great deal of opposition from Pharaoh, Moses finally succeeded in leading his people out of Egypt, to search for the land God had promised them. On Mount Sinai, Moses spoke directly with God and received the Ten Commandments and other laws.

During the 40 years of exile in the wilderness, Moses remained loyal to his people and to his God. Despite the Israelites' regular lapses of faith in God and their rebellions against Moses's own leadership, he stood by them, frequently pleading to God for mercy on their behalf. When Moses's own sister, Miriam, complained about him, claiming that God had spoken to her as well as to Moses, God rebuked her, explaining that although he appeared to other people in visions or dreams, the way in which he appeared to Moses was different. He said, "With him will I speak mouth to mouth, even clearly, and not in dark speeches" (Numbers 12:8).

Although he devoted his whole life to God, Moses was not above sin himself. On one occasion, in the wilderness, he used his rod to bring forth water from a rock, instead of just speaking to the rock, as God had ordered. For this disobedience, he was forbidden entry into the Promised Land, though he did climb Mount Nebo to view it from a distance, shortly before his death.

A man of God

Throughout his life, Moses's faith in God never wavered. He was a trusting and obedient servant until the day he died. Despite all his achievements, and his status as God's chosen one, he remained meek, humble and patient, always putting his people's needs before his own. He was both a great man and a great leader.

The death of Moses

The book of Deuteronomy describes the death of Moses, finishing with the following words about one of the greatest of Old Testament prophets. "And there has not arisen in Israel a prophet since like Moses, whom the Lord knew face to face, none like him for all the signs and wonders which the Lord sent him to do in the land of Egypt, to Pharaoh and to all his servants and to all his land, and for all the mighty power and all the great and terrible deeds which Moses wrought in the sight of all Israel."

Deuteronomy 34:10-12.

The Battle of Beliefs

ON their arrival in the land of Canaan, the Israelites fought many battles with the local people, in an attempt to take over their land. Alongside the war over land, another war was also being fought – a war of religion.

God had instructed the Israelites to drive the Canaanites away from their lands. He knew that the local people worshipped different gods, and that their religion might influence the Israelites. At first, the Israelites obeyed God, but as the years went by, they grew tired of constantly fighting the Canaanites and began to live alongside them as neighbours. As God had predicted, they also began to worship their gods.

Statue worship
Many Israelites were attracted to the Canaanite gods because they could worship statues, which was forbidden by their own God.

Destroying the altar
Gideon destroyed his father's altar to Baal and built a new altar to God. He went on to defeat the hordes of invading Midianites with an army of only 300 men.

Gideon and the angel
In this picture, the angel of the Lord commands Gideon to destroy his father's altar to Baal, together with its statue. Gideon was appointed by God as one of the Judges who would save the Israelites from their enemies.

Canaanite gods
These are three of the main Canaanite gods. Dagon is believed to be a god of grain or vegetation. Baal, which means lord, is a weather god associated with thunderstorms and rain. He is often shown holding a bolt of lightning. Asherah is a fertility goddess associated with Baal.

DAGON   BAAL   ASHERAH

One aspect of Canaanite religion that the Israelites would have liked was the idea of worshipping an image, such as a statue, of a god or goddess. It would have been far more satisfying to worship something they could actually see, as the Israelites were forbidden to worship idols by Moses's second commandment.

The other reason the Israelites turned to the local gods was their apparent control over the fertility of the land. Once the Israelites settled down to become farmers, their crops were very important to them. Many of the Canaanite gods were linked to nature and fertility, and, because of this, they seemed to the Israelites to have more direct influence over their daily life than their own God did. The Canaanites were very successful farmers; some took this as evidence of the superiority of Baal.

Battling on
While the physical battles of clashing swords and shields raged noisily around Canaan, the quieter battle of beliefs was also going on.

The Judges

THE officials called Judges were originally appointed by Moses during the wilderness years. His father-in-law, Jethro, suggested that they could take some of the burden of responsibility from Moses' shoulders. These were not Judges in the legal sense, in the way that people use the word today. After the death of Joshua, no single leader took over, and the Judges took on the role of rulers in peacetime and military leaders in wartime. So the word "judge" came to mean "leader" or "governor".

Ehud and Eglon
Ehud was one of the early Judges. He saved the Israelites from the Moabites by killing their king, Eglon.

Deborah's wisdom
Deborah used to sit under a palm tree and hand out advice to Israelites who came to her for help with settling their disputes.

The Book of Judges in the Old Testament tells of the lives of these Judges. Their main role was to save the Israelite people from their enemies and to try and keep them faithful to God's laws. During the time of the Judges, a pattern of events kept repeating itself. The Israelites turned away from God and started to worship the Canaanite gods so God punished them by letting them fall into the hands of a foreign ruler. The people repented and begged for mercy, promising to change their ways so God appointed a Judge to save them. For a period of time, the people mended their ways, but after the death of the Judge, they slipped back into their sinful habits.

There were 14 Judges, the first being Othniel and the last Samuel. Some ruled for a very short time and achieved nothing of great importance. Others were more significant, including Deborah, a woman Judge who, together with Barak, saved the Israelites from the Canaanite General Sisera. Gideon took on the mighty army of the Midianites with a force of only 300 men, and there was Jephthah, a brigand who defeated the Ammonites. The most famous Judge is Samson, who made many attacks on the Philistines. Under Samuel, the last Judge, and the first Kings, the nation of Israel was eventually brought together and the Philistines were finally defeated.

TIMELINE 1400BC TO 1000BC

• Moses receives the Ten Commandments, but finds the people worshipping the golden calf and smashes the tablets.

THE ISRAELITES CROSS THE RIVER JORDAN

• Moses, Israel's greatest leader, dies.

• Joshua is appointed leader of the Israelites.

• Joshua takes the Israelites across the River Jordan into Canaan, and leads them in victory against Jericho.

1400BC   MOSES SMASHES THE STONE TABLETS

1300BC

12

Samson and the Nazirite Laws

THE Judges were chosen by God to lead and judge his people. It is confusing, therefore, to see that some of these appointed leaders, who are held up as examples to their people, lived their own lives in a way that was far from what people might expect, and seemed to disregard many of God's laws.

The most obvious example is Samson. He was a Nazirite which meant that he was dedicated from birth to the service of God by special vows. Nazirites were not allowed to cut their hair nor to come into contact with dead bodies. Samson broke most of his Nazirite vows, by eating honey from the carcass of a lion he had killed and by allowing Delilah to cut off his hair.

Although it is hard to accept the behaviour of Judges like Samson in positions of authority, we must remember that all the Judges are instruments of God and their actions are part of God's plan. For example, it is because Samson allows Delilah to cut his hair that he is captured by the Philistines. In their temple God gives him back his strength so he can kill several thousand of them at once. God's purpose for Samson is to defeat the Philistines, so He allows some of His laws to be broken in order to achieve something more important.

Forbidden food
Samson broke his Nazirite vows by eating honey from a nest bees had made in a lion's carcass.

The strongest man
When Samson was found in Gaza, he escaped by uprooting the city gates and walking away with them.

Tricked by a woman
Delilah tricked Samson into revealing the secret of his strength and then betrayed him to the Philistines.

• Joshua renews the Israelites' covenant with God before he dies.

ISRAELITES' WEAPONS AND A SHEKEL

• After the death of Joshua, the Israelites lose their faith in God. They begin to worship Canaanite idols, and fall into the hands of Canaanite rulers.

• Deborah and Barak rescue the Israelites from the army of Sisera.

• Gideon rescues the Israelites from the Midianites.

DEBORAH DEFEATS SISERA

JEPHTHAH'S DAUGHTER

• Jephthah defeats the invading Ammonites, but pays for his foolish vow to God when he returns home.

1100BC

• Samson the Nazirite judges Israel and defeats the Philistines.

• Ruth and Naomi make their journey to Bethlehem. Ruth marries Boaz, and Obed is born.

PHILISTINE WARRIOR'S COFFIN

1000BC

THE GREAT KINGS

The Israelites appoint their first king, Saul. Like the monarchs who follow him, he has great strengths as a leader, but also many imperfections. The stories follow the varying fortunes and behaviour of the Israelites and their leaders, from David, who started off as a shepherd boy, to Solomon, who was known for his wisdom.

Introduction

HERE you can read about the Israelites' battles amongst themselves and with their neighbours, and follows the rises and falls of their faith in God. This section covers the period of time from Samuel through the reigns of the first kings of Israel, to the division of the kingdom into two nations, Israel and Judah.

The story starts with the story of Samuel, who, brought up by Eli the High Priest, was called by God as a prophet at an early age. He went on to rule Israel as a Judge, a ruler of Israel called by God. Under Samuel's leadership the Israelites' faith in God was restored. When he got older the people asked him for a king, so God instructed Samuel to anoint Saul the first king of Israel.

Saul was very popular with his people and successful in war, but things soon started to go wrong. Saul disobeyed God several times. He was eventually punished when God rejected him as king, and Samuel anointed a shepherd boy called David as Israel's next king. David became very popular after killing the Philistine giant Goliath. Saul became so jealous that he tried to kill David who escaped to safety in the wilderness where he lived for many years. He only returned to Israel after Saul and his four sons died during a battle with the Philistines.

After Saul's death, David eventually became king over all Israel. He captured the city of Jerusalem and made it his capital, setting up the tabernacle there, and bringing back the ark. It was David who wanted to build a temple, a permanent home for the Ark of the Covenant containing their sacred laws, but God decreed this would be done by the next king, David's son, Solomon.

Jerusalem
David decided when he became king that he wanted Jerusalem as his capital. It is now known as the "City of David".

When Solomon took the throne on David's death, his main aim was to maintain the peace that his father had achieved. Solomon concentrated on developing trading links with his neighbours, and he channelled his energies into huge building projects, the most important of which was the temple in Jerusalem. As part of his plan to forge links with his neighbours, he married many foreign women, but his wives reintroduced pagan gods into Israel and Solomon joined them in their worship. God's punishment to Solomon was to split the kingdom in two, and only two of the 12 tribes were given to his son. The other ten crowned a government official called Jeroboam as their ruler.

Until the era of the kings, the Israelites had been led by Judges or priests. The first king, Saul, was requested by the people. Samuel tried to persuade them to be content to worship God as their king, but they wanted to be like their neighbours. God gave His consent, but warned that a king would make demands on his people, and a king would not be as forgiving as God had been.

The king's role developed as it passed from Saul, to David, to Solomon. Saul was a fine warrior king but never quite established his position as religious leader – it was Samuel who performed this role during his lifetime. David was very successful, he was in many ways the ideal king. He established Israel as a nation state and founded a dynasty that lasted for over 400 years. Because he had been involved in warfare he was not allowed to build a temple – that role fell to Solomon who was wise, peaceful, but was not, and could never be, perfect.

David is very significant in Jewish history. The Star of David is the symbol of Judaism and features on the Israeli flag today. After David's death, the Jews hoped for a Messiah (an "anointed one"), a righteous leader descended from David, who would reunite the tribes of Israel and restore Israel's position in the world. The message of the New Testament is that this hope was fulfilled in Jesus Christ, and the lineage from David to Jesus is traced at the beginning of Matthew's gospel.

David and Jonathan
The fugitive David was the closest of friends with Jonathan, even though Jonathan was the son of King Saul, who wanted to kill him.

Judea and the Dead Sea
The Salt Sea, now called the Dead Sea, and the River Jordan are at the centre of the Promised Land, and have been important since the miraculous crossing of the river by Joshua. The shores of the Salt Sea are actually 400m below sea level.

Israel in the Time of Samuel

THERE were great changes to the state of Israel during the life of Samuel. When he was first called by God, the Israelites had long since fallen into sinful habits. They were worshipping other gods, the same gods that the Lord told them never to worship when they first arrived in Canaan under the leadership of Joshua.

When Samuel became the last Judge of Israel, the Israelites were fighting a losing battle with the Philistines, one of the tribes already living in Canaan. The Philistines were one of the first people to use iron in their weapons. They had a better organized army and were winning land from the Israelites. This stopped when Samuel took command. His first battle with the Philistines, with help from God and the Israelites with their renewed faith, was a huge success. For the rest of Samuel's life the Philistines were forced further and further east towards the sea.

All the lands around Israel at this time were kingdoms, and most were successful in battle, much of the time against the Israelites. Many of the people thought that this was because the Israelites did not have a single, strong leader to stand at the head of their army. They asked Samuel for a king, and he anointed Saul.

Saul won his first victory against the Ammonites who were laying siege to the city of Jabesh-gilead. This was the first of many victories for Saul, who won many cities for Israel. He won a great victory in the battle at Michmash, when his son Jonathan led the outnumbered Israelites against the powerful Philistine army. Saul also met with success in the south of the kingdom, winning battles with other tribes like the Edomites and the Moabites.

Despite his military successes for the Israelites, Saul was never as successful in leading the Israelites in their worship of God. Samuel was always the religious head of the country. This led to problems for Saul, who offended God and Samuel time after time. God eventually abandoned Saul as king, and blessed David instead. After Saul's death at Gilboa, and a brief civil war for the crown between David and Saul's surviving son, Rehoboam, David ruled the whole of Israel as the sole king.

David first made sure that the land Saul had gained from the surrounding tribes was safe, and went on to win more land, from the Philistines, the Edomites, the Ammonites, the Moabites, and the Arameans in the north. When he captured Jerusalem and made it his capital, the Israelites' conquest of Canaan was finally complete.

David did not stop there. He had extended the kingdom, but he also expanded the 'vassal territories' of Israel. These were states or kingdoms that paid sums of money to David so that he would not attack them, and David would also provide them with protection from other invading states. David extended the empire from Ezion-geber in the south, to Damascus in the north. At his death, he handed on to his son Solomon an empire larger than any that the Israelites would ever see again.

Solomon was not the man of war that his father had been. He secured the lands that his father had gained, and made peace treaties with the surrounding powers to ensure that his kingdom was safe. Solomon divided his kingdom into twelve districts, each with its own governors to collect taxes and organize the forced-labour schemes, where people had to leave their land and work for Solomon for one month in three. By getting the country organized like this, he could claim taxes from the people, which funded his building work. But the heavy taxes and forced labour made him unpopular.

When his son, Rehoboam came to the throne and told the people he would be even worse than his father, ten of the tribes rebelled and crowned Jeroboam, one of Solomon's governors, their king. This split Israel into two countries. The northern country kept the name of Israel, and built their capital city at Samaria. The southern country was made up of the two tribes of Benjamin and Judah. They took the name of Judah, with their capital at Jerusalem.

The Promised Land
The picture on the left is an old map of the Promised Land. It shows the Salt Sea, the River Jordan and the Sea of Chinnereth on the right-hand side. You can also see Egypt and the River Nile on the left.

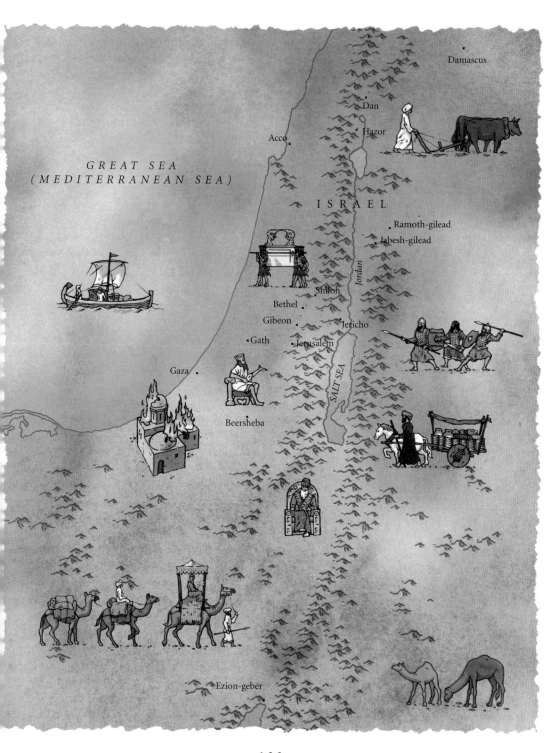

Damascus

Dan

Hazor

Acco

GREAT SEA
(MEDITERRANEAN SEA)

ISRAEL

Ramoth-gilead

Jabesh-gilead

Jordan

Shiloh

Bethel

Gibeon

Jericho

Gath

Jerusalem

Gaza

SALT SEA

Beersheba

Ezion-geber

The Birth of Samuel

AFTER the Israelites had settled into the Promised Land, they began to forget God. People ignored the warnings of the Judges. They sank into sinful habits, worshipping false idols. Eventually, few God-fearing families were left. Even old Eli – the high priest in the tabernacle at Shiloh – had two wicked sons. Hophni and Phinehas were priests themselves, but they had no respect for God. They were dishonest and violent, and even took the sacrifices worshippers brought for the Lord, beating up anyone who resisted.

Only a few people still kept the Lord's commands. Among them were Elkanah and his two wives, Peninnah, who had many children, and Hannah, who had none. Each year, the family would travel from their home in the hills to worship God in the tabernacle at Shiloh. And each year, Hannah would pray with all her heart that the Lord would grant her children. One year, after Peninnah had teased her about being childless, Hannah was more distressed than usual. She stood in the house of the Lord begging God to answer her. "Lord," she vowed, "if you'll grant me a son, I promise I'll give him into your service."

When Eli noticed her muttering under her breath, he was furious. He was always having to throw thugs out of the shrine, and now a drunk had wandered in. "Get out of God's house and don't come back till you've sobered up!" he yelled furiously at Hannah.

"Please forgive me, my lord, I'm not drunk," sobbed Hannah, and poured out her heart to the old priest.

"Go in peace," he said kindly, "and "may you have your wish. I'll add my prayers to yours."

Imagine Hannah's joy soon after when she realized she was pregnant! She called the boy Samuel, and a couple of years later, she kept her promise to God. Hannah went back to Shiloh and gave the boy into Eli's hands. God rewarded Hannah's loyalty by sending her five other children, and each year she returned to Shiloh to see her firstborn son.

Samuel grew up pure-hearted and strong. He loved the old priest as if he were his real father, and Eli was as proud of Samuel as he was ashamed of his own sons. "Why do you commit these terrible crimes?" Eli raged at Hophni and Phinehas. But they just ignored the old man and carried on regardless.

One day a man arrived in Shiloh, asking for Eli. The days of great prophets such as Moses and Joshua were long gone. However, Eli knew the stranger was a prophet. The prophet's message made Eli's blood run cold.

"Centuries ago, God appointed your family as priests to serve Him for ever. Now your sons are sinning against

✤ ABOUT THE STORY ✤

The birth of Samuel showed the Israelites that God always tries to bring His people back to obey and love Him. God never gives up on them completely, but He sends a leader to help them. Samuel is one of several people in the Bible who were born for the special purpose of leading the Israelites. But it took time for him to learn and to grow before he was ready for his task.

Priests and worshippers
As priests, Eli's sons were entitled to some of the sacrificial offerings brought to the tabernacle. They abused their position by taking more than their proper share, and because of their sinful acts, God put a curse on Eli's family.

Him. Know then that sickness, poverty and misery will soon arrive at your door. Both your sons will die on the same day, and the Lord will raise up a new, faithful priest who will serve Him truly."

From then on, Eli had a heavy heart. And as his spirit sank, he started to lose his sight, but Samuel was always close at hand to help the old man.

One night when Samuel was lying in bed he heard someone calling his name. Samuel ran to the high priest straight away. But the old man was puzzled.

"I didn't call you," Eli said. "Go and lie down again."

Samuel had just settled down when the voice came again. "Samuel! Samuel!" Once more, Samuel leapt up and raced round to Eli's room.

> **" I will fulfil against Eli all that I have spoken concerning his house. "**

"Here I am, father," he told the old man.

"I didn't call, my son," replied Eli. "Go back to sleep now." But when it happened a third time, a shiver ran down Eli's spine. He suddenly realized what was going on.

"Go and lie down," he told Samuel gently. "If someone calls you again, say, 'Speak, Lord, for your servant is listening.'"

When Samuel heard the voice again, he replied just as Eli had told him, and the Lord spoke clearly into his mind.

"I am about to punish Israel for their lack of faith. Also tell Eli I am about to punish his family, because of his sons' evil deeds, which he knew about but failed to stop."

Samuel was worried. How could he possibly give the old man such dreadful news? "You must tell me everything that the Lord said," Eli insisted. Sadly, he listened to everything that was going to happen. He sighed wearily. "It's the Lord's will," murmured Eli. "He must do whatever He sees fit."

Sacrificial fork
This sacrificial fork would have been used by the priests to scoop up the parts of the sacrifice to which they were entitled.

Hannah's song
When Hannah took Samuel to Shiloh and gave him into God's service, she sang a song of praise and thanksgiving to the Lord. The words of the song suggest that she was a prophetess. Hannah's song has been compared to that song that Mary sang when an angel told her she would become the mother of Jesus.

∼ THE SONG OF HANNAH ∼

THE LORD MAKES POOR
AND MAKES RICH;
HE BRINGS LOW, HE ALSO EXALTS.
HE RAISES UP THE POOR
FROM THE DUST;
HE LIFTS THE NEEDY
FROM THE ASH HEAP,
TO MAKE THEM SIT WITH PRINCES
AND INHERIT
A SEAT OF HONOUR.
FOR THE PILLARS OF THE EARTH
ARE THE LORD'S,
AND ON THEM HE HAS SET
THE WORLD. ∼

Home of the tabernacle
This is Shiloh, where the tabernacle was kept, and where Hannah went to pray. Its modern name is Seilun. The tabernacle was set up here by Joshua when the Israelites conquered Canaan and did not move until the time of King David.

Philistines Capture the Ark

As Samuel grew up, he became known far and wide as a true prophet. Eli the high priest was getting frail and blind. His one hope was that Samuel would prove to be God's chosen new leader. Everything else looked gloomy.

The Philistines wanted to win back their land and were about to attack once again. The Israelite army was going to meet them, confident that God would be with them and give them victory. However, despite Samuel's rousing preaching, many people still worshipped idols. In the past, whenever the Israelites had turned away from God, God had turned His back on them too. Now, He left them to face their worst enemy alone.

At the end of the first battle 4,000 Israelite soldiers lay dead at the feet of the cheering Philistines. The elders were shocked. "Why did God allow us to be crushed like this?"

they groaned. "We'll have to bring the Ark of the Covenant here. We must have God with us on the battlefield if we are to be saved from our enemies."

The two wicked sons of Eli brought the holy ark from Shiloh. As the ark entered the camp, the soldiers cheered so loudly that the Philistines heard it in their own base. When they found out the cause of the commotion, they shook in their shoes. "The Israelite God who struck down the mighty Egyptians has come to help them!" they howled. "We're doomed!" However, instead of waiting in despair, they looked death straight in the eye. "Fight, Philistines!" came the command from their generals. "Don't be taken like slaves, but die with honour!" The soldiers launched a sudden, courageous attack.

Later that day, Eli was sitting worrying about the ark. "I should never have let them take it," he murmured. Then, he heard wailing, and footsteps hurrying towards him. "I come from the battlefield," the messenger panted.

Eli gripped his seat and tried to steady himself. "What's happened?" he asked.

"There's been a terrible slaughter!" the messenger wept. "30,000 foot soldiers have been slain and your sons are among them!"

Eli's heart was pounding. "What news of the ark?" he yelled, in a frenzy.

The messenger looked up at the high priest. "It has been

❖ ABOUT THE STORY ❖

The Ark of the Covenant contained the Ten Commandments that God had given to Moses. It symbolized God's presence, so when it was captured it seemed as if God Himself had left the Israelites. But He did not intend people to think that the ark had any magical properties. This event was like a visual aid to show that God was more powerful than Dagon, the false god of the Philistines.

Travels of the ark
The ark was moved from Shiloh when the Israelites wrongly tried to use it as a good luck charm in battle. The Philistines captured the ark at Eben-ezer, but plagues infested each city it was kept in, so it was sent back to the Israelites at Beth-shemesh.

captured!" he whispered. Eli gasped and toppled backwards as if he'd been punched. There was a snap as the old man's neck cracked and Eli died, God's judgement on his family fulfilled.

The Philistines carried the ark to Ashdod, where their lords displayed it in the temple of their god, Dagon. However, next morning, the people found the statue of Dagon fallen face down on the floor before the ark. The Philistines set their god back in its place and dusted him off. The following day Dagon was again found lying in front of the ark, with his head and hands broken off. Soon ordinary people discovered lumps growing inside them and their skin breaking out in boils. Then thousands of rats scuttled into the city. "It's the ark!" the people wailed. "Get rid of it!"

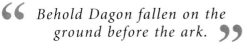

> **“** *Behold Dagon fallen on the ground before the ark.* **”**

"They may be right," the lords agreed. "We'll send the ark to Gath instead."

The people of Gath fared no better. No sooner was the ark within their walls than the tumours and boils began to plague them too. "Take it away!" the inhabitants screamed.

The people of Ekron heard of plans to transfer the ark to them, and immediately they sent a committee to stop them. "Don't you dare send us that cursed thing!" they raged.

The Philistine lords sighed. "There's only one thing for it: we'll have to give it back to the Israelites."

The lords consulted magicians on how to return the ark. They built a cart to carry it, with an offering of ten golden statues. They hitched up two cows that they'd separated from their calves. "Set the cart off without a driver," the magicians instructed. "If the cows go to the border, it will prove the Israelite God really is in charge. If they return to their calves, we'll know it's all a load of rubbish."

The Philistines were stunned to see the cows plod straight down the road to the Israelite city of Beth-shemesh, just as if the cart had an invisible driver. The Israelites in the fields couldn't believe their eyes. Weeping with joy, they ran to receive their nation's treasure. And the ark stayed in a safe-house at nearby Gibeath-kiriath-jearim for 20 years, for the people dared not move it.

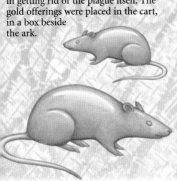

Plagues
The offering of golden statues mentioned in the story included five gold rats, each one representing one of the five Philistine rulers. The Philistines hoped that by sending out statues of the rats that were carrying the plague, they would succeed in getting rid of the plague itself. The gold offerings were placed in the cart, in a box beside the ark.

S OME PEOPLE REFUSE TO HONOUR OR SERVE GOD. THE BIBLE TELLS US THAT EVENTUALLY EVERYONE WILL HAVE TO ADMIT THAT HE EXISTS AND IS WORTHY OF WORSHIP. ALL WILL BOW BEFORE HIM – AS THE STATUE OF DAGON DID.

Ark in battle
The ark was the Israelites' most precious possession. By using the sacred ark as a talisman to protect them from the Philistines, the Israelites showed disrespect to God. Their punishment was to lose both the battle and the ark.

Samuel in Command

SAMUEL grew up a strong man, full of faith in the Lord. He became the Judge, or leader of Israel, just as Eli had hoped. The great prophets of the past – Abraham, Moses and Joshua – had all spoken to the nation and inspired the people, and Samuel was no exception. One of the very first things he did was to call a huge meeting at Mizpah. "There is only one God," he told the hundreds of thousands of people gathered there. "You have seen what dreadful things you bring upon yourselves when you abandon the Lord. Now, if you really want to turn back to God, you must get rid of all the pagan idols you've been worshipping. You must beg the Lord's forgiveness and feel truly sorry in your hearts. Make up your minds that you're going to serve the one true God. Do your very best to obey every single one of His commandments and laws. Then the Lord will save you all from the threat of the Philistines and raise the whole nation of Israel above all its enemies."

As the people listened, they looked up with awe at the young man who stood in front of them. Samuel's eyes shone as he spoke of God, his whole body was alive with passion. "It's true!" they shouted. "We've sinned against the Lord! Help us to find forgiveness!"

Filled with hope, Samuel gave great thanks to God. Then he instructed the nation that everyone was to begin a long fast right there and then as part of their penance, and Samuel led the crowd in prayer.

Meanwhile, news of the massive gathering was reaching the ears of the Philistine lords. "You'll never get another chance like this," the spies reported. "Nearly all of the Israelites have gathered together in one place, and they're mostly unarmed! To top it all, Samuel is there too!" Without a moment's delay, the Philistine lords mobilized their troops and marched on Mizpah.

Samuel was right in the middle of making a sacrifice when a terrified Israelite scout came dashing up to him with word that the full might of the Philistine army was drawing near. Panic rippled through the crowd like wildfire. The people began to jump up in terror, turning this way and that, not knowing which way to run. Samuel, however, calmly continued making his offering to God. He didn't flinch even when the Philistine soldiers suddenly appeared on the crests of the hills all around, endless dark figures against the sky.

> **The hand of the Lord was against the Philistines all the days of Samuel.**

As the Israelites' screamed, the Philistines began to charge down the slopes towards them, spears aloft, swords glinting in the sun. At the very last minute, when the Philistines were close enough for the Israelites to see their faces, Samuel finished his sacrifice and looked up to heaven, praying for help. The wave of roaring troops suddenly disintegrated into a confused mob of bent figures, who stumbled about with their hands to their ears. The Israelite screams died away into a stunned silence. While they heard nothing but the beating of their own

hearts, the Philistines rolled on the earth in agony at the mind-splitting thunder that came from the skies.

Once the Israelites had recovered from the shock, they rushed on the soldiers with renewed confidence that the Lord was with them. And victory was theirs. It was a sign that God was willing to forgive the sinning nation.

For the rest of Samuel's life, the Israelites defeated the Philistines in every battle they fought. All the cities the Philistines had won back were recaptured by Israel, too. The nation's other enemies sensibly stayed well away.

The Israelites looked up to Samuel as one of their greatest ever leaders; they respected him as someone very close to God. But Samuel didn't keep his distance from the people. Each year he toured round the country, going from place to place among them. And the prophet won back the Israelites' hearts for the Lord.

Samuel

Not only was Samuel a Judge and a prophet, but his name is also given to the two books of *Samuel* in the *Old Testament*. When he was a baby, his mother dedicated him to God and he was brought up by the high priest, Eli, at the temple at Shiloh. He was first called upon by God while still a child. His leadership was later challenged by those who wanted a king as leader instead of a Judge. After some resistance, Samuel anointed Saul as the first king of Israel. He later anointed David as the next king. Samuel died in a place called Ramah, north of Jerusalem, and was buried there.

❖ ABOUT THE STORY ❖

Samuel gives us here the perfect example of the supreme faith in God that the Israelites have been lacking. Even as the Philistines bear down on the unarmed Israelites, Samuel knows that the Lord will protect them, so he puts the Lord first, completes his sacrifice and God saves them.

Saul is Made King

IN his old age, Samuel made his two sons, Joel and Abijah, Judges over Israel. But like the sons of Eli, they were corrupt. They took bribes from the people, and ignored the way the rules should have been applied. Bad actions were frequently said to be right and good deeds to be wrong.

Eventually the elders of Israel visited Samuel at Ramah. "Samuel, you are a great man. But we know that you are too old to lead us now," they told him. "However, your sons are dishonest. We don't want Judges anymore, we want a king to govern us, like all the other nations."

When the elders had gone, Samuel wearily closed his eyes. "A king, Lord," he sighed. "You'd think that to have you for a king would be enough."

"The Israelites are rejecting me, just as they have before," God replied. "If the people want a king, they shall have one. But make sure they know what they're getting."

Samuel called a great assembly of the people. "Listen to the Lord's warning," he told the Israelites. "A king will force you to work as his servants. He will tax you and take a tenth of all your grain and wine, flocks, and workers. You will weep and wail at how your king rules over you, but the Lord will not answer your cries. For in having a king, you are pushing God aside."

"All the other nations have a king," the people protested. "Why shouldn't we?"

Samuel realized they weren't going to listen. Inside his head he heard the Lord's voice. "Give these Israelites what they want," God said.

Samuel shook his head. "Go home, all of you," he said quietly.

Months later, up in the hill country, a landowner called Kish told one of his sons, called Saul to track down some escaped donkeys. Saul searched for days without any luck until his servant told him that Samuel happened to be nearby. "He might help us," he said.

As the two men approached the city gates, they were surprised to see a stranger coming out to meet them. They were even more shocked when the old man said, "I am Samuel, who you are looking for. God told me yesterday that you would be coming. Your donkeys have been found, so stop worrying about them. In any case, a few donkeys are nothing compared to the whole of Israel." Saul was puzzled. Whatever did Samuel mean? He was even more puzzled when Samuel took Saul and his servant to be guests of honour at a great feast, and insisted they stay the night with him.

Next morning, the prophet anointed Saul with oil. "The Lord has declared that you are to be king of Israel," Samuel announced. "You will rule over all the people and

save them from their enemies. As a sign that this message comes from God, on your way out of the city two men will give you news about your donkeys. At the large oak tree at Tabor, three men will offer you bread. Finally, near the Philistine garrison at Gibeah, you'll meet a group of prophets singing hymns. Then I'll meet you at Mizpah."

Everything happened just as Samuel had predicted, but Saul was no longer amazed at these strange events. He had changed and had a new faith in the Lord.

Nevertheless, at the meeting the prophet called at Mizpah Saul was terrified. He'd never seen so many people in one place before. "Hear me, Israelites!" Samuel shouted to the crowd. "It is time to select your king." He told the people to draw lots, so everybody would know that nothing unfair had gone on. Although it seemed like chance, Samuel knew that God was in control. First, the Israelites drew lots for the tribe the king should come from – Benjamin was chosen. Next, the tribe drew lots – and the Matrite families were picked. Out of all the Matrite families, Kish's was chosen. And finally, from Kish's family, Saul's name was pulled out of the hat.

> We will have a king over us
> that may govern us and go
> out before us and fight
> our battles.

Saul was nowhere to be found! The excited Israelites searched the area for their new king. Finally someone spotted him hiding among a heap of bags, and he was pushed forward. "Here is the king God has chosen for you!" bellowed the prophet.

The kingdom of Saul
This map shows the extent of Israel during the reign of King Saul. The Israelites had held on to a lot of Canaan, but they had never defeated the Philistines or the tribe of Moab.

Horn of oil
Samuel anointed Saul by rubbing a special holy oil onto him. This ceremony was a sign that Saul had been chosen by God. Samuel would have used olive oil mixed with spices, such as cinnamon and nutmeg. The oil would have been contained in a horn made of ivory and gold.

Sometimes people do things which they shouldn't. This story reminds us that God allows us to use our free will to make mistakes. He always stays with us to help when things go wrong and when we are in need.

♦ ABOUT THE STORY ♦
God had intended the Israelites to be a model nation, showing others what it was like to trust God completely. But the Israelites found it hard to trust God when they couldn't see Him. They thought a king would be better, but forgot that kings are often selfish.

Saul's First Victory

NOT long after Saul became king, part of his new kingdom found itself in trouble. When the Israelites had first arrived in the Promised Land, they had conquered many territories belonging to the Ammonites. Ever since, the Ammonites had been intent on taking back their land, and sometimes they attacked Israel's borders. Now, under the command of Nahash, Ammonite warriors had

besieged the Israelite city of Jabesh-gilead. The outnumbered citizens tried to save themselves by making a treaty with the Ammonites. "If you allow us to surrender peacefully," the Israelite messengers pleaded with Nahash, "we promise to serve you as slaves."

But Nahash was ruthless. "We will allow you to live," he announced coldly, "on one condition: that we put out the right eye of every Israelite in the city."

The inhabitants of Jabesh-gilead were devastated, and the elders begged for seven days to think about it. What a terrible choice they had to make: either face starvation and eventual slaughter by the Ammonites; or suffer torture, endure life in bondage, and bring utter shame on the whole nation. Messengers raced out of the city towards Gibeah and King Saul, knowing that the lives of their families and friends depended on their getting through.

When the panic-stricken riders burst into King Saul's palace, he wasn't at home. Even though Saul was king, he still worked as a farmer and he was busy in the fields. That evening, as Saul returned from his ploughing, he heard weeping and wailing in his courtroom.

> ❝ *The Spirit of God came mightily upon Saul and his anger was greatly kindled.* ❞

Hearing the news from Jabesh-gilead, Saul's anger rose with the outrage of God Himself at the brutal Ammonite threat. With his own hands, he slaughtered two oxen and hacked them into pieces. Then he sent them to every tribe

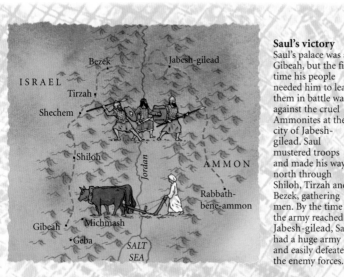

Saul's victory
Saul's palace was at Gibeah, but the first time his people needed him to lead them in battle was against the cruel Ammonites at the city of Jabesh-gilead. Saul mustered troops and made his way north through Shiloh, Tirzah and Bezek, gathering men. By the time the army reached Jabesh-gilead, Saul had a huge army and easily defeated the enemy forces.

Working the land
At this time, farmers like Saul would have used wooden ploughs. Poorer farmers had no metal, but wealthier ones had ploughs with iron blades. As a pair of animals (usually oxen) pulled the plough along, the blades turned the soil over and cut furrows in it so that seeds could be planted there. A light plough was an advantage as the fields were often stony. It was useful to be able to lift the plough over boulders. Large stones were used instead of fencing to mark the boundaries of a field.

Meanwhile, Saul split his forces into three battalions. Early next morning they attacked the Ammonite camp and took the tribespeople completely unawares. Just as the king had promised, by midday the fighting was finished. The ground was littered with the lifeless bodies of the Ammonites, and the people of Jabesh-gilead wept with relief at their narrow escape.

How the Israelites rejoiced! They had hoped for a king who would put their enemies to rout. Saul was the answer to their prayers. "Where are those unfaithful few who refused to pay our king tribute?" the people began to shout. "They should die for their lack of loyalty!"

"Calm down!" cried Saul. "You're not going to lay hands on anyone. This day is a day of celebration, for the Lord has saved Israel once again." The soldiers marched triumphantly back to Gibeah, with their glorious king at their head. They sacrificed peace offerings to the Lord and carried on the celebrations.

in Israel with the message: "Anyone who doesn't follow me into battle will find the same thing happens to his herds."

Israelites across the country felt the Lord was calling them to defend the land. Every fit man came out to fight. When Saul mustered his army at Bezek, he had 300,000 Israelite troops to face the 30,000 Ammonite soldiers.

Within the city, the terror among the people was growing quickly. "Don't be afraid," came the reassuring message from their new king. "By midday tomorrow, I promise you that it will all be over."

The people of Jabesh sent an envoy to tell Nahash that they would surrender the next day at noon. At best, the message would trick the Ammonites into a false sense of security. At worst, they would have to give themselves up and face the appalling consequences.

Defending a town
Towns in ancient times had to be carefully defended because of constant battles over land. Most towns were surrounded by walls which were 3 m wide and 6–9 m high. The walls prevented enemies from entering and formed a platform from which to attack. The picture shows a battering ram being used against the walls of a besieged city.

> ❖ **ABOUT THE STORY** ❖
> *This victory helped the Israelites to see that they could rely on God to rescue them from their enemies. It also reminded them that He did not want them to become slaves again, as they had been in Egypt. Unfortunately, although this victory was entirely due to God's help, Saul began to think he had special powers too – and this pride led to his later downfall.*

Saul and Jonathan

SAUL'S son Jonathan inherited his father's fighting spirit, and his battalion of 1,000 soldiers took the Philistine garrison at Geba. The nation's hopes soared. They could recapture more of the land taken by the Philistines! All Israel followed Jonathan's example and rallied to their king. But the Philistines sent for reinforcements, and soon 30,000 chariots and 6,000 cavalry had amassed at Michmash, vastly outnumbering Saul's army. Many of the Israelite volunteers lost their nerve and hid in the hills.

Saul didn't move until the prophet Samuel arrived to offer sacrifice to the Lord. After waiting a whole week, Saul decided to delay no longer. Even though only priests were allowed to offer sacrifices, he'd have to do it himself.

Just as he finished, Samuel arrived. "You have done a very foolish thing," the angry prophet told Saul. "Because you have gone against the Lord's commandments, He will take the kingdom away from you and your sons. Instead, a new king will be crowned." Then Samuel left the camp.

Things were bad. Only 600 Israelite soldiers remained, and only Saul and Jonathan had proper weapons – everyone else had axes and scythes from their farms. The Philistines were in no hurry to attack; they knew they could crush the Israelites at any time.

Jonathan could not bear the waiting any longer. "Let's go over to the Philistine garrison and see what happens," he urged his armour-bearer one day. Trusting the Lord, Jonathan decided that if the Philistines challenged them to come up to the camp, it would be a sign that God was with him, and they would defeat the Philistines.

The Philistine look-outs laughed when they saw the two Israelites approaching. They were sure they had nothing to fear. "Come here!" they mocked, drawing their swords. "We've got something to show you!"

Jonathan felt a surge of confidence. "God is with us!" he whispered. The two men attacked and soon 20 Philistine soldiers lay dead. They turned and began to make for the main Philistine camp.

At the sudden sight of the two Israelites, the Philistines were thrown into utter confusion. It seemed as if the enemy had appeared out of nowhere. The Philistines ran to and fro in panic, and in the chaos they ended up fighting each other.

❧ ABOUT THE STORY ❧

When Saul became king, Samuel explained that God was still in charge; Saul was simply His servant. Therefore, the human king had to obey God's laws. To show that he did, the king was not allowed to offer sacrifices – that was the job of priests. Saul, however, decided that he could do what he liked. He tried to take God's place, and as a result lost the right to be king.

SCYTHE ADZE CHOPPER SICKLE

Israelite weapons
These are some of the tools the Israelites might have used as weapons. A scythe was normally used for cutting the crops at harvest time. An adze was a tool with a wooden shaft and a metal blade used for planing large pieces of wood to a smooth finish. An axe was used mainly for cutting down trees and chopping wood roughly into shape. The sickle here was also used to cut crops. It is made of wood with flint teeth.

Next day, King Saul went with a priest to ask God for guidance. Saul's prayers were met by silence. "Someone has sinned and so the Lord has closed His ears to us," the king announced. "Whoever it is will die." Imagine Saul's horror when he found out that it was Jonathan who had disobeyed him. The army yelled, "We don't want Jonathan to die for his mistake! Our victory over the Philistines is all due to him." The whole army fell on their knees, praying to God and offering all they had as a ransom for Jonathan. The king's son was spared, and the soldiers carried him home in triumph.

> **Cursed be the man who eats food until it is evening and I am avenged on my enemies.**

Back in the Israelite camp Saul noticed the commotion, and sent his troops on the attack. When the Philistines saw Saul's soldiers coming, they ran for their lives. "No one is to stop for food until every Philistine is dead!" cried Saul. On and on went the battle until nightfall when, faint with hunger, Saul was forced to make camp. But Jonathan hadn't heard his father's command not to eat. When he found some honeycomb as they marched he ate it.

Saul's disobedience
Saul's arrogance in taking over the role of the prophet and offering a sacrifice cost Saul dearly – his sons would not inherit their father's throne. The picture above shows priests offering a sacrifice.

SAUL'S COMMAND NOT TO STOP FOR FOOD WAS FOOLISH. IT CAUSED PEOPLE TO SUFFER AND NEARLY COST JONATHAN'S LIFE. THE BIBLE TELLS US NOT TO SAY THINGS WE MIGHT LATER REGRET. IT IS IMPORTANT THAT WE ARE HONEST WITH OURSELVES AND OTHERS, BUT WE MUST BE AWARE OF OTHER PEOPLE'S FEELINGS AND RESPECT THEM.

Jonathan
This story illustrates the courage of Jonathan as a warrior, but he is mainly remembered for his loyalty to his friend David, who succeeded Saul as king of Israel. Jonathan was the eldest son of King Saul, and his loyalty to David conflicted with his duty to his father, who wanted David dead. Although Jonathan made several attempts at peacemaking, he was forced to disobey Saul to protect David. Jonathan died with his father during a battle against the Philistines at Mount Gilboa.

Saul the Warrior King

KING Saul went on to win victory after victory. But he and Samuel hadn't spoken since the day the king had offered his own sacrifices at Michmash. So Saul was surprised when the prophet Samuel arrived at the palace. Samuel had a message from God. "When Israel moved from Egypt to Canaan, the Amalekite people attacked us.

God now commands you to go and destroy them. Have no mercy. Don't even spare their cattle or possessions."

Saul marched 210,000 fighting men to a valley near Amalek. He attacked the city and killed the people.

However, the Amalekite king, Agag, begged Saul to spare him. Saul also had second thoughts about slaughtering the Amalekite sheep and cattle. He added them to his own flocks.

Even before the king returned, the Lord had told Samuel that

S AMUEL'S STATEMENT "TO OBEY GOD IS BETTER THAN TO SACRIFICE" IS OFTEN REPEATED IN THE BIBLE. IT MEANS THAT RELIGIOUS ACTS ALONE DON'T PLEASE GOD: WE MUST OBEY HIM IN OUR DAILY LIFE. ∽

Destruction of Amalek
This picture shows the destruction of Amalek. The Amalekites had been enemies of the Israelites since their years in the wilderness. God ordered Saul to destroy them as a punishment for their repeated attacks on His people. He also wanted to ensure that the Amalekites would no longer be a threat to Israel.

Sparing the Kenites
The Kenites were a tribe who had once shown kindness to the Israelites by guiding them in the desert. Because of this, they were spared by Saul. The name "Kenite" means "smith". The region the Kenites inhabited was known to contain copper, shown above, so they are thought to have been coppersmiths.

Saul had defied God. At once Samuel set off to find Saul.

"I've done it!" Saul lied. "I did what the Lord wanted."

"Why then can I hear the noises of cattle?" said Samuel.

Saul piled lie upon lie. "We took the animals so we can sacrifice them to God." he said.

"Stop!" Samuel bellowed. "You've disobeyed the Lord's commands! Why did you take some things for yourself, when you knew it was wrong?"

Saul still wouldn't own up. "I *have* obeyed God," he insisted. "My mission was to crush the Amalekites. King Agag is in my control, and I've wiped out his city. We've left the best of the livestock to sacrifice to the Lord."

Samuel was furious. "You should know that to listen to God and obey Him is much more important than offering Him sacrifices! Rebellion and stubbornness are terrible sins. You have rejected the word of God, and He has rejected you as king."

At that Saul panicked. "I'm sorry. I have sinned," he confessed, falling on his knees before the wise old prophet. "I know I should have listened to the Lord, and not worried what the people thought. I beg you, please ask God to forgive me."

The prophet was stony-faced. "The Lord no longer sees you as the king of His people." Samuel turned to go and Saul tried to stop him. He caught the edge of the old man's robe and it ripped. "Just as you have ripped my robe," Samuel declared, "so today the Lord has torn the kingdom from you. He is going to give it to a better man."

Even though Saul was king, Samuel was still the Judge of all Israel. He called for a sword and killed Agag, king of the Amalekites, on the spot.

Samuel returned to his home and Saul went back to Gibeah. The prophet grieved for Saul, but he would have nothing further to do with him. God was sorry that He'd ever chosen Saul to be king of Israel.

> " *And Samuel hewed Agag in pieces before the Lord in Gilgal.* "

God's rejection of Saul

Samuel ordered Saul to destroy all the Amalekites, including all their livestock – their cattle and sheep. Instead of killing the Amalekite king, Agag, Saul took him prisoner. He also kept the best of the animals for himself instead of destroying them. Because of this disobedience, Saul was rejected by God as king and Samuel never saw King Saul again. Samuel had predicted that if Israel had a king, troubles such as this would arise. However, instead of being pleased at his accurate forecast, he grieved for Saul. The picture shows God telling Samuel that He is rejecting Saul as king, while Saul looks on.

❖ ABOUT THE STORY ❖

Saul had grown greedy. He wanted to add to his wealth, and it seemed wasteful to destroy everything. He had not understood that God had ordered the complete destruction of the Amalekites to show that He is a God who punishes sin – the Amalekites had opposed God in the past. Before the battle, Saul had spared the Kenites who lived among the Amalekites, because they had once helped God's people.

The Choosing of David

THE time came when the Lord told Samuel to stop feeling sorry for Saul. "He is no longer king of Israel," God told the elderly prophet. "I want you to take some holy oil to Bethlehem. Visit Jesse, for I have chosen one of his sons to be Israel's new king."

Samuel was worried. "If Saul hears about this, he'll kill me," he told the Lord.

"Pretend that you are in Bethlehem to make an important sacrifice," the Lord suggested. "Invite Jesse to the ceremony and then I will show you what to do."

When the elders of Bethlehem heard that the great prophet was coming, they hurried to meet him, wondering why he had come. "Welcome," they greeted Samuel. "We hope there's nothing wrong." Everyone feared the awe-inspiring man of God.

"Of course there's nothing wrong," Samuel assured them. "I'm here to hold a special prayer service and offering, and you're all invited."

The leaders of Bethlehem must have been surprised to see that the prophet invited Jesse's household, a mere family of farmers to the important service. However, they must have been even more jealous when, after the prayers and the singing and the sacrifice were all done, Samuel drew Jesse and his family to one side for a quiet word. "I'd like to meet your family," the prophet said. The embarrassed farmer felt very honoured, and introduced his sons one at a time.

First was Eliab. As soon as Samuel laid his eyes on Jesse's broad-shouldered, good-looking eldest son, he thought to himself, "Surely this is the new king of Israel." But God immediately spoke clearly into his mind.

"Don't be deceived by how handsome or tall these young men are. Remember Saul – he looks like a hero, but he's not a true king. I see people differently from the way you see each other. I value someone not on their outward appearance, but on their inner worth. I look at human hearts and judge people on what they're like inside."

Next, Abinadab came forward. The prophet studied his face. "No, not this one," he thought.

Then Jesse called Shammah. Again Samuel thought, "No, not him either."

Four more of Jesse's sons passed under the all-seeing eyes of God's faithful servant, but Samuel knew that none of them was the right man. "There must be someone else," thought Samuel to himself, and said out loud to Jesse: "Are those all your sons?"

"There's one more," the puzzled farmer stuttered. "My youngest, David. But he's out looking after the sheep."

"Go and fetch him," Samuel urged gently.

When David arrived, the prophet at once heard the voice of the Lord saying, "Get up and bless him, for this is the one." So, to the complete shock of Jesse and his family, Samuel drew out his precious ceremonial horn filled with holy oil and anointed Jesse's youngest son David as the future king of Israel.

> ❝ *The Spirit of the Lord departed from Saul, and an evil spirit tormented him.* ❞

After the prophet had gone, Jesse's family remained puzzled by what had happened. However, no one could deny that David seemed different, wiser, and sure of himself, with a strange fearlessness.

At the same time that David was filled with God's grace, the Spirit of the Lord left King Saul. Instead, an evil demon came to drive him mad with worries, doubts and fears, and thrust him into deep, black depressions.

Saul's servants suggested a companion to lift his spirits. "David, the son of Jesse of Bethlehem, can play the harp quite brilliantly. He's also a brave young man – a good fighter. And above all, people say that he's close to God."

Saul sent for Jesse's youngest son to come to the palace, never dreaming that the boy would one day replace him on the throne. David seemed to be the only person who could relieve the king of any of his depression, and Saul grew to love him dearly. He made David his honoured armour-bearer and kept him close by his side. Whenever Saul felt gloomy, David would play the harp and bring some moments of peace to the troubled king.

Anointing
This picture shows Samuel anointing David as king by rubbing holy oil on to him. In the Old Testament, a person was anointed to show that they were in some way holy or special to God. Objects such as pillars, shields and the tabernacle, could be anointed too. It was a sin to use anointing oil for any other purpose. Anointing was an act of God and, because of this, was a solemn and important event. In the New Testament, Jesus anointed sick people as a way of healing them.

❖ ABOUT THE STORY ❖
The Bible implies that David did not know exactly why he was anointed. If it had been known, Saul would have tried to kill David, and others could have tried to capture the throne for David. The young shepherd still had much to learn before he was ready to be king.

David and Goliath

IT wasn't long before the Philistines waged war on Israel again. King Saul gathered the army together, and young men from all over the country hurried to the king's camp.

David returned to his former job of looking after Jesse's sheep while three of his older brothers enlisted with Saul. Jesse worried about them continually; his eyes always looked dull and tired. One day, David noticed his father packing some grain, bread and cheeses. "Take these things to your brothers, David," Jesse urged his youngest son. "Then hurry home and tell me how they're doing."

When David reached Saul's camp, he found the soldiers retreating in a panic, running from the battle line as fast as they could. David couldn't believe his eyes. He was nearly trampled underfoot as the last soldiers swarmed past him. Then he saw the enemy, and he understood. On the far side of the battlefield, standing alone, was the biggest man David had ever seen. He was nearly as tall as two men with colossal legs like tree trunks. He carried a spear the size of a battering ram, and his mighty body was clad in enormous bronze armour. "Who is that?" David gasped, rooted to the spot. The soldiers nearby explained.

"It's Goliath of Gath," they told David. "Each time we're ready to attack, he strides out and challenges us to settle things by a duel. He says that if any puny Israelite can beat him, then the Philistines will be our slaves. If he beats our champion, then the Philistines will take all of us into slavery. The king has offered a huge reward to anyone who'll fight him, including his daughter's hand in marriage. But who could beat such a giant?"

"I'd give anything for the chance!" shouted David defiantly, and he went to find the king.

At first, Saul was reluctant to let the young shepherd face the huge warrior. But there was something about the way David spoke that convinced the king he might not be sending the boy to his death after all. "God has given me the strength to fight lions and bears when I am looking after my father's sheep," David said, "and now I know He'll give me the strength to beat this giant!" So Saul gave David permission to go and try.

The king dressed the shepherd for the battle, but David wasn't very big and Saul's armour totally swamped him. David could hardly move. And the weight of Saul's hefty sword and shield made his arms ache. So David took off all the equipment again, until he stood there in his simple shepherd's robe, holding only his sling, his crook and a bag of five smooth, round stones.

When he saw the tiny figure coming out to meet him, Goliath threw back his head and laughed. "Am I a dog, that you come with a stick to beat me?" he roared. "Come on then," he taunted. "I'll mince you into little pieces and feed you to the wild beasts." David was completely unruffled by the huge soldier.

> **"** *David prevailed over the Philistine with a sling and a stone and killed him.* **"**

"You may have mighty weapons, but I'm armed with the most mighty weapon of them all, the name of the

---

❧ ABOUT THE STORY ❧

David's anger was because Goliath was mocking God, not just frightening the people. The Israelites had forgotten that God was more powerful than any enemy. David had known God's protection and help in the past and was convinced that God would not let him down. David's faith in the power of God meant that, armed only with a sling and stones, he could single-handedly do what the whole Israelite army could not.

Single combat
The practice of single combat was sometimes used to decide who should win a war or battle. In single combat, each side chose an individual to represent them. The above picture shows two knights fighting this sort of duel, with the armies facing each other.

country, Saul's subjects loved David more than ever before. The king just became more and more jealous.

One day, the scheming king was presented with the perfect plan to remove David for good. Saul discovered that David and his daughter, Michal, were in love. To David's utter astonishment the king said he'd like them to get married. After all, he was only a farmer's son. There was no way he could afford the traditional expensive present, especially for a king's daughter.

Saul grinned. "All I ask in payment for the bride is that you single-handedly slay 100 Philistines." The wicked king was sure that this time David would not survive. Once

> *Saul thought to make David fall by the hand of the Philistines.*

again, David did the impossible. He killed not 100, but 200 Philistines. And Saul was forced to watch David marry his beloved daughter.

For Saul, this was the last straw. Now, above everything else, the king wanted David dead. He no longer cared how it was done or by whom. He was even ready to do it himself, never mind that it was a sin. Saul began to draw up a murderous plot with his courtiers.

Jonathan heard the palace rumours and raced to tell his best friend that his father wanted to kill him. He hid David away and then begged his father not to go ahead with his terrible plan. Although the king's icy heart

melted at first, it wasn't long before he was being driven mad with hatred again. Saul sent officers to arrest David and then, without a trial, to kill him.

Saul's daughter Michal was suspicious. She noticed strangers hanging around outside the house one night and immediately warned her husband. "My father's spies are everywhere. You must go," she wept. After a tearful farewell, David quietly climbed down a rope from the window and escaped into the night.

Next morning, when soldiers battered down the door, all they found in David's bed was a life-size statue wearing a goat-hair wig. David was far away, in the safe hands of God's faithful old servant, Samuel.

Evil spirits

After Saul disobeyed God, the Spirit of God left him and evil spirits began to torment him by whispering in his ear. These evil spirits were sent by God to punish Saul. Saul lost control of his mind and became depressed and violent. His jealousy towards David drove him to attempt to kill him. David was no longer able to soothe the king's troubled mind with his harp-playing.

David's harp

There were several different types of harp. The picture shows a Jewish harp, also called a nebel. It is made out of animal skin stretched over a round soundbox. The word "nebel" means "skin bottle". Another type of harp is the kinnor, a small stringed instrument with a wooden frame. David's harp could have been either of these.

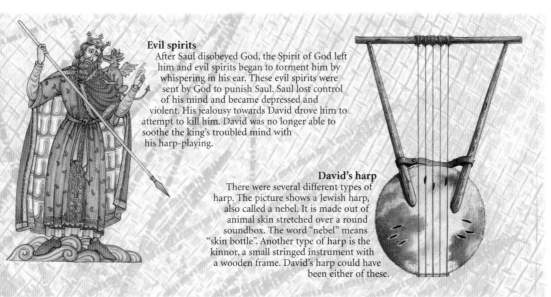

A Faithful Friend

SAMUEL sent David to a safe house at Naioth in Ramah. But Saul found out and sent soldiers after him. When they didn't return, the baffled king sent another group ... and then another ... Finally, wild with frustration, he set out after his son-in-law himself. But when Saul reached Naioth, he met the same strange fate as his soldiers. God's Spirit overcame him and he fell into a trance and took off his clothes. Allowing David to escape.

Apart from his wife, Michal, and the prophet, Samuel, there was only one other person David could trust to help him: the king's own son, Jonathan. He arranged a secret meeting with his best friend.

When the two men met safely, they hugged each other. "What have I done to make your father hate me so much?" David asked Jonathan.

Jonathan shook his head in dismay. "I still can't believe that my father wants you dead. If there's anything I can do to help, just say the word." David had an idea.

✧ ABOUT THE STORY ✧

Many of the Bible's teachings are revealed in practical situations rather than given as a series of ideas. One of its chief teachings is that God is faithful to His people and that He expects us to be faithful to Him and to each other. In this story, Jonathan shows that faithfulness in a dramatic way. The story encourages us to trust God and to care for each other as Jonathan cared for David.

Bows and arrows

Jonathan's bow would have been made of wood, together with animal horn and sinews. His arrows were probably made of reed, with metal tips. Arrows were carried in a leather holder called a quiver, which held about thirty arrows.

Saul's trance

When Saul arrived in Naioth, the Spirit of the Lord came over him and he went into a type of trance. God made him strip off his clothes because they were symbolic of his royal status, whereas in God's presence he was powerless. The Bible describes Saul's behaviour as "prophesying", which means revealing or interpreting God's will.

"It's simple!" he cried. "The new moon festival begins tomorrow and Saul will expect me at court. I'll stay here in the country. If your father asks where I am, say that I asked your permission to go and make a sacrifice with my family. If this doesn't bother him, I'll be reassured that I'm no longer in danger. However, if he's angry, then I'll know that I've spoiled some evil plan to get his hands on me."

"Yes!" cried Jonathan, eagerly. "I'll wait and see how he reacts, then I'll go out for my archery practice. Hide near the range. Once I've shot my arrows and my servant is collecting them, listen carefully to what I shout to him. If I yell, 'The arrows are near you,' it's a sign you have nothing to fear. But if I say, 'The arrows are further on,' then you're in danger and must get away fast." The two friends made a vow in the name of God that they would always remain loyal to each other, no matter what might happen.

Next day, at the feast, David's place at the king's table was empty. Saul didn't let it spoil his fun, but on the third day, when the king saw David's vacant chair, he exploded. "Where is David?" he demanded. Jonathan told his father the excuse David has asked him to give Saul.

David and Jonathan's plan didn't fool him. "You traitor!" he raged. "I know you're best friends! As long as he's alive, you'll never ascend to the throne that's rightfully yours!" Saul brandished a spear. "Bring David to me!"

Jonathan was seething. Stubbornly he replied, "Why should I? What has he done?"

The king roared and hurled his spear at his own son.

Next morning, full of sadness, Jonathan went out to the archery range. He shot his arrows past his servant, and as the lad searched for them, Jonathan called out, "The

> 66 *'The Lord shall be between me and you for ever.'* 99

arrows are further on. Hurry up, don't hang about."

Jonathan sent the servant away, and David came out. Instead of greeting his friend with the usual embrace, David bowed low. It was the only way he could show Jonathan his gratitude for the great loyalty he had shown. The two friends knew it might be the last time they ever saw each other. "Go in peace," Jonathan said, "and may the Lord keep our friendship firm for ever." Then the two men turned away from each other and went their separate ways, Jonathan went back to his tyrant father at the palace, and David, the outcast, to life on the run.

❁ RELIGIOUS FEASTS ❁

During religious feasts people gave thanks to God, repenting of their sins and offering sacrifices. These are the main feasts mentioned in the Old Testament:

The Feast of Weeks *was later known as Pentecost. It was celebrated on the fiftieth day after the Sabbath that began the Passover. It was marked by the offering of sacrifices.*

The Feast of Tabernacles, *which was also called the Feast of Booths, lasted for seven days. It commemorates 40 years in the desert at the time of Moses. Fruit was gathered and people lived in booths, or tents, made of branches.*

The Day of Blowing of Trumpets, *begins the new year. Sacrifices were offered and work stopped.*

The Day of Atonement *is when the high priest makes sacrifices to God to make up for peoples' sins. It took place on the tenth day of the seventh month.*

The Feast of Purim *commemorates the events of the book of Esther, when Queen Esther saved the Jews from a plot by the prime minister to kill all the Jews.*

David the Outlaw

WHEN David left Saul for good, he disguised himself as an ordinary Israelite and fled to Nob. The head priest Ahimelech recognized him instantly and was suspicious. David pretended he had come without all the pomp of the royal household on the king's business. Ahimelech believed him.

Unfortunately, David saw in Nob, another of Saul's officers called Doeg. David knew Doeg recognised him, and David was unarmed. "The king sent me off in such a hurry that there wasn't time to gather my equipment," David pretended to Ahimelech. The only weapon the priest possessed was Goliath's sword. It was the sharpest and most deadly David had ever seen. David was pleased as he himself had won the sword from Goliath in battle.

It wasn't safe to stay in Nob, so David decided to hide among Saul's enemies. He fled to King Achish, the Philistine king of Gath, but his fame had gone before him. "Isn't this Israel's champion?" Achish's servants murmured, hauling David before the throne. He was among his enemies, and in grave danger, so he pretended he was mad. Luckily Achish believed David was mad, and threw him out of the court.

David was so famous that no matter how he disguised himself, he risked being recognized. He tried to avoid people altogether by going to the wilderness around Adullam. But first his brothers hurried to him, and then runaways sought him out. Eventually, David found himself leading about 400 men, many on the run, just like David.

Saul was furious that David was still free. One day he commanded everyone to assemble before him. The king strode up and down the ranks, his face as black as thunder. "You are all so loyal to David that not one of you will tell me where he is?" he accused his men, in a cold rage. Doeg seized his chance to gain favour.

"I saw David at Nob," he told Saul. "Ahimelech gave him some food, and Goliath's sword." Saul's face lit up.

"You will be well rewarded," the king promised the smug Doeg. "Go and kill Ahimelech and his priests, then slaughter everyone else in the treacherous city," he commanded, "or die yourself."

Only one citizen in Nob managed to escape Doeg and his murdering troops, that was Abiathar, Ahimelech's own son. He brought the outlaws news of the terrible massacre. David wanted revenge at once, but the Israelite city of Keilah was besieged by the Philistines and God asked

❧ ABOUT THE STORY ❧

This story shows the readers the contrast between Saul and David. Saul, appointed by God as king, is behaving selfishly. David, who was told by the prophet Samuel that he will be king one day, is willing to wait and refuses to take the law into his own hands. He will not kill Saul to make Samuel's promise come true, because he believes it is wrong to do so.

Cave shelter
The cave where David and his men hid, and where he cut off part of Saul's robe, was at a place called En-gedi, a fresh water spring west of the Salt Sea. The Hebrew word "en-gedi" means "spring of the kid" A "kid" here means a young goat. The place was home to wild goats, but the rugged ground and availability of water made it equally good as a hiding place for people. During excavations that took place in 1949 and 1961-5, several fortresses and a synagogue were discovered on the site.

The king broke down and wept. "You have repaid evil with kindness," he sobbed, "and you will truly be a great king one day. I ask you only to vow that you won't destroy my family for the evil that I have done to you." David gladly gave Saul the promise he wished for and the two men parted in peace, at least for the time being.

> ❝ *The Lord gave you today into my hand in the cave, but I spared you.* ❞

David to rescue it. David's fighters saved hundreds of Israelites, even though they were risking their lives by leaving their hiding place in the hills.

Saul was overjoyed. "How stupid David is to walk into a walled and gated city," he laughed. Saul sent soldiers to Keilah, to capture David, but David and his band raced away. God had warned them of the king's approach.

Saul kept looking for David. As he was walking out of a dark cave he heard a familiar voice shout his name. Shocked, he spun round to see David at the cave-mouth, waving a piece of cloth. The outlaws had been hiding in the gloom, and David had crept up to the king and cut off a piece of Saul's robe without him knowing. David bowed down, as always. "Why do you listen to those who say I would hurt you?" he called out to Saul. "See, today I could have cut your throat, but I cut only your robe instead."

I T IS OFTEN TEMPTING TO GRAB IN A WRONG WAY SOMETHING WE BELIEVE SHOULD BE OURS. THE BIBLE TEACHES THAT WE CANNOT ACHIEVE GOOD ENDS BY USING BAD MEANS.

David runs from Saul
David escaped from Saul at Gibeah and was taken by Samuel to Ramah. He met his friend Jonathan at Horesh, before he fled to Nob. After seeking refuge with the Philistine king at Gath, David hid in the wilderness around Adullam, before he rescued the town of Keilah. He finally found Saul in the cave at En-gedi.

Mizpeh
Ramah
Gibeah
Nob
Bethlehem
Gath
Adullam
Keilah
Hereth
SALT SEA
Ziph
En-gedi
Horesh

David and Abigail

THE time came when the elderly prophet
Samuel knew that death was near. Samuel
was revered through the all Israel.Grief-stricken
people gathered at Samuel's house in Ramah one
last time to hear what he had to say.

"I have listened to all your complaints and answered
your request for a king," the old man wearily told the
crowds. "Now your king walks before you, leading you on,
and I must stop here. Always remember that God was
deeply offended by your demand for a king on earth. You
must still strive to serve God as best you can, or He will
sweep you aside as he would a pestering fly, both you and
your ruler. As a sign that what I say is truly the word of
God, the Lord will today send thunder and rain to destroy
your wheat harvest."

Later that day, colossal black clouds blotted out the
skies and towered over the land. Spears of lightning
stabbed through the gloom, thunder rumbled like chariot
wheels across the heavens and raindrops like arrows
flattened the crops in the fields.

The people of Israel trembled. King Saul shuddered.
Samuel, the prophet and last Judge of Israel, passed away.

When David heard the news of his old friend's death,
he was deeply saddened. He was also now in even
more danger. With the great
prophet gone, there was no one
with any power to stop King Saul
doing exactly what he
wanted. Even though
Saul had called off
the hunt for his
rival, David knew
that the

demons which tormented the king wouldn't leave him
alone for long. It was only a matter of time before they
drove him mad with jealousy and fear once again, and
then Saul would surely set out once more to find his rival
and kill him.

David told his band of men to move camp. They set off
never staying too long in one place and living off their
wits. Sometimes they would risk approaching a nearby
village to ask for food and drink. At other times, they
would simply plunder flocks of sheep and herds of cattle
that were grazing out in the open, taking animals they
thought their owners could spare.

When the outlaws reached the pasturelands around
Carmel, they encountered many shepherds, each with a
massive flock, who all said that they worked for an
important farmer called Nabal. David could have simply
allowed his hungry outlaws to help themselves to a few of
Nabal's sheep. After all, the farmer seemed to own
thousands! He thought it would be better to strike a
bargain with such a wealthy man, rather than make
enemies by stealing from him. David sent ten men to the
sheep-shearing at Carmel to find the landowner and
politely put forward their requests.

Now Nabal was a thuggish type of man, puffed up
with his own importance and used to throwing his
weight around. When David's messengers were shown
in by his servants, he hardly gave them a glance. "Who
is this David? I don't know any 'son of Jesse'," he scoffed
pretending not to have heard of the great hero. "He's
probably just another runaway servant. Do you really
expect me to welcome a complete stranger and his band
of criminals into my home and invite them to share
my food? Now go away and don't come back!"

Nabal's servants were shocked. How could
their master humiliate the great hero like this?
David was putting out his hand in friendship,
and Nabal was slapping it away. The servants
knew that Saul's former army commander

wouldn't put up with their master's insults. Though they begged Nabal to change his mind the stubborn man wouldn't listen. The servants imagined how David and his men would be putting on their weapons and galloping towards them at that very moment. In desperation, one of Nabal's servants went to confide in their master's wife, Abigail.

Abigail was as good-natured and beautiful as her husband was arrogant and ugly. She knew that Nabal's rudeness would be the cause of all of their deaths, unless she went quickly to beg for mercy. Hurriedly, she loaded several donkeys with 200 loaves, five sheep, sacks of raisins, grain and fig cakes, and two wineskins. And without telling her husband, she set off down the mountain towards David's camp.

Abigail had not got very far when she saw a cloud of dust approaching. As David and his men drew into sight, she leapt down from her saddle and knelt before them, begging forgiveness for what her husband had done.

David was touched by the beautiful young woman's pleas. "Go in peace," he told her kindly. "I am glad that the Lord sent you to me this day."

Abigail raced home, full of relief that she'd saved her whole household from death, but cross that her husband had put them in such a desperate position in the first place. She was even more angry to find that Nabal was completely unconcerned; in fact, he had thrown a great feast. There he was, right in the middle of all the merry-making, and roaring drunk. Fuming with rage, Abigail pursed her lips and stormed off. Next morning, when Nabal was sobering up with a head-splitting hangover, she told her husband what she had done. Nabal was instantly filled with a cold fury. His face turned white, his eyes glazed over, his hands gripped the arms of his chair like icy claws, and his spluttering mouth froze into silence. He was paralysed like stone, and he died ten days later.

> " *Nabal's wife told him these things, and his heart died within him.* "

When David heard that Nabal had died, he simply nodded. "The Lord has repaid Nabal for his own evil-doings," he said. "Things have come to a just end." But he couldn't get thoughts of Nabal's wife out of his head. David had lost his wife, Michal, because when he had first gone on the run, the outraged King Saul had forced his daughter to marry another man. Now David was reminded of Michal by Abigail's loyalty and beauty. It wasn't long before the outlaw began to woo Nabal's widow, and soon Abigail became his wife.

WINESKIN   FIGS   BREAD

Supplies for the outlaws
This picture shows the food and drink that Abigail gave to David. To the left is a wineskin, above are figs, which were dried and made into cakes, and bread. David could have just stolen Nabal's sheep from the fields, but chose instead to befriend the shepherds and make an honest request. Abigail's quick action saved her husband's life temporarily, but he died later, punished by God for his wickedness.

❖ ABOUT THE STORY ❖

David had been forced by Saul to live on the edge of the law. He never wanted to steal from anyone unless there was no alternative. He offered many landowners protection from the Philistines in return for food and drink for him and his men.

The Witch of Endor

King Saul once more lapsed into an angry, black depression and once again he ordered his troops to find and kill his rival.

The king fared no better than before. Under cover of darkness, David and two of his men crept boldly into Saul's base, right up to Saul's very bedside. Neither Saul nor his soldiers stirred. His army commander Abner and royal bodyguard slept all around him. Once again, David chose not to slay Saul. Instead, he stole the spear and water jar from his bedside.

Next morning, David called across the valley. "Abner! Why weren't you watching over the king properly last night?" Both Saul and his general trembled at David's mercy and goodness in sparing Saul's life.

Back at their hideout, David told his followers, "Saul will hunt me down wherever I go within Israel. The only way for us to have any sort of freedom is if we go and live among our enemies, the Philistines." So David returned to King Achish of Gath, this time as the leader of a 600-strong band of soldiers. Achish had no reason to think that David was trying to trick him as they were both enemies of King Saul. The cunning king gave the outlaws land on the border of Gath and Israel. He hoped that David would stir up trouble by raiding Israelite settlements for supplies. David was also crafty. He attacked Philistine towns instead, and made sure that there were no

survivors left alive to report the events. When Achish asked him who he had been attacking, he lied. The king trusted David completely. He thought David had begun to attack his own country and his people would never forgive him.

One day the Philistine leaders joined forces to attack Israel, and Achish asked David to ride with his army. David pretended that he was pleased. Achish rewarded him by appointing him his personal bodyguard.

Meanwhile, in the Israelite camp, Saul watched the arrival of the enemy forces with growing dread. His own army was hopelessly outnumbered, and his prayers were unanswered. He felt that God had abandoned him, and he could no longer ask Samuel for advice. He was desperate. According to God's law, Saul had banished everyone who practised magic, but now he sent his servants to seek out someone with magic powers. They found a clairvoyant at Endor who claimed she could talk with the dead. Saul disguised himself and hurried with two men to the medium's house. "I'll pay you well for a message from the spirit world," Saul told her. But the woman was wary.

"If the king hears that I have been practising witchcraft, I'll be put to death," she protested. Saul swore in God's name that no harm would come to her. Nervously the woman asked who he wanted to contact.

Swallowing hard, Saul whispered, "Bring up Samuel." The woman shivered at the name. All her instincts told her not to try, but Saul insisted. So the woman closed her eyes.

Suddenly she leapt up away from Saul in alarm. "You've tricked me!" she gasped. "You're the king himself!"

"Have no fear. Please tell me what you see," Saul begged.

Trembling all over, the woman shut her eyes once more. "I see an old man wrapped in a robe," she replied. "He wants to know why you've disturbed his rest." The king bowed down. Though he couldn't see Samuel, he knew it was the holy man.

> **Samuel said, 'Why then do you ask me, since the Lord has become your enemy?'**

"I face my biggest battle with the Philistines yet," Saul said to Samuel. "God no longer speaks to me through either prophets or dreams. So I've come for your advice."

Samuel's reply was grim. "Since the Lord has turned away from you, why do you come to me for help? The Lord has already told you He has taken the kingdom away from you and given it to David. Moreover, the Lord is about to give Israel into the hands of the Philistines. Tomorrow, you and your sons shall find yourselves here with me!"

Saul was shocked to the core. If Samuel was right, then nothing in heaven or earth could save him or his nation. Samuel had never been wrong before.

Magic

In the Bible, magic is defined as attempting to influence people and events by supernatural means. Black magic, such as witchcraft, tries to achieve evil results. White magic tries to undo curses and spells, and to use supernatural forces for the good of oneself and others. According to the Bible, all kinds of magic are wrong and must be overcome by the power of God. Magic is not compatible with a relationship with God and living a life that pleases him. This picture shows a breastplate that was worn by Egyptian magicians.

✣ ABOUT THE STORY ✣

The Israelites had been forbidden by God to consult people who claimed to be able to influence the course of events through magic. They were to rely on God alone. Asking spirits questions was dangerous, as it could bring the Israelites into contact with evil forces.

The Death of Saul

THE Philistine and Israelite armies hurried to prepare for battle. Tension rose in both camps. The Philistine commanders boiled with rage when they saw David and his men riding with King Achish of Gath. "What are these Israelites doing here?" they demanded.

"I can vouch for him completely," Achish explained. "David is Saul's greatest enemy and has lived in my lands for years now." The Philistine chiefs weren't convinced.

"We don't trust him," they said determinedly. "For all you know, he might make it up with Saul and turn on us in the fighting. Send him away at once, where he can be no risk to us!"

The king of Gath couldn't change their minds so he told David that he was to have no part in the fighting. David was secretly relieved. He hadn't wanted to fight Saul.

Everything happened as Samuel had warned Saul through the witch of Endor. A Philistine victory was never in doubt. Their mighty army slew the Israelites in their hundreds. Among the dead and dying were three of Saul's four sons, including Jonathan, David's best friend. Saul himself had fallen under the showers of Philistine arrows, and was terribly injured. Saul's armour-bearer struggled to lift him up and help him limp away, but Saul was bleeding badly and in too much pain. "I'd rather die than be taken alive by the enemy," he groaned to his servant. "If you love me, help me to kill myself and escape being tortured by these ungodly savages." His armour-bearer broke down, unable to carry out the dreadful task. So Saul summoned the last dregs of his energy. Moaning with agony, he

hauled himself to his feet and heaved up his sword. Then with one final effort, he fell forward on to the sword, gasping his last breath. Once Saul's armour-bearer was sure the king was dead, he killed himself too.

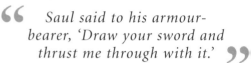

> " *Saul said to his armour-bearer, 'Draw your sword and thrust me through with it.'* "

As the news spread that their leader was dead, the exhausted Israelites turned and fled. The Philistines hacked off Saul's head and stripped his corpse of his armour, sending the trophies in triumph to the temple of their god, where they were put on display. Then they hung the dead king and his sons high on the town walls of Beth-shan.

Next morning, the royal bodies were gone. The brave people of Jabesh-gilead had made their way through enemy territory in the night to rescue the corpses, remembering how Saul had saved them many years ago from having their right eyes put out. The body of the first king of Israel was returned to his country and buried honourably among his grieving people.

David was devastated when he heard the news, yet he could see how God's hand was behind everything. The Lord had prevented David from having any part in the death of the king. Now he mourned Saul, who had both loved him and hated him at the same time, who had grown arrogant with power and turned away from God, and who had been driven mad in the knowledge that God

DAVID'S LAMENT FOR SAUL MAY SEEM ODD. BUT DAVID TRUSTED GOD AND DID NOT ALLOW HIMSELF TO BECOME BITTER. IT IS AN EXAMPLE OF HOW GOD WANTS PEOPLE TO TREAT EACH OTHER.

The last days of Saul
Saul, worried about what would happen in the battle with the Philistines, found a witch at Endor to talk to the dead proph Samuel. Samuel said he could not win as God was against him. Saul went with his army to meet the Philistines in the Valley of Jezreel, where he died.

had abandoned him. And David grieved for Jonathan, the friend he loved even more than his own brothers, who had defied his father to stay loyal to David.

David remembered how the king had loved to hear him play the harp, the one thing that was able to bring him peace. He thought of the perfect tribute for Saul and his son. He would compose a beautiful song in their honour, telling all about the mountain battle.

The song began:
"Thy glory, O Israel, is slain upon thy high places! How are the mighty fallen!"
When David sang his song, gently plucking at the strings of his harp as he had done so many years ago in the palace for the king, he wept with sorrow that Saul would never again hear him play. He wept for the loss of his closest friend, Jonathan, a loss to David himself and to all Israel.

◈DAVID'S LAMENT◈

SAUL AND JONATHAN, BELOVED AND LOVELY!
IN LIFE AND IN DEATH THEY WERE NOT DIVIDED;
THEY WERE SWIFTER THAN EAGLES,
THEY WERE STRONGER THAN LIONS.
JONATHAN LIES SLAIN UPON THY HIGH PLACES.
I AM DISTRESSED FOR YOU, MY BROTHER JONATHAN;
VERY PLEASANT HAVE YOU BEEN TO ME;
YOUR LOVE TO ME WAS WONDERFUL.

Philistine figurine
This figurine was found in the Philistine city of Ashdod, and it represents one of the Philistine goddesses, probably a fertility goddess that they believed made all things grow, such as their crops.

David's lament
The song David wrote for his two friends, Saul and Jonathan, has been described as one of the most beautiful pieces of poetry in the Bible. It expresses great sadness at the loss of the men both as national figures and as personal friends of David.

◈ ABOUT THE STORY ◈

Once again, David had a lucky escape, reminding him that God was always protecting him. He could not get out of fighting with the Philistines without appearing disloyal and risking being killed by them as a traitor. God helped him and used the Philistines themselves to get David out of a tight spot. After this, few would question David's loyalty to Israel or his right to be king.

David Becomes King

WHEN Saul was dead, David prayed for guidance. He heard the Lord telling him to go back to Israel, to the south, and settle in Hebron. The people of Judah welcomed the hero with open arms, crowning David as their king.

The eleven other tribes in Israel did not accept David as their ruler. The general of Saul's army, Abner, with the backing of his troops, had set Saul's surviving son, Ishbosheth, on the throne to rule the rest of Israel.

King David ruled Judah and King Ishbosheth ruled the rest of Israel for several years. But everyone knew that Israel should be united with only one king.

One day the two armies fought, and David's soldiers won. Abner escaped, pursued by Asahel, brother of Joab, David's commander. Abner was forced to fight him and he stabbed Asahel with great regret.

After this there was full-scale civil war. Gradually support for David grew stronger. Ishbosheth was a weak ruler. He had never expected to be king as Saul had been grooming Jonathan for the throne. But power had gone to Ishbosheth's head. Eventually, Ishbosheth even confronted his most ardent supporter, Abner, because he had married one of Saul's concubines. Ishbosheth was trying to control everything. The general erupted. "After all I've done for you," he yelled, "you're rebuking me about a private affair!" Abner had only respected Ishbosheth because he was Saul's son; now he lost even that little regard. Abner did admire David as a servant of God and a great leader. "From now on, I'm going to support David," Abner bellowed.

"And God help me if I don't do everything I can to put him on the throne over all Israel." Ishbosheth stood trembling as Abner stalked off.

David threw a great feast to welcome Abner and Michal, his first wife, to the palace. Abner promised David that he would speak personally to the leaders of the 11 tribes and win their support for David. Abner set off immediately after the feast.

Soon afterwards David's commander, Joab arrived. He was appalled that the king had befriended the killer of his younger brother, Asahel. "David, Abner's deceiving you!" he cried. "He'll always remain true to the house of Saul." When David refused to listen, Joab sent a messenger to tell Abner to return. When the general arrived, Joab asked him

The murder of Abner
Abner was Saul's nephew, so he supported Saul's son, Ishbosheth, in preference to David. However, after quarrelling with his master, Abner transferred his loyalty to David. David's army commander, Joab, was angry when he heard that David had welcomed Abner, because Abner had killed his brother, Asahel. Without David's knowledge, Joab murdered Abner. The picture shows a medieval altar detail of the scene, dating from 1181.

Hebron
Hebron is situated 30km southwest of Jerusalem and is the highest town in Palestine. Many important figures in the Old Testament were buried there. So, apparently, were all the sons of Jacob, except for Joseph. Hebron was King David's capital for seven and a half years, until he moved to Jerusalem.

> **All the tribes of Israel came and said, 'You shall be prince over Israel.'**

for a private word. As Abner bent to Joab's ear, Joab stabbed him. "Now I am revenged for my brother's death!" Joab hissed.

David was furious. He cursed Joab and honoured Abner with fasting, and people tore their clothes in grief.

More tragedy followed. Two of Ishbosheth's captains had realised that without Abner Ishbosheth couldn't rule for long. They wanted to gain favour with David, so they crept into Ishbosheth's house and stabbed him. Then they ran to David and proudly told him of their crime. To their shock, David was horrified. "Ishbosheth had done nothing wrong," he groaned. "You have killed an innocent man in his own house. You will die for your wickedness." The traitors were executed.

David was now the sole contender for the throne. The elders gathered together and anointed him. At last, the king God had chosen ruled all Israel.

Anointing oil
The oil used for anointing would have been oil from olives (below), mixed with myrrh and spices such as cinnamon (right) and cassia (bottom right). The recipe was made from instructions given to the prophet Moses. Ordinary olive oil was used in cooking, in lamps and as a medicine, but it was a sin to use the special anointing oil for any other purpose.

> ❖ **ABOUT THE STORY** ❖
>
> *Once again the writer wants to show how David lived according to God's laws. In ancient times, rulers often killed potential rivals, and took revenge on their enemies. Joab was like that, but David wasn't. He didn't want to force his way to power. He knew that human life is precious. He had killed people in war, but when he had the chance to "live and let live" in peace time he did.*

Bringing the Ark to Jerusalem

KING David wanted to mark the beginning of a new era for the unified country. He thought it would be wrong to remain at Hebron or move to Saul's palace at Gibeah. He decided to make Jerusalem his new capital city.

The Jebusites who lived there were afraid of being thrown out of their homes so they barred the gates against him. David sent some of his soldiers up a large water pipe into the heart of the city, and soon the gates were open. The king's men streamed in, and from that day onwards Jerusalem was known as the City of David.

Once David's new palace had been built, he wanted to make a proper home for the ark in Jerusalem. The holy chest containing the Ten Commandments had been kept in a village near the border of Israel ever since the Philistines had returned it.

David declared that the day the priests moved the ark should be a public holiday, and the people of Israel poured into the streets. The people sang and played tambourines, flutes and cymbals as the ark rolled along on its ceremonial chariot. King David himself led the way.

Then disaster struck! The oxen pulling the chariot stumbled on the rocky road, and the man guiding the cart, called Uzzah, reached out to steady the precious ark. Only the priests were allowed to touch it. As soon as Uzzah touched the ark, he fell lifeless to the ground. The shocked Israelites fell silent, reminded of God's holy power. The festivities were over for that day.

Uzzah's death made even King David nervous, and for three months he left the ark in the care of Obed-edom the Gittite. When he tried again to move it, he held a prayer service and offered sacrifices before the procession set off. The people came out to celebrate with even more energy than before. They sang and danced in the greatest carnival they'd ever held. Even King David took turns dancing with them. Quite carried away, he stripped off his clothes and leapt for joy before the ark of the Lord.

> " *David danced before the Lord with all his might.* "

Not everyone was enjoying themselves. Since Michal had returned to be the king's wife, she'd grown jealous of the other wives David had taken in her absence. She felt superior because she was King Saul's daughter, and she thought it beneath her to go and mingle with the common people in the streets. As the ark entered Jerusalem she stayed in her room in the palace, looking down on the revelry with disdain. Imagine her horror when she saw her husband, the king, half-naked and singing and dancing with everyone else! Things were never the same between Michal and David again. For the king loved his subjects and his subjects loved him, and he thought it right that he should be among them to pay homage to the God who ruled over all.

David and the priests brought the ark to where the tabernacle had been set up, the richly embroidered tent in which it had rested since the time of Moses. The king offered more sacrifices and prayers, and blessed the people. Then he distributed a gift of bread, meat and raisins to every person to commemorate the occasion.

❧ ABOUT THE STORY ❧

When Uzzah died, David was partly to blame. The ark should never have been put on a chariot. It was meant to be carried on poles, which the priests rested on their shoulders. That was how they carried it the second time. Uzzah's death showed the people that it was important to follow God's commands fully. David had thought he could improve on what God had said. He was wrong.

Surprise attack
Because of Jerusalem's position on a high plateau surrounded by deep ravines, the Israelites had never before succeeded in capturing the city. The Jebusites felt safe but David took them by surprise by entering the city via a water shaft. The picture above shows the possible route taken by David and his men.

When David was quietly resting in his palace, he thought, "Beautiful as the tabernacle is, we need a permanent temple. My own house is made of cedar wood and covered in gold and silver. The tabernacle is only a tent." He shared his idea with Nathan, a prophet. The next day, Nathan told David that God had spoken to him in a dream. "The Lord says that the tabernacle will do for now. You are a man of war, and you should not build the holy temple. But one of your sons will be a man of peace, and he will build a temple to the Lord so glorious that people far and wide will hear of it." At this prophecy from Nathan, David was content.

Death of Uzzah
Uzzah made the mistake of touching the holy ark, which not even the Levites were allowed to handle. God was so angry with Uzzah that He punished him with death. The second time David tried to bring the ark into Jerusalem, he made sure that the Levites carried it according to the instructions that had been laid down by Moses.

Jerusalem
This view of modern Jerusalem shows the city walls, the old quarter, which is the oldest part of the city and the mosque called The Dome of the Rock.

David and Bathsheba

KING David ruled justly and fairly. He won victories over his enemies, but was capable of great acts of mercy, too. Saul's son Jonathan had himself left a son, called Mephibosheth, who was crippled in both feet. David commanded that Mephibosheth and Ziba, the servant who looked after him, be brought to the palace. "I'm giving back to you all the lands that belonged to your grandfather, Saul," David told the amazed boy, kindly. "Ziba will look after it for you while you live here at the palace with me. For I loved your father as my brother, and so I will love you as my son."

Although David was a good and great king, he was still just a man, capable of sinning like everyone else. The day

finally came when David offended God, during a time when the Israelites were fighting a tribe called the Ammonites. The king had put the army in the capable hands of his commander Joab, while he stayed in Jerusalem to take care of things at home. David liked to stroll on the flat roof of his palace in the evening, looking out over the houses and hills of his beautiful capital city. Late one afternoon, he was pondering matters of state and admiring the view as usual when his thoughts were interrupted. Bathing in a pool in one of the gardens below was the most beautiful woman he had ever seen. For the whole evening afterwards, he found it impossible to concentrate. He couldn't rest until he knew who she was.

David discovered that the woman's name was Bathsheba and that she was married to Uriah, a soldier in his army, safely away at the war. David gave in to temptation and began to woo Bathsheba. For several months the two

Amman – ancient Rabbah
Uriah and the rest of David's army were away fighting at Rabbah, the capital city of the Ammonites. Today, the city of Amman, the capital of Jordan, lies on the same site. The Ammonites had become a powerful people, but David and Joab succeeded in defeating the city and putting its inhabitants to forced labour. Later, after the death of Solomon, David's son, the Ammonites resurfaced as a threat to Israel. Today, many archaeological remains exist in and around Amman. Elsewhere in the city are ruins of cities from many different ages, including Roman and medieval. Among these ruins, sculptures and inscriptions from the 700s and 600s BC have been found. This picture shows a view across Amman from the citadel in the city. You can see the amphitheatre in the foreground.

Perfume pot
After bathing, Bathsheba would have rubbed perfumed oil into her skin. Perfume was a luxury and was kept in special containers like this pot dating from the 900s to 800s BC.

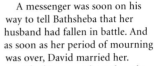

lovers enjoyed a secret, romantic affair, until Bathsheba told David that she was expecting his baby. The king panicked. If Uriah found out, he would know that the baby was not his because he had been away. Everyone would soon know that David had sinned by sleeping with another man's wife.

The anxious king tried to disguise his sins. He sent a message to his commander Joab to send Uriah home, pretending that he wanted an update on the war. Uriah gave the king his report, and David sent him home. But next morning, the king found that the gallant officer had not slept at home with his wife. He had vowed not to return home while his men were still fighting, so he'd slept at the door of the palace.

Next day the king held a banquet for the soldier and plied him with alcohol. Surely if Uriah was drunk, he'd forget his resolution and go back to his wife? That way, Uriah would not know that the child was not his. But Uriah curled up on one of the king's couches instead.

David could not own up to his terrible sin. However, his next plan involved committing an even worse one. When Uriah went to rejoin his troops, David gave him a letter for Joab, the army commander. It said: "I command you to put Uriah in the frontline. When he is in the thick of the fighting, withdraw your troops so he is left alone among the enemy." Joab did just what David had ordered.

A messenger was soon on his way to tell Bathsheba that her husband had fallen in battle. And as soon as her period of mourning was over, David married her.

The king must have thought that he had got away with his crime, but God sees everything. The prophet Nathan came to see him. "Listen to this story," he told David. "Once upon a time a rich man owned lots of sheep, and a poor man had one little lamb, which was like a pet. One day, when a visitor came, the rich man took the poor man's lamb and roasted it for dinner."

David was angry. "He deserves to die for this. Who is he?" he cried.

> " *Set Uriah in the forefront of the hardest fighting that he may be struck down, and die.* "

"You," the prophet said. "And the Lord will punish you. You have sinned in private, but all Israel will see you suffer. In the future, your own children will rebel against you. But first, the baby will die." Sure enough, Bathsheba's baby was born weak. Though David prayed and fasted, begging God to save its life, a week later the infant died.

Uriah's death
David's sin in sleeping with Bathsheba led to the second sin of murder. If Uriah had gone to his wife, the child could have been passed off as his and David would not have killed him. David hoped once Uriah was dead, no one need know what had happened. But Nathan exposed the truth, and David was punished.

O NE REASON DAVID SINNED MAY HAVE BEEN BECAUSE HE WAS TIRED — HE SHOULD HAVE BEEN OUT WITH HIS ARMY. TEMPTATION IS OFTEN GREATEST WHEN OUR RESISTANCE IS LOW AND WE BECOME WEAK.

❖ **ABOUT THE STORY** ❖

Until now, David has been shown as always loyal to God and anxious to do the right thing. In this case, though, it is Uriah who is right, and David who is very wrong. His lament over Saul could now be applied to himself: "How are the mighty fallen." The Bible never hides the failings of its greatest heroes. The stories are told to warn readers that everyone, even someone as great and as devoted to God as David, is vulnerable to sin.

Absalom the Rebel

NATHAN'S prophecy that King David's children would rebel against him soon came true. David had many wives and children and was used to them all arguing among each other. But when his son Amnon attacked his daughter Tamar one day, it was serious. The family took sides and didn't forget the row. Two years later, another of David's sons, Absalom, took revenge for Tamar. He killed Amnon and fled to Egypt.

The king grieved for both his lost children. He couldn't bring back Amnon, but he could bring back Absalom. After five long years, David sent word to his son saying he was forgiven and that he could return safely to Israel, but on condition that he wasn't allowed to contact him at the palace.

For Absalom, this was worse than living in exile. He found it unbearable to think of all his brothers and sisters living as royal princes and princesses, while he lived in the same city as an outcast. Eventually, after three years had passed, David sent for Absalom. Absalom threw himself at the feet of the king, begging his father to receive him back into the family. David's heart melted, and he raised his son to his feet, hugging and kissing him. Absalom was disappointed not to feel the gladness he thought he'd feel. He remained full of a bitterness that wouldn't go away, and over time it grew and grew until it finally turned him against his father.

Secretly, Absalom decided to try to win the support of David's subjects for himself and overthrow his father. He was already a favourite with the people because he was a very handsome young man with long, thick hair. Each morning he presented himself at the city gate, standing on a horse-drawn chariot with fifty attendants around him. He would talk to the people and listen to their complaints, winning their hearts as a royal who did not mind shaking hands with ordinary people. "It's a shame the king doesn't come and chat to you all like this," Absalom would tell them. "He doesn't know about your problems like I do." And he'd heave a big sigh. "If only I were in charge, I'd fix things right away."

More and more people began to pledge their allegiance to the king's son, including those in the government such as David's trusted counsellor Ahithophel. Finally, even the bold Absalom thought that he was being a little too daring in organizing a rebellion right under the king's nose. He made an excuse to leave the city, telling his father that he wanted to go to the family city of Hebron to offer prayers and sacrifices for forgiveness. Then secretly he sent messengers to all the tribes telling his followers to come and gather there, for he was about to proclaim himself king.

However, many people still remained true to David, and word came to him of what his son was up to. He immediately fled out of danger by taking his court and leaving Jerusalem. Absalom moved in straightaway and set himself up on the throne. But what next? "Let me take some men and catch up with David," Ahithophel urged. "Your father will be unprepared and I can kill him without dragging anyone else into it. That way, you'll avoid civil war and your new subjects will be all the more pleased with you."

But a counsellor called Hushai gave quite the opposite advice. "No, you should bide your time," he told Absalom. "Your father is an experienced warrior and is probably hiding somewhere safe, away from his troops altogether. You have the throne now. Why not wait and gather a proper army around you? Then you can lead your men into battle and win all the glory for yourself."

Absalom liked the sound of that, and chose to follow Hushai. But unbeknown to him, the counsellor was one of David's men, working under cover to trick him with bad advice. And the king's son had fallen headfirst into the trap. Absalom's delay gave the king the breathing space he needed to rally his troops.

> " The king cried with a loud voice, 'O my son Absalom.' "

Even after all his treacherous son had done to him, David couldn't find it within himself to stop loving his son. And on the day that the two armies finally clashed, the king instructed his captains to take Absalom alive and not to harm him.

The battle took place in the thickly wooded forest near Shiloh, a dangerous place full of quicksands, poisonous snakes and wild animals that claimed almost as many lives as the fighting itself. When countryman had finished slaying countryman, and the victory was David's, over 20,000 men lay dead among the trees.

Absalom was not one of them. He had leapt on to a mule and tried to escape. It proved impossible to dodge the branches that barred the galloping animal's way. As the terrified mule turned this way and that in the dense undergrowth, Absalom's hair got caught in the trees. And when his mount finally found a direction in which to bolt, the king's son was left dangling from a branch while the animal shot away from under him.

Back at David's palace everyone was rejoicing, except for the king himself who was waiting anxiously at the gate for a messenger to bring news of his son. When he heard that his own army commander Joab had found Absalom and killed him, despite his orders, he broke down and wept uncontrollably. "My son, my son!" he wailed. "I wish that I had died instead of you." David was paying a terrible price for sinning with Bathsheba.

In the years ahead there was more trouble to come, God sent a famine and then a plague to make the job of establishing peace within the nation extra hard. There was some happiness, too. Bathsheba gave birth to another baby boy called Solomon, who comforted his mother and father a little for the children they had lost. David loved Bathsheba as his favourite wife, and Solomon was to become his most beloved son.

Royal advisers
Kings were often dependent on their advisers to help them make decisions. Absalom takes the wrong advice when he listens to Hushai.

THE BIBLE ENCOURAGES ITS READERS TO WAIT PATIENTLY FOR GOD TO GIVE US NEW OPPORTUNITIES, AND TO BE CONTENT WITH WHAT WE HAVE. IF WE TRY TO FORCE OUR WAY, MANY PEOPLE CAN GET HURT.

❖ **ABOUT THE STORY** ❖

Absalom may have had his father's fighting spirit, but he had none of his patience and faith. Absalom became hungry for power and tried to force himself on to the throne. The writer wants us to notice that Absalom never asked what God wanted.

The Death of David

WHEN David was very old, he told everyone that he wanted Solomon to be king when he died. Another of David's sons had his own ideas. Adonijah wanted to be king and he talked several influential people into supporting him, including Joab, David's army commander, and Abiathar, the priest.

Adonijah thought that the old king no longer understood what was going on outside the palace walls, so he held a coronation ceremony for himself. Most of the royal officials of Judah attended the event. Nathan the prophet, who hadn't been invited, soon heard of it. He warned David's wife Bathsheba, and she went straight to David, who lay ill in bed. "You said our son

> ❝ *All the people said, 'Long live King Solomon.'* ❞

Solomon would be your successor," she said, "yet Adonijah has made himself king. People are confused."

David took immediate action, which was quite the opposite to what Adonijah expected. Soon, Solomon was mounted on the king's own horse, wearing the king's crown, parading to Gihon with Nathan and Zadok the priest. There, they anointed Solomon as the new king, God's chosen successor to David. The appointment of the new ruler was proclaimed all over Israel.

People up and down the country celebrated. Adonijah heard the noise when he was in the middle of a party for his own coronation. As soon as his guests realised that the shouts of "Long live the king!" were for Solomon, they sneaked away. When David died and the rightful heir Solomon took the throne, no one dared argue with him.

❖ ABOUT THE STORY ❖

Although the Israelites' request for a king had not been according to God's purpose, this story reminds readers that God did not abandon His people. He continued to guide them in the choice of the next king. The Bible teaches that God keeps His "covenant" or agreement with His people even when they are unfaithful to Him. God had a very special purpose for the new King Solomon.

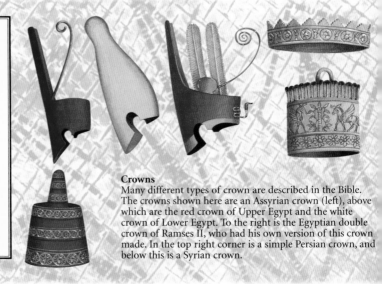

Crowns
Many different types of crown are described in the Bible. The crowns shown here are an Assyrian crown (left), above which are the red crown of Upper Egypt and the white crown of Lower Egypt. To the right is the Egyptian double crown of Ramses II, who had his own version of this crown made. In the top right corner is a simple Persian crown, and below this is a Syrian crown.

The Wisdom of Solomon

SOLOMON was only young when he became king. But he was ready to rule. He knew how the civil wars and the strife with Israel's neighbours had taken their toll on the nation, and he wanted to keep Israel at peace. First he had his rival Adonijah and his supporters executed. Then he married the daughter of one of his major enemies, Pharaoh, ruler of Egypt.

Solomon trusted God, just as his father had done. One night, during a religious festival at Gibeon, God spoke to the young king in a dream. "What gift would you like me to give you?" the Lord asked. Solomon thought hard.

"Lord," he replied, "I wish to rule well. Therefore give me wisdom, so I can judge between right and wrong, and govern my people with fairness." The Lord was delighted with Solomon's answer.

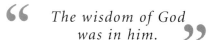

> ## The wisdom of God was in him.

"Because you didn't ask for anything for yourself," God told him, "only for something that will benefit Israel, you will have your wish. I will also give you wealth, honour and long life."

One day, two women came to the king, begging him to settle an argument. They had both given birth, within three days of each other. But one night one of the babies had died. The first mother claimed that the other woman's child had died, and that she had swapped the dead baby for her live one while she slept.

"No I didn't!" the second mother yelled. "The living child is mine!"

"Enough!" bellowed Solomon. "Fetch me a sword." The two women waited. "The living baby will be cut into two and half given to each of you," he announced.

While the second woman nodded her agreement, the first woman fell on her knees before the king, weeping uncontrollably. "No, no, my lord! Do not kill the child," she wailed. "Please give it to her instead."

"Take your baby," Solomon smiled, laying the child in the first woman's arms. The king knew that the real mother would rather give up her child than allow it to be killed.

People were amazed by the king's good judgment, and he soon became known as "Solomon the Wise".

Royal wedding
Instead of marrying for love, Solomon used his marriage as a way of maintaining peace in Israel. He chose Pharaoh's daughter as his bride, as Pharaoh was unlikely to declare war on his son-in-law.

❧ ABOUT THE STORY ❧

In the Bible "wisdom" is the ability to understand, do and say the right thing, it isn't simply knowing things. Wisdom is always seen as a gift from God (in the New Testament the apostle James tells his readers to pray for it). In a holy sense, wisdom is knowing what God wants in any situation, and making decisions based on the way in which God wants people to live, not on what is easiest at the time.

Building the Temple

KING Solomon had new plans for almost everything, taxes, employment, the armed forces, trade, building. His greatest plan of all was for a great temple at Jerusalem, just as his father had wanted, a glorious home for the ark. It took four years just to lay the foundations of the temple. It was a similar design to the tabernacle, but twice as big. To complete the temple took another three years.

An enormous workforce was employed. King Solomon ordered many Israelites to leave their lands for one out of every three months to work for him. He also forced prisoners of war to become slaves. Soon thousands of men were cutting stone to size at the quarry. The great blocks were then heaved to the building site and hoisted into place so that not a single hammer or pickaxe was heard inside the holy building during its construction. For the really skilled work, Solomon hired expert joiners, carvers and metal workers from overseas.

Only the very best building materials were used. Rafts of the finest cedar and pine wood were floated down the coast from King Hiram of Tyre in Lebanon and taken inland by camel train. Merchants went to distant lands to trade Israel's foodstuffs and oil for gold and silver, rich fabrics and precious stones.

Eventually, all was finished. The temple was amazing. The walls and ceilings were made of elegant, sweet-smelling wood beams and planks. Rooms were lined with pure gold and carved with winged cherubim. Intricately carved doors of olive wood separated the sacred innermost chamber, the Holy of Holies from the outer room, the Holy Place, together with a shimmering veil that hung from delicate chains. The altar itself was made of gold.

Solomon dedicated the temple to the Lord with a grand ceremony. There were prayer services, and animals were sacrificed. The king prayed that God would make the temple a place that would inspire all who saw it to follow the Lord. He told the people that if ever they fell into the hands of enemies, they should look to the holy building, remembering what it stood for and who it served.

Finally there was a great procession as priests and elders of the tribes, with King Solomon at their head, brought the sacred ark of the covenant to its new resting place. As the priests laid it gently in the Holy of Holies, a cloud of God's glory filled the inner sanctuary. The Lord was present in the new house just as he had been in the tabernacle. The whole nation rejoiced.

> 66 *The glory of the Lord filled the house of the Lord.* 99

When the celebrations were over, Solomon heard God say to him, "I have heard your prayers and requests and I have accepted this house you have built me. If you keep my commandments, I will establish your royal throne over Israel for ever, just as I promised your father, David. But if you turn aside from following me and worship other gods, then I will cause this temple to be destroyed and everyone will wonder how and why such a thing happened."

Tools of the trade
These pictures show an Egyptian stonemason's mallet (far right). Stonemasons cut and shaped blocks of stone. They used many of the same tools as carpenters, including saws, mallets, chisels and an adze, used like a modern plane, (right).

The temple's rooms
The temple was divided into three areas: the entrance porch, the outer room (or Holy Place) and the inner room (or Holy of Holies). The outer room was a larger space, used by the priest for rituals and ceremonies. The inner room was smaller and was rarely used. Both rooms had wooden walls and doors, covered in decorative carving and overlaid with gold. Around the outside of the temple there were store rooms.

Holy of Holies
The Holy of Holies was the sacred inner room of Solomon's temple. This was where the ark of the covenant was kept. When the ark was taken into the Holy of Holies, the whole room filled with cloud, which signified that God was present.

Worship is not only a matter of going to a religious service or ceremony. We worship God whenever we do something just because we love Him and want to honour Him.

❧ ABOUT THE STORY ❧

Solomon's temple must have been a beautiful place. The king did not build it to show off his skill and wealth, but because he wanted to give the best he had to God. The temple became a symbol both of God's presence among the people, and also of God's blessings to them. It was an act of worship in itself, because Solomon and the people sacrificed time and money to build it.

Wealth and Splendour

ONCE the glorious temple was finished, Solomon's building plans were far from over. He built a new palace with a massive hall where he could sit in judgement. With splendid royal living apartments as well, the palace was even bigger than the temple. The mountain quarries swarmed with labourers. Sparks flew from the desert blast furnaces, the roads groaned at the weight of materials going in and out of Jerusalem. The magnificent palace was made entirely of cedar wood and the finest marbles, with three tiers of windows to let the sun stream in and high ceilings held aloft by rows of pillars.

Then Solomon started work on a mighty wall to circle Jerusalem, thick and high enough to stand firm against foreign armies. He sent his surveyors to oversee the reconstruction of cities such as Gezer that had been destroyed in Israel's many wars. New strongholds sprang up from these blackened heaps of rubble. They were even greater than before, with thriving markets and public buildings. Solomon built new store cities to hold all of Israel's supplies and treasures. The Israelites filled new warehouses with sacks of grain, nuts and figs, which Israel's farmers paid as taxes to the king. They stacked cellars with barrels of wine and vats of oil, and heaped treasures and gems into locked safe-houses. Housing and training grounds were built for King Solomon's 1,400 gleaming chariots and 12,000 horsemen. On the Red Sea coast, Solomon built an entire fleet of merchant ships that travelled far and away to seek treasures, and returned with cargoes of apes, peacocks and ivory, rare woods and metals, and gleaming jewels.

As Solomon's subjects heard each new demand from their king, it seemed he was asking them to perform the

❊ TREASURES FROM ABROAD ❊

The Israelites traded with many other countries and brought back all kinds of exotic treasures, such as gold, silver, jewels and ivory.

Bronze figure
This is a Babylonian bronze statuette of a figure carrying a basket full of building materials. Figures like this were put in the foundations of temples.

Stone lion's head
This stone lion's head came from Assyria. It might originally have been attached to the handle of a fan.

Silver goat
This silver goat is thought to have come from Persepolis in Persia. It dates from the 400s BC.

impossible. They grumbled and groaned at the high taxes and the enforced labour. The king certainly wasn't loved by his people as David had been. Even so, everyone was impressed and overawed. The sailors and traders carried news of the king's greatness abroad, so that even people who weren't sure where Israel was heard rumours of its wealth, splendour and its greatest marvel of all – Solomon's wisdom. The king seemed to know all there was to know about anything. He could recite over 1,000 poems and quote over 3,000 proverbs. Statesmen and philosophers travelled to Solomon's court from far away, to listen to the king and ask his advice.

> " *God gave Solomon wisdom*
> *beyond measure.* "

One of the visitors was the Queen of Sheba from Arabia. She had heard all the rumours about the king and wanted to know if they were true. So she came to see for herself, travelling with a great retinue of servants and carrying gifts of gold and jewels.

Solomon showed the queen everything, from his golden palace, throne and dishes; to how he ran his court with fairness and administered justice to the people. He showed her how the Israelites worshipped in their glorious new temple. He said he could answer any question she asked. The Queen of Sheba was left speechless. "Israel is lucky indeed to have such a magnificent king," she told Solomon. When she returned home, Solomon gave her many souvenirs from Israel's treasure houses.

Solomon's kingdom
During the rule of Solomon, Israel was more wealthy than it had ever been before. On this map the orange colour shows the lands of Israel. The dark brown colour shows the lands that paid tribute to Solomon. By this time, the Ammon, the Moab and even Philistia had all been conquered.

Trading ship
This picture shows a stone relief of a Phoenician trading ship. The Phoenicians were neighbours of the Israelites and, along with the Philistines, were leading powers at sea. The Israelites had little experience of the sea, so Solomon used Phoenician ships manned by Phoenician sailors to carry out his trading activities. The Israelites looked upon the ship as an object of wonder, and a safe journey was thought to be a demonstration of God's goodness and power.

❖ ABOUT THE STORY ❖
Solomon had prayed for wisdom rather than riches, but God promised him riches as well as a special sign of His blessing. At this time, people assumed those who became wealthy were favoured by God. Later, they realized this is not always the case.

Fall of Solomon

ONE of the ways that all kings in ancient times showed how great they were was by having many wives. Just as Solomon outdid everyone in the splendour and scale of everything around him, he also outdid everyone in the number of women he married. Including Pharaoh's daughter, Solomon had 700 wives altogether. He also had 300 mistresses. It was not just because he was greedy. The king knew that all his plans for making Israel great rested on peace. The only way to keep the peace was to make treaties with his enemies abroad. And over the years, Israel had made many enemies. So Solomon kept his ministers of foreign affairs busy negotiating deals at meeting after meeting, while he himself married princess after princess. After all, it was unlikely that one country would attack another if the rulers were father- and son-in-law ...

There was only one problem. King Solomon's wives were from peoples such as the Moabites, the Ammonites, the

Syrian storm-god
Solomon had wives from many foreign lands, such as Moab, Edom and Syria. These women continued to worship their own gods, instead of the Israelite God. This is a stone relief of the Syrian storm-god, Hadad, standing on a bull and holding his symbol of a forked bolt of lightning.

The Edomites
This is an impression of the king of Edom's seal, from 800BC. The Edomites were one of the tribes that attacked Solomon during his reign.

SOLOMON MAY HAVE JUST BEEN BEING TOLERANT OF THE OTHER RELIGIONS SO THAT HE COULD KEEP ORDER. BUT THE BIBLE TELLS US WE CANNOT BE TOLERANT OF ANYTHING THAT GOES AGAINST GOD. KEEPING THE TRUTH IS MORE IMPORTANT THAN KEEPING THE PEACE. ∾

Edomites, the Sidonians and the Hittites. These were all nations with whom the Lord had forbidden the Israelites to mix. God had commanded this from the first days of the Israelites' arrival in the Promised Land. The foreign tribes worshipped pagan gods, and the Lord knew that if the Israelites intermarried with them, they would be tempted to follow the pagan ways.

King Solomon was no more able to resist this temptation than anyone else. As he grew older, he allowed his beautiful, loving wives to sway his judgement. He allowed them to perform their own pagan rituals and worship their own idols (burning holy incense and offering sacrifices as only the priests were allowed to do), and he even built special places in which to do it! First, there was a temple to Chemosh, the god of the Moabites. Then there was a temple to Molech, the god of the Ammonites, which Solomon had built on the mountain east of Jerusalem, within sight of the mighty Israelite temple itself! Soon pagan temples were being built all over the country, and every one of them with the full knowledge, and even with the approval of the king. Even worse, the wives persuaded Solomon to go and worship with them too. He didn't stop going to the temple of the Lord, but he was also often seen praying at the temple to Ashtoreth, goddess of the Sidonians, and Milcom of the Ammonites.

God was furious with him. How could the man on whom He had bestowed the gifts of wisdom, wealth and honour, turn away from Him so easily! The Lord spoke to the king angrily. "Solomon!" He thundered, striking fear into the king's heart. "You have not kept my covenant and laws as I commanded you to! I promised to establish your royal throne over Israel for ever if you lived by my laws, but you have worshipped pagan idols. I am therefore going to tear your kingdom away from you. However, for the sake of your father David, I will not make you suffer this in your lifetime. I will do it to the son who succeeds you on the throne. He will be left with only a small part of your kingdom, while one of your servants will rule over the rest."

> **When Solomon was old, his wives turned away his heart after other gods.**

Even though Solomon was the most knowledgeable man in the world, he had no idea who the "servant" was that God was speaking of. It was a bitter pill to swallow. Instead of the kingdom he'd worked so hard to build going to his son, most of Solomon's efforts would be enjoyed by a stranger. Yet the king understood he had sinned. He had no choice but to accept the Lord's punishment and beg His forgiveness. The king realized that the period of peace, unity and prosperity he had brought to Israel was about to come to an end, all through his own fault. Despite all the efforts Solomon had made to live peacefully with his enemies, the last years of his reign were plagued with unrest. Two rulers in particular continually raided Israel, King Hadad of Edom and King Rezon of Damascus. The king knew that it was the way things would be for Israel in the future.

Shishak
The kings of Edom and Damascus were not the only ones to attack Israel during Solomon's reign – the Pharaoh Shishak also invaded. Shishak is the first Pharaoh to be mentioned by name in the Bible. This is a small silver pendant showing the Pharaoh, possibly worn on a necklace as jewellery.

Burning incense
This picture shows an incense burner from the 10th century BC. Incense was commonly used during religious ceremonies, as an offering to God. The word "incense" refers both to the substance used for burning (usually a spice or gum) and to the characteristic smell that is produced.

✦ ABOUT THE STORY ✦

Solomon failed God by allowing his wives to draw him away from God. Other nations worshipped many gods, and the temptation was great for the Israelites to do the same. Solomon, who loved God, foolishly allowed these other gods to be introduced into Israel.

The Kingdom is Divided

THERE was a high-ranking official in Solomon's government called Jeroboam, a very capable man who carried out his work quickly and efficiently. The king rewarded Jeroboam with promotion, making him minister over all the forced labour schemes in the territories that belonged to the tribe of Joseph.

Jeroboam was delighted. He immediately packed up his house and belongings, and set off out of Jerusalem to move to his new job. However, he hadn't long been on the road when he saw the prophet Ahijah coming towards him. To Jeroboam's astonishment, the prophet stripped off the new robe he was wearing and ripped it into twelve pieces. "I am here with a message for you from the Lord," Ahijah declared. "God is about to tear the kingdom away from Solomon and rip Israel apart, for the king has forsaken Him and turned to worshipping false idols. Solomon's son will rule over only two of the tribes, and the Lord will make you king over the other ten."

Jeroboam was amazed. Though he was an ambitious man, he had never dreamed of being on the throne of Israel. How on earth was all of this going to happen, he wondered? He was an important man in the kingdom, but surely he wasn't important enough to be king.

Jeroboam knew that the dramatic prophecy was best kept to himself, but he couldn't resist confiding in his family and friends. They found it hard to keep the exciting

secret, and the news leaked out until people all over the country were whispering the rumour. Soon word reached the ears of the king himself. Solomon realized with dread that Jeroboam was the "servant" God had chosen to take over the kingdom. In desperation, the king sent men to kill Jeroboam, but he managed to escape and fled to the distant country of Egypt.

Finally, after reigning over Israel for forty years, King Solomon died and his son Rehoboam took the throne. Even though Solomon had made Israel a wealthy, famous country, life under him had been terribly hard. The exhausted people wanted to make sure that their new ruler would be less demanding than his father had been. They searched for a spokesperson to approach the new king, and there was no one more suitable than Jeroboam, who had returned from Egypt after Solomon died.

Rehoboam asked his counsellors what they thought he should do about the people's request. First he went to the advisers who used to be at his father's side. These old men knew how the people had suffered under Solomon's rule. They wisely advised the king to win the favour of his new subjects by showing them mercy and reducing the levels of taxation and forced labour.

Then Solomon's son went to his new advisers. They were inexperienced and counselled the king to show the people his authority by imposing laws that were even harsher than those of his father.

> 66 *'My father chastised you with whips, but I will chastise you with scorpions.'* 99

The king thought for a while. Rehoboam was an arrogant young man who liked the idea of his subjects cowering in fear before him. He foolishly chose the advice of the younger men over that of his father's more experienced counsellors and advisers. "You have asked me to lighten your yoke," he announced to the anxiously waiting people. "Hear this. My father lashed you with whips, but I am going to lash you with scorpions!"

The tyrant had expected the Israelites to shut up and meekly shuffle away at this cruel threat. He was shocked to find that it had quite the opposite effect. Labourers all over the country downed tools and sat at home, refusing to work. On top of this general strike, there were demonstrations and organized protests. Several protests broke out into violent scuffles with the king's men, who had been sent to keep the rioting workers under control. In one demonstration the king's minister in charge of Israel's forced labour, Adoram, was stoned to death. "We will no longer serve the house of David," the people shouted. "We want a new king!" The ten tribes in the north of Israel crowned Jeroboam as their new ruler.

Only the tribe of Judah and the tiny tribe of Benjamin, in the south of the country, remained faithful to Solomon's son. From them he gathered 180,000 warriors to go and fight Jeroboam for the throne. A prophet called Shemaiah stopped him, bringing word from God. "The Lord says that no one shall fight against his countrymen. Everyone must return home, for this division in the kingdom has been brought about by the Lord himself."

So the kingdom that David had unified, and that Solomon had spent years building up, was once again split into two. The ten tribes of the north kept the name Israel, and the two small tribes of the south were called Judah.

The divided kingdom

God punished Israel heavily for Solomon's disobedience. The two new kings ruled their separate tribes. Judah and Benjamin followed Solomon's son, Rehoboam, and all the other tribes crowned Jeroboam as their new king. Two kings were not as strong as one king would have been, and they lost land to the surrounding tribes.

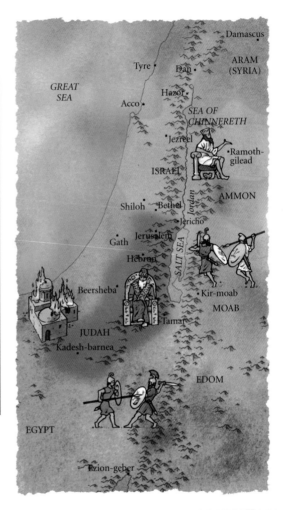

Jeroboam's seal

In around 930BC Jeroboam became the first king of the separate Israel. The son of a wealthy landowner, he worked his way up in the royal court until he was in charge of many of Solomon's building projects. During one of these projects, Jeroboam led the workforce in a rebellion against the king's heavy-handed practices. Because of this, he was banished to Egypt, where he remained until Solomon's death. The picture shows Jeroboam's seal.

The Book of Proverbs

FROM earliest times there were people in Israel and across the ancient world who studied what was called "wisdom". The writers of the book of *Proverbs* and other wisdom literature in the *Old Testament*, such as the books of Job and Ecclesiastes, discussed such difficult questions as: What is the purpose of life and why is there death, suffering and evil in the world? Some of these reflections on life are collected in the book of Proverbs.

Proverbs are short sayings that are easy to remember and which teach something about life and how people should live. They are general sayings, which means that they mean something to everyone and are relevant to all people in many situations.There are proverbs in many cultures all over the world.

Many of the wise sayings in *Proverbs* are basic common sense, but they are underpinned by the belief that wisdom comes from God:

"Trust in the Lord with all your heart and lean not upon your own understanding." (3:5–6)

The structure of the book of Proverbs varies.

Wisdom in Proverbs
The writers give a vivid picture of wisdom:
"Length of days is in her right hand, and in her left are riches and honour. Her ways are ways of pleasantness and all her paths are peace. She is a tree of life to them that lay hold upon her, and happy is everyone that retaineth her."

WISDOM

Sometimes several proverbs are linked by a single theme, such as the family or laziness.

Here are some examples of wise sayings from the book of *Proverbs*:

> *Let not loyalty and faithfulness forsake you.*
> (3:3)

> *He who seeks good finds goodwill, but evil comes to him who searches for it.*
> (11:27)

> *Even in laughter the heart is sad, and the end of joy is grief.*
> (14:13)

> *A soft answer turneth away wrath, but a harsh word stirs up anger.*
> (15:1)

> *Better a meal of vegetables where there is love than a fattened calf with hatred.*
> (15:17)

> *Pride goes before destruction and a haughty spirit before a fall.*
> (18:18)

> *Train up a child in the way he should go and when he is old he will not depart from it.*
> (22:6)

> ❝ *A word fitly spoken is like apples of gold in a setting of silver.* ❞
>
> (25:11)

> ❝ *Like cold water to a thirsty soul, so is good news from a far country.* ❞
>
> (25:25)

> ❝ *Do not boast about tomorrow for you do not know what a day may bring forth.* ❞
>
> (27:1)

> ❝ *As water reflects a face, so a man's heart reflects the man.* ❞
>
> (27:19)

SOLOMON AND THE BOOK OF *PROVERBS*

It is generally agreed that the book of *Proverbs* was compiled during the days of Israel's first kings, although editing continued for some centuries after this. It is not

> ❝ *Let another praise you, and not your own mouth* ❞
>
> (27:2)

known exactly what Solomon's role was, but the book is introduced as 'The proverbs of Solomon, the son of David'. His name appears again at the beginning of chapters 10 and 25, and the collections of proverbs from 10:1 – 22:16 and 25:1 – 29:27 are usually attributed to him. Solomon was famous throughout the ancient world for his outstanding wisdom. Unlike the kings before and after him, he was wealthy, he had many international contacts and he was not engaged in warfare. He was able to collect and compose thousands of proverbs and songs. His court became an international centre for the exchange of learning.

❖ THEMES IN *PROVERBS* ❖

The themes dealt with in the book of *Proverbs* cover all aspects of life, including home, work, relationships, justice, attitudes and everything people do, say or even think. The sayings are based on practical observations of everyday life, and there is an underlying belief behind all the proverbs that wisdom comes from God.

The wise man and the fool
This is the main theme of the whole book and forms the subject of the first nine chapters. The proverbs highlight the contrast between the wisdom of obeying God and the folly of wilfully going one's own way.

The righteous and the wicked
The wise person will lead a good, or righteous, life, whereas the fool will always be tempted by wrongdoing – in other words, he will become wicked. God loves and protects righteous people and is angry with those who are wicked. Although they may succeed for a while, it is only a matter of time before they arrive at death and destruction.

Laziness and hard work
Many of the proverbs describe the downfall of the lazy person. These people only realize their error too late, when they have achieved neither wealth nor status.

The family
This theme covers marriage, including unfaithfulness. It also covers the relationship between parents and children, including how they should be disciplined. Many of the sayings on this theme are still relevant today.

The Temple

ALTHOUGH it was King David's great ambition to build a temple, his son, Solomon, actually ordered the work to be done. Solomon built the temple in Jerusalem as a permanent home for the Ark of the Covenant – the wooden chest containing the Ten Commandments. The temple took seven years to complete. It was built as a house for God, rather than as a place to hold big gatherings of people. We have a good idea of what it looked like because there are detailed descriptions in the Bible. Solomon may have based his temple on the temples of the pagan tribes of the time. Ruins of these have been excavated that are similar in style to the Bible descriptions.

Solomon's temple was a rectangular building. It was about 30m long, 10m wide and 15m high. The temple probably stood on a platform above the level of the courtyard in which it was built, and was reached by a flight of steps. In the courtyard, in front of the temple, was a huge bronze altar for sacrifices and

an enormous bronze basin supported by twelve bronze bulls, which was used for ritual washings. There were store rooms along three sides of the building, which were probably used to keep sacred objects. The front entrance porch had a doorway with a giant bronze pillar on each side. These pillars were called Jachin and Boaz. It is not known what purpose they served as they were not part of the structure of the temple.

A pair of folding wooden doors led from the entrance porch to the outer chamber of the temple, which was known as the Holy Place. This was the larger chamber where the high priest performed ceremonial duties. The chamber was lit by five pairs of golden lampstands, and by a row of latticed windows high in the walls on each side.

A second pair of wooden doors led from the Holy Place to the inner chamber, which was known as Holy of Holies. This was a very sacred place. The doors

Solomon's temple
This picture shows the finished temple. In the Holy of Holies, the t guardian cherubim can be seen, their outstretched wings meeting above the Ark of the Covenant

to it were probably only opened once a year, for the high priest at the atonement ceremony. The Ark of the Covenant lay in the Holy of Holies, guarded by two wooden cherubim, each about 5m tall. When the ark was first put in place, the Holy of Holies was filled with a cloud, which signified the presence of God.

Both the Holy Place and the Holy of Holies had walls panelled with cedarwood and floors covered with cypress planks. The walls and doors were carved with flowers, palm trees and cherubim, and inset with gold. None of the underlying stonework was visible at all.

Solomon was assisted by neighbouring tribes in the building of the temple. He already had a friendship with King Hiram of Tyre, in Phoenicia. This alliance was strengthened by the agreement that Hiram would supply many of the materials for the temple, in particular the wood, and would take charge of the building work. In return for this, Solomon would provide him with foodstuffs, such as wheat, barley and oil.

Ancient cherubim
The figure shown on the right is actually what the cherubim in Solomon's temple would have looked like. Today we think of cherubim as looking like little children, but this figure has more in common with an Egyptian sphinx.

The tabernacle
The tabernacle was built during the Israelites' wilderness years, as a home for the Ark of the Covenant. It was a portable temple, which could be carried wherever they went. After the Israelites settled in Canaan, the tabernacle was kept at Shiloh, Nob and Gibeon, before Solomon built his temple, and the ark was transferred there.

The skill of many craftsmen, including stonemasons, carpenters and bronze-workers, was used to build the temple. Stonemasons sawed, hammered and chiselled stone blocks into shape, to make the basic structure. The blocks were worked on before being brought to the holy site so that no unnecessary noise was made. Even during the building stage, the place was regarded as holy. Ordinary woodwork was done by carpenters, but the woodcarving, such as the cherubim and the panelling on walls and doors, was carried out by specially skilled craftsmen. For the basic woodwork, local woods, such as cedar, cypress, oak, ash and acacia, were used, but for the carving work, hard woods, such as ebony, sandalwood and boxwood, were imported from abroad. King Hiram supervised much of the bronze casting himself, including the two decorative pillars for the entrance to the temple, and the huge basin, which was able to hold nearly 45,000 litres of water.

DAVID IS MADE KING

• Death of King David

• Solomon is made king of the united kingdom of Israel

DAVID AND NATHAN

• Solomon is blessed with wisdom by God

• The Queen of Sheba visits Solomon

• Death of King Solomon

• Solomon's son, Rehoboam becomes King of Judah

WEALTH OF SOLOMON

950BC

ASSYRIAN LION'S HEAD

• Jeroboam, Solomon's servant, becomes king of Israel

• The prophet Shemaiah tells Rehoboam he must not try to invade Israel

900BC

EXILE AND RETURN

The divided kingdom of Israel is constantly under the threat of invasion from enemy empires in surrounding lands. The Israelites are driven from their land and undergo a long exile in Assyria and Babylonia. Throughout these troubled times, prophets such as Elijah struggle to keep up the Israelites' faith in God. Finally the exiled people, now known as Jews, return to their homeland.

Introduction

THIS section tells of the rise and fall of the kingdoms of Israel and Judah, of the people who lived there and the kings who reigned over them. It describes the enemy empires – Syrian, Assyrian, Babylonian and Persian – that posed a constant threat to the Israelite nation. It also follows the lives of the prophets, from Elijah to Ezekiel, who struggled through these difficult times to sustain the Israelites' faith in God.

The two main prophets who lived in the kingdom of Israel were Elijah and Elisha. Elijah received his calling from God during the reign of King Ahab. Ahab had been persuaded by his wife, Jezebel, to join her in worshipping the Phoenician god, Baal. As more and more people followed the king and turned to Baal and other pagan gods, Elijah had his work cut out trying to turn them back to God.

Nebuchadnezzar's Palace
These are the remains of the palace of Nebuchadnezzar in Babylon. The exile was when the Israelites were forced from their homes in Judah to live in Babylon, but it is also the time when the Jewish faith was properly established.

Even after Elijah proved God's supremacy in a contest, Ahab continued to sin against God. When a man called Naboth refused to sell him his vineyard, the king had him stoned to death, then took the land. Elijah reminded him that, in refusing to sell his birthright, Naboth had been obeying God, and predicted that Ahab and his family would die in dishonour. His prediction came true, when Ahab was killed in battle, and his blood licked up by stray dogs.

Elijah is one of only two people in the Bible not to die – the other is Enoch, a man who enjoyed a particularly close fellowship with God. When the time came for Elijah to go to heaven, he was carried upwards in a flaming chariot. This amazing spectacle was witnessed by Elijah's assistant, Elisha. As Elisha picked up the cloak dropped by his master, the mantle of power passed to him.

Beth-shan, Israel
There were two important pagan temples here that stood at the time of the good King Josiah.

Elisha continued the work of Elijah, but when he failed to eliminate Baal worship God was forced to punish the Israelites. The mighty Assyrians besieged Israel's capital, Samaria, for three years and eventually took control of the city. The kingdom of Israel had come to an end, and its people were scattered throughout the vast Assyrian Empire.

Meanwhile, the smaller kingdom of Judah was facing the same problems. Despite the efforts of the prophet Isaiah, the people continued to worship pagan gods, and most kings didn't stop them. There were some exceptions – God rewarded the loyalty of King Hezekiah by stopping the Assyrians taking over Judah and giving the king an extra 15 years to live.

Then the Babylonians besieged Judah's capital, the holy city of Jerusalem, for two years. They destroyed the temple, burned the city to the ground and took most of the inhabitants to Babylon as exiles, ending the kingdom of Judah.

The exiled people of Judah became known to the Babylonians as Jews. A prophet called Ezekiel gradually managed to get the Jews to pull together and follow the laws of Moses in an attempt to preserve their own identity. They were rewarded by God and their lives began to improve. Ezekiel predicted that they would return to the Promised Land to rebuild their temple. This came true when the Babylonian King Cyrus eventually decided to allow the exiled Jews to return to Jerusalem. They rebuilt the temple and the city, and threw out all the non-Jews living there. God's people were back in the Promised Land. They had their temple and holy city and they were once again one nation under God.

This section ends with the stories of Daniel, the prophet who interpreted the dreams of kings and survived being thrown into a den of lions; Esther, the beautiful young wife of King Xerxes, who saved the Jews from destruction by appealing bravely to her husband; and Jonah, the unwilling prophet, who was swallowed by a whale as a punishment for disobeying the call of God.

The main thread running through this section is the lives and teachings of the prophets. The role of these people was to remind the Israelites of the covenant they had made with God during the time of Moses, and to warn them of the consequences of disobedience. Prophets were known as "men of God", but God often referred to them as His servants. The person usually held up as the best example of a prophet was found in Moses. He received a specific and personal call from God. He was warned in advance of events and of their significance by God. He was concerned about the welfare of his people. He played an active role in the affairs of the nation. His prophesying was made up of a combination of proclaiming about the present situation and predicting the future.

God usually spoke to His prophets by simply making them aware of His message, but He also used dreams and visions. A prophet was often associated with a group of disciples, some of whom may have been called by God, while others joined the prophet to learn from his wisdom. It is most likely to have been these disciples who recorded the words of their masters in the books of the Bible.

Jerusalem at the centre of the world

The picture on the right is an ancient map of what was known of the world at the time of Ptolemy, an Egyptian ruler who lived in AD100. Even at this time Jerusalem, capital of Judah, was a very important city. This world map places Jerusalem at its centre.

❧ EXILE AND RETURN ❧

This section covers the lives of two of the greatest prophets, Elijah and Elisha, and tells the stories of the later kings of Israel and Judah.

THE LIFE OF ELIJAH
First Book of Kings, Ch. 17 to 22.
Second Book of Kings, Ch. 1 & 2.
THE LIFE OF ELISHA
Second Book of Kings, Ch. 3 to 17.
KINGS OF ISRAEL AND JUDAH
Second Book of Kings, Ch. 11 to 25.
THE PROPHETS
Isaiah Ch. 1 to 9.
Jeremiah Ch. 1 to 36.
THE EXILE
Jeremiah Ch. 40.
Ezekiel Ch. 18 to 37.
Daniel, Ch. 1 to 6.
THE RETURN FROM EXILE
Ezra, Ch. 1 to 10.
Haggai, Ch. 1.
Nehemiah, Ch. 1 to 6.
ESTHER
Esther, Ch. 3 to 8.
JONAH
Jonah, Ch. 1 to 4.

Divided Kingdoms and Exile

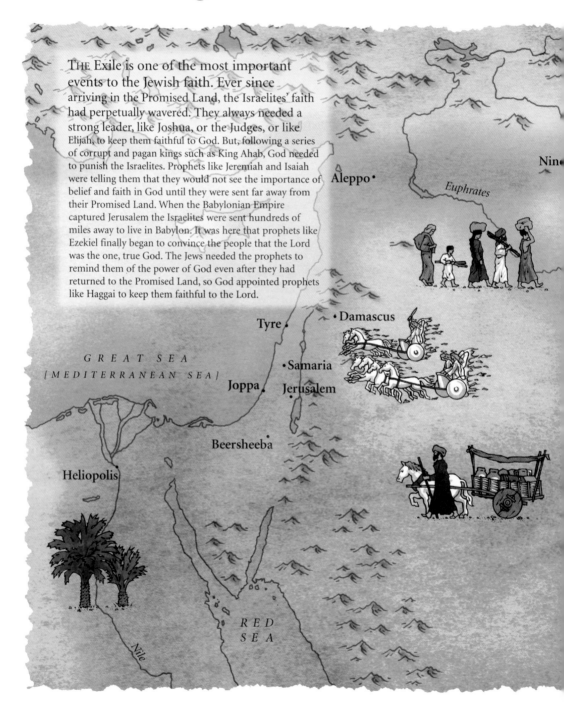

THE Exile is one of the most important events to the Jewish faith. Ever since arriving in the Promised Land, the Israelites' faith had perpetually wavered. They always needed a strong leader, like Joshua, or the Judges, or like Elijah, to keep them faithful to God. But, following a series of corrupt and pagan kings such as King Ahab, God needed to punish the Israelites. Prophets like Jeremiah and Isaiah were telling them that they would not see the importance of belief and faith in God until they were sent far away from their Promised Land. When the Babylonian Empire captured Jerusalem the Israelites were sent hundreds of miles away to live in Babylon. It was here that prophets like Ezekiel finally began to convince the people that the Lord was the one, true God. The Jews needed the prophets to remind them of the power of God even after they had returned to the Promised Land, so God appointed prophets like Haggai to keep them faithful to the Lord.

Aleppo •

Nin

Euphrates

Tyre •

• Damascus

GREAT SEA
[MEDITERRANEAN SEA]

• Samaria

Joppa •   Jerusalem

Beersheeba •

Heliopolis

RED
SEA

Nile

shur

Tigris

• Babylon
• Nippur

HYRCANIAN
SEA

LOWER
SEA

Persepolis

King Ahab the Bad

AFTER the reign of King Solomon, the Promised Land split into two kingdoms. The ten northern tribes kept the Promised Land's name – Israel. The smaller kingdom of Judah, formed by the two southern tribes, kept the capital, Jerusalem, and the temple built by King Solomon.

King Jeroboam of Israel was worried. He knew that his ten tribes would want to travel to the temple at certain times, as was the custom. And if his subjects felt that God's home was in Judah, wouldn't they eventually want to be ruled by the king of Judah instead? Jeroboam decided to set up two massive altars in his own country, at

Bethel and Dan, with a huge golden statue of a calf for each one. He appointed his own priests, with new prayer services and feast days. Then he appointed a new capital city for Israel, Samaria.

But in fact King Jeroboam need not have worried. The Hebrews in Judah were deserting the temple in droves and taking up pagan religions, which seemed to be much more fun. At pagan festivals the people ate and drank what they wanted, and danced with who they wanted – their gods didn't seem to mind at all. So statues of idols began to pop up all over Judah and their king did nothing to stop it.

For years, evil king followed evil king in both kingdoms. But Ahab, the sixth king of Israel, was one of the very worst. Ahab married Jezebel, the daughter of the king of Sidon, who worshipped the pagan god Baal. Jezebel persuaded Ahab to worship Baal too, and soon nearly all the Hebrews in Israel were worshipping Baal at a huge temple that Ahab built in Samaria.

> 66 *And Ahab did evil in the sight of the Lord more than all that were before him.* 99

But not everyone abandoned God. The Lord called a faithful man named Elijah to take a message to King Ahab: "I am the God of Israel, whom you have forgotten. There will be no rain in the country until I say so."

The king just laughed. But before long, the weather got drier and drier. Ahab got angrier and angrier, and the Lord told Elijah to hide. Elijah headed east, as God instructed,

Jezebel
Jezebel was a Phoenician princess, married to King Ahab of Israel. When she arrived in Samaria, she continued to worship her native god, Baal. Jezebel encouraged her husband, his court and the whole of Israel to turn away from their God towards Baal. Ten years after Ahab died, Jezebel came to a violent end – she was thrown from the window of her palace by her servants, under the orders of King Jehu.

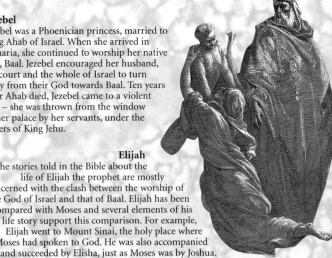

Elijah
The stories told in the Bible about the life of Elijah the prophet are mostly concerned with the clash between the worship of the God of Israel and that of Baal. Elijah has been compared with Moses and several elements of his life story support this comparison. For example, Elijah went to Mount Sinai, the holy place where Moses had spoken to God. He was also accompanied and succeeded by Elisha, just as Moses was by Joshua.

next day... and the next day... in fact, every day that Elijah was there. But despite the plentiful food, her son fell sick with a fever and, after several days, died.

"You say you're a man of God," she cried to Elijah. "Have I done anything wrong to deserve my son's death?" The prophet took the lifeless body to his own bed. He laid the boy down and knelt beside him. Three times Elijah cried out to God to give back the child's soul, and three times he listened for the child's heart to start beating again.

Soon, when Elijah carried the boy downstairs to his mother, he was alive.

ntil he reached the brook of Cherith. There, Elijah ound a cave for shelter. The drought was so bad that here wasn't an animal or a blade of grass in sight. But he Lord didn't let Elijah go hungry. Morning and vening ravens arrived at the cave carrying meat and read for him in their beaks. Then the brook dried up in he sweltering sun. "Go to Zarephath," came the Lord's oice. "There's a widow there who will look after you."

Sure enough, Elijah was taken in by a very poor vidow who had only a handful of flour and a little oil ft for herself and her son to eat. Nevertheless, she ade Elijah a meal and resigned herself to starving to eath. Yet the next day she was amazed to find that her our jar and oil jug were full once again... and the

od the provider
his picture shows Elijah being fed by vens. God demonstrates His superiority He is able to provide for Elijah even in e heartland of Baal worship.

Samarian ivory
The building of Samaria was begun by King Omri and continued by his son, Ahab. This piece of ivory from the palace dates from the 9th century BC and shows the Egyptian god Horus.

> ❦ **ABOUT THE STORY** ❦
> *The reason why the people preferred Baal to the true God was that worshipping him was much easier and less demanding. However, the story of Elijah reminds readers that God always keeps a few people faithful to Himself and uses them to challenge others to return to Him. Believers may be few in number at times, but they are all very important to God's purposes.*

Elijah's Challenge

As God had commanded there had been no rain for three years. Elijah heard God telling him to go and find the furious King Ahab before Ahab found him. The king hated to obey Elijah, but he followed all his instructions: he needed the rain. He summoned the 450 priests of Baal and also the 400 priests of Asherah (Jezebel's other god) and ordered all his subjects to go to Mount Carmel.

The prophet was waiting for them. "The Lord God has brought this terrible drought upon Israel because you are sinning against Him and worshipping idols," Elijah told the king, sternly. "Let's settle this once and for all. I challenge your priests to a contest. Tell them to prepare a bull for sacrifice to their gods and I'll prepare another for sacrifice to the Lord. But no one must set either offering alight.

We'll all pray to our gods to miraculously light the fire themselves. And whoever has their prayer answered will obviously be worshipping the true god."

When everything was in place, Ahab and Jezebel's priests began to call upon Baal to light the offering. All morning they prayed, chanting themselves into a trance and dancing themselves mad. In their frenzy, they even slashed themselves with their sacrificial knives. But it was no use. Not a spark, not even a puff of smoke.

> " *They raved on but there was no voice; no one answered, no one heeded.* "

❧ ABOUT THE STORY ❧

Baal was said to be a god who controlled the weather and sent storms. So he already looked weak because there had been no rain. Then, when the fire (perhaps a lightning bolt) hit Elijah's sacrifice, it proved to everyone that Baal didn't really exist, but that the true God did. Elijah ordered the execution of the priests because they had led people away from God. This was a very serious offence in Israelite law.

Mount Carmel
This is a view down Mount Carmel, which is also the name given to a group of mountains in north-west Israel. It is believed to be the site of Elijah's contest with the prophets of Baal. In Bible times, it was covered in oak and olive groves.

Jezebel's seal
This picture shows a seal from the 9th-8th centuries BC. The name 'Jezebel' has been added in Phoenician letters. Jezebel was a Phoenician princess.

command," the prophet called aloud. There was a mighty roar as the sodden heap burst into flame, and everything was burnt to ashes: not just the bull and the firewood, but the stones and the soil too! The terrified crowds were beaten back by the immense heat and fell to the ground to worship the one true God. Elijah pointed at the trembling priests of Baal and Asherah. "Kill them," he ordered. "Make sure not one of them escapes, for they have led you all into sin." At once the Israelites fell on the evil men.

King Ahab was enraged. But the prophet simply ordered him to calm down and have a meal.

Meanwhile, Elijah prayed while his servant watched the sky for rain. Suddenly Elijah's servant shouted out. "A little cloud as small as a man's hand is heading this way!"

"It is the rain," smiled Elijah. "Quick, Ahab! Get in your chariot and drive home before the storm overtakes you!" The king raced down the mountain as black thunder clouds chased him all the way to his royal city of Jezreel. As for Elijah, he was filled with the spirit of the Lord, and ran so fast that he beat the king back to the palace.

Elijah enjoyed watching the priests make fools of themselves. "Shout louder," he mocked. "Maybe your god is having a nap!" At midday the priests of Baal and Asherah gave up, exhausted. It was Elijah's turn. First Elijah took 12 large stones, one for each of the tribes of the Promised Land, and he rebuilt the altar to the Lord that had once stood at the top of Mount Carmel. He arranged the firewood and laid his bull on it, then he dug a deep trench all around. Elijah ordered the Israelites to fetch water and pour it over the altar. The astonished Israelites drenched the animal and the wood until the water filled the trench.

Then Elijah stood before the altar and prayed. The thousands of waiting men and women fell silent. "Lord, show these people that you are the one true God, and that I am your servant and have done everything at your

Fire from God
The illustration shows Elijah's sacrifice bursting into flames, while the prophet himself prays beside it. The sacrifice of the priests of Baal was not set alight.

Fleeing from the storm
In this picture, Ahab and Elijah are shown fleeing from the storm. Because the spirit of God came upon Elijah, he was able to run very fast and reached Jezreel before Ahab.

The Still Small Voice

WHEN King Ahab told Jezebel about Elijah's show of power on Mount Carmel, the queen turned purple. She shook with rage. She spat, she spluttered and finally exploded. "Find that trouble-making prophet!" she screamed at a messenger. "Tell him that by tomorrow he'll be in exactly the same place as my dead priests!"

In fear for his life, Elijah fled; first south into the kingdom of Judah and then into the desert. How depressed and worn out he was! All his efforts before the people at Mount Carmel had not been enough. He'd failed to turn the king and queen back to the Lord, and the Israelites would soon be back to worshipping their pagan idols once again. The prophet didn't have the will to go on any longer. He sank down under a broom tree. "Lord, I've had enough," he groaned. "Let me die right here." Exhausted, he fell into a deep, troubled sleep.

The touch of a gentle hand brought Elijah back to consciousness. Through his bleary eyes, he saw that the hand belonged to an angel, and at once the prophet was wide awake. "Get up now," the angel said, kindly. "You must be hungry." Elijah turned to look where the angel indicated and saw that a jug of fresh water stood next to some freshly baked loaves of bread. The smell was irresistible, and Elijah gratefully tucked in. With his stomach full and his mind much comforted, the prophet drifted off once more. But this time his dreams were easy. And when he awoke, the angel was there again. "Come and eat," came the soft voice, "or you won't be fit to make the journey." The journey that the angel wanted

Elijah to make was a long one – 40 days and 40 nights through the desert. But the special food and drink had revived Elijah more than he would ever have imagined, and he made it safely to Mount Horeb, the holy place where Moses himself had spoken to God. It was the perfect place to hide and wait for the Lord's instructions.

> " *And behold, a voice said, 'What are you doing here, Elijah?'* "

Day after day Elijah sat inside a cave and wondered what would happen next. The prophet had totally lost track of time when he heard the Lord's voice calling him. It took him completely by surprise. "Elijah! Elijah!" God said. "What are you doing here?"

The prophet leapt to his feet and spoke aloud into the darkness. "Of all the people in Israel, only I remain faithful to you, Lord," Elijah called. "Because of this, they want to kill me."

"Go from this cave and stand outside on the mountain," God ordered.

Elijah had hardly stuck his nose out into the

open when the wind began to blow. First, a brisk breeze lifted the fallen leaves and swirled them around; then the wind howled into a gale that plucked trees out of the ground and ripped rocks from the mountainside and tossed them around like pebbles. And Elijah stood safe and unafraid with the hurricane roaring round him. He did not feel that God was in the wind.

Next, the ground underneath the prophet began to tremble... then to shake... then to shudder... and with a mighty crack, the mountain split in two. Elijah stood safe and unafraid on the heaving soil. He did not feel that God was in the earthquake.

All at once there was a blaze of flame and a rush of heat as every tree, plant and blade of grass caught fire. Elijah stood safe and unafraid while the flames licked all around him. He did not feel that God was in the inferno either.

Finally, the wind dropped, the earth juddered to a halt and the flames died away. Elijah was left alone in the silence of the mountainside. Then he heard a still, small voice speaking quite clearly into his mind – and he felt the Lord was there. Deeply afraid, he hid his face in his cloak and listened. "Go to Damascus in Syria and find two men: Hazael and Jehu. Anoint them as future kings: Hazael, king of Syria, and Jehu, king of Israel. They will wreak terrible destruction on King Ahab and his sinning subjects, and I will be avenged by them for the wrongs the Israelites have done me. When you have finished in Syria, go and find Elisha, the son of Shaphat. He is to be your assistant and will take over from you when your work for me is done. And do not be discouraged. There remain 7,000 people in Israel who have not worshipped Baal and who are true to me."

Elijah set off for Syria with renewed energy and hope. No matter how gloomy things looked, God had shown him that He was always there and would deal with things in His own good time. And with Elisha for a companion, Elijah would no longer have to face the sinning Israelite nation on his own.

ELIJAH WAS UPSET WHEN HIS LIFE WAS THREATENED. HE PANICKED AND RAN AWAY. HE WAS VERY TIRED. PEOPLE MAKE BAD DECISIONS WHEN THEY ARE TIRED. WHAT THEY NEED TO DO IS STOP AND PRAY.

The journey of Elijah
Elijah travelled all over Israel to follow God's commands. He first heard God speak to him in Tishbe, and had his competition with the Baal prophets after going to Zarephath. He then fled to Mount Sinai, before going up to heaven on the chariot of fire.

❧ ABOUT THE STORY ❧
Elijah was used to seeing God act in spectacular ways. Wind represented His powerful Spirit, the earthquake was a sign of His judgement and fire was what He had spoken through on Mount Carmel. Elijah had to learn that God works in many different, quieter, ways too. God had quietly kept other people faithful to Himself, but Elijah had been too busy to notice.

Ahab Strikes a Deal

When Ahab was king of Israel, the strongest nation in the region was Syria, under King Benhadad. Benhadad wanted to take Ahab's kingdom for himself. He gathered together his armies, marched into Israel, and soon reached Samaria. King Ahab's capital city was besieged; thousands of soldiers were ready to attack.

Ahab despaired. But a prophet arrived with a message from the Lord. "I will give these enemies into your hands. By this, you will know that I am the one true God. Send the servants of your district governors out to fight."

The king was mystified, but armed the 232 servants and pushed the shocked men outside the city walls to face the full might of the Syrian army.

Ahab couldn't believe his eyes. The servants hacked their way through the enemy lines. He sent reinforcements and soon Benhadad's men were either dead or scattered.

Ahab was overjoyed, but the prophet warned him that Benhadad had escaped and that Syria would attack again. Sure enough, in the spring, the Syrians appeared again. Once more the prophet told Ahab: "The Lord will again give you victory to prove He is the one true God."

By sunset, the smaller army of Israel had slain 100,000 Syrians. The stunned invaders tried to flee to the city of Aphek, but in the jostle to get through the gates the city wall collapsed, crushing many to death. King Benhadad was one of the lucky few who made it through. To try and escape with his life, the defeated king offered to return all the Israelite cities he had conquered, and let the Israelites trade with Syria. Ahab accepted, and the deal was sealed.

The Israelite king was triumphant, but a prophet gave him a grave message. "The Lord is angry with you for sparing this enemy," he said. "God will take your life instead of his, and your people instead of his." Ahab's heart sank, and he resented the word of the Lord.

❧ About the Story ❧

Nothing seems to be enough to convince Ahab that the Lord is all-powerful. Unconvinced by the contest on Mount Carmel, the Lord shows Ahab his power by helping him win two great victories against armies that were better trained and far outnumbered his own. Rather than humiliating Ahab in front of his own people the Lord helps him, but the king still does not accept the word of the Lord and remains completely unrepentant.

Syrian prince
This statue from around 800BC shows a Syrian prince, seated on a throne, with his feet on a footstool. He is armed with a dagger and wears a necklace with symbols of the sun and moon. It is possible that King Benhadad might have looked like this.

Trading places
In return for saving Benhadad's life, Ahab was allowed to set up trading places in Damascus. The jewellery being bought and sold there might have looked like these necklaces, made of gold, lapis lazuli and cornelian.

Naboth's Vineyard

IN Samaria, next door to King Ahab's palace, there was a beautiful vineyard which belonged to a man called Naboth. Every day the king would look out of his window and dream of the wonderful fruits and vegetables he would grow for himself if only he owned the fertile earth.

One day a royal messenger knocked on Naboth's door. "The king wants your vineyard," he said bluntly. "You can either swap it for any vineyard you want or the king will pay you good money for it."

Naboth pondered for a moment. "This land has belonged to my family for generations," he thought. "I wouldn't part with it for any sum of money, and besides, the Lord says that it's a sin to sell someone your birthright." Naboth looked at the messenger. "Tell the king he can't have my vineyard," he said firmly. "It's God's law that I can't part with it."

The king was extremely annoyed. He lay in his bedroom in a mood, refusing to eat anything. "Cheer up!" Jezebel laughed. "I'll get you the vineyard." The wicked queen wrote a letter to each of the elders in the city. She forged Ahab's name and sealed each letter with the king's royal seal. The plot was set.

Some weeks later there was a great ceremony in the public square. As Naboth stood on the platform in front of all the citizens, two men began to lie that they had heard him curse both God and the king. "Treason! Treason!" cried the corrupt elders and nobles, stirring up the crowd into a frenzy. And the innocent, bewildered Naboth was dragged outside the city and stoned to death.

The delighted king trotted off to claim the vineyard. However, as he strutted round it the prophet Elijah came striding up to him. "The price you have paid for this vineyard is your very soul," the furious prophet thundered. "Because of your crimes against the Lord, you and all of your family will be wiped out. The dogs will lick up your blood and the birds will peck at your bones."

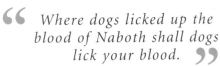

> **" Where dogs licked up the blood of Naboth shall dogs lick your blood. "**

Ahab was terrified at the words of the great prophet. He wept and tore his clothes. He put on sackcloth and fasted, all to try and earn some mercy from God. When the Lord saw that Ahab was at last taking some notice of Him, He promised to show him a little mercy, but as for complete forgiveness – it was far too late for that.

Breaking the law
According to God's law, it was forbidden to sell land that had been inherited from one's ancestors. The picture above shows Ahab and Naboth in the vineyard.

Ahab's seal
This is a picture of Ahab's seal. It is a bronze ring and the inscription on it reads "Ahab, king of Israel". Jezebel would have used this seal to forge Ahab's signature on the letters she wrote.

> ◆ **ABOUT THE STORY** ◆
> *Ahab knew that the law said he couldn't take Naboth's vineyard. But Jezebel, who cared nothing for God's law, believed the king could do anything. But she knew that simply taking the vineyard would cause a riot, so she lied and murdered to get it. The Bible has many stories about people who misused their power, and shows that God's law is to be obeyed by everyone, however famous, rich or powerful they are.*

The Death of Ahab

It didn't take long for Elijah's prophecies of disaster to start striking the royal family. And it was King Ahab himself who met his doom first. The king of Israel had become friendly with his rival, King Jehoshaphat of Judah. Ahab suggested that he and Jehoshaphat should together attack Syria to win back the city of Ramoth-gilead, which was in the hands of King Benhadad. "What do you think?" Ahab asked the king of Judah. "You can consider my forces your own," Jehoshaphat assured him. "Only let's first consult the Lord about this plan."

King Ahab called all the prophets in Israel to the palace. "We want to know whether we should fight the Syrians for Ramoth-gilead," King Ahab said. The prophets all agreed. "The Lord says yes..." said some. "The Lord will give you victory..." urged yet more. One of them, Zedekiah, even approached the thrones wearing a horned battle helmet! But for some reason, Ahab felt uneasy about the prophets' enthusiasm. He looked around the room. Someone was missing.

"Where's Micaiah?" the king said slowly. "Bring him here at once." Ahab explained why to Jehoshaphat. "Micaiah is a troublesome prophet," he sighed. "He never tells me what I want to hear. But because of this, I tend to believe him more than the rest. They just seem to agree with everything I say."

When Micaiah arrived, he at first went along with the other prophets.

✤ ABOUT THE STORY ✤

This story shows how weak Ahab was. He knew Micaiah told the truth, but he was afraid to call the battle off – after all, he had suggested it himself. As a result, he lost his life and Israel and Judah lost the battle. The point of the story is that it is better to lose face and listen to God than to ignore God and bring trouble on oneself and others.

Preserved armour
This coat of mail found at Nuzi, in Iraq, dates from around 1400BC and is made of overlapping bronze scales. This is the sort of armour Ahab would have worn.

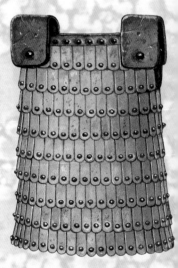

Coat of mail
Coats of mail were worn by archers who were unable to protect themselves with shields. They were more protective than leather armour and lighter than plate armour. Their weak point was the joints of the sleeves, which is probably where the arrow that killed Ahab entered.

"Go and triumph," he told the king, "God will grant you victory." But Ahab looked him in the eye.

"Come now, Micaiah," he insisted. "Tell me the truth."

Just as Ahab feared, Micaiah then prophesied doom and gloom. "I have seen all Israel scattered upon the mountains like sheep with no shepherd," he began.

Ahab groaned and turned to Jehoshaphat. "You see, I told you so. He never has a good word to say for me."

Micaiah continued, "I saw the Lord in heaven, wondering how He could persuade you to attack the Syrians. One of the angels said He'd put lies in the mouths of your prophets so they'd advise you to go to battle."

Zedekiah flew into a fury. He struck Micaiah across the face. "How dare you say that God lies to us and yet speaks truthfully through you?"

"You'll see that I'm right on the day that you run and hide in the face of defeat," Micaiah answered.

At the mention of the word "defeat", King Ahab decided he'd listened to quite enough. "Arrest this man!" he cried to his guards. "Keep him in prison on bread and water until I return victorious and decide what to do with him."

Micaiah remained completely unruffled. "If you return victorious, my name's not Micaiah," he said calmly.

Despite the Israelite king's outward show of confidence, he was inwardly very worried by Micaiah's words. Ahab let Jehoshaphat go into battle dressed in his king's robes and riding in his royal chariot, while he disguised himself as an ordinary soldier. Benhadad of Syria had ordered his chariot regiment to attack no one but the king of Israel, and they nearly killed Jehoshaphat by mistake, thinking that he was Ahab.

However, one of Benhadad's archers, firing at random, delivered the king of Israel's mortal wound. An arrow pierced a chink between the plates of metal and embedded itself deep in his flesh. A faithful horseman carried the wounded king out of the fighting, and all day he lay in his chariot, watching his troops being slaughtered. After sweltering and bleeding all day in the hot sun, that evening King Ahab died and his troops disbanded and fled.

> **" They washed the chariot by the pool of Samaria, and the dogs licked up his blood. "**

Ahab's body was taken home to Samaria and buried there. But it was at a spot near to where Naboth had been stoned to death that his chariot was washed clean. And as Ahab's blood streamed out of the chariot floor, stray dogs came and licked it up, just as Elijah had said they would.

Micaiah
Micaiah was a prophet during Ahab's reign. Apart from this story of his meeting with the king, little else is known about him. He may have been brought out of prison to prophesy in this case. He had obviously prophesied regularly before as Ahab was already aware of his gloomy, but truthful and accurate, predictions.

Cleaning the chariot
The above picture shows people cleaning out Ahab's chariot after his death. The blood is being licked up by stray dogs, fulfilling Elijah's prophecy.

Elijah's Chariot of Fire

ELIJAH sighed. He had to go on a journey, and he knew it would be his last. "God is sending me to Bethel," he told his assistant, Elisha. "Don't come with me. I won't need you this time." But Elisha sensed what lay behind his master's words and he insisted on keeping Elijah company.

When the two companions reached the far-off town, Elisha found out that he wasn't the only one who knew what was about to happen. The prophets living at Bethel whispered to him worriedly. "Do you know that the Lord is going to take Elijah from us?" they gasped.

"Yes, I know," Elisha reassured them. "Keep it to yourselves." And he hurried back to his master.

"Why don't you stay here, Elisha?" the older prophet urged. "The Lord has told me that I've got to go further on, to Jericho."

"You're not getting rid of me that easily," smiled the young man, striding out determinedly.

They drew near to Jericho and saw the prophets of the city waiting for them. Once again, Elisha was beckoned aside. "The Lord is going to..." they began.

"Hush, now," interrupted Elisha. "I know. Now try to keep it quiet." And he dashed back to his master.

"Honestly, Elisha," insisted the older prophet, "I really think you should stay here. God now says that I've got to go all the way to the River Jordan."

"As long as the Lord's above and you're alive down here, I'll never leave you," said the faithful young man. And the companions went on down the road, followed by a group of about 50 prophets, who hung back nervously.

Elijah and Elisha reached the Jordan. Elijah took off his cloak, rolled it up and struck the waters with it. The river parted, leaving a dry path. The two men crossed without even getting their feet wet.

Then Elijah turned to Elisha and smiled sadly. "You know that I'm going to be taken from you," he said. "Is there anything you'd like to ask me or do for you?"

"Master," Elisha said, "I need a double share of your spirit in order to do your job."

Crossing the Jordan
The crossing of the River Jordan that Elijah and Elisha made reminds us of the miracle that Moses performed when he parted the waves of the Red Sea. When Elisha also performed the same miracle, it showed that he had indeed taken over from Elijah.

❧ ABOUT THE STORY ❧

This great vision was God's way of telling Elisha that he was called to a very special job, carrying on the work that Elijah had started. Elijah wasn't able to promise the "double share" of his power, because only God could give that, but he believed God would answer Elisha's prayer. There was nothing magical about Elijah's cloak, but it is symbolic of the fact that Elisha is taking over Elijah's role.

Elijah shook his head. "That's something I can't promise to give you," he replied. "However, if God allows you to see me taken up to heaven then I'm sure He will give you what you ask."

Elisha saw everything. It started as a glimmer in the sky that swirled and glowed until it became a flaming chariot drawn by horses of fire that landed between them. Elisha watched in awe as Elijah got in and raised one hand in farewell. Then the horses began to gallop in circles until everything was a blazing whirlwind. The chariot rushed upwards and was gone.

> ❝ *Behold, a chariot of fire and horses of fire separated the two of them.* ❞

Elisha knew that he'd never see his master again and began to mourn. Then he noticed Elijah's cloak lying on the ground. Rolling up the cloak, he cried aloud, "Where is the God of Elijah?" He struck the waters of the River Jordan and once more the river parted to let him through.

When the 50 prophets saw Elisha's miracle, they knew that the spirit of Elijah had come on him, and they bowed down before him. But they found it hard to accept that the great prophet was really gone. "May we go and look for Elijah?" they begged. Elisha was reluctant to let them go, but realized they hadn't seen what he had seen.

After three days of searching, the prophets returned. They knew in their hearts that Elijah was in heaven and wouldn't be coming back.

A first-born son
Elisha is not being greedy or arrogant when he asks Elijah for a "double share". A first-born son usually inherited a double portion of a parent's estate, so it is more that Elisha wants to be recognized as Elijah's spiritual heir.

Elisha, Elijah and the prophets
The Bible tells us that a group of prophets followed Elijah and Elisha round the country. The "prophets" in this case are not the same as Elijah and Elisha. They are people who try to live good lives, but God does not speak directly to them.

Elisha and the Women

ELISHA travelled and spread the word of God, working many miracles that established his reputation as a great prophet.

In Jericho, he purified the foul-tasting water that gushed from the city's main spring.

Elisha also helped a woman so poor that she had only a single jar of oil. She was deep in debt, and her creditor was about to take her children into slavery as settlement. Elisha told her to borrow empty jars and begin pouring her own oil into them. To her astonishment, as long as there were jars to be filled, the oil kept flowing. She had more than enough oil to sell to pay off her debts.

In Shunem, a rich woman made Elisha and his servant, Gehazi, welcome in her house. The prophet wondered how he could repay her kindness. Then Gehazi mentioned that the wealthy couple didn't have a child. "This time next year, you will have a son," Elisha told them. And to the couple's great joy, they did.

Some years later, Elisha was praying at Mount Carmel with Gehazi when the woman came hurrying up, weeping her heart out. "My son is dead!" she sobbed. "He was brought home this morning with a bad headache and by lunchtime he was lifeless in my arms! You're a holy man, please do something!" At once, Elisha hurried to the woman's home.

> 66 *As he stretched himself upon him, the flesh of the child became warm.* 99

When they got there, Elisha quietly shut the door to the dead child's room and prayed. Then he stretched his hands out over the small, stiff body. Elisha sensed his skin gradually warming up and felt gentle breath on his face. "A-choo!" the child sneezed. "A-choo! A-choo!" God had answered the great prophet's prayers to bring the dead boy back to life.

Oil jar
The Bible refers to the use of oil a great deal, and it usually refers to olive oil. Oil was used for cooking as much in Elisha's time at it is now, but it was also an offering to God, used for trade and as fuel for lamps.

MIRACULOUS STORIES OF PROPHETS HEALING THE FAITHFUL REMIND US THAT GOD PROTECTS HIS PEOPLE. THESE STORIES ENCOURAGE FAITH WHEN TIMES ARE HARD. ~

The widow's oil
This is an illustration of the story based on a picture in a 13th-century Spanish Bible. Many Bibles throughout history have been very lavishly illustrated, not only with pictures but with decorated letters.

Naaman the Leper General

WHEN the Syrians took some of the Israelites captive, they heard the amazing stories of Elisha. The general of the Syrian army, Naaman, was particularly interested. He had leprosy, a terrible skin disease. His wife's Israelite maid was sure that Elisha would be able to cure him, so Naaman asked the king if he could go to find the prophet.

> *He was a mighty man of valour, but he was a leper.*

When Naaman and his royal entourage arrived at Elisha's house, Naaman was annoyed to find that the prophet wouldn't come out but sent a servant instead. "Elisha says to tell you to bathe seven times in the River Jordan," Gehazi said. "Goodbye." And he shut the door.

Naaman was furious. He'd come all this way to see the holy man, and he'd brought magnificent gifts, too: sacks of silver, bags of gold and ten very expensive robes. "All Elisha had to do was pray a bit!" he raged. "If it's just a matter of washing, we've got better rivers back at home!" Humiliated, he was about to head straight back to Syria, when one of his attendants stopped him.

"Sir, you've nothing to lose," he said. "You've come all the way here, and it's an easy thing to do. Why not try?"

Once... twice... three times Naaman washed himself in the Jordan. The sores were there just the same. Four... five... six – nothing. But as he rose from the waters for the seventh time, he knew something was different. He looked down and saw that his skin was as smooth as a child's.

Naaman jumped for joy, then ran to thank Elisha. "Now I know that your God is the true God," he said. "May I take some earth to worship him when I return home?"

"Of course," said the delighted prophet, but he wouldn't accept a single gift that Naaman tried to press upon him.

When Naaman had left, Elisha noticed that Gehazi was missing. Instantly, he knew his servant had gone to tell Naaman that his master had changed his mind about the gifts, so he could take them for himself.

When Gehazi returned the prophet knew what he had done and was unforgiving. "Now you have Naaman's wealth, you can have his leprosy too," Elisha thundered, and the horrified servant felt his skin begin to bubble.

Arean architecture
The Syrians were known at this time as "Arameans", and Syria was called "Aram." The picture shows the base of a column from an Aramean palace. The sphinx is a mythical animal that is seen in art and architecture all over the world. Solomon had sphinxes, called cherubim in Israel, in the temple he built at Jerusalem.

Earth from Israel
At this time people believed that a god could only be worshipped on their "home" land. In order to carry on worshipping God, Naaman asks Elisha if he can take some of the earth of the Promised Land home with him to make a holy place in Syria.

Saved from the Syrians

THE king of Israel relied on Elisha to help him with the continuing Syrian attacks. The prophet sent detailed warnings to the palace, outlining the Syrians' battle plans. He'd tell the king exactly where and when the Syrians would hit next, so the Israelites were always ready.

The Syrian king grew frustrated. "It's as if the king of Israel can read my mind!" he raged.

"Elisha the prophet knows the secrets you whisper in your bedchamber," his servants replied. "It's he who tells the king."

"He has to be stopped!" the king roared. "Where is he?"

"In the Israelite city of Dothan," came the answer.

"Go there at once and seize him," the king bellowed.

In Dothan, Elisha's servant woke up and flung open the door. "Master, master, look!" he screamed. "The Syrian army is right here, in Dothan!"

Stretching into the distance were gleaming chariots and armoured men. "Never mind," he reassured Gehazi. "There are more of us than there are of them." Elisha prayed, and Gehazi could see chariots and horses of fire all around their house. Then Elisha prayed again. "Lord, please strike the Syrians blind – just temporarily." And he set off down to the Syrian camp.

Samaria
This piece of ivory furniture from Samaria is decorated with a carving of a lion fighting with a bull. The city was besieged and captured by the Assyrians in 722BC and this signalled the end of the northern kingdom of Israel.

Siege craft
During a siege, the attacking army surrounded the city. The army would try to cut off supplies of food and force the inhabitants to surrender.

The blinded Syrians were stumbling about, terrified. When Elisha arrived and told them to follow him, they were only too pleased to hear someone who seemed to know what was going on, and they marched on until Elisha told them to stop. There was a short silence while he prayed, and then suddenly the soldiers found they could see again. To their horror they found they were in Samaria, the capital city of Israel.

The King of Israel was just as confused as the troops. "What shall I do?" he asked Elisha. "Shall I kill them?"

> ## " The king said to Elisha, 'My father, shall I slay them?' "

"No," laughed the prophet. "Show how great you are by giving them a huge feast and then sending them all home."

After that the Syrians didn't attack Israel again for a long time. But eventually King Benhadad decided to lay siege to Samaria and starve the Israelites into defeat so he surrounded the city. No one could get in or out. Traders and merchants bringing food and wine to the city were turned away, and people got hungrier and hungrier.

Inside Samaria, things grew desperate. The people would eat anything – weeds, mice, beetles. Each day the Israelite king walked around the city walls. When he even saw people arguing over eating each other, he stormed off to Elisha. "Your God has done this to us!" he yelled.

"Tomorrow there will be plenty of food on sale in this city, and all at the right price," Elisha yelled back. "Trust me." Then he began to pray.

Later that night, four starving lepers sneaked out of the city to the Syrian camp. They were dying anyway, so weren't risking much by asking the enemy for food. But they couldn't see a soul or hear a sound. The camp was deserted.

The Lord had filled the ears of every soldier in the camp with the sound of a mighty army on the move. Thinking that a huge army of Israelite reinforcements was heading straight for them, the panicking soldiers hadn't hung about to strike camp. They had just fled, leaving everything exactly where it was.

The lepers went wild, dashing from one storehouse to the next, shoving food into their mouths, cramming it into their pockets, running off and hiding it. Then they thought they'd better go and tell the king. And the next day, food was on sale in Samaria just as Elisha had said – more than enough for everyone.

The journeys of Elisha
After Elisha witnessed Elijah being carried to heaven by the flaming chariot, he travelled around a great deal, but he spent a lot of time in Samaria. In the capital city of Israel he brought God's message to the kings and people. It was near Samaria that Elisha's servant saw the vision of the heavenly army.

❧ ABOUT THE STORY ❧
In the days of Elisha there were far fewer maps. Most people who travelled had little idea what the places they were aiming for looked like. The roads were mostly tracks and there were no signposts. So the Syrians were blind in the sense that they were lost! Also, they didn't really know what Elisha looked like – there were no photographs – so they didn't recognize him. They hardly expected their enemy to walk up and introduce himself!

Jehu the Avenger

A commander in the Israelite army called Jehu was sitting in the officers' room one day when a messenger came from Elisha, asking to talk to him in private. Jehu took the rather agitated man out of the room. The man took out a bottle of sacred oil and said, "I anoint you king of Israel. You will strike down every last one of the royal family belonging to King Ahab, fulfilling the great Elijah's prophecy." Then he dashed away.

Now Jehu knew that King Joram of Israel, Ahab's son, lay very ill in bed, but he certainly wasn't dead yet. And why ever would he, Jehu, be chosen as the next king?

"Is everything all right?" his friends asked, as he returned pale-faced to the mess.

"Yes, everything's fine," Jehu replied, his mind obviously elsewhere.

"So why did that mad fellow come to see you then?" the other officers began. They pressed him so hard to find out what had happened, that eventually Jehu gave in and told them. Roaring with delight, they laid their cloaks down so Jehu wouldn't have to get his feet dirty, and took him out to show the other soldiers. They trumpeted loud fanfares to proclaim Jehu their new ruler, then raced off to get rid of King Joram.

The king's guard on the watchtower in Jezreel looked down and saw a group of charioteers in the distance, speeding towards the city in a cloud of dust. The racing chariots showed no sign of slowing, and the lookout soldiers guessed that Jehu was at their head – he was well

known for driving everywhere at top speed.

King Joram realized that if one of his highest-ranking officers was dashing to see him, it must be serious; and he raised himself up out of his sick bed to go out and meet him.

"You're too ill to go alone," said Joram's nephew, King Ahaziah of Judah, who had come to visit his sick uncle. "I insist on coming too."

Joram was too weak to argue. "Prepare our royal chariots," he croaked to his servants, as he staggered out on Ahaziah's arm.

Face to face the chariots thundered nearer and nearer. When they were within shouting distance, King Joram gathered his remaining strength and yelled, "Do you come in peace, Jehu?"

"How can I come in peace," came the reply, "when your mother, Queen Jezebel, is worshipping idols, practising black magic and leading our whole country into sin?"

Joram's heart began to pound. "Treachery, Ahaziah!" he cried, and the two kings wheeled their chariots back in the direction of the palace. But it was too late. Jehu reined his horses to a halt, drew his bow and fired an arrow that pierced Joram right between the shoulder blades. The king sank down dead in his chariot and his driverless horses careered over the bumpy ground. Jehu paused just long enough to order his men to catch the chariot and fling Joram's body on to the ground, abandoning it to the birds and the

beasts. Then he pursued the fleeing king of Judah and shot him dead, too.

Next, Jehu turned back to the city of Jezreel. Queen Jezebel was waiting for him at the palace, adorned in her finest regalia and hanging over the balcony, screaming insults. Jehu looked up at the trembling servants who stood next to her. "Are you with me?" he shouted. The men didn't hesitate to please their new king. They grabbed hold of the queen and hurled her out of the window.

Jehu had had a busy day. He strode into the palace and instructed the servants to prepare him something to eat and drink. He rested and ate his meal, recovering from his exertions. By the time he felt refreshed enough to get round to ordering the servants to clear away the queen's body, stray dogs had eaten her and there was nothing left.

> ## *Jehu slew all that remained of the house of Ahab in Jezreel.*

The avenging king's work wasn't over. During the months that followed, he ordered his officers to bring him the heads of all of Ahab's 70 other sons. Then he laid plans to kill all Ahab's counsellors, friends and priests. Finally, the whole of King Ahab's house lay dead, just as Elijah had prophesied.

Face at the window
This ivory carving is believed by some to be Jezebel looking out of her palace at Jezreel.

EHU WAS FOLLOWING GOD'S ORDERS WHEN HE WENT OUT AND TOOK REVENGE ON AHAB'S FAMILY FOR ALL THE WRONG THEY HAD DONE. IT IS NATURAL FOR PEOPLE TO FEEL ANGRY ABOUT THOSE WHO DO WRONG. THE NEW TESTAMENT SAYS THAT FOLLOWERS OF JESUS ARE NOT TO TAKE REVENGE LIKE THIS. THERE'S A BETTER BUT MUCH HARDER WAY TO RID THE WORLD OF EVIL: BY LOVING OUR ENEMIES.

⟡ ABOUT THE STORY ⟡

This bloodthirsty story comes from a time in history when there was not the kind of legal and police system we have today. People who were wronged had to take revenge themselves. Ahab and Jezebel broke God's law so blatantly that God took His revenge through Jehu, and there was no way he could be stopped. This story shows that Ahab and his supporters got what they deserved in the end.

The End of Israel

KING Benhadad of Syria was ill – so ill that he thought he might be dying. He remembered how the Israelite prophet Elisha had cured Naaman of leprosy, and told his servant, Hazael, to ask him if it was God's will that he should recover, too.

Elisha knew just why Hazael had come. "You can tell your king that he will get better," the prophet said, "but God has told me that he's going to die." Hazael was more than a little confused by this answer, but he didn't question it because Elisha was staring at him so strangely. Then the prophet began to weep. "I am grieving because you will bring great suffering to Israel," Elisha explained. "You will set on fire our fortresses, slay our men, batter our women to death and crush our children."

Hazael was appalled. "What am I, a wild animal?".

"You are to be the next king of Syria," Elisha said quietly.

On the long journey back to Damascus, Hazael had plenty of time to think about what the prophet had said. The day after he returned, he took a blanket and suffocated Benhadad while he slept. Then he took the throne for himself.

Meanwhile, in Israel, King Jehu was busy putting right the wrongs of King Ahab and his son King Joram. He did his best to wipe out the worship of Baal and other pagan gods from his land, directing his subjects back to the Lord. But he didn't go quite far enough. He allowed King Jeroboam's two golden calves to remain on their altars at Bethel and Dan. And the Lord began to punish Israel, using the king of Syria to do so. Hazael continually attacked Israel and took more and more land.

When Jehu and Hazael died, their sons carried on in their footsteps. Jehu's son Jehoahaz continued the worship of the calves at Bethel and Dan, and angered the Lord still further. In turn, God continued to give Hazael's son military success. The king of Syria slaughtered so many of Jehoahaz's

❧ ABOUT THE STORY ❧

The fall of Israel was a very sad event. The ten northern tribes were never re-united. The Bible writers say that this last defeat was God's punishment for the nation's refusal to worship Him alone, and for people's desire to follow wrong religious practices. The end was a long time coming, however; God had warned them for several centuries. This story shows that God is a judge, but that He is also very patient.

Bowing to the king
This limestone relief shows Jehu, or one of the ambassadors of the king, bowing down in front of the conquering King Shalmaneser, which was the usual gesture of defeat. Behind the kneeling figure, Israelite attendants carry the gifts requested by Shalmaneser. The stone dates from around 840BC and originally stood at Nimrud in Assyria.

Winged sphinx
This statue of a winged sphinx was a common image in Assyrian art. Statues like this were put at the gates of their palaces as they believed they had the power to ward off evil spirits.

troops that in the end there were no more than 10,000 foot soldiers, 50 horsemen and 10 chariots left in the Israelite army. By the time King Jehoahaz died, the whole land of Israel was very nearly destroyed by the might of the Syrian army.

It was left to Jehoahaz's son, King Jehoash, to fight back. By now Elisha was a very old man. As he lay dying, he called Jehoash to him for the last time. "Take a bow and arrows and open the window to the east," the frail prophet asked Jehoash. Then Elisha laid his hands over the king's hands and told him to shoot an arrow out of the window in the direction of Syria. "That is the Lord's arrow of victory, the victory you shall have over your enemy," the holy man told him. "Now take the other arrows and strike the floor with them." Jehoash hit them on the floor three times. Elisha's face fell. "You should have struck more times, for then you would have defeated Syria completely," he told the king. "Now you will win only three battles." Nevertheless, these three battles were enough to recover several Israelite cities and keep the Syrians at bay.

Over the years that followed, the Israelites fell back into worshipping pagan gods and ignoring the Lord. Weird idols and strange altars reappeared all over the countryside, with all sorts of seances, black magic and even human sacrifice taking place. And the Lord made sure that each Israelite king had an increasingly hard struggle to hold on to his lands.

> *So Israel was exiled from their own land to Assyria.*

At the same time, a greater threat than Syria was rising: the cruel, merciless Assyrian Empire. They conquered country after country, and soon the Assyrian King Shalmaneser turned his eyes towards the Promised Land. Shalmaneser said he would leave Israel alone as long as King Hoshea, the last king of Israel, paid the Assyrians a vast amount of gold and silver each year. The desperate Hoshea sent messengers to Egypt begging for help, but Shalmaneser heard of his plot and the vast Assyrian army swooped down to lay siege to Samaria. The capital city was besieged for three nightmarish years before it finally fell. The kingdom of Israel was no more.

The Assyrians rounded up the Israelites and scattered them across their empire. Samaria became filled with foreigners from other lands conquered by the Assyrians. They became known as Samaritans.

Idol worship
The Samarian golden calves were set up by Jeroboam, the first king of the divided Israel, to try to stop his subjects going to the temple in Jerusalem to worship.

Assyrian Empire
The Assyrian Empire, at its height, stretched across the whole of the 'fertile crescent'. This is a crescent-shaped area of land that is very good for growing all kinds of crops. The crescent followed the routes of the three great rivers of the area: the river Nile in Egypt, and the rivers Tigris and Euphrates in present-day Iraq.

Kings of Judah

W HEN Jehu the avenger killed King Ahaziah it left the kingdom of Judah without a ruler. The king's mother, Athaliah, wanted to be queen. So she set about killing everyone else in the royal family. Soon, Athaliah ruled unchallenged over Judah – or so she thought. For an heir still remained. Ahaziah's sister had smuggled one of his sons, Joash, into the temple in Jerusalem, where her husband, Jehoiada, was high priest. There the little boy grew up unharmed, while his grandmother wreaked havoc as queen.

When Prince Joash was seven years old, Jehoiada

told his secret to the senior army officers and some elders of Judah. Under heavy guard, the young boy was crowned the new king of Judah.

"Treason!" Athaliah cried, when she saw her subjects bowing to the child. Jehoiada told the guards to take her out of the temple, and they killed her in her own home.

At first Joash was a good king who loved the Lord. He was upset that the temple built by Solomon had fallen into disrepair, so he set up a collection box for donations of money to restore the building. But when the high priest died, evil officials talked Joash into worshipping pagan idols. The king even sent money from the temple fund to King Hazael of Syria, to pay him not to attack. Prophets warned the king that his sins would bring Judah down, but he refused to listen. Once, Jehoiada's son, Zechariah, climbed to the top of the temple and began preaching. "Why have you all forsaken the Lord?" Zechariah shouted. "God says that because you've abandoned Him, He's going to abandon you."

Leprosy
This picture shows King Uzziah in the temple, burning incense on an incense altar. For this sin, he was struck down with leprosy. Today, leprosy is known as a contagious disease that affects the skin, the inside of the mouth and the nerves. The Hebrew word for leprosy is less specific. Some of the features of leprosy described in the Bible do not occur in the disease that we call leprosy today.

Household gods
This is a statue of an Assyrian god called Lahmu, which means 'the hairy one'. Lahmu was one of the household gods who guarded homes and kept out evil spirits. The Assyrians put figures of these gods under the floors of their houses. Lahmu is just one example of the pagan gods the Judeans turned to at this time.

The crowds began to drag Zechariah down. King Joash chose not to call a stop to the riot. Instead, he watched as the prophet was beaten to death. The king went to check he was really dead. Zechariah's eyes suddenly opened. "May the Lord see and avenge!" he whispered.

That year the Syrians attacked Jerusalem. They slaughtered many people and plundered the capital. Joash was killed by his own men. They knew that he had brought the trouble upon them.

Under Joash's son, King Amaziah, the country went from bad to worse. He worshipped pagan idols as well as the Lord. And instead of attacking Syria, he turned on his neighbour, Israel. As God's punishment, Judah was defeated and Amaziah captured. The wall of Jerusalem was broken and the treasures in the temple seized.

Amaziah's son, King Uzziah, determined to do better. He worshipped only God, and the Lord helped his army win many victories over his enemies. But success went to his head and Uzziah grew arrogant. When he tried to burn incense in the temple, a job only priests were allowed to do, the Lord punished him by striking him with leprosy.

> ❝ *And the Lord smote the king, so that he was a leper to the day of his death.* ❞

Uzziah's grandson, Ahaz, was the worst king of all. He abandoned all pretence of worshipping the Lord and turned openly to worshipping the pagan gods. He worshipped idols and even burned his own son alive as a sacrifice. He smashed all the holy objects in the great temple in Jerusalem and replaced the great altar with a pagan one, then he eventually locked its doors forever.

God was furious. First He allowed the king of Syria to march into Judah and take hundreds of captives back with him into Damascus. Then He let the king of Israel massacre Judah's army and return to Samaria with over 200,000 prisoners. Other tribes in the Promised Land such as the Edomites and the Philistines took towns and villages in Judah. Eventually Ahaz found himself facing the might of the ruthless Assyrian King Tiglath-Pileser.

❖ ABOUT THE STORY ❖

The kings of Judah had a great advantage over the kings of Israel – the temple was in their capital to remind them of God and His laws. But even good kings were weak, led astray by their officials and forgetting that God had helped them succeed. These stories are in the Bible to show how important it is for leaders to live in God's ways. When they don't, the whole country suffers.

King Tiglath-Pileser
This stone relief from Nimrud in Assyria shows King Tiglath-Pileser standing in his chariot with a driver and an attendant. The relief dates from around 740BC.

Damascus
The kingdoms of Israel and Judah were often attacked by the Syrians, and many of their treasures ended up in Damascus, the Syrian capital. This picture shows goods for sale in modern-day Damascus.

Isaiah Shows the Way

IN the year that King Uzziah died, the prophet Isaiah had a vision in the temple. He saw the Lord sitting on a throne. Above Him were angels called seraphim who sang a beautiful song in praise of God:

"Holy, holy, holy is the Lord of hosts, The whole earth is full of His glory." The temple trembled and was filled with clouds of smoke.

> " *Holy, holy, holy is the Lord of hosts.* "

"Help!" cried Isaiah. "I have seen the King, the Lord of hosts. How can I live with being the sinning, flawed person I was before?"

One of the seraphim flew to the prophet, touching his lips with a burning coal that he'd taken from the altar. "Your sins have been forgiven," the angel told him.

Then came a voice that made Isaiah's heart leap. "Who is there that will take my message for me?" God asked.

Without a moment's hesitation, the eager prophet sprang to his feet. "Here I am, Lord!" he cried. "Send me."

"Then go and speak to my people," said the Lord. "But you will find they will not listen or understand till they have been scattered far from the Promised Land."

God spoke to the prophet throughout his lifetime. He spoke of trouble, but also of great hope. "For to us a child is born," Isaiah said, joyfully, "to us a son is given." He was speaking of the coming Messiah, Saviour of the world.

ISAIAH'S VISION REVEALED GOD'S HOLINESS – HIS PERFECTION. BIBLE WRITERS TELL US THAT GOD CAN NEVER DO WRONG, AND THAT WE ARE TO TRY TO BECOME LIKE GOD, HOLY IN SPEECH AND CONDUCT. ❧

Seraph
A seraph has six wings, two to fly, and a pair each to cover its face and feet. The task of the seraphim Isaiah saw was to guard the throne of God.

Isaiah
Isaiah was a prophet who lived in Jerusalem in the 8th century BC. He prophesied during the reigns of several kings, from Uzziah to Hezekiah. Most of his prophecies concentrated on the futures of Judah and Jerusalem. Isaiah is important as the prophet who foretold the coming of the Messiah, the Saviour of the Jewish people.

King Hezekiah the Good

JUDAH had held out against the Assyrians for 20 years after Israel had been conquered. God was rewarding Judah's good king, Hezekiah, who had destroyed all the pagan altars and kept the Lord's laws. Then the Assyrian king, Sennacherib finally attacked. Hezekiah was afraid and offered Sennacherib all his gold and silver to keep out of Jerusalem. Hezekiah even had to strip the temple itself in order to make the payment. But the ruthless Assyrian went back on his word and marched on Jerusalem anyway.

Sennacherib's spokesman tried to talk the citizens into surrendering, speaking in Hebrew, to make sure that everyone understood. "Hezekiah may say that your God will save you, but no nation has been saved from the Assyrians by their god. Make peace instead," he shouted.

The king told his subjects not to listen to the Assyrian lies, and went to the temple to pray. "Don't worry," Isaiah told him. "The Assyrians will never be allowed to enter Jerusalem, for it is God's city and he will certainly defend it."

That night, the Lord sent an angel over the Assyrian camp, and many of Sennacherib's troops died. Then news came that the African country of Ethiopia had suddenly attacked Assyria and the king was needed back home. And on returning to his capital, Nineveh, Sennacherib was murdered by his sons.

The saving of Jerusalem was not the only miracle God worked for the good Hezekiah. Once, when the king was very ill and was near death, he begged the Lord to repay his faithfulness with a little more life. Isaiah brought the news that his prayers had been answered, God was granting him 15 more years of life.

But no matter how hard the king tried not to sin, he could not lead a blameless life. Years later, when the king of Babylon's son came to visit, Hezekiah proudly boasted about all the treasures he once again possessed. He showed the pagan prince every single precious gem, piece of gold and chest of spice he owned.

Isaiah was not pleased. "God says the time will come when all you have shown to this prince will be carried off to his kingdom," he prophesied, "and your sons will be servants in the Babylonian king's palace."

God's angel of death
This medieval-style picture shows an angel flying over the Assyrian camp, striking the soldiers dead. God sent the angel to save the king of Judah, Hezekiah, because he had been a faithful worshipper of God.

❖ **ABOUT THE STORY** ❖
This story shows that God is completely fair and just in every possible way. When Hezekiah most needs the care and support of the Lord, God is there for him, and is able to give him as much extra life as He wishes, to reward Hezekiah for his loyalty. But when Hezekiah makes a mistake, he is punished by God. It may seem harsh to punish the king for this mistake, but God has very high standards of behaviour for all His people.

Josiah and the Law

WHEN King Hezekiah of Judah died, his 12-year-old son, Manasseh, came to the throne. Manasseh was as bad as his father had been good. He not only rebuilt all the pagan altars that Hezekiah had destroyed, but built new ones too. He even set up statues of idols in Jerusalem's great temple! He had witches and wizards as counsellors and he took part in all sorts of evil rituals.

The next king, Amon, was just as wicked and cruel as his father. The people killed him, and put his eight-year-old son Josiah on the throne instead.

Like his great-grandfather, Hezekiah, Josiah loved God even when he was a very young boy. It saddened him to see how the temple had been dishonoured and vandalised over the years, and at the age of 26 he ordered the great house of the Lord to be repaired.

Craftsmen cleared every dusty corner, restoring the building wherever possible, and knocking down and rebuilding wherever it was not. Sacred objects, that had been flung aside for years, again saw the light of day and were polished up, good as new.

One day, the high priest, Hilkiah found a soft cloth. Inside was a hole was a bundle wrapped in richly embroidered material. When Hilkiah unwrapped the package, he gasped. Inside lay an ancient scroll containing laws that God had given to Moses long ago in the wilderness. Trembling, he took it straight to the king.

Josiah read the scroll at once. He didn't stop until he'd taken in every single word. And he was horrified. King after king in Judah had led the people in breaking every law there was to break. And the scroll told of the dreadful punishments that God promised to those who sinned. Josiah broke down and wept, tearing his hair and ripping his clothes. "My people!" he cried. "Is it too late to be forgiven for our sins?" The king sent his officials to ask a prophetess, Huldah, what he could do to put things right. Her answer was solemn: "All you have read in the holy scroll will come true. Your people have sinned and the Lord will take vengeance upon them. But because you are full of repentance, God will allow you to live in peace. Your eyes will not see the misery of Judah's punishment."

> 66 *And when the king heard the words of the book of the law, he rent his clothes.* 99

Josiah ordered everyone in Judah to come to a great meeting at the temple. Loud and clear, Josiah read the scroll of the law to his subjects. His face was stern, his eyes deadly serious. You could have heard a pin drop. Not a sneeze, not a cough, not a whisper came from the huge throng while the king was reading. Then Josiah rolled up

Scroll of law
The Hebrew laws, also called the law of Moses, are God's instructions to His people as to how they must worship God and live their lives.

Josiah and Huldah
This picture shows Josiah's officials asking advice from the prophetess, Huldah, as to how they could make amends for past errors.

At last, the Lord was the one and only God worshipped in Josiah's kingdom, and the king led his people in a festival which had been forgotten for many years – the feast of the Passover – which they celebrated just as it said in the scroll of the law. Everyone in the country spoke about the wonderful things the young king had done. But it was not to last, because 13 years later Josiah was killed in battle and his reforms were to die with him.

the scroll and held it aloft, so everyone could see. "From this day onward," he thundered, "I swear with all my heart and soul to live by every single law in this scroll and walk in the path of the one true God." The crowds before him leapt to their feet. "We are with you!" they cried. "We will obey the Lord!"

Then Josiah told the priests to burn the pagan idols in public. He ordered all the heathen priests in Judah to be slain, and then went the length and breadth of the country, smashing every single one of their altars into dust. He cleared the places where human sacrifices had been offered and filled them with the bones of the dead, and no one went there any more.

Josiah
This picture shows Josiah reading the scroll. Although Judah was ruled by Assyria, their hold on the land was weakening. This meant Josiah could ignore the Assyrian gods he was told to worship.

Assyrian bronze demon
This is a bronze statue of an Assyrian demon, called Pazuzu, who was believed to carry disease. It is 15cm high and dates from around 800BC.

Jeremiah's Warnings

JEREMIAH was the son of a priest, and a quiet young man. He was stunned when he heard the Lord talking to him. "I want you to speak for me to the people," God said, "to remind them what dreadful fates will befall them if they continue to do wrong. It will be difficult, because they won't want to listen and they won't believe you. But don't get downhearted. Tell them everything I say, and I will give you the strength to cope."

The Lord told Jeremiah to go to a potter's house and watch him moulding his clay. As the wheel span, the water jar the potter was making suddenly collapsed into an ugly, squat shape. The potter stopped what he was doing and squashed the clay into a wet ball. Then he threw it back on to the wheel and began again, shaping it into another quite different vessel that stood tall and upright and beautiful. "Go and tell the people of Judah that they are like clay in my hands," the Lord told Jeremiah. "At any time, I can crush a nation that is becoming evil and destroy it. But if it repents, I can change my mind and allow it to flourish into something strong and good."

Jeremiah bought one of the potter's earthen flasks and set out for the valley of Hinnom, where many of the locals had turned once again to pagan worship. In front of all the people, he raised the flask up above his head and then dashed it to the ground, where it smashed loudly into a thousand tiny pieces. "The Lord says that the day is coming when this place will be called the Valley of Slaughter," he cried. "Because you have forsaken the one true God, your enemies will slay you here in your homes. The Lord will shatter Judah like this broken flask, so no one can repair the kingdom."

So Jeremiah's mission began, travelling from village to village with the same message, for the Lord wanted to give His people one last chance to mend their ways. But everywhere he went, he was shouted down by the angry locals and chased out of town – some of them even tried to kill him. Yet the lonely prophet didn't give up, and the Lord gave him enough courage to stand and preach in Jerusalem in the temple itself: "Listen to the word of God!" he shouted, above all the jeers and insults. "The Lord will destroy this very city and all the towns through the whole of Judah. For you stubborn, stupid people are refusing to heed his warnings."

> ❛ *Behold, like the clay in the potter's hand, so are you in my hand, O house of Israel.* ❜

The high priest, Pashhur, pushed his way through the mob. "How dare you cause this commotion in the house of the Lord!" he spat, striking and kicking Jeremiah until he lay cowering on the ground, and then hauling him away for a night in the stocks. But Jeremiah had a personal prophesy ready for Pashhur when he came to release him the following morning: "The Lord says that you will bring terror unto yourself and onto all your friends. Your enemies will kill all those you love while you look on, helpless. Judah will fall into the hands of the king of Babylon, and you, Pashhur, and all your family shall be carried away to live there in captivity. You will die in exile for failing to lead the people in the true ways of the Lord."

When God saw that Jeremiah wasn't having much success with talking to the people, He told him to write down every single word He'd said on a scroll. Perhaps then the warnings would seem more 'official' and the people might take notice of them. So Jeremiah called his loyal servant, Baruch, and dictated everything God had ever said to him. It was a long and tricky job. Everything had to be remembered perfectly and written down just so. But finally it was finished. "Baruch, you must read this to the

people," Jeremiah told the exhausted scribe. "I can't do it; I am not allowed to go to the temple. If I do the officials will arrest me. Go to the temple and, slowly and clearly, read out the whole scroll. Don't miss out anything."

One of the men who heard Baruch reading in the temple was Micaiah, a high-ranking official in the king's government. The words left him shaking in his shoes and he went straight to the royal court to tell his superiors what he'd heard. Baruch was immediately sent for and told to read the scroll all over again. The nobles were just as worried as Micaiah. "Are you sure this has all come from the mouth of the man of God?" they asked.

"Every word came from Jeremiah's lips and was written down by my hand," Baruch assured them.

"Then go and hide with your master, out of reach of King Jehoiakim's anger," the nobles urged him. They took the scroll to the king's secretary for safekeeping, and nervously went to Jehoiakim's chamber to tell him the most important bits. To their surprise, the king seemed to take it all quite calmly. "Really?" he remarked, looking concerned. "All Jeremiah's work, eh? He says it's the word of God, does he?"

When the king asked if he could see the scroll for himself, the nobles were pleased. "Of course," they agreed. "We're so glad you're taking an interest in it. We really do feel that there's something in these words of Jeremiah's." But to the nobles' horror, as each chapter of the scroll was read out to the king, Jehoiakim merely cut it off and threw it into the fire.

And when the last piece had burned away, the king sighed and wiped his hands. "That's sorted that," he said.

The Lord spoke to Jeremiah. "Never mind," He consoled the dejected prophet. "You'll just have to write it all out on a new scroll." And Jeremiah began to dictate to Baruch all over again.

Jeremiah

Jeremiah is seen here with his scribe, Baruch. Jeremiah was first called as a prophet in his early twenties. His prophesying continued for 40 years and spanned the reigns of the last five kings of Judah: Josiah, Jehoahaz, Jehoiakim, Jeconiah and Zedekiah. Jeremiah's prophecies did not always please the kings and priests of the time and, as a result, he was persecuted, plotted against and imprisoned. He spent much of his life struggling with the dilemmas that his prophetic calling imposed upon him.

> ### ❖ ABOUT THE STORY ❖
>
> *Jeremiah is sometimes called 'the weeping prophet'. The state of his country and the attitudes of the people upset him terribly. His message was not all doom and gloom; he offered hope to people who trusted God. The fact that he was made to suffer by people who rejected his message reminds later readers that following and serving God is sometimes very hard. It is sometimes necessary to face imprisonment and even death.*

The End of Judah

KING Nebuchadnezzar of Babylon conquered nation after nation, growing so strong that he crushed even the mighty Assyrian Empire. He swept into Judah and surrounded Jerusalem, leaving King Jeconiah (Jehoiakim's brother) begging for mercy. Nebuchadnezzar agreed to leave Judah alone, but on drastic terms. First, Jeconiah and the royal family would be taken into captivity in Babylon, along with all the elders and priests. Secondly, Nebuchadnezzar would also take into exile many of Judah's skilled craftspeople, whom he could use in his own kingdom. Thirdly, Judah would have to pay a massive yearly tribute of treasure in return for peace. And fourthly, Nebuchadnezzar got to choose his own king: the youngest of the good King Josiah's sons, Zedekiah, who would have to obey his every word if Judah was to be left alone.

The stunned people left in Judah could hardly believe what had happened. They were deeply shocked at losing their leaders, and their own future hung in the balance.

Jeremiah wrote a letter of comfort to the exiled people in Babylon: "God says make the most of this bad situation. Do all your usual things and enjoy life. Don't grumble and be nasty to the Babylonians. Look after their cities and the Lord will look after you. For He has told me that in 70 years' time, He will bring you back to the Promised Land where you will again live happily."

Jeremiah started wearing an oxen's harness to show the people in Judah that being captured by the Babylonians was not a bad thing. They would be happy living under someone else's rule, as the ox was. "This is the Lord's work," the prophet said. "Judah's punishment is unfolding as it should."

The Lord showed the prophet a vision of two baskets outside the temple: one full of plump, juicy figs and the other full of overripe, stinking fruit. "The exiles in Babylon will eventually ask me for forgiveness and I will make sure that they flourish like the good figs," God explained. "But anyone who struggles against my will and tries to remain in Judah will rot like the fruit in the second basket." After this, Jeremiah went to King Zedekiah himself to warn him to put all thoughts of rebellion out of his head. "You must not try to resist Nebuchadnezzar," he warned, "or you will lose everything."

"Just whose side do you think you're on?" cried Zedekiah, and locked him up. But Jeremiah's faith didn't waver. He believed that the Lord would one day restore Judah and, to prove it, he invested a large sum of money in buying a piece of land.

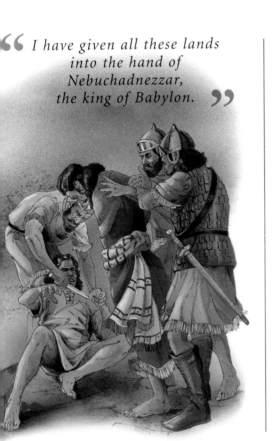

> ❝ *I have given all these lands into the hand of Nebuchadnezzar, the king of Babylon.* ❞

Even under house arrest, Jeremiah kept on sending out messages. "Anyone who stays in Jerusalem will die by sword, starvation and disease," he told them. "But those taken into exile by the Babylonians will live and prosper."

"This is ridiculous," thought the nobles of Jerusalem, "we have to shut him up." They threw Jeremiah into a deep, dark, mud-filled pit and left him there to die. But the king secretly sent a servant to haul him out and bring Jeremiah to him. "I need you to tell me the truth," he said to the prophet in private.

"Promise not to kill me and I will," replied the exhausted, starving prophet. The king anxiously agreed.

"God says that if you surrender to Nebuchadnezzar, the lives of you and your family will be spared and this city will survive," said Jeremiah. "However, if you try to fight against the Babylonians, Jerusalem will be burned to the ground and you will not escape from their hand."

Several years later, despite all Jeremiah's warnings, Zedekiah made a deal with the Egyptian army to try to defeat King Nebuchadnezzar and the Babylonian army. But the Egyptian king went back on his word and withdrew his troops, leaving Jerusalem to stand alone. The Babylonians pounced and Zedekiah barricaded the city. It withstood the siege for two years before the starving people finally gave in. The king was caught and forced to watch his sons slaughtered before he was blinded. He was led in chains to Babylon, along with many of his subjects. Only a few of the very poorest people were allowed to remain in Judah. Nebuchadnezzar's army smashed the walls and pulled down the temple before burning the city, just as Jeremiah had said they would.

Babylonian Empire
After the Assyrian Empire, the Babylonians became the greatest military force in the region. They conquered the Assyrians to occupy the important area of fertile ground around the River Tigris in the east, and the River Jordan in the west.

❧ ABOUT THE STORY ❧

The final destruction of Jerusalem took place in 587BC. This incident is one of the most important in the whole of the Old Testament. It marks the end of Judah as an independent country; there were never again any real kings to rule it and it was always dominated by a larger nation. Its destruction showed people that God had meant what He said – He hated rebellion against Him.

Ezekiel and the Exiles

WHEN the Babylonians were taking their captives from Judah into exile, they asked Jeremiah whether he would like to go or stay. Times were dangerous in the tiny, weak country, and he chose to stay to help Gedaliah, the governor the Babylonians had appointed to rule over the few people who remained. But the pagan tribe of the Ammonites saw their chance to take back land they had lost centuries ago to Moses and Joshua and they murdered Gedaliah. "Stand your ground against the Ammonites," Jeremiah told the terrified Judeans. "If you remain in Judah, the Lord will one day make you strong again. But if you are tempted by the thought of fleeing to Egypt, and wilfully abandon the Promised Land, you'll have only

death to look forward to." But the people of Judah fled, forcing Jeremiah to go with them, and the last remnants of the nation were swallowed up by the Egyptian civilization.

Meanwhile, among the exiled people of Judah – now called "Jews" by the Babylonians – a new prophet had arisen, a man called Ezekiel. Before Jerusalem had fallen, the Lord had told him that it would be up to him to try to keep the Jews together as a nation and turn them back to the one true God.

It was an extremely difficult task. The Jews were now scattered throughout a foreign country, among a strange people who had their own religions and customs. The Jews had no Promised Land, no elders, no kings. And the great temple in Jerusalem, where they thought God lived, had been destroyed.

Ezekiel had to teach the Jews two very important lessons – first, that God is everywhere, and secondly, that God judges everyone on who, not what, they are. For at first the Jews thought that simply being one of God's race of chosen people was enough to be given back the Promised Land one day.

"Here you are among pagans," Ezekiel said. "You're worshipping their idols, eating their food and sacrificing to their gods. Do you really think that the Lord will reward you? Each one of you is responsible for yourselves. If your father has sinned, you won't necessarily be damned for it. If your children commit crimes, God won't consider it to be your fault. The Lord is here, watching you in exile, and judging each one of you on your own, purely on what you do and how you live."

Ezekiel
The prophet Ezekiel was taken to Babylon as an exile. Five years after this, he received his call as a prophet. His prophecies were not generally popular but he still managed to reach a position of honour.

The Exile
This map shows Babylon, where the exiles were taken. This was a very important time in the history of the Israelites. In Babylon, under the leadership of prophets like Ezekiel, they became a united nation. This was where they were first called Jews.

Haran
Aleppo
Hamath
Asshur
GREAT SEA
Tadmor
Damascus
Tyre
Samaria
Jerusalem
Babylon
Nippur
Beersheeba

> **As I prophesied, there was a noise, and behold, a rattling; and the bones came together, bone to its bone.**

Gradually, the Jews began to take Ezekiel's teaching to heart. Far from their homeland, living among strangers and surrounded by foreign religions, they began to pull together as a nation and turn back to worshipping the one true God. And as soon as they did so, they began to enjoy life and prosper, just as Jeremiah had hoped they would. Jewish craftsmen began to be recognized for their skilled work. Jewish farmers were employed by Babylonian landowners at excellent rates of pay, and Jewish officials rose to prominent positions in government.

God was pleased and he began to grant Ezekiel visions of the restoration of the Jewish people and the rebuilding of the temple in the Promised Land. "The Lord has shown me that our nation lies dead like a skeleton," Ezekiel told the people. "But we have only to ask God to breathe on us and we will live. The scattered parts of the skeleton will connect together, bone to bone. And the Lord will join the two peoples of the Promised Land into one kingdom with one king, and raise us up to life as one nation."

❖ ABOUT THE STORY ❖

Prophets like Jeremiah had been told by God that the Israelites would prosper living in Babylon, and also that the nation of the Jews would be properly created after the Israelites had been taken far from their homeland. Under the leadership of Ezekiel this begins to happen. God's long term plan for his chosen people is coming to fruition, and the Jews are learning to love God and live by his laws, and they are reaping the benefits.

The father of Judaism
This picture shows Ezekiel teaching the Jews in exile. He is thought of as the founding father of Judaism as it is today, as it was he who drew together the exiles from Israel and Judah and made them into a faithful and devoted people.

Nebuchadnezzar's Dream

IT wasn't just God who was pleased with the way the Jews worked hard and lived good lives in Babylon. King Nebuchadnezzar was pleased too. So pleased that he took the most promising young people to the palace to learn Babylonian culture and language.

Four of the students were Daniel, Shadrach, Meshach and Abednego. They worked hard and God rewarded them with exceptional talents in letters and wisdom, and the gift of understanding dreams for Daniel. At the end of the course they amazed the king who gave them important jobs on his royal staff.

The king often had bad dreams and would ask his advisers to tell him what they meant. These "wise men" consulted oracles and conjured up spirits, then told Nebuchadnezzar what they thought he wanted to hear. But after one dream the king decided to test them. "This time, I don't just want an interpretation," he said. "I want you to tell me what I dreamed, too."

Panicking, the advisers made a wild stab at lying. The king was enraged. "Put them all to death!" he fumed. Unfortunately, that included Daniel and his three friends. When Daniel heard, he ran to the king. "I'm sure I can tell you about your dream," he begged.

Nebuchadnezzar remembered how Daniel had impressed him before. "Come back tomorrow," he demanded, and Daniel dashed home to pray.

Next day, he returned confidently. "No human, however wise, can tell you your dream," Daniel began. "But last night the Lord showed me. You dreamed of a huge statue –

Brick-making

The furnace in the story was probably used for making bricks. A brick is a piece of straw and mud or clay (usually rectangular) that is dried hard in the sun or baked in a kiln. In Bible times, bricks were used more than any other material for building. At first, bricks were shaped by hand, but later wooden moulds were used. In Babylon, bricks were often stamped with the king's name. The picture, from a tomb near Thebes, shows brick-makers at work.

Book of Daniel

This is a fragment on a Greek papyrus manuscript of the book of Daniel from around AD250. This Greek version of the Hebrew Old Testament originally contained the books of Ezekiel, Daniel and Esther and was one of 11 books from a Christian library found in Egypt.

the head was gold, the chest and arms silver, the belly bronze, the legs iron and the feet half iron, half clay. A huge rock smashed the statue into pieces that blew away on the wind. Then the rock grew into a great mountain which filled the world."

Nebuchadnezzar gasped. "The body parts stand for five empires," Daniel explained, "that will come after yours. But God's kingdom will eventually destroy all human empires and will stand for ever."

> ❝ *The mystery was revealed to Daniel in a vision of the night...* ❞

After that, Daniel was appointed chief royal adviser and his three friends were made provincial governors. The other district officials were filled with jealousy. But they didn't have long to wait to get their own back.

Nebuchadnezzar made a huge golden statue. He ordered a fanfare to be played at certain times, and whenever the people heard the music, they were to fall down in the direction of the idol and worship it – or be thrown in a furnace. The jealous district officials told Nebuchadnezzar that Shadrach, Meshach and Abednego refused to pay homage. They were arrested and brought to Nineveh.

"Do what you will. We cannot bow down to an idol," the friends told the king. The king ordered that the furnace be made seven times hotter than usual, and that the friends should be bound and thrown into the blazing furnace immediately.

But when Nebuchadnezzar went to check that the men had been burned to a cinder, he was utterly baffled. The servants who had thrown the Jews into the white hot flames were killed by the searing heat. But inside the furnace, the three men were walking around freely, chatting to what looked like an angel. "Come out!" Nebuchadnezzar roared. The three men stepped out of the blaze without a single hair on their head singed.

The shocked king sent a decree through the whole of Babylon. "No one may say anything against the God of the Jews, for no other god is as powerful as theirs."

The meaning of the dream
The kingdoms described in Daniel's interpretation are believed to be Babylon (represented by gold), Persia (silver), Greece (bronze) and Rome (iron). The rock that grew into a huge mountain represents the everlasting kingdom of God.

❖ ABOUT THE STORY ❖

These stories were included in the Bible to encourage the exiles to stand firm for God and not to lose their faith when they were being threatened in Babylon. The stories showed that God could save His people from terrible things, just as He had done in the past. People in ancient times were very interested in dreams; Daniel's experience reminded them that God understood everything even if people did not.

Belshazzar's Feast

THE next king to seize the Babylonian throne was Belshazzar. He loved to show off just as much as Nebuchadnezzar, and was especially fond of holding massive feasts to impress everyone. Belshazzar planned one grand banquet for a thousand guests. The huge banqueting hall was decorated with the richest hangings and ornaments from the royal treasure houses. Hundreds of waiters, musicians and dancers were booked. Belshazzar employed the very best chefs in Babylon and brought rare delicacies from the furthest corners of his empire for their elaborate menus. He ordered the most expensive wines from his cellars. The king took care of every single detail.

The feast was a complete success. The guests applauded and cheered the performance of the entertainers. They gasped as the waiters brought in platters of magnificent food and placed jewelled pitchers of wine on every table. Then Belshazzar called for silence. "Ladies and gentlemen," he announced proudly, "tonight is a very special night. You are in the greatest city in the world, being entertained by Nineveh's top performers, tasting the best food and wine that money can buy." Belshazzar's guests gave a loud cheer. "It is only right," the king continued, "that you should be eating and drinking from the finest plates and cups." Belshazzar turned to his servants. "Bring out the holy goblets we mighty Babylonians took from the Jews' temple in Jerusalem!"

The guests loved it. "Let's drink to our own gods!" they cried, drunkenly. "Here's to the gods of gold and silver!" They turned to toast the king himself and raised their glasses. "Cheers Belsha..." Their voices died away as they saw that the king was pale-faced and still, staring like a statue at a mysterious hand writing on the wall. The ghostly finger traced several words and Belshazzar sank wobbly-legged into his seat. "Guards! Guards!" he cried. "Fetch my advisers immediately!"

Belshazzar's magicians were totally baffled. Not one of them could tell what the mysterious writing said. "Call Daniel," advised the queen mother. "My husband Nebuchadnezzar used to say he was the wisest man in the entire world."

> **They drank wine, and praised the gods of gold and silver.**

The king promised to make Daniel the third most important man in the empire. "Keep your promotion," replied Daniel. "You're not going to be pleased with what I have to tell you. The first word – *mene* or 'number' – means that you have reached the full number of days God is granting you as king. The second word – *tekel* or 'weight' – means that God has weighed out what you are worth in His eyes, and it isn't much. The third word – *parsin* or 'divided' – means that your kingdom will eventually be split up. God is going to give half to the Medes and half to the Persians."

The party was definitely over. That very night, King Belshazzar was murdered. And Cyrus, king of the Medes, took the empire of Babylon for himself.

MANY PEOPLE TAKE FAITH IN GOD LIGHTLY AND MAKE FUN OF PEOPLE WHO WORSHIP GOD. THIS STORY REMINDS BELIEVERS THAT ONE DAY GOD WILL JUDGE EVERYONE ON EARTH. ❧

Hanging Gardens
The Hanging Gardens of Babylon did not literally 'hang', but were built on the roof on stepped levels called terraces. King Nebuchadnezzar is said to have built the gardens to please his wife who missed the greenery of her home in the mountains of Media. The Hanging Gardens were well known throughout the ancient world and in the 2nd century BC were listed as one of the Seven Wonders of the World.

Persian Empire
The Persian Empire stretched from Egypt in the west right across to the banks of the river Indus in what is modern Pakistan. Persia was the largest of the three empires, the others being the Assyria and Babylonia, that ruled Palestine and beyond.

Return from Exile

KING Cyrus was a man with new ideas of how to run an empire. He told all the peoples who had been captured by the Babylonians that they were free to go home. He had a special message for the Jews. "It is your God who has made me emperor over all the earth. Now go and rebuild His house in Jerusalem. Anyone who wishes to remain in Babylon can help by giving money and supplies to those who are returning." Cyrus even gave back the treasures Nebuchadnezzar had taken from the temple.

Not all the Jews wanted to leave. They had been in exile for many years, and a lot of them knew no other life than in Babylon. But some began to pack. The prophets Isaiah, Jeremiah and Ezekiel had foretold that the Jews would one day rebuild Jerusalem, and they decided that now the time had come, it was up to them to do it.

The Jews found Jerusalem still in ruins. They built an altar out in the open air for the Feast of Tabernacles, and offered prayers and sacrifices. Then work on the temple began under two new leaders: Jeshua (a priest) and Zerubbabel (a descendant of King David). The day the foundations were finished was a day of great emotion. The priests led the celebrations with singing and dancing, and there were tears of sadness from those who remembered the former great temple of Solomon, as well as tears of joy.

> " *The returned exiles celebrated the dedication of this house of God with joy.* "

The work went on, very slowly. The peoples brought to the Promised Land by the conquering Assyrians and Babylonians came to look. "We want to help," they volunteered. "We've been following your religion as best we can. Let us help with the building and then we can all worship your God together." But the Jews wouldn't have any of it. During their years in exile, they'd followed their religion very strictly. They were afraid that if they let foreigners join in – some of whom still worshipped pagan idols – they would be led into breaking

Samaritans
After the Assyrians captured Samaria and the Israelites were sent away, Samaria was filled with people from other lands who became known as Samaritans. The Jews always resented them for taking their kingdom. Here the Jews are sending away the Samaritans.

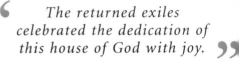

❧ ABOUT THE STORY ❧

The exiles returned from Babylon to Jerusalem in 538BC, but the temple was not finished until 516BC – almost exactly 70 years after Nebuchadnezzar had destroyed it. This was the second Jewish temple to stand in Jerusalem; the Temple of Solomon was the first. The second temple was not as big or grand as Solomon's first temple. It stood until the Roman General Pompey destroyed it in 63BC.

some of their laws. "You can have nothing to do with our God or our temple," the Jews told the Samaritans. The rioting that broke out was so bad that the exiles were forced to down tools, and the temple was left unfinished.

With the passing years, times grew harder in the Promised Land. "Look at what's happening," a prophet called Haggai told the Jews. "Our crops are failing, the water is drying up, our clothes are falling to bits and money seems to run through our fingers. It's because we've built ourselves houses to live in, but we haven't finished off the house of the Lord."

"The Lord has told me that we should be strong and complete the building of the temple," another prophet, Zechariah, agreed. "He says that as soon as we've done it, there'll be bumper harvests and plenty of rain, and we'll live peacefully and prosper."

This encouraged the Jews to go back to work. But the envious Samaritans went to the governor of the province to cause trouble. "Who gave you permission to build here?" he demanded angrily.

"We're building at the command of Emperor Cyrus himself," the Jewish elders explained. "If you write to the new king, Darius, he'll tell you it's the truth." When the governor received a reply from Nineveh that, yes, Darius had indeed found such a decree signed by Cyrus, the Samaritans were forced to back off and the temple was finally finished. The Jews celebrated by holding the great feast of Passover and sacrificed 12 goats among the many offerings – one for each of the scattered tribes of the Promised Land. At last, the surviving Jews felt they had made a new beginning.

Palestine after exile
When the Jews returned to Israel their great ideas for rebuilding the city and the temple gradually became less important. They felt that building houses and farming the land for food were more urgent. The prophet Haggai reminded them that God would care for them if they rebuilt the temple in His honour.

Haggai's message
The prophet Haggai told the Jews that their lives would not improve until they got their priorities right and started putting God first, instead of themselves.

Rebuilding Jerusalem

THE Promised Land remained a province
of the empire of the Medes and Persians
for many years, under Darius's successor King
Ahasuerus and then King Artaxerxes. Stories
about the few Jews who had left the comfort and
security of Babylon and had returned to their homeland
used to make their way across the empire to the many
people who had stayed in Babylon and Persia. The news
was not always good. Rumours reached a priest called
Ezra that the Jews in Israel were slipping into bad habits,
mixing with the pagans and becoming lazy in their
worship of the Lord. He at once begged the Persian
King Artaxerxes to let him go to sort it out. Now Ezra
was very persuasive. The king found himself not only
giving permission for Ezra, his fellow priests and a
couple of thousand Jews to return to the Promised
Land, but also found himself giving money to help
them on their way. He wrote an official decree that told
the provincial governor to support Ezra in any laws and
judgments he thought fit to impose on the people.

The minute Ezra arrived in the Promised Land, people
came running to him to tell of Jews who had married into
the pagan communities and were living according to their
ungodly customs – it turned out that the priests and the
community leaders were the worst offenders of all! Ezra
sat down in front of the temple and wept, crying out in a
loud voice, confessing everything the people had done
wrong. It was as bad as he had feared. But the determined
holy man didn't stay downhearted. He made the priests
swear to amend their ways and called everyone to attend a
meeting of the utmost importance. Soon a crowd of Jews
stood in the open square of the temple, while Ezra told
them in no uncertain terms that they had to give up
everything to do with pagans and turn back to God's law.

It wasn't just Ezra whom King Artaxerxes allowed to
return to the Promised Land with his blessing. Some years
later the king noticed that his butler was moping around
with a long face and he asked him what was wrong.

"Sir, I've heard that my countrymen, the Jews, have
raised a new temple in Jerusalem," Nehemiah explained.
"But the city all around it is a disgrace. It's still lying
utterly in ruins."

> ❝ *Come, let us build the wall*
> *of Jerusalem, that we may*
> *no longer suffer in disgrace.* ❞

"I shall write a letter to the provincial governor,
Sanballat, to tell him that I'm putting you in charge of
rebuilding the city, and you must go at once," said the
king. "Just promise me that you'll come back as soon as
you've finished."

Of course, Sanballat and Tobiah, his second-in-
command, gave Nehemiah a very frosty reception. The
king had sent them a Jew who had been given equal
powers to their own, and they had been given no part to
play in the rebuilding of the important walled city.
Nehemiah knew from the start that the government
officials were going to make life difficult for him, so he
surveyed the ruins of Jerusalem late at night, sorting out
in secret what needed to be done.

As soon as Nehemiah got down to work, Sanballat and Tobiah did their best to cause trouble. First, in front of the provincial army, they taunted and ridiculed the Jews as they scuttled back and forth over the charred heaps of rubble. Then, as the walls began to take shape, they tried different tactics. "The ramparts and turrets are for shutting you out of the city," the officials told the local people, trying to make them angry. "Are you going to just sit back and watch?"

Sanballat and Tobiah were delighted when the furious Samaritans began to attack the workers on the walls at every opportunity. But Nehemiah simply split the working Jews up into teams, and put two teams on each shift: one to stand watch with weapons and fight if necessary, the other team to carry on building the walls.

Under Nehemiah's leadership, the Israelites finished the walls in only 52 days. Even the local people who had tried to tear them down were impressed. "Their God must have had a hand in it," they whispered, as they stood beneath the towering walls in awe and watched the Jews sing and dance their way right round the city in a great ceremony of dedication.

While the Jews were completing the inside of the city, they didn't take any risks with the Samaritans, who were getting more and more worried as the city neared completion. Each day, they kept the gates firmly shut against attack as they built house after house, until there were enough people living inside Jerusalem to defend it. Then, just as Sanballat and Tobiah had feared, they cast out anyone who wasn't Jewish through and through. At last the descendants of the kingdoms of Israel and Judah felt they could hold their heads up high again. They were back in the Promised Land, one nation under one God.

Ahasuerus and Darius
This section of a stone relief shows the Persian King Darius on his throne. Behind him stands his son, Ahasuerus, who was also known as Xerxes. This relief was found in Persepolis, in Iran. It is around 2.5m high and dates from 521 to 486BC.

❖ ABOUT THE STORY ❖

Nehemiah is one of the great heroes of faith in the Bible. His job in Persia was very important – he had to make sure the king wasn't given poisoned wine! He combined his practical common sense with a deep faith in God which he expressed through prayer. Whenever a problem arose, Nehemiah didn't just think up a solution, he prayed for God's help and wisdom too.

Daniel and the Lions

DANIEL was one of the Jews who felt too old and settled to leave Babylon. Instead of returning to the Promised Land, Daniel remained at the palace, a trusted adviser to King Cyrus of the Medes and Persians. Cyrus's successor, King Darius, relied on Daniel even more. Darius made Daniel one of the most powerful people in the

whole empire. He appointed him as one of three ministers to rule over his kingdom. Daniel did a much better job than the others. Darius began to trust him more, consulting him privately and giving him special responsibilities. The two other ministers were jealous. They began to seek a way to bring about Daniel's downfall, eager to find any little mistake they could blow up into something big. But Daniel was such a God-fearing man that he seemed to live a perfect life. He didn't lie or swear. He didn't gossip and spread rumours. He always dealt with people fairly, and was polite and helpful. The two ministers were soon at their wits' end.

They plotted together, and went to King Darius with a clever plan. "We need a new law," one of the men told him, looking serious. "Nobody should be allowed to ask for anything from any god or man except you for a period of 30 days."

"And anyone who breaks the law should be flung into a den of lions," added the second, eagerly. "All the district officials agree."

"Oh all right then," Darius sighed, stamping his royal seal on the law. The two men hurried away to spy on Daniel, rubbing their hands with glee.

It wasn't long before they were back at the palace, demanding to see the king.

"We think you should know about Daniel," they said. "He gets down on his knees three times a day and prays to his God, facing Jerusalem. What are you going to do about it?"

King Darius realized he had been tricked and was furious. "Get out of my sight!" he roared, kicking

King Cyrus
This marble head from the 6th century BC shows King Cyrus, who ruled Persia from 558 to 530BC. It was Cyrus who conquered the Medes in 549BC.

Medes and Persians
This stone relief dating from around 485 to 465BC shows a row of Medes and Persians. The Medes are wearing rounded hats and short tunics, whereas the Persians are dressed in full-length robes and tall crowns.

the two ministers as they grovelled before him. The worried king spent all day striding back and forth, desperately trying to think of a way to get Daniel off the hook. But it was no good.

"The law's the law," the officials insisted.

So Darius very reluctantly sent his guards to arrest his best minister.

The king shuddered as he stood at the top of the pit, listening to the lions roaring hungrily below. He turned to the old man who stood beside him and placed his hand on his arm. "Daniel, my friend," he said to his trusted adviser. "May your God – whom you serve so faithfully – save you." The royal guards lowered Daniel down towards the snarling lions, then blocked off the pit with a huge stone. Darius marked the entrance with his royal seal, so no one would dare tamper with it, and then trudged back to the palace. The sad and anxious king wouldn't eat or talk to anyone. He shut himself up in his room and spent a sleepless night alone, worrying, and furious that he'd been tricked by his ministers.

> " *The king said to Daniel,*
> *'May your God, whom you*
> *serve continually,*
> *deliver you.'* "

As soon as the sun rose, Darius was back at the pit, demanding it be uncovered. "Are you down there, Daniel?" he cried, as the guards began heaving away the stone. "Are you all right?"

To his great relief, a familiar voice came floating up from the darkness. "My king, I am alive. An angel has been here with me, and the lions have done me no harm."

The emperor nearly wept with joy. "Quick," he yelled at his guards. "Get him out of there at once!"

Later on, the lions got their dinner after all. The king ordered that the two wicked ministers be thrown into the pit along with their families, and the animals tore them to bits. Then Darius sent a proclamation out to every corner of the Medean empire announcing to all the nations that Daniel's God should be worshipped by everyone as the one true God. "He saves all of those who believe in Him," wrote the emperor, "and His kingdom will last for ever."

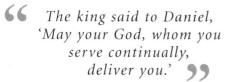

Lion of Babylon
This picture shows a detail from a reconstruction of the gateway into Babylon. Lions were associated with kings and power.

Marduk
In this picture from a carved cylinder found at Babylon, the Babylonian god, Marduk, is shown standing on a creature which has the body of a serpent. This creature was his symbol. Marduk wears a crown and holds a rod and a ring, which are symbols of authority.

❖ ABOUT THE STORY ❖

The book of Daniel was written especially to encourage Jews to be faithful to God at a time when they were being persecuted by people who did not believe in God. No one finds it easy to admit they believe in God when they know they could be killed for it. Daniel's example was meant to show them that even in such terrible situations, God could still help and rescue them, but that even if He didn't, they should still be faithful to Him.

Esther the Beautiful

DURING the reign of the next emperor, King Xerxes, there were still many thousands more Jews living in Babylon and Persia than had returned to the Promised Land. The civilization of the Medes and Persians was still the greatest in the world, and Xerxes was immensely proud of his empire, which stretched all the way from India to Ethiopia. He decided to hold a massive banquet in his capital, Susa, to celebrate his magnificence. First, he invited every single one of the princes, army chiefs, nobles and governors in his empire to a feast the likes of which no one had ever seen before. In immense marble halls bedecked with banners of the finest silks, his honoured guests lay on golden couches and ate off jewelled platters while every single one of the priceless valuables in Xerxes' treasure houses were paraded before them on velvet cushions. It took 180 days for the stunned VIPs to admire all Xerxes' splendours. Then the generous king threw his doors open to his subjects too, holding a magnificent garden party for a further week in the grounds of the palace itself. The ordinary people were stunned, they had never seen such magnificence! There were refreshing fountains tinkling in the sunshine, the perfume of sweet-smelling flowerbeds, mosaics underfoot of mother-of-pearl and precious stones – and as much free wine as everyone could drink!

By the seventh day the king was feeling exceedingly merry. "I've not only got the most beautiful palace in the world," he thought, "I've also got the most beautiful queen too." He summoned his seven chamberlains and ordered them to go and fetch the queen at once. "Tell her to put on her best dress," he demanded. "I want to show her off to everyone."

Now Queen Vashti was giving her own party for all the women, in another part of the palace. She was a strong, independent woman, besides being beautiful, and she refused to come. "I can't leave my guests so rudely," she told the chamberlains. "Whatever would they think? And besides, I don't want to be paraded about like something from one of my husband's treasure houses."

When the chamberlains told the king that Vashti wouldn't come, he was mad. Xerxes' courtiers were far too frightened of the raging emperor to tell him to calm down. In fact, they all nodded their heads and agreed that he was very right to be so angry. "Whatever are you going to do about Vashti?" the most senior of them urged. "You can't possibly let her go unpunished. What will happen if other women get to hear of it? We'll have wives all through the empire rebelling against their husbands. And where will that leave us?"

> **Let the maiden who pleases the king be queen instead of Vashti.**

"You're right," decided Xerxes. "Vashti will have to go. Kick her out and find me a new queen to take her place – one who's even more beautiful."

A royal proclamation soon went out through all the land, announcing a competition. All the young maidens in

the kingdom were to present themselves at the palace. The most beautiful would be chosen to stay for lessons in skincare, hairstyling, make-up and how to behave like a queen. And at the end of a year, the king would choose the one he liked best to replace Vashti.

In the back streets of Susa there lived a servant in the royal household called Mordecai, an old Jewish man who was one of those who had chosen to stay in Babylon rather than return to the Promised Land. Mordecai was the guardian of his orphaned cousin Esther, whom he had brought up as his daughter. "No one could be more beautiful or queenly than you," he told her, giving her a hug. "Hurry along to the king's palace and enter the competition– but make sure you don't tell anyone you're Jewish. The king might not be so keen on that."

Esther easily made it on to the short list of the most beautiful maidens in the country and she was hurried off to new living quarters in the palace, where all the young women were to be groomed for a year. Every day, Mordecai would make sure he had an errand to do that would take him past her chambers. And every day, he was more and more pleased with what he saw of Esther's progress. She was such a well-mannered and good-natured girl that she quickly became the favourite of Hegai, the courtier in charge of the competition. He made sure that Esther had the very best face creams, the finest food from the royal kitchens and the most skilled maids to help her with her hair and advise her on her clothes.

The time came for the young women to parade, one by one, in front of the king. They were all trying very hard to impress him. In the end, though, there wasn't much of a competition at all. Esther was by far the winner, and the delighted Xerxes held a lavish great banquet in honour of his lovely new queen.

Make-up and jewellery
Wealthy women wore jewellery, like this gold armlet which is decorated with griffins, a mythical animal with an eagle's head and a lion's body.

THIS STORY SOUNDS A BIT LIKE THE STORY OF CINDERELLA – SOMEONE FINDING THEIR DREAMS COME TRUE, AND GETTING FAMOUS AND RICH. BUT THIS STORY IS NOT JUST ABOUT ESTHER HAVING FUN AND ENJOYING HER NEW ROYAL LIFE. IT REMINDS US THAT WHEN GOD DOES ALLOW SUCH THINGS, HE GIVES US RESPONSIBILITIES TOO. ESTHER WOULD HAVE A VERY DIFFICULT, BUT ALSO IMPORTANT, JOB TO DO AS QUEEN.

❧ ABOUT THE STORY ❧
This story is really about God's protection of His people and the timing of His purposes. It seemed pure chance that Esther was chosen, and she kept very quiet about her nationality. But God knew that soon she would be the only person who could avert a tragedy. The Bible shows God working behind the scenes so that everyone is in the right place at the right time when it really matters.

Esther Saves the Jews

NOT long after Esther had become queen, Mordecai heard two palace servants in the palace plotting to kill the king. He hurried to tell his daughter and she went straight to her husband. Xerxes ordered the men to be arrested, tried and hanged.

After this, the king decided he could do with a right-hand man. He chose Haman, who was an arrogant man who ordered everyone to bow when they saw him coming.

"I'm not paying homage to anyone but God," Mordecai said. Haman wanted revenge for being embarrassed. He decided to punish not only Mordecai, but his entire race.

"Sir," Haman said to Xerxes one day, "there are a people in your empire who refuse to live by your laws. They ignore your government officials and only take notice of their own priests and elders.

If you don't put a stop to it, you'll soon have a full-scale rebellion on your hands. Why don't you let me exterminate them?"

"Order what you think best," Xerxes said, handing him his royal seal. "Have these troublemakers wiped out."

"The prime minister's proclamation includes you," Mordecai wrote to Esther. "Go to your husband and beg him to do something."

But it wasn't that simple. Esther replied, "It's the death penalty for anyone who enters the king's presence uninvited. But if I am to die for my people, then so be it."

After three days of fasting and praying, the brave young queen went to the king. Luckily his face brightened into a smile. "What can I do for you?" he said, and held out his sceptre to her, ushering her in.

Festival of Purim
The Jewish festival of Purim is held in spring to commemorate the defeat of Haman's plot to massacre the Jews. At the festival, the book of Esther is read aloud and it is customary for the congregation in the synagogue to cheer Esther's name, but shout and boo whenever Haman is mentioned.

The king's sceptre
Esther was risking her life when she went to see the king. This was an offence punishable by death, unless the king held out his sceptre. This law allowed the king some privacy and protected him from would-be murderers.

Casting lots
Haman threw lots, rather like modern dice, to determine a day to carry out his plan to exterminate the Jews. Small stones and pieces of pottery, like the ones above, were often used as lots. The word *purim* is the plural of the word *pur*, which means "lot".

"Sir," Esther said, "will you have dinner with me tomorrow? And will you bring the prime minister?"

The king was delighted. Haman smirked smugly. "No one else in the entire empire is as important!" he bragged to his friends. But one thought left him glowering. "Still that Mordecai refuses to bow."

"Don't put up with it," everyone urged. "Get the king to build a gallows and hang him. Then you can enjoy tomorrow's dinner unspoilt."

The king had been unable to sleep and he'd been reading his official records all night. "Look here," Xerxes remarked to his advisers, "there's no record of how we rewarded Mordecai for foiling that murder plot. We must put things right straightaway." The King called Haman. "If you were king, how would you reward your most loyal servant?" the king asked.

> *And Haman said to himself, 'Whom would the king delight to honour more than me?'*

Haman thought the king was talking about him. "Dress the hero in your robes and crown and set him on your horse. Then give him a parade through the streets with a noble leading the way, shouting, 'The king is delighted to honour this man!'" he said.

The king clapped his hands. "Brilliant!" he cried. "Hurry along and do it for Mordecai the Jew."

It was the beginning of the end for the miserable Haman. That night, at dinner, Esther made her plea. "Oh my king, I am Jewish," she sobbed, "and orders have been given for me and my people to be put to death."

Xerxes was outraged. "Whose orders?" he bellowed.

"His!" Esther wept, pointing at the evil prime minister. Just as Haman had wanted, the king demanded that gallows to be built as quickly as possible – but it was the prime minister who was hanged on them, not Mordecai. Esther confessed that the faithful servant was her foster father and Xerxes rewarded him with Haman's old job. At once, Mordecai sent out an edict which cancelled the former prime minister's commands and, thanks to Esther, thousands of Jewish lives were saved.

Esther
This painting shows Queen Esther dressed in her royal robes. She was very brave and risked her life to save her people. But the Bible does not commend her when she encourages the Jews to massacre their enemies.

ESTHER PUT GOD AND OTHERS BEFORE HERSELF. SHE COULD HAVE DONE NOTHING AND DIED WITH HER PEOPLE. INSTEAD, SHE RISKED HERSELF TO SAVE THEM. IT IS AN EXAMPLE OF HOW GOD WANTS US TO LIVE.

✦ ABOUT THE STORY ✦

The Medes and Persians had very strict laws. Once a law was made, no one – not even the king – could change it. So when Haman was hanged, the order to kill the Jews still stood. The new law which Mordecai drafted allowed the Jews to defend themselves against anyone who attacked them. That way, no one would bother to comply with the original law.

Jonah and the Whale

IN the days of the great Assyrian Empire, there was a prophet, Jonah, who was not very pleased when God called him. "Jonah, I want you to go to the Assyrian capital, Nineveh," the Lord told him. "Preach to the pagans there. They're doing nothing but sinning against me." Now Nineveh was a long way away, the Assyrians were a hard, cruel race and Jonah – a Jew – didn't really care about foreigners anyway. "I'll run away to somewhere the Lord can't find me," he thought, packing a bag. Soon he was boarding a ship and setting off on a long voyage in quite the opposite direction to Nineveh – to Tarshish in Spain.

No sooner had the ship left harbour and reached open waters than the skies darkened and the wind began to blow up. Great gusts whipped up the sea, rain lashed the masts and the ship was tossed up and down the towering waves, threatening to break up at any moment. Terrified, the sailors threw as much of their cargo overboard as they could to lighten the load, but the ship still bowed and cracked in the full force of the storm. "On your knees!" cried the captain. "Each one of you beg your gods to save us!" and he ran around the ship to check that everyone was praying.

Then the sailors superstitiously cast lots to find out which of the passengers had brought the wrath of the gods upon them. They picked Jonah, who was soon surrounded by the angry crew. "Which god do you serve?" they demanded. "What have you done to bring this storm raging down upon us?"

"I'm a Hebrew," Jonah gulped. "The only thing that's going to save everyone is if you throw me overboard." Even though the sailors were desperate, they weren't murderers, and they did their best to row to shore. But it was impossible. With every stroke of their oars, the wind seemed to blow more strongly. In the end, they had no choice but reluctantly to throw Jonah off the ship. As soon as the prophet had splashed into the water, the gale began to die down and the waves to subside. And as Jonah drifted away from the ship on the swell, he heard the captain and the sailors praying once more – but this time to the one true Lord, not to their pagan gods.

> ❝ ... and Jonah was in the belly of the fish three days and three nights. ❞

Just when Jonah thought things couldn't get any worse, they did. One minute he was bobbing up and down in the water like a cork; the next minute, he was swimming around inside a dark, wet cave – a huge fish had swallowed him up. For three days and nights Jonah was in the pitch black darkness of its belly. "Oh Lord," he prayed, "I'm dreadfully sorry. If you get me out of here, I promise to obey you in future." A little circle of light appeared in the distance and very quickly widened. There was a rumbling and a roaring and a rushing of water, and the fish coughed him out of its mouth. Choking and spluttering, the prophet felt himself dropped onto a firm bed of sand. "Thanks be to God!" he cried as the waters drew back leaving him in warm sunlight blinking on the dry land.

happened. The sun set on the 40th day and still nothing had happened. "We have been saved," cried the people of Nineveh. "God has forgiven us!" They sang and danced and rejoiced, offering prayers and sacrifices to God – all except Jonah, who stomped off into the desert.

"Why have you spared them, Lord?" he moaned up to heaven, stacking a few sticks together as a shelter from the heat. "They aren't even Jewish! If you're going to save sinners like these, I'd rather be dead than serve you."

God taught Jonah one last lesson. Overnight, a broad, shady tree grew over Jonah that guarded him from the burning sun till evening and kept him cool. But next morning, the disappointed prophet found that the tree had withered away. And Jonah needed its protection more than ever. All day long, not only did the sun blaze down but a scorching wind also blew across the sands. "Lord, the death of that tree is the last straw," Jonah groaned. "Please let me die."

"How can you be so upset about the death of a tree you didn't plant or water," the Lord scolded, "when you're cross with me for not killing the thousands of people in Nineveh?" Jonah finally realized that God created all the people of the world, and He cares for people from all nations, not just his own; that the Lord's kingdom stretches over the whole earth.

The Lord's voice boomed at him: "Now are you ready to go to Nineveh for me? Tell those pagans that unless they beg my forgiveness for their sins, in 40 days' time I will destroy the city." Jonah trembled before the power of God, and set off at once.

The city of Nineveh was so big that it took Jonah three whole days to work his way across it, shouting himself hoarse as he went. But to his great surprise, the ruthless Assyrians listened to what he had to say. When the king himself got to hear Jonah's message, he sent out a royal proclamation ordering everyone to begin praying and fasting at once. When dawn broke on the 40th day nothing

A reluctant prophet
Jonah tried to escape from the purpose that God had for him by fleeing on a boat from the port of Joppa. He could not escape the will of God, though, and when the sailors threw him overboard to try to save their ship, he was swallowed by a big fish, which left him on the shore. From there he went to Nineveh.

❖ ABOUT THE STORY ❖

The point of this story is that God cares about people of all races and wants everyone to love and worship Him. Jonah started with a very narrow view of God's purposes. He thought that God had given the Jews, and the Jews alone, the right to be saved. Jonah's experience changed his view. This story also encourages people to obey God even when they don't see the reasons for the instructions. Everything will always work out as God intends.

The Old Testament Prophets

ELIJAH was a prophet of Israel who lived in the 9th century BC, during the reign of King Ahab. Nothing really is known about his background. Six episodes in the life of Elijah are related in the Bible: his prediction of drought, the contest on Mount Carmel, his flight to Mount Horeb, also called Mount Sinai, the story of Naboth, the oracle about King Ahaziah, and Elijah's ascent to heaven. All these episodes, except for the last, are concerned with the clash between the worship of the God of Israel and that of Baal. It was King Ahab's wife, Jezebel, a Phoenician princess, who encouraged Baal worship among the Israelites.

In the first episode, after Elijah announces to King Ahab that there will be a drought, he escapes, first to the brook at Cherith and then to Zarephath, in Phoenicia, where he performs a miracle by healing a sick boy. In both places God provides for Elijah.

In the second episode, Elijah presides over a contest between God and Baal on Mount Carmel. Elijah's sacrifice to God bursts into flames, whereas the sacrifice of Baal's priests remains unlit. After this victory, there is a mighty storm as God puts an end to the drought by bringing the rain. In doing so, He shows Himself to be superior to Baal.

Elijah then flees to Mount Horeb, the mountain where God gave Moses the Ten Commandments. Elijah's journey to this holy place is important as Elijah is returning to one of the most important places in the Jewish faith.

The fourth episode tells the story of a man called Naboth. He refuses to sell his vineyard to King Ahab because he knows it is forbidden by God to sell inherited land. When Ahab has Naboth stoned to death and takes his vineyard, Elijah announces that he will be punished.

In the fifth episode, Elijah reveals that God will punish King Ahaziah for worshipping the Syrian god, Baal-zebub.

Finally, Elijah is taken up to heaven in a chariot of fire and his role as prophet passes to Elisha.

It was Elijah that was to appear to Jesus, along with Moses in what is called the Transfiguration. Elijah remains to this day one of the most important of the Old Testament prophets; a place is still set for him at the table for some of the Jewish feasts.

Elijah and Moses

Elijah has been compared with Moses. Elijah is accompanied and succeeded by Elisha, just as Moses was by Joshua. Elijah's demonstration of God's power on Carmel was like Moses receiving the law on Mount Horeb.

The chariot of fire
This picture shows Elijah being taken away to heaven in a chariot, watched by Elisha. The taking of someone to heaven, while still alive, is called a translation. Only two people in the Bible are said not to die: Elijah and Enoch.

ISAIAH was a prophet in Judah from around 740-700 BC. Most of his prophecies concentrated on Judah and, in particular, on its capital, Jerusalem. He prophesied from the reign of King Uzziah to the reign of King Hezekiah.

These were troubled times for the Jewish people as, not long after Isaiah was called as a prophet, the Assyrians took over the state of Judah, making it part of their empire.

Isaiah's prophetic life began when he had a vision in the temple at Jerusalem, of God sitting on a throne, surrounded by angels called seraphim. God told him to go out and speak to the people, passing on the message that they should put their trust in Him alone, they should not worship other gods, they should keep His laws, and should listen to His prophets.

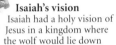

Isaiah's vision
Isaiah had a holy vision of Jesus in a kingdom where the wolf would lie down with the lamb.

From ancient times, Isaiah has been thought of as the greatest of all the Old Testament prophets. He has been called, amongst other things, "the prophet of holiness" and "the eagle among the prophets". He is perhaps most important as the prophet who foretold the birth of the Messiah, who would be descended from King David and would come to save the Jewish people. Isaiah prophesied that the present Assyrian Empire of violent rule would be replaced by a peaceful kingdom of God. He described the Messiah as a king of Israel who would free his people from the Assyrians. Christians, though, believe that Isaiah's words foretell the coming of Jesus Christ, who would save everyone, Jews and Gentiles alike, from sin.

Isaiah says, "For unto us a child is born, unto us a son is given: and the government shall be upon His shoulder: and His name shall be called Wonderful, Counsellor, the mighty God, the everlasting Father, the Prince of Peace."

❧ KINGS OF ISRAEL AND JUDAH ❧
The single nation ruled by Saul, David and Solomon split into two after Solomon died.

Israel (north)
Jeroboam *931-910BC*
Nadab *910-909BC*
Baasha *909-886BC*
Elah *886-885BC*
Omri *885-874BC*
Ahab *874-853BC*
Ahaziah *853-852BC*
Joram *852-841BC*
Jehu *841-814BC*
Jehoahaz *814-798BC*
Jehoash *798-782BC*
Jeroboam II *793-753BC*
Zechariah *753-752BC*
Shallum *752-752BC*
Menahem *752-742BC*
Pekahiah *742-740BC*
Pekah *752-732BC*
Hoshea *732-723BC*

All dates for kings are approximate.

Judah (south)
Rehoboam *931-913BC*
Abijah *913-911BC*
Asa *911-870BC*
Jehoshaphat *870-848BC*
Jehoram *848-841BC*
Ahaziah *841BC*
Athaliah *841-835BC*
Joash *835-796BC*
Amaziah *796-767BC*
Uzziah *791-740BC*
Jotham *750-732BC*
Ahaz *735-716BC*
Hezekiah *729-687BC*
Manasseh *696-643BC*
Amon *643-640BC*
Josiah *640-609BC*
Jehoahaz *609-609BC*
Jehoiakim *609-597BC*
Jehoiachin *597-597BC*
Jeconiah *597-597BC*
Zedekiah *597-587BC*

❧ PROPHETS ❧
The Old Testament prophets worked in specific regions. Some even prophesied in foreign countries.

Israel
Samuel *1050-1010BC*
Elijah *870-852BC*
Micaiah *870-852BC*
Elisha *855-798BC*
Amos *760–780BC*
Hosea *760-722BC*

All dates for prophets are approximate.

Judah
Joel *810-750BC*
Isaiah *740-700BC*
Micah *742-687BC*
Zephaniah *640-610BC*
Huldah *610-605BC*
Habakkuk *605BC*
Jeremiah *626-587BC*
Ezekiel *593-570BC*
Nahum *630-612BC*

Jeremiah　　Ezekiel　　Samuel　　Micaiah

The Book of Psalms

THE Book of Psalms in the Old Testament, also known as the Psalter, is a collection of 150 religious verses which are sung or recited in both Christian and Jewish worship. According to tradition, 73 of the psalms were written by King David, a musician and a poet. Other authors named in the titles are King Solomon and the prophet Moses.

O Lord, our Lord, how majestic is Thy name in
all the earth!

Thou whose glory above the heavens is chanted
By the mouth of babes and infants, Thou hast founded a
bulwark because of Thy foes,
to still the enemy and the avenger.

When I look at Thy heavens, the work of Thy fingers
the moon and the stars which Thou hast established;
what is man that Thou art mindful of him,
and the son of man that Thou dost care for him?

Yet Thou hast made him little less than God, and dost
crown him with glory and honour.
Thou hast given him dominion over the
works of Thy hands;
Thou hast put all things under his feet,
all sheep and oxen,
and also the beasts of the field,
the birds of the air, and the fish of the sea,
whatever passes along the paths of the sea.

O Lord, our Lord, how majestic is Thy name in
all the earth!

Psalm 8; A psalm of David

The Lord is my shepherd, I shall not want;
He makes me lie down in green pastures.
He leads me beside still waters; He restores my soul.
He leads me in paths of righteousness for His name's sake.

Even though I walk through the valley of the
shadow of death,
I fear no evil; for Thou art with me;
Thy rod and Thy staff, they comfort me.

Thou preparest a table before me in the
presence of my enemies;
Thou anointest my head with oil, my cup overflows.

Surely goodness and mercy shall follow me all
the days of my life;
and I shall dwell in the house of the Lord for ever.

Psalm 23

Make a joyful noise to the Lord, all the lands!
Serve the Lord with gladness!
Come into His presence with singing!

Know that the Lord is God!
It is He that made us, and we are His;
We are His people, and the sheep of His pasture.

Enter His gates with thanksgiving,
and His courts with praise!
Give thanks to Him, bless His name!

For the Lord is good;
His steadfast love endures for ever,
and His faithfulness to all generations.

Psalm 100

TIMELINE 1000BC TO 400BC

• Solomon's kingdom is divided into Israel in the north and Judah in the south. Jeroboam rules Israel, and Solomon's son Rehoboam rules Judah.

DECORATIVE FURNITURE FROM
SAMARIA, CAPITAL OF ISRAEL

1000BC

• Ahab becomes king of Israel, with Jezebel as his queen.

ELIJAH'S
CONTEST WITH THE
PROPHETS OF BAAL

900BC

• Isaiah is prophet to King Ahaz and King Hezekiah.

• Samaria falls to the invading Assyrians.

ISRAEL'S CAPITAL, SAMARIA, IS CAPTURED,
AND IS OCCUPIED BY THE ASSYRIANS

800BC

The Trials of Job

THE Book of Job tells the story of a rich man called Job, who was faithful to God and blessed by him. One day, a member of God's heavenly council suggests that Job's faith should be tested. He makes a bet with God that if Job were to suffer great misfortune, he would lose his faith. To find out if he is right, God gives permission for Job to be robbed of his wealth, his ten children and his health. Job's family and friends assume that his misfortunes are God's punishment for some terrible sin, and throw him out of the town.

As Job sits outside the city gates, three of his friends (known as Job's comforters) come to console him. After seven days of silence, Job pours out his feelings in a bitter lamentation and there follows a long, heated discussion about the reason for his plight which forms most of the book. Although his friends' lack of understanding drives Job to distraction, it also turns him to God. Despite his suffering, he refuses to curse God and continues to pray to Him. In the end, Job's prayers are answered. He is made twice as wealthy as he was before, he is cured of his disease, he has ten more children and goes on to live a long and happy life.

The book of Job has been called "one of the most original works in the poetry of humankind". It deals with human experience in general and, in particular, with suffering. Although in the end Job's misfortunes disappear, the story seems to contradict the basic principle that those who have faith in God will have good fortune, and people that do not will suffer. The question Job keeps asking is why God is treating him in this way. One suggestion is that Job needed to realize that he did not know everything about God, and that he could not predict God's actions. By the end of the story, Job has understood that God's wisdom and greatness are such that no human can ever fully grasp them. Job's mistake was that his idea of God was too small. When he realizes the greatness of God, his problems disappear.

Discussing the problem of suffering
This picture shows Job with his three comforters. The phrase "a Job's comforter" has come to mean a person who makes a situation worse, while apparently trying to give comfort.

• King Josiah restores the worship of God to Judah while they are occupied by the Assyrians.

• Jerusalem is captured by the Babylonians, and the Exile begins as the Jews are taken to Babylon.

KING JEHOIAKIM BURNS BARUCH'S SCROLLS

700BC

• With God's guidance, Daniel rises to a position of power in Babylon, and he is saved from the lions in the pit.

FRAGMENT FROM THE BOOK OF DANIEL

• Ezekiel brings the Jews together into a nation, worshipping God.

EZEKIEL TEACHING

600BC

• Under the guidance of God the Jews re-establish themselves in the Promised Land.

JEWS CELEBRATE COMPLETING THE NEW TEMPLE

500BC

400BC

A CHILD IS BORN

*The stories cover the events leading up to the birth of
Jesus in Bethlehem, and the immediate threats to
His life. Jesus is noticed as a remarkably wise
12-year-old, but then nothing is recorded of His life
until He is about 30. His gathering of the disciples
and first miracles herald the start of His ministry.*

Introduction

ABOUT 2,000 years ago an event happened that was to change the world for ever. Jesus Christ was born. From His birth the modern calendar is dated (although the actual year of Jesus's birth was probably 7BC or 4BC, not the year 0, because a medieval monk made a mistake in his calculations!). Every time we look at a calendar and write down the number of the year, we are reminded of the birth of Christ and the existence of the Christian Church since then.

The story of Jesus's birth and His early years is also very familiar. Even today, when many people are less religious than they used to be, many public Christmas displays will include a Christmas crib with the baby Jesus, Mary, Joseph, the shepherds and the wise men, some angels and a few animals nosing around.

The birth and beginning of Jesus's ministry, or teaching, is one of the most important parts of the Bible story with a clear link to modern times. Yet most of Jesus's early years are completely obscure. Only a few events are recorded in the Gospels. There are so few details that, later, people added to the stories to make them more interesting or exciting, or to make a point. Many of these stories though, have no basis in history.

Even the familiar Christmas story owes more to tradition than to the facts that we are given in the Gospels. The only evidence for Jesus's birth in a stable is the fact that Mary laid him in a manger, which was the normal cot for a newborn child in an ordinary Israelite home. A baby was safer there than on the floor where everyone else slept!

The Christmas story also features the amazing sights of the chorus of angels singing to the shepherds, and a new star appearing in the sky. The events have led

Jesus in the temple
When Jesus was separated from Mary and Joseph in Jerusalem, He went to His father's house, God's temple in Jerusalem, where He amazed the religious elders with His knowledge.

many people to question the truth of these stories. However, the gospel writers include these details to make an important point. The baby Jesus was not an ordinary child. He was the Son of God who came into the world as a human to share human life. His aim was to bring humans and God back together in a relationship of trust and service.

The miracles of Jesus's birth continue as Jesus begins His ministry. The paralysed man is healed outwardly and has his sins forgiven. The madman is made mentally and spiritually healthy again; the centurion's servant is healed, even though many people at the time thought that God did not care for Gentiles (people who were not Jewish). In each case the story enlarges on Jesus's mission: to bring God's forgiveness and to break through the barriers of human pride.

The miracles finish with the great act of stilling the storm. With the voice of the Creator's authority, Jesus bids the waves to be still. "Who is this?" cry the amazed disciples in fear and trembling. The message of the gospel writers is clear: "We believe He is the Son of God." They leave their readers to decide if they are right.

Dead Sea and the wilderness
Before Jesus could begin His ministry in Galilee, He was tempted by the Devil in the wilderness around the Dead Sea. When it was proved He could resist temptation, He began His ministry.

❧ A CHILD IS BORN ❧

This section covers the birth and early life of Jesus, His baptism by John the Baptist, His temptation by the devil, and the early part of His ministry in Galilee

JUDEA BEFORE JESUS
Luke, Ch. 1.
THE BIRTH OF JESUS
Matthew, Ch. 2; Luke Ch. 2.
JESUS'S EARLY LIFE
Matthew, Ch. 2; Luke Ch. 2.
JESUS BEGINS HIS MINISTRY
Matthew, Ch. 3 & 4; Luke Ch. 4.
THE FIRST MIRACLE
John, Ch. 1 & 2.
JESUS'S MINISTRY IN GALILEE
Matthew, Ch. 8 to 14.
Mark, Ch. 1 to 6; Luke Ch. 3 to 9.
John, Ch. 5.
SERMON ON THE MOUNT
Matthew, Ch. 5 to 11.
Luke, Ch 6 & 11.

Mary and the baby Jesus
This is a fresco (a painting on a wall of a church) of the Virgin Mary and the baby Jesus. Both are shown with haloes, a sign that they are sacred figures.

Jesus and His Early Life

THE birth of Jesus is one of the most recognized stories from the Bible. Every December millions of people celebrate the birth of the Messiah, God's anointed saviour. In many cases, though, the religious significance of this event, and what it has meant for Christians since, has been forgotten by many people.

The sources for two of the gospels, Matthew and Luke, were probably different. The story of the birth of Jesus in the gospel of Matthew is told very much from Joseph's point of view. Luke's gospel focuses very closely on Mary, mother of Jesus, and on Elizabeth, who was Mary's cousin and the mother of John the Baptist. There is a great deal of detail in Luke's account of the birth of Jesus that relates specifically to Mary. This has led some people to think that Luke's source may have been Mary herself. The writers of Matthew and Luke both agree on the divine part of Jesus's origin, that God Himself was Jesus's father.

There is a huge contrast between the amazing events surrounding Jesus's birth, and the surroundings in which these events took place. The Bible indicates, although does not actually say, that the Son of God was born in a stable surrounded by farm animals. He was laid in a manger, from which animals ate. While there, though, He was visited by the magi, wise men and astrologers from the east, from Babylon or Arabia. The Bible tells us that these men followed a new star to find the baby Jesus. Elsewhere, a great chorus of angels announced the birth of Jesus to the shepherds.

When His parents presented Jesus in the temple, as was the custom, they met Simeon and Anna, two prophets whom God had told of the Messiah's birth, who proclaimed Him the saviour of all the people of the world.

After the events surrounding His birth in Bethlehem, Jesus returned with Mary and Joseph to their home town of Nazareth. This was a small, unimportant town in Galilee, although it was close to several of the main trade routes for the Roman Empire. Jesus spent about the first thirty years of His life there, before He was rejected by the people.

Jesus's mission properly began with His baptism in the River Jordan. He was baptized by his cousin, John the Baptist. At the baptism, God gave a sign to everyone present that Jesus was special. The Holy Spirit descended to Jesus in the form of a white dove, and the voice of God announced that Jesus was His son. These messages from God said two things. God announced to the world that Jesus was the Son of God. He also introduced Jesus to the world as His servant. God was saying that Jesus was the person sent by God to deliver the people of the world from sin and evil.

Before Jesus could begin His ministry, He had to undergo a test. He went into the wilderness around the Jordan valley, and was tempted three times by Satan. The temptations of Jesus explored the idea of what it was to be the Son of God. Jesus's replies to Satan's various challenges strengthened His knowledge of His role and what He would have to do. When Jesus refuses to turn stones into bread to eat, He is putting His trust in God to provide what He needs to survive. Jesus says that we should all forget about obtaining earthly goods. We should trust God to provide us with what we need. Satan also tells Jesus that He should throw Himself off of the roof of the temple. Jesus refused to put God to the test in this way. Jesus shows that He did not need to put God to the test in order to trust Him.

There is also another important point that the writer of the Bible makes in this story. Jesus proved that He had learnt the lessons that God had been trying to teach the Israelites since the time of the Exodus. When Moses was leading the Israelites out of slavery in Egypt, they spent forty years wandering in the desert before they were allowed to enter the Promised Land. They had not learnt to trust God in every way. The answers that Jesus gives to Satan's temptations come from the book of Deuteronomy. They show that He has learnt these lessons, and is ready to begin His ministry.

This map shows the area of Jesus's birth and early life. You can see Nazareth, from where Mary and Joseph set out on the long journey to Bethlehem, where Jesus was born. Jerusalem is where Jesus was presented in the temple, and where Simeon and Anna prophesied His great role.

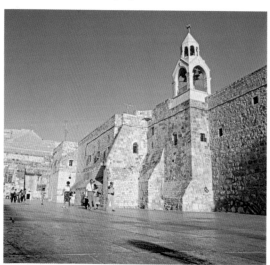

Bethlehem
The Manger Square in Bethlehem is the place of Jesus's birth. The ancestors of King David lived in Bethlehem. Joseph was a descendant of David, born in Bethlehem, so he had to return there for the Roman census, where the Romans counted the population.

MEDITERRANEAN
SEA

•Ptolemais

•Cana

•Nazareth

SEA OF
GALILEE

•Hippus

•Sennabris

•Scythoplis

Caesarea•

•Sebaste

Jordan

Joppa

•Emmaus

•Jericho

•Jerusalem •Bethany

•Bethlehem

•Bethabara

DEAD SEA

A Son for Elizabeth

IN the days when King Herod ruled the land of Judea, there was a priest called Zechariah whose wife was Elizabeth. They both tried to live faithfully by the laws of the Jewish religion, but they had one great sadness in their life. They had reached old age without having any children. Still, they always tried to make the most of any happy occasion that came along. One of these occasions was when Zechariah was chosen to be the priest allowed to enter the sacred holy place in the great temple in Jerusalem and burn incense to the Lord. It was a great honour.

The day of the festival arrived and Zechariah dressed in his splendid ceremonial robes, his hands trembling. He could hear his fellow priests singing outside the temple, leading the crowd of worshippers in prayer.

> **66** *They were both righteous before God.* **99**

Eventually, Zechariah stood before the incense altar in the holy place itself. With his eyes cast humbly downwards, the aged priest began to burn the sacred incense. And as he spoke aloud the holy passages he had learnt by heart, Zechariah suddenly had the strangest feeling. He was not alone. Someone else was there too, joining him in prayer. Very nervously, Zechariah looked up – and straight away crumpled to the floor with fear. An angel was standing to the right of the altar!

"Don't be afraid, Zechariah," the angel said. "I have come to tell you that your prayers have been answered. You and your wife are going to have a son, whom you must call John. He will bring great happiness not only to you, but also to many other people. The Lord will love him dearly and will send His Holy Spirit to fill your son's heart even before he has been born. Through John, many souls will turn to God. He will prepare the people for the Lord's coming."

The angel Gabriel
A 14th-century stained-glass window shows Gabriel, the angel who announced the news of John's birth. He also told Mary she would have Jesus. Gabriel's name means 'Mighty man of God', and he is one of only two angels named in the Bible (the other is Michael, the warrior angel). He is an archangel who stands in God's presence and takes only special messages into the world.

MOST PEOPLE WOULD FIND IT HARD TO BELIEVE AN ANGEL. THE MESSAGE OF THIS STORY IS THAT GOD EXPECTS HIS PEOPLE TO BELIEVE WHAT HE SAYS, WHICH TODAY IS WRITTEN IN THE BIBLE. ◡

Wailing (Western) Wall
This huge wall in modern Jerusalem is a place of prayer for Jews. It is all that remains of King Herod's temple after the Romans destroyed it. They often leave papers with prayers on them tucked into the gaps between the stones.

Zechariah was totally stunned. "But... Why... How..?" he stuttered. "We're too old to have children. How can this be true?"

"I am Gabriel," the angel thundered, and Zechariah cowered in terror. In heaven, the angel Gabriel stood at the side of God Himself. "I have been sent by the Lord to bring you this good news," he said. "Because you don't believe what I say, you will be struck dumb until these things come to pass." And he vanished.

Outside the temple, thousands of worshippers were waiting for Zechariah to finish burning the sacred incense and come out of the temple. They waited and waited. Murmurs began to run through the crowd. "Where's the priest? Maybe he's fallen ill. Shouldn't someone go and check? " Elizabeth started to get worried.

Then a shout went up from the people at the front. "Here he comes!" and

everyone saw the shape of the elderly priest emerging from the shadows of the temple out into the sunlight. The cheering crowd fell quiet, waiting for Zechariah to speak. Although the priest's lips moved, no sound came out of his mouth. The puzzled men and women looked at each other. What had happened to Zechariah in there? They watched as the priest moved his hands back and forth, silently demonstrating that he had seen a vision from heaven but could no longer speak. The crowd were stunned.

As they stood there, gasping in shock, Elizabeth pushed her way through the throng to her husband's side. And quietly, she led him away from all the fuss.

Not long afterwards, Elizabeth discovered she was expecting a baby. She knew she'd be the talk of the town if people discovered that such an old woman was having a baby. So she tried to keep in the house, out of sight, where she kept her joyous secret to herself. The couple wouldn't let anything spoil their happiness.

Incense shovel
Priests burning incense at the temple used a shovel like this to move burning coals from the altar of burnt offering outside the temple to the smaller incense altar inside.

Altar and incense
The altar for burning incense in the temple was probably this shape, but it would have been made from bronze. It follows the standard pattern, with four horns at the corners on which blood was sprinkled to purify the altar. The incense was made from 13 different ingredients which created smoke – a symbol of the people's prayers going up to heaven.

> ❧ **ABOUT THE STORY** ❧
>
> *This happy story about a couple having their prayers answered illustrates what the Bible generally teaches about prayer. God did not give them what they asked for just because they were holy people and He thought they deserved it. He answered because the birth of John the Baptist was part of His bigger plan for the world.*

A Son for Mary

ABOUT six months after Zechariah's vision in the temple, God sent the angel Gabriel on another important mission. This time his message was for Elizabeth's cousin, Mary.

Mary lived at home with her parents in the region of Galilee, in a town called Nazareth. She was engaged to Joseph, a carpenter who was descended from the great King David, the greatest king of Israel. Every day, as Mary swept and cooked, she looked forward to when she would marry and have a home of her own.

One day, Mary was doing her chores as usual when a light suddenly flooded the room where she was working. She looked up and saw a beautiful man standing in front of her, his face and clothes bright with radiance.

> *You will bear a son, and you shall call His name Jesus.*

"Hello Mary," the man said. "Know that God is with you; I am His messenger, the angel Gabriel. I have come to tell you that the Lord has chosen you above all other women for a very special blessing."

Even though Gabriel had spoken gently, Mary was still petrified. She was always careful to follow God's laws, but she had never expected the Lord to take any notice of a village girl. Priests and elders were far more important than her, and they didn't have angels suddenly appearing in their kitchens.

Gabriel saw the fear on Mary's face.

Nazareth
In Jesus's day Nazareth was a small and obscure town. It was in the north of Judea, overlooking the fertile Plain of Esdraelon. The Church of the Annunciation, on the site where Mary is thought to have seen the angel, is in the centre of the picture.

MARY'S RESPONSE TO THE ANGEL WAS DIFFERENT TO ZECHARIAH'S. SHE DID NOT KNOW HOW IT COULD HAPPEN, BUT HER FAITH WAS FIRM. SHE HAS BEEN A MODEL FOR FAITH EVER SINCE. ❧

Annunciation
When the angel announced to Mary what God intended to do, it was called an annunciation. The event is marked by a service in many churches, on 25 March.

"Don't be afraid," he said, kindly. "God loves you. He's going to send you a son, whom you must call Jesus. He will be ruler over all the Lord's people and His kingdom will have no end."

Poor Mary was even more confused. Nervously, she whispered to the angel, "How can I have a child? I'm not married yet."

"God is going to send His Holy Spirit to you, to grace you with His own Son," the angel replied. "Remember that nothing is impossible for the Lord. Indeed, your cousin Elizabeth has also been blessed and is going to have a baby – even though she's past the age for having children."

Mary was astounded. "How wonderful!" she gasped. As she thought of what the angel promised her she told herself, "It's not right to be afraid, Mary. If the Lord has indeed selected you for this special gift, you should accept it with joy and give thanks for it." With her heart thumping, she said. "I am ready to serve the Lord. Let everything happen to me just as you have said." Gabriel smiled at her and disappeared.

Once the angel had gone, Mary's first thought was to congratulate her cousin. She packed a bag and set off.

Mary couldn't wait to embrace her cousin. "Hello!" she cried as she got closer. "Congratulations!"

As Elizabeth heard her cousin's voice, she felt as if her baby had jumped up inside her to greet Mary. Elizabeth suddenly knew Mary was pregnant, and that the baby would be God's own Son. "Mary, you are the most blessed of all women!" Elizabeth exclaimed, throwing her arms around her. "And what an honour to have the mother of my Lord come to visit me!"

Carpenter's tools
Joseph was a carpenter, and would have used tools like these. They were made with wooden frames and metal (iron or bronze) cutting edges. Here (clockwise from top) is a saw, mallet, plane and axe. Carpenters made furniture for homes, farm tools such as carts , and helped build houses by making door frames and roof beams.

Mary
This is a woodcut of the angel speaking to Mary. The Bible does not tell us what either of them looked like. It is likely that Mary was young, possibly in her late teens.

❖ ABOUT THE STORY ❖

The birth of Jesus was carefully planned by God. He decided exactly when, where and how Jesus would be born. Christians see in this story a sign that Jesus really was the Son of God. Because He had no human father but was conceived by the Holy Spirit, Jesus was both fully divine (from His heavenly Father's side) and fully human (from His mother's side).

The Birth of John

MARY stayed with Elizabeth for three months. She was no doubt a great help to her older cousin when she was heavily pregnant with her unborn baby and, of course, the two women shared the amazing secret of how they had each been blessed by the Lord. However, Mary began to worry that she had been away from home too long, and eventually the day came when she sadly told Elizabeth that she must say goodbye. Not long after Mary had gone, her cousin gave birth to a baby boy, just as the angel Gabriel had told Zechariah she would.

Like all proud parents, Elizabeth and Zechariah thought they would burst with happiness. Their friends and relations gathered round to help them celebrate. "What are you going to call him?" someone asked, as they all took turns in cuddling the tiny bundle.

"Oh, they're sure to call him Zechariah after his father," said a family friend, tickling the child under the chin.

"Yes," a relative agreed. "After all, it's the tradition to name him after the father."

"Well maybe they might like to call him after another member of the family," butted in one of the baby's many uncles, while he grabbed the child out of someone else's arms. "For instance, they might like to call him after me!"

"Wait! Wait!" Elizabeth laughed, holding up her hand for silence. She could see that a family argument was about to break out. When everyone was quiet, she said very firmly, "We're going to call him John."

"JOHN!" everyone repeated in shock. "Why ever are you going to call him John?"

The argument began all over again.

"The first boy is always named after his father..."

"There's not a single person in the entire family who's called John..."

Elizabeth stood her ground.

"I'm sorry," she smiled, completely unfussed. "He's going to be called John, and that's that."

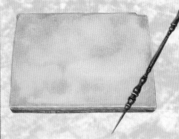

◆ ABOUT THE STORY ◆

Names in the Bible were not just labels for people. Often names were given to describe something about them. Jesus was so called because He was 'the Saviour'; His name means 'God saves'. John's name means 'The Lord is gracious', and shows that through him God was preparing to start an important work.

Writing
Most people at this time wrote on a wooden board covered with a layer of wax, which was written on with a stylus, a pointed wooden stick. The wax could later be melted and smoothed over, ready for use again. Parchment and papyrus were too expensive for most people.

Scribes
In biblical times, not everyone could read and write. Scribes were used to write letters and business documents. Their main job, however, was to copy out the religious texts and teach them to the people. They also taught in the schools attached to local synagogues.

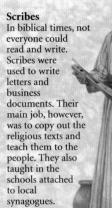

e took her baby back into her own arms, where he lay
ite content and peaceful.
The relatives and friends wouldn't give up.
"What does Zechariah think?" they urged.
"Surely he can't be happy about this John business?"
Elizabeth sighed.
"Why don't you ask him yourself?" she suggested.
Everyone looked at each other, slightly embarrassed.
"He might not be able to speak," Elizabeth said loudly,
tting a little red in the face, "but he hasn't lost the ability
think or write."

66 *He shall be called John.* 99

The friends and relations found a writing tablet and a
n, and crowded round the elderly priest in anticipation.
"WHAT DO YOU WANT HIM TO BE CALLED?" one of
em yelled in Zechariah's face.
"He's not deaf either, you know," Elizabeth murmured.
Slowly and carefully, in big, clear letters, Zechariah wrote
t 'His name is John'.
There was utter commotion as the relatives and friends
ad Zechariah's words.
"Well, I don't believe it!" one remarked.
"John!" another spluttered. "John!"
"Yes," said Zechariah, above the hubbub. "His name is
hn." There was a gasp of astonishment as all heads
rn d to look at the priest. His eyes widened and he
pped his hands over his mouth in surprise. "I can talk!"
whispered. "My voice has come back!" he shouted.

"Thanks be to God!" And he grabbed hold of the laughing
Elizabeth and whirled her round, dancing and singing.
After that, there wasn't a single person in the whole of
the hill country of Judea who didn't get to hear of the
child who had been born so late to Elizabeth and
Zechariah, and the miracle of how the priest's voice had
returned. Everyone knew that the Lord must have had a
hand in the amazing events, and they waited in awe to see
what kind of man the child would grow up to be.

Jewish motifs
Jesus was born and raised as a Jew, and
worshipped in the Jewish synagogue. This
mosaic depicts several Jewish motifs. In
the centre is the seven-branched
candlestick (the menorah). Also shown
here is a shofar (a ram's horn,
bottom right) which priests blew to mark
the start of the Sabbath and other holy
days. Above it is an incense shovel.

Benedictine faith
When Zechariah could speak again, he
uttered a prophetic poem about the
ministry of his son John. This poem is
called the Benedictus, and is still sung in
some church services today. Later, Saint
Benedict founded the Benedictine order
of monks and nuns, shown here.

The Birth of Jesus

WHEN Mary told Joseph that she was expecting a baby, he was very worried. They weren't yet married and there was sure to be a scandal. That night, Joseph had a vivid dream. An angel said, "Joseph, don't be afraid to take Mary as your wife. The baby growing within her is the Son of God. He is the Saviour whom the prophets said would one day come to save everyone from their sins. When the child is born, call Him Jesus. Raise Him as if H were your own son." Joseph awoke much comforted.

As the time drew near for the baby to be born, another problem arose. The Emperor Augustus Caesar ordered a census. This meant that very man had to go to where he was born, together with his family, to be put on a register

Joseph had to travel to Bethlehem, a long way from Nazareth. Mary was heavily pregnant. It was not a good time for her to be travelling.

By the time they arrived, the city was full to bursting. There wasn't a single room to be had. Joseph and Mary trudged from place to place, exhausted, dirty and starving. And Mary began to fe that the baby was on its way.

Bang! Joseph thumped on the door of an inn.

"We haven't any room," said the burly innkeeper from behind the door.

"Wait!" Joseph yelled. "Please! We just need a tiny corner somewhere, somewhere warm and dry. It doesn't matter where. My wife's about to give birth!"

> ❝ *She wrapped Him in swaddling clothes, and laid Him in a manger.* ❞

The innkeeper said, a little more gently, "All my rooms are completely full. I can offer you the stable, if you don't mind the animals. You're welcome to stay there if you like."

Augustus
The Emperor who ruled at this time was Augustus. His real name was Octavian. He became the first Emperor of Rome in 27BC, when he was given his name. He was a great administrator, and ordered several censuses. His aim was to govern the entire empire from Europe to Judea firmly but fairly.

J OSEPH DID WHAT GOD WANTED, BUT HE HAD TO DO WHAT THE AUTHORITIES WANTED TOO. GOD MADE SURE THAT DESPITE THE EMPEROR'S ORDERS, HIS SON WOULD BE BORN SAFELY.

Mary, mother of Jesus
The Bible tells us very little about the Virgin Mary. Like Joseph, she was descended from David. Many Christians believe that she remained a virgin throughout her life. She is regarded as the most important of all the saints.

Joseph accepted the offer gratefully, so it was in the innkeeper's stable, with the oxen, sheep and chickens looking on, that the Saviour of the world was born. Mary had no crib in which to lay her precious bundle, so she nestled Him among the straw of a manger from which the animals fed. There the baby Jesus stayed. He was safe and warm and sheltered, and He had His loving mother and father at His side.

Joseph

In New Testament times an engagement between two people was regarded as binding as marriage itself. The only way to break it was to get a divorce. It was also thought to be sinful if someone had a sexual relationship before they were married. So Joseph probably thought Mary had been unfaithful to him. The angel told him it was a miracle, and so he loved Mary and cared for her.

❧ ABOUT THE STORY ❧

The story of Jesus's birth is very moving. It reveals important truths about God's plans for the world. Jesus was born in a borrowed room, not in a king's palace, even though He was the 'King of kings' before whom everyone should bow in honour. It teaches that Jesus came into the world to show God's love for people who feel they have nothing. God has known the same sadness that they know.

The Visit of the Shepherds

WHILE Bethlehem was full to bursting with people, the fields around the city were quiet and empty, except for a few shepherds and their flocks. As usual, the men were spending the night under the starry sky, taking turns at sleeping and watching, so that no sheep would go astray, stolen by wolves or even bears. It was a cold and lonely job. They had only the dying flames of the campfire to keep them warm. Apart from its flickering, and the pale glow of the moon and stars, all was calm, all was still.

Suddenly the night sky above blazed as if it were on fire. It was like trying to look into the full glare of the

Praising God
In churches today, a choir sings hymns, psalms and songs as part of worshipping God. Music is a powerful way of praising Him. The pictures of heaven given in the Bible describe angels and people singing God's praises.

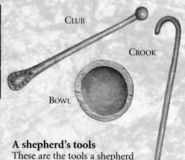

CLUB

CROOK

BOWL

A shepherd's tools
These are the tools a shepherd would have used. The club was for fighting off attacking wolves. He also had a food bowl from which he could eat. The crook was used for rescuing lost sheep.

A shepherd's cloak
Sheepskins would have been made into coats. These were to keep shepherds warm as they stayed up to guard their sheep.

scorching desert sun. The shepherds fell back, trying to shield their eyes as high overhead a figure appeared.

"Do not be afraid," came its voice, speaking clearly into the mind of each of the shepherds. "I have news that will bring great joy to everyone on earth. Today in Bethlehem, the city of David, a Saviour has been born who is Christ, the Lord. You will find Him wrapped up in swaddling clothes and lying in a manger."

> 66 *To you is born this day a Saviour, who is Christ the Lord.* 99

The sound of countless singing voices filled the air. The heavens were filled with angels.

"Glory to God in the highest," they sang, "and peace to His people on earth."

Then suddenly the singing died away and the light faded. The dazed shepherds were left staring up at the sky. The gleaming moon and stars now seemed only an echo of the real beauty of the heavens, which they had glimpsed for a while and had now disappeared.

The shepherds hurried off to Bethlehem, leaving only a couple of men behind to guard the flocks. They were excited. The prophets had spoken of a Christ, or Messiah, whom God would send to save the world from its sins. Had this most amazing person now been born?

The shepherds searched from place to place in the packed town until they heard the crying of an infant coming from a stable behind an inn. The shepherds found Mary and Joseph huddled over the manger, attending to a baby wrapped in swaddling clothes.

"It is indeed the Saviour! Christ, the Lord!" the shepherds gasped, approaching the little family and falling on their knees. They told the startled parents about the visit from the angels and what they had said. When the shepherds had paid their tributes and gone, singing praises to God as they went, Mary and Joseph began to wonder and marvel at everything that had happened.

Medieval nativity
Many pictures have been painted of the first Christmas. This one shows the shepherds together with the wise men. Mary and Jesus have haloes round their heads. Artists used this device to show people who were specially blessed by God.

❖ **ABOUT THE STORY** ❖

Shepherds were despised by most people. They were thought to be liars and couldn't give evidence in court. Only people with no hope could be shepherds. This story reminds readers that God has shown Himself specially to people who everyone else despises and who think they are not good enough for God. The good news of Christianity is for everyone, regardless of background.

Jesus is Presented in the Temple

WHEN their baby was eight days old, Mary held a naming ceremony according to God's laws. From then on, the baby was called Jesus, just as the angel had told Mary He should be. Then, according to the custom, Mary and Joseph travelled up from Bethlehem to the temple in Jerusalem to present Jesus to the Lord and to offer a sacrifice of two doves or pigeons.

Now there lived in Jerusalem an old man whose name was Simeon. Simeon had always done his best to lead a good life and was well known by everyone in the city to be a very holy man. As the people of Jerusalem watched him make his way to and from the temple every day, his lips moving in constant prayer, they never dreamed that he had a precious secret. The Holy Spirit had promised Simeon that, as a reward for his faithful, lifelong service to God, he would not die before he had seen with his own eyes the Messiah who would save the world. Simeon felt he had been blessed with the highest of honours, and he looked forward with his whole heart to the moment that he would meet his Saviour.

> *Mine eyes have seen thy salvation which thou hast prepared in the presence of all peoples.*

When Mary and Joseph arrived in the temple with Jesus, Simeon was already there. That morning, the Holy Spirit had once again spoken to him, telling him that

---

⬩ ABOUT THE STORY ⬩

To most people, Jesus was just another baby. To those who were trying to look at the world through the eyes of faith, He was someone special. Even today, some people, like Simeon and Anna, are gifted with a kind of spiritual second sight that helps them to discern God's purposes behind events. They are called prophets. This event helped Mary and Joseph to know more about Jesus.

Mary weeps
When Mary took Jesus to the temple, Simeon prophesied that she would suffer much grief because of what would happen to Jesus.

Taking Jesus to the temple
The Jewish law said that after 40 days a woman who had a son must offer a sacrifice at the temple. The proper sacrifice was a lamb and a pigeon, but poor people were allowed to bring two pigeons. The ceremony dates back to Old Testament times when eldest sons used to have to become priests. Then when the Levites took this role, the Israelites would symbolically 'buy back' their sons from God, from the priesthood, by making a sacrifice as Mary does here.

today was the great day when God's promise to him would be fulfilled. With his heart pounding in his breast, Simeon had prepared himself with great haste and hurried to the temple as fast as he could. And as soon as the old man laid eyes on the baby, he knew who He was.

"May God almighty bless you," Simeon cried, holding out his trembling arms to hold the child. "I have long dreamt about this day. Now I can die in peace, for my eyes have seen the one who will save the world. This child will be the glory of Israel and the light of hope for all the peoples of the earth."

Simeon turned to the stunned parents. "This child is a sign from God, but many will not listen to His message," the old man said to Mary. "Because of this, a great sadness will pierce through your heart like a sword," he continued. "However, He will also win many hearts for the Lord."

While Simeon was speaking, a woman even older than Simeon shuffled up. It was Anna, the prophetess. She had spent much of her life in the temple, devoting herself to fasting and prayer.

"Allow me the blessing of holding my Saviour," she said. A curious crowd was beginning to gather around the family and Anna lifted her voice aloud, thanking God for allowing her to see the holy child and telling everyone that the infant was the hope of the world.

As soon as Mary and Joseph had made their offering, they said goodbye to Simeon and Anna and hurried away from the eyes of the temple worshippers. They were more than a little embarrassed by all the fuss, and naturally felt bewildered by the strangeness of everything that had happened since their son's birth.

Simeon and Anna
Simeon and Anna were people of faith who were expecting God to do something special. They didn't know what to expect, but prompted by the Holy Spirit they recognized Jesus.

The journey
The distance from Nazareth to Bethlehem was about 129km. Mary and Joseph walked there. It does not say in the Bible that Mary rode on a donkey, but it is quite likely that she would have done. There were well-trodden tracks between towns, but no paved roads. Bethlehem was a short distance from where the temple was in Jerusalem.

The Wise Men Find Jesus

FAR away in the east, some learned priests were puzzled to see that a strange star suddenly appeared one night in the sky. Not only was it a star they had never noticed before, but it shone brighter than any other. The wise men hurried off to consult their writings. They agreed that the brilliant star was an unmistakeable sign. The saviour had been born. Now all they had to do was find Him.

The wise men spread out their maps and plotted a route from the position of the star. Finally, they chose

gifts for the child who was King of the whole earth. Then they mounted their camels and set off across the desert.

News reached King Herod that strangers from the orient were searching Jerusalem. "They're looking for a child that has been born king of the Jews," the king's spies told him.

"Are they, indeed?" murmured Herod, stroking his beard thoughtfully. After all, he was king of the Jews. Somewhere in Judea, a rebellion was brewing. He kept calm and summoned the chief priests and scribes to a meeting. Herod pretended that he was curious to learn more.

"Where do your scriptures say that the Christ child is to be born?" Herod asked innocently.

"The prophets say that the Messiah will be born in Bethlehem," the priests replied.

Herod nodded, interestedly. He had the answer that he needed.

As soon as the priests and scribes had gone, the king called for the most trusted officers in his army.

"Find these wise men from the east," he ordered, "and bring them to me. Only do it in secret, or the people will really start to take notice of these rumours."

Soon, the wise men were ushered into the presence of the king of Judea. They had heard that Herod was a ruthless, harsh ruler and were worried. However, Herod was politeness itself.

"When exactly did this star appear?" the king asked. The wise men told him all they knew about the child.

The magi
Most pictures show three wise men, or magi, because they brought three gifts, although this number is not used in the Bible. It is likely that there were more than three as people tended to travel in larger groups. They were learned priests, not kings as is sometimes suggested.

Astrologers
The magi priests were also astrologers. In ancient times, astronomy (the study of planets) and astrology (giving advice based on the stars) were practised by the same people. The Jews were not to use astrology – God alone was their guide.

The wise men did indeed find Jesus in Bethlehem. The star shone biggest and brightest over the town and led the travellers to where Mary and Joseph were now staying. They were surprised at the arrival of the splendidly dressed guests, just as the wise men were to find the holy family in an ordinary house. They had no doubt, though, that the baby was the king of all kings. They bowed their heads to the floor and paid tribute, then they unlocked their jewelled caskets and offered Mary their gifts of gold, rarest frankincense and myrrh.

The night before the wise men set off on their return, they had a dream which deeply disturbed them. "Herod must not be told," they agreed. They took a different route home, so that the evil king could not find them.

In turn, Herod seemed most helpful.

"Try Bethlehem instead of Jerusalem," he suggested.

The wise men bowed down and thanked Herod for his generous help. There was no time to waste.

"Oh, by the way," Herod added, "when you have found the child, would you be so kind as to tell me where He is? I must of course go and worship Him myself."

> 66 *They offered Him gifts, gold and frankincense and myrrh.* 99

"Consider it done, O King," the wise men agreed.

As soon as the door closed behind them, Herod thumped his fist down on his throne.

"As soon as I know where this 'king' is, I will make sure He is killed!" he snarled.

Casket and gifts

The gifts brought by the magi may have been in a casket like this. The gold was the sign of royalty, frankincense was a sign for a priest and myrrh was a sign of death and burial.

Arabia

This is the town of San'aa in Yemen. The Bible tells us that the magi came from the east. The most likely places were Arabia or Babylon.

❖ **ABOUT THE STORY** ❖

The wise men were gentiles (non-Jews). Their appearance in only Matthew's Gospel is of great significance to Christians. The message is that Jesus has come into the world for all peoples. Matthew, in fact, is the most Jewish of the Gospels so this story is a reminder of Jesus's wider ministry. This event is celebrated in many churches as the Feast of Epiphany (6 January).

Escape to Egypt

MARY and Joseph marvelled at how far the wise men had travelled to see their son. So many strange things had happened since He had been born. Maybe the departure of the wise men would mark an end to all the amazing and unusual events for a while...

That night, Joseph once again dreamt that an angel came and stood by his side.

"You must take Mary and the baby and hurry away from here at once," came the angel's urgent message. "Flee into Egypt and stay there until I come to tell you it is safe to return. King Herod of Judea is going to search for the child. He is determined to kill Him."

Next morning, Joseph gently shook Mary awake and told her to get Jesus ready. He lifted his wife and her precious child on to the donkey and the family crept away unnoticed through the quiet streets of Bethlehem.

Meanwhile, in Jerusalem, King Herod was waiting for the wise men to return. Every day, he grew more and more frustrated and more and more angry.

"Surely those wretched astrologers must have found the child by now?" he'd bellow at his trembling advisers.

The days turned into weeks, and still Herod grew more and more furious. Finding his rival, the baby Christ, was top of his agenda. The thunder-faced king could think of nothing else. How could he enjoy life, knowing that rumours were spreading about another king of the Jews? Besides, if the wise men were right, and this baby really

was the Messiah spoken of in the scriptures, He would soon have supporters up and down the country. And that would leave Herod at serious risk of losing his throne.

One sunset, as yet another day ended with no word from the wise men, King Herod finally snapped. "Bring me the general of the royal army!" he howled with rage.

The burly army commander was at once ushered in.

"Order your men to go through every single household in the Bethlehem area and find every male child under two years old," Herod spat, "then kill them all."

A gasp went around the court room.

The blood drained from the general's face and he fell to his knees before the ruthless, cruel monarch.

"But... but... sire, surely..." he stuttered, falling silent as Herod bent down to whisper in his ear.

"If I hear that there is even one male child under two years old left alive, I shall hold you personally responsible," hissed the king, and he swept away to his private chambers, leaving the army general grovelling miserably on the cold palace floor.

> **" Herod is about to search for the child, to destroy Him. "**

Soon, the sound of screaming rose up over Bethlehem. No one could escape the heartbreaking shrieks that tore the air. Panicking parents ran desperately to and fro, trying to secrete away their tiny sons. The soldiers marched like machines into every possible hiding place. They trampled over those who threw themselves to the ground and begged for them to have mercy. They turned deaf ears to pleading and crying of men and women beside themselves with grief.

At last, when there was not a single male child under the age of two left in the whole of the area around Bethlehem, Herod was satisfied. So much then for the supposed Messiah, king of the Jews!

In fact Jesus was long gone. Joseph kept Him and His mother safe in Egypt until the angel told him that Herod had died and it was time to return home to Judea. So finally the family returned to the quiet town of Nazareth in the remote district of Galilee, where Jesus grew up far away from the evil eyes of Herod's son, King Archelaus.

THE FACT THAT JESUS EVENTUALLY RETURNS TO ISRAEL FROM EGYPT TO SAVE THE PEOPLE THERE ECHOES THE WAY THAT THE ISRAELITES FLED EGYPT WITH MOSES HUNDREDS OF YEARS BEFORE.

Flight into Egypt

The Gospel of Matthew tells us that as soon as Joseph was told by the angel that Jesus was in danger he took his family out of Israel to Egypt. It was a long and difficult trip for the family to make, especially as Jesus was so young.

❖ ABOUT THE STORY ❖

Herod the Great is known to have been a violent and cruel man, who was greatly afraid of rivals. He even had two of his own sons put on trial, convicted and executed because of an alleged family plot against him. There is no record outside the New Testament of the killing of the male infants but it would have been typical of Herod to order it.

Lost and Found

In the sleepy town of Nazareth, Jesus grew up just like all the other children. Mary and Joseph taught Him to obey all the laws of their religion and made sure that He learned all the teachings of the holy scriptures.

Every year, Mary and Joseph travelled to Jerusalem to celebrate the great festival of Passover, as all Jews tried to do. One year, when Jesus was 12 years old, the family went as usual to share the wonderful experience of praising God in the temple at this important time of the year.

When it was time to go home, Mary and Joseph found a crowd of travellers planning to go their way. Jesus disappeared among them. Like all children His age, He

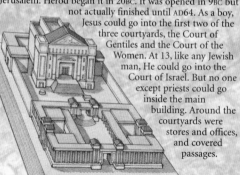

didn't want to walk by His parents' side. He wanted to talk with His own friends. Mary and Joseph weren't worried. They knew their son was sensible enough to keep close by.

After the first day's journey, when the tired, dusty travellers were getting ready to make camp for the night, Jesus was nowhere to be seen.

"Jesus! Jesus!" called Mary and Joseph, at the tops of their voices. The boy didn't come running.

The anxious couple hurried from group to group.

"Has anyone seen our son?" they asked. "He has very dark eyes; He's about this high; He's very gentle and well-mannered; a quiet, thoughtful boy."

Everyone just shook their heads.

Joseph looked very serious. Mary was close to tears.

"There's nothing more we can do now," the carpenter told his wife, putting his arm around her. "First thing in the morning, we'll retrace our steps."

Neither Mary nor Joseph managed to sleep for worry. Anything could have happened to Jesus. What if He had been kidnapped by bandits or eaten by wild animals? It didn't bear thinking about.

> **" All who heard Him were amazed at His understanding and His answers. "**

As they went back to Jerusalem, Jesus's parents grew more anxious. There wasn't a single sign as to what had happened to Him. The boy had just disappeared.

People milled everywhere in the narrow streets, jostling

Herod's temple
This was the greatest of all three temples which had been built in Jerusalem. Herod began it in 20BC. It was opened in 9BC but not actually finished until AD64. As a boy, Jesus could go into the first two of the three courtyards, the Court of Gentiles and the Court of the Women. At 13, like any Jewish man, He could go into the Court of Israel. But no one except priests could go inside the main building. Around the courtyards were stores and offices, and covered passages.

Bar and Bat Mitzvah
When Jewish girls reach the age of 12 they have their Bat Mitzvah, Jewish boys have a Bar Mitzvah aged 13. This is a ceremony when in the eyes of their religion, they become adults, and take on the religious duties of a Jewish adult.

shoulder to shoulder. It was looking like an impossible task. Several times they thought they saw Jesus, but each time it turned out to be another boy about His age. They couldn't leave without their precious son. They would hunt high and low until they found Him, hopefully alive and well. By the third day the only place the desperate parents hadn't searched was the great temple itself.

Wearily, Mary and Joseph climbed the great stone steps and entered the huge courtyard. Some type of meeting was going on in one of the porticoes. They could see elders and priests, deep in discussion. They tiptoed forwards. Then Mary's voice rang out loud and clear.

"Jesus!" she gasped, pushing her way through the learned men to where Jesus stood in the middle of them.

"Please excuse us," Joseph explained. "We've been looking for Him all over the place."

To his utter astonishment, the leaders all shook his hand.

"We cannot believe your son's understanding of the scriptures," they told him. "And He has raised searching questions that few people ask."

Meanwhile, Mary's relief at finding her son was giving way to anger.

"Jesus, we have been worried sick!" she scolded. "How could you just go off on your own and leave your father and me wondering where you were?"

"You should have known that you would find me in my Father's house," Jesus said, calmly.

Mary was taken aback at Jesus's strange answer, but she didn't have the time to puzzle over His mysterious words. All she wanted to do now was get back home safely. Later, she remembered Jesus's strange reply. And, of course, she hadn't forgotten the angel, the shepherds and the wise men, Simeon and Anna in the temple. It was all very mysterious indeed...

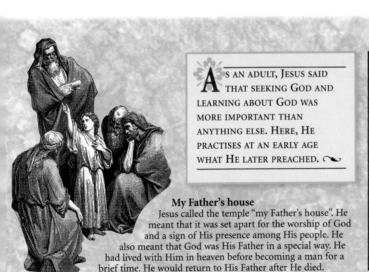

AS AN ADULT, JESUS SAID THAT SEEKING GOD AND LEARNING ABOUT GOD WAS MORE IMPORTANT THAN ANYTHING ELSE. HERE, HE PRACTISES AT AN EARLY AGE WHAT HE LATER PREACHED.

My Father's house

Jesus called the temple "my Father's house". He meant that it was set apart for the worship of God and a sign of His presence among His people. He also meant that God was His Father in a special way. He had lived with Him in heaven before becoming a man for a brief time. He would return to His Father after He died.

✦ ABOUT THE STORY ✦

We know little about Jesus' boyhood, and nothing about how He looked or how He behaved. Some legends were made up in the 3rd and 4th centuries, but none of them can be traced any earlier. This story shows that Jesus was aware of His special relationship with God from an early age. It also shows that He learned to obey His parents in His preparation to obey God.

Jesus is Baptized

JESUS's cousin, John, grew up to devote his life entirely to God. When he was a young man, he went off on his own into the wilderness around the River Jordan. John just wrapped a rough camel skin around him and ate locusts and honeycombs that he found in the wild.

When John was around 30 years old, a change came upon him. Instead of keeping himself to himself, he began to preach to all the peoples who lived near the river.

"I have heard the word of God!" he would yell. "You must think about your sins and be truly sorry for them. I hear you say that you're Abraham's descendants, God's chosen people. I tell you that God could raise these very stones up to life, if He wanted. Beg the Lord's forgiveness and be good. For the day is coming when the Lord will judge sinners."

> **❝ I have baptized you with water; but He will baptize you with the Holy Spirit. ❞**

People began to travel to the Jordan to hear what John had to say. All kinds of men and women came, common folk, noblemen, priests, tax collectors, even Roman soldiers. No matter who they were, John's message was the same. He said people should turn back to God, be kind, don't cheat or lie, and don't hurt anybody with harsh words or violence.

Every day, people would line up by the River Jordan, eager to be forgiven for their wrongdoings and wanting to make a new start. One by one, John would take them into the river and submerge them, blessing them as they rose up from the water cleansed of their sins.

As the weeks passed, rumours began to spread among the people of Galilee.

"Maybe this John is the Messiah spoken of by the prophets..." people would murmur.

"Surely this holy man is the Christ!" exclaimed others.

John was always very clear about the truth.

❖ ABOUT THE STORY ❖

This event marks the beginning of Jesus's public ministry. Through it He received confirmation that He was indeed the Son of God, and He received the spiritual power He needed to do His work. His baptism was also a way of identifying with the people He came to die for. He was saying that He was willing to take people's sin on His shoulders, which He did on the cross.

Baptism
Baptism is a ceremony in which a person is submerged beneath water, or sprinkled with water, as a sign that they want to follow Jesus and turn away from their sins. Most churches use it as the main ceremony to make someone a church member.

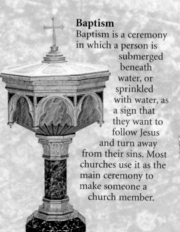

John
We do not know where John grew up. It seems possible that his parents, Zechariah and Elizabeth, died when he was young, and that he grew up in a religious community in the desert. His work was foretold in the Old Testament, and he was likened to Elijah. Here you can see John baptizing Jesus.

"I am not the Messiah, or Elijah, or any other prophet. I am merely one voice crying out in the wilderness, trying to prepare the way for the Lord," he said. "I'm baptizing you with water, but there is one coming soon who will baptize you with the fire of the Holy Spirit. He is much greater than me – so great that I'm not even fit for the job of cleaning His sandals."

When Jesus himself arrived among the crowds at the banks of the Jordan, John knew who He was immediately, and he told everyone who was there.

"Here He comes!" he cried, falling on his knees. "The one God has promised us! The one who will take away the sins of all the world!"

Jesus laid a hand gently on his cousin's arm and looked deep into his eyes.

"Will you baptize me too, John?" He asked.

"My lord," John gasped. "I can't baptize you! It should be you who baptizes me!"

However, Jesus insisted.

"We should each of us do what God has given us to do," He said, quietly.

And so John led Jesus down into the Jordan.

At the very moment that John blessed Jesus as He rose from the waters, the two men heard a mighty thunderclap. John looked up to see the clouds of the heavens parting, and a dove came gliding down bathed in heavenly light. John knew that the Holy Spirit was descending on his cousin. Then a voice spoke that seemed to come from everywhere and nowhere all at once.

"This is my beloved Son," the voice said, "with whom I am well pleased."

Locusts and honey

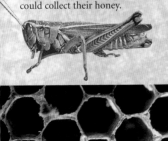

Locusts are large grasshoppers which can breed into great swarms. They are very nutritious and are still eaten today. Wild bees made nests in rocky places. John could collect their honey.

Sadducees

Most Sadducees were priests, but not all priests were Sadducees. They were a group within Judaism. As a group they were very snobbish and mostly came from the upper classes. They despised ordinary people. In Jesus's time, they were the major group in the Sanhedrin, the Jews' ruling council. However, they often had to follow the Pharisees because the latter were popular with the ordinary people. They accepted only the written laws of the Old Testament, and not all the extra ones the Pharisees made up. They did not believe in life after death, or that God could or would guide a person's life. The Sadducees died out after the temple was destroyed by the Romans in AD70. No one is sure how they started, whether as a political, religious or aristocratic group.

Tempted in the Wilderness

JESUS knew He was the Son of God, the Messiah the prophets had said would come to save the world from its sins. Now He had to prepare for the job He had been sent to do.

Led by the Holy Spirit, Jesus went into the wilderness where He could be on His own to pray. There He talked to God for 40 days and 40 nights, asking for guidance in the difficult days that lay ahead. He ate nothing, and as Jesus grew weak with hunger and exhaustion, the devil came to Him in His thoughts.

"If you really are the Son of God," Satan whispered, "why don't you turn these stones into bread?"

Jesus knew this would be wrong on several counts. First, He had heard the voice of the Lord calling Him His Son. He knew He should have faith that this was true, not try to work a miracle to prove it. Second, eating was far less important than obeying God. Jesus realized that His body would die if He didn't eat, but His body would die one day anyway. It was far more important to look after His soul by not doing anything that would offend His Father in heaven. Besides, He should trust God to look after Him. After all, long ago, Moses had led the starving Israelites through the desert. He had trusted the Lord, and God had sent them food from heaven.

Jesus summoned up His strength.

"No," He told the devil. "People can't live on bread alone; we need to listen to the words of God to survive."

Satan was annoyed. However, he tried not to let it show. Instead, he put a picture of the holy city of Jerusalem in Jesus's mind. It was as if Jesus was standing right on the top of the great temple, looking down on the streets and houses all around. Balancing so high up made Jesus dizzy and His head began to whirl and spin.

"If you really are the Son of God," Satan challenged, "don't be afraid to fall off. The angels will come and catch you. They'll make sure you don't even bruise a single toe."

It was a very tempting thought. Why struggle to do things the hard way, fighting Satan, when there was a quick solution? Jesus knew it would be wrong. His life as the Messiah was going to be dangerous, sad and lonely. There would be no easy way out. His Father in heaven wanted Him to live as a human, to show people the right way to God – even if it was the most difficult way of all.

∻ ABOUT THE STORY ∻

Jesus was tempted in the same way as everyone else. The first temptation was to put the satisfaction of His own needs and desires before God's will. The second was to take a short cut to do God's work, rather than do it in God's way. The third was to grab power over people for Himself. The message is that we should not just be concerned with the end result, but also how we get there.

The Judean Desert

This area is wild and inhospitable. There are oases (for water), but it is hot in the day and cold at night, and there is little shelter. Jesus was here about six weeks. The desert is often thought of as a place of testing because it is a place of extremes.

J ESUS RESISTED TEMPTATION BY QUOTING FROM GOD'S WORD, WHICH IS A GOOD WAY OF DEALING WITH IT. IF THOUGHTS AGREE WITH THE BIBLE, THEY ARE FROM GOD; IF NOT, THEY COME FROM THE DEVIL. ∾

"No," He told the devil, firmly. "It is wrong to put God to the test like this. The easiest thing to do is by no means always the best."

Satan was furious, but he didn't give up. Instead, he whisked Jesus's thoughts away to the highest mountain in the world. As if Jesus were an eagle, flying high up in the skies, He could see the whole earth spread out below Him. How beautiful His Father had created everything! Waving fields of crops grew out of pink and brown soil. Wide carpets of green grass and sweet-smelling forests covered plains and hills. Deserts glowed yellow and ice caps shone blue-white. Rivers rippled and sparkled down to seas as broad as the skies above. The devil showed Jesus all the

wonders of the world. Images of golden palaces, splendid temples and treasure houses overflowing with all the riches of the earth arose in Jesus's mind. There were magnificent armies of brave-hearted warriors and rows of gleaming chariots led by prancing horses. There were fleets of ships laden with exotic cargoes from mysterious lands...

"Take a good look!" urged Satan. "All this can be yours. I will give it all to you – if only you will bow down and worship me."

Jesus knew that the devil was indeed mighty, for he had hold of many people's hearts. Those who turned to Satan to make them powerful ended up cruel, dishonest and selfish. They ruled by crushing others, and kept themselves happy by making others miserable. Those who followed the Lord might not become rich or famous, but they would find love and happiness and be truly at peace. Besides

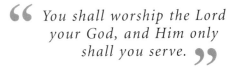

> **You shall worship the Lord your God, and Him only shall you serve.**

which, Jesus knew that all kingdoms of the world will one day fade to dust and that only the kingdom of God will last for ever.

"No," He told the devil, in disgust. "Get away from me! People should worship only the Lord God."

Satan nearly exploded with frustration. He had tempted Jesus with all he had. Raging wildly, the devil disappeared. And as Jesus sank down in the sands of the desert, utterly worn out, angels came to look after Him.

Satan
Satan is often pictured with horns (like a raging bull) and a forked tail (like a snake's tongue). These are symbols of what he is like. He is vicious in attitude and poisonous in intent. The Bible tells us very little about Satan. It seems he was an angel in heaven who became jealous and proud. He rebelled against God and was thrown out. Now he seeks to oppose God and his people in any way he can. He is not as powerful as God, however, and Jesus came to destroy the grip Satan has on people.

The First Miracle

JESUS left Judea and travelled back to Galilee. It was time to begin teaching the people what they had to do to enter the kingdom of God. Several of John the Baptist's followers went along with Jesus, wanting to help. As soon as Jesus arrived home, He and His mother had to go to a wedding in Cana. Weddings were always big, important celebrations and often lasted several days.

Perhaps the steward in charge of the wedding reception hadn't ordered enough wine for such a large feast. Or maybe the guests were drinking more than usual. Whatever the reason, Mary noticed halfway through the wedding reception that the wine had almost run out. While the guests were all munching and slurping their way through each delicious course, nervous, red-faced servants were scurrying off with empty wine jars.

"Look. There's no more wine left," Mary quietly said to her son.

Jesus was concerned. He knew how embarrassing it would be for the bride and groom if they had nothing to offer their thirsty guests to drink.

"I'm sorry, but I can't do anything about it," He whispered back. "The time is not yet right for me to show the powers my Father has given me."

Mary just held His hand and nodded, reassuringly. Then she turned to the servants nearby.

"Excuse me," she said, politely. "I couldn't help noticing that you're almost out of wine. My son can help you. Just do exactly as He says."

Jesus looked at His beloved mother and smiled. Then with a sigh, He said to the servants, "Fill your empty jars up to the brim with water."

> **66** *The steward of the feast tasted the water now become wine.* **99**

Very puzzled, they hurried off to carry out his instructions. And soon they were back, struggling under the weight of their full urns.

"Now draw out some of the water into a goblet," Jesus told them, "and take it to the steward for tasting." (It was the custom for the steward to check every jar that came out of the cellar, to make sure that the wine was good.)

Well, the servants were mystified. They were sure that their boss would think they had gone mad when they took him water to test, pretending it was wine. They didn't dare refuse to carry out one of the guest's instructions. And besides, there was something about the man's kind eyes and His mother's gentle manner that made them trust that everything would be all right.

Now the steward was an expert wine taster. And he knew all the tricks of

Cana
This was a small village north of Nazareth. We are not sure of the exact site today. The town pictured may be built near it.

Water jars
Water jars were usually used for the ceremonial washing of people's feet. It was the custom to wash a visitor's feet when they came to your house; they wore open sandals. Many Jews also insisted on ritual washings before they ate, as a religious act.

his trade, such as serving the best wine first and bringing out the cheaper wine later, when the guests were less aware of what they were drinking. So when he drank this time from the servant's goblet, he was amazed. This new wine was even better than the wine they had served at first! Before the servants could explain where it had come from, the steward hurried off to congratulate the groom on his good taste and generosity.

Jesus had worked the first of many miracles He was to perform throughout His life. His followers had seen Him do the impossible, and they believed more strongly than ever that He truly was the Son of God.

MARY'S WORDS – "DO EXACTLY AS HE SAYS" – ARE ADVICE WHICH EVERYONE CAN FOLLOW. IN ORDER TO LIVE IN GOD'S WAY, CHRISTIANS BELIEVE THAT WE HAVE TO DO EVERYTHING HE SAYS.

Wine tasting
This shows the steward tasting the wine. Wine in the New Testament can also stand for Jesus's blood, which He shed on the cross for the sins of the world. It is significant that Jesus's first miracle involved wine, as if looking forward to His greater miracle of salvation.

❖ ABOUT THE STORY ❖

Jesus sometimes said that His teaching was like new wine, or that He came to bring to people the new wine of the kingdom of God. He meant that He brought the new life of the Holy Spirit to people who would follow Him. As with many of His teachings, Jesus illustrated His words by His miracles. God's new life is plentiful, like the supply of wine at Cana. There is plenty of it.

Followers Flock to Jesus

JESUS began to travel around Galilee, teaching from synagogue to synagogue.

"Beg the Lord to forgive your sins," He urged, just like His cousin John the Baptist. "For the time is near when the doors of God's kingdom will be thrown open. The Holy Spirit has sent me to bring the good news that captives will be set free, the blind will see and the poor will no longer have to suffer."

Everyone who heard Jesus was amazed at the way He spoke. He didn't simply read out the scriptures, as other scribes did. He interpreted them as if He were sure He knew what they were all about.

Jesus's actions were pretty astounding too. Jesus was preaching one day in Capernaum, when a madman suddenly flew into a crazy fit.

"I know who you are," the madman yelled at Jesus. "You're the Holy One of God! What do you want with us? Have you come here to destroy us all?"

Jesus remained calm. He said firmly, "Be quiet!" He stared at the madman. "Leave him!" He commanded.

At once, the man crumpled into a heap on the floor. At Jesus's command, the demons left him.

❖ ABOUT THE STORY ❖

There was something "different" about Jesus. It was not just what He said nor was it just what He did – there had been miracle workers before. He was in a class apart, and people could see it. However, He wouldn't explain it. Jesus silenced the one person who really knew – the madman. He wanted people to learn to trust Him in the ordinary things of life.

The miraculous catch of fish
This had a special impact on Peter. He knew that fish went to the bottom of the lake in the daytime, where the water was cooler. If Jesus had the power to make the fish come into the net, He could do anything. The miracle spoke to Peter in terms he understood.

The worshippers were left in shock.

"Who on earth is this man?" they whispered.

Reports spread like wildfire about what had happened. Even though it was nearly dark, everyone who heard about the captivating stranger with the special powers came at once to find Him. Sick and injured people came flooding from the nearby towns and villages to be healed by Jesus.

> ❝ *I know who you are, the Holy One of God.* ❞

He laid His hands on them, filling them with a sense of forgiveness and hope, curing each and every disease.

"You will stay with us, won't you?" the people pleaded.

"I'm afraid I can't," Jesus explained. "I must move on to other places. I have to tell everyone how they can find happiness by turning to God. It's what I was sent to do."

One day, Jesus was preaching to a crowd on the beach when He noticed Peter and Andrew, who were fishermen, washing their nets. Jesus jumped into their boat and asked them to take Him a little way offshore. There He sat and spoke to the people from a safe distance.

When Jesus finished preaching, He asked Peter to steer the boat into deeper waters and to lower his nets.

"Master, we fished all night last night and caught nothing," Peter protested. "As it's you who's asking, we'll have another go."

When the brothers tried to pull up their nets, they were so heavy with fish that they could hardly lift them. They had to call to James and John in another boat for help.

When the two boats were nearly sinking under the weight of the catch, Peter knelt at Jesus's feet.

"Lord," Peter said, "I'm not worthy to be one of your followers. I didn't really trust you. I didn't really believe that we'd catch anything."

"Don't be afraid," Jesus said. "From now on, all of you are going to be catching people instead of fish."

The men left behind everything they had and dedicated their lives to following Jesus.

Jesus and the disciples

A disciple is someone who learns from another person and seeks to do what they say and live how they live. There were many disciples of Jesus. He chose 12 of them to do special work for God.

Fishermen

Many people who lived around the Sea of Galilee were fishermen. They fished from boats at night, or waded into the waters in the day to throw nets over the smaller fish in the shallows by the shore, in the same way as the fishermen shown here. The Sea was well stocked with many kinds of edible fish that were sold locally.

Demons

Some people who seemed insane, or mad, were thought to be possessed by demons. People believed demons to be beings who wanted to stop God's work.

Jesus the Healer

PEOPLE far and wide got to hear about Jesus. So many men and women came to see Jesus that the synagogues weren't big enough to fit them all in. With everyone lining up to be healed, Jesus could hardly find a moment to Himself to go off and pray. The authorities began to grumble at how whole towns would grind to a halt when the exciting new preacher arrived. Everyone would down tools and go off to hear Him talk.

Jesus didn't mean to cause trouble. He was just concerned to spread His message to as many folk as possible and help all those who were in need.

In one city, a leper crept up to Jesus one day and knelt at His feet. "Lord, I know that if you want to, you can cure me," the poor man begged, his skin crumbled and deformed with the terrible disease.

"Of course I want to," said Jesus, gently. "Be clean." And Jesus reached out and touched his skin.

The leper was shocked. After all, his deadly disease was so infectious that most people ran off screaming if they saw him coming. Then he realized that Jesus was smiling at him. The leper looked at his fingers. He felt his face. He peered down at his legs. He couldn't believe it! He was cured! His skin was smooth and healthy! Weeping with joy, he thanked Jesus over and over again.

"Don't tell anyone about this," Jesus said. "Go straight to the priest and make an offering of thanks to God."

The overjoyed leper couldn't contain himself. He went leaping about the streets on his brand new legs, waving his healthy arms in the air, telling everyone he met about how the wonderful Jesus had cured him.

So Jesus's reputation spread even further afield and even more people came travelling to see the extraordinary man. Instead of going to towns, Jesus began to preach in the wide open spaces of the countryside, where there was room for everyone.

On another occasion, Jesus was preaching in a private house to a crowd that included many important teachers of the law. Priests, elders and Pharisees had come from towns and cities all over Galilee and Judea, and even from the great city of Jerusalem itself, to question Jesus. They wondered who He really was. A trickster? A prophet with healing powers like Elijah and Elisha? Could He possibly be the Messiah, as so many people were claiming?

> " *Great multitudes gathered to hear and to be healed of their infirmities.* "

As usual, there wasn't even standing room inside the little house. People were crammed together so tightly that they couldn't even raise a hand to scratch their nose. Others spilled out into the passage that led to the street.

While Jesus spoke, four latecomers began struggling to push their way inside. Their job was made even more difficult because they carried a friend of theirs on a stretcher, a man who was paralysed. The ranks of spectators were too dense. There was only one thing for it.

Sweating with the strain, the men carried their friend up the outside stairs on to the flat roof of the house. They tied ropes to the stretcher and removed some of the roof covering. Then, very slowly and carefully, they lowered the stretcher through the gap and down into the room where Jesus was teaching.

Jesus was extremely moved at the friends' faith and at the plight of the paralysed man.

"Take heart, my son," he said, "your sins are forgiven."

All the Pharisees and Saducees present were horrified. It was one thing to have the power of healing, but how could anyone have the power of forgiveness? Only God had that! It was blasphemy!

Jesus soon put a stop to their grumblings.

"I know just as well as you that anyone can say, 'Your sins are forgiven,'" He said. "After all, no one can see whether they really have been or not. To prove to you that God has granted me this power and has healed this man's soul, I shall heal his body too."

Jesus turned again to where the man lay stiff and still on his stretcher.

"Rise up and walk," He commanded.

To everyone's amazement, the man immediately stood up and rolled up his stretcher. Then, praising God, he hurried off to show his family, his grateful friends cheering and slapping him on the back.

The priests, elders and Pharisees didn't dare say a single word more. How could they? What they had just seen was truly astonishing. In fact, everyone agreed they had never seen anything like it before.

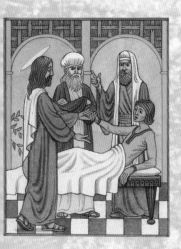

JESUS COULD SEE THE MAN HAD A DEEPER NEED THAN JUST TO HAVE HIS BODY HEALED. EVERYONE NEEDS FORGIVENESS FOR THEIR SPIRITUAL 'SICKNESS' – THE SIN THAT KEEPS THEM AWAY FROM GOD.

Pharisees
They were a group of powerful religious leaders who believed that the only way to be right with God was to keep every one of His laws all the time. Pharisees were sincere people, but they hindered others' faith, so Jesus often criticized them.

❖ ABOUT THE STORY ❖

This story shows that Jesus wasn't out to get lots of publicity, His main concern was for the people He helped. Jesus's miracles were not a way of seeking attention, He wanted what was best for people. Jesus knew that people might be attracted to Him by miracles. He also knew, though, that such things would not make them want to trust their lives to God, which was what He wanted.

Matthew is Called

JESUS was walking down a road one day with His many disciples when He looked into an open window and saw a man working at a desk. The man was Levi, later known as Matthew, and he was working in the tax office.

At that time, Judea was under the rule of the Roman empire. The Jews hated everything to do with the conquering nation and its army. They had to pay the Romans in taxes, and the people who collected the taxes for the Romans were seen as traitors. As a result, if you became a tax collector, people you had been friends with for years suddenly stopped talking to you. Even members of your own family didn't want to know you any more. Complete strangers would shout at you in the street, calling you names.

Matthew was one of these hated tax collectors. And while many citizens in the town had taken the day off to see Jesus, Matthew knew he wouldn't be welcome among the crowds of the city. He stayed indoors, busily hunched over his tax records.

Matthew was trying hard to concentrate on his work, when he suddenly felt that someone was watching him. The hair bristled on his neck and he swung round. Matthew found himself looking straight at a stranger who was staring in at

him through the open window – a stranger with the kindest face and deepest, darkest eyes he'd ever seen. Matthew knew it was Jesus.

"Follow me," He said.

Matthew didn't need telling twice. Without a word, he got up out of his chair. He didn't even close his books or put away his pen. He just left everything exactly where it was and hurried off eagerly to join Jesus's disciples.

That night, Matthew insisted that he repay Jesus's kindness by having Him to stay at his house. It was his way of showing how much Jesus meant to him. When

Women disciples
There were also female disciples who were following Jesus. They looked after the practical needs of the twelve. They also listened to and learned from Jesus.

Metal cup
Most ordinary people drank out of pottery cups or out of small bowls. Silver cups like this would be used only by rich people and in the temple.

Tax collectors
Tax collectors were in charge of collecting a wide variety of taxes for the Romans, that they used to pay for their empire.

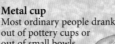

it. Surely, they thought, Jesus should be sitting down to eat with us, rather than with the common folk? And not just peasants, but tax collectors! Sinners!

The Pharisees grew even more annoyed when Jesus told them off for their moaning.

"Those who are well have no need of a doctor," He explained. "It is those who are ill who need to be healed. I have not been sent to look after good people; it is sinners who have most need of me."

> 66 *Jesus said to Matthew,*
> *'Follow me.' And he rose*
> *and followed Him.* 99

"We try so hard to live good, strict lives!" they protested. "Our followers often fast and pray, as do the disciples of John the Baptist. We never see yours doing the same. Your followers always eat well and drink merrily, as if they're at an eternal banquet! What's it all about?"

"Would you expect guests at a wedding not to celebrate while the bridegroom is present?" Jesus scolded. "There will be plenty of time for fasting when the bridegroom is taken away from the guests."

Jesus's mysterious answer infuriated the Pharisees all the more. Even His disciples didn't really understand. They didn't mind too much. Jesus often seemed to talk in riddles. He always seemed to know more than He was letting on. His followers realized that He explained everything He thought they needed to know. They trusted that the rest would all unfold in its own good time.

Jesus had invited him to go along with His followers, Matthew hadn't wanted anyone to notice him. He hadn't jumped up and down for joy, shouting aloud for all to hear. Inside, his heart was dancing. And he was sure that Jesus somehow knew how he felt.

Matthew threw the greatest feast that he could offer Jesus and His disciples. He didn't really have any friends of his own to share the joyous occasion with, so he invited other tax collectors along instead. For the first time ever, Matthew's house was full of guests enjoying themselves – and he loved it.

When the Pharisees got to hear of it, they were very jealous! The Pharisees were devoutly religious and considered themselves better than other people because of

The Roman Empire
Jesus lived in Galilee under the rule of the Roman Empire. This was the largest empire in the world at the time. Emperor Augustus brought stability to the Empire and secured the borders.

> ✢ **ABOUT THE STORY** ✢
>
> *Jesus was known as a friend of tax collectors and people who were regarded as sinners. To have a former tax collector as one of His inner circle of disciples made Him even more odious to the religious leaders, who regarded such people as beyond God's help. Jesus said He came to call all sorts of people to follow God, and this was shown in His choice of disciples.*

The Faithful Centurion

JESUS befriended many people who were despised by other Jews. One day, He helped a non-Jewish officer in the Roman army.

It all began when a group of elders came hurrying up to Jesus when He was preaching one day in the town of Capernaum.

"Sir, we have been sent to find you by a Roman centurion," one began.

"He has a loyal servant who he's grown to love like his own son," interrupted another.

"But the servant is very ill," butted in yet another.

"You really should help him out," another elder added. "Even though the centurion is a gentile and an enemy of Israel, he's always been very good to us Jews. He even helped to build our synagogue..."

> *He is worthy to have you do this for him, for he loves our nation, and he built us our synagogue.*

Even before they had finished talking, Jesus was already striding along on His way to the centurion's house.

Jesus had very nearly reached the centurion's house when some people came dashing out of it.

"We have a message for you," they told Jesus. "Our friend says he's not worthy to have you honour his home with your presence, and that is why he never dreamed of coming to see you himself. He begs you not to trouble yourself any further. Instead, he says that if you simply say

Chemists
Although Jesus healed many people, most of the time people had to rely on the medicine of the time. Chemists used herbal remedies for everything, because there were no drugs. Some of these may have been useful, but others were not. Many chemists were con-men, and would just cheat the people.

JESUS OFTEN USED HIS MIRACLES TO TEACH SOMETHING AS WELL. HE SAID PEOPLE SHOULD TRUST GOD AND ACCEPT HIS WORD. THAT IS WHAT FAITH IS ALL ABOUT, TODAY AS WELL AS THEN. ◆

Surgical instruments
Compared with modern standards, Roman surgery was very crude, but for the time it was well advanced. The bronze instruments shown here are (from top to bottom) forceps, a spoon, a spatula and a scalpel.

the word of command, his servant will be healed. After all, he's a centurion. He's used to giving orders and finding that everything then happens just so!"

Jesus's face lit up with happiness.

"I tell you, I haven't found such faith among any of you Jews," He told the crowds who were following Him. "There will be people from far-off nations who are allowed to enter the kingdom of heaven, while many from the nation of Israel will be left outside in the darkness, to howl and gnash their teeth in despair."

Jesus turned away and the centurion's friends began to hurry back to the house. They found the servant was completely recovered, just as if he had never been ill.

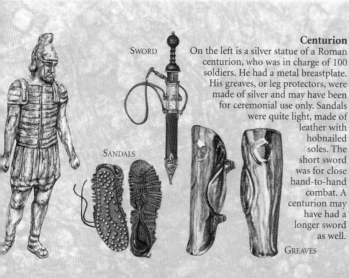

Centurion

SWORD

SANDALS

On the left is a silver statue of a Roman centurion, who was in charge of 100 soldiers. He had a metal breastplate. His greaves, or leg protectors, were made of silver and may have been for ceremonial use only. Sandals were quite light, made of leather with hobnailed soles. The short sword was for close hand-to-hand combat. A centurion may have had a longer sword as well.

GREAVES

Trouble Begins to Brew

DAY by day, as Jesus's friends grew in number, so did His enemies. Jesus first came up against opposition in Nazareth. You might think that the people of His home town would be proud of the famous local boy. When they heard Him preaching in the synagogue, telling them all kinds of new things they should and shouldn't be doing, they were irritated and envious.

"Where on earth did He get all this wisdom and the knowledge to do all these amazing things?" they scoffed.

"He's only the son of Joseph the carpenter, after all. We know His family: Mary, His mother, and all His brothers and sisters! He's just a normal person like us!"

Jesus was deeply saddened by their lack of belief. There was nothing He could do but turn His back on Nazareth. The people had wasted their chance to hear His message.

Elsewhere, Jesus couldn't help offending other people because His teachings were so new and fresh. The priests and elders, Sadducees and Pharisees, had spent their lives studying the ancient scriptures, but Jesus often presented them in a very different light.

"It's all right to eat all kinds of food," Jesus preached. "It's not what goes into people that is unclean, but what comes out of them, such as evil thoughts, pride, violence. You don't have to stick to all the traditional washing rituals, either. They don't cleanse your soul, as the Pharisees believe they do. They only cleanse your body."

> 66 *But they were filled with fury and discussed with one another what they might do to Jesus.* 99

Of course, the holy men who had been doing their best to follow these laws for years, believing they were doing the right thing, were furious to hear Jesus telling them it wasn't necessary. And sometimes He even criticized them openly, saying that they had lost sight of what God's commandments were really all about and that they were just practising meaningless traditions.

What annoyed the Jewish leaders most was the way in which – in their eyes – Jesus broke the laws of the Sabbath. One Sabbath morning, some Pharisees were with Jesus and His disciples walking through a cornfield. Now even though no Jews were allowed to eat until later in the day, Jesus's hungry followers were pulling the heads off the stalks and eating the grain.

"Don't you remember what David once did when he was desperate for food?" Jesus told the angry Pharisees. "He ate the holy bread that only priests are allowed to eat. You should make sure you remember that the Sabbath was made for people, not people for the Sabbath."

Jesus regularly healed people on the holy day. The Jewish elders considered this to be work and therefore a sin. On one occasion, He healed a crippled woman who had been bent double in terrible pain for 18 years.

"None of you would think anything of untying a donkey or ass on the Sabbath to let it drink," Jesus explained, "so shouldn't I set this woman free from her bonds?"

Another time, Jesus healed a man who had a dreadfully deformed and paralysed hand.

"Do you think it's right to do good or evil on the Sabbath?" He challenged the fuming holy men and scribes. "Do you think

hat on God's holy day we should save
fe or destroy it?"

One Sabbath, Jesus went to the pool
f Bethesda, where lots of sick and
njured people used to gather in the hope
f a miraculous cure. It was said that now
nd again an angel would stir up the water
nd the first person then to plunge into the
ool would be cured. Jesus knew that one
rippled man in particular had been
aiting by the pool for a long time. For
henever he saw ripples on the water, he
ouldn't drag himself to the pool fast
nough and someone else always beat him
here. Jesus was filled with pity and simply
aid, "Pick up your bed and walk." To the
nan's delight, he found he could do exactly that.
Many of the Jews who saw and heard about the
niracle weren't so pleased. They were sure that His
ealing on the Sabbath was breaking God's
ommandments. Jesus's answer annoyed them even more.
My Father doesn't stop working on the Sabbath and
either do I," He told them.

"How dare He call God His Father!" the priests and
lders gasped, totally outraged. "It's blasphemy!"

Jesus just shrugged.

"It is God my Father who has given me the authority to
erform miracles such as these, to raise the dead to life
nd to judge sinners. I warn you that the day is coming
oon when everyone will hear the voice of the Son of God
alling them to be judged – even the dead will come forth

to be either rewarded or punished."

The Jewish leaders were fuming, but Jesus carried on.

"You search the scriptures to find out how to win eternal
life. Even though Moses wrote that I would be coming,
you refuse to follow me. If you don't believe Moses, how
do you expect to believe what I am telling you?"

So it was that many of the priests and elders, Pharisees
and Sadducees, became Jesus's enemies. Little by little,
more and more of them began to gather together in secret
to plot ways in which they might get rid of Him...

JESUS DID NOT BREAK
GOD'S LAW, BUT HE DID
BREAK THE RULES PEOPLE HAD
ADDED TO GOD'S. HIS ACTION
REMINDS PEOPLE TO CHECK THAT
THEIR TRADITIONS DON'T STOP
PEOPLE KNOWING GOD.

Pool of Bethesda
Bethesda was like a health spa. The pool
is probably one of two which can be seen
near St Anne's Church in Jerusalem
today. Legend said that the first person to
enter the pool after it was touched by an
angel would be healed.

⚜ ABOUT THE STORY ⚜

*The Sabbath (the seventh day
of the week, our Saturday) is
special for the Jews. God was
said to have rested from
creation on the seventh day.
People were commanded to rest
and remember God on that day.
Jesus was later raised from the
dead on Sunday, the first day of
the week and for Christians
Sunday has become their
"Sabbath". Jesus said the day
was for everyone's benefit.*

The Apostles are Appointed

THERE came a time when Jesus said He needed to be alone for a while. Everywhere He went, people clamoured to see Him. So eventually Jesus went on His own up a mountain to pray. All night long the disciples waited for Him to return. At last they saw the familiar figure of Jesus striding towards them.

Jesus called out 12 names: the brothers Peter and Andrew, James and John, Matthew the tax collector, Philip, Bartholomew, James, Thaddaeus, Thomas, Simon the Zealot, and Judas Iscariot. Then He took the puzzled men away from the rest of the disciples, where He could speak to them in private.

"I have something very important to ask of you," Jesus said, seriously. "I need you to help me carry out my mission. I want you to split up and go off on your own into the countryside. Preach my message as you go. Tell all the people that the kingdom of heaven will soon be here. I am going to give each of you special powers. I want you to heal the sick as I do, to raise people from the dead for me, to cleanse lepers and to cast out demons from those who are possessed by evil."

The 12 men looked at each other anxiously.

"Furthermore, I want you to do all this for nothing," Jesus continued. "You mustn't take any payment from anyone. I don't want you to take anything with you – not even a bag with a

THE APOSTLES HAD TO RELY ON GOD FOR EVERYTHING. TODAY, WE TEND TO ASK GOD ONLY FOR WHAT WE CAN'T GET OURSELVES. THIS STORY ENCOURAGES US TO RELY ON GOD AND NOT TO WORRY. ~

The 12 apostles
This mosaic from Italy is one artist's attempt to show what the 12 apostles looked like. The word apostle means "one who is sent". With the exception of Judas Iscariot, they all became leaders of the Christian Church after Jesus died.

hange of clothing or a spare pair of sandals. You must
ely on finding good people in the towns you visit who
vill put you up and look after you."

The friends all nodded, listening very carefully.

"It will not be an easy job," Jesus went on. "You have
lready seen the problems I face. If anyone refuses to
sten, don't get dismayed. Just go on your way and shake
ff your disappointment, just as you shake the dust from
our shoes. However, be wary all the time. I know that I'm
ending you out like sheep heading straight for a pack of
volves. There will be people who will hear you and follow
ou, but there will be others who make up their minds to
ate you because you are my representative. They will try
nd arrest you, and they'll haul you before royal courts to
rder you to stop spreading my message. Don't be afraid.
t times like these, the Holy Spirit will give you courage
nd tell you what to say. You shouldn't fear people,
ecause they can hurt only your body, not your soul. Have
reat fear of the Lord, for He can destroy both your body
nd soul in the fires of hell. My Father in heaven will be
ooking after you all the way."

> **And they departed and went
> through the villages, healing
> everywhere.**

Jesus was pleased to see that the 12 men He had chosen
ooked determined.

"Don't think that I have come to bring peace on earth,"
le told them. "I have come to bring a sword that will

carve up the righteous from the wicked. Anyone who does
not take up his cross and follow me, bearing the
responsibilities that go with this, will not find heaven. If
you give up your lives to me – even perhaps dying for my
sake – you will be given new lives."

From that day onwards, the 12 men were known as the
apostles. And for several weeks, they went out on their
own around the countryside, teaching and healing. And
when they returned, they were full of the wondrous
miracles they had been able to perform in Jesus's name.

⟡ ABOUT THE STORY ⟡

*Jesus spent much of His time
with the 12. He gave them more
teaching than the rest
of the disciples, and He trained
and equipped them to take
over His mission when He
died. Despite all their
experience with Jesus, they
still didn't fully understand
His mission until after His
resurrection. Then it became
clear, and they were ready for
their special work.*

The Sermon on the Mount

ONE day, Jesus went up a mountain so everyone could hear Him.

"Blessed are all those people who realize that God is missing from their lives, for heaven will be theirs. Blessed are those who are full of sorrow, for they will be comforted. Blessed are the gentle, for they will be given the earth. Blessed are those who hunger and thirst for goodness, for they will receive what they desire. Blessed are those who are merciful, for they will have mercy shown to them, too. Blessed are those with pure, true hearts, for they will see God. Blessed are those who strive for peace; God considers them His own children.

> 66 *If anyone strikes you on the right cheek, turn to him the other also.* 99

Blessed are all those who are made to suffer because they are trying to do right, for theirs is the kingdom of heaven. If others mock you and make your life miserable because you follow my teachings, you should rejoice and be glad, for you will win a wonderful reward in heaven! You are the light of the world, so shine like beacons to lead others to God."

The crowds were amazed at Jesus's words.

"Don't think that I'm telling you to forget the law or abandon the teachings of the prophets," Jesus continued. "I'm not. You need to pay more attention to them than ever. The law says that you should not kill anyone; I'm

Church of the Mount of Beatitudes
This church is built where Jesus is believed to have preached the Sermon on the Mount. The sayings that begin with the word "Blessed" at the beginning of the sermon are known as Beatitudes.

The Lord's Prayer
Jesus gave this prayer as a model, rather than simply a prayer to be recited. In it are all the main elements of prayer. It addresses God as Father, who can be trusted to provide all we need. It worships Him and puts His will first. It seeks forgiveness and thinks well of others. It asks for God's protection, as well as for His provision of our basic needs.

~THE LORD'S PRAYER~

OUR FATHER WHO ART IN HEAVEN,
HALLOWED BE THY NAME.
THY KINGDOM COME,
THY WILL BE DONE,
ON EARTH AS IT IS IN HEAVEN.
GIVE US THIS DAY OUR DAILY BREAD;
AND FORGIVE US OUR TRESPASSES,
AS WE FORGIVE THOSE WHO
TRESPASS AGAINST US;
AND LEAD US NOT INTO TEMPTATION,
BUT DELIVER US FROM EVIL.
FOR THINE IS THE KINGDOM, THE POWER
AND THE GLORY, FOR EVER.
AMEN.

telling you that you shouldn't even argue with anyone. The law says that you shouldn't go off with another person's husband or wife; I'm telling you that you shouldn't even think about it. If what you can see is leading you to sin, then gouge out your eyes. It's better to lose part of your body than have your whole body burnt in the fires of hell because you have sinned. The law says that you are entitled to take revenge on someone who wrongs you. I'm telling you that you should do nothing to get your own back. In fact, if someone hits your right cheek, turn the left towards them so they can strike that too. The law says love your neighbours and hate your enemies. I'm telling you to love your enemies, too. You should be kind and generous to all people, no matter who they are."

The crowds looked up at the preacher in awe.

"Now," Jesus went on, "many people like everyone to know that they give money to the needy and they go every day to the synagogue, making sure that everyone knows about it. God will not reward these people in heaven, for they have already received the admiration of those on earth. Don't show off your good works and boast about them. Do your fasting and giving to charity in secret, not so everyone knows, and when you pray, use these simple words..."

And Jesus taught the crowds to pray.

"Also, don't bother with wealth. The riches of this world can easily be stolen or turned to rust. Instead, build up the treasure of good thoughts and deeds that thieves can't get and that won't decay. And don't worry about what you're going to eat or wear. If you put your efforts into searching for God, He'll make sure that you're looked after."

Jesus stretched His arms out to the hundreds of people who were patiently listening, entranced.

Everyone who follows these words of mine will be like a wise man who builds his house on rock, so it stands firm. Anyone who hears what I say and yet takes no notice will be like a fool who builds his house on sand. The winds will blow it down and the rains will wash it away."

olid foundation
sus wanted to make sure that people
new that those who built their "house",
r life, on the foundation of faith in God,
ill be safe and secure.

Andrew and James
Andrew had been a disciple of John the Baptist before he became one of the apostles. James is believed to be the brother of John. They, together with Peter and Andrew, seem to have been fishing partners.

The Parables of the Kingdom

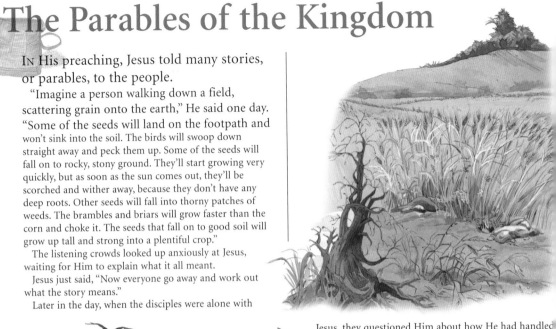

IN His preaching, Jesus told many stories, or parables, to the people.

"Imagine a person walking down a field, scattering grain onto the earth," He said one day. "Some of the seeds will land on the footpath and won't sink into the soil. The birds will swoop down straight away and peck them up. Some of the seeds will fall on to rocky, stony ground. They'll start growing very quickly, but as soon as the sun comes out, they'll be scorched and wither away, because they don't have any deep roots. Other seeds will fall into thorny patches of weeds. The brambles and briars will grow faster than the corn and choke it. The seeds that fall on to good soil will grow up tall and strong into a plentiful crop."

The listening crowds looked up anxiously at Jesus, waiting for Him to explain what it all meant.

Jesus just said, "Now everyone go away and work out what the story means."

Later in the day, when the disciples were alone with Jesus, they questioned Him about how He had handled the crowds.

"Jesus, why do you tell the people parables and then leave them to try to understand for themselves?" the disciples asked. "When you're with the 12 of us in private, you always explain everything."

Jesus sighed. "You have been given the gift to understand all the secrets I tell you about the kingdom of heaven," He explained. "Other people, who haven't been privileged in this way, wouldn't understand. So I teach them through stories. This way, the more carefully they listen and the harder they try to understand, the more they will get out of them and the closer they will get to the kingdom of heaven. For many of them look at me, but they don't really see who I am. They listen to me, but they don't really hear what I'm saying. They think they're taking in my words, but they don't really understand."

And He explained to the disciples what the parable of the sower meant.

> ❝ And He told them many things in parables. ❞

"The seed is the word of God. The footpath stands for those who hear the word of God but who don't take it in. The devil will swoop down straight away and steal the message away from them. The rocky ground represents those who pay attention to the word of God and take it on board for a short while. Because the message hasn't sunk deep enough into their hearts, any difficulties that arise will overcome them and they will give up on it. The weed

e those who hear the word of God but ho are either too worried about their aily problems, or simply too busy aving a good time, to do anything bout it. The good soil stands for nose who absorb the word of God eep within themselves. They give it a lace to grow, and over time they bear ood fruit."

Jesus explained other parables to the isciples. He told a story about a sower, hose enemy had secretly planted weeds nong his crops. When the sower's rvants saw the shoots appear, they asked im if he wanted them to go and pull them ut. The sower was worried that they'd get onfused and pull the good plants out with the ad ones. "Leave it till harvest time," he told them. Then I'll tell my reapers to pull out the weeds first nd burn them, leaving the corn to be safely gathered in." sus explained that the sower was the Son of God and the eld was the world. The seeds were people who loved God nd the weeds people who opposed God. He said that at ne end of time, the Son of God would send His angels to ast the bad people into hell, leaving the good people to ve happily in the kingdom of heaven.

Once, Jesus compared the kingdom of heaven to a grain f mustard. "It is a small seed," He said, "but it will grow nto a massive bush and birds will nest in its branches."

Other parables showed how determined people had to e to enter the kingdom. They needed to be like a pearl

merchant who sees the most precious pearl of all and sells everything he has in order to buy it. Or a person who discovers buried treasure in a field. He covers it up again, and he rushes away to sell everything that he owns, just so that he can buy the field. God's kingdom is like the treasure, you must want it more than anything else.

Jesus warned everyone to listen hard to the stories He told. "No one goes out to buy a lamp and then covers it up or puts it under the bed, so its light is hidden," He said. "So having come to hear me, make sure you don't ignore my teachings. For what I am telling you, everyone will one day know to be the truth."

Grain sieve
Grain was always sifted in a shallow basket like this before being ground to make flour for bread. Some weed seeds might be mixed in with it which would poison the bread. Some weed seeds were picked out by hand and the contents of the basket shaken so that any remaining seeds which were smaller than the grain, would drop out of the holes.

Sower's bag
Farmers sowed their seed by hand. They ploughed the soil then walked up and down throwing handfuls of seed from the bag slung over their shoulder. Usually, they then ploughed the field again, or drove animals over it, to push the seed into the soil.

> ❖ **ABOUT THE STORY** ❖
>
> *These parables built up a picture of what the kingdom of God was like. It isn't something that could be illustrated in one simple picture. Together the parables show that it is God's rules working in people's lives. Therefore the kingdom of God can be anywhere. It grows as more people learn to serve God and influence others for good. It is worth more than anything else because it lasts for ever.*

Jesus Stills the Storm

JESUS was exhausted. He'd been preaching all day by the Sea of Galilee to crowds that were bigger than ever. His throat was hoarse and His legs and back were aching. He'd already tried to tell the people that He'd finished for the day.

Even though it was now growing dark, it was obvious that many didn't want to go home. They were still lurking about in groups, waiting to see where Jesus was going next, so they could follow Him.

"Let's sail over to the other side of the lake," Jesus said to His disciples. "We might be able to be on our own there for a while."

They splashed along the seashore to their boat and pushed off, raising the little sail. As the boat cut through the waters, Jesus sank into a deep sleep down at the back of the boat, rocked by the rise and fall of the waves and lulled by the swish of the sea.

While Jesus dreamed, the disciples were horrified to notice dark clouds racing across the sky and heading straight for them. Before they'd even had time to furl the sail, the wind began to whip up around them. It wailed and howled, stirring up the waters into great peaks that tossed the little boat into the air and then plunged them down towards the depths.

> **"** *Why are you afraid, O men of little faith?* **"**

Of course, Peter, Andrew, James and John were used to storms like this. They were fishermen and had often been caught in them.

"Don't worry," Peter called out cheerfully, "it's just a little breeze. Nothing to be sick about!"

He showed them how to tie the sails down, and how to bale out the water which splashed over the side and made their feet cold.

However, it wasn't just a little breeze. It was the most horrendous storm they had ever known. It was as if a giant hand was shaking the boat, trying to make it sink.

"I'm scared!" shouted one of the disciples.

"I can't swim!" cried another.

Soon, even Peter was terrified. Some clung on to the sides of the boat and the mast for dear life, drenched by the waves that came crashing on to the deck, threatening to wash them overboard. Others were thrown to and fro as they rushed back and forth, trying desperately to bale out the water that swamped the boat. Through it all, Jesus went on sleeping undisturbed.

"Master! Master!" the terrified disciples cried, their voices nearly drowned out by the screaming of the gale. "Wake up! We're all going to drown!"

Jesus opened one eyelid and sat up, sleepily. He yawned and stretched, then stood up in the front of the boat to face the full force of the storm.

"Peace!" He thundered, reaching His arms up towards the black, raging skies.

"Be still!" He bellowed, stretching His hands out over the billowing waters.

At once the howling died away, the wind dropped and the sail hung limply in the still air. The sea suddenly flattened into a glassy mirror, its surface barely disturbed by a single ripple. The clouds were blown from the evening skies, until a still, starry night hung over the peaceful little boat.

Jesus turned to face the trembling disciples.

"Why were you afraid?" He asked the astounded men, as they cowered away from Him in complete awe. "You have such little faith."

Then He lay down once more and drifted off to sleep, just as if the danger had never happened.

As the disciples stirred themselves from their shock and turned the boat back on track for the far shore, they couldn't stop whispering about what they had witnessed.

THE DISCIPLES FORGOT ONE IMPORTANT FACT: GOD WOULD NOT LET HIS SON PERISH IN AN ACCIDENT BEFORE HIS WORK WAS COMPLETED. INSTEAD OF PANICKING, THEY SHOULD HAVE TRUSTED GOD.

Storm on Sea of Galilee
The Sea of Galilee is surrounded by steep hills. During the afternoon, the hot air which rises off the lake cools over the hills and can form storm clouds. This then rushes down the steep hills and whips up the lake into a boiling cauldron.

⟡ ABOUT THE STORY ⟡

Jesus teaches two things through this extraordinary storm. One is that He trusted the disciples to look after the boat, which is why He was asleep. The second is that He showed Himself to be Lord of creation. He has complete power over natural forces. The message is that with Jesus "on board" a person's life, there is nothing to fear.

Legion and the Swine

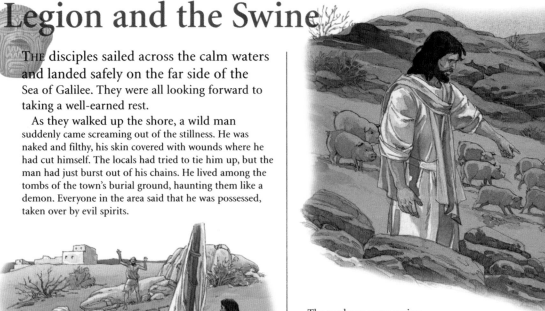

THE disciples sailed across the calm waters and landed safely on the far side of the Sea of Galilee. They were all looking forward to taking a well-earned rest.

As they walked up the shore, a wild man suddenly came screaming out of the stillness. He was naked and filthy, his skin covered with wounds where he had cut himself. The locals had tried to tie him up, but the man had just burst out of his chains. He lived among the tombs of the town's burial ground, haunting them like a demon. Everyone in the area said that he was possessed, taken over by evil spirits.

The madman came racing towards Jesus and flung himself at His feet. He seemed to know His name.

"Jesus, Son of the Most High God, what do you want with me?" the madman slobbered.

Jesus knew that it wasn't the man himself who was really speaking; it was the demons inside him.

"What is your name?" Jesus demanded.

"Legion," the demons inside the madman replied. "For there are whole legions of us inside of him."

Jesus began to tell the evil spirits to get out of the man

Demon possession
People at the time believed that sometimes evil spirits took over a person's life. Examples have been seen in many cultures. Casting out demons is known as exorcism. This is a sculpture of a demon leaving someone's mouth.

Burial ground
Most cultures respect their dead. This is a Middle Eastern burial ground. The one Legion lived in was probably a network of underground caves.

put on clothes, and was sitting calmly by Jesus's side. The townspeople couldn't understand what had happened. Who was this stranger to command evil spirits like that?

> 66 *The whole herd rushed down the steep bank into the sea, and perished in the waters.* 99

"Keep away from us!" the nervous locals yelled. Jesus sighed and picked Himself up and went back to the boat.

Legion ran after them. "I can't thank you enough! Please, take me with you," the grateful man begged.

Jesus took his hand. "Go back to the home you once had," He said. "I want you to tell everyone how much God has done for you."

and leave him alone.

"Don't send us into hell!" shrieked the demons. "Let us live somewhere else, such as in those pigs."

Jesus looked at the snuffling animals nearby.

"Go!" He commanded the demons.

At once, the pigs began to grunt in terror. Then they galloped wildly down the slopes to the cliff edge and dived to their deaths on the rocks below.

The petrified herdsmen fled in terror. Soon they were back with anxious townspeople. Legion had washed and

Monastery at Kursi
The exact site where this story took place is unknown, but this Byzantine monastery at Kursi was built where tradition said Legion had been cured.

Demon mask
This terracotta mask comes from Babylon. It shows the giant Humbaba. Masks like this were the Babylonians' way of trying to keep the demons away.

Healed by Faith

ONE day, a synagogue leader called Jairus pushed his way through the hundreds of people surrounding Jesus and knelt down at the surprised preacher's feet.

"Master," he pleaded, ignoring those jostling him from all sides. "My little daughter is only 12 years old and she is dying." He looked up at Jesus with a tear-stained face. "I beg you to come and lay your hands on her to make her well again."

Jesus immediately stood up and set off after Jairus. And as usual, the massive crowd went with Him, surrounding Him on all sides, pulling and elbowing each other out of the way to be as close as possible to the great teacher.

They hadn't gone very far when, without any warning, Jesus suddenly stopped and span round. The startled crowd fell silent.

"Who touched me?" He said, scanning the rows of anxious faces. "Who reached out and touched my robe?"

The people hung their heads and waited for the person to step forward.

"Master," said Peter quietly, "there are people pressing in on you from all sides. You are struggling to walk along because everyone's pushing you back and forth. How can you ask who has touched you?"

"Somebody in particular reached out for me," Jesus

explained. "I felt power go out of me."

Jesus's eyes singled out a woman in the crowd.

"Don't be afraid," He said. "Come here." And the people fell back to let the trembling lady through.

> **❝** *The girl is not dead, but sleeping.* **❞**

The woman had been ill for 12 years with a painful disease. She had been to many doctors in the hope of a cure, but if anything, they had made her worse. Yet she had great faith in Jesus. She had truly believed that He had the power to cure her. Even if she couldn't get to see Him or speak to Him, she had been determined to get close enough to touch Him, for that, she had felt, would be enough. As the crowds had pushed and shoved round Jesus as He walked along, the woman had seized her chance. She had pressed her way forwards as near to Jesus as she could, then thrust her arm out between the people in front of her. Her fingers had just scraped the edge of Jesus's robe.

"My daughter," Jesus said to the woman, gently. "It is your faith that has made you well."

All this time, Jairus was waiting anxiously. Please hurry up, he was thinking, or it will be too late. Just as Jesus was finishing speaking to the woman, Jairus saw one of his

servants approaching. His heart sank.

"My lord," the servant said gently.
"Don't trouble the preacher any further.
I'm afraid that your daughter is dead."

Jesus had overheard. He put His hand
on the heartbroken Jairus's arm.

"Don't worry," He said. "Trust me.
She'll be all right."

When Jesus, Jairus and the crowd of
followers reached Jairus's house, the
mourners were already there, weeping
and wailing outside.

"Don't be so upset," Jesus told them.
"The girl isn't dead at all. She's just in a
deep sleep."

The mourners scoffed at His kind
words. Some of them even laughed.
Jesus took no notice. Taking only Jairus
and his wife, and His three friends
Peter, John and James, He made His way
to the room where the body lay, stiff
and cold. Tenderly, Jesus held the little
girl's hand.

"My child," He whispered, "it's time
to get up now."

The girl opened her eyes wide and
sat up on the bed.

Even though Jesus told the overjoyed
parents not to tell anyone what he had
done, it wasn't long before news of the
miracle was all over the countryside.

Jesus and hope
This mosaic shows
Jesus wearing a
blue robe. The
artist showed
Jesus wearing
blue because it
is the colour of
hope. This is
because it
resembles the
sky. It was this
faith and hope
that Jesus liked
and admired,
and wanted
people to have.

> **❖ ABOUT THE STORY ❖**
>
> *The sick woman demonstrated
> her true faith in Jesus. She
> knew that if she touched Him
> she would be cured. But she
> delayed Jesus so much that
> Jairus's daughter was dead
> before Jesus got to her. Many
> people would say that Jesus
> got His priorities wrong. By
> doing what He did, Jesus
> meets the needs of young
> and old equally.*

The Death of John the Baptist

JOHN the Baptist was thrown into prison by King Herod Antipas of Judea because he had criticized the king's marriage to his niece Herodias. The marriage broke the law of Moses because the couple were related, and they had both had to divorce their partners in order to marry.

John was all alone in prison and his mind was troubled. He sent his followers to ask Jesus if He really was the one the world was waiting for.

"Tell John everything you have seen," Jesus told John's disciples. "The blind see, the lame walk, lepers are healed, the deaf can hear, the poor are cheered in spirit, and the dead are raised to life."

He paid tribute to the great preacher.

"John the Baptist is the greatest person ever born," He told them, "but many people have refused to listen to him, just as they now fail to listen to me."

King Herod's new wife had tried to make King Herod execute John. Herod did not dare kill such a righteous man, no matter what he had said.

One day, the king threw a massive banquet and his daughter, Salome, danced for him.

Herod clapped his hands in delight.

"That was wonderful," he gushed. "What can I get you to say thank you? Anything you want. You just name it."

Greek dancers
Dancing was a favourite pursuit at ancient banquets. Salome's dance followed in a long tradition that went back hundreds of years. This is a painting from a vase of Greek dancers, from 500BC. Salome's dance has often been portrayed in music and dance since. A composer called Richard Strauss wrote a whole opera called *Salome*.

Symbol of Rome
The eagle, seen here on a round base, was the symbol of the Roman Empire.

Wedding statue
This Roman relief shows the bride and groom holding hands while a third person reads out the legal contract.

The best the king could do was to return John's body to his followers. His horrified disciples buried him and then told Jesus the news.

> ❝ *Herodias had a grudge against him, and wanted to kill him.* ❞

Herod couldn't forget what he had done. And when news came to him of a strange preacher who healed the sick and raised the dead to life, Herod trembled. He thought that perhaps Jesus was John the Baptist risen from the dead.

"Anything?" asked Salome, her eyes opening wide. She dashed off to tell her mother.

"Mother says that I should ask you for the head of John the Baptist," Salome murmured, when she called back.

Herod gasped. He'd made a promise in front of all his guests. He'd have to keep his word, and he ordered John executed. Later that day, Salome took her cruel mother the head of John the Baptist on a plate.

HEROD PAID THE PRICE FOR HIS OWN FOLLY. HE SHOULD NEVER HAVE PROMISED SALOME 'ANYTHING'. MAKING RASH PROMISES IS RARELY A GOOD IDEA. THINGS CAN HAPPEN TO MAKE US REGRET THEM. ❧

The harp
The harp was a popular instrument throughout biblical times and would have been played at Herod's banquet. However, the instrument used in biblical times was more properly called a lyre, because it had fewer strings than a harp.

❧ **ABOUT THE STORY** ❧

The coming of John the Baptist was foretold in the Scriptures. People were looking for Elijah as the scriptures had said he would return, but Elijah was reborn as John. The fate that John meets foreshadows the death of Jesus Himself. John is executed because of the silly dislikes and jealousy of one person. Jesus is a victim of the jealousy and dislike of a whole group of people.

Jesus's Time and Place

LIFE in Judea at the time when Jesus lived was dominated by the occupying Roman army. Soldiers were everywhere, patrolling the streets to keep law and order as there was no police force.

The soldiers had wide powers. They could order people to do anything for them. Ordinary people could be told to feed soldiers or give them somewhere to sleep. If soldiers were marching somewhere, they could force people to carry their bags or just walk in to their homes and take an ox-cart or pack animal.

The Romans had an efficient system of government. Ruling over the whole empire was the emperor (called Caesar in the Gospels, which was a title rather than a name). Jesus was born during the reign of the great Emperor Augustus, who organized the empire with great efficiency. The emperor during Jesus's ministry was Tiberius. He was a bad emperor. He hardly ever went to Rome and lived a life of indulgent luxury and splendour.

Each province and district had a senior Roman official in charge, usually appointed directly by the emperor. Two such governors are mentioned in the Gospels. Quirinius was in charge of the province of Syria, and Pontius Pilate, who was prefect of Judea and who sentenced Jesus to death by crucifixion. From records outside the gospels we know that Pilate was a cruel man.

The Romans allowed the Jews some freedom, and to have kings in various parts of Judea. All of these were members of the Herod family. Herod the Great had started to build the temple in Jerusalem for the Jews. He died about the time Jesus was born, and his area was split between three of his sons, all of whom are named in the Gospels: Herod Philip, Archelaus and Herod Antipas. They had limited, but real, powers to govern aspects of life.

The Roman occupiers were hated. The Herods, though, were thought to have more sympathy with the Romans than with their countrymen, and they were too powerful to displease. The people who collected taxes for

the Romans from merchants and ordinary householders, however, were despised and seen as traitors.

The greatest critics of tax collectors were the Pharisees, a group of about 6,000 men. They were very traditional in their beliefs and practices. Jesus often came into conflict with them because they taught that the only way to be right with God was to practise all the tiny laws which they said were contained in the scriptures. The Pharisees were very fussy. Jesus said that they had lost sight of the real meaning of the law. They were so busy sticking to all the tiny little laws that they ignored all the big ones.

Sometimes allied with them were the Sadducees who were a snobbish group of leaders, mostly priests, who only accepted the written laws of the scriptures, not the others

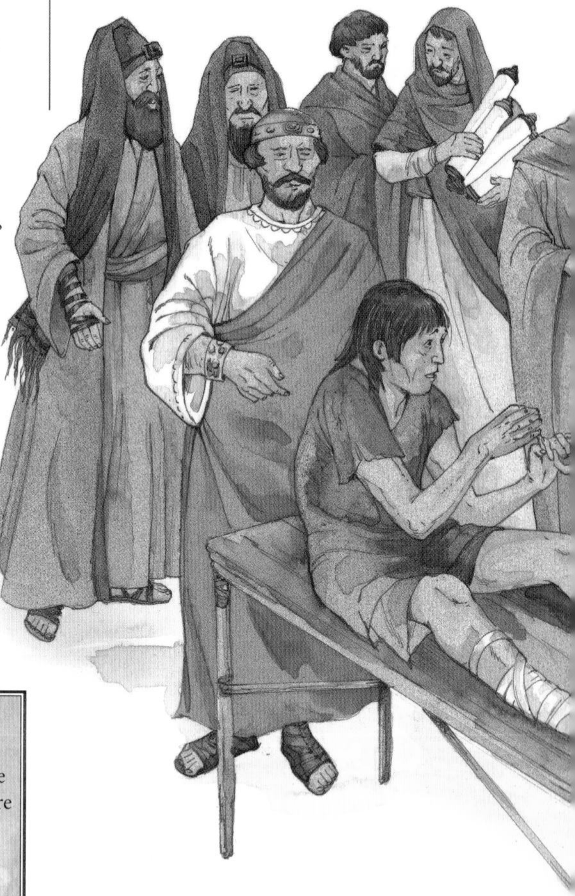

> ⚘ **PEOPLE AT THE TIME OF JESUS** ⚘
>
> This picture shows Jesus healing a paralysed person (centre). Watching him are a number of people who we encounter in the Gospels. From left at the back there are two Pharisees and two Sadducees. In the blue robe is a tax collector. Roman soldiers stand at the back, and on the far right are two Essenes. In the foreground is a local governor (left), such as Herod Antipas, and a Roman emperor (right).

which the Pharisees had added. Unlike the Pharisees at the time, they did not believe in life after death.

Other religious groups existed in the area but are not mentioned directly in the Gospels. Among them were the Essenes. They were scattered in monastic communities all over Judea, but their most famous community was at Qumran near the Dead Sea, where the Dead Sea scrolls were found. They had a strict rule of life. It is sometimes thought that John the Baptist grew up among the Essenes but there is no direct proof of this.

Dead Sea scrolls

The "Shrine of the Book" is in a museum in Jerusalem where some of the Dead Sea scrolls are kept. They were found in 1947 in caves near Qumran by the Dead Sea and were the library of the community that once lived there. The scrolls contain ancient copies of all the Old Testament books except the Book of Esther.

Roman Worship
This is the Temple of Castor and Pollux, the twin gods who the Romans believed helped them win battles. The Romans worshipped many gods, and built temples to them through the Empire.

Gladiators in Rome
The Roman Emperors were famous for putting on grand shows for the Roman citizens. This is the Colosseum, where the Romans made men, called gladiators, fight wild animals and each other.

The Apostles

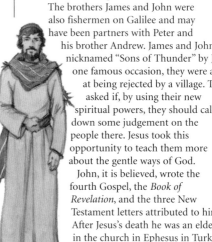

JOHN

Jesus had many disciples. The word means "one who learns". They were people who followed Jesus about the countryside whenever they could. They thought about His teaching, watched His actions, and tried to live in the way He taught. At some point early in His ministry, Jesus selected 12 particular disciples to become an inner core, that He would teach to become leaders in the church.

Later, they were called apostles, which means "one who is sent". They were Jesus's agents sent into the world to spread His teaching. At least some of them, such as Peter and Matthew, had been called as individuals first. Jesus taught the apostles privately, and restricted some of His more significant miracles (such as the stilling of the storm) to them alone.

Within the circle of twelve, there was an even smaller inner circle of three: Peter, James and John. We do not know much about the backgrounds of the disciples, but certain things do stand out.

Peter's birth name was Simon, which means "stone" in Greek. He was dubbed Peter (the rock) by Jesus. He was the spokesman of the group. Peter often opened his mouth before thinking, and as a result sometimes offended people. Passionate, impulsive and dedicated, he seems to have been the sort of person who would be your friend for life if he liked you.

He was a fisherman from Lake Galilee, and owned a boat which Jesus used

PETER

from time to time for transport and also as a floating pulpit when he preached to large crowds by the lakeside. At the crucifixion, Peter denied ever knowing Jesus. Filled with remorse he was forgiven, and became the leader of the first Christians. He also became the first disciple to take the gospel to non-Jews. He was martyred in Rome by the emperor Nero about AD66. It is believed that he was the source of information behind Mark's Gospel.

The brothers James and John were also fishermen on Galilee and may have been partners with Peter and his brother Andrew. James and John were nicknamed "Sons of Thunder" by Jesus. On one famous occasion, they were angry at being rejected by a village. They asked if, by using their new spiritual powers, they should call down some judgement on the people there. Jesus took this opportunity to teach them more about the gentle ways of God.

John, it is believed, wrote the fourth Gospel, the *Book of Revelation*, and the three New Testament letters attributed to him. After Jesus's death he was an elder in the church in Ephesus in Turkey. He was later exiled to the prison island of Patmos in the Aegean.

JAMES

ANDREW

TIMELINE 10BC TO AD30

• Jesus is born to the Virgin Mary and Joseph in Bethlehem

• Herod orders the death of all baby boys under the age of two in an attempt to kill the baby Jesus.

10BC   THE BIRTH OF JESUS

• Jesus is presented in the Temple

EMPEROR AUGUSTUS 29BC-AD14

• Jesus is found in the temple talking to the religious elders

JESUS IN THE TEMPLE

James was to become one of the first Christian martyrs, executed by King Herod in about AD43. He is not the same James as the one who later led the church in Jerusalem and wrote the New Testament letter bearing his name.

Andrew, Peter's brother, was not one of the inner circle, but deserves a special mention. He comes across as the most gentle and caring of the disciples. It was Andrew who first brought Peter to Jesus. "Come and see!" he'd cried excitedly to his (probably elder) brother. It was Andrew who saw the possibility of using the five loaves and two fish to feed the 5,000. And it was Andrew who, with Philip, brought some non-Jews to Jesus, too. He was a man of vision. It is believed that he was crucified in Asia Minor in about AD60.

Matthew was a tax collector, also called Levi, and he gave up his despised job to become a disciple. He did not, however, become the treasurer of the group. That job fell to Judas Iscariot, who became infamous later as the one who

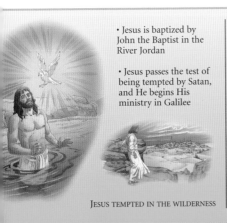

JUDAS

LIP

MATTHEW

THOMAS

handed Jesus over to the rulers. Why he did this has remained a mystery. The Gospels indicate he was prompted by the devil. We know that when he saw that Jesus was to be executed, he gave back the money he had been paid to betray him and committed suicide.

Thomas, known as the doubter, was missing from the group when Jesus first appeared to them after the resurrection. He refused to believe their stories. Only later, when he was able to see and touch Jesus for himself, did he believe in His resurrection. The experience was life-changing; it is believed that he went on to form the church in India.

Little is known of the others. There is even some confusion over their names in the Gospels (like Peter, many of them seem to have had more than one name). They were Bartholomew, another James, another Simon (also called "the Zealot"), Thaddeus (also called Judas) and Philip.

THADDEUS

BARTHOLOMEW

SIMON

JAMES

• Jesus is baptized by John the Baptist in the River Jordan

• Jesus passes the test of being tempted by Satan, and He begins His ministry in Galilee

JESUS TEMPTED IN THE WILDERNESS

• Jesus performs His first miracle, turning water into wine at the wedding in Cana

THE FIRST MIRACLE

JOHN THE BAPTIST EXECUTED

• John the Baptist is executed by Herod at the request of his step-daughter, Salome

AD30

THE MAN OF MIRACLES

After gathering His disciples, Jesus travels widely in the lands around the Sea of Galilee, preaching His message. He tells stories to make what He has to say easier to understand, and performs miracles that show that He is indeed the Son of God. Many people begin to follow His teachings, but there are also those who question whether He really is the Messiah.

Introduction

JESUS spent much of His time in Galilee, the northern part of the country where He had grown up. He worked His way southwards, possibly visiting Jerusalem briefly several times. Here you can read about some of His teaching and miracles in Galilee, and then in Jericho and elsewhere.

Among the outstanding things He did were: feeding 5,000 people with just five loaves and two small fish; walking across the choppy waves of the sea; appearing to three of His disciples in His heavenly glory; and raising Lazarus from the dead.

Much of His teaching was in parables, simple stories based on everyday events which contained deep truths about God and His plans. Jesus used parables because it was easier for the people around Him to understand what He was saying in the form of a story. Some of Jesus' most famous stories are included here: the good Samaritan who cared for a stranger; the lost sheep that was found by a loving shepherd; the prodigal son who came home to say sorry; the proud Pharisee and the humble tax collector; and the unmerciful servant who didn't do to others what had been done to him.

Jesus's teaching remains as relevant today as it was 2,000 years ago. Among the subjects He covered were how to handle money and possessions, how to regard people we don't like, what God's plans are for life after death and how to get ready to meet God.

Jesus was a legend in His own time. People didn't know what to make of Him. Some thought He was just a great prophet, others thought He was one of the past

Jesus Christ
This painting of Jesus shows Him with a halo, a bright circle of light, around His head. Haloes like this first appeared in artwork in the 400s. The circle symbolizes perfection.

Judea and the Sea of Galilee
Jesus spent about three years travelling around Galilee teaching and healing the people that He found. He performed many miracles on and around the Sea of Galilee, such as walking on water, and feeding the 5,000 people.

prophets come back to life. He was watched with great interest because people in 1st-century Judea did believe that the promised Messiah, God's specially chosen servant, would come to them soon.

Jesus's followers were called disciples. Jesus had chosen twelve of these as His special companions, who are sometimes called apostles. One day, when Jesus was talking to His 12 disciples, He asked them who they thought He was. Peter, who acted as spokesman for the group, blurted out, "You are the Christ! The Son of the living God!" He got it right, although he hadn't worked it out for himself. Jesus said that it had been specially revealed to him by God.

However, even Peter and the others didn't really know exactly what that meant. The Messiah they expected was a military liberator who would chase the Romans out of Judea and set up a Jewish state which would be the envy of the world. The Romans had conquered all of Judea as part of their great empire, and they had left soldiers to keep the people of Judea in order. Some rich people made the best of the presence of the soldiers. Also, tax collectors were employed to collect money for the Romans, but this meant they were hated by the normal people. Most people resented the presence of the Romans, and wanted them out of their country. When Jesus arrived, saying He was the Messiah people expected Him to rid them of the Romans, but that was not Jesus's aim.

Jesus set about showing them, as well as explaining to them, who He really was. Soon after Peter's "confession" Jesus took Peter, with James and John, up a mountain where He was "transfigured" or transformed in front of their eyes. He glowed with heavenly glory. "That's the sort of Messiah I am," He was saying. "God's Son from heaven, not a soldier from earth."

When He fed the 5,000 with five loaves and two fish, He was demonstrating that as the Son of God He was also the Creator of all things and could provide what people needed. It was a lesson in both religion and faith. And when He walked on water, He was showing that nothing on earth was beyond His power to control.

His healing miracles showed that God cared for people in every part of their lives. With His raising of Lazarus from the dead He showed that death is not the end. Even this doesn't defeat God. There's something more to come.

Some people were so offended by the way Jesus wanted to change the old traditions and re-interpret the law of God that they dismissed Him as a trickster and a false teacher. Jesus was saying that important people had been misinterpreting the teachings of the Bible for generations. Although most people struggled to understand Him, no one who really watched Him or listened to Him with an open mind was ever quite the same again. And Christians today would say that hasn't changed down the centuries, either.

❖ THE MAN OF MIRACLES ❖
Here you can read the stories of Jesus's teaching and miracles throughout Galilee, and in Jericho

FEEDING THE FIVE THOUSAND
Matthew, Ch. 14, Mark Ch. 6, Luke, Ch. 9, John, Ch. 6.
JESUS WALKS ON WATER
Matthew, Ch. 14, Mark, Ch. 6.
JESUS'S MINISTRY IN GALILEE
Matthew, Ch. 16 to 25, Mark, Ch. 9 & 10, Luke, Ch. 10 to 19.
OPPOSITION TO JESUS GROWS
John, Ch. 6 & 7.
LAZARUS RAISED FROM THE DEAD
John, Ch. 11.
JUDGEMENT DAY
Matthew, Ch. 25.

The woman from Samaria
The Samaritans had been hated by the Jews since the time of the Exile when the Samaritans had taken over the sacred city of Jerusalem. Jesus, though, preached to Samaritans as well, extending the word of God to everyone.

Jesus and the Sea of Galilee

THE Sea of Galilee, and the region that surrounds it, are where Jesus spent much of His time, preaching to the people of the area, and teaching them about the new ways that He wants them to live their lives.

The Sea of Galilee is actually a lake, through which the River Jordan flows. This supply of fresh water means the Sea of Galilee is home to great numbers of fish, such as carp and tilapia, also known as Saint Peter's fish. The fishing grounds in the Sea of Galilee were famous throughout the Roman Empire, so the people of Galilee were able to export a lot of their catch, they would sell it to other countries. The Sea of Galilee is 211m below sea level and is surrounded by steep hills. This means that fierce storms can start on the lake at almost any time. Jesus and His disciples were sometimes caught out on the lake in these storms, but Jesus was miraculously able to calm the waves and get everyone safely to shore.

The fact that Jesus grew up in Galilee is reflected through all the Gospels. Many of His miracles and His parables relate to the type of work that ordinary people at this time would have done, and relate to the sorts of agriculture that would have been familiar to people at the time. Not only is Jesus drawing on the sort of experiences He would have had growing up, but He is telling His stories using characters and places with which His audience are familiar. When Jesus performed a miracle and fed 5,000 people with five loaves of bread and two fish, the fish that He used were almost certainly tilapia or carp, caught by local fishermen in the Sea of Galilee.

Throughout Jesus's parables we see a similar situation. He talks about agriculture, about farmers, and vineyards, and He uses the relationship that the Jews had at the time with people like the Samaritans to make His point. Ever since the time of the Exile, the Jews had hated the Samaritans, who were the people that the conquering Babylonians had moved to the sacred city of Jerusalem. Jesus uses this in His parable of the good Samaritan. He chose someone that His audience believe will not help the injured man to make the point that race and colour do not matter in God's kingdom, that the hated Samaritan who helped is more the man's neighbour than the priest and the Levite who did not.

Jesus's ministry in Galilee was a mission of preaching and healing. He healed a wide range of problems, from paralysis and blindness to leprosy and demon possession. He even raised people from the dead. There were many people at the time who claimed to be able to cure people of these problems – Jesus was different not only in that He could genuinely cure them of their illnesses, but He did not use the sort of elaborate rituals that many people would have used to try to impress the audience. Jesus's power and authority over evil is unquestionable, so a single word of command was enough.

Jesus is also remarkable in that most of the miracles that He performed are not in order to show how powerful He is. He pities people for their suffering, and because He is the Messiah, the son of God, He is able to cure these people miraculously. When He is not healing people He is still helping them, such as when He feeds 5,000 people with five loaves and two fishes, or when He calms the storm, or even when He turns water into wine at the marriage in Cana. He is not reserved about what He is able to do, He helps miraculously because He is the Christ.

There are, though, exceptions to this. When Jesus walked across the water to reach His disciples, He was not helping anyone. But in this case He was teaching His disciples, He was making it clear to them who He was, and making it clear to Peter that faith can achieve anything.

We can see on this map the areas of some of Jesus's miracles, and some of people He healed and the events in His life.

Roman influence

The influence of Rome runs through the whole of the New Testament. Jesus was raised during the occupation, and was crucified according to Roman law. While there were problems with the Romans, as far as the people of Judea and Galilee were concerned, they gave a great deal to the people. Their buildings were very advanced for the time, for example, this is a magnificent Roman amphitheatre. By AD200 the Romans had built over 80,000km of good roads through their empire.

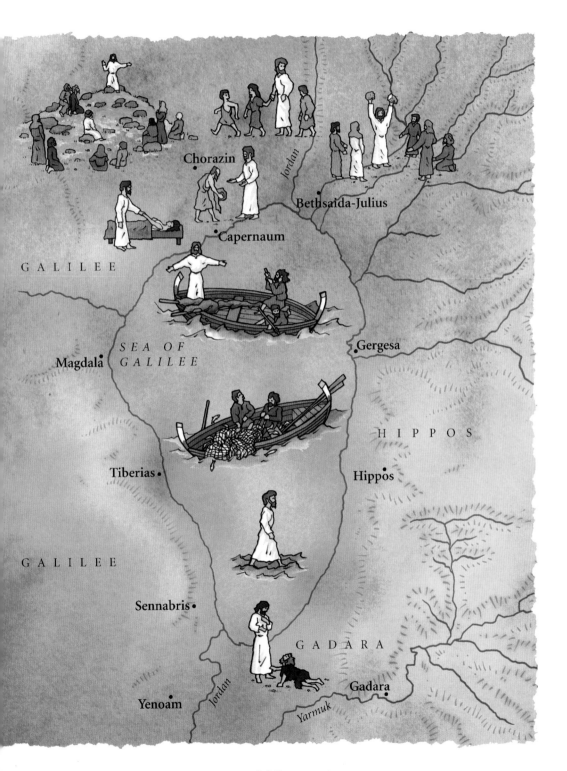

Chorazin

Jordan

Bethsaida-Julius

Capernaum

GALILEE

SEA OF
GALILEE

Magdala

Gergesa

HIPPOS

Tiberias

Hippos

GALILEE

Sennabris

GADARA

Yenoam

Jordan

Gadara

Yarmuk

Feeding the Five Thousand

THE twelve disciples had accompanied Jesus on His travels for many months. They had also spent several weeks in pairs on the road. Without Jesus present, they taught His message, healed lepers and cured diseases. By the time they rejoined their master, they were exhausted.

Times were even more trying for Jesus. The crowds grew bigger every day. However, many of the Pharisees and Sadducees refused to accept Jesus's teaching. They longed to get Him out of the way. Finally, on top of everything else, Jesus's cousin, John the Baptist, had been executed after spending several months in King Herod's dungeons.

One day Jesus and His 12 friends got into a little boat and sailed away from the crowds across the Sea of Galilee towards the quiet northern shore. They all urgently needed some rest and some peace and quiet.

At last it was peaceful! The sounds of the crowds were blown far away by the wind. Jesus and the disciples could hear nothing but the comforting swish of the sea, the gentle flap of the sail and the friendly cries of the seagulls.

However, the hundreds of people on the shore weren't going to be put off. On foot and on donkeys, they set off at once racing round the coast, joined by others they saw on the way. By the time Jesus's boat reached the far shore, to his surprise there was a massive throng waiting in anticipation for Him.

Instead of getting angry, Jesus just sighed.

"Look at them milling about," He said gently. "They're like sheep without a shepherd."

As the disciples guided the boat in the people started clamouring for Jesus to heal them. Even though Jesus was tired, He agreed to stay and the crowd settled down. Putting His exhaustion aside, Jesus began to speak. . .

Jesus was still preaching to the massive crowd when it began to grow dark.

"Master," said the disciples, "it's getting late now and we're a long way from anywhere. You should tell everyone to leave and find some food and a place to stay."

"You give them something to eat," Jesus replied bluntly.

The disciples looked at each other anxiously. They thought there must be over five thousand people listening to Jesus. How were they going to be able to feed them?

"We have only 200 denarii between us," they protested.

Washing rituals
The Pharisees had many religious ceremonies. This is one of the ritual baths they used for washing as a sign of spiritual purity. Jesus taught that people became pure by saying sorry to God and by living His way, not by taking part in ceremonies.

Popular catch
The carp fish, shown above, was one of the main fish living in the Sea of Galilee at this time, so it was a fish often caught by fishermen. It may well have been the sort of fish Jesus had in the story.

Loaves and fish
This ancient mosaic shows the kind of loaves and fish Jesus might have used. The picture reminded people that Jesus could provide for all their physical needs. It also reminded them that anything offered to Him, however small, could be used by Him to do good.

"Even if we find somewhere to buy bread, we would need a fortune to be able to buy enough food for everyone here. There won't be anywhere near enough to go around."

"All we've got at the moment is what this lad has brought with him," Andrew added, guiding a young boy with a basket through the crowd. "Five loaves of bread and two fish. But they're not going to go very far among this many people!"

"Tell everyone to sit down," Jesus said quietly, taking the basket from the boy. When everyone was settled, He said a blessing over the loaves and the fish and broke them into

> **"** *Taking the five loaves and the two fish he looked up to heaven, and blessed and broke the loaves.* **"**

pieces. "Now share them out among the people," He instructed His disciples calmly.

To everyone's utter astonishment, there was more than enough bread and fish to satisfy everyone. It soon became clear that there would be enough leftovers to fill 12 whole baskets.

Baking bread
In Bible times, fire was usually lit inside the stone oven rather than underneath it. When the stones were hot, the fire was raked out and dough placed on the sides (sometimes even on the outside) of the oven where it baked. The bread came out looking like flat rolls, or fat pancakes.

Fishing nets
The fish Jesus used were caught in the Sea of Galilee. Fishermen either dragged nets behind their boats or cast them from the shore.

> ✢ **ABOUT THE STORY** ✢
>
> *Jesus was the host at this gathering, and took the responsibility of feeding all of the people. His miracle reminds us that Jesus, the Son of God, is the Creator and Sustainer of all things and that we are dependent on God for all our needs. It also reminds people that Jesus not only cares for the physical needs but also our spiritual needs.*

Jesus Walks on Water

THE news rippled through the crowd that Jesus had used only five loaves and two fish to feed them.

"A miracle! Jesus must be the prophet that was promised to us," came the delighted cries. "Let's make Him our king!"

The people began to shout for Jesus to speak again. So Jesus turned back to the disciples huddled round Him.

"They're obviously not going to let me go for a while," He said to his 12 friends, kindly. "Why don't you start back without me?"

"But Lord, how will you..?" the disciples protested.

"Don't worry, I'll catch up," Jesus reassured them.

Wearily, the friends went down to their boats, climbed aboard and sailed away from the crowds.

Eventually people went home. Jesus wanted to talk to His Father, so He climbed into the hills to pray.

Meanwhile, the disciples were in trouble. A strong wind had blown their boats off course, into the choppy open waters. The night grew darker. They lost sight of the shore and the stars. They felt lost and afraid. As they searched for the glimmer of the dawn, they saw a pale glow in the darkness that lengthened into the white form of a man.

"It's a ghost!" the disciples cried, shrinking away in fear.

Then a familiar voice called to them above the gusting wind and the crashing waves.

"Don't be afraid!" it said. "It's me, Jesus!"

The disciples didn't know what to think. So many strange things had happened to them recently! Nothing was as it seemed any more.

Fishing boat
Boats like this were used on the Sea of Galilee. They were powered by a single sail and by oars. They were large enough to carry about a dozen men.

Sea food
This plate from Roman times is decorated with images of sea foods. People using decorations like this shows how important the sea was to people in Biblical times. Not only was it used for food and water, but also transport and trade.

PETER LEARNED AN IMPORTANT LESSON: HE COULD DO WHAT JESUS WANTED WHEN HE HAD COMPLETE FAITH IN JESUS AND TRUSTED HIM ENTIRELY. PEOPLE NEED GOD'S HELP TO DO HIS WILL. ❧

Anchor
Just as an anchor stops a ship drifting, so God's promises to us are firm and secure. They will keep us safe from harm.

Peter peered forwards, squinting through the darkness. "Lord, is it really you?" he cried. "If it is, tell me to come to you across the water."

"Come! Come!" Jesus's voice floated across to them.

> ❝ *When they saw Him walking on the sea they thought it was a ghost.* ❞

Peter swallowed hard and stood up. Gingerly, he made his way to the edge of the rocking boat and looked down into the swirling water. Then he lifted his head and focussed on the white shape in the distance. "It is Jesus, my friend," he said to himself. "Jesus has told me to come to Him." Peter stepped out of the boat.

The other disciples couldn't believe it. Far from plunging into the depths, Peter was walking away from them on the water! Step by step across the tossing waves he went, as steadily as if he was strolling along the sand on the shore, not walking across the sea itself in a storm.

But when Peter looked down at the seething water beneath him, his courage suddenly deserted him. "Help me, Lord!" he yelled in a panic. "I'm sinking!"

Jesus reached out a hand and heaved Peter up. "You have such little faith in me! Why did you doubt me?"

Jesus put His arm around His friend and guided him back to the boat. Instantly, the waves and wind fell calm. The other disciples in the boat had seen it all.

"Lord!" they cried, falling at Jesus's feet. "We know you truly are the Son of God!"

Navigation
At this time people used the stars to guide them at night. This picture shows the Pole Star and Ursa Minor at the centre, with the constellations (going clockwise from the left) Draco, Cephius, Cassiopeia, and Camelopardus.

High places
Mountains and hills in Judea provided many places to go to, to pray alone. It is not likely that the Jews felt they were nearer to God in high places, but that mountains reminded them of God's power.

❖ ABOUT THE STORY ❖

This is one of Jesus's strangest miracles. Most of His miracles helped people by healing or feeding them. This one is meant to teach the disciples about Jesus. No one can walk on water, and only God could overrule the laws of nature. Hence Jesus was showing them, in a way they could not doubt, that He was God in human form.

Peter the Rock

ONE day Jesus and His disciples were on the road to Caesarea Philippi. For once, there was no one else around and they could talk freely. Jesus seized the opportunity to have a very important conversation.

"I sometimes call myself the 'Son of Man'," Jesus said, as they tramped along the dusty path. "What do people think I mean by that? Who do people think I am?"

The disciples shrugged.

"Some say you are John the Baptist..." one began.

"Or the great prophet Elijah come back to us..." interrupted another.

"Or one of the other prophets from the old days, like Jeremiah," suggested another.

Jesus shook His head and sighed.

"But who do you think I am?" He asked quietly.

Peter replied without a moment's hesitation. "You are the Christ, the Son of the living God!" he said.

Jesus smiled.

"You have been blessed, my friend," He told Peter. "My Father in heaven has helped you to understand this."

Jesus rested His hand on Peter's shoulder.

"You are Peter the rock," said Jesus, "the rock on which I will build my church – a church that nothing will be able to destroy, not even death. Peter, I will give you the keys to the kingdom of heaven, and whatever laws you lay down on earth will stand in heaven too." Jesus looked around at the little group.

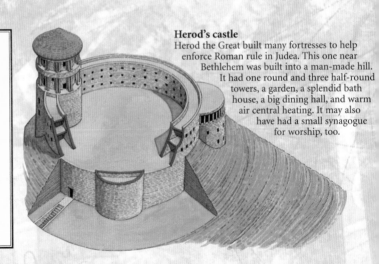

✧ **ABOUT THE STORY** ✧

When Jesus called Peter "The Rock" he was playing on the meaning of Peter's name, which is "stone". The message he and the others preached was like a "rock", strong and firm. Peter also became the first leader of the church and the first disciple to preach to non-Jews. Peter was an effective foundation upon which the church could be built.

Herod's castle
Herod the Great built many fortresses to help enforce Roman rule in Judea. This one near Bethlehem was built into a man-made hill. It had one round and three half-round towers, a garden, a splendid bath house, a big dining hall, and warm air central heating. It may also have had a small synagogue for worship, too.

"It is most important that you tell no one that I am the Christ. No one at all. But since you all know who I am, I should tell you what is going to happen to me."

Jesus's tone was deadly serious. He breathed a deep sigh.

"The time is coming soon when I will have to go to Jerusalem, and things will become extremely difficult there. The elders and the chief priests and the scribes will make a great deal of trouble for me and I will have to go through a lot of suffering. Eventually, they will even put me to death." The disciples gasped. "But," Jesus said, holding up His hand to silence them before they could protest, "on the third day after my death I will be raised back to life again."

> ❝ And He began to teach them that the Son of Man must suffer many things. ❞

Peter couldn't get over what Jesus had just said.

"God forbid, Lord!" he cried, absolutely horrified. "Such dreadful things should never happen to you!"

Jesus drew Himself up, straight and determined.

"To take an easier way would be to give in to the devil's temptations," he explained. "Peter, you are seeing things through human eyes. You aren't seeing them as God does."

Peter sadly hung his head.

"Now," Jesus announced to all the friends, His voice kind but firm. "Anyone who wants to follow me is going to have to sacrifice all their pleasures and comforts. They will have to be prepared to face danger and hardship, pain and suffering. To follow me even to the death, if needs be."

Jesus looked at the disciples' anxious faces.

"But I tell you this," He assured them. "Anyone whose main concern is to keep safe and content will lose the chance of eternal happiness. Yet anyone who gives up their life for the sake of me and my teachings will live for ever in heaven. For what good is it if you win the whole world, but lose your soul in getting it? And what could be more precious to someone than their soul? Believe this – the Son of Man will one day come again in heavenly glory, and everyone will then be repaid for all they have done."

As they walked on, the disciples' minds were perplexed and their hearts heavy with dread at what Jesus had warned lay ahead.

Jesus and His disciples
This carving depicts the moment when Jesus told the disciples that He would be killed and then raised in Jerusalem.

Peter and the keys
This painting shows Jesus giving Peter the keys of heaven. This shows that the disciples had the "key message" which enabled people to find God.

Herod's coins
The Romans allowed the Jews to mint their own coins. The coins here were minted by Herod the Great, Herod Agrippa or Herod Antipas. Usually Jewish coins had pictures of plants or man-made objects on them.

A Vision of Glory

ABOUT a week after Jesus's solemn conversation with the disciples, He asked Peter and the brothers James and John to go with Him up a mountain to find a quiet place to pray. They left the other disciples at the foot of the slopes with a bustling crowd. The four friends reached a peaceful spot and settled down to pray.

Peter, James and John were so wrapped up in their prayers that they had no sense of time passing. It could have been minutes, it could have been hours.

As Jesus prayed, His face turned towards heaven. He was utterly motion-less, like a living, breathing statue. It was as if He was present only in body and not in spirit; as if He couldn't hear the birds wheeling and crying overhead nor the wind gently ruffling His hair.

When the three disciples had finished praying they turned to watch Jesus, not daring to move or speak. They waited and waited... and still Jesus went on praying. After a while, Peter, James and John felt as if they were sinking into a trance themselves. Then something seemed to stir them. They shook themselves awake to an amazing sight.

Jesus's face began to shine with an inner glow. It grew lighter and lighter until it was more radiant than the sun.

His robes began to glisten and gleam – brighter and brighter until they were a dazzling white. While Peter, James and John shielded themselves from the glare, two other glimmering figures appeared. Jesus opened His eyes and stood up to talk to them.

To the three disciples' astonishment, they realized that the heavenly newcomers were Moses and Elijah – the mighty law-giver and the greatest of the prophets! They heard them discussing with Jesus the terrible trials He was to face in Jerusalem – what He was going to suffer and the way He was going to die. And as Peter, James and John watched and listened – totally transfixed – they saw the great prophets Moses and Elijah start to move away, gradually beginning to fade into the distance.

> ❝ *His face shone like the sun, and His garments became white as light.* ❞

"Master!" Peter cried out urgently, not wanting the magnificent vision to end. "It's wonderful that we're here. Allow us to make three shrines – one for you, one for Moses and one for Elijah..."

Mount Tabor
This is one possible site of Jesus's transfiguration, where He appeared as a heavenly being to Peter, James and John. There was a town on its top even in Jesus's day, so it wouldn't be easy to be alone there. Some scholars think that the transfiguration happened on the more remote Mount Hermon.

P ETER WANTED TO BUILD SHRINES BECAUSE HE WANTED TO KEEP THE FIGURES ON EARTH. HE HAD TO REALIZE THAT SPIRITUAL EXPERIENCES CANNOT BE PRESERVED. ∾

As he was speaking, a cloud surged above them, blotting out the luminous skies and throwing darkness over the ground. A voice boomed down from heaven, saying, "This is my Son, my Chosen One; listen to Him!"

At the sound of the almighty voice, the three disciples fell on their faces in terror. When it had finished speaking, they felt the cloud's shadow lifting from over them. They felt Jesus's gentle touch upon them and heard His familiar voice saying, "Get up. Don't be afraid."

When Peter, James and John looked up, Jesus was alone – just a seemingly ordinary man, as before.

As the three stunned disciples followed their master down the mountain, Jesus told them not to tell anyone at all what they had seen and heard, not until He had risen from the dead.

Peter, James and John were bewildered. There were so many things that the three of them didn't understand.

"What do you mean, you will 'rise from the dead'?" they asked Jesus. "Besides, why should the Son of Man suffer and be condemned to death? And why does it say in the scriptures that Elijah must return before all this is to happen?"

"Elijah's return is to prepare the way for the Son of Man – and in fact he has already been here," Jesus explained. "But the people did not recognize him. They

did to him exactly what they liked, just as they will do to the Son of Man." At last the three apostles realized with a shiver that Jesus was speaking of John the Baptist.

Jesus with Moses and Elijah
Moses gave the Old Testament law to the Jews, and Elijah was the greatest prophet of the Old Testament. Jesus came to complete their work.

John the Baptist
John the Baptist was Jesus's cousin, who prepared the way for the coming of Jesus. He was executed when Herod promised his step-daughter anything she wished after she danced for him. Her mother told her to ask for John's head because he had criticized her marriage to Herod.

> ✦ **ABOUT THE STORY** ✦
>
> *Jesus had taught that He came from heaven, and this incident showed the disciples what heaven was like. It helped them to believe that He really was the Son of God, as Peter had declared a few days earlier. They saw the purity and holiness of heaven as a bright light. Visions of God's holiness often make people realize just how sinful they actually are.*

Moving Mountains

JESUS, Peter, James and John came down from the mountain to find a noisy crowd surrounding the disciples who had remained behind at the foot of the slopes. The companions hurried to find out what was going on. Suddenly Jesus was swamped by people all shouting at once.

Jesus raised His hands and motioned for everyone to be quiet. Then He spoke. "Will someone please tell me what you are squabbling about with my disciples?"

An anxious-looking man immediately stepped forward. "Teacher, I came with my son to find you. He's ill. It's like there's an evil spirit in him which suddenly throws him to the ground. He foams at the mouth and jerks horribly, then stiffens like a board. I asked your disciples to cast out the evil spirit from my son, but they couldn't."

Jesus looked around at the nine embarrassed and deeply puzzled disciples. Thanks to Jesus's gift of healing powers, they had been able to perform many miraculous cures on their own. But each disciple had tried to heal this particular boy, and no one had had any success.

"My faithless friends! How long must I put up with you?" Jesus scolded. "Now bring the child to me."

Jesus had barely laid eyes on the boy when he collapsed.

"How long has he been like this?" Jesus asked.

"From childhood," the boy's father sobbed. "It's very dangerous, too. It's like the evil spirit wants to kill him! My son has fallen onto the fire and even into water."

The child moaned and tossed.

"I beg of you," the upset man continued, "if it's possible to do anything, please help us."

> **❝** *All things are possible to him who believes.* **❞**

"My friend," Jesus replied, "anything is possible if you only have faith."

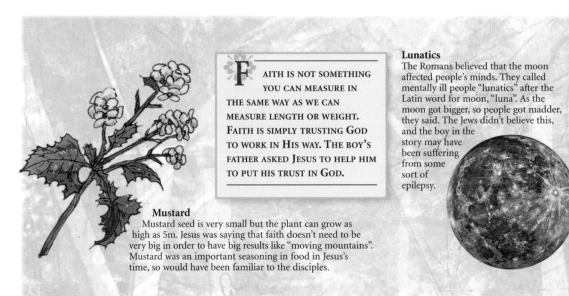

FAITH IS NOT SOMETHING YOU CAN MEASURE IN THE SAME WAY AS WE CAN MEASURE LENGTH OR WEIGHT. FAITH IS SIMPLY TRUSTING GOD TO WORK IN HIS WAY. THE BOY'S FATHER ASKED JESUS TO HELP HIM TO PUT HIS TRUST IN GOD.

Lunatics
The Romans believed that the moon affected people's minds. They called mentally ill people "lunatics" after the Latin word for moon, "luna". As the moon got bigger, so people got madder, they said. The Jews didn't believe this, and the boy in the story may have been suffering from some sort of epilepsy.

Mustard
Mustard seed is very small but the plant can grow as high as 5m. Jesus was saying that faith doesn't need to be very big in order to have big results like "moving mountains". Mustard was an important seasoning in food in Jesus's time, so would have been familiar to the disciples.

down and took the boy's hand in His own. At once, the child's fingers quivered. Then they tightened around Jesus's grasp. Finally, he opened his eyes, and Jesus helped the dazed child to stand up.

While the crowds were still with them, the disciples said nothing to Jesus about the healing. But as soon as they were on their own, they asked Jesus why He could cure the boy when they couldn't.

"It's because you have so little faith," Jesus explained. "Even if you had faith the size of a mustard seed, nothing would be impossible for you. You would be able to move mountains."

The father's eyes lit up with hope. "I believe you can help my unbelief!" he cried.

Jesus turned to the writhing body of the boy.

"Spirit! I command you to come out of him!" He ordered, sternly. "Never enter him again!"

Immediately, the boy began to thrash more violently than ever. Fits convulsed him, his arms flayed in the empty air and his legs juddered. The onlookers gasped as the boy gave a final groan and collapsed into a crumpled heap.

His father was left motionless with shock, appalled and terrified. But the crowd began to whisper.

"He looks as though he's dead," someone muttered.

Everyone fell silent as Jesus stepped closer. He bent

Charms
The Romans used lucky charms like this bulla to ward off evil spirits. The Jews did not believe that charms could defeat spirits. Jesus often cast evil spirits out of people to show that God was always more powerful than evil.

Fire
Fire was essential to life, but it was not easy to light so people kept them burning all the time. The boy could have fallen in at any time. This model is of an Egyptian fanning a charcoal fire to make it burn brighter.

Jesus and the Children

JESUS's disciples had a lot to learn. While they were following Jesus down the road to Capernaum one day, they began a silly argument.

"Which one of us is the best, then?" was the question that started it all.

"Well," someone piped up, "I've known Jesus the longest..."

"Ah, but that doesn't necessarily make you the greatest," someone else quickly protested.

"I reckon it's him," came another voice, "because he's done the most miracles."

"No, no, no," another voice insisted. "I think it's whoever prays hardest..."

And so they went on... and on... and on.

The disciples didn't think that they had been overheard. But when they had reached their destination and had settled into their lodgings, Jesus asked them, "So what were you discussing on the way down here?"

The 12 men fell into an embarrassed silence. None of the disciples could look Jesus in the eye. Some of them shifted awkwardly from foot to foot and began to fidget.

It was as if Jesus had heard every word. Or maybe He just knew what was in all of their hearts.

"If you want to be considered great before God," Jesus said, "you must put others first and yourself last. Here on earth, the greatest people are thought to be those who have the most servants to run around after them. But in the kingdom of heaven, the greatest people will be those who have willingly done the most to help others."

> ❝ *Let the children come to me, and do not hinder them.* ❞

Jesus reached out to a little child that was running by and she smiled as He drew her toward Him.

"Look at this simple, earnest child," He said. "Unless you give up your worldly values and become like this little girl

❖ ABOUT THE STORY ❖

There was nothing sentimental about Jesus's attitude to children: He knew they could be as awkward as anyone else. He also knew they could teach people something about trust. He wanted to stop the disciples from discriminating against people. They did not think of children as fully human yet; Jesus accepted them, and everyone else, just as they were.

Capernaum
This was an important town on the north-west shore of the Sea of Galilee, close to where the River Jordan enters it. It was the home of Peter and other disciples, and was where Jesus began His ministry. He preached in the synagogue there shortly after He was baptised.

ou will never even set foot in the kingdom
f heaven. It is those who are selfless and
iving like children who are the greatest
n the kingdom of heaven. Their angels see
God face to face. Always respect those who
ave a simple, childlike faith. For in doing so
ou'll be honouring me and my Father. If you sneer
nd look down on them, you'll end up wishing that
ou'd drowned yourself in the depths of the sea."

But the disciples didn't remember their
esson for long. Some weeks later, after Jesus
ad been preaching for the whole day, the
isciples saw that some people were
ringing their children to Jesus so He
ould bless them. While some of the
ttle ones were shy and hung back,
iding behind their parents' legs,
thers ran round boisterously. The
isciples began to shoo the children away,
eeling sure that, at the end of such a long
ay, they must be annoying the weary
reacher. But Jesus stopped them. "Don't
end the children away. Let them come to
he," He scolded, "for the kingdom of
eaven belongs to them." Jesus bent down
mong them so the children could wrap
heir arms round His neck and climb onto
His lap. "Unless you are like this – able to
ive yourselves wholeheartedly – you will
ever be able to enter the kingdom
f heaven."

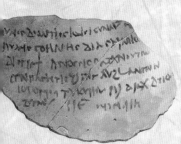

God's provision
This is a receipt issued by a Roman tax
ollector. Jesus told people not to get
vorried about money and possessions,
out to have the simple faith of a child
nd trust their heavenly Father to provide
or their needs.

Children
Jesus used children as an example of
faith and trust. Children do not usually
have the same worries as adults, and
took Jesus at His word.

God's children
This picture shows that all people are
God's "children". That is, He cares for
them like a good parent.

The Rich Man's Question

JESUS stood up and drew His robes around Him, ready to take to the dusty road once more. But before He and His disciples were quite ready to set off, a man came running up to them.

"Wait!" he was crying. "I beg you to wait!"

The friends stood patiently while the man dashed up and knelt at Jesus's feet. The disciples were a little surprised, as the man was well-spoken and dressed in what were obviously very expensive clothes. It was strange to see such a wealthy person kneeling to anyone!

"Good teacher," the man panted, trying to catch his breath, "please tell me what I have to do to win eternal life."

"Why do you call me 'good'?" Jesus asked gently. "No one is good but God alone."

The man looked puzzled, so Jesus just answered his question with a kind smile.

"You know the commandments," He said, "Do not kill, do not pursue another man's wife, do not steal, do not lie, respect your father and mother, and love your neighbour as yourself."

"Master, I have tried my hardest to keep all these commandments ever since I was a little boy," the man said.

"Then there is only one other thing you must do," Jesus said, His voice low. "You must sell everything you possess and give every penny of all the money you make to the poor."

Dyeing clothes
Rich people in Biblical times, as today, liked to wear richly coloured clothes. Wool (and linen for rich people and priests) was dyed in vats like this.

The eye of the needle
Jesus's humorous saying about camels passing through the eye of a needle means that people who trust in their wealth or status cannot get into heaven. Only people who trust God – rich or poor – can enter His presence.

The man's eyes widened. Then his face fell, and he [bo]wed his head. "Thank you, master," he said and slowly [go]t to his feet and turned away.

> ❝ *Sell what you have, and give to the poor, and you will have treasure in heaven.* ❞

The disciples watched the man trudge off down the [ro]ad. He was deep in thought, his shoulders slumped and [hi]s heart heavy.

Jesus understood that He had just told the man to do a [d]rastic, life-changing thing. He realised that it would be [ex]tremely difficult for him to carry out the instruction. Yet [H]e also knew that it was a necessary for him to do to get [to] heaven. He sighed.

"How difficult it is for those who are wealthy to enter [th]e kingdom of God!" Jesus remarked. "In fact, it is easier [fo]r a camel to pass through the eye of a needle than for a [ri]ch person to reach heaven."

The disciples were worried. After all, most people [w]orked hard to be comfortably off. Very few people would [fi]nd it possible to give away all that they owned.

"Surely no one will be saved then?" they asked Jesus.

"There are things that are impossible for people," He [re]plied, "but with God, there is always a way."

As Peter listened and pondered, a thought struck him.

"Lord, we have left everything to follow you – our [fa]milies, our homes, our possessions, our jobs," he said. [Is] this enough?"

"Anyone who has done what you have done will receive a reward a hundred times better than what they have left behind," Jesus assured them, "and eternal life will be theirs."

he colour purple
[T]he best and most expensive dye for [cl]othes came from the murex, a shellfish [in] the Mediterranean. It gave a deep [p]urple colour. Only rich people, [li]ke the man in the [st]ory, could [af]ford it.

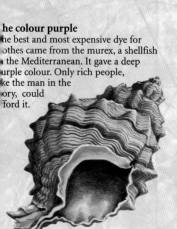

Flax
Flax grows in many parts of the world and has blue flowers. The stem of the plant can be soaked in water and its fibres separated and woven to make linen. Linen was more expensive than wool, and was woven in several grades from coarse to fine – fine linen was the most expensive.

❖ ABOUT THE STORY ❖

This story does not mean that rich people can't go to heaven. Jesus did not discriminate on the basis of wealth. People who have a lot of possessions tend to focus their life on what they have and can get. God then takes second place in their lives. Jesus said that God had to be first. Sometimes that's easier if you have nothing. You then trust Him for everything.

The Good Samaritan

JESUS seemed to know the scriptures and the law of Moses so much better than anyone else. The experts who had dedicated their lives to studying God's teachings were jealous of Jesus, and were always trying to catch Him out.

One day, a lawyer came to Jesus to put him to the test. "Teacher, what must I do to win eternal life?" he asked.

"What does the law tell you to do?" Jesus asked.

"It says to love the Lord God with all your heart and soul," the lawyer reeled off pat. "And to love your neighbour as much as you love yourself."

Jesus looked the lawyer firmly in the eye. "Correct," He said. "So there's your answer."

The lawyer wasn't satisfied. "Ah, but who is my neighbour?" he asked smugly.

Jesus answered the question with a story. "A man was travelling from Jerusalem to Jericho," He began, "when bandits attacked him on the road. There was no one around to hear the man's shouts for help. The bandits beat and kicked the man to the ground, until he lay bleeding in the dust. They stripped him of all his possessions and ran off, leaving him for dead."

The lawyer winced at the terrible crime and drew his cloak a little more closely around him.

"Some time later, a priest came along," Jesus went on. "But as soon as the priest saw the dreadfully injured man, he quickly crossed over to the other side of the road and hurried on past, trying not to look."

The lawyer was shocked. How could such a holy man have ignored someone in such need?

"The next traveller to come by was a Levite," Jesus said.

The Levite is sure to help, thought the lawyer. Levites are good people – so good that God rewarded their tribe with the highest positions of office in the temple.

"But the Levite did just the same as the priest," Jesus continued. "He took one look at the naked, bruised body and dashed by on the other side of the road."

The lawyer was appalled. He would have expected such behaviour of a Samaritan – one of the hated people who had taken over Samaria when the Jews were sent to Babylon – but not a Levite!

It was almost as if Jesus had read the lawyer's mind.

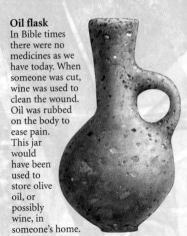

Oil flask
In Bible times there were no medicines as we have today. When someone was cut, wine was used to clean the wound. Oil was rubbed on the body to ease pain. This jar would have been used to store olive oil, or possibly wine, in someone's home.

The priest and the Levite
Although the story sounds amazing to us – we would expect religious leaders to help someone – there was a twist in it which Jesus's hearers would have understood. Neither of the leaders would dare touch a dead body, because it would make them "unclean" and unable to do their work for a while. They were thinking of themselves, not caring for their neighbour.

"The third person to see the dying man was a
[S]amaritan," Jesus announced.

[...] Well, that's it then, the lawyer thought, pulling a face. I
[b]et he goes over to see if there's anything to steal and then
[k]icks him when he finds there isn't!

> ## ❝ *When he saw him, he had compassion.* ❞

Jesus said, loud and clear, "The Samaritan was horrified
[t]o see the injured man and rushed over at once to help."

The lawyer couldn't believe his ears!

"The Samaritan cleaned the man's cuts and bandaged
the wounds. Then he put the man up on his donkey and
went to the nearest town. The Samaritan gave an
innkeeper some money to look after the man until he was
better. 'If you spend more than that,' the Samaritan told
the innkeeper, 'I'll pay you back when I next come this
way.' Which of these three travellers would you say was the
neighbour of the man who was attacked?" He asked.

"The one who helped him," mumbled the lawyer.

"Yes," said Jesus. "Then go and behave the same way."

IT IS ALWAYS EASIER TO DO
WHAT WE WANT THAN TO
DO SOMETHING THAT IS BETTER
FOR OTHERS, BUT IT IS ALSO
COSTLY. THIS STORY TELLS US
THAT GOD'S WAY IS SOMETIMES
THE HARD WAY.

Lawyers
The lawyers who opposed Jesus were also
called "scribes". They were people who
copied out the religious law and taught it
to others. Jesus said that they had failed
to apply their own teaching in the way
God intended.

❖ ABOUT THE STORY ❖

*This parable is probably one of
the best known of all of Jesus's
stories. People today still talk
about a kind person as a "good
Samaritan". Jesus wanted
people to live out their faith in
practical ways. He also implied
that we cannot please God just
by caring for our neighbour
and ignoring God. The two
commandments belong
together: love God, love others
as much as you love yourself.*

Joy Over Repentance

FOR centuries, the Jews had always looked up to their religious leaders with the utmost respect. However, these leaders often looked down their noses at the Jewish people.

Jesus's new style of religious leadership was dramatically different. He was often to be found visiting the poor and the sick, laying his hands on lepers or dining at the houses of the hated tax collectors. He not only walked, talked, ate and slept among the common folk, he genuinely seemed to enjoy their company, too. And, in turn, He won vast numbers of their hearts. Jesus never turned anyone away – no matter how lowly their position was in society or how hated they were because of their race or job. Jesus even befriended liars, thieves and vagabonds. Indeed, He often said that He had not been sent to meet good people, but to search out as many sinners as possible.

The Jewish leaders hated Jesus for mingling with those they saw to be the dregs of society. They couldn't understand how a holy man could bring himself to mix with sinners, criminals and down-and-outs. How degrading it was, they thought, to all those who tried hard to uphold the strict religious laws – and degrading most of all, to God.

One day, when a particularly poor crowd had gathered round Jesus to hear the word of God, the Pharisees and scribes began to grumble and complain even more loudly than usual. Jesus soon quietened them by telling a couple of stories.

"A shepherd had a flock of 100 sheep," Jesus began. "But when he came to round them up at the end of the day, he saw that one sheep must have wandered off and got lost. Without a moment's hesitation, the shepherd left his flock in the sheepfold and went off over the fields to look for the one missing sheep. He searched high and low for a

Beer jug
Most of the people Jesus met drank wine which was cheap and easy to make from the grapes grown locally. Beer was not widely drunk in Palestine. This beer jug is unusual and perhaps belonged to a rich person.

Silver ingots
In Old Testament times, people used silver ingots like this as money. The value depended on the weight. By New Testament times this was becoming less common for everyday trading, as there were many coins in circulation.

long time, and when he finally heard a lonely bleating he was overjoyed. The shepherd returned home with the stray animal, knocking on all his friends' and neighbours' doors to share the good news with them.

"And there was a woman who owned ten pieces of silver. Then, one night, one of them went missing. Determined to find it, she lit a lamp and searched through the house, sweeping every nook and cranny, turning out every corner and cupboard, shifting every piece of furniture, until she found it. 'Hooray!' she cried to her friends and neighbours. 'I have found my lost piece of silver!' And they all celebrated with her."

At first, the disgruntled Pharisees and scribes were puzzled at the stories. They didn't see what lost sheep, or a woman losing her money, had to do with them. But their faces grew red with embarrassment when they heard Jesus's explanation.

> **Just so, I tell you, there is joy before the angels of God over one sinner who repents.**

"Like the shepherd's joy over his one lost sheep, there will be more gladness in heaven over one sinner who repents than there will be over 99 good people who do not need any forgiveness. And like the woman's happiness at finding her single piece of silver, there will be great celebrations in heaven for each and every sinner who repents – no matter how common or humble they are."

I T IS VERY EASY TO LOOK DOWN ON PEOPLE WHO ARE LESS WELL OFF THAN US OR WHO HAVE "STRAYED" FROM GOD'S WAYS. CHRISTIANS ARE CALLED TO LOVE SUCH PEOPLE JUST AS GOD LOVES THEM.

Palestinian house
Most houses in New Testament times were quite small and often only had one room (on two levels). Jesus would have lived in such a house, and visited many others. Animals were kept on the lower level; the family ate and slept in the raised area. The flat roof might be used for drying crops or eating and sleeping on in summer. Cooking was usually done outside. The windows were narrow and had no glass.

The Story of the Prodigal Son

JESUS had a powerful parable for the snooty religious elders about showing forgiveness to sinners. "Once upon a time," He began, "there lived a wealthy farmer. He had two sons who worked beside him on the land and he was content that they would inherit the farm when he died and would look after it well. However, one day the younger son came to him with a proposition.

"'Father, I'm old enough now to choose my own path,' the lad said, 'and I want to go off and see the world.' He shifted about from foot to foot, looked down at the floor and nervously cleared his throat. 'I was hoping you could perhaps give me my share of the farm now, in cash.'

"The farmer was more than a bit taken aback by this unusual request but, being a generous man who loved his sons dearly, he agreed. And as soon as the money was in the younger son's hand, he packed his bags and set off, looking for excitement and adventure.

"Unfortunately, the lad wasn't as mature and capable as he had thought. He managed to travel a long way, saw lots of sights and eventually made it safely to a distant city. But there he fell in with a bad lot of friends, who were only too willing to help him squander his money. Before long, the boy found his purse was empty. Of course, the moment the farmer's son hit hard times his "friends" disappeared. He found himself alone and penniless.

"He knew there was nothing else for it but to try to find a job. However, a dreadful famine suddenly swept the country and everyone tightened their belts. It was no good begging for scraps or rooting for leftovers – there weren't any.

And the only work the boy knew how to do – farming the land – was scarce. The desperate young man was thankful to get a job as a lowly swineherd.

"Every day as the farmer's son drove the pigs out to feed he had to fight off the urge to eat some of the pigswill for himself. He was miserable and starving.

"'On my father's farm even the hired hands have enough to eat,' he moaned to himself, 'and they still have food left over. Why, oh why did I leave home!'

"Bit by bit, the lad swallowed his pride.

"'I want to go home,' he finally decided. 'I'll go back to my father and beg his forgiveness for being such an arrogant fool. I won't even dare ask him to accept me back as his son, but perhaps he'll take me back as one of his labourers – and that's more than I deserve.'

"The farmer's head had been filled with thoughts of his son every single day he had been away. He had worried over him and missed him, and hadn't stopped loving him for one second. When the landowner saw his child's familiar figure approaching from the distance he ran to meet him as fast as his ageing legs would carry him.

> ❝ *Father, I have sinned and I am no longer worthy to be called your son.* ❞

"'Father,' the trembling boy wept, as his father enveloped him in a huge bear-hug. 'I have sinned against God and against you. I am no longer worthy to be called your son.'

"'Bring out my best robes!' the farmer interrupted, calling to his servants. 'Dress my son in my best clothes! Put my ring on his hand and new shoes on his feet! Bring that calf we were saving for a festival and cook it up into something really special! We're going to celebrate and feast like never before. My long lost son has come home!'

"While the younger son was filled with repentance and gratitude, his older brother was furious.

"'Father, what do you mean by all this?' he demanded angrily. 'How am I supposed to feel? I have stayed here and worked with you all these years and you've never thrown a feast for me! But as soon as this loser shows up again, having wasted all your hard-earned money, you give him the best of everything you own!'

"With tears of joy in his eyes, the farmer took his eldest son by the hand.

"'Son, you don't know how much it means to me that you have remained by my side. And everything I have is yours. But today is a day to be glad. For your brother was dead to me and now he is alive; he was lost and now we have found him again!'"

Signet ring
The ring given by the father to his son was probably like this one, a signet ring. It might have had a family symbol on it. It was a sign of authority and honour, rather than being just a piece of jewellery. Rings were commonly worn by both men and women in Biblical times.

Ploughshare
Today, ploughs have steel "shares", the part that digs into the earth and turns it over. In ancient times they probably had iron blades which were fixed to the forked branch of a tree. Ploughs were pulled by oxen, often yoked together in pairs. The farmer walked behind, steering the plough by the handle. Ploughing was essential to preparing hard soil for the seed.

> ❖ **ABOUT THE STORY** ❖
>
> *This moving story is not really about the son at all, but about his father. The older man is always looking for the boy, and when he comes at last, the father is ready to forgive and forget his sins. Jesus meant that as a picture of God. He wants people to come back humbly to Him, and He will forgive what ever they have done that is wrong.*

Heaven and Hell

ALTHOUGH Jesus spoke often about the coming kingdom of God, many people didn't understand what He meant. They thought of the great rulers of the time who had magnificent palaces of gold and silver, treasure houses full of jewels, armies of golden chariots and armoured footsoldiers, and ranks of slaves to do their bidding. They pictured Jesus as the proclaimed king of the Jews and at the head of a mighty army, which would come marching through Judea, flags flying, to take charge of the country. The Pharisees once challenged, "So when is the kingdom of God coming, then?"

Jesus replied, "The kingdom of God will not come with great announcements and fanfares, nor will there be anything splendid to see. For the kingdom of God is inside you." Jesus was talking about a spiritual kingdom that exists through life and after death, where both good and wickedness will grow until the end of time. Then God will cast out everything that is evil, leaving only goodness.

As well as not understanding what the kingdom was like it was also difficult for people to accept Jesus's teachings on what they had to do to enter it.

"Everybody wants lots of money, a big house, an important job and expensive possessions, don't they?" they would wonder. "But Jesus tells us that none of these things are important in the kingdom of God – in fact, they can even stop you getting there!"

> ❝ *And at his gate lay a poor man named Lazarus.* ❞

"Yes," others would agree. "Jesus says that if we want to enter the kingdom, instead of envying those who have lots of servants, we should give our lives willingly to helping others. Instead of trying to get rich, we should give away everything we own to those who are poor."

One day, Jesus told the people a story that He hoped would help them understand before it was too late. "There was once a very rich man who lived in a huge house. Every day he dressed in the finest clothes and dined at a table overflowing with the best food. Each day a wretched beggar called Lazarus would crouch outside the gates of the mansion, dreaming of what it would be like to taste

A triumphant emperor
This is the sort of leader many people expected Jesus to be, a commander of an army riding into a city in a triumphant procession, such as the Roman emperor shown above. Instead Jesus came meekly, riding on a donkey.

Riches
These are Roman coins from the first century. The rich man was so greedy that he didn't think about God at all, and ended up separated from God in hell.

Judea
Judea was the name that the Romans gave to the area that the Jews called Judah. It was ruled by a Roman governor until after Jesus's death.

some of the rich man's leftovers. Lazarus was all alone,
starving and in rags. He was so miserable he barely
noticed the stray dogs who licked his filthy skin, or the
flies that crawled over his skinny body.

"Eventually, the poor man's suffering came to an end
and he died. And as he left the dirt and poverty of his life
in this world, angels hurried to carry his soul to heaven.

"Now it so happened that soon afterwards the rich man
died as well – but his soul was taken straight to the fires of
hell. As he suffered in torment, the rich man cast his eyes
heavenwards and saw the beggar standing side by side with
the great Abraham, father of the Jewish people.

"'Abraham!' the rich man screamed. 'Have mercy on me
and send Lazarus to cool my burning tongue with a few
drops of water! I am being burnt alive!'

"Abraham remained unmoved and his voice was stern.

"'Son, remember that on earth you surrounded yourself
with luxury and comfort, leaving Lazarus in the cold. Now
he is being comforted while you suffer. Besides, it's
impossible for those in heaven to be cast into hell, and for
those in hell to escape to heaven. Hell is an eternal
punishment.'

"The rich man groaned in despair. Too late, he began to
think of other people.

"'Then please at least send Lazarus to my father's house.
I have five brothers and they're all like me. They need
warning, or they'll all end up here!'

"Abraham shook his head.

"'No!' he bellowed. 'They have the words of Moses and
the prophets. If they don't heed those great people, they
won't take notice of any other voice from the dead.'"

WE CANNOT EXPECT GOD TO
GIVE US GOOD THINGS IF
WE NEVER SHARE OUR GOOD
THINGS WITH OTHERS. IN FACT, IF
WE DON'T LEARN TO GIVE, WE
WILL BECOME GREEDY AND SHUT
OFF FROM GOD'S LOVE.

Dogs
In New Testament times, Jews did not
have dogs as pets. They roamed the
streets and scavenged scraps. They
regarded them as vermin and "unclean".
So being licked by dogs made Lazarus a
complete outcast in Jewish eyes.

❖ ABOUT THE STORY ❖
*This story is about having right
attitudes to money and people
in this life. It refers to life after
death in the popular terms of
the day. It is not intended to
teach us more about eternity
than that some people go to be
with God and others don't. It
does show that we "reap" in the
next life what we "sow" in this
one, however. It encouraged
Jesus's hearers that God loves
those who are despised.*

Opposition to Jesus Grows

JESUS's preaching was sometimes so bold that it outraged many of the Jews.

"He says to us, 'I have come down from heaven'. How dare He!" many of them exclaimed. "This is just Jesus, after all, the son of Mary and Joseph!"

"He says to us, 'I am the living bread from heaven'!" others scoffed. "What on earth does He mean?"

Even some of Jesus's faithful followers were offended when He said, "He who eats my flesh and drinks my blood has eternal life, and I will raise him up on the last day."

"It's the spirit that's important," Jesus explained, "not the flesh that surrounds it. My words promise life."

After this, many of Jesus's disciples gave up in disgust.

"What about you?" Jesus asked His 12 closest friends. "Do you want to leave me too?"

Peter spoke up determinedly for all the disciples.

"No, Lord," he reassured Jesus. "You speak to us of how to win eternal life and we believe you. We have all come to know that you are God's Chosen One."

> ❛❛ The chief priests and Pharisees sent officers to arrest Him. ❜❜

"Yes, and I chose you," Jesus reminded them. "But I have to tell you, one of you will turn to evil."

The disciples were shocked, but Jesus would say no more.

By the time of the feast of Tabernacles, Jesus had

Soldiers
Roman soldiers were based in Judea to keep the peace. The chief priests also had their own guards and it was probably these who tried to arrest Jesus. However, it was the Romans who finally crucified Him.

❧ ARMOUR OF GOD ❧

The apostle Paul described to early Christians the armour that they would need to fight the power of the devil. He described it to them as if it were the armour of a Roman soldier.

Equipment	Meaning
Belt	Truth
Breastplate	Righteousness
Sandals	Gospel of peace
Shield	Faith
Helmet	Salvation
Sword of the Spirit	Word of God

offended so many of the elders that going publicly to Jerusalem was highly dangerous. But he was determined to celebrate the occasion properly. When the news spread that Jesus, a wanted man, was preaching openly in the temple, the Jews were amazed.

The chief priests and the Pharisees ordered his immediate arrest as a rabble-rouser. But the officers came back empty-handed.

"Where is He?" cried the chief priests and Pharisees. "Why haven't you brought Him to us?"

"He's an extraordinary man!" the officers answered sheepishly. "We've never heard anyone speak like Him. The crowds love Him. Everyone's talking about Him and wondering what He means! But even though He speaks strangely, He hasn't done anything wrong. What can we arrest Him for?"

The chief priests and Pharisees decided they'd have to trick Jesus into openly defying one of the laws and then He'd *have* to be arrested.

Next day, Jesus was teaching in the temple when the scribes, priests and Pharisees strode in to talk to Him.

"Teacher," they said to Jesus, dragging forward a frightened woman. "This woman is a sinner. She has been seen with another woman's husband. Now, the law of Moses says she should be stoned to death. What do you think we should do with her?"

Jesus stood up and faced the hostile officials. "Let him who has never sinned throw the first stone," He said.

Jesus's answer completely thwarted the authorities. He hadn't interpreted the law of Moses as they did, but His answer hadn't broken it either. After all, all of them had sinned in some way; they were only human. Lost for words, they stormed out.

Holy Communion
In this service, Christians eat bread and drink wine, which symbolize Jesus's body and blood, reminding people of Jesus's death on the cross for their sins.

Pens
These pens come from Roman times and may have been the sort used by the scribes in Judea. Scribes wrote letters for people and also copied the scriptures.

Bull sacrifice
The Jews sacrificed a bull in the temple once a year to show they were sorry for their sins. The New Testament says that 'the blood of bulls' cannot take away people's sins; only Jesus can do that.

Ungrateful Lepers

WHEREVER Jesus went, His fame as a healer spread before Him. One day ten figures, tattered and misshapen, stumbled into the path ahead. They stood a little way off and held up their hands. The disciples realized that the group was infected with leprosy.

"Jesus, master, have mercy on us," they moaned.

"Go and show yourselves to the priest," Jesus said.

Filled with hope, they did what He told them. The lepers hadn't gone far when they felt their skin tingle. They looked at each other in disbelief. Trembling, they felt the smoothness of their skin. They were cured! Weeping tears of happiness, they ripped off their bandages and danced with joy. They were cured!

> ❝ *Then said Jesus, 'Were not ten cleansed? Where are the nine?'* ❞

Some time later, Jesus and His disciples saw a stranger running towards them.

"Thanks be to God who healed me!" the man wept.

The astonished disciples realized he was one of the lepers, now totally cured.

"You're a Samaritan, aren't you?" said Jesus. "Tell me, where are the other nine I healed? Are you the only one who's come back to give thanks and praise God?"

❧ ABOUT THE STORY ❧

When the man came back, Jesus told him that his faith had made him well, that is "whole". He was healed not only in his body but in his spirit because he had come to worship God. Jesus healed people because He cared about their physical needs. But He also cared about their spiritual requirements and their life as a whole.

Lourdes

Healing is a mysterious thing. Even doctors don't always know why some people get better and others don't. Christians believe that people who are ill should pray for God's healing as well as go to doctors. Some make pilgrimages to special places such as Lourdes (seen here) where they believe God sometimes performs special miracles of healing.

The Power of Prayer

JESUS often said how important it was to pray – and He didn't just mean reciting long verses in the temple. He meant having private conversations with God about everyday worries and asking for personal guidance. This was a new idea for many people.

"If your child asked you for a fish or an egg to eat, would you give them a snake or a scorpion?" He said. "Of course not! Well, if you give good gifts to your children, think about all the wonderful things your heavenly Father knows how to give you if you only ask Him!"

> ❝ *And He told them a parable, to the effect that they ought always to pray and not lose heart.* ❞

Jesus realised that some people would misunderstand Him, and would expect to pray for something one day and have it the next. So He told a story to show that people should never stop talking to God, even if they felt their prayers weren't being answered.

"There was once an arrogant judge who had no respect for either God or people. He simply didn't care if justice was being done or not. However, every day a good woman would come to his house and bang on the door.

"'I am being wronged by my neighbour!' she would yell. 'Please come with me and consider the case, then you can give me a just verdict.'

"Day after day the judge ignored her. But she still turned up. 'She's never going to give up!' the judge finally burst out. 'She's going to plague me for ever!' And he went and sorted out her problem for her – just so she wouldn't bother him again."

Jesus told His disciples, "The woman was so determined that even the corrupt judge gave her what she wanted. So imagine how much faster the heavenly Father will respond to the pleas of those He cares for."

Votive hand
The Romans often sought healing by visiting the temple of their favourite god. They would make offerings to the god and say a prayer. Sometimes they would leave a model of the part of the body they wanted to be healed, such as this hand. This was called a votive offering. Some people left models of ears, which we assume was because they were deaf.

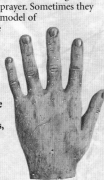

Physician and child
On this marble tombstone a doctor is seen examining a child. Medicine in the first century was very crude. On the ground is a cup for collecting blood, possibly taken to try to cure the child.

❖ **ABOUT THE STORY** ❖

Jesus taught that prayer isn't about trying to make God do what we want Him to do, but about finding out what God wants us to do. Jesus showed that God always wants the best for people, that is by getting to know and trust God even when life is difficult. God may know that wealth or healing is best for someone, but Jesus didn't promise that either were ours by right.

The Pharisee and the Tax Collector

THE Pharisees had been brought up from birth to think that they were special – different from common Jews and way above the likes of foreigners. And none of the lessons that Jesus taught through His stories managed to get through to them. The Pharisees took great pride in the way in which they carefully observed every single rule of the faith, and it blinded their eyes, sealed their ears, closed their minds and hardened their hearts. When Jesus preached how good people should befriend sinners and forgive them, the Pharisees merely scoffed. When Jesus taught that the wealthy should give all they had to the poor – even if they were ungodly, undeserving people – the Pharisees just sneered. It was impossible to shake their confidence in the righteousness of their own beliefs and habits.

Still, even though the Pharisees were Jesus's worst enemies, He never gave up trying to warn them about how they were falling unwittingly into sin.

"Once upon a time," He told His disciples, "two men went into the temple to pray. One was a Pharisee..."

The Pharisees in the crowd looked smug. How good we are, they thought, making sure we pray at all the right times!

"The other man was a tax collector," Jesus went on.

The Pharisees bristled. How dare a Roman-loving traitor venture into the holy temple before God, they thought.

Jesus saw the Pharisees' self-satisfied faces change to looks of disgust, but He went on regardless.

"The Pharisee strode straight into the centre of the temple, in full view of everyone. He made a great, solemn show of lifting his eyes and arms up towards heaven and then he began to pray out loud.

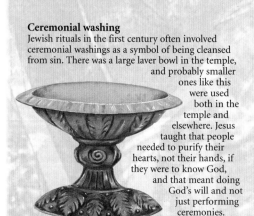

Ceremonial washing
Jewish rituals in the first century often involved ceremonial washings as a symbol of being cleansed from sin. There was a large laver bowl in the temple, and probably smaller ones like this were used both in the temple and elsewhere. Jesus taught that people needed to purify their hearts, not their hands, if they were to know God, and that meant doing God's will and not just performing ceremonies.

Roman gods
The Romans who had invaded Judea worshipped many gods, although they did not build temples to them in Judea and the Jews were not especially aware of them. Later, Christians encountered them a great deal. Jupiter (far left) was the king of the sky and god of thunderstorms. Minerva (left) was the patron goddess of craft and wisdom. She was also the patron goddess of the Emperor Domitian, who persecuted Christians.

'God, thank you for making me different from everyone else,' he announced. 'Thank you for lifting me above all the liars, thieves and scoundrels. I fast twice a week, I give a percentage of all I earn to charity and I'm glad about it. God, thank you for making me better than people like that no-good tax collector who crept in with me,' he cried.

"The tax collector was hiding behind a pillar in the furthest, darkest corner of the temple. He didn't dare venture out where anyone might see him. He hung his head and wrung his hands. His heart was heavy with the anguish of wrongdoing and the burden of regret.

"'Oh Lord, I am a sinner,' he whispered, looking at the floor in shame. 'I beg you to have mercy on me.'"

> ❝ *But the tax collector would not even lift up his eyes to heaven.* ❞

Jesus paused for a moment and looked round at the waiting faces of the crowd. He saw that the Pharisees were scowling, angry at how he had portrayed them as pompous, conceited windbags to everyone that was listening. But nevertheless, He looked them straight in the eye and He finished the story.

"I tell you, that day it was the tax collector who went home blessed by the Lord," Jesus said. "For all those who set themselves high will eventually fall, and all those who consider themselves lowly will be raised up."

The Pharisees stood up, fuming with cold rage. They turned on their heels and stalked off, their elaborate robes swirling out behind them.

Animal sacrifices
Many ancient religions offered sacrifices of animals. The Romans did it only occasionally, but butchers often slaughtered meat using special pagan ceremonies, and this caused the first Christians real problems of conscience. This sacrificial knife would have been used to slit animals' throats. It has an ornate lion's head on the handle.

Seat of Moses
Synagogues often had a stone seat at the front called the "Seat of Moses". The scribe who taught the law of Moses sat there, and in a sense was sitting in Moses's place. This ancient seat was found in a synagogue in Chorazin, in Galilee.

❖ **ABOUT THE STORY** ❖

This is an important parable because the attitude of the Pharisee is one which still exists in our society today. Jesus is saying that it doesn't matter how good a particular person is, they can never be good enough for God. This is because everyone has sinned in some way. Jesus told people not to compare themselves with others, but with God instead.

Martha and Mary

JESUS and His disciples were gradually drawing nearer to the capital city, Jerusalem. The 12 friends brooded on the awful things Jesus had told them would happen to Him when He got there.

One of the villages Jesus stopped at on His way to Jerusalem was Bethany. A woman named Martha invited Jesus to come and stay at her house.

Martha made sure that Jesus and His friends were cool and comfortable, and at once set about serving the weary people with refreshments. As she bustled in and out, carrying in jugs of wine, pitchers of water, drinking goblets and plates of nibbles, another young woman crept out of an inner room and quietly sat down.

> *Mary sat at the Lord's feet and listened to His teaching.*

"Mary, come and give me a hand!" Martha hissed at her sister, as she deposited another tray of food among the hungry guests. But Mary just shrugged and turned back to Jesus, listening intently to every word He had to say.

Martha stood there, hands on hips, more than a little bit annoyed. She too would like to sit with the great preacher and chat. But if she did that, everyone would be left hungry and thirsty. After all, someone had to get the

dinner... The dinner! She remembered with a shock the pot she had left boiling over the flames and hurried back to attend to it.

Martha made trip after trip to and from the kitchen, carrying in course after course of delicious food and taking out load after load of empty cups and plates. When the final morsel was laid on the table, she went to join Jesus and His friends. But how left out Martha felt by then! The disciples were deep in a conversation she couldn't follow; she had no idea what they were talking about or laughing at. And there was scarcely room for her to sit down at the very edge of the group!

Martha had been determined to show Jesus and His friends the very best hospitality she could provide – but in doing so she'd hardly seen anything of the great preacher she so admired. She looked at her lazy sister sitting there at Jesus's feet, gazing up at Him in awe! Martha's face was flushed, her arms were aching and now her lip began to tremble.

"Lord!" she burst out sobbing. "Don't you care that my sister has left me to do everything? Why don't you tell her to get up and help me?"

While Mary hung her head in shame and the disciples fell into an embarrassed silence, Jesus got up to comfort the poor woman.

"Martha, Martha," he soothed, "you have

concerned yourself with preparing and cooking all these different dishes when we only needed one to satisfy our hunger. Your sister has chosen the best dish of all – listening to me – and it will not be taken away from her."

Bethany
Bethany was a small village about 3km east of Jerusalem, towards Jericho. Jesus seems to have stayed here quite often and was very close to Mary, Martha and their brother Lazarus. This painting, found in a church in Bethany, shows Jesus raising Lazarus from the dead.

Tableware
Romans in the first century used elaborate plates and cups at their meal tables, although the Jews tended to use plainer ones. The potter was an important person in every town, because everyone needed his wares. Cups generally didn't have handles. There were no knives or forks, either – Jesus and His friends would have picked food out of dishes and eaten it with their fingers.

❖ ABOUT THE STORY ❖

Jesus is gently teaching Martha about priorities. She thinks that the most important thing is to entertain her guests, but it stopped her from learning about God through Jesus's teaching. She wasted a unique opportunity to be fed spiritually, because she was too concerned about physical food. Jesus taught that God was more important than food because life with Him lasted for ever.

Lazarus is Brought Back to Life

MARTHA and Mary had a brother, Lazarus, and they all became firm friends with Jesus. But the time soon came for Him to move on once again.

Some weeks later Jesus was preaching and healing far away when a messenger came to Him with an urgent request.

"Lazarus is seriously ill," the messenger explained, "so ill that Martha and Mary fear he is dying. They beg you to come as quickly as you can to make him well again."

The disciples knew how fond Jesus was of the family and expected Him to drop everything and hurry off. To their surprise, Jesus just remarked, "This will not end in Lazarus's death. He has been struck down as a way for God to show His glory through me." And Jesus calmly stayed where He was, continuing His work.

Two days later Jesus announced that He was heading back to Bethany. But the disciples were worried.

"Master, you have many enemies there," they said. "Some people have even sworn to stone you! Surely you shouldn't go back there."

"It is not time yet for my life to end. I will be safe for the moment," Jesus replied. "Now our friend Lazarus has fallen asleep and I must go and wake him."

"Lord, if he is sleeping, he will wake up on his own," the disciples protested, not quite understanding.

"Lazarus is dead," Jesus sighed, "and I am glad that I was not there when he died. Because of this, your belief in me will grow." Jesus smiled at His bewildered followers. "Now let's forget these fears and go to him right away."

By the time Jesus arrived at Bethany, Lazarus had been dead for four days. A pale-faced Martha came out of the village to meet Him.

"If only you had been here, Lord, my brother would not have died," said Martha, her voice cracking. "But I know that God will do anything you ask."

Jesus was filled with compassion at Martha's faith. He said to her, "I am the resurrection and the life.

Sarcophagi
This is an elaborate stone coffin. Only a few rich people in Judea were buried in them, however. Most dead bodies, including Lazarus and later Jesus, were wrapped up in bandages and placed on a ledge or on the floor of a natural cave or tomb cut out of a rocky hillside.

Sleeping
Jesus said that Lazarus was not dead, only sleeping, an image often used in the Bible. Jesus uses this image to teach His disciples that physical death is not the end, but leads to a new spiritual life.

Anyone who believes in me and dies will live again, and anyone who believes in me and lives will never die." He held Martha's gaze. "Do you believe this?" He asked.

"Yes, Lord," Martha whispered in awe. "I believe that you are the Christ, the Son of God." And she ran back to the house to fetch her sister.

As Jesus watched Mary and her grief-stricken friends, a shadow clouded His face. Mary fell at Jesus's feet and sobbed as if her heart was breaking.

Jesus asked her gently, "Where have you buried him?"

And as Jesus was shown the way to Lazarus's tomb, He too broke down and wept for His dear friend.

Lazarus had been laid in a cave, with a large rock rolled across the entrance to keep out wild beasts or bandits.

Jesus's voice was low and firm.

"Take away the stone," He ordered.

Martha gave a little gasp. "Lord, he has been dead for four days now. His corpse will smell."

"Didn't I promise you that if you only believe, you will see the glory of God?" Jesus replied. "Roll away the stone."

As Martha and Mary's friends began to heave the huge rock, Jesus began to pray.

"Father, I thank you for hearing my voice," he said. "I know that you always hear me. But I want everyone here to know and believe that it is you who sent me."

The friends heaved one last time and the rock moved aside. Jesus took a step forward and shouted into the gloomy interior.

"Lazarus!" His voice echoed. "Come out!"

No one moved a muscle.

All was perfectly still and silent.

And then they heard the sound of muffled footsteps coming towards them from the depths of the cave, and the dead man came slowly walking out into the sunlight, all wrapped up in a shroud. He stopped in front of Jesus.

> " *The dead man came out, his face wrapped with a cloth.* "

"Unbind him," Jesus ordered, "and let him go."

And the overjoyed Martha and Mary did just that.

CHRISTIANS STILL USE JESUS'S WORDS "I AM THE RESURRECTION AND THE LIFE" AT FUNERALS. IT REMINDS THEM OF THEIR BELIEF THAT THEY WILL RISE FROM THE DEAD WHEN JESUS RETURNS TO EARTH. ᴄ⟋

Tomb of Lazarus
Many years after New Testament times, people built this monument to Lazarus at the place in Bethany where they think his tomb was.

The Unmerciful Servant

MOST of the astonished men and women who had seen Lazarus walking out of his tomb believed they had witnessed a miracle. However, a few troublemakers thought it was a trick. They hurried to the chief priests and Pharisees, calling an emergency council meeting at once.

"What on earth are we going to do?" they grumbled. "It doesn't really matter whether He's genuine or not. If we let Him keep on like this, soon everyone in Judea will believe in Him. The Romans will think that there's a serious threat, crush the whole nation and destroy our religion."

The high priest Caiaphas had a different opinion.

"This Jesus will die for the good of us all," he prophesied. The chief priests and Pharisees wouldn't listen. From that moment on, they made up their minds that it was more important than ever to find a way to have Jesus put to death.

Jesus was well aware that He wasn't liked by everybody, but He always preached that people should forgive their enemies, such as the time when Peter came to him with an important question.

"Lord, how many times should I forgive someone who does me wrong?" Peter asked. "Up to seven times?"

Jesus replied, "Not just seven, but seventy-seven – forgive them every single time." And he told a story to explain why.

"There was once a generous king who had kindly lent money to several of his servants. The time came for the servants to repay their debts, and the king called them in, one by one. One servant in particular had borrowed a vast

sum of money – ten thousand talents, in total. And when it was this servant's turn, he stood in front of the king ashen-faced, his knees knocking. He had failed to make enough money to pay back what he owed.

"The king followed the terms of the contract and ordered that the loan should be made good by selling the servant, his wife and his children into slavery, and auctioning all of his possessions. The devastated man fell on his knees, sobbing and begging forgiveness.

"'My lord!' he cried. 'Have mercy on me! Bear with me a little while longer and I promise I will find every last penny that I owe you.'

"The good king took pity on the poor man and agreed to give him some more time to pay. Trembling with relief at his narrow escape, the servant rushed from the throne room. As he left the palace, he came across one of his

Prisoners go to work
This ancient stone relief shows prisoners handcuffed to each other and escorted by guards. They may be going to work. Most prisoners in ancient times worked in labour camps rather than being kept in jails.

Restraint
When prisoners were kept in a jail, they were usually shackled in some way. Having their feet locked in a kind of "stocks" was the most common form of restraint. Sometimes prisoners were chained to their guard to stop them escaping.

work colleagues, a man who owed him the rather small amount of one hundred denarii. The servant was desperate. Grabbing his frightened friend around the throat, he pushed the man up against the wall and threatened him. 'Give me my money!' the servant demanded. 'I need it now – or else!' Just as the servant had done, the man broke down and begged for more time to pay. The servant was ruthless. He had the man immediately flung into prison until he found a way to come up with the money.

"When the other palace employees heard about the servant's behaviour, they went to tell the king. Soon, the cruel man found himself back in the throne room. This time, the king wasn't smiling, he was frowning angrily.

"'You wicked servant!' the king roared. 'You begged me to be merciful, to not sell your belongings and put you in prison, and I gave you more time to repay your debt. Don't you think you should have shown similar forgiveness to your friend?' And the king had the hard-hearted servant thrown into jail at once."

> **❝** *Should not you have had mercy on your fellow servant, as I had mercy on you?* **❞**

Jesus explained what the parable meant. "The king is like my heavenly Father," he said. "And if you don't find it in your heart to forgive people, your punishment will be the same as the unmerciful servant's."

THE UNFORGIVING SERVANT WAS SELFISH. HE GRABBED HIS OWN FREEDOM BUT DENIED SOMEONE ELSE THEIRS. JESUS USED THIS AS AN EXAMPLE TO SHOW THAT PEOPLE SHOULD BE KIND TO EACH OTHER.

Forgiveness
This painting of Jesus offering forgiveness and a welcome into heaven reminds people that any sin is a sin against God. The New Testament teaches that forgiveness is offered freely by God as an act of grace.

⬥ ABOUT THE STORY ⬥

In this story Jesus wants His listeners to see how great God's forgiveness is, and to learn to treat each other as God treats them. It is hypocritical to accept His forgiveness yet not offer it to others, because people who love God are called to imitate His ways in their lives. Indeed, if people did not forgive each other, Jesus warned, they would be unable to appreciate what God had done for them.

Zacchaeus is Forgiven

ZACCHAEUS was a fat little man. A fat little man whom nobody liked very much. For Zacchaeus was Jericho's chief tax collector. And by collecting his countrymen's hard-earned money for the hated Romans – and taking extra for himself – he had made himself very rich.

"Here comes that traitor, Zacchaeus," people would say as they saw him walking down the road, and they'd cross over to the other side of the street.

"Here comes that crook, Zacchaeus," people would sneer as they saw him out shopping, and they'd shut up their market stalls to avoid serving him.

"Here comes that liar, Zacchaeus," people would whisper as they saw him entering the synagogue to pray, and they'd turn their backs as he went past.

All Zacchaeus's ill-gotten wealth couldn't make up for the hatred people felt towards him and for the loneliness of his life.

Just like all the other citizens of Jericho, for many months now Zacchaeus had heard stories of an amazing holy man called Jesus of Nazareth, who preached the most inspiring sermons and performed miracles of healing. And when Zacchaeus heard people gossiping outside his window of how Jesus would be passing through Jericho that very day, Zacchaeus was determined not to miss the opportunity to see Him. He locked up the tax office at once and went out into the street. It wasn't difficult to work out where Jesus was going to be. He could already hear a buzz of excitement coming from the other side of the city. Zacchaeus hurried off at once, as fast as his short legs would carry him.

By the time Zacchaeus reached the route that Jesus was expected to take, crowds of people had already lined the streets – ten or twelve people thick in places. Zacchaeus jumped up and down, trying to see over their shoulders, but he was too small. All he could see was row

upon row of the back of people's heads. So Zacchaeus tried pushing. He set his shoulder to the jostling wall of bodies in front of him and heaved, trying to squeeze through. All he got was his toes stamped on and an elbow in the eye. He was just as shut out of the ranks as before.

Then Zacchaeus had an idea. Huffing and puffing in the hot noonday sun, he set off again running – right down the pavement behind all the crowds. Hurry, hurry, he thought to himself. Hurry or you might miss him. Zacchaeus didn't quite know why he wanted to see Jesus so much, but he knew he did. He realized with surprise that nothing else would have got him running so fast through the streets of Jericho.

> 66 *And he sought to see who Jesus was, but could not because he was small of stature.* 99

Just when Zacchaeus thought that his legs were going to give way and his heart was going to burst inside his chest, he reached what he was looking for – a tall, thick sycamore tree that he used to climb as a boy. Come on, Zacchaeus, the panting chief tax collector thought to himself, you can still do it if you put your mind to it. And he reached up on tiptoe into its branches.

How everyone would have laughed if they had seen the fat man scrambling up the tree trunk in a most undignified way. No one was taking any notice. They were far too intent on peering into the distance to catch the first glimpse of Jesus coming down the road.

As Zacchaeus balanced himself uncomfortably among the branches, the crowd began to cheer and jump up and down. Way above their heads, Zacchaeus could see everything. Making their way slowly through the clamouring, grabbing people was a group of very simply-dressed men. And in the middle of them was a man with the kindest face he had ever seen.

Zacchaeus knew he had to be Jesus of Nazareth. The way Jesus smiled so gently at the noisy rabble all around Him made Zacchaeus feel truly ashamed of the swindling he had done in the past, and he longed to jump straight down from the tree and join him.

Jesus was drawing nearer and nearer, until He was right underneath Zacchaeus's sycamore tree. And the chief tax collector nearly fell off his perch with shock, for Jesus suddenly stopped, peered up through the leaves right at him and said his name.

"Zacchaeus, hurry up and come down," Jesus said. "I'm on my way to stay with you."

The crowd fell silent. They weren't just amazed to see Zacchaeus the chief tax collector nesting in a tree, they were also stunned that the holy man had even lowered Himself to speak to him – let alone say that He wanted to visit his house.

"What about us?" they began to murmur. "Why does the preacher want to go and stay with a nasty man like that?"

The delighted Zacchaeus didn't give them a chance to persuade Jesus to change His mind. The little man leapt out of the tree and bowed down before Jesus.

"Lord," Zacchaeus said, "you know that I am a sinner. However I stand before you today a changed man. I intend to give half of everything I own to the poor. And I'm going to look back through my records and give anyone that I've ever cheated four times as much as I owe them."

Jesus smiled and laid His hand on Zacchaeus's arm. "I have come to find people just like you," He said.

With that Zacchaeus eagerly escorted Jesus to his house.

PEOPLE WERE AMAZED THAT JESUS SHOULD TAKE ANY NOTICE OF A BAD PERSON SUCH AS ZACCHAEUS. BUT JESUS SHOWED THAT BAD PEOPLE OFTEN WANT TO BE LOVED AND ACCEPTED, AND THAT WHEN THEY ARE, THEY CAN CHANGE FOR THE BETTER WITH GOD'S HELP. HE CALLED HIS FOLLOWERS TO LOVE AND ACCEPT OTHERS, AND NOT TO JUDGE THEM.

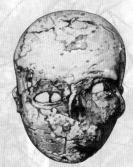

Jericho
Zacchaeus lived in Jericho, believed to be the oldest walled town in the world. This plaster-covered skull dates from about 7000BC. It was made when the people of Jericho prayed to their ancestors.

❖ ABOUT THE STORY ❖

Zacchaeus responded to Jesus with great generosity because he appreciated His forgiveness. The Jewish law said that a thief should pay back twice what he had taken, but Zacchaeus paid back four times as much. This is an example of "repentance": showing our sorrow by what we do. It was a sign that Zacchaeus had changed.

The Workers in the Vineyard

WHEN people came to see Jesus, and he was able to forgive them their sins, they had the chance to start again with a clean slate. One of Jesus's parables gave people a life-changing sense of freedom and hope. "There was once a land-owner who went out early one morning to the market place to hire workers," Jesus began. "He saw that there were many labourers waiting to be hired and he offered them the usual fee of one denarius per day. The men agreed and got down to work picking the grapes.

"Three hours later, the landowner went out again to the market place. Just as he had expected, several latecomers were hanging around hopefully.

"'If you're looking for work, go to my vineyard. I'll pay you a fair rate at the end of the day,' the landowner said.

"The pleased men hurried off straight away.

"At midday, the landowner went again to the market place and found workers who were delighted to be hired. And he went once more in the middle of the afternoon and picked up yet more grateful labourers.

"When there was only about one hour left before the

Treading grapes
In order to make wine, grapes need to be pressed to get the juice out. This was done by putting them into large vats and treading on them, as shown in this Byzantine mosaic from Beth-shan.

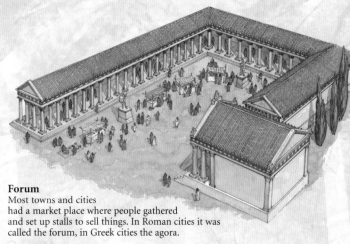

Forum
Most towns and cities had a market place where people gathered and set up stalls to sell things. In Roman cities it was called the forum, in Greek cities the agora.

abourers were due to down tools, the landowner hurried o the market place one last time, and soon there were ven more workers in his vineyard. He didn't want them o feel unwanted and go home without any wages.

"As the sun set, the landowner told his steward to hand ut the wages. The hot, exhausted men who had been vorking in the vineyard all day long were surprised when he landowner said, 'Pay the last shift of workers first.'

"'Evening shift – one denarius!' the steward announced, ressing a shiny coin into each of the worker's hands. The nen were startled and delighted. A whole day's pay for less han an hour's work. How generous the landowner was!

"The mid-afternoon shift stepped forward. If those who ave done less work than us have been paid one whole lenarius, they wondered, how much will we be getting?

"'Mid-afternoon shift – one denarius!' the steward cried.

"At first, the labourers were disappointed. But they soon heered up. We've still got a whole day's wages for less han a day's work, they thought.

"'Mid-day shift – one denarius!'

"This time the workers weren't at all pleased. Is this a oke? they wondered. We could have turned up at the very ast minute and still have been paid the same!

> ❝ *Now when the first came,*
> *they thought they would*
> *receive more.* ❞

"And then the steward called out for a final time. 'Early-norning shift – one denarius!'

"There was nearly a riot. 'What do you mean by all this?' demanded the men. 'You've paid these shirkers the same as us, yet we've toiled in the scorching heat all day long!'

"The landowner was calm and kind. 'Friends,' he said. 'I'm not cheating you. Didn't we agree that you'd be paid one denarius? It's my choice to give these latecomers the same wages as you. Can't I spend my money as I like?'"

When Jesus explained the parable, his audience's hearts leapt. "The kingdom of heaven is like the landowner and his vineyard," Jesus said. "Even if you only find your way to God at the last minute, you'll still be as welcome as those who have been with God a long time."

Grape picking
Vineyards, places where people grow grape vines, were important in Israel. Vines grew well in the sunny climate, so grape production was an important part of the economy. They were eaten as fruit, and pressed to make wine. They were also dried to make cakes of raisins. This Egyptian wall painting shows grape pickers harvesting the crop.

> ❧ **ABOUT THE STORY** ❧
>
> *Jesus intended this parable to be applied in two ways. First, it applied to the newcomers to the faith who were despised by the "old guard". Secondly, it applied to those who would come to trust Jesus later from outside the Jewish religion. In heaven, He was saying, all are equal. This is not to encourage people to delay believing in Him, but to reassure those who realize at the last minute.*

Blind Bartimaeus

EVERYBODY in Jericho knew Bartimaeus the beggar. He had been blind from birth and lived rough on the streets. Clutching his rags around him, he'd lift his dull eyes whenever he sensed people approaching and would hold out his begging bowl in hope. Occasionally, someone would take pity on him and drop a denarius into it. Bartimaeus was such a familiar figure that the people of Jericho had stopped thinking about his sad plight a long time ago.

One day used to seem very much like another for Bartimaeus. Every day he'd wake in darkness, sit by the roadside in darkness and then go to sleep in darkness.

But one morning, Bartimaeus got up to find that things were different. The road he sat beside was much busier than usual, and there were excited crowds hanging about all around him.

"What's going on?" Bartimaeus cried, as hordes of people swept past him in both directions. "Who are you waiting for?"

"Jesus of Nazareth is going to pass by here on His way out of Jericho," said a voice.

Bartimaeus's pulse began to race. He had heard people talking about Jesus of Nazareth before. Bartimaeus thought that the man sounded amazing. People said that you had only to hear Him talk and your spirits would be lifted. They said that He healed lepers, cured paralytics and even raised dead people back to life! Bartimaeus had longed to encounter the preacher for himself. He was sure that if the great man could do all these wonderful things, He'd be able to make him see, too. But he had never dared to dream that he might actually get the chance to meet the holy man.

Now, hope suddenly flooded into the blind beggar.

"Son of David!" he began to shout, forgetting everyone around him in his desperation. "Have pity on me!"

From somewhere, Bartimaeus found a strength he never knew he had. He raised his voice louder, determined that Jesus should hear him. As he did so, the noise of the crowd grew more excited all around him, and Bartimaeus knew that the holy man was nearby.

"Jesus of Nazareth, please have mercy on me!" he yelled, his cries ringing out above the hubbub.

"Shut up, Bartimaeus!" came voices from all around.

❧ ABOUT THE STORY ❧

When Bartimaeus used the term "son of David" he was recognizing that Jesus was not just a remarkable man but that He was also the Messiah. It was this "faith" which Jesus commended. The blind man's prayer, too, was one of faith and dependence. He asked first and foremost for mercy. He knew that before God, everyone was a spiritual beggar, whether they were rich or poor.

Hebrew calendar
Bartimaeus didn't live by the calendar because every day was the same to him. This is a fragment of a Hebrew calendar. It is divided into twelve months, but they are different from ours.

Jesus healing
This old painting shows Jesus healing Bartimaeus. Healing was one way in which Jesus showed people God's love and compassion in action.

"Oh Lord," the beggar gasped, "please let me see." Bartimaeus felt gentle fingertips on his eyelids and immediately the gloom began to lift into a thick fog that swirled and cleared into a world of bright colours, the beauty of which he had never been able to imagine.

> ❝ *He said, 'Lord, let me receive my sight.'* ❞

"Go in peace," Jesus said, "your faith has made you well." There was no way that the grateful beggar was going to leave the man who had given him such a precious gift. Joining on behind Jesus's disciples, Bartimaeus danced down the road, weeping aloud with joy and praising God.

We can't hear what he's saying."

But Bartimaeus just shouted louder than ever. "Jesus, son of David, take pity on me!"

"Bartimaeus, be quiet!" the voices came again – but this time they were filled with surprise. "Be quiet and listen! Jesus is calling for you. Quickly! Go to him."

In his hurry to get up, Bartimaeus got in a terrible angle in his tattered cape. He ripped it from around him and threw it away, groping his way forwards. All of a sudden, he sensed Jesus was there, right in front of him. "Bartimaeus, what do you want from me?"

FAITH IS BELIEVING THAT GOD CAN DO WHATEVER HE WISHES, AND TRUSTING HIM TO DO WHAT WILL BRING HONOUR TO HIM AND BE BEST FOR US. FAITH LETS GOD DECIDE WHAT THOSE THINGS ARE. ☙

Begging

Beggars were sadly a common sight in Bible times. They were often treated like vermin by some religious people, who believed that God had cursed them. Jesus went out of His way to help and heal poor people.

The Wedding Feast

JESUS once said, "Many that are first will be last, and the last first." By this, He meant that some of the most important and distinguished people on earth will eventually be considered worthless by God; and many people who are looked down on and despised on earth will be precious in God's sight. If you were someone who always seemed to be down on your luck, Jesus's words were very comforting. If you fell into the "important and distinguished" category though, like the Pharisees, His words were deeply disturbing – not just a criticism, but a warning, too.

One night when Jesus had been invited to eat at the house of a Pharisee, Jesus told a story that He hoped would help His host to reach heaven.

"Once upon a time there lived a king who had a dearly beloved son. The prince was about to get married, and the king gave orders for a fantastic wedding banquet to be thrown. Only the very best would do for his son! Menus were discussed, recipes were tasted, wine was ordered, entertainment was booked, invitations were sent out, seating plans were drawn up, the silver was polished, flowers were arranged. And after months of preparation, all was finally ready. The delighted king sent out his servants to summon the guests to the celebrations.

"But they all returned alone. Trembling, they ventured before the king one by one and gave the guests' pathetic excuses. One guest said that he'd just bought a field and he really had to go out and plough it straight away. Another said that he'd just bought a herd of oxen to do some urgent work on his farm. A third said he couldn't come because he'd only just got married himself, and he couldn't leave his wife! And so it went on…

"The king was deeply offended and disappointed by the rudeness of his friends and relations.

"'Go and invite them again!' he roared, and sent the servants scurrying off once more.

"But yet again, not a single soul would come.

"'That's it! I've had enough of that ungrateful lot!' the king bellowed. 'They don't deserve to come and enjoy themselves here anyway.'

"He called for his servants one more time.

"'Go out into the streets and lanes of my kingdom,' he told them, 'and bring me all the homeless people you can find. The poor, the lame, the blind – invite them all! I'm going to give them the party of their lives! And give everyone a special robe to wear in honour of the occasion.'

"The banqueting hall was soon filled with the joyous sounds of feasting. And on the top table, the king was the happiest of all. He sat and watched the total strangers with the utmost pleasure. They seemed to be enjoying his hospitality far more than his friends and relations had ever done, and they were certainly more grateful.

"Suddenly, among the rows of guests with their richly decorated and brightly coloured clothes, the king's eyes fell on a man dressed in rags. His plate was piled high with food and he was tucking in, oblivious to everything and everyone around him. The king sprang angrily to his feet and marched down the rows of guests to where the man was seated.

"'Where is your robe?' the king demanded. 'Everyone invited by my servants was given a robe as a gift. Get out of here! You're an impostor!'

"While the man mumbled and spluttered, searching in vain for an excuse, the furious king called for his guards.

"'Tie him up and sling him outside into the darkness!' the king ordered. Then he gave the signal for the party to carry on…

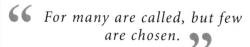

> **For many are called, but few are chosen.**

"Remember," Jesus told the alarmed Pharisee who had invited Him to dinner, "many receive a special invitation to join God's kingdom, but only those who whole-heartedly want to be a part of it will be allowed to enter."

Wedding entertainment
Weddings in every culture often include singing and dancing. In Judea people sang and danced to the music of pipes and lyres. These are Egyptian musicians.

Hammurabi
Hammurabi was a king in Babylon about 1,800 years before Christ. He is pictured at the top left of this 2.5m obelisk, receiving laws from the god Shamash. Engraved on this obelisk are 280 laws relating to such things as marriage, as the King's son in this story, and murder. Some, but not all, of them are like the laws that God gave to Moses.

❧ **ABOUT THE STORY** ❧

The picture of the kingdom of God as a wedding party shows that heaven is a joyful place, where people are united with God and can celebrate his love. They also need to be "clothed" in this life with his love, too, and not be wrongly "dressed" in bad ways of behaving, like the man in the story. Jesus said people couldn't expect to get to heaven if they just pleased themselves.

The Wise and Foolish Bridesmaids

IT was only natural that after listening to Jesus preach about the coming of the kingdom of heaven, people should ask, "Lord, when will this happen?"

Most of Jesus's disciples assumed that judgement day would be in the next few years, and certainly within their lifetimes. But Jesus explained to them in parables that only God knew when the end of the world would be.

"Picture ten bridesmaids at a wedding reception, waiting for the bride's new husband to arrive," Jesus told His disciples. "Darkness is falling, and the bridesmaids are standing outside with lamps to welcome the bridegroom in.

But five of the bridesmaids have been foolish. They haven't thought to take flasks of spare oil with them.

"Unfortunately, there's no sign of the bridegroom. He's taking such a long time that the bridesmaids' legs begin to ache from standing up for so long, and they all sink to the floor for a short rest. One by one, their lamps grow short of oil and flicker out. In the quiet darkness, the weary bridesmaids all drift off to sleep.

"Suddenly they're being woken by a shout. 'The bridegroom is on his way! The bridegroom is on his way!'

"They spring to their feet. The wise bridesmaids refill their lamps with the oil they've brought and light them up. The foolish bridesmaids are left looking rather daft.

❖ ABOUT THE STORY ❖

Jesus said that when He returned to earth, the world as we know it would end. Evil would be punished, justice would be seen to be done and God's people would be united with Him for ever. Before that, He said, there would be many troubles that His people would need to be ready for. This story tells Christians to keep alert so they are ready for whatever God wants to them do.

A modern wedding
Marriage is a sign that a couple are leaving their old family and setting up a new family or household together. They pledge their faith to each other and also to God. This is a modern Jewish wedding similar to the one Jesus's story is about.

IT WAS DIFFICULT FOR THE DISCIPLES TO UNDERSTAND THAT ONLY GOD KNEW WHEN JUDGEMENT DAY WOULD BE. JESUS SAID WE COULD BE JUDGED BY GOD AT ANY TIME, SO WE MUST ALWAYS BE READY. ❧

the five remaining bridesmaids hold their lamps high to light the way. Everyone bustles the laughing bridegroom into the house and when the last guest is inside, the door is closed behind them.

"When the five foolish bridesmaids return, their lamps lit once again, they are dismayed to find that they're locked out of the party. They bang on the door.

"'I'm sorry,' calls a voice, 'but I don't know you. I can't be sure who you are.'

"And the girls are left outside in the cold darkness.

"Don't be foolish like the five forgetful bridesmaids," Jesus warned His disciples urgently. "Make sure you're always prepared for God's coming, because you can never have any idea when it will be."

"'Please lend us some of your oil,' they ask their friends, somewhat sheepishly.

"The five sensible girls refuse. 'We're sorry, but we can't,' they explain. 'The bridegroom may still be a little way off yet, and if we share our oil with you, none of our lamps will last long enough. Why don't you hurry off and buy some more oil?'

> **And while they went to buy, the bridegroom came.**

"The bridesmaids do as their more thoughtful friends suggest, and it just so happens that while they're gone, the bridegroom arrives. The guests all come out of the house to meet him, and amid much joyous singing and dancing,

Torchlight procession
At Jewish weddings in biblical times, the groom usually went to the bride's house, then took her to his house for the party, accompanied by an ever-growing procession of friends and relatives. Sometimes the party was held at the bride's house. Often the procession was at night, hence the need for the lamps, as there were no street lights.

Oil lamps
Oil lamps provided the main form of lighting in Bible times. The shallow bowl was filled with olive oil, and a wick was draped over the lip and lit. In the house they were placed on ledges.

The Parable of the Pounds

DESPITE all Jesus's teachings, as he drew nearer and nearer to Jerusalem some of His disciples became more and more convinced that the kingdom of God was about to appear. They still expected Jesus to lead a revolution in Jerusalem to overthrow the Romans. Jesus knew, as He'd already told His disciples, that far from gaining political power, He was going to be arrested, tried and eventually put to death.

"While you wait for the coming kingdom of the kingdom of God," Jesus said, "make the most of everything God has given you." Then Jesus told them this parable.

"A prince had to travel far away to claim a kingdom that was his rightful inheritance. As he would be away some time, he called his trusted servants to him.

"'Will you look after things for me while I am gone?' he asked them, and he gave them his bags of money for safe-keeping – five bags of gold to one servant, two bags to another servant and one bag of gold to a third servant. Then the prince left to claim his kingdom, leaving the men to decide what to do with their borrowed fortunes.

"Year followed year, and the servants heard no word from their prince. Finally, he returned home, now a king, with a kingdom and all the fine trappings that went with it! The celebrations went on for weeks! Eventually he

...lled his three trusted servants to him to ask them ...bout his money.

"'Now, tell me what you did with my savings,' the ...ing said, excitedly. 'Did you put them to good use?'

"The first servant hauled in ten sacks of coins.

"'Your highness,' he said. 'I decided to trade with ...our five bags of gold. I worked hard at it and I have ...ade you another five bags on top.'

"The king was overjoyed. His servant had repaid his ...ust better than he could ever have imagined. 'Oh ...ell done!' he cried. 'I shall reward you by ...aking you governor over ten of my new cities.'

"Then the second servant came forward, heaving ...our bags of coins before the king. 'Your highness,' he ...id. 'I traded with your money, too, and have also ...oubled the sum. Here are four bags of gold.'

"The grateful king clapped his hands in delight. 'My ...anks and congratulations to you, too!' he beamed. 'How ...ould you like to be governor over five of my new cities?'

> ## 66 *For to every one who has will more be given.* 99

"Then the third servant stepped forwards, with only ...ne, quite grubby, sack of money. He looked down at his ...et and mumbled, 'Your highness, I didn't do anything ...ith your money. I've seen how ruthless you can ...ometimes be and I was afraid. So I just hid the coins ...afely in the ground.' And the servant handed back the ...ngle bag of gold with which he had been entrusted.

"The king was hurt and annoyed. 'You mean to tell me that you have done nothing with my gift,' he boomed. 'How can you have been so idle? Even if you didn't feel able to trade with it yourself, you should have taken it to my bankers. They could have invested the money, so it was still being of some use.

"The king swung round to his guards.

"'Take the money off this servant and give it to the man who made ten bags of money,' he commanded, 'then kick the worthless servant out. For those who are deserving and have worked hard for their reward will receive more. Those who haven't bothered to try, will have what little they possess taken away from them.'"

Banking
The Romans had a banking system, part of which was licensed by the state. The Jewish bankers tended to be moneylenders rather than savings bankers. This stone relief shows a Roman banker at his desk, perhaps in a market place.

Burying money
There were no banks for Jews to use at this time, no safe places to deposit metal ingots, coins or jewellery. People who wanted to hide their wealth buried it in the ground.

❖ ABOUT THE STORY ❖

This parable is often called "The parable of the talents" because the money or "pounds" were, in the original, "talents" which were units of weight for precious metals. And because we use the word "talent" to mean "what you are good at", it is an encouragement to use everything we have (not just money) to honour and serve God.

Judgement Day

"AT the end of the world, the Son of Man will come in all His glory, surrounded by angels," Jesus promised His disciples. "He will sit on his magnificent throne and all the peoples of the world will gather before Him. Every last soul who has ever walked the earth will be there; every single man, woman and child God has created since the very start of time; all human beings from all nations.

"The Son of Man will call each person forward one by one – there will be no hiding from Him. 'Go to the right,' he will say to one. 'Go to the left,' to another. And everyone will find they have no choice but to obey. So the Son of Man will separate out the vast crowd of souls into the righteous and the wicked, just as a shepherd separates out the sheep and the goats among his flock.

> 66 *He will separate them one from another as a shepherd separates the sheep from the goats.* 99

"When every last soul has been accounted for, the good people will all be gathered at the Son of Man's right hand. He will smile at them and throw His arms open wide, saying, 'Come with me! You have been blessed by my Father. It's now time for you to enter the kingdom that has been being prepared for you since the beginning of the world. For when I was hungry, you gave me food; when I

Jesus the shepherd
Pictures of the shepherd and his sheep are found in churches, because Jesus called Himself "the good shepherd" who looked after His people. Hence, in the parable, people who love in the way He wants are called "sheep" as opposed to the goats who did not serve Him.

Christian charity
This aid worker is helping sick people in Africa. Christians believe that it is essential to do something practical to help people as an expression of their faith.

was thirsty, you gave me drink; when I was a stranger, you befriended me; when I had no clothes, you bought me new ones; when I was ill, you came and held my hand; even when I was in prison, you came faithfully to visit me.'

"The righteous will turn to each other in bewilderment.

"'Lord,' they will say, 'when did we do all these things for you?'

"And the Son of Man will explain, "Whenever you said a kind word or did a generous deed for any one of your fellow men and women – no matter who they were – it was just as if you were doing it for me.'

"Then the Son of Man will turn to the evil souls on His left. They will cower away before His gaze and tremble in terror at the sound of His voice.

"'Be gone from my presence,' He will command. 'For when I was hungry, you let me starve; when I was thirsty, you let me choke; when I was alone and needed a friend, you made no effort to get to know me; when I shivered in rags, you let me freeze; when I was sick, you let me suffer; when I was locked up, you abandoned me.'

"The appalled souls will cry out in despair, 'But Lord, when did we come across you being hungry or thirsty or a stranger or naked or sick or cast into a dungeon? When did we ignore you?'

"'Whenever you walked past someone who needed your help,' the Son of Man will reply, 'it was just as if you were doing it to me.'

"And they will be driven into hell, where they will be punished for ever. But the good people will be carried straight to heaven, where they will live in happiness for ever more."

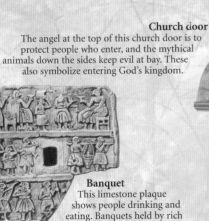

Church door
The angel at the top of this church door is to protect people who enter, and the mythical animals down the sides keep evil at bay. These also symbolize entering God's kingdom.

Banquet
This limestone plaque shows people drinking and eating. Banquets held by rich people were often excessive, and so were condemned by Jesus.

❖ **ABOUT THE STORY** ❖

On a previous occasion, Jesus had said, "By their fruits you shall know them." He meant that people who claimed to follow Him but acted selfishly were betraying their Lord. This parable stresses that point. In the book of James it says that faith without action is dead. However, Jesus is not saying that kindness alone, without any faith, will get someone to heaven.

Teachings of Jesus

PEOPLE have always admired the teaching of Jesus in the Gospels. Some of His sayings have become part of everyday life: "Turn the other cheek"; "Go the second mile"; "Do to others as you would have them do to you". Jesus taught a lot of other things besides how to get on with our (sometimes difficult) neighbours. In fact, He mostly taught about God – what He is like and how we can get to know Him.

His key teaching was about the kingdom of God, which He said had arrived when He started His ministry. This wasn't a physical place; rather it was anywhere that God's rule was obeyed. He said it was growing from small beginnings like a big plant grows from a tiny seed, and that it grew alongside the kingdoms and values of this world like wheat growing among weeds. God's people – those who truly belonged to His kingdom – would be separated out from the rest on the day of judgement and spend eternity in heaven with God.

In order to enter the kingdom, people had to believe in Jesus. "Faith", to Jesus, was about trusting God. So He taught that God was like a loving parent who really did care for a child. Some people at the time thought God was a bit of an ogre. Not so, said Jesus in the Sermon on the Mount. If you know to give your child some bread to feed him when he's hungry, and not a stone to choke him, surely God will give us His loving gifts too.

Jesus taught His disciples to pray, asking God for all the things they needed and trusting Him to supply them. But He also warned them that they couldn't have everything they wanted. The Christian way, He said, was "a narrow way". It meant self-sacrifice – saying no to our desires in order to serve God and others first.

Part of that self-sacrifice was to be kind and loving to our neighbour, and in His parable of the good Samaritan, Jesus defined our neighbour as "anyone in need". He also said that a rich person should go and sell all his possessions and give the money to the poor. Jesus did not say that to every rich person, but in this case (as in others) the man's wealth was more important to him than God's kingdom. Jesus constantly challenged people to get their priorities right. Who was in charge of their life – them or God? What drove them – the desire to be rich and famous or the desire to honour God?

That was the point of the most famous collection of Jesus's teaching in what is known as the Sermon on the Mount. Some of it is repeated in the Sermon on the Plain in Luke 6, and both sermons are unlikely to have been taught at any one time. The Gospel authors have collected together some of Jesus's sayings into one place – He probably repeated them on many occasions.

The Sermon on the Mount begins with a reversal of normal human values and goes on to remind Christians that their role in the world is to be like salt, preserving it from going bad and being God's "flavour" or influence within it. Their "light" – their faith, applied in life – is to be seen, not hidden. Christianity, He is saying, is a public religion not a private philosophy.

In order to be salt and light in the world, Jesus's followers are to obey God completely and to aim for perfection, which is God's standard. People that are perfect in this way do not harbour anger against others, even if they have wronged them. They respect others, not treating them as objects who exist only to satisfy their desires.

Sermon on the Mount
The sermon that we are told in the gospel of Matthew that Jesus gave "on the mountain" has been described by some people as the first text on what it means to be a Christian and how one can lead a life following Jesus. It is as part of the Sermon on the Mount that Jesus teaches the people "The Lord's Prayer", and tells them that they can address God as the "heavenly Father".

Jesus and the apostles

Within His large group of followers Jesus chose a special few to whom He gave extra teaching. These men are normally called "apostles". The apostles were not always able to work out exactly what Jesus meant in His parables, so Jesus would explain to them what He meant.

Throughout the Bible, God is shown to keep His promises absolutely and to forgive sinners willingly. The person who follows Him is to be faithful and true as well, willing to help others and not to seek revenge or to stand in unfair judgement of others. They will then become generous to others, and their religious practice will be sincere, coming before all personal ambitions. Such an attitude is likely to experience real answers to prayer.

Jesus taught that if God really is in charge of your life, and you are seeking Him and His love above all else, then you'll discover the one thing everyone seeks: happiness. You won't have to worry, because you'll know that God is in charge and that He will provide all you need, even if He doesn't give you all you want.

You can also be assured that He'll help you at all times, even at the hardest times when you think you cannot carry on. Towards the end of His short life, Jesus told the disciples to expect to receive the power and help of God the Holy Spirit. He would help them to understand what Jesus had taught and would reassure them of God's loving presence at all times. He would also go ahead of them in their ministry, making people aware of their need for God.

In other words, being a follower of Jesus affected every part and every moment of a person's life. Jesus sometimes pictured the kingdom of God like buried treasure found in a field. The finder went and sold all he had in order to buy the field – and get the treasure. It was that valuable, and that important.

❖ THE BEATITUDES ❖

This well-known series of short sayings starts off Jesus's Sermon on the Mount. They are a guide for the people who wish to enter the kingdom of God. They start with the word "Blessed", which some versions of the Bible translate as "How happy". It means, "If you do what follows, you will receive God's kindness and blessing." Each is then followed by a promise. Probably the most famous of these is "Blessed are the meek, for they shall inherit the earth".

Beatitude	Means: If you are...	Then you will...
Poor in spirit	aware of your deep need of God	enter God's kingdom
Mourning	really sorry for your sins and the world's sin	know God's forgiveness and comfort
Meek, gentle	obedient to God in all ways	receive God's good gifts
Hungry for uprightness	longing to know God and do His will	be spiritually satisfied for ever
Merciful	sorry for others and helping them in their need	experience God's kindness
Pure in heart	sincere in every way	stay in touch with God
Peacemaker	helping enemies to become friends	be doing God's most important work
Persecuted	suffering for God's cause	be welcomed into heaven as a hero

Women in the Bible

THE Gospels deal with women in very different ways to how people would have expected at the time. The first announcement of the expected birth of Jesus, the promised Messiah, was to a woman (His mother) and after His birth, to shepherds. And the first appearance of Jesus after His resurrection was to women. Yet women and shepherds were regarded as inferior citizens. Their word was not trusted in a Jewish court. In a demonstration of the "good news of the kingdom", the Gospels show that Jesus came especially to show God's love to people who were despised by others.

During His lifetime, Jesus demonstrated that same concern and compassion. Although He did not break with His culture to the extent of having any women among His closest disciples, in all His dealings with them He treated women with dignity, respect and love. Indeed, without a large group of mostly anonymous women who provided food and shelter , the disciples would have had a much harder time. Some women, however, play a more prominent part in the Gospels.

Mary Magdalene

This Mary had a troubled past, but we are not told the details. Jesus had cast seven demons out of her, and she was devoted to Him with gratitude for the new life He had given her. She was at the cross when He died, and was the first to see Him alive three days later, although she at first thought He was the gardener.

Martha and Mary of Bethany

With their brother Lazarus, these two women were especially close to Jesus. They were probably unmarried (or possibly widowed) and invited Jesus to make their home a base when He was in the south of Judea.

One day Martha scurried around getting supper for Jesus and His disciples, annoyed that Mary, her (probably younger) sister, didn't help, but instead sat with the men listening to Jesus. Mary, Jesus said, had chosen the best option, taking advantage of a unique opportunity to learn about God. Her knowledge would remain for ever, but food could wait.

However, later at the tomb of Lazarus, Martha made a statement of faith in Jesus which is equal to that of Peter: "You are the Christ, the Son of the living God".

Salome

Salome is believed to have been the wife of Zebedee and mother of James and John, two of Jesus's closest disciples. She may also have been the sister of the Virgin Mary, and hence Jesus's aunt. She too was at the cross and witnessed the resurrection of Jesus.

TIMELINE

• Jesus performs the miracle of feeding five thousand people

JESUS FEEDING THE FIVE THOUSAND

AD30

LAVER BOWL

• Jesus walks over the Sea of Galilee towards the disciples' boat. Peter walks on water also, but loses his faith in Jesus and sinks

JESUS AND PETER

• Jesus calls Peter "the Rock" on which He will build His church

• The disciples Peter, James and John, witness Jesus transfigured into a heavenly being with Moses and Elijah

THE TRANSFIGURATION

Unnamed women Jesus helped

The "sinner" who anointed Jesus's feet while He ate supper in a Pharisee's house is not named in the Bible, but her devotion was commended and her faith brought her wholeness and healing.

So too did the woman caught in adultery (John 8:1–11). Here was an example of the double standards of the time. She was sentenced to death, but the man she had been with was not. Jesus simply said, "Whoever is without sin can cast the first stone", upholding the law but making it impossible for anyone to execute its sentence. Then, forgiving her, He said, "Go and sin no more." She had a new start.

The Virgin Mary, mother of Jesus

Pre-eminent among the saints, she conceived Jesus while a virgin as a unique sign that her child was the "Son of God" and also fully human at the same time. She was probably quite young at the time and was a woman of clear and trusting faith. During Jesus's childhood, when strange things happened (as when He remained for three days in the temple when He was twelve), Luke tells us that she "treasured these things in her heart" (Luke 2:51).

She was present at the cross, grieving at His death, and Jesus showed His great love and compassion for her by asking John to take Mary and look after her. She was also one of the first witnesses of His resurrection. However, she is not mentioned in the rest of the New Testament.

⚜ WORSHIPPING MARY ⚜

Later in church history Mary was declared to have been taken bodily into heaven (without dying). Many people pray to her today as one of the saints.

Shrine
This is a traditional shrine to Mary that has been built at the side of the road.

JESUS AND THE
SINNING WOMAN

• Pharisees send soldiers to arrest Jesus, but they return without Him

• Jesus teaches the people about the power of prayer

• Jesus tells the stories of the prodigal son and the good Samaritan

• Jesus cures ten lepers, but only one Samaritan man comes to thank Him

JESUS AND THE LEPERS

• Jesus forgives the corrupt tax collector Zacchaeus in the city of Jericho

JESUS AND MARY

LAZARUS RAISED FROM
THE DEAD

• Jesus visits His friends Mary and Martha in Bethany and raises Lazarus from the dead

AD33

DEATH AND RESURRECTION ·

Jesus is warmly welcomed by the people into Jerusalem, but there is opposition from religious leaders and the authorities are afraid of His popularity. The scene is set for Jesus's last days on earth, His arrest and trial, and His death. However, Jesus miraculously returns to His followers after death and encourages them to continue to spread His teachings.

Introduction

HERE you can read about Jesus's last days on earth, from His arrival in Jerusalem to His betrayal by Judas which led to His arrest, trial and death. It ends with the story of His miraculous resurrection and His ascension to heaven, where He was reunited with God His Father.

Via Dolorosa
This carving shows Jesus on the way to Golgotha just outside Jerusalem. It is situated on the Via Dolorosa, the "Way of Sorrow" in Jerusalem, along the route Jesus would have taken. It shows Simon of Cyrene helping Jesus with His cross.

The story begins with Jesus's last visit to Jerusalem. Jesus Himself was already aware that His entry into the city would lead to a final confrontation with the authorities, finishing with His own death. He told His disciples exactly what would happen, but they found it hard to believe His words. The visit took place during Passover time, so the streets were crowded with thousands of pilgrims. Instead of slipping in unnoticed, Jesus made a dramatic entry, riding on a donkey. This was interpreted as a fulfilment of the prophecy that the Messiah would enter Jerusalem on a donkey.

On His arrival in the city, Jesus immediately threw out of the temple the traders who were making money out of the pilgrims and increasing the profits of the corrupt temple officials. During the days that followed, Jesus preached in the temple area, while the religious leaders did their best to trick Him into incriminating Himself with statements of blasphemy, speaking against God. As the conflict escalated, the Jewish elders grew more determined to remove this troublemaker once and for all.

At the end of Passover week, Jesus held a farewell meal for His disciples. During this Last Supper, He gave some final instructions to His closest followers, and also revealed that He knew there was a traitor in their midst. After the meal, Jesus went to pray in the Garden of Gethsemane. He begged God to spare Him from His suffering and God sent an angel to give Him strength. Shortly after this, Jesus was arrested. The disciple Judas had betrayed Him to the Jewish elders, and had led them to the garden, showing them who Jesus was with a kiss.

Immediately after His arrest, Jesus was tried by the Jewish court, the Sanhedrin, and found guilty of blasphemy. Under Jewish law, blasphemy was punishable by death. At this time, though, only the Roman governor could pass the death sentence. Under Roman law,

Mount of Olives
In the hours before Jesus was arrested, He went to the Mount of Olives, shown here. He often went to the Garden of Gethsemane, which was on the Mount, to find peace from the bustle of Jerusalem itself.

the charge of blasphemy was not even recognized. Because the Jewish leaders wanted Jesus dead, they brought Him before the Roman governor, Pontius Pilate, on a charge of treason. Although Pilate could find no case against Jesus, he bowed to public pressure and condemned Him to death by crucifixion.

Before the crucifixion took place, Jesus was savagely beaten and cruelly mocked by the Roman guards. The crucifixion itself involved a slow and very painful death. Throughout His ordeal, Jesus prayed to God to give Him the strength to bear the pain. One of the two thieves crucified alongside Jesus was impressed by His words of forgiveness and concern for others, even during His dreadful suffering. When Jesus died with a final cry of "It is finished", His body was taken down from the cross and buried in a nearby tomb.

According to the Bible, Jesus's tomb was found to be empty on the Sunday morning after His crucifixion. It was a group of women who made the discovery and, shortly afterwards, one of them, Mary Magdalene saw Christ alive again. For some weeks after this, Jesus made several appearances to His disciples, both in Galilee and Jerusalem. When He had convinced them that He had overcome death, and assured them that He would continue to help them even when He was no longer physically present, He departed, leaving them to carry on His work. The disciples watched in amazement as their master ascended to heaven, to return to His Father.

Throughout these stories we can see Jesus's suffering, and His strength in the face of that suffering. Jesus accepted His death and never denied God. Christians believe that when Jesus died, He took upon Himself the sins of everyone, so that anyone could be forgiven by God and live with Him for ever. They believe that Jesus accepted the pain of death to show, by His resurrection, that God and His love are not defeated by death. Christians try to follow Jesus's example, living their lives according to God's purpose of saving the world through love.

The other important aspect is Jesus's miraculous resurrection. The Christian idea of resurrection was different from the beliefs of other religions at the time. Christians thought of the body as being resurrected, and of it being transformed so that it was suitable for the eternal life to follow.

The Greeks were different. They thought of the body as a hindrance to true life and believed that after death, the soul would leave the body behind entirely. Their concept of life after death was in terms of a soul that never died. The Jews believed in resurrection, but thought it would be with the same body.

The resurrection has been of central importance to the Christian faith since the earliest preaching began. Right from the start, Christians believed that Jesus had risen from the dead, and that they too would rise after death to be with God eternally. Jesus said, "I am the resurrection and the life; he who believes in me, though he die, yet shall he live".

✦ DEATH AND RESURRECTION ✦

Here you can read of Jesus's last days, His crucifixion, resurrection and His final ascent to heaven

JESUS TEACHING IN GALILEE
Matthew, Ch. 20, Mark Ch. 10, Luke, Ch. 7 & 18, John, Ch. 12.

JESUS IN JERUSALEM
Matthew, Ch. 21, 22, 24 and 26, Mark, Ch. 11 to 14, Luke, Ch. 19 to 22, John, Ch. 2, 11 to 14

JESUS ARRESTED AND CRUCIFIED
Matthew, Ch. 26 & 27 Mark, Ch. 14 & 15, Luke, Ch. 22 & 23 John, Ch. 17 to 19

JESUS'S RESURRECTION
Matthew, Ch. 28, Mark, Ch. 16 Luke, Ch. 23 & 24, John, Ch. 20 & 21, Acts Ch. 1.

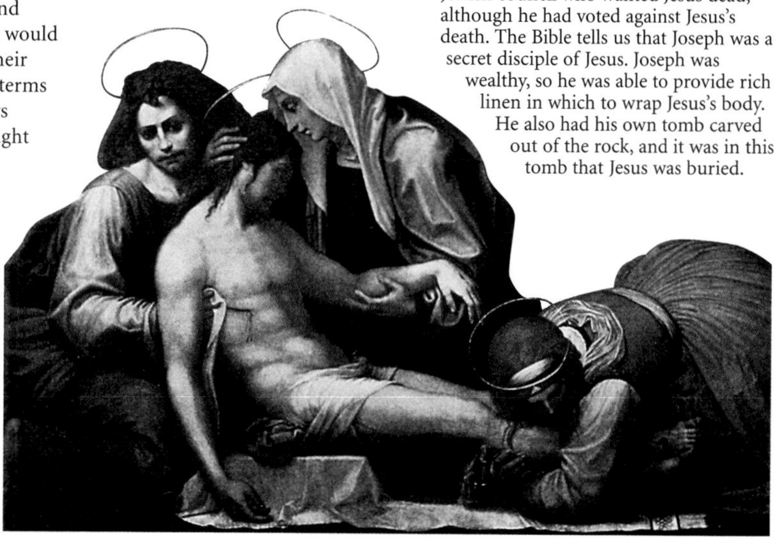

Jesus taken from the cross
After He died, Jesus was taken down from the cross by Joseph of Arimathea, seen here with Mary Magdalene, and Mary, mother of James and John. Joseph was a member of the Sanhedrin, the ruling Jewish council who wanted Jesus dead, although he had voted against Jesus's death. The Bible tells us that Joseph was a secret disciple of Jesus. Joseph was wealthy, so he was able to provide rich linen in which to wrap Jesus's body. He also had his own tomb carved out of the rock, and it was in this tomb that Jesus was buried.

363

Jesus in Jerusalem

THE CITY OF JERUSALEM, where Jesus was tried and crucified, was, even at this time, a very important city. Its history can be traced back to at least 3000 years before the birth of Jesus, and today it is considered sacred not only to Christians, but to followers of Judaism and Islam as well. The first part of its name means "foundation". The second part, *salem*, probably originally referred to Shalem, a Canaanite god or goddess. The Canaanites were the race of people that lived in this area before the Israelites arrived. So the original meaning of the name was probably "foundation of Shalem". Over the years, though, the second part of the name probably came to be associated, in the minds of the Jewish people living there, with the Jewish word *salom*, meaning peace.

Since the start of His ministry, Jesus had known that He would meet His death in Jerusalem. He had told His disciples many times that this would be the case, but they had never entirely believed him. Jesus wanted to make sure that as many people as possible heard and understood His message, so His last days in Jerusalem are full of symbols that the people could have picked up on, and that would give them clues as to His mission.

Jesus deliberately made His final trip to Jerusalem at the time of the Jewish festival of Passover. During this feast the Jews remember the events that took place when their ancestors were slaves in Egypt. Before the pharaoh of Egypt would release the Israelites from slavery, God, through Moses, had inflicted nine plagues upon the pharaoh and his country. In the tenth and final plague God killed all the first-born children and animals in Egypt. However, He "passed-over" the houses of the Israelites who had followed special instructions for the first Passover meal given to them by God through Moses.

When Jesus enters Jerusalem during Passover week, not only is the city more crowded than usual because of the all the pilgrims who have come to the holy city to celebrate, but these people are already thinking about death and being saved by God, as it is the reason that many of them are in Jerusalem.

Jesus made a highly symbolic entry into the holy city. The Old Testament tells how a Messiah would come and save the Jewish people. This Messiah, the Bible says, would enter Jerusalem on a donkey. Jesus knew exactly what message He was giving the people. Throughout His ministry, Jesus had told only His disciples that He was the Messiah, and He had told them not to tell anyone. At this stage, though, He is arriving in Jerusalem to fulfil the role on earth that God gave Him and can He tell everyone that He is the Messiah.

Soon after entering Jerusalem, Jesus went to the temple and again fulfilled Old Testament prophecies by clearing the traders from it, as He had done once before. By making His anger and displeasure publicly very clear, Jesus was making known His anger at the religious authorities of the time, the Sadducees and the Pharisees, for allowing, and sometimes encouraging, the traders and the money-changers into the grounds of the temple.

Jesus's time in Jerusalem is traced on this map. The Bible tells us that He was staying in Bethany, and came every morning of Passover week to the temple to teach the people. You can see the site of the Passover meal that Jesus took with His disciples, the Last Supper, before the group followed Jesus out to the Garden of Gethsemane for Jesus to pray. In the Garden, Jesus was betrayed, as He knew He would be, by Judas to the authorities. Jesus was arrested and taken for an unofficial trial at the house of Annas, the former High Priest. Jesus was then taken to the house of Caiaphas, the high priest, where He was tried for blasphemy, speaking against God, by the whole Sanhedrin, the Jewish council. The punishment under Jewish law for this crime was death, but the Jewish authorities could not order Jesus's execution, only the Roman governor could do that. The elders had a problem, though. They knew that Pontius Pilate, the Roman governor, would not recognise a charge of blasphemy as he was not concerned with the Jewish religion. In order to get Jesus executed, they changed the charge, they told Pilate that Jesus was trying to stir people up to fight against the Romans. The elders hoped that the governor would not be able to ignore a charge of this sort. Even though Pilate could find no charge on which he could find Jesus guilty, the elders had done such a good job of stirring up hate among the people of Jerusalem that Pilate eventually bowed under the pressure from the public and allowed Jesus to be led away. Jesus was taken to Golgotha, outside the city walls, where the Romans crucified Him.

Death of Christ
The death and the resurrection of Jesus are the most important events in the Christian faith. Christ's suffering is sometimes used symbolically, such as in this image of a peasant praying before Christ. The peasant, dressed as he is, could not have been present for the real crucifixion. He is praying to the forgiving spirit of Jesus.

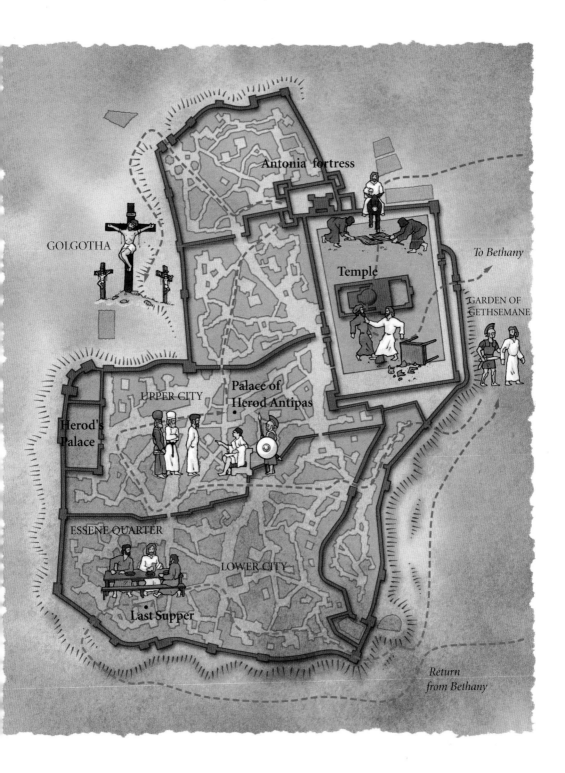

Antonia fortress

GOLGOTHA

Temple

To Bethany

GARDEN OF GETHSEMANE

UPPER CITY

Palace of Herod Antipas

Herod's Palace

ESSENE QUARTER

LOWER CITY

Last Supper

Return from Bethany

Jesus Turns for Jerusalem

THE 12 disciples had been travelling around Judea for three years. Every day they had walked for hours, relying on the goodness of strangers to feed and shelter them. Every day, they had dealt with the masses of pushing, shouting people who had come to see Jesus. The disciples had listened to hundreds of people pour out their problems. They had given the downcast men and women new hope by preaching Jesus's message of God's kingdom. They had seen people with terrible illnesses and diseases, taking many to Jesus for healing and healing others themselves. They had stood up against the anger of the religious authorities, who insisted that Jesus was a wicked hoaxer

leading the people into sin. They had faced the violent mobs who came to stop Jesus and His disciples by force. In private, the disciples had struggled to understand as Jesus explained His teachings. Each one of them had carried in his heart the great secret Jesus had told them: that He was the Messiah, God's chosen one, the one the prophets said long ago would be sent to save the world from its sins.

It was hard work, and one night's sleep was never enough. However, the disciples were dedicated. They believed wholeheartedly in Jesus and were determined to follow Him, no matter how difficult it was.

One morning, Jesus was already up and saying His prayers. The disciples hurried to join Him. Then they sat back and waited for Jesus's instructions. Jesus's words were strange and worrying.

"It is time for me to go to Jerusalem," He explained.

Jesus looked around and saw both excitement and worry in the disciples' faces. He had told His 12 helpers

❧ ABOUT THE STORY ❧

Jesus had probably been to Jerusalem several times during His three-year ministry. He knew that this time would be different. The opposition had grown to fever pitch. He must have been afraid, because He knew it would be painful. He also knew that this was why He had come into the world. So Jesus set out to do God's will, because He knew that God's will was the best for Him, and for everyone.

The Messiah
In the Old Testament, it is prophesied that the Messiah will come to save the Jewish people. In the New Testament, Jesus is described as the Messiah, come to save mankind. The word "messiah" comes from the Hebrew word meaning "anointed one". The Greek word for anointing, "christos", is the origin of Jesus's title, "Christ".

long ago that they were working their way towards Jerusalem, and the disciples were well aware of the dangers that lay ahead there. Although the Romans were governing Judea, the elders in Jerusalem had great power and they wanted Jesus out of the way. Once Jesus was in the capital city, it would be much easier for the priests, scribes and Pharisees to get their hands on Him.

Jesus looked at His anxious friends and smiled sadly.

"I've already told you what will happen to me there," He said, "but I know that none of you have been able to believe it. Yet my words are true. In Jerusalem, everything that the ancient prophets said would happen to the Son of Man will finally come to pass. I will be handed over to the chief priests and scribes. They will condemn me to death and give me to my enemies to be mocked and tortured. Finally, I will be put to death by crucifixion and three days later, I will be raised up to life again."

The disciples all began to speak at once, clamouring and questioning and protesting. Jesus held up His hand for silence. As the twelve men brooded, their eyes downcast and their minds troubled, the mother of James and John came hurrying up and knelt before Jesus.

> 66 *Grant us to sit, one at your right hand and one at your left, in your glory.* 99

"Lord," she said. "Please let my two sons sit beside you in your kingdom – one at your right hand, the other at your left."

Jesus's voice was low and firm.

"Only my Father can grant that," He replied. "However, I can tell you that anyone who would be great in my Father's kingdom must be a humble servant to others here on earth. I myself came here to serve others – not to have others serve me – and to give up my own life to save the lives of many."

Brooch
The Romans wore many types of jewellery including brooches like this one. Brooches were often ornate and were worn by both men and women. They had safety pins on the back and were used to fasten clothes, such as cloaks, at the shoulder.

Jesus's journey to Jerusalem
During His ministry in Galilee, Jesus visited Jerusalem several times. The journey that He made from Capernaum to Jerusalem was a long one, nearly 160km on foot.

Christian symbol
The cross is a sign of Christianity because it represents the cross on which Jesus was crucified. Some Christians wear a cross, usually around the neck, as a sign of their commitment to Jesus.

Jesus is Anointed

ON His way to Jerusalem, Jesus stopped at the little town of Bethany to stay with His close friends, Mary, Martha and Lazarus.

The two sisters and their brother were overjoyed to see Jesus. They had every faith in His teachings and loved Him dearly, not least because Lazarus owed his life to Jesus. Once, after a sudden illness, Mary and Martha's brother had died. Four days later, Jesus had arrived and brought Lazarus walking out of his tomb alive and well.

Now the little family welcomed Jesus with open arms, each providing the best hospitality they could. Martha rushed around in the kitchen, preparing a delicious meal. Lazarus was the perfect host, keeping all his guests entertained and happy while they sat waiting at the table. Mary saw how weary the travellers were from their journeying, and slipped away to fetch something to soothe and refresh Jesus. She decided on a tiny bottle of scent she had been saving – the most rare and expensive perfume that money could buy. Mary didn't give Jesus just a few dabs of it. Instead, she cracked open the precious alabaster flask and let every last drop of the cool, beautiful perfume trickle over His hot, tired skin.

Several of the disciples leapt to their feet in shock at the very extravagant gesture.

"What are you doing, woman?" cried Judas Iscariot,

totally appalled. "You would have been better off selling that perfume and giving all the money to the poor!"

"Leave Mary alone," Jesus scolded. "You will always have poor people to show generosity to, but you will not always have me. By anointing me with this beautiful perfume, Mary has in fact prepared my body for burial."

> ❝ *In pouring this ointment on my body she has done it to prepare me for burial.* ❞

The disciples looked at each other in puzzlement and began to whisper about what Jesus could mean by speaking of burials and of not always being with them. Jesus Himself stayed silent, wrapped up in memories of another time, not too long before, when a woman had shown Him a similar kindness.

Once, when He had been dining at a Pharisee's house, a woman He had never met before had hurried to see Him. The woman had been a terrible sinner all her life, but she had heard Jesus speak of love and repentance, and she had felt something inside her change. From then on, all she had truly wanted was to be forgiven and to be able to make a new start.

The woman had sat behind Jesus and cried. Her tears had fallen on His feet, dusty from the road, and had washed them clean. She had dried Jesus's wet feet with her hair and tenderly kissed them. She opened up an expensive bottle of perfume that she had brought with her especially, and scented His skin.

Jesus had been very touched by the woman's kindness, which was quite the opposite of His host's. The Pharisee hadn't gone to any trouble at all to make Jesus feel welcome. When he had seen that Jesus was allowing the sinning woman to touch Him, the Pharisee had practically turned up his nose and shifted his seat further away in disgust.

At this, Jesus had told His host a story. "Two men owed money to a moneylender," He had said. "One owed a large amount and the other owed a small amount. Neither man was able to repay what he had borrowed, and the moneylender let them both off their debts. Which man would feel more grateful?"

"The one who owed more money," the Pharisee had replied.

"Exactly," Jesus had agreed. "Compare yourself with this sinning woman. You gave me no water to wash with, but this woman has washed my feet with her tears. You gave me no towel to dry them, but she has dried them with her hair. You gave me no kiss of greeting, but she has covered my feet with kisses. You gave me no scent to freshen up with, but this woman

has brought me expensive perfume. I can tell you that all her sins are forgiven, and so she shows me much love."

The other guests had murmured angrily, "Who does this man think He is, to say that He can forgive sins?"

But Jesus hadn't taken any notice of the offended guests' remarks. Instead, He had simply turned to the young woman and smiled. "Your faith has saved you," He had said, gently. "Go in peace."

Alabaster
The perfume bottle in the story is made from a translucent stone called alabaster. Alabaster is very soft and easy to carve, this Turkish relief is made of alabaster. Only expensive perfumes would have been kept in alabaster bottles. Everyday perfumes were kept in pottery jars.

Precious perfume
Perfumes were made from many kinds of plants, herbs and spices and were imported into Palestine from countries such as India and Egypt. When Mary anoints Jesus with her best perfume, she is honouring Him as a special guest and showing her devotion to Him.

> ❧ **ABOUT THE STORY** ❧
> *The Pharisees thought that by keeping all their religious ceremonies they would be good enough to please God. They forgot that sometimes there was anger, hatred and greed in their hearts. That was a sin against God. This woman knew she had sinned and so said sorry. She could be forgiven. People who did not think they had done wrong could not please God. They had to say sorry for their sins, too.*

The First Palm Sunday

It was the week before the great feast of the Passover. Jews from all over Judea were hurrying to Jerusalem for the celebrations, and the authorities were desperate to know whether Jesus would dare visit the temple with all the other worshippers. The chief priests and scribes and Pharisees had given out strict orders that if anyone knew where the "trouble-making" preacher was, they should let them know immediately, so they could arrest Him.

Jesus and His disciples were at Bethany with Mary, Martha and Lazarus. By the time the authorities heard, hundreds of people had left Jerusalem to see Jesus.

The Jewish elders were furious. They couldn't possibly seize Him in the middle of His supporters. Instead, the chief priests and scribes and Pharisees gathered their spies to them once again.

"We'll have to wait and see if Jesus comes to Jerusalem for Passover," they hissed. "Keep a sharp eye out. He'll probably try to mingle unnoticed among the crowds."

They needn't have gone to such trouble. The Sunday before Passover, Jesus and His disciples set off quite openly for Jerusalem, surrounded by a cheering crowd. The disciples sang Jesus's praises aloud as they accompanied their master to Beth-page, which lay close to the capital city on the Mount of Olives.

"Go into the village," Jesus instructed two of His disciples. "There you will find a donkey tethered to a doorway. Untie it and bring it to me. If anyone asks what you're doing, just say that the Lord needs it."

The men hurried off and, sure enough, they found the donkey, just as Jesus had said. As soon as the owners found out who it was that wanted to borrow the animal, they threw their robes on its back for a saddle and gladly brought it to Jesus themselves.

"Be careful though," the owners told Jesus. "He might be quite wild. No one has sat on him before."

When Jesus mounted the donkey, it stood still and calm and obedient. It was on the gentle, grey animal's back that Jesus set off again, heading for the holy city.

At this, a new wave of excitement rippled through the crowd accompanying Jesus. The ancient prophets had foretold that the Messiah would one day enter Jerusalem on a donkey! This must be Him, they thought.

Hundreds of men, women and children came running out to greet Jesus, cheering excitedly. Some took off their robes and spread them out over the road, while others paved the way with broad palm leaves and flowers.

"Hosanna!" they shouted. "Blessed is He who comes in the name of the Lord! Hosanna in the highest!"

All the way to Jerusalem, people poured out to welcome Jesus. When Jesus saw the city itself, He began to weep.

> ❝ *So they took branches of palm trees and went out to meet Him.* ❞

"Oh Jerusalem!" He murmured. "Though you greet me now, you will fail to believe that God has come to you. Because of that, you will be utterly destroyed."

Everyone was far too excited to notice Jesus's sorrow, as the joyful procession wound its way around the city.

Jesus entered Jerusalem like a victorious king. But the victory still had to be won. He would defeat sin and His death on the cross when He rose from the dead. ❧

Palm Sunday
Here is Jesus on the donkey, making His way to Jerusalem. The people lining the route are laying palm leaves on the ground in front of Him. Many churches celebrate Palm Sunday today with processions in which branches of palms are carried.

"Hosanna to the son of David!" they cried. "Blessed is the King who comes in the name of the Lord! Hosanna in the highest!"

"This is outrageous!" the purple-faced Pharisees yelled at Jesus. "These people think that you're the Messiah! Tell them to stop at once!"

"Even if they were silent," Jesus replied, "the very stones would cry out."

Passover meal
Jesus entered Jerusalem in the week before the great Jewish feast of the Passover. People now date the Christian Easter celebration in the same way the Jews decide the date of Passover, based on the Jewish cycle of the moon.

The graceful palm
A palm is a tall tree with a straight, narrow trunk and a cluster of huge feathery leaves at the top. Palm leaves were a symbol of grace and victory. They were laid down in front of Jesus as a mark of respect.

❧ **ABOUT THE STORY** ❧
King David and his family had ridden on donkeys (or mules) in Old Testament times. There was an Old Testament prophecy that said the Messiah would enter Jerusalem like this. So Jesus was showing that He had come to fulfil the prophecies and that He claimed to be David's successor. It was a powerful visual message. Some people, though, like the Sadducees, did not believe the fulfilment of the prophecy before their eyes.

Jesus in the Temple

JESUS was horrified to find that the great temple of Jerusalem was being used as a market place. Money-changers were transferring foreign coins into Jewish shekels and making handsome profits for themselves. Stallholders were selling sacrificial animals to the pilgrims at ridiculously high prices. Instead of the reverential silence Jesus expected, His ears throbbed with the buzz of bartering, the lowing of livestock, the shouting of friends and everyday chit-chat.

Jesus had seen the temple dishonoured in this way a couple of years ago. With a furious cry of, "Take these things away! You will not make my Father's house into a business place!" Jesus had driven all the traders out by force. It had not taken them long to return.

Now Jesus exploded with even greater anger.

"The temple should be a house of prayer for all the nations of the world!" He roared. "You have made it into a den of thieves!"

Jesus went through the courtyards like a whirlwind. He pushed over the money changers' tables, sending coins spilling on to the floor and cascading down the steps. He smashed open the bird cages, releasing doves into the air. He flung the livestock traders into the dusty streets, sending their cattle and sheep stampeding after them.

Finally, the temple was cleared. It didn't stay empty for long, though. Crowds of people soon flooded back in to see Jesus, packing the courtyard.

"Tell us about God's kingdom!" came the shouts. "What must we do to have our sins forgiven?"

Other voices cried out for healing.

As soon as Jesus began to speak, the temple fell silent as everyone concentrated on His every word.

Each evening through Passover week, Jesus would return to Bethany. Then, every morning, He would go straight back to the temple in Jerusalem. He would stand until nearly dusk, preaching His message of hope and salvation, and laying His hands on whoever was in need, making them well again.

When the Jewish elders saw the wonderful things Jesus did and heard the excited children crying out, "Hosanna to the Son of David!" they couldn't stand it. They came stomping right into the middle of the crowds and shook their staffs in Jesus's face.

"By whose permission are you teaching here?" the Jewish dignitaries raged. "Who has given you the authority to stir up the people like this?"

> **Hosanna to the Son of David!**

"Let me ask you a question, and if you can answer it, then I'll tell you," Jesus replied calmly. "Now, who gave my cousin John the right to baptize? Did God want him to do it or was it just the people?"

The Jewish elders scratched their heads.

"If we say God, Jesus will ask us why we didn't believe John's teachings," they argued. "However, if we say the people, the crowds here will probably stone us. For they believe that John was a true prophet from God."

"We don't know!" they spat, their faces like thunder.

USUALLY, PEOPLE GET ANGRY WHEN THEY HAVE BEEN HURT PERSONALLY. JESUS'S ACTION SHOWS THAT GOD FEELS ANGRY AND HURT WHEN PEOPLE DO NOT TAKE HIM AND HIS WORSHIP SERIOUSLY.

Temple traders
Roman traders in the temple are selling doves to be used as sacrifices to God. Jesus is angry when He sees this going on, as this sort of behaviour is wrong in a place of worship. To make matters worse, the traders are taking advantage of the pilgrims' faith by charging high prices for the birds.

They knew that they could not give either answer.

"Well, if you can't tell me that," replied Jesus, "then I can't tell you by what authority I say and do these things."

Once again, Jesus had managed to keep the hostile Jewish authorities at bay. However, they weren't about to give up and leave Him alone. For the chief priests, scribes and Pharisees, plotting Jesus's death had become their number one concern.

Pilgrims
People who travel to a holy place for religious reasons are called pilgrims. Many of Jesus's followers travelled long distances to see Him and listen to His teachings. These pilgrims are in Jerusalem during Passover week.

Weighing their wares
This bronze steelyard was hung by its upper hook and used by traders for weighing their goods. The object to be weighed was attached to the lower hook and the acorn-shaped weight was moved along the long arm until it balanced in a straight line.

❧ ABOUT THE STORY ❧
This story shows that Jesus was not always gentle, meek and mild. Here, He is like one of the Old Testament prophets calling down God's judgement on people. Jesus often taught about God's judgement, as well as about His love. He warned people who took God's love for granted that they could be in for a big shock when God shut them out of His kingdom. He does judge and He does forgive. Both truths are important.

The Wicked Tenants

BY Tuesday of Passover Week, everyone in Jerusalem knew Jesus was speaking out against the authorities.

"Once upon a time," Jesus preached, "a man planted a vineyard. When all the work was done, he had to leave for another country. So he brought in tenants to look after the vineyard.

"Time passed, and the owner sent a servant to bring back some of the first crop of grapes for him to sample. The servant returned empty-handed and covered in bruises. The tenants had refused to hand over any crops, and had beaten up the servant. The vineyard owner tried again. However, the second servant came back more severely wounded than the first. The third time the vineyard owner sent a servant,

he didn't return at all. The tenants actually killed him.

"Still the vineyard owner didn't give up. He kept on sending servants. The tenants beat up some and murdered others, until there was only one man left: his own son, whom he loved dearly. Surely they will respect him, the vineyard owner thought. To his great sorrow and regret, the tenants butchered his son just like the others.

> **❝ I will send my beloved son. ❞**

"Now, I will tell you what the vineyard owner will do next," Jesus announced to the crowds in the temple. "He will come and destroy the wicked tenants and give the vineyard to others who deserve it."

Everyone knew Jesus meant the tenants were the Jewish elders and the vineyard was the kingdom of God. The elders seethed to hear it.

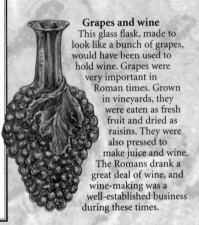

❧ ABOUT THE STORY ❧

Jesus is not just telling this story against the religious leaders of His day. It includes their ancestors too. It is a sad story that sums up how people had treated God's servants for many centuries. The tenants are the leaders in every age. The servants are prophets who God sent to call people back to Himself. So often, these servants were ignored or got rid of. Soon, this generation of leaders will kill God's Son, Jesus.

Grapes and wine
This glass flask, made to look like a bunch of grapes, would have been used to hold wine. Grapes were very important in Roman times. Grown in vineyards, they were eaten as fresh fruit and dried as raisins. They were also pressed to make juice and wine. The Romans drank a great deal of wine, and wine-making was a well-established business during these times.

Jesus as the son
In this story, Jesus is using the death of the vineyard owner's son to symbolize His own death, as the son of God, at the hands of the Sadducees and Pharisees.

The Barren Fig Tree

ONE morning when Jesus was hurrying from Bethany to Jerusalem, His stomach began to rumble. He had left so early to get to the great temple to begin preaching and healing that He and His disciples had had no time for breakfast. So when Jesus caught sight of a fig tree growing by the roadside, He called a halt for a few seconds and went over to pick some of its juicy fruit for Himself and His companions to eat.

However, when Jesus drew closer to the tall, leafy tree, He was dismayed to find that there wasn't a single fig among the branches.

"May you never grow any fruit ever again!" He cried.

The disciples stood and watched open-mouthed as all at once its leaves faded to yellow, then crinkled to brown, then fluttered from the branches to the ground. The tree that had been alive and green just a few moments ago now stood bare and dry and withered.

> " *Jesus answered them, 'Have faith in God...'* "

The 12 men gasped. Even though they had witnessed Jesus perform many dramatic miracles, they had never seen Him use His powers except to help people in some way. In fact, whenever anyone had challenged Jesus to prove Himself by performing a miracle "just for show", He had always refused. Now all of a sudden He had destroyed a harmless tree.

"Why?" the stunned disciples spluttered.

"To show that if you only have faith in God, you will find that you can make anything happen," Jesus replied. "I tell you that when you pray, if you truly believe that God has heard you and will answer you, you will surely receive whatever you prayed for. Remember, always forgive others who do you wrong. For then, in turn, your Father in heaven will be able to forgive the things that you yourself do wrong."

Deep in thought, the disciples continued with Jesus on their way...

FAITH IS NOT LIKE KNOWLEDGE. IT CANNOT BE TESTED IN AN EXAM TO SEE HOW MUCH WE HAVE GOT. WE EITHER HAVE IT, OR WE DO NOT, BECAUSE FAITH IS SIMPLY TRUSTING GOD.

Picking figs
This picture shows a man picking ripe figs from a tree. Together with grapes and olives, figs were an important fruit. The common fig is mentioned more than fifty times in the Bible and the Hebrew language has four different words for "fig". Figs were eaten as fruit, pressed into fig-cakes and also used in medicine.

❖ ABOUT THE STORY ❖

This is a strange thing for Jesus to do – He did not usually destroy things. It was even harder to understand because it was not the right time of year for figs! Jesus is acting out a parable. God's people are meant to bear fruit – that is, to do what God wants. He is saying that the fig tree stands for God's people who have rejected Him and that they will wither away like the tree. Sure enough, in AD 70, the Romans destroyed Judea.

Jesus is Put to the Test

THE Jewish authorities were desperate. "There must be something we can do to stop this Jesus of Nazareth!" the highest Jewish officials discussed in secret. "We can't get rid of Him by force because He's always surrounded by adoring crowds. If we went to arrest Him and they turned on us, we'd be totally outnumbered.

"We've warned everyone that Jesus isn't even a prophet, let alone the Messiah, and we've told the people that He's turning them away from our true religion. They're so bewitched by Jesus that they're not taking any notice.

"We can stand in the middle of the temple and shout and yell and stamp our feet as much as we like. It doesn't seem to have the slightest effect on Jesus."

After a lot of scheming, the chief priests and scribes decided to try a different tack. They ordered their spies to go and mingle with Jesus's

supporters in the temple. They were told to try and lead Him into saying something that would break the law. The Jewish elders rubbed their hands with glee at the thought of finally catching Jesus out. Their enemy would soon be hauled in front of the Roman provincial governor for judgement and punishment – and the harsher the better!

"Teacher," the spies wheedled from among the temple crowds. "We know that you truly teach the way of God. He is the only leader you respect and the law of heaven is the only law you follow. So what should we do about earthly leaders and earthly laws? For instance, the Roman Emperor Caesar demands that we give him taxes. Should we pay this tribute or not?"

"Why are you putting me to the test?" Jesus said. He wasn't fooled for one second.

> ❝ *Knowing their hypocrisy, He said to them, 'Why put me to the test?'* ❞

"Look at this coin," Jesus instructed, showing a piece of Roman money to the spies. "Whose head and inscription does it have on it?"

"Caesar's," the spies mumbled.

"Exactly," replied Jesus, flipping the coin at them. "So give to Caesar the things that belong to Caesar, and give to God the things that belong to God."

With his answer, Jesus had dashed the plans of the Jewish elders yet again. Despite their bitter frustration and disappointment, even they couldn't help but be awed by the wisdom of the carpenter's son from Nazareth.

❧ ABOUT THE STORY ❧

One of the big debates among the Jews of the 1st century AD was how they should regard the Romans who occupied their country. Some wanted to rebel and fight the Romans. Others accepted the invaders in order to make life easy. So this was a clever question. If Jesus sided with the Romans, He was a traitor to the Jews. If He sided with the Jews, He was a traitor to the Romans. He still got out of it!

The Roman battlefield
The taxes that Caesar demanded were used to run the empire. This included paying for the hated Roman army pictured here in a battle with barbarians.

Roman standard
The Roman standard was the ceremonial emblem, carried on a pole, by soldiers in the army. The Roman army was the most efficient in the world and the standard was a symbol of power and strength.

Jewish Elders Try a Trick

THE Sadducees tried to trip Jesus up and expose Him as a fraud. They thought up the trickiest question they could imagine and strode confidently to the temple to put it to Jesus.

"If a woman has been widowed seven times," the smug Sadducees asked Jesus, "which of the seven men she married will be her husband in the life after death?"

The Sadducees didn't know the answer to questions like these, so they had come to the conclusion that life after death couldn't exist. They still thought they were cleverer than everyone else for having come up with the questions at all.

Yet Jesus wasn't at all foxed.

"You know nothing of the scriptures or the power of God," He replied bluntly. "When people are raised from the dead, they are not married. They are like angels in heaven. As for life after death, haven't you read in the scriptures that God said, 'I am the God of Abraham and Isaac and Jacob'? As you know, He's not the God of the dead, He's the God of the living!"

After that, the stunned Sadducees didn't dare ask Jesus any more questions. The Pharisees did.

"What is the greatest of all of God's commandments?" they asked Jesus.

"To love God with all your heart and mind and soul," Jesus replied at once. "Second most important is to love your neighbour as you love yourself. All the other commandments rest on these two."

The Pharisees were dumbstruck. Jesus didn't just know the scriptures better than anyone else, he understood them better, too.

"Now let me ask you a question of my own," Jesus said. "If the Christ is the son of King David, how come in the scriptures David calls the Christ 'Lord'?"

Of course, the Pharisees didn't know the answer. And, as they stood gaping open-mouthed, they heard titters of laughter ripple through the temple crowds.

"This man is making us look like fools!" the chief priests, scribes, Sadducees and Pharisees raged in private. "We have to get rid of Him if it's the last thing we do!"

Jesus and the saints
This stone carving shows Jesus surrounded by symbolic representations of the saints, Matthew, Mark, Luke and John. These saints wrote the four Gospels, the books in the Bible that tell us about Jesus's life and teaching.

> ❧ **ABOUT THE STORY** ❧
> *The Sadducees only accepted the first five books of the Old Testament and they would not believe anything that was elsewhere in the Bible. They were very unpopular and acted in a very superior way. They loved intellectual arguments, which were of no help to people who wanted to know God better. They were not open to what God might say; they just wanted to prove Jesus was not one of them.*

The Great Denunciation

THE trouble between Jesus and the Jewish authorities had reached boiling point. It was as if the temple itself was split into a battlefield, with the chief priests and scribes mustering their forces on one side, while Jesus roused His loyal troops on the other.

"The scribes and Pharisees follow in the footsteps of Moses," Jesus preached, in a loud clear voice. "So do as they say." He paused for a second, to make sure He had everyone's full attention. "However, make sure you don't do as they do, for they are hypocrites!"

The hundreds of listeners gasped as if with one voice.

Jesus's eyes sparkled with anger. His hair bristled with outrage. "Everything they do is for show!" He roared. "They recite long elaborate prayers many times a day, but they stand in full view of everyone to do it, to make sure that they are seen and admired by all. They wear long, fancy robes to make sure that everyone notices them. They make sure they sit up front at feasts and at the synagogue, so that everyone knows they are there. They tell you to address them as 'Rabbi', so they can feel that they're superior to you all."

Both murmurs of agreement and gasps of shock came from the crowd.

"Well," Jesus went on, "I tell you to call no one 'Rabbi'. You have one master, who is the Christ. You have one teacher. You have one father – our Father in Heaven – and you are all brothers and sisters. I can assure you that whoever sets themselves up as superior to others will one day find themselves the lowest of the low. Whoever does their best to serve others, will one day find themselves honoured with greatness."

Jesus shook His head sadly. "Yes, I feel sorry for the scribes and Pharisees," He cried, "for they will never see heaven themselves. Worst of all, these blind fools are leading you, the general public, astray, so they're shutting the gates of the kingdom not just against themselves but against others, too."

The crowd erupted into a clamour of outrage.

"Let me give you an example," Jesus said. "They tell you that an oath on the temple is meaningless, but an oath on the sacred temple gold is binding. This is ridiculous! For which is greater: the gold or the temple which made the gold sacred? Similarly, they tell you that to swear by the altar means nothing, yet to swear by a holy altar sacrifice is to make a solemn vow! Nonsense, again! For which is greater: the sacrifice itself or the altar which makes the sacrifice holy?"

The listening men and women looked at each other. It was hard to argue with that type of logic...

Jesus continued, "So I tell you that anyone who swears by the temple swears by it and by Him whose house it is!"

Ripples of applause broke out among the stunned crowd. The temple was full, and everyone was listening intently to Jesus's words.

"Furthermore," Jesus went on, "the scribes and Pharisees tell you that the hundreds of tiny rules they follow are vitally important. By doing so, they put a heavy burden on the shoulders of anyone who wants to follow God. Moreover, their preoccupation with minor matters means that they neglect the weightier matters of the law, such as justice and mercy and faith! I tell you that the scribes and Pharisees are like whitewashed tombs, which from the outside appear beautiful, but on the inside are full of dead men's bones. They are the sons of those men who, through history, were so blinded by their own self-righteousness that they refused to listen to the prophets. Even today, they are persecuting, driving out and killing the very people sent by God to help and warn them. O Jerusalem! How many times have I tried to show you the way to salvation? Yet your house is tumbling into ruins! You will not see me again until you say, 'Blessed is He who comes in the name of the Lord.'"

Jesus looked around at the hundreds of faces in the crowd. Angry discussions were breaking out between those who agreed with His criticism of the elders and those who thought He had gone too far. Jesus could see that many of the men and women hadn't really grasped what He meant.

His eyes fell on a tiny, bent-over old woman, hobbling to the temple collection box on crooked legs. Younger, richer people were sweeping past her, nearly knocking her over. One by one, they dropped in their handful of silver or gold with a smile of self-satisfaction and stalked away, head held high. Eventually, the poor widow reached the collection box for her turn. She shoved a shaky hand into her tattered pocket and brought out two coppers – the only money she had left in all the world. She dropped the coins into the box without a moment's hesitation and stood for a while, saying a silent prayer, before hobbling away.

Jesus smiled, and pointed the poor and feeble woman out to everyone in the crowd that had gathered around Him.

> ❝ *Truly, I tell you, this poor widow has put in more than all of them.* ❞

"That widow has done more good than all the scribes and Pharisees put together," He told the hushed throng. "For they only donate as much as they reckon they can afford, making sure they still have riches left over. This woman has very little, yet she has given it all for the love of God."

Synagogues
A synagogue is the Jewish place of worship. It also serves as a centre for the Jewish community. There are religious services three times a day, with readings and prayers. The religious teacher at the synagogue is called the rabbi. Synagogues may date back to the exile in Babylon in the 500s BC, when the people were far from Jerusalem and had no temple. By the time of Jesus, most Jews outside Jerusalem came together on the sabbath at their local synagogue.

❖ ABOUT THE STORY ❖

Many people think that pleasing God is a matter of keeping certain rules. That is quite natural. Rules give us a structure for daily life. Jesus never said we should ignore God's rules; He encouraged people to keep them. The rules the Pharisees kept had been made up by them. They were customs. The main rules that God and Jesus want us to keep are to love God from our hearts, and to love others as we do ourselves.

The End of the World

JESUS headed back to Bethany for the night. His footsteps were heavy as He trudged wearily along the road, His mind full of the troubles that He knew were close at hand. Jesus began to silently pray to His Father in heaven, asking for guidance and courage. Suddenly His thoughts were disturbed by gasps of awe from His disciples behind Him.

"Look, Master!" came their voices. "How wonderful!"

Jesus spun round to see what His disciples were marvelling at – a fantastic view of the whole of Jerusalem, glowing in the setting sun. The huddles of whitewashed houses nestling in the hills were shimmering pink and orange. The gardens that overflowed down the slopes were flooded with rosy light. Towering over everything, the holy temple itself was ablaze against the skyline, golden fire rippling across its pillars.

"The house of God is truly magnificent!" the disciples cried. "Absolutely breathtaking!"

Jesus nodded His head sadly.

"Take a good look," He said, "and remember. For I tell you that the day will come when not a single stone of all this will remain standing."

With that, Jesus turned back on His way, leaving His disciples puzzled, murmuring among themselves.

"Whatever can He mean?" they wondered, hurrying to catch up. "How would the temple be destroyed? When? Who would dare to pull it down?"

Later, Peter, James, John and Andrew drew Jesus to one side and spoke with Him in private.

"Lord, can you tell us when the end will be?" they asked Jesus. "What signs will there be to show us that it's about to happen?"

Jesus sat quietly for a while, His all-seeing eyes gazing far off into the distance. Then He looked at His friends and sighed.

"The end will not come," He said, "until nation has risen against nation, and kingdom against kingdom. There will be wars and earthquakes and famines, and this will still only be the beginning. Before the time draws near, my gospel must be preached throughout the world to all peoples. You who follow me and who spread my teachings will be persecuted for my sake – even by those whom you most love. You will suffer being beaten and put on trial and even executed. You must have courage to be my witness in spite of it all. The Holy Spirit will tell you what to

ay and will give you the strength to endure through verything that is sent to test you. In the end, whoever has tood firm will be saved.

"Be very careful that no one leads you astray. There will e many who come in my name, saying, 'I am the Christ', ut you must not listen to these false prophets. They will

work wonders and show you great signs and warn you that the end is about to come – all to get you to abandon me and follow them. Do not believe them. Remember that I told you all this would happen, and take heart.

"When the end of time finally draws near, the sun will darken and the moon will no longer give out light. The stars will fall from the skies and the seas will rise up against the earth. People everywhere will tremble with fear and faint with terror at what is happening, for the very powers of the heavens will be shaken. But my faithful followers should not be afraid. It is then that you should raise your heads and look up with glad hearts. For your salvation will then arrive. The Son of Man will come riding on the clouds in all His glory with all the angels. He will send them out on the winds to all four corners of the earth, and He will gather every single good person to Him.

> **Take heed, watch; for you do not know when the time will come.**

"When exactly this will happen, I cannot tell you. No one knows – not the angels in heaven, not the Son of Man – only the Father Himself. Be ever watchful. You do not want God to come suddenly and find you sleeping. For if the Lord comes on a day you do not expect, and you have left it too late to prepare yourself, there will be no hope for you. You will be cast out into hell, where souls suffer eternal punishment, and you will be left to weep and wail for ever in the darkness of utter despair."

❖ ABOUT THE STORY ❖

Jesus taught a lot about the future, but He never gave people enough detail to enable them to work out exactly what would happen when. In fact, "the end time" in the Bible is really the whole period between Jesus's resurrection and His return or "second coming". He says people are not to waste time trying to work out what the future will be, but to use their time wisely so that they are ready for anything.

Destroying the temple
As Jesus predicted, the temple in Jerusalem was destroyed by the Romans in AD 70. This stone relief shows them plundering the temple and stealing its treasures.

The end of the world
This is the explosion of a nuclear bomb. In the story, Jesus warns His disciples that the world will come to an end, and tells them to be prepared for this. Today, many people see the image of a nuclear explosion as a symbol of the end of the world brought about by humankind.

Judas Plots Betrayal

THE chief priests and scribes, Pharisees and Sadducees, were at their wits' end. They had tried to trick Jesus and it hadn't worked. The crafty Nazarene troublemaker had foiled every trap they had laid. No, cunning was no good. The Jewish elders would have to go back to their first option – force. They still had the same old problem – Jesus's crowds of supporters felt so passionately about their teacher that they'd fight tooth and nail to defend Him. Even though the authorities desperately wanted Jesus out of the way, they didn't want to risk their own lives in doing it.

Secretly, the Jewish elders gathered together in the palace of the high priest, Caiaphas. They brainstormed and schemed and argued long into the night, and came up with just one possibility. Sooner or later, they decided, Jesus would be on His own, without the support of His disciples. They would have to seize the moment with both hands. They would approach Jesus by surprise, backed up with troops, and arrest Him swiftly and without any fuss. The elders were determined that nothing would go wrong this time. The opportunity would be rare and they might only get one chance.

One big hurdle still remained. Even with their spies in the crowds, the Jewish dignitaries couldn't watch Jesus every minute of every day and night. After all, He was closely flanked by His 12 disciples at all times and they disappeared off together now and again in private. However were the elders going to be able to find out where and when to make their move?

Who knows, the Jewish authorities might never have got the chance at all if it hadn't been for a traitor inside the camp. Months before, Jesus had warned the disciples that one of them would turn to evil. The shocked men hadn't been able to believe it and had instantly laughed it off. Even so, the thought had haunted them for a while. Which one of them was Jesus talking about? What kind of evil could they possibly turn to? As time had passed, each one of the twelve had pushed the ridiculous thought further and further to the back of their minds until they had all totally forgotten it.

Roman atrium
Wealthy men such as Caiaphas would have received guests in a large hall, called an atrium, inside the front door. This picture of an atrium in Pompeii shows that the roof was open to the sky, to let in light. An atrium often contained a pool, which helped to keep it cool, as well as plants and statues.

Caiaphas's house
This picture shows the stone steps that lead up to Caiaphas's house. Caiaphas was the Jewish high priest and, as such, was the head of the Sanhedrin (the Jewish high court). Meetings such as the one described in this story may have been held in Caiaphas's house in order to keep them secret.

Yet Satan hadn't forgotten. He had been niggling away t the heart of Judas Iscariot for some time now, playing n his weaknesses, eating away at his doubts, filling him up with the poison of jealousy. On the fateful night that he elders sat plotting in Caiaphas's palace, Judas found hat a wicked idea popped into his head as if from nowhere.

> *Then Satan entered into Judas called Iscariot, who was of the number of the twelve.*

The chief priests and scribes, Pharisees and Sadducees, ever found out what made Judas Iscariot do what he did. n any case, they didn't care. In the end, they were just ;lad that he came knocking on their door, although at irst they glowered at him with suspicion.

"Everyone knows that you're after Jesus of Nazareth," Judas swaggered. "Well, I'm one of His most trusted friends."

"Y-e-s," the high priest uttered in a low voice. "Go on…"

Under Caiaphas's stony gaze, beads of sweat began to break out on Judas's forehead. His dull eyes blinked shiftily.

"Surely I'm exactly what you need. Someone who can get closer to Jesus than you ever could," he blustered, "if the price is right, of course."

An excited murmur went round the table and eager smiles lit up the elders' wrinkled faces. They could hardly believe their good fortune! Urgently, the corrupt officials huddled together and discussed for a while.

It seemed like a lifetime to Judas, all alone in the middle of Caiaphas's great hall, with his heart pounding inside his chest. Finally, the Jewish elders settled themselves back into their chairs and arranged their robes around them.

"We will pay you thirty pieces of silver for delivering Jesus of Nazareth into our hands," they announced haughtily. "No more and no less."

Judas swallowed hard.

"Done," he said.

After a quick drink with his new friends to seal the matter, he hurried off into the night. There wasn't a moment to lose if he was going to claim that reward.

Love of money
The Jewish priests hand over the money to Judas. Judas is prepared to betray Jesus to satisfy his own greed. The Bible states that you cannot serve both God and money, and that money should be valued for what can be done with it, not in its own right.

❧ ABOUT THE STORY ❧

No one knows exactly why Judas betrayed Jesus. He seems to have been a loyal member of the disciples up until now. He was probably motivated by several reasons, money being the least of them. He may have been very mixed up about who Jesus was and what He had come to do. Maybe he thought this action would help. His betrayal, though, warns readers that even those closest to Jesus can turn against Him.

Jesus Faces His Betrayer

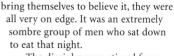

JESUS knew that time was running out. He would very soon be leaving the troubles and wickedness of this world and would return to His Father in heaven. He was filled with great sadness at the thought of leaving behind all those He loved on earth. He and His 12 closest friends would be able to share just one more evening together – the Passover supper. Yet in order to enjoy each other's company for the last time, the arrangements had to be highly secret, so Jesus's enemies couldn't find Him.

"Go into Jerusalem and watch for a man carrying a pitcher of water to pass by," Jesus instructed two of His disciples. "Follow him and he will lead you to a certain house. Ask the owner of the house to show you where your teacher is to celebrate the Passover. You will then be taken to a large upstairs room where you'll find all you need to make everything ready."

Later that evening, the disciples made their way cautiously to the appointed meeting place. Their mood was serious. It certainly wasn't going to be the joyful Passover supper of previous years. This time, everyone was deeply worried. Only two days before, Jesus had warned His friends once again that He was soon to fall into the hands of His opponents and that they would put Him to death. Even though the disciples still couldn't bring themselves to believe it, they were all very on edge. It was an extremely sombre group of men who sat down to eat that night.

The disciples were stirred from their grim thoughts when Jesus suddenly stood up, took off His outer robes, tied a towel around His waist and filled a bowl with water. They realized with shock that He was preparing Himself to wash the dust from their feet – a job usually done by the lowliest servants.

When Jesus came and knelt down beside Peter, who was horrified.

"Master, I can't allow you to do that for me!" Peter cried, laying hold of Jesus's hands.

"You don't understand now what I'm doing," Jesus replied, "but trust me – later you will." Peter was adamant and swung his legs out of reach.

"I'll never let you wash my feet, Lord," he said, firmly.

"Then I can't call you my friend," Jesus said to him with a sad smile.

"Well, in that case, wash my head and hands too!" Peter urged his friend and master.

"No," said Jesus, gently wetting Peter's feet. "Anyone who bathes needs only to have their feet washed to take away the dust from the road."

Jesus busied Himself with the towel.

"All of you are clean – except for one," He said to

Jesus the servant
Jesus took on the role of a servant and washed His disciples' feet. He taught His followers to serve each other as equals.

Footwashing
Most people wore open sandals, so their feet quickly became dirty. It was therefore customary for guests to have their feet washed on arrival at a house. A servant would usually carry out this task, using a water bowl like the one shown here.

Himself. He moved around the group of friends, attending to them in turn, and returned to His place at the table.

"You call me 'teacher' and 'Lord'," He said to the 12 companions, "and that's what I am. Just as I have stooped to wash your feet, so you should humble yourselves before others. Remember that a servant is not greater than his master, and always show other people the kindness, care and respect that I have shown you today."

Jesus paused for a moment and sighed a heavy sigh. His brow grew furrowed and His face darkened.

> ## For He knew who was to betray Him.

"One of you will betray me," He said in a low voice.

Hurt cries of protest went up from all around the table, and Jesus held up His hand for quiet. He refused to say anything more and motioned for everyone to return to their meal.

As the disciples went back to their eating and chatting, Peter found he had suddenly lost his appetite. He signalled to John, who was sitting nearest to Jesus.

"Please ask Jesus to tell us who He means," Peter whispered.

John leant over for a moment and murmured to His master, and the hushed answer came back, "The one to whom I will give this bread."

Peter watched as, slowly and deliberately, Jesus tore off a piece of His bread, dipped it into the dish in front of Him and offered it to Judas Iscariot.

"Do what you have to do," Jesus said quietly, "but do it quickly."

Without a word, Judas got up from the table and left the room.

The disciples who noticed him go thought that Jesus was sending him on some sort of errand – perhaps to buy some more wine, or to go to distribute some food to the poor. They didn't give him more than a sideways glance.

Yet Jesus had looked deep into Judas's eyes. He had seen that they were cold and hard.

Teachers and pupils

Much of Jesus's teaching took place in the temple, which was officially used as a school for Jewish children. Many Roman children, though, did not go to school as they had to work. Richer children went to a primary school between the ages of six and eleven. After this, some boys went to a secondary school.

The Last Supper

JESUS motioned for His 11 friends around the table to fall quiet. Soon, all attention was fixed firmly on Him.

Jesus reached out for a hunk of bread. He shut His eyes and lifted the bread up heavenwards. Loud and clear, He said a blessing over it, giving thanks to God. Then Jesus broke the bread into pieces and handed it round to each of the disciples.

"Take it... eat it..." He said, pressing the bits of bread into His friends' hands. "This is my body, which will be given up for you."

The wide-eyed men did as their master instructed.

Next, Jesus poured some wine. He reverently lifted the goblet up and blessed it, praising aloud to God. Then Jesus held the brimming cup out to His friends. "Take this, all of you, and drink from it," He said. "This is my blood, the seal of a new and everlasting promise from God. My blood will be spilt for you and for all people so that your sins may be forgiven."

> **This is my body which is given for you. Do this in remembrance of me.**

One by one, the disciples took the goblet to their lips and drank.

"I am giving you a new commandment," Jesus told them. "To love each other as I have loved you. Then everyone will know that you are my followers. May my peace always be with you. Don't let your hearts be troubled, and don't be afraid. Just follow everything that I have told you and be joyful. For you will know that I am alive in the Father, that you are alive in me, and that I am alive in you. If you keep my commandments, you will show that you truly love me. My Father in turn will love you."

Jesus rose to His feet. "Now come," He said, opening His arms and smiling at His friends. "Accompany me to the Mount of Olives. I should like to pray for a while in the Garden of Gethsemane."

As they walked through the moonlight, Jesus continued to talk. He had many things still to tell the disciples and only a little time left in which to say them.

"I want you to do the things I've done tonight as a way of remembering me," Jesus told the disciples. "For I will be with you only a short while longer and then I must go away. Where I am going, you cannot follow."

The disciples turned to each other in disbelief.

"Lord, where are you going?" Peter cried.

"I will not leave you for ever," Jesus consoled. "I am going to prepare a place for you in my Father's house. I will return a while, and then I will have to go away again. Even though you won't be able to see me anymore, I'll always be with you – inside your hearts. Later on, when the time comes, you will follow me and we will all be together again."

Peter couldn't bear the thought of Jesus leaving them. "No!" he insisted, stopping in his tracks. "Why can't we follow you now?"

Jesus looked at His companions sadly. "By the end of the night, you will all have deserted me," He said.

Site of the supper
Jesus's last meal with His disciples is traditionally believed to have been held in the building shown above. It is called the Coenaculum and is situated on Mount Zion in Jerusalem.

The Holy Grail
In medieval legend, the Holy Grail is the cup used by Jesus at the Last Supper, or the dish that was on the table during the meal. The medieval knights of the Round Table went on quests to find the Grail, which are described in the stories of King Arthur, written from the 1200s onwards. The word "grail" comes from the Old French word "greal", meaning a kind of dish. The image of the Grail is also used to represent the human body containing the Holy Spirit.

CHRISTIANS HAVE DIFFERENT VIEWS ABOUT THE WAY THEY SHOULD CELEBRATE THIS LAST SUPPER. SOME CALL IT MASS, OTHERS EUCHARIST OR HOLY COMMUNION, SOME THE LORD'S SUPPER OR BREAKING OF BREAD. FOR ALL THEIR DIFFERENCES, THEY AGREE THAT THIS IS THE CENTRE OF WORSHIP. IN SHARING BREAD AND WINE, THEY SHOW THEY DEPEND ON GOD AND WANT TO DRAW ON HIS GRACE FOR THEIR LIVES. ❧

"Not me!" Peter cried. "I will never desert you! I would lay down my life for you!"

There was a chorus of agreement from the other disciples, who were just as shocked.

"Would you, Peter?" Jesus said softly. "My friend, before you hear the cock crow to greet the dawn, you will have denied three times that you know me."

Peter almost wept.

"I will never deny that I know you," he gulped, "even if it means that I have to die with you."

❧ ABOUT THE STORY ❧

The Last Supper took place during a Jewish Passover meal. During the meal, there were a number of symbolic actions which reminded people of what God had done for them. Among these actions were the sharing of bread and wine. Jesus took these and gave them a new meaning. God was making a new agreement with His people, sealed by the death of Jesus and setting them free from slavery to sin and death.

Remembering Jesus
This is a picture of the Last Supper by the Italian artist Leonardo Da Vinci. Christians today commemorate Jesus's last meal with His disciples by eating and drinking holy bread and wine. The bread and wine are referred to as the body and the blood of Christ.

In the Garden of Gethsemane

IN the Garden of Gethsemane, the disciples yawned wearily. "Stay here and rest," Jesus said kindly to the disciples.

As the grateful men began to collapse to the ground, Jesus stopped Peter, James and John.

"My friends, I know you are tired too," He said, "but would you keep me company?"

The three disciples saw that Jesus's face was creased with sorrow and His eyes sparkled oddly. They accompanied Him further on. They had never seen Jesus so sad and troubled before. "I must be on my own to talk to my Father," He said. "My heart is so heavy, I fear it is breaking. Will you watch over me while I pray?"

Peter, James and John looked on helplessly as Jesus sank to His knees, clutching His head in His hands.

"Oh my Father!" Jesus cried out from His soul.

He felt the sins of all the world pressing in on Him from all sides, and He knew the horror of what lay ahead. "Father, nothing is impossible for you. I beg you, please take away the suffering that I have to face."

Jesus prayed for a long while and Peter, James and John were overcome by sleep. "Couldn't you have stayed awake just one more hour for me?" Jesus whispered to them. "Be careful of temptation," He said, softly. "Your spirits are willing, but your flesh is weak."

Again He prayed, "If this torment must come, then I will endure it. Your will, not mine, should be done."

Eventually Jesus arose and went back to His friends.

"I beg you, wake up!" He whispered urgently.

The three exhausted men stirred, but didn't wake. Trembling, Jesus returned to His lonely prayers.

"Father, I know the hour has come," He groaned. "Give me the strength to die gloriously. Holy Father, look after these people so they may reach you safely. I pray also for those whom I haven't met, but who believe because they hear about me through others."

> 66 *Judas, would you betray the Son of Man with a kiss?* 99

Jesus returned one last time to Peter, James and John.

"Are you still sleeping?" He murmured. "No matter. It's time. Look, my betrayer is here."

Suddenly, flaming torches came flashing through the dark. Shadows loomed forwards from all around.

The disciples woke and dashed to Jesus's side. They faced a band of armed men – hired hands of the elders.

WE DON'T OFTEN THINK OF JESUS NEEDING US, ONLY OF US NEEDING HIM. HOWEVER, ON THIS OCCASION, WHEN HE NEEDED HIS FRIENDS TO ENCOURAGE AND HELP HIM THEY FAILED. TODAY, JESUS NEEDS PEOPLE TO BE HIS HANDS AND HIS VOICE IN THE WORLD. EACH TIME HE IS LET DOWN, HIS TEARS FLOW AGAIN. ∽

Jesus's retreat
The Garden of Gethsemane was situated to the east of Jerusalem, near the Mount of Olives. In Hebrew, "Gethsemane" means "oil press", and this is where the mountain olives were brought to be pressed into oil.

Kneeling to pray
Jesus and his disciples often went to pray in the Garden of Gethsemane. The way Jesus went down on his knees to pray gave rise to the Christian custom of kneeling to pray.

"Who are you looking for?" Jesus asked.

"Jesus of Nazareth!" the men shouted angrily.

"I am He," announced Jesus.

There was something so powerful in His voice and manner that the thugs shrank back nervously.

Then a face the disciples knew well came forward.

"Master!" said Judas Iscariot, greeting Jesus with his usual embrace.

"Oh Judas," Jesus sighed sadly, "must you betray me with a kiss?"

It was the sign the thugs had been waiting for and they leapt forwards to seize their enemy.

Jesus didn't resist, but the disciples flung themselves at the soldiers. Peter had brought a sword, but his wild slashes only cut off the right ear of the high priest's servant.

"Enough!" roared Jesus. "Put away your sword, Peter, for those who use violence die by violence. If my Father meant for me to be protected, armies of angels would speed to my rescue."

Jesus touched the wound. At once, the ear was healed.

Then Jesus turned to the mob.

"Am I a criminal, that you come to take me like this?" He demanded. "Every day I was there in the temple. Yet this fulfils the prophecies. It is evil's greatest hour."

With that, Jesus was marched away. Panic broke out among his followers, and as the remaining guards turned on the yelling crowd, the disciples fled for their lives.

Betrayed with a kiss
When Judas kisses Jesus, he is giving a signal to the soldiers. Jesus is sad that His disciple has betrayed Him with a kiss, which was normally given as a sign of affection or respect.

Christ's passion
Jesus expressed His anguish at His fate in a prayer to God. He knew that His mental pain would be even worse than the physical punishment He was to endure.

❧ ABOUT THE STORY ❧

Jesus knew, and He had always known, that He would be crucified in Jerusalem. He had foretold it often enough to his apostles, but knowing it did not make it any easier. Crucifixion was a horrible, painful way to die. The human side of Jesus almost opted out of His divine calling. Despite His struggle with His natural human fears, He knew that God's eternal will was more important than His short-term suffering.

Peter's Denial

MARCHING along to the soldiers' rhythm, Jesus saw the mighty city of Jerusalem rearing up in front of Him. Guards held Him tight on either side and lowered spears were aimed at the ready at His back. Without slowing the pace, the soldiers tramped straight through the city gates and along the streets to the grand house of Caiaphas, the high priest. All the time, following behind them was Peter, cloaked by the night. He made sure he kept at a safe distance, but he didn't let Jesus out of his sight for a single instant. Peter even followed the soldiers right into Caiaphas's courtyard. Then he could go no further. Jesus was taken through Caiaphas's huge front doors and they slammed shut. Peter's friend had disappeared from view and he himself was shut out in the cold.

Peter turned and found himself looking into the curious faces of strangers. The high priest's servants and maids had built themselves a fire in the middle of the courtyard, and they were huddled around it to keep warm. Trying not to draw any more attention to himself, Peter drew his robe further over his face and lowered his head. He edged nearer the circle of people to join them and did his best to enter into the general conversation.

Even though Peter was now standing near to the blazing fire, nothing could take away the cold fear that grasped his heart. Ice seemed to be running through his veins and it was as if an empty blackness was eating away at his stomach. Peter shuddered, and a serving maid peered at him through the flickering flames. A look of recognition crossed her face and she pointed her finger at him.

"You're one of the prisoner's followers, aren't you?" she blurted out.

Peter's heart began to race. Here he was, all alone in the midst of his enemies.

"Of course not!" he muttered. "I don't know what you mean."

Very gradually, Peter shifted into the shadows a little.

As he sat alone and shivered, footsteps drew near.

"You are," said another serving maid, looking hard into Peter's face.

She raised her voice to her colleagues around the fire. "This man was with Jesus of Nazareth," she cried.

"No I wasn't," Peter insisted frantically. "I don't know anyone of that name."

He gathered his robes more tightly round him and hoped desperately that no one would notice he was breaking out into a cold sweat.

"You must be one of Jesus's followers," said a servant, coming right up close. "You speak with a Galilean accent."

The crowing of the cock
Many people kept poultry, and the sound of a cock crowing at dawn would have been a familiar one. It was a signal that the night was over and the next day was beginning.

Peter
When Peter denies knowing Jesus it is an example of human weakness. Even the most dedicated followers of Jesus are vulnerable when their loyalty is tested. This reminds us that only God can provide us with the strength to avoid temptation.

Galilee
The area in northern Israel where Jesus and Peter grew up is called Galilee. It is mostly hilly, with a large lake known as the Sea of Galilee. Galilee was a much wealthier region than Judea, having made the most of the Roman occupation, and its people were not popular in Jerusalem. The people who accused Peter recognised his strong Galilean accent.

"Yes," said another, moving in towards them. "Didn't I see you in the garden with Him?"

> ❝ *Peter again denied it and at once the cock crowed.* ❞

Peter sprang to his feet in terror. His voice was high and shrill. "I've told you!" he cried. "I don't know the man!"

As the servants nervously backed away, a raucous noise ripped through the air – the sound of a cockerel. Peter's heart began to pound in his chest as he remembered Jesus's words: "My friend, before you hear the cock crow to greet the dawn, you will have denied three times that you know me." Then the tears began to pour uncontrollably from Peter's eyes and, filled with utter misery and sadness, he stole away to be on his own with his shame.

Peter's weakness

Peter denies that he knows Jesus. When Jesus had predicted this, Peter had been adamant that he would die before denying Him. However, concern for his own safety took precedence and Peter was not strong enough to stand by his master and friend. Jesus had known this would happen.

Armed with spears

The soldiers who arrested Jesus would have carried spears similar to the ones shown here. Earlier spears had now been replaced by the heavy javelin (called a *pilum*), which had a sharp, narrow point. The javelin was thrown through the air and its point could pierce the shield and even the armour of an enemy.

❖ ABOUT THE STORY ❖

While he was with Jesus and the other disciples, Peter was brave and determined. Once he was on his own, his courage melted away. He was confused and frightened. This story shows the human side of one of Jesus's greatest followers. It shows that even the best can fail, when they expect to succeed. Peter's mistake was to stop trusting God just when he needed that trust most. The good news was that later, Peter was forgiven.

Trial Before the Sanhedrin

CAIAPHAS's palace was filled with a sinister silence. Jesus's footsteps echoed as he was marched down the long corridors, then through a big, heavy door. Jesus found himself in an important looking chamber. Annas, the former high priest, was standing at the window. "So this is the famous Jesus of Nazareth," he said.

He looked Jesus straight in the eye.

"I've heard so much about you," he said, with a stony smile, "but I'd rather hear it from your own lips."

Then the questioning started. What did Jesus think about the scriptures? What miracles did He claim to have worked? Who did He think He was? Throughout it all, Jesus remained quiet and calm. He didn't say a word, even when Annas peered closely into His face. Finally, the former high priest lost his temper.

"Answer me!" he spat. "Or I'll have you thrown into prison until you find your tongue!"

"I have always spoken openly," Jesus replied softly. "I have preached in public. I have never taught in secret, so why ask me about my work? Why don't you ask any of the people who came to hear me?"

SMACK! A guard's hand stung Jesus's cheek. "Is that how you talk to your betters?" the soldier raged.

"If I have said anything wrong, explain to me what it is," Jesus said. "If not, why have you hit me?"

Annas had had enough. He was getting nowhere.

"Take him away!" he barked.

Jesus was marched off to Caiaphas, the high priest, and the council of Jewish elders, the Sanhedrin. The officials

Money-changers
The priests in the story are described as corrupt because they took advantage of their positions to increase their own wealth. They insisted that only one currency was used to pay taxes at the temple and to buy sacrificial animals. Money changers exchanged currency for the worshippers at the temple, charging them for this service. The priests claimed part of the proceeds for themselves, and this was one of the things for which Jesus condemned them.

Public meetings
Jesus used to preach a great deal in public places. He often used open spaces in the countryside so all the people could hear Him. The Romans built these buildings called amphitheatres specifically for large meetings, and to hold plays and games.

began to fire false accusations at Jesus. They even brought out false witnesses whom they'd bribed with money. Yet no two witnesses could be found to agree on a story.

Eventually, a couple of men came forward.

"We both heard this man say that He could destroy the temple of God and rebuild it in three days," they agreed.

Jesus had said this, but He had been referring to His own body. He was foretelling that He would be raised up to life three days after His death. The men, like most people, had misunderstood.

> ## I have said nothing secretly

"Have you nothing to say to that?" Caiaphas raged. Still Jesus didn't move a muscle.

"Right!" Caiaphas yelled, losing all patience. "I order you to tell us, under solemn oath, whether you think you're the Son of God!"

When Jesus spoke, there was majesty in His voice.

"I am," he said, "and one day you will see the Son of Man seated at the right hand of the Father in Heaven."

"Blasphemy!" Caiaphas bellowed, purple with fury. "He has insulted God! What shall we do with Him?"

"Put Him to death!" the elders roared.

At long last, they had Jesus where they wanted. They blindfolded Him and spat on Him, and punched and kicked Him, saying, "Let's hear you prophesy, now, Christ! Tell us who it was that struck you!" Their laughter rang through the night.

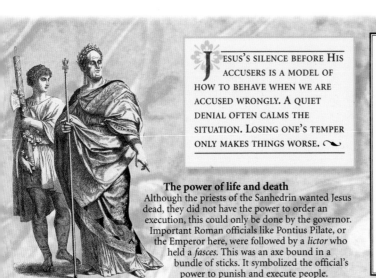

JESUS'S SILENCE BEFORE HIS ACCUSERS IS A MODEL OF HOW TO BEHAVE WHEN WE ARE ACCUSED WRONGLY. A QUIET DENIAL OFTEN CALMS THE SITUATION. LOSING ONE'S TEMPER ONLY MAKES THINGS WORSE.

The power of life and death
Although the priests of the Sanhedrin wanted Jesus dead, they did not have the power to order an execution, this could only be done by the governor. Important Roman officials like Pontius Pilate, or the Emperor here, were followed by a *lictor* who held a *fasces*. This was an axe bound in a bundle of sticks. It symbolized the official's power to punish and execute people.

❖ ABOUT THE STORY ❖

When Jesus first mentioned to His apostles that He was the Son of God, He made it clear to them that they were not to tell anyone. He did this because people were expecting the Messiah to be an earthly soldier and leader who would fight the Romans and force them to leave Judea. However, now Jesus knows that the time for Him to reveal the truth has arrived. He can tell the truth, and the prophecies will be fulfilled by Him.

Pontius Pilate

EVEN though the chief priests and scribes had passed sentence, one more hurdle lay in front of them: an execution could only be ordered by the Roman governor, Pontius Pilate. They didn't have a moment to waste...

The whole of Jerusalem awoke that morning to the news that the elders had condemned Jesus of Nazareth to death. When the gossip reached the ears of Judas Iscariot, he was totally appalled at what he had done. Filled with shame and remorse, he tore to the temple as fast as he could to try to put things right.

"I have committed a terrible sin!" he cried to the chief priests. "Jesus is innocent and I have betrayed Him!"

The Jewish officials just stared at Judas coldly.

"That's not our problem," they said. "It's yours."

Despair flooded over Judas. He threw his thirty pieces of silver onto the temple floor and ran out into the city streets. Later, Judas Iscariot's body was found hanging. He was too disgusted with himself to go on living.

Meanwhile, in another part of the city, Jesus was standing in Pontius Pilate's judgement hall. The Roman governor looked at the weary, bruised man and then said, "So, are you the King of the Jews?"

"Are you asking me this for yourself," Jesus replied softly to the governor, "or because you've heard other people say it about me?"

Pilate looked away from Jesus's steady gaze. "Look," he said seriously, "your own people and priests have handed you over to me. Tell me what you've done."

"My kingship is not of this world," Jesus said. "If it were, my servants would have fought to prevent me being handed over to the Jews."

"So you are a king?" the intrigued Pilate challenged.

"Yes," said Jesus. "I was born for this and I came into the world to bear witness to the truth."

Pilate paused for a while, deep in thought.

"The Jewish elders tell me that you've been plotting against the Roman government," he said.

Jesus said nothing.

"They say that you're rousing up the Jews against us," Pilate continued, "that you're encouraging them not to pay Caesar's taxes, and setting yourself up as their leader."

Again, Jesus remained silent.

Roman Robur
When Jesus was beaten by the Roman soldiers, He was probably taken to a robur like this one. It was a pit, deep underground, for beating prisoners.

Pilate's judgement
This picture shows Jesus standing in front of the Roman governor, Pontius Pilate. Only Pilate had the authority to sentence him to death. Under Roman law, blasphemy was not a crime. So, in order to persuade Pilate to pass the death penalty, the Sanhedrin told him that Jesus was guilty of treason against Rome.

"Hmmmm," said Pilate. He strode out, leaving Jesus with the guards.

"I find that this man has done nothing wrong," Pilate announced to the elders.

> ❝ *For he knew that it was out of envy that they had delivered him up.* ❞

"He's a troublemaker!" they insisted. "He's been stirring up people all the way from His home in Galilee to Judea!"

"Galilee!" Pilate suddenly spotted a way out of this situation. "Well, if He's from Galilee, then it's Herod who should deal with Him."

Herod happened to be in Jerusalem that week, so Pilate hurriedly had Jesus marched over to see him. Jesus was soon back in Pilate's palace, though. Herod was unable to find Jesus guilty of any crime either. On top of everything, Pilate's wife said, "Last night, I had a dream about Jesus of Nazareth. He is innocent of everything that the Jews have accused Him of. Have nothing to do with Him."

That settles it, Pilate thought. The Jewish elders have delivered this man up out of envy. He strode out and found that a huge crowd had gathered outside.

"This man has done nothing to deserve death," Pilate announced to the Jewish elders and the people. "I shall have Him flogged and let Him go!"

With that, Pilate's guards dragged Jesus away to be soundly whipped.

The praetorium
The military headquarters and palace where the Roman provincial governor, such as Pontius Pilate, lived was called the praetorium. It had a large tower at each corner, as in the picture. Two of these towers overlooked the main temple. Pilate's soldiers brought Jesus to the palace's private judgment hall, where he was tried.

✥ ABOUT THE STORY ✥

The Sanhedrin have to send Jesus for trial to the Roman governor, as they do not have the power to order His execution themselves. However, they realise that Pilate will not listen to their complaints about Jesus's religious claims, so they tell Pilate that Jesus has been plotting against the Roman government, thinking he will be more likely to convict Jesus. The governor realises that the charges are unfounded, and releases Him.

Condemned to Die

THE Jewish authorities had done their work well. They had mingled with the crowds, persuading them that Jesus was a blasphemer and a liar. As Pilate turned to walk away into his judgement hall, the citizens of Jerusalem cried out in protest. "No!" the hundreds of men and women cried out to Pilate. "Kill him! Kill Jesus of Nazareth!"

Pilate was totally taken aback.

"Why?" he said. "Whatever has he done?"

The Roman governor felt sure that Jesus was innocent. All at once, he had an idea that would help him get Jesus off the hook. Pilate had remembered that it was the custom at Passover to release a prisoner of the people's choice. He knew that there was a murderer in the cells by the name of Barabbas. Pilate felt sure that the people of Jerusalem would much rather have Jesus walking among them in the streets than a bloodthirsty killer.

"Who would you rather have me release?" Pilate asked the crowds. "The King of the Jews or Barabbas?"

"Not Jesus of Nazareth!" the shouts came back. "We want Barabbas released! Give us Barabbas!"

Meanwhile, the Roman governor's soldiers were taking great delight in punishing their Jewish prisoner. They had gathered the whole battalion to come and join in the fun. Armed with cruel barbed whips, they rained down blow after blow, lashing Him with all their strength. Each soldier only stopped when he was out of breath and the sweat was dripping off his forehead, then another immediately stepped forward to take his turn. Every time Jesus was forced to His knees by the constant pain, the guards hauled Him up roughly to withstand more. Their leather thongs ate into Jesus's flesh. The blood streamed off His body and ran along the floor. Even then, the

❧ ABOUT THE STORY ❧

The charge that Jesus was the Son of God made Pilate afraid. Like many Romans, he was superstitious. He believed there were many gods, and that it was a good idea not to get on the wrong side of any of them. However, he was more concerned about getting a bad report from the Jews, which could stop him getting promotion. (Judea was not a very important posting.) So he sacrificed Jesus for himself.

Punishment before death
Jesus is flogged by the Roman soldiers. The punishment of flogging was often used before putting someone to death.

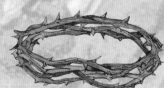

Crown of thorns
In Roman times, a crown was a symbol of royalty and kingship, just as it is today. Crowns were usually made of gold, or other precious metals, but the Roman soldiers made a crown by weaving together the stems of a thorny plant. By putting this on Jesus's head, they were making fun of the idea of Him as a king.

soldiers hadn't had enough. They plaited a crown of thorns, pressed it into Jesus's scalp and threw a regal purple cloak around His shoulders. The Roman guards gave Jesus a reed to hold for a royal sceptre, and propped Him up in the midst of them.

"Hail, King of the Jews!" they mocked, knocking Jesus to the floor and spitting on Him.

Suddenly, Pilate himself strode in.

"Help the man to stand and bring Him out here with me," he ordered. "Immediately!"

So Jesus was brought bleeding in His crown and cloak before the jeering crowds.

"Look!" bellowed Pilate. "Look at this man! I have not found Him guilty of anything!"

The chief priests and elders began to cry, "Crucify Him!" and the crowds quickly picked up the chant.

> ## The chief priests answered, 'We have no king but Caesar.'

"Take Him yourself and crucify Him!" Pilate roared, knowing that under Roman law they couldn't. "In my eyes, He's done nothing wrong!"

"By Jewish law He should die!" the Jewish officials shouted back. "He says He's the Son of God."

At that, a look of terror came over Pilate's face. Straight away, he had Jesus marched inside again so he could speak to Him in private one last time.

"Who are you?" he urged, lifting up Jesus's drooping head. "Where have you come from?"

Jesus didn't answer.

"Why won't you speak to me?" Pilate moaned. "Don't you know that I hold in my hands the power to have you either put to death or set free?"

Jesus raised His eyes.

"You would have no power at all over me if it hadn't been given to you from above," He said quietly. Pilate made up his mind.

"I shall release this man!" he announced to the crowds.

A deafening roar of disapproval went up all around the Roman governor.

"Then you will be no friend of Caesar's," warned the chief priests. "Anyone who says they're a king is flaunting their defiance of Rome!"

The last thing Pilate wanted was to get into deep water with the emperor himself. Trembling with nerves, he called for a bowl of water and a towel. As the Roman governor washed his hands in front of everyone, the clamouring crowds fell into an expectant hush.

"I cleanse myself of this man's blood," Pilate declared.

This time, the noise that went up from the crowd was that of cheering.

Minutes later, Barabbas the murderer was released and Jesus was led out to be crucified.

Washing away the guilt
Pilate washes his hands before Jesus's crucifixion. By doing this, he was telling the crowd that he did not want to be held responsible for Jesus's death.

POLITICIANS TODAY VALUE PUBLIC OPINION. THEY OFTEN MAKE POLICIES TO WIN THEM VOTES. THE BIBLE REMINDS US THAT PLEASING GOD IS MORE IMPORTANT THAN PLEASING PEOPLE.

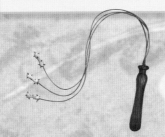

Tortured and mocked
This Roman whip is similar to the one that would have been used to flog Jesus. It consists of three leather cords attached to a handle. After Jesus had been flogged, the soldiers mocked Him by dressing Him in a purple tunic. This colour was normally worn by royalty.

Crucifixion

THE slumped figure was hardly recognizable as Jesus. The crown of thorns cut into His head. Blood ran down His battered face. His robes were stained from His wounds. Yet Jesus's kind eyes still shone with compassion. His tormentors had not broken His spirit.

The guards heaved in a solid wooden cross, twice the size of Jesus, and laid it on His back. Slowly, Jesus dragged it off through the packed streets of Jerusalem. Each step took every bit of His strength and will. Eventually, He stumbled and collapsed into the dirt, the cross crashing down on top of Him. The soldiers hauled Jesus to His feet and heaved the cross onto His back. Jesus's knees buckled and He sank to the floor, unable to move any further.

The infuriated soldiers turned towards the crowd of onlookers and dragged out a broad-shouldered man, called Simon of Cyrene. He had no choice but to carry the vicious cross on his back. Jesus staggered along behind him with two condemned thieves.

People lined the roads to see the criminals. They yelled insults and spat. Running desperately among the crowds were Jesus's friends. Many women wept bitterly, unable to turn their eyes away from Jesus's suffering, even though they could do nothing to help.

"Don't weep for me," Jesus told them, "but for yourselves and your children for the destruction which is to come."

Eventually they reached Golgotha. A soldier offered Jesus wine and pain-killing herbs, but He refused. Then came the agonising hammering – one long nail through each hand and one piercing both feet.

"Father, forgive them," cried Jesus, "for they don't know what they are doing!"

A placard was fixed above Jesus's head, reading: 'Jesus of Nazareth, King of the Jews' in three languages.

"It shouldn't say that!" the elders yelled in protest. "It should say, 'This man said, "I am King of the Jews".'"

Pontius Pilate silenced them with a glare, and they turned their attention to taunting Jesus instead.

"If you're the Son of God, come down from the cross!" the chief priests mocked.

"He said He saved others, now He can't save himself," scoffed the Pharisees.

"You said you could destroy the temple and rebuild it in three days," yelled the elders, "so why can't you get free?"

> " *Father, forgive them; for they know not what they do.* "

While the officials yelled their jibes, two other crosses were raised, one either side of Jesus's twisted body.

"You said you were the Christ," sneered one of the thieves. "So save yourself and us too!"

"How dare you!" gasped the other thief. "We deserve our punishment, but this man is innocent! Lord, remember me when you reach your kingdom."

"I promise you," Jesus whispered, "today you will be with me in paradise."

Suddenly darkness fell over the whole land. A cold wind screeched, drowning out the soldiers at the foot of the cross who were casting lots for Jesus's clothes.

All those who loved Jesus clung together in grief, as close to the cross as they dared. Among them were Jesus's mother Mary, the disciple John, and Jesus's friends Mary Magdalene and Salome.

"Mother," came Jesus's voice, "look after John as your son. John, take care of my mother as your own."

For three long hours, the weeping friends watched Jesus's silent agony. Then suddenly His voice rang out: "My God, my God! Why have you abandoned me?"

One of the mourners rushed to lift a stick with a sponge of wine on the end for Jesus to drink.

"Father, I give up my spirit into your hands," He cried loudly. "It is finished!" His head drooped

At that moment, a great storm broke. The ground shook and rocks split open. The veil which hung in the temple ripped into two. Some people later swore that they saw graves open and spirits rise out of them.

The Roman centurion at the foot of the cross gasped, "This man truly was the Son of God."

And terror struck the hearts of everyone at Golgotha.

❖ ABOUT THE STORY ❖

This story is packed with symbolism. Jesus refuses the wine to dull the pain, because He has to carry the weight of sin without help. Darkness falls as a sign that Jesus has been cut off from God. Pilate is more accurate with his placard than the religious leaders realized.

Golgotha
It is not known exactly where Golgotha was, but it is often thought to be this hill outside Jerusalem.

Simon of Cyrene
The man who carried the cross for Jesus, Simon of Cyrene, was probably a pilgrim visiting Jerusalem for the Passover. Cyrene was a city in North Africa, with a large Jewish population.

Jesus is Buried

THE dead body of Jesus hung on the cross until evening was drawing near. Then the Jewish elders began to grow rather agitated. Sunset would mark the start of the Sabbath, and the holy day would be made unclean if the men weren't taken down from their crosses, and the thieves that had been crucified with Jesus were still alive.

The Roman soldiers didn't need much encouraging. Glad to speed things up, they marched over to the thieves and broke their legs with a couple of savage blows. The robbers sank down under their own weight, making it impossible for them to breathe. Within minutes, they had suffocated to death.

The soldiers didn't bother doing the same to Jesus – everyone knew that He was already dead. As the Romans walked away, one soldier spitefully thrust his spear as deep as he could into Jesus's side, just for good measure. Jesus's watching friends saw blood and water gush from the wound. They shuddered and turned away in horror.

As dusk began to fall on the city of Jerusalem, Pontius Pilate sat alone, brooding on the death of Jesus of Nazareth. A servant disturbed the Roman governor from his troubled thoughts to tell him that a wealthy member of the Sanhedrin was begging to see Pilate at once.

When the visitor was ushered in, Pilate was mightily relieved to find it was Joseph of Arimathea, a Jewish official widely held to be good and just and fair.

Joseph bowed low. "Sir," he began, "I come to confess a secret. I myself am one of the followers of Jesus of

Roman burial urn
Jesus's body was buried, but some Romans at this time had their bodies cremated and the remains put into urns. This marble burial urn contains the ashes of a woman called Bovia Procula. The inscription on the urn describes her as a "most unfortunate mother". This may mean that she died during childbirth, as many women did at this time.

Jesus and Nicodemus
This bronze carving shows Jesus talking to Nicodemus, a Pharisee who came to Him for secret teaching. Not much is known about Nicodemus, but he was probably a member of the Sanhedrin.

Harrowing of Hell
This Greek Orthodox icon shows Jesus going down to Hell after His death. In medieval times, this episode was called the "Harrowing of Hell".

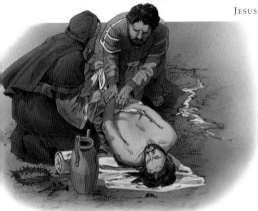

Joseph had prepared for his own burial – and they laid Jesus inside. Then Joseph and Nicodemus rolled a heavy stone in front of the tomb to close it up. There was nothing more that could be done, and at last everyone went their own sad way into the night.

Meanwhile, an extremely annoyed Pilate was busy giving an audience to yet more callers from the Sanhedrin.

"Sir, when that imposter was alive, He said He'd rise up to life again after three days," the officials said. "Therefore, order a guard to be set around the tomb until the third day, so His friends can't come and steal the body and trick everyone into thinking His words have come true."

"You have your guard!" roared Pilate.

By the time darkness had fallen, armed guards were the only living things in the garden of graves where Jesus lay.

Nazareth," Joseph continued, "although I did not tell my colleagues who, as you well know, envied and hated Him. I was one of the few on the Sanhedrin who voted against this innocent man's death. Now I have come to ask a favour. Please allow me to take Jesus's body down from the cross and bury it."

> ❝ *Joseph took the body and laid it in his own new tomb.* ❞

Pilate didn't have to think twice. "Very well," he said.

So it was that, in the dim evening light, a member of the very Council that had bayed for Jesus's blood, tenderly recovered His body from the cross. A friend called Nicodemus had brought burial spices of myrrh and aloes, and he and Joseph hurriedly wrapped Jesus in a linen shroud. Together, the two men carried Jesus's body to a nearby garden cemetery, and the women who had been friends of Jesus followed close behind, wailing aloud. A small cave-like tomb had been carved out – the tomb that

Myrrh and aloes
In the story, Nicodemus provides expensive spices for Jesus's burial. Myrrh is a sweet-smelling gum from the bark of a tree. Aloes is the bitter juice of the aloe plant. Before burial, the body was washed and wrapped in a linen cloth, and the head was wrapped in a linen square. The spices would have been put between the folds of linen.

Joseph of Arimathea
Joseph of Arimathea carries two flasks containing Jesus's sweat and blood. With Nicodemus, Joseph prepared Jesus's body for burial.

❖ ABOUT THE STORY ❖

There was no doubt that Jesus died. Roman soldiers had seen many dead bodies; they knew all the signs. The blood and water is a sign for later readers, however. It showed that the red and white cells of Jesus's blood had begun to separate around the heart, which happens after death. There was no trickery or mistake which caused Jesus to live on. Furthermore, the Gospel writers saw Jesus's death as a fulfilment of Old Testament prophecy.

Jesus Disappears

THE torches of the Sanhedrin's guard flickered outside Jesus's tomb all night of that first Good Friday. Sitting in the cemetery among the dead, the soldiers were very glad when they saw the light of Saturday finally dawning. They kept watch all that next long day, through the evening and into Saturday night. As it grew closer to the dawn of the third day after Jesus's death, the soldiers became increasingly jumpy. The Sanhedrin had assured them that they only had to fear the living, not the dead. They were on the lookout only for Jesus's friends coming to steal the body, not for ghosts. No, those haughty Jewish officials certainly didn't believe that a dead man was going to come walking out among them – but then they weren't sitting in front of the tomb, were they?

> ❝ *Tell people, 'His disciples came by night and stole Him away while we were asleep.'* ❞

When the first light of the sun crept over the horizon on Sunday morning, the soldiers kept their eyes open, brandishing their spears and swords at the slightest rustle of the birds among the bushes.

Suddenly, the earth began to tremble under the soldiers' feet. It began to shake so violently that the guards were flung headlong on to the ground. A searing white light blazed out of the sky and descended over the tomb, dazzling the soldiers where they lay. They peered through their fingers and saw with astonishment that a man as luminous as lightning, as white as snow, was rolling away the massive stone from the entrance of the tomb. Nearly paralysed with fear, the cowering soldiers managed to scramble to their feet and flee for their lives.

At the same time, a group of sorrowing women were making their way to the tomb, among them Jesus's devoted friends Mary Magdalene, Mary the mother of James and John, and Salome and Joanna. They had seen how hurriedly Joseph and Nicodemus had had to prepare Jesus's body before sundown brought the Sabbath, and the kind women meant to attend to the body properly, anointing it and wrapping it with all the customary care and attention. As the grieving friends walked along through the earliest rays of the morning sun, they worried that they might not be strong enough to move away the huge stone. When they drew close to the spot, their pulses began to race. They could see that someone had already

Easter parade
Here you can see a Good Friday procession in Jerusalem. Christians are gathering to re-enact Christ's walk to Golgotha with the cross.

Ossuary
In Roman times, there were two stages to a Jewish burial. First the body was wrapped, anointed and placed in a tomb. Later, when the flesh had decayed, the family gathered up the bones and put them in a stone box called an ossuary.

Meanwhile, the terrified guards had taken their amazing story straight to the chief priests and an emergency meeting of the Sanhedrin was called. There was much shouting and arguing, thumping of tables and blaming of each other. In the end, a desperate decision was reached.

"Take this for your troubles," the elders soothed, pushing bags of coins into the sweating hands of the pale soldiers. "When people ask you what happened, tell them that you all fell asleep on duty in the night, and that Jesus's disciples crept up on you and stole the body. If Pilate himself somehow gets to hear of this mess, we'll buy his silence too. Don't worry, just say what we've told you and we'll make sure you don't get into trouble."

That was the story that was soon spread around the Jews of Jerusalem.

done it. Hearts pounding, the women raced to the tomb. Wherever were the soldiers who had been set to guard the body? Which wicked people had got there before them? What terrible things were they doing to their beloved Jesus's body, even at that very moment?

When the first couple of women reached the tomb and squeezed inside, they screamed. Jesus's body was gone, and sitting where His body should have lain, there were two shining men in radiant clothes.

"Why are you looking for the living among the dead?" came the men's voices. "Don't you remember that the Son of Man said He'd rise on the third day?"

The startled women nearly fell over each other in their hurry to get out of the tomb. Pushing their friends before them and sobbing an explanation, they ran away as fast as their legs could carry them.

JESUS HAD TOLD THE DISCIPLES THAT HE WOULD RISE FROM THE DEAD, BUT THEY HAD NEVER UNDERSTOOD OR BELIEVED HIM. REAL FAITH TAKES GOD AT HIS WORD, AND EXPECTS HIM TO FULFIL IT.

Mary Magdalene
When she first met Jesus, Mary Magdalene was possessed by evil spirits. When Jesus cured her of this "illness", she became a devout follower of His. It is not clear from the Bible whether her illness was physical, mental or moral, or some combination of the three.

❧ ABOUT THE STORY ❧

The Bible writers do not tell us what happened to Jesus between His death and resurrection. There is one hint in Peter's second letter which suggests Jesus told the good news of His victory over sin and death to the people who had died before and were waiting in "Hades", or Hell. The Bible writers focus instead on the supernatural elements of the resurrection. This action, they are saying, is a miracle of God.

The Women Meet Jesus

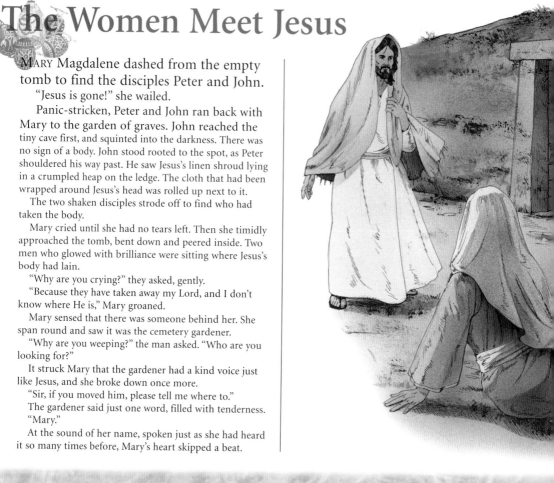

MARY Magdalene dashed from the empty tomb to find the disciples Peter and John.

"Jesus is gone!" she wailed.

Panic-stricken, Peter and John ran back with Mary to the garden of graves. John reached the tiny cave first, and squinted into the darkness. There was no sign of a body. John stood rooted to the spot, as Peter shouldered his way past. He saw Jesus's linen shroud lying in a crumpled heap on the ledge. The cloth that had been wrapped around Jesus's head was rolled up next to it.

The two shaken disciples strode off to find who had taken the body.

Mary cried until she had no tears left. Then she timidly approached the tomb, bent down and peered inside. Two men who glowed with brilliance were sitting where Jesus's body had lain.

"Why are you crying?" they asked, gently.

"Because they have taken away my Lord, and I don't know where He is," Mary groaned.

Mary sensed that there was someone behind her. She span round and saw it was the cemetery gardener.

"Why are you weeping?" the man asked. "Who are you looking for?"

It struck Mary that the gardener had a kind voice just like Jesus, and she broke down once more.

"Sir, if you moved him, please tell me where to."

The gardener said just one word, filled with tenderness. "Mary."

At the sound of her name, spoken just as she had heard it so many times before, Mary's heart skipped a beat.

The Garden Tomb
It is not known exactly where Jesus's tomb was situated. The Bible tells us only that it was in a garden near where the crucifixion took place. Christians believe its most likely location is here, a place called the Garden Tomb, in Jerusalem.

Easter eggs
In many European countries, people celebrate Easter by decorating eggs and giving them as gifts. Eggs and flowers are a symbol of new life.

"Teacher," she cried and sank to her knees, gazing up adoringly at the man she loved above all others.

"Go now," Jesus smiled. "Find my disciples and tell them that I will soon be returning to my Father."

Meanwhile, the other women who had seen the stone rolled aside were still scurrying home together in fear. All at once, they saw the dim form of a man appear in front of them in their path, and they sprang back in alarm.

"Good morning," said the figure.

The women couldn't believe their ears at the familiar voice. They fell to the ground with amazement.

"It can't be!" they whispered. "Jesus, is it really you?"

"Don't be afraid," Jesus smiled, holding His arms out towards His friends. "Go and tell my disciples to travel to Galilee, and I will meet them there soon."

> **" Mary Magdalene went and said to the disciples, 'I have seen the Lord!' "**

The vision disappeared as suddenly as it had arrived.

A little later, Mary Magdalene burst into the room where the disciples sat together in grief, red-eyed and miserable. Her face was flushed with excitement.

"I have seen the Lord !" she cried and, in a joyful tumble of words, told them everything that had happened.

The disciples shook their heads sadly. They wanted to believe Mary, but they had seen Jesus hanging on the cross with their own eyes. There was nothing anyone could say to change that.

❖ ABOUT THE STORY ❖

Many attempts have been made to "prove" that Jesus did not truly rise from the dead, and that this was a "spiritual" experience like a vision. The Gospel writers include little details that have a ring of truth. The grave clothes are lying as if the body has passed through them; Jesus did not just take them off. Grave robbers are not so careful. Mary failed to recognize Jesus because she was upset, not in a spiritual state of hope.

Jesus appears to Mary Magdalene

This painted wooden statue, dating from the 1600s, shows Mary Magdalene meeting Jesus, after He has risen from the dead. Mary Magdalene was the first person to see Jesus after the resurrection. She set off for the tomb with a group of women, but apparently ran ahead of them and arrived before them. When she discovered the tomb was empty, she immediately went to find Peter and John. After they had gone to search for the body, Mary remained alone at the tomb, weeping. It was then that she saw two angels, followed by Jesus Himself, risen from the dead.

On the Road to Emmaus

LATER on that morning of the third day, two of Jesus's disciples began walking out of Jerusalem on their way to Emmaus, a little village about eleven kilometres away. The subdued companions trudged along with heavy hearts, going over and over Jesus's sudden capture, unfair trial and terrible death. As they walked, a stranger caught up with them on the road and asked to walk with them.

"Of course, friend," replied one of the disciples, Cleopas, and then carried on with the conversation as before.

The stranger seemed puzzled.

"Can I ask what you're talking about?" He said.

Cleopas stared at the man, stunned.

"You must be the only person in the whole of Jerusalem who hasn't heard about the events of the past few days," the disciple remarked.

The stranger shrugged His shoulders innocently.

"What events?" He asked, His eyes twinkling.

"The things that have happened to Jesus of Nazareth, the greatest prophet who ever lived," replied Cleopas, reverently. "You must have heard of how our chief priests and elders seized Him, persuaded the Roman governor to condemn Him to death and then had Him crucified?"

The stranger shook His head.

"All our hope was in Jesus of Nazareth," Cleopas went on. "We had believed that He was the one sent to save us."

He paused and swallowed hard.

"Besides all of that," Cleopas continued, waving his disappointment aside, "it is now the third day since His death. Earlier on, some of the women in Jesus's company of friends brought us an amazing story about having found His tomb empty and having seen a vision of angels, who said that He was alive!"

The stranger's eyes grew wide with surprise.

"Of course," Cleopas explained, "some of us dashed straight there to see for ourselves. All we saw was that the body had indeed gone – nothing else."

The disciples hung their heads gloomily.

Suddenly the stranger seemed to know more than He

❧ ABOUT THE STORY ❧

Once again, two disciples fail to recognize Jesus. Luke brings out two important points. One is that Jesus was recognized in the breaking of bread. Christians today claim that they "meet" Jesus in a special way when they "break bread" in communion. Secondly, Jesus was known for His "burning" teaching: it gave them hope and challenged them. Today, Christians meet to hear His teaching read and explained, and to "hear" Him through it.

The resurrection
"Resurrection" means to bring a dead person back to life. "Resuscitation" can mean this too, but a resuscitated person will die eventually. Christians believe when someone is resurrected, their soul enters a new body, in which they will spend eternity.

had previously let on.

"Don't you understand what the prophets had foretold?" the man rebuked the disciples gently. "It was necessary for Christ to suffer, in order for Him to be glorified."

The stranger went on to explain the mysteries of the scriptures as the disciples had only heard Jesus explain them before. Cleopas and his companion were so fascinated by the stranger's knowledge that when they reached Emmaus and the stranger made to bid them goodbye, they begged Him not to travel on down the road but to stop with them for the evening.

So it was that the two disciples came to be having supper with the stranger. When the man took some bread and blessed it, broke it into pieces and gave it to them, the disciples at last realized who He really was.

"Jesus!" they gasped, pushing back their chairs and springing to their feet.

The stranger vanished before their very eyes.

"We should have known!" the disciples scolded each other as they hurried straight back to Jerusalem through the darkness. "Didn't your heart burn strangely within your chest as He explained everything to us?"

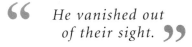

> " *He vanished out of their sight.* "

When the disciples reached the city, they found the disciples in a buzz of excitement. Before Cleopas and his friend could even get a word out, the disciples cried, "Peter has seen the Lord!" and dragged them into the room to tell them how Jesus had appeared to Peter and chatted with him. When the two disciples finally managed to explain how they too had met with Jesus, the room erupted in a riot of cheering and praying and weeping for joy. It seemed that Mary Magdalene's story was true, after all!

Emmaus
It is not known exactly where the village of Emmaus was situated, but some people believe it was here, at the village of Amwas, about 11km west of Jerusalem.

Jesus's last days
The Bible tells us that Jesus was resurrected on the third day. He appeared to Peter and to all the disciples, including Cleopas and his companion as they walked to Emmaus. Jesus used this time to visit His disciples, to reinforce their faith and to prove to them all that He was resurrected, that His prophecies had come true.

Doubting Thomas

JESUS's followers were jubilant, and everyone in the room wanted to talk to Peter and Cleopas and his friend at once. The disciples crowded round the three men, firing questions and praising God, begging to hear them tell again and again exactly what Jesus looked like and each word of what He said.

All at once, the hubbub died away into silence. Everyone stood stock still, staring open-mouthed at the newcomer among them. No one had heard anyone knock. No one had seen anyone enter. Yet there He was. It was Jesus.

> 66 *Jesus said to them, 'Come and have breakfast.'* 99

"Peace be with you," Jesus said, softly, greeting His friends with a familiar raise of the hand.

Everyone shrank back in fear.

"Be careful, it's a spirit!" came murmurs from the back of the room.

A frown creased Jesus's brow. "Why are you frightened?"

He asked. "I am no ghost. Look here, see the wounds on my hands and feet. It's me, Jesus."

A few of the disciples began to creep nearer, cautiously.

"Yes," urged Jesus. "Don't be afraid to touch me. See, spirits don't have flesh and bones, as you can feel that I have."

As the first trembling hands touched Jesus's warm skin, the faces of Jesus's followers brightened into delight.

"Master!" they cried. "It's really you!"

Laughing at their amazement, Jesus sat down at the table in the midst of them. Together, everyone shared a meal, just as they had done so many times before.

Now there was one disciple who wasn't present to see Jesus for himself. When Thomas later heard his friends' story – even though he saw their gladness and joy – he found the news too hard to accept.

"Unless I can touch the mark of the nails in His hands with my own fingers, and put my own hand into the wound in his side, I can't believe it," Thomas whispered.

No matter how hard he tried, he couldn't get rid of the doubts that nagged away inside him.

Eight days later, Jesus's followers were again gathered together in private, doors tightly locked against the prying

eyes of the Jewish council's spies. Just as before, halfway through the evening Jesus appeared silently among them. No one noticed His arrival.

> ❝ *'See my hands and my feet, that it is I myself'* ❞

"Peace be with you," He greeted his friends and turned straight to Thomas, who had shrunk back, thunderstruck.

Jesus reached out and took the terrified disciple's hands.

"Here," Jesus said, holding Thomas's fingers against the nail wounds in His palms. "Feel the wound in my side. Don't doubt any longer. Have faith. It is true."

As Thomas's fingers sank into Jesus's flesh, he broke down and wept.

"My Lord and my God!" he cried.

"You believe now because you have seen me for yourself," Jesus said, gently. "Even more blessed are those who don't see me and yet still believe."

M OST PEOPLE HAVE DOUBTS. IN FACT, IT WOULD BE TRUE TO SAY THAT FAITH IS NOT REALLY FAITH IF THERE IS NO RISK OR DOUBT AT ALL. FAITH IS NOT THE SAME AS CERTAINTY. WE CANNOT PROVE TO OTHERS THAT GOD EXISTS OR THAT HE LOVES US. WE CAN ONLY DISCOVER GOD'S LOVE FOR OURSELVES AS WE SEE GOD AT WORK IN OUR LIVES, AND EVEN THEN ONLY WHEN WE TRUST HIM TO SHOW US. 〜

Doubting Thomas
Thomas was a believer but his faith was mixed with uncertainty. He could not believe Jesus was alive again unless he saw and touched the scars. The phrase "a doubting Thomas" has come to mean a person who refuses to believe something without proof.

❖ ABOUT THE STORY ❖

This story shows that even a close friend of Jesus could doubt what had actually happened. It could be said that those who believe today are in a way showing more faith than Thomas and the others. There is plenty of evidence to convince us that it did happen – the evidence of the disciples written down for us and the generations of Christians since.

The Appearance at Galilee

SEVERAL of the disciples gathered one evening by the Sea of Galilee. The men looked out over the water at the beauty of the setting sun. They shared fond memories of all the precious times they had been on the lake with Jesus, floating in private in Peter's little boat, far from the crowds of disciples on the shore.

Now, once again, the ex-fisherman pushed his boat into the sea and his friends jumped in: James, John, Thomas and Nathaniel among them. They unfurled the sail and felt the wind push them into deeper waters. Under the stars, they cast their nets and sat quietly together, waiting.

All night long the men fished, but time and again they raised their nets to find them empty. There was still nothing in the nets by the time the dawn began to show itself over the glassy water.

"Have you caught anything?" came a voice, floating over the waves to the fishermen.

The disciples looked towards the shore and made out the small figure of a man on the beach.

"No! Nothing!" they hollered back.

The man cupped His hands to His mouth and called back, "Try casting your nets to the right of the boat!"

Peter and his friends decided they may as well try the stranger's advice. As they lowered the nets over the side, they felt them grow heavy with fish. In fact, it took all the disciples' combined effort to heave them back up again!

As John watched the hundreds of slippery bodies wriggling on the floor of the boat, he remembered a time when Jesus had given similar advice, and exactly the same thing had happened. Of course! he thought, turning to Peter and beaming broadly. "It's the Lord!" he cried.

At once, Peter's face lit up and he dived straight off the

Jesus the shepherd
This statue of Jesus as the Good Shepherd comes from Turkey and dates from the 300sAD. Jesus saw Himself as a shepherd, with people as His flock. He said, "I am the good shepherd. The good shepherd lays down His life for His sheep. I know my sheep and my sheep know me".

Catching fish
In Jesus's time, people caught fish with nets, like the disciples in the story, or with a hook and line. The fish-hook shown here is made of bronze, but earlier ones were made from bone or iron. Fish were an important source of protein, as not many people ate much meat. Although fishermen often made a good living, they worked very hard. After fishing for most of the night, they then had to haul in the catch, mend the nets and sails, and dry, salt or pickle the fish ready to be taken to markets in other towns and villages.

boat into the water. Laughing with delight, the disciples watched as Peter splashed out for the shore in his eagerness to reach Jesus. Turning the sail into the wind, they headed for the beach themselves.

Peter ran dripping up the beach to find that Jesus was busy getting a little fire going.

"Go and bring some of the fish!" Jesus yelled. "Then come and have some breakfast!"

The overjoyed Peter immediately ran back down the shore to where his friends were landing the boat.

"Hurry up!" he yelled, practically jumping up and down with excitement.

Minutes later, together again with their master, Jesus's friends enjoyed the most delicious meal they had ever tasted, in the warmth of the early morning sun.

After they had all eaten their fill, Jesus turned to Peter and looked deep into his eyes.

"Peter," He asked, seriously, "do you love me?"

"Yes, Lord," the disciple replied, "of course I do!"

> **66** *Lord, you know everything, you know that I love you.* **99**

Jesus asked the question twice more. Each time, Peter grew more offended that Jesus felt He had to ask again. Peter didn't realize that each time he told Jesus he loved Him, his friend was forgiving him for having denied he knew Jesus on the night He was arrested.

At the third time of asking, Peter cried, "Lord, you know everything! You know very well that I love you!"

"I want you to look after my people like a shepherd looks after his flock," Jesus replied, "and follow me."

PETER'S EXPERIENCE TELLS PEOPLE TODAY THERE CAN ALWAYS BE A NEW START WITH JESUS WHEN WE LET HIM DOWN. HE DOES NOT FORSAKE US WHEN WE FAIL HIM. IT IS POSSIBLE TO WORK FOR HIM AGAIN.

Fishers of men
This picture shows Jesus speaking to the disciples as they fish from their boat. Jesus said, "Come, follow me and I will make you fishers of men." In this story, the disciples are actually fishing, but Jesus is telling them that by teaching others the ways of Christianity, they would be acting as fishermen of people.

The Ascension

FINALLY, it was time for Jesus to leave the world. He tenderly gathered His disciples together and walked with them once more to the Mount of Olives. It was there, among the groves in which the companions had walked and talked so often, that Jesus said His farewells.

"Don't leave Jerusalem yet," Jesus told His 11 friends. "For John baptized you all with water, but in a short while you will be visited by the Holy Spirit, who will baptize you again. With the powerful gifts my Father will send you, I want you to go and tell people about me through all nations of the world. Preach my gospel to the whole creation, to the very ends of the earth. Baptize all those who believe as my followers, in the name of the Father, and of the Son, and of the Holy Spirit, and teach them everything that I have taught you. For all those who believe and are baptized will be saved from their sins."

Jesus looked around at His friends' sad faces. He lifted up His hands and blessed them.

> " *While He blessed them, He parted from them and was taken up into heaven.* "

"Don't forget," He said, softly. "I am with you always, even until the end of time."

As Jesus spoke, He was lifted up into a dazzling cloud of glory that blazed from up above and hid Him from the disciples' view. All at once, the cloud faded to a glimmer of light, and then it disappeared. Jesus was gone, and the disciples were left gazing up into the blue emptiness of the Jerusalem sky. Their minds were filled with awe and their

hearts were heavy with sorrow.

Voices from nearby brought the staring disciples back to earth with a bump.

"Men of Galilee," they said, "why do you stand looking up to heaven?"

The disciples shook themselves and looked round. They saw two strangers standing nearby in gleaming white robes.

"Jesus has gone from you and is now in heaven. But one day He will return, and He will be just the same as now, when you have seen Him go."

Overcome by wonder and strangely comforted, the disciples slowly made their way back to Jerusalem. In their heart of hearts, each man knew for sure that he wouldn't be seeing Jesus any more. Yet the friends also knew for certain that one day Jesus would return again in glory. After all, Jesus had proved that He never broke a promise, no matter how impossible it seemed.

Olives
In the story, Jesus walks with His disciples among the olive groves. Olives were one of the main crops of ancient Israel. Some fruit was eaten whole but most of the crop was pressed to extract the oil. Olive oil was used in cooking, in lamps and as a lotion to soothe the skin.

The Holy Trinity
Christians believe that there are three persons in God: the Father, the Son, or Jesus, and the Holy Spirit.

❧ ABOUT THE STORY ❧

This is the last resurrection appearance. The "ascension" of Jesus is an acted parable, a picture. It is supposed to make it clear to the disciples that Jesus is going where they cannot follow yet, to heaven. We use symbolic language in the same way. Heaven is not a place up in the sky. Heaven is a completely different form of existence to anything that we know or can experience on earth.

Christian Art Around the World

JESUS was crucified by the Romans, who ruled Israel at that time. He had been handed over to them by the Jewish priests, because of His refusal to submit to their authority. Although the Roman governor, Pontius Pilate, could not find Jesus guilty of any crime, he eventually bowed to pressure and sentenced Jesus to death.

The crucifixion took place outside Jerusalem, at the time of the Passover, just before the Sabbath. Jesus was 33 years old. Crucifixion was a common method of execution at that time, involving a slow, very painful and very public death. First, the Roman guards flogged Jesus and taunted Him, forcing Him to wear a crown of thorns on His head. After this, He was too weak to carry His own cross to the place of execution, so it was carried by a pilgrim called Simon of Cyrene. When He arrived at Golgotha, Jesus was stripped and nailed to the cross, where He died after about six hours.

Three days after the crucifixion, according to the Bible, Jesus rose from the dead just as He had promised He would. A group of women went to the tomb where His body had been buried and discovered it was empty. One of the women, Mary Magdalene, was the first person to see the risen Christ. Over a period of forty days, Jesus appeared to His disciples in Jerusalem and Galilee, and continued to teach them, just as He had done before His death. He commanded them to tell everyone the gospel, or "good news", that His death had made forgiveness and new life possible for all. Then He rose up, or "ascended", to heaven, returning to His Father.

Jesus's death is seen by Christians as the ultimate sacrifice. They believe that He gave his life to pay the price for all the sins of mankind. Because of the resurrection, Christians think of Jesus not as a dead hero, but as a living Saviour who has overcome death. They believe that He helps and guides those who follow Him and that, by offering them the chance of eternal life after death, He makes it possible for them to overcome sin and death, just as He did.

During the reign of Constantine, the first Roman Christian emperor (306–337), the cross became a symbol of Christianity. At first, the cross was empty, which symbolised Christ coming back to life. More recently, the crucifix has become more important. This is a cross with Jesus still on it. As a symbol, this emphasises how Jesus suffered for people's sins.

In the 1500s and 1600s Catholic missionaries, mainly from France, Spain and Portugal, travelled all over the world, spreading the Gospels to people who would not otherwise come into contact with Jesus and His teachings. This has meant that today, Christian art is found all over the world.

Mount of Olives, Jerusalem
This is a picture of Jesus chalked on the floor near the Mount of Olives, at the very heart of Christianity. It shows a heavenly, glowing Jesus before the cross. This emphasises Jesus's resurrection, and His promise of eternal life for all who believe in Him.

Guatemala
This lady is carrying a picture of Jesus as part of an Easter procession. Processions like this one, which recreate Jesus's walk with the cross to be crucified, happen in Christian communities all over the world at Easter. This one is in Guatemala, a small country in Central America.

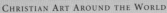

Far Eastern Christianity

This shrine is in Tacloban City, in the Philippines. It is made up of carved, wooden images. Christ is in the centre. Around him are Matthew, Mark, Luke and John, who wrote the Gospels.

India

This is a painting of Jesus, held by children in the city of Madurai, in India. Most of the people in India are Hindu, but the first Christian missionaries arrived in the 1500s. A missionary is a religious person who travels around the world trying to convert people in other countries to their religion.

Crucifixion

This is the sort of scene of the crucifixion that is most often seen in Christian art. It shows Christ on the cross, and important people gathered around Him. On the left is a Roman centurion, and on the right of the picture are Mary Magdalene, Mary, mother of Jesus, and Salome.

Ethiopia

The strong history of Christianity in Ethiopia, in Africa, that is shown in this decorated altar piece, stems in part from the Bible story where the apostle Philip, baptizes an Ethiopian minister. Tradition in Ethiopia claims that this minister, who was probably a royal treasurer, was the first person to spread the Gospel in Ethiopia.

Faith in Peru

Peru is a country on the western coast of South America. It has a strong Christian tradition. The majority of the people are Roman Catholic. The first Catholic missionaries arrived in Peru in the 1500s.

The Gospels

THE word "gospel" literally means "good news". In the New Testament the gospel is the good news that God has fulfilled His promises to Israel by sending His Son, Jesus Christ, to save mankind. The first four books of the New Testament are known as the Gospels but, strictly speaking, they are four different accounts of the same gospel written by four early Christians.

Most of the material contained in the four Gospels would have been passed around by word of mouth before it was written down. The first person to spread the gospel was Jesus Himself. After His death, the disciples carried on teaching people about His life. As those people alive during Jesus's lifetime began to grow older and die, the need was felt for a written record of events. The four books known as the Gospels were written during the second half of the 1st century AD. Three of them – Matthew, Mark and Luke – contain common material although they present it in different ways. The fourth, John, stands apart from the others. Together the four books give a full picture of Jesus.

The first Gospel, Matthew, is presented in a very orderly way and has an emphasis on Jesus's teaching. It was traditionally believed that the author of the first Gospel was the disciple Matthew, but this view is no longer widely held.

Matthew includes most of the stories told in Mark, together with many sayings of Jesus and some other stories. He links the New Testament with the Old Testament much more closely than the other Gospels do, focusing on Jesus as the fulfilment of the prophecies about the coming of a Messiah. Matthew also describes the Christian church as 'the new Israel', explaining that because Jesus was rejected by so many of the Jews, Israel has been expanded to include non-Jews, or Gentiles. He stresses that whereas in Judaism it was the law that was supreme, in Christianity, it is Christ Himself.

The second Gospel, Mark, is usually thought to be the earliest. The author is traditionally believed to be John Mark of Jerusalem, a companion and interpreter of the disciple Peter. In fact, Mark's Gospel has sometimes been called Peter's Gospel, because the influence of the disciple is so apparent.

Mark is shorter and simpler than the other three Gospels, and there is a noticeable lack of detail. One explanation for this may be that Mark's Gospel has its roots in the oral tradition, word-of-mouth story-telling. When stories are repeated from

TIMELINE

JESUS, THE GOOD SHEPHERD
• Jesus turns and heads for Jerusalem.

<u>AD33</u>

JUDAS ACCEPTING HIS SILVER FOR BETRAYING JESUS

• Jesus enters Jerusalem on the back of a donkey, fulfilling the Old Testament prophecies of the Messiah.

• Jesus clears the temple of traders and money lenders.

THE LAST SUPPER

• Jesus and His disciples eat their Passover meal, The Last Supper. Jesus breaks the bread in the ceremony that becomes the Communion.

• The disciples go with Jesus to pray in the Garden of Gethsemane, on the Mount of Olives near Jerusalem.

JESUS IS FLOGGED BY THE ROMANS

memory, they become simplified. Mark's purpose in writing his Gospel was not to produce a work of literature, but to summarize the facts and communicate the truth. His Gospel is best understood as a written record of Peter's teaching.

The author of Luke, the third Gospel, was a well-educated man, with a knowledge of medicine. Through his close contact with Paul and other early Christian leaders, Luke had the opportunity to acquire first-hand knowledge about the life of Jesus and the history of the early Christian church. Luke's Gospel, like Matthew's, includes nearly all the material contained in Mark, but it has been rewritten in a more complex and professional style. It also includes much of the teaching of Jesus which is found in Matthew, together with other information. Luke also intends his Gospel to be seen as a historical work. He does not simply tell the stories but tries also to demonstrate their reliability. More than the other Gospels, Luke focuses on the human interest aspects, such as Jesus's concern for social outcasts. He also emphasizes Jesus's role as Saviour.

It is generally believed that the fourth Gospel was written by the disciple John, or at the very least by a disciple of John's, using his memoirs as a basis. This direct link to Jesus gives the book of John a special importance. John was probably the last Gospel to be written, and the author was likely to have been aware of the contents of the other three. However, the material contained in John is quite different. Unlike the other Gospels, it focuses less on incidents that took place at Galilee and more on Jerusalem. None of the parables are included, but John includes a lot of material that does not appear in the other Gospels. One significant difference is that Jesus often speaks in long dialogues unlike anything found in any of the other three Gospels.

John's Gospel is often seen as more of a personal interpretation of Jesus, rather than a straightforward account of His life. Instead of just telling the story of Jesus's life on earth, John brings out the meaning of it for his readers. His main purpose is to reveal the glory of Jesus as the Messiah, or Saviour, and the Son of God. His aim is to convert his readers to this belief and so to bring them into eternal life.

THE
HOLY
GRAIL

• Jesus is tried by Pontius Pilate. Although Pilate cannot find Him guilty of anything, He is condemned to death.

• Jesus is crucified. Christians believe he was dying for the sins of all the world's people.

JESUS APPEARS AT GALILEE

Jesus is arrested in the garden.

Peter is accused of being a follower and colleague of Jesus. He denies knowing Jesus, and the cock crows.

JESUS BEFORE THE SANHEDRIN

THE HARROWING
OF HELL

• Jesus blesses the disciples, His friends and companions, and He ascends to Heaven to take His place by God.

AD33

SPREADING
THE WORD

These are the stories about what happened after Jesus had ascended into heaven, leaving His apostles to spread the Christian message on earth. Fired by their faith and by the Holy Spirit, the apostles are able to heal illness and perform miracles in the name of God. Their life is not easy, however. As they lay the foundations of the Christian Church, they are opposed and persecuted, threatened and thrown into jail, or even killed.

Introduction

WHEN Jesus died at the time of the Jewish Passover, there were many people who hoped that they would hear no more of His teaching, which had challenged so many established ideas. The apostles, Jesus's closest followers, were disillusioned and disappointed. Their hopes had been dashed.

Foreign gods
This is the Temple of Apollo in modern Turkey. The apostles met great resistance from some people on their travels. All the places they visited already had gods of their own, with great temples built in honour of them, such as this one. They did not want to give up the gods they had been worshipping, sometimes for thousands of years.

With the news of His resurrection, hope returned to the apostles, and fear to the authorities. Yet it was scarcely believable. The apostles struggled to make sense of the resurrection. The authorities explained it away or ridiculed it. Then something amazing happened.

It was another Jewish Festival, 50 days after Passover, the festival of Pentecost. The apostles had been told to wait for an event which they would only recognize when it happened. That day God came upon them in a way they had never known before. They felt His presence and were filled with boldness to preach the message of Jesus.

The Christian church was born. It got off to a flying start, there were 3,000 conversions in a single day. The authorities soon cracked down, though. Prison awaited the disciples when excited crowds rioted after a spectacular healing. It did not deter them or the growing numbers who recognized the real hand of God upon the apostles.

Just as the church was getting itself organized, and people were learning to share responsibility and to meet for worship regularly, Stephen, one of the strongest of the new believers, was arrested, tried and stoned to death for blasphemy. Christians fled in all directions as, flushed with success, the authorities made one last effort to stamp out the Christian church for good. However, not even prison could stop the disciples preaching – especially when, on a couple of occasions, the apostles were freed in what could only be described as a miracle. One disciple, Philip, fled north to Samaria and led a

Paul's base of operations
Ephesus was, at this time, the most important city in the Roman province of Asia, in what is modern Turkey. Paul's final missionary journey had Ephesus as its goal, and he stayed there for over two years. He eventually made Ephesus the base for bringing Christianity to the whole region.

powerful mission in which many people turned to Christ. Others, not named, spoke about the gospel wherever they went, starting small communities of Christians across Judea, Syria and beyond.

Leading the opposition campaign was a Pharisee named Saul. Well learned in the scriptures, he knew all the stories about God's powerful deeds in the past. Little did he expect to experience one for himself. Thrown to the ground by a thunderbolt, blinded by a heavenly light, he was confronted by the risen Christ Himself and was suddenly converted to Christianity.

The new convert to Christianity used his Roman name, Paul, from then on as a sign of his change. After a period of study and reflection, thinking about his experiences, he was found by one of the church leaders, Barnabas, and called in to help the church at Antioch in Syria. It became his base, and from there he set off on three remarkable missionary journeys.

He trekked on foot and by sea all over what is now Asia Minor and Greece, starting churches and looking after the new converts. Although a Jew himself, he became the apostle to the Gentiles, the non-Jewish people, but he was not the first to recognise their rightful place in Jesus's church. That had been Peter, the leader of the apostles since the crucifixion of Jesus.

After an eventful life in which he was shipwrecked several times, beaten by persecutors and muggers, stoned almost to death, and suffering illnesses and deprivation, Paul was finally arrested and shipped to Rome for trial before the Emperor Nero. The remainder of his life is uncertain, except that he was executed some four years after his arrival in Rome.

While he travelled, he also wrote thirteen of the New Testament books. These were mostly letters to people he had met, but they included a couple of essays on religion. He was not the only one to write, however. The New Testament ends with a remarkable vision, written by John, full of powerful symbolism, about the state of the world in the period between Christ's resurrection and future return. The book captures the hope of the first Christians which caused them to face appalling hardships, persecution and the threat of death, all for the sake of Jesus Christ.

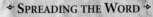

❖ Spreading the Word ❖

This is the history of the early Christian Church, the acts of the apostles in the time after Jesus's death

The Early Church
Acts Ch. 1 to 5, Ch 9 to 13.
Peter's Journeys
Acts Ch. 3 to 5.
The First Christian Martyr
Acts Ch. 6.
The Conversion of Saul
Acts Ch. 8 & 9.
Paul's Missionary Journeys
Acts Ch. 11, 13 to 28.
The Vision of John
Revelation.

The Book of Revelation

Tradition says that the last book in the New Testament was written by the apostle John, shown here, who also wrote the fourth Gospel. The book is described as apocalyptic. This means that it says that God will eventually intervene and destroy the world to bring about his will. The book uses lots of symbolism, such as describing evil as a horned beast.

The Early Church

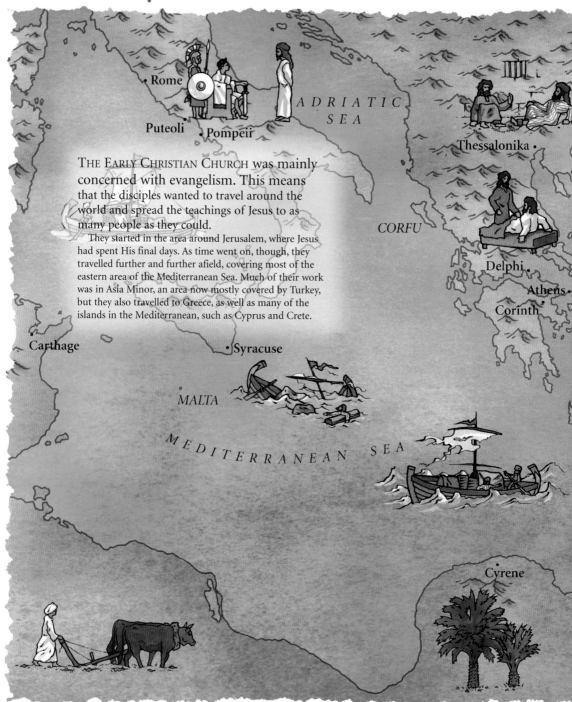

Rome

Puteoli · Pompeii

ADRIATIC
SEA

Thessalonika ·

CORFU

THE EARLY CHRISTIAN CHURCH was mainly concerned with evangelism. This means that the disciples wanted to travel around the world and spread the teachings of Jesus to as many people as they could.

   They started in the area around Jerusalem, where Jesus had spent His final days. As time went on, though, they travelled further and further afield, covering most of the eastern area of the Mediterranean Sea. Much of their work was in Asia Minor, an area now mostly covered by Turkey, but they also travelled to Greece, as well as many of the islands in the Mediterranean, such as Cyprus and Crete.

Delphi ·

Athens ·
Corinth ·

Carthage

· Syracuse

MALTA

MEDITERRANEAN SEA

Cyrene

BLACK SEA

MEDITERRANEAN SEA

Ancyra

Iconium

Ephesus

Miletus

Derbe

Tarsus

Antioch

Myra

Rhodes

CYPRUS

Salamis

Salmone

Paphos

CRETE

asea

Sidon

Damascus

Caesarea

Jerusalem

Alexandria

Memphis

Twelve Once More

AFTER Jesus had been taken up into heaven, the disciples followed His instructions and went back to Jerusalem to wait for the Holy Spirit to come and baptize them. The friends were more than a little nervous. They had seen many extraordinary things since they had met Jesus. His miraculous return from the dead had crowned everything. Even so, the disciples couldn't imagine how the Holy Spirit would visit them, and they had no idea when it might happen. Still, the amazing events since Jesus's death had inspired new faith in the disciples. They realized that everything Jesus had ever said would happen had come to pass just as He had foretold. Even though

Jesus was no longer among the disciples, their belief in Him and His teachings was unshakeable. They didn't doubt for one second that Jesus would one day come back to the world in all His glory, to establish God's kingdom on earth.

While the disciples were waiting for the Holy Spirit, they gathered together in a house in Jerusalem with Jesus's mother, Mary, the other women who had been close friends of Jesus, Jesus's brothers and many dedicated followers – about 120 people in all. Everyone thought it best to lie low for a while. Now that the officials had succeeded in having Jesus executed, they were looking for an excuse to wipe out all His followers, too. They

Tree of life
This engraving from the 1500s shows Jesus being crucified on the Tree of Life. The tree was said to be growing in the Garden of Eden. John sees a vision of it in Heaven, as he describes in the book of Revelation. It is a symbol of God's eternal life, a way of saying that Jesus lives for ever.

The light of the world
The disciples' message was that Jesus was the only way to God. Jesus had called Himself the light of the world, that is, the one who shows people the way to God. In this painting by English painter Holman Hunt, Jesus 'the light of the world' is standing outside the door of someone's life, waiting to be invited in.

were determined to stop the spread of Jesus's teachings, which they felt sure were leading people away from the law of Moses. So Jesus's followers kept out of the way of any possible trouble, and devoted themselves to praying.

There was just one thing that Peter felt had to be done.

"Jesus chose twelve of us to be His special helpers – one for each of the twelve tribes of Israel," Peter reminded the disciples one day. "Now there are only eleven of us."

The disciples hung their heads in shame and sadness as they remembered how Judas Iscariot had betrayed Jesus. Judas had waited until Jesus was in a quiet, vulnerable spot, then he had led the authorities straight to Him so they could arrest Him, all for 30 pieces of silver.

"Yes," the disciples agreed. "You are right, Peter. We feel it is what Jesus wants us to do. Who should we pick?"

> 66 *And they cast lots for them, and the lot fell on Matthias; and he was enrolled with the eleven disciples.* 99

The friends prayed and discussed, discussed and prayed, and finally agreed that the new disciple should be someone like them. They wanted someone who had followed Jesus right from the time when His cousin John first baptized Him and He started to teach, to the moment when He was taken up to heaven.

Out of all Jesus's followers, there were only two men who would do – Joseph and Matthias. Deciding between them was a very serious business. The disciples had to be absolutely sure that they chose the man that Jesus wanted. They prayed long and hard for guidance, and in the end Matthias was chosen. The disciples were twelve again.

Christian baptism
Baptism is a ceremony in which a person is sprinkled with, or immersed in, water. It is a sign that God forgives and cleanses people of their sins. Sometimes it includes (or is followed later by) laying-on of hands to receive the gifts of God's Spirit. This tomb from the AD 200s shows the priest laying hands on a child after baptism in Rome. The Holy Spirit is represented by the dove.

THE DISCIPLES PRAYED HARD FOR GUIDANCE. GOD LEADS HIS PEOPLE, BUT IT IS NOT ALWAYS EASY TO FIND OUT WHAT HE WANTS. PRAYER IS A WAY OF OPENING OURSELVES TO GOD AND HIS WILL.

⚜ **ABOUT THE STORY** ⚜
There was nothing magic about the number twelve, but it was an important sign to the first Christians. It showed them that God was making a new start. The Jewish race had started from the twelve sons of Jacob. The Christian Church begins with twelve disciples. The choice of the twelfth person had to be made by God, to show that the church was a spiritual fellowship, and not simply a human organization.

Tongues of Fire

THE disciples waited and prayed for a sign that the Holy Spirit was with them.
Eventually, 50 days after Passover and the death of Jesus, it was time for the feast of Pentecost. This was the harvest festival when Jews celebrated God's giving of the law to Moses. As usual, Jerusalem quickly filled with Jews from all over the world who were coming to worship at the temple.

On the day of Pentecost itself, the disciples met together to worship. Their thoughts were suddenly disturbed by a rushing noise. They had never heard anything like it before. It was like a wind tearing through the room. They felt energy and passion blaze

through them. The twelve friends turned to each other with joy, and saw that a tiny flame was hovering steadily over each man's head.

"The Holy Spirit is with us!" they cried.

To their utter astonishment, they heard each other speaking in foreign languages.

"Praise be to God!" they shouted. "We are blessed with special gifts from the Lord!"

The disciples ran out into the streets. They couldn't contain their excitement. Some disciples found themselves yelling praises to God in Greek. Others were shouting prayers in Arabic. Some heard themselves singing hymns in Latin and Persian, and other languages besides.

> " ...we hear them telling in our own tongues the mighty works of God. "

The hordes of Pentecost worshippers passing by were startled by the commotion and stopped to see what was going on. A crowd soon gathered around the disciples. Egyptians, Persians, Greeks, Romans, Libyans, Parthians and Phrygians were all amazed to hear the disciples speaking perfectly in their own languages.

"Who are these men? They can understand and speak our language!" the foreign worshippers gasped.

Others simply scoffed at the strange sight.

"They're just talking gibberish!" some people mocked. "They must have been at the wine!"

At this, Peter called for silence.

Church of the Holy Spirit
Pentecostal churches encourage members to use the 'gifts of the Holy Spirit'. Their worship is usually very lively.

THE HOLY SPIRIT IS GOD GIVING HIS POWER TO PEOPLE SO THAT THEY CAN SERVE HIM. THE DISCIPLES HAD TO WAIT TO RECEIVE HIM. WE CANNOT ORDER GOD TO DO WHAT WE WANT. ❧

The fire of the Spirit
The disciples saw the Spirit as tongues of flame above their heads. This medieval altar panel shows them waiting for the flames coming from the hands of God. Fire was a symbol of purity. The Spirit purified the disciples so they could work for God.

"We are not drunk!" he yelled, his face lit up with exhilaration. "We are devout Jews and have been worshipping, just as we should do at Pentecost. This is the fulfilment of the prophecy of the prophet Joel," he cried.

The crowds scratched their heads as they tried to remember the Scriptures.

"Joel said that the time would come when God would pour out His Spirit over people and they would prophesy, and that in those days, anyone who turned to the Lord would be saved from punishment for their sins."

Many people in the crowd gasped and remembered.

"Israelites!" Peter continued. "We are Jews like you, yet we follow the teachings of Jesus of Nazareth. You all know that He was put to death unjustly. This was all according to God's plan. For God raised Him from the dead. We have seen Jesus alive with our own eyes! What has happened to us today is the work of the Holy Spirit flowing from Him!"

A murmur of amazement went around the crowd. It wasn't just Peter's rousing words or sudden ability to speak new languages that stirred them, it was also the disciples' happiness and passion.

"What do we have to do?" voices began to cry out.

"Be truly sorry for your sins," Peter roared. "Beg God's forgiveness in the name of Jesus Christ. Then you will receive the gift of the Holy Spirit!"

"Yes, we want to be saved through Jesus Christ!" shouted the crowd. "We want to obey Jesus's teachings!"

That very day, 3,000 people were baptized into the new Christian Church as followers of Jesus.

Judaism at the time of Christ
The first Christians were Jews or Gentiles, non-Jews who had embraced the Jewish religion. Some who were in Jerusalem on the day of Pentecost took the message of Christ to their home countries. Areas with a Jewish population are shown here in orange.

❧ ABOUT THE STORY ❧
Pentecost had originally been a celebration of the barley harvest and also of the 'first fruits' – the first pickings of the fruit trees. So it was a significant day when the 'first fruits' of the Holy Spirit – the people who became Christians – were 'harvested'. It had also become a celebration of God giving the law to Moses. Christians saw the Holy Spirit as God giving a new way of life to His people.

Peter the Healer

IN the days after Pentecost, the excitement in Jerusalem grew. Crowds came to hear the twelve preach and see them perform miracles in the name of Jesus of Nazareth. Every day more people believed that Jesus really was the Christ, the Son of God sent to save everyone from their sins, and that through Him all sinners could be saved.

One day, Peter and John were on their way into the temple to pray, when a lame beggar sitting at the Beautiful Gate called out to them, "Kind sirs, do you have a few pennies you can spare?"

Peter and John stopped and stared at him.

"Look at us," Peter said kindly. "We have no silver or

gold – but what we do have, I will give you."

Peter stretched his hand towards the beggar.

"In the name of Jesus Christ of Nazareth," he said, "get up and walk."

Peter took the beggar by the hand.

Immediately the beggar touched Peter's fingertips, he felt new strength in the leg muscles and joints that had been useless for so long. His eyes lit up and without thinking, he sprang to his feet.

He took a few steps, then a few skips, then a few jumps. "I'm healed!" he yelled. "I'm healed!"

The beggar began to leap about and dance in delight. He followed Peter and John into the temple, praising God at the top of his voice. Worshippers hurried to see what the commotion was all about, and were astonished to see the beggar who had sat at the Beautiful Gate all his life.

The Beautiful Gate
Scholars are not certain where exactly Peter and John met the beggar in this story, but most think it was where the Corinthian Gate now is, on the east side of the Temple of Jerusalem. It led into the part of the temple called the Court of the Women. It would have been a good place to beg as many people passed it.

MIRACLES IN THE BIBLE ARE NOT ENDS IN THEMSELVES. THEY WILL ALWAYS POINT TO SOME TRUTH ABOUT GOD. IN THIS CASE, PETER USED THE HEALING TO PREACH ABOUT GOD'S SALVATION. ❧

A time for prayer
The Bible tells us that Peter and John were going to the temple at prayer time, 3 p.m. At this time there were set times for prayer in the temple. The morning and evening sacrifices were at 9 a.m. and 3 p.m. and there were prayer times to coincide with these. There were final prayers at sunset.

Before long a great crowd gathered around Peter, John and the beggar in the temple courtyard.

"Why are you so amazed?" Peter asked the stunned onlookers. "Why do you look at us as if we're filled with strange magic powers? For it is God who has done this through us. The God of Abraham and Isaac and Jacob – and the Father of Jesus Christ – whom you put to death."

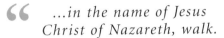

> ## ...in the name of Jesus Christ of Nazareth, walk.

In a loud voice, Peter began to proclaim that God had brought Jesus of Nazareth back to life from the dead, that they had seen Him with their own eyes, and that it was their faith in Jesus Christ that had made the beggar well.

"Repent!" Peter cried at the crowds. "Turn again to God, that He may forgive your sins. Then, when Jesus Christ returns in all His glory at the end of the world, you will be blessed for ever instead of eternally damned."

The crowds suddenly fell back with fear. Temple guards armed with spears pushed through the people and marched up to the two disciples, followed by a group of angry priests and Sadducees, the religious elders.

"What are you doing?" the holy men thundered. "How dare you cause this rumpus in the temple!" They turned to the guards. "Arrest these men at once!"

Peter and John were hauled away to prison.

Statue of a sick man
This Egyptian statue dates from about 1200BC. From the Egyptians through biblical times there was little help for sick people. Many died young through disease.

Peter and John heal the beggar
This engraving shows the lame man just getting to his feet. Peter and John had only been able to heal him because God was working through them.

❖ ABOUT THE STORY ❖

Being a beggar was a miserable life. There was no social security system by which disabled or chronically sick people could get help from the government. They depended entirely on their families and the gifts of kind people. Peter and John could bring the gift of health and new life in every sense of the word – physical and spiritual. It was a sign that God was interested in every part of human life.

Arrested

PETER and John watched the sun set through a prison window. They weren't surprised or downhearted. Jesus had warned the disciples that they would suffer opposition and danger as they tried to spread His word.

After a damp and dirty night in the cells, the two disciples were dragged before an emergency meeting of the Jewish high council, the Sanhedrin.

"Now," Caiaphas the high priest said, holding them in his icy stare. "Tell us by what power or in whose name you healed this lame beggar yesterday."

It was more of a challenge than a question, just as if Caiaphas was daring them to say the name "Jesus Christ".

Peter remembered that Jesus had promised that He would give His followers the words to argue against His

enemies. Peter knew he was filled with the Holy Spirit, and he had a new courage to face the high priest.

Peter said, "We healed him through Jesus of Nazareth. You tried to destroy Jesus, but God raised Him back to life. He is the only path to heaven."

The elders leapt to their feet at the disciple's boldness.

"These men are peasants!" some of the elders yelled. "They are uneducated fishermen from Galilee."

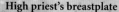

> **By what power or by what name did you do this?**

"Jesus of Nazareth was intelligent!" others cried. "It's amazing he even spoke to these simple people. They probably can't even read or write."

"That may well be the case," others bellowed, "but the

Jerusalem is central
This medieval map shows Jerusalem at the 'centre of the world'. Jerusalem is central to the Bible story. It was where the first temple was built, where Jesus was crucified and where the disciples first received the Holy Spirit. From Jerusalem, the message spread throughout the world.

High priest's breastplate
The high priest, Caiaphas, would have worn a breastplate like this. It was studded with twelve semi-precious stones, one for each tribe of Israel. Inside the breastplate was a pocket, where high priests in Old Testament times kept the Urim and Thummim, sacred stones which may have been engraved with 'yes' and 'no'. They were used to discover God's will.

fact remains that somehow they healed the beggar. What are we going to do about this miracle?"

The councillors argued amongst themselves.

"Listen!" the Jewish officials spat at last. "We order you never to mention Jesus of Nazareth again or do any type of miracles in His name. Do you understand?"

"We understand," nodded Peter and John quite calmly, "but we can't do what you ask. We have to do what God wants us to do, not what you people want us to do."

At that, there was total uproar.

"How dare you defy the command of the Sanhedrin!" the enraged councillors yelled, and Peter and John were hauled away.

The elders were at their wits' end. They couldn't charge Peter and John with having broken any law and, to their immense frustration, they had no choice but to let them go with only a warning.

Back with their anxious friends, the two disciples praised God and prayed for strength and guidance.

"Lord, see how the elders have threatened us and grant us the courage to spread your gospel boldly, gracing us with the power to heal and perform miracles through Jesus Christ."

Despite the Sanhedrin's warning, the disciples carried on preaching and baptizing just as before.

Peter arrested
Peter was arrested on more than one occasion. This is an early statue showing him being dragged away.

Teaching the believers
Peter and John teach the early Christians. It is likely that as well as formal sermons, much of the teaching was based on questions people asked.

The Early Church Community

EVERY day, the Jews who had become followers of Jesus prayed in the temple and also broke bread in their homes as Jesus had done at the Last Supper, remembering Him just as He had asked them to do. Followers old and new told everyone how they had found new happiness and peace thanks to Jesus of Nazareth and how they had received the gifts of the Holy Spirit through baptism. Their excited neighbours and friends would beg to join the new Jewish group too.

Being baptized as a follower of Jesus Christ wasn't an easy path to follow. Jesus's followers were expected to follow the disciples' leadership and live as Jesus had done. This meant giving up everything they had previously held

dear. They had to sell all their possessions and give their money to the disciples to be donated to the poor. Most followers did this willingly. They believed that it wouldn't be long before Jesus would return in glory – perhaps a matter of months, maybe a matter of years, but certainly within their lifetimes. What was the use in holding on to their possessions? Besides, they felt they had changed inside when they were baptized. They embraced the idea that they were now part of a church, a community of brothers and sisters. They were happy to share anything they needed, and found comfort and fulfilment in being kind and generous to others instead of self-centred and thoughtless.

However, others found it more difficult to give up everything they had worked so long and hard for. A man called Ananias and his wife Sapphira obediently sold everything they owned after they were baptized. Yet when Ananias went to give the money raised from the sale to the

The church goes on
The word church simply means a gathering. Its focus is on a group of people, not the building in which they may meet. From early on, Christians have gathered together to worship God and to learn about Him. The pattern of services may vary greatly from church to church, and from place to place, but they all have the same end in view, the worship of God.

Church building
Early church buildings were not unlike many of those seen today, as this mosaic from around AD400 shows. During New Testament times, though, there were no special church buildings. People met in the homes of Christians, outside or in hired halls. Later the apostle Paul uses the image of a building. He says that Christians are built into a new community like stones are built into a temple.

disciples, he didn't take all of it. He and his wife decided to keep some back for a rainy day.

As Ananias laid down his sacks of money before the disciples, Peter frowned at him.

"Ananias, why has the devil filled your heart?" Peter challenged. "You are lying to the Holy Spirit and keeping back some of your money!"

Ananias and Sapphira had not breathed a word to anyone of what they had done. Ananias realized that Peter couldn't possibly have known, unless God Himself had told him! The terrified man stood open-mouthed and

> **And great fear came upon the whole church, and upon all who heard of these things.**

spluttered. Words stuck in his throat, and he began to choke and gasp. A cold fear clutched at his heart and squeezed it with icy fingers. Then he fell down dead.

Sadly, the disciples carried him out to bury him. Three hours later, while they were still away, the unsuspecting Sapphira arrived.

"Where is my husband?" she asked, cheerily.

Then her face fell. Sapphira saw that Peter looked grim. She felt that the atmosphere in the room was stony. Sapphira realized that something was wrong.

"First, tell me how much you have sold the land for," Peter asked her.

Sapphira swallowed hard and lied about the amount, feeling her face begin to flush with shame.

Peter's eyes flashed fire. "Why have you and your husband joined together in sin?" he groaned. "Why do you think you can deceive the Holy Spirit?"

Sapphira hung her head.

"Listen," said Peter, growing angrier by the second. "Do you hear footsteps? They are the footsteps of those who have just buried your husband. They're coming to do exactly the same to you!"

With a scream, Sapphira fainted and fell stone dead on the floor.

When the disciples came in, they found they had another body to bury. All the followers who heard of God's wrath trembled in fear. How glad they were that they had found salvation through Jesus Christ! God's punishments on sinners were terrible.

Caring for the needy
The first Christians cared for each other. They were not afraid to sell possessions and give the money to help others. They did this because Jesus had given up everything, including His life, for them. They also believed God would bless them spiritually.

Teaching in Jesus's Name

PETER became famous as a healer. People from towns and villages all over Judea began to put sick people out on the pavements, in case Peter passed by. They believed that if even his shadow fell on them, they would be healed.

The officials of the Sanhedrin were worried. Even though Jesus was dead, it was in His name that people were being stirred up. Even some of the priests had been baptized as followers.

"We must put a stop to this!" the officials raged.

Once again they had Peter and John arrested and flung into the city prison with murderers, robbers and thugs.

Peter and John weren't behind bars long. That night, an angel of the Lord came and released them.

"Go to the temple and tell everyone about salvation

through Jesus Christ," the angel told them, before he disappeared. That's exactly what Peter and John did.

Meanwhile, the Sanhedrin members were waiting for the guards to bring Peter and John before them. Caiaphas sat impatiently drumming his fingers.

Down in the dungeons, the guards were panicking. Peter and John were nowhere to be found. The baffled guards trembled with fear as they returned to Caiaphas.

"The prisoners have gone," the guards mumbled.

"What do you mean, gone?" the high priest roared.

The cowering soldiers shrugged.

"The sentries were on guard and the doors locked, but Peter and John weren't there."

Remains of Peter's house
These remains in Capernaum are believed by some scholars to be of the house where Peter lived. It was used as a church for some 300 years and later a church was built over part of it, which suggests that the first Christians thought it special.

Leader of the disciples
Peter was the spokesman for the twelve disciples during Jesus's lifetime and afterwards. He often spoke up when the others were afraid.

"Right!" screamed Caiaphas. "That's it! You're going into the dungeons yourselves until..."

Luckily for the guards, a servant burst in.

"Well?" snarled the high priest.

"My lord, we've heard that your two Galilean prisoners are preaching in the temple!" the servant panted.

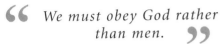

> ❝ *We must obey God rather than men.* ❞

Thunder-faced, Caiaphas sent his guards off to arrest Peter and John again, and the next day the disciples found themselves facing the fury of the Sanhedrin.

"We expressly forbade you to mention the name of Jesus of Nazareth!" the councillors screamed.

"We must do what God wants," Peter and John insisted. "God has filled us with the Holy Spirit so we can testify that Jesus is the Saviour of the world."

The members of the Sanhedrin were enraged.

"Put them to death!" the Jewish officials screamed. "They have no regard for us or our laws!"

One voice rose over the uproar. "Calm down! Take the prisoners away while we discuss things properly."

It was the Pharisee, Gamaliel, a teacher of the law for whom everyone had the utmost respect.

"Friends, listen," Gamaliel continued. "In past years, several so-called holy men have risen up and tried to set up religious sects to rival the worship of God. Look what happened to them. One by one they came to a sticky end and their followers were all killed. It is bound to be the same with this Jesus of Nazareth."

The Jewish officials murmured their agreement.

"There is another reason not to overreact," Gamaliel went on. "There is a possibility – although we are all agreed that it is highly remote – that Jesus really is who His disciples say He is: the Son of God. If this were true, nothing anyone could do would stop His followers. In the end, we might even be found guilty of opposing God!"

The scowling elders could see the sense in Gamaliel's words. Grudgingly, they agreed to let Peter and John go. However, first, they had the disciples beaten, and ordered them once more never to speak the name of Jesus of Nazareth again.

Reaching a verdict
The Sanhedrin was the Jews' supreme court of law. Verdicts were reached by voting. In Greek courts, jurors used voting disks like these, which come from around 300BC. Those with a solid hub meant the person was not guilty, those with a hole meant guilty.

Prisoner in agony
This silver and bronze figure shows a Libyan prisoner in Egypt between 1580 and 1200BC. Throughout history people have invented ways of hurting and torturing people they don't like, as the authorities did with Peter and John.

> ❖ **ABOUT THE STORY** ❖
>
> *Gamaliel's common sense saved the Sanhedrin from another miscarriage of justice. They had condemned Jesus illegally as they had not allowed a day to pass before a guilty verdict was announced. They were about to do the same again. Luke, who wrote this story, is showing that God was in control. Jesus had to die, to fulfil God's purpose. The disciples could not die yet. They had work to do for God to fulfil His purpose.*

Stephen the Martyr

As the number of people who wanted to follow Christ increased, so did the number of helpers the disciples needed. The disciples chose seven men to distribute money and food and preach Jesus's gospel. One assistant, called Stephen, soon stood out as being especially learned and courageous. He was full of faith and the Holy Spirit, and had the power to work miracles. He spoke with such wisdom that the teachers in the synagogues found they had met their match. Eventually, the elders bribed people to say they had heard Stephen speak out against Moses and God. Stephen was put on trial before the Sanhedrin.

"We've heard this man Stephen say Jesus of Nazareth will destroy the temple and will change the laws that Moses gave us direct from the hand of God," people lied.

Stephen listened to all the lies without blinking or saying a word. His face grew bright and shone like the face of an angel.

The high priest tried to ignore the glow of Stephen's face. "Is this so?" he questioned. "Tell us now!"

The Holy Spirit helped Stephen speak. He spoke of the Jewish people, from the moment God had chosen Abraham to found the Jewish faith and guided him to Israel. Stephen said that God had sent Jesus of Nazareth as the fulfilment of His plan. In the past, the elders had persecuted prophets for speaking the truth, and they had done exactly the same thing to Christ.

"Jesus is the Saviour of the world, sent to you by God Himself," Stephen cried. "You murdered Him!"

The Sanhedrin were outraged. They exploded with hate.

To their immense annoyance, Stephen seemed totally unaware of it all. The young man stood gazing upwards, a blissful smile on his face.

"Look!" he gasped. "I can see the heavens opening!"

Stephen fell to his knees, oblivious to the riot around him.

"I can see the Son of Man sitting at the right hand of God!" Stephen gasped, with tears of joy in his eyes.

"What is this rubbish?" the Jewish officials yelled, looking up and seeing nothing but the bricks of the roof. Stephen's calmness enraged them even more.

"This man reckons he can see God!" the elders cried. "It's blasphemy – and the punishment is death!"

The officials clapped their hands over their ears so they wouldn't have to hear any more of Stephen's vision.

> **They chose Stephen, a man full of faith and of the Holy Spirit.**

"Take him away!" they yelled to the guards.

The soldiers dragged Stephen through the streets of Jerusalem and out of the city gates, with the furious Sanhedrin following, picking up rocks as they went. They reached the spot where stonings took place and stood Stephen up against a wall.

"Forgive them, Lord," Stephen murmured as the elders backed away. "Don't hold this sin against them."

The elders took off their cloaks and gave them to an eager young Pharisee called Saul to hold. Then they rolled up their sleeves and began to throw stones with glee.

"Lord Jesus, receive my spirit," Stephen cried aloud, as he sank down under the rain of rocks.

At last, Stephen lay dead. He was the first person to die in the name of Jesus Christ.

The stoning of Stephen
Stoning was the usual method of execution used by the Jews. Their law allowed it for many offences. Jewish law said the chief witnesses had to cast the first stone.

Stephen's gate
This street in Jerusalem is said to be where Stephen was stoned.

❧ ABOUT THE STORY ❧

Stephen was the first Christian martyr. The word comes from a Greek word which means witness. A martyr is someone who believes in his or her faith to the extent of being willing to die for it. During his trial, Stephen had spoken of the history of the Israelites in which people had regularly disobeyed God. Now, he said, they had ignored God's message once again, by crucifying Jesus.

Saul and the Christians

THE very same day that Stephen was stoned, the Sanhedrin decided that enough was enough. They marvelled that the followers of Jesus Christ were so loyal that they were even willing to die for Him. There were more followers than ever. Every day, the disciples were turning hundreds of Jews towards the new ideas of Jesus of Nazareth. The officials had to put a stop to the spread of Christ's word, and fast. They had tried ordering and threatening, and it had done no good. The Sanhedrin decided that force was the only avenue left.

Only a few hours after Stephen died, temple soldiers and the officers of the Jewish elders went marching into every house in Jerusalem, hunting high and low for

followers of Jesus Christ. They upturned every house, questioned anyone who looked the slightest bit suspicious, and managed to haul off many followers. One of the keenest officers was the young Pharisee, Saul, who had held the Sanhedrin's cloaks at Stephen's stoning. Saul wished with all his heart that he hadn't been lumbered with holding the garments. He would have liked to have been able to throw a few stones himself.

Saul hated the followers of Jesus Christ with a vengeance. He had been brought up a very strict Jew and he felt that Jesus's disciples were busy undoing everything that he had always believed was important. Saul made up his mind that he would make the Sanhedrin's command his life's work. It didn't matter how long it took, he would

PERSECUTION IS WHEN A PERSON OR GROUP ARE MADE TO SUFFER FOR SOME REASON. CHRISTIANS HAVE ALWAYS FACED SUFFERING, FOLLOWING THE EXAMPLE OF JESUS, BUT THOSE WHO FLED SAUL'S MEN HELPED TO SPREAD JESUS'S WORD ABROAD. ∾

Early spread of Christianity
Jesus told the disciples that they were to take the Christian message to 'Judea, Samaria and the rest of the world'. The early chapters of Acts show how Philip (shown in mauve) and Peter (shown in red) travelled around the whole region.

Samaria
This city was despised by traditional Jews at the time of Christ. The city had existed since King Jeroboam had made it Israel's capital after the kingdom split under King Solomon. Herod the Great built a temple dedicated to the Roman Emperor Augustus there shortly before Christ was born.

stop at nothing until every last follower of Jesus Christ was locked up, and preferably killed. Saul decided that he wouldn't stop at Jerusalem, either. After turning the holy city upside down, Saul commanded his disciple-hunters to sweep through the whole of Judea.

Never in his wildest dreams did Saul think that he was actually part of God's plan to spread the word of Jesus Christ. In forcing Jesus's followers to flee, the gospel was taken to many thousands of people who wouldn't otherwise have heard it. In every region the escaping followers passed through, they told the locals the good news of Jesus's promise of salvation. Jews everywhere begged to be baptized.

> " *Now, those who were scattered went about preaching the word.* "

The disciple Philip had great success in the city of Samaria. He preached passionately and worked great miracles. He healed those who were paralysed and cured others with terrible sicknesses that wracked their bodies with pain and tormented their minds. Crowds hurried to see Philip's amazing powers and hundreds were baptized. One of the new followers was a man called Simon, who for years had conned the locals into thinking he was a magician by performing tricks and conjuring. Simon knew

real power when he saw it. He realized immediately that Philip wasn't a simple trickster like himself but had real power given to him from God.

There were so many people in Samaria who flocked to hear Philip's message that he couldn't cope with the numbers, so Philip's friends and fellow disciples of Jesus, Peter and John, journeyed down to help him. When the two disciples arrived, they laid their hands on those who had been baptized and prayed that they might receive the gifts of the Holy Spirit.

"How amazing!" cried Simon, when he saw what Peter and John were doing. "You have magic in your hands! I'd give anything to have power like that!"

The ex-magician scrabbled through his bag and pulled out the last of his money.

"Look, take this!" he cried, holding out a handful of coins. "Give me some of your magic power, too!"

Peter turned on Simon in fury. He didn't often get angry, but when he did, it was terrifying.

"May your silver be damned along with you!" Peter roared, dashing the money to the ground. "You can't buy gifts from God!"

For the first time in his life, Simon was truly humbled before Peter. He made up his mind to make the most of what he was and not strive to be anything else or to envy others their special gifts.

"I am truly sorry," he said. "Please pray for me that my sins are forgiven through Jesus Christ."

Philip
God gave Philip the gift of preaching, to spread the Christian message and to bring people to personal faith. This mosaic from the 1100s shows him casting a demon from a man.

❧ ABOUT THE STORY ❧

According to Tertullian, a Christian writer in the AD300s, 'the blood of the martyrs is the seed of the church'. The church has grown most during times when Christians are being persecuted. This is partly because people decide that Christianity must be true if it is worth dying for. No one would die for a lie. It is also because early Christians amazed observers by their love for each other.

Philip and the Ethiopian

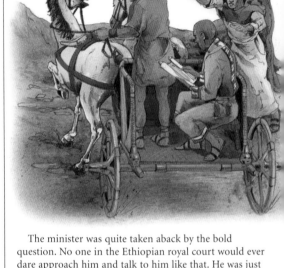

AFTER Peter and John had helped Philip in Samaria, they returned to Jerusalem. They preached the word of Jesus in many Samarian villages along the way. Philip didn't go with them. An angel of the Lord spoke to him and told him to go south instead, down the road from Jerusalem to Gaza. So, Philip obediently set off down the hot, dusty, desert road. He didn't know exactly where he was going, but he remembered that Jesus had said so many times before that God would always show the way.

As Philip trudged along, he saw a chariot come slowly rumbling by with an important-looking passenger inside. The chariot bore the symbol of the queen of Ethiopia, in Africa, and Philip realized that its passenger must be one of the queen's government ministers, who was returning home after worshipping in the temple in Jerusalem.

As Philip marvelled at the splendid sight, he heard a voice speaking to him, urging him gently.

"Philip, go and meet the man in the chariot," the voice said, and Philip knew it was the Holy Spirit.

Straight away, Philip ran to the chariot and greeted the minister with a respectful bow.

"Good afternoon," said Philip.

The minister turned his head haughtily. He was reading a scroll of the teachings of the prophet Isaiah, and he didn't look too pleased at being interrupted. Still he was well brought-up and polite, so he said "Good afternoon" back, before returning to his reading.

Philip didn't give up, though.

"I see you're reading Isaiah," he said, cheerily. "What do you think of it? Can you understand the prophecies?"

The minister was quite taken aback by the bold question. No one in the Ethiopian royal court would ever dare approach him and talk to him like that. He was just about to scold Philip when he noticed the kindness and honesty in his eyes. There was something about Philip that made the minister bare his heart and speak quite openly.

"No, I don't really understand much of it," the minister confessed in a whisper. "How can I, when I don't have anyone to help me?"

"Well, I understand it," said Philip, with a grin.

"Do you?" said the minister excitedly. "Do you really? Then you'd better come and join me."

Philip clambered up into the regal chariot and sat

beside the Ethiopian minister. Philip picked up reading from the point where he had interrupted him. As they continued the journey together he explained the Scriptures and told the Ethiopian minister all about the good news of Jesus.

> ❝ *Beginning with this scripture, he told him the good news of Jesus.* ❞

The minister was entranced. Every word that Philip said rang true in his heart. The way of life Jesus preached was surely the only way to heaven. Jesus of Nazareth was surely the Christ foretold by the ancient scriptures!

Suddenly, the minister yelled "STOP!" at the top of his voice. The horses slowed to a halt and the minister jumped out of the chariot.

"Look!" he said excitedly, pointing across the road. "There's a pool. I want you to baptize me as a follower of Jesus Christ right away."

He grabbed Philip's hand and hurried him across the road as fast as his legs would carry him, splashing into the water. He listened intently to Philip's prayers, joining in with them in his heart. Then came the great moment. Philip dipped him down under the water and the minister was washed clean from all his sins. He emerged new-born, ready to begin a new life as a

follower of Christ. Philip was gone. The beaming minister looked all around, but couldn't find him anywhere. Still, nothing could dampen his spirits. He went on his way, singing God's praises and rejoicing at his new found faith and salvation.

As for Philip, he had been mysteriously whisked away by the Holy Spirit and taken to another town where he was needed to preach the gospel. He continued to preach the word of Jesus and convert people all the way down the road to Caesarea.

A Holy King
This minister was probably a royal treasurer for the queen mother. In Ethiopia at this time it was the queen mother who ruled the country from day to day as the king himself was thought to be too holy.

Ethiopian
In biblical times, the country of Ethiopia was in fact Nubia, which is now part of Sudan and Egypt, in northern Africa.

❧ ABOUT THE STORY ❧

The Ethiopian was a Gentile who had adopted the Jewish religion. He would not have been allowed to take part in Jewish ceremonies, because he was foreign. There was a Jewish community in Upper Egypt, from whom he had probably first heard about God. He is evidently very keen to find out more. This story shows how God met his spiritual need by inspiring Philip to be in the right place at the right time.

The Road to Damascus

THE YOUNG Pharisee soldier Saul had been having great success in his mission to wipe out the followers of Christ. Jerusalem's prisons were full to bursting with followers, all thanks to him. Saul was feared far and wide. Day and night, capturing followers was all he thought about.

When Saul had stormed from Jerusalem through every town and village in Judea, he went to the high priest and asked permission to extend his search to Damascus. The high priest gave Saul letters to take to all the synagogues, telling them that Saul had the authority to arrest whoever he pleased.

As the city of Damascus loomed in front of him, he rubbed his hands together eagerly. There should be plenty more followers of Jesus to hunt down there...

Suddenly Saul was struck by a flash of lightning that knocked him off his horse and left him cowering on the ground.

"Saul, Saul, why are you persecuting me?" a voice boomed.

"Who are you?" Saul stammered.

"I am Jesus, your sworn enemy," the voice roared.

Saul shook with fear. Deep in his heart, he knew it was the truth and he groaned aloud.

"Now rise," the voice ordered. "Continue into the city and wait there."

Saul sensed the light fading from all around him. He lowered his hands from his face and opened his eyes. Everything was pitch black.

"I'm blind!" he yelled, scrabbling around in a panic. "Help! Help! I'm blind!"

"Sir, whatever happened?" the soldiers asked, as they helped Saul up. "Why did you fall off your horse? What was that strange sound?"

"Did you not see anything?" Saul gasped. "Did you not hear the voice and what it said?"

"We heard something, Sir," the guards said. They looked at each other worriedly. Had Saul been working too hard?

Slowly and carefully, the soldiers led Saul into the city and found a room where he could stay. Saul would say nothing further to anyone. He wouldn't eat. He wouldn't drink. He hung his head, his sightless eyes gazing blankly

❧ ABOUT THE STORY ❧

This was a unique event. We do not know exactly what happened, except that Paul later said the people with him heard something, but did not see the light. Only Paul himself heard the full message and actually saw Jesus in the shining light. Paul later became an apostle – one who had seen the risen Jesus. Many visions of God include bright light, because light is a symbol of purity.

Thirteen disciples
This engraving shows thirteen disciples. Matthias has replaced Judas, and Paul (far left) has joined them. The disciples were the recognized authorities of the early church. Their teaching was regarded as coming from God.

at the ground, completely absorbed in his own thoughts.

Two whole days passed like this. The soldiers did not know what to do. On the third day, there was a knock at the door. It was a stranger called Ananias.

"The Lord told me to come and find you here," said Ananias, helping the wobbly Saul to his feet. "I know that you are the enemy of Jesus Christ, but He says that He has chosen you to spread His teachings – not just to the Jews, but to the Gentiles, too."

With that, Ananias laid his hands on Saul's trembling head. At once, scales seemed to fall away from Saul's eyes and he found he could see once more. Totally overcome with relief and joy, Saul fell on his knees and gave thanks to God. Then, to the utter astonishment of his soldiers, he begged to be baptized. He wanted to become one of the followers of Jesus Christ who he had sought to wipe out!

> 66 *Saul, Saul, why do you persecute me?* 99

Once Saul had got his strength back, he went to the synagogues in Damascus and proclaimed Jesus as the Son of God. People couldn't work out if the famous Saul,

persecutor of Christians, really had been converted, or if it was some kind of trick. At first, only the Jews who refused to believe in Jesus Christ decided that Saul was sincere. They felt that their greatest ally had betrayed them and, in their disappointment, they plotted to kill him. Suddenly Saul found himself being persecuted for the sake of Jesus Christ, just as he had persecuted so many others! Luckily, Saul heard of the plan and escaped.

It proved harder to convince the followers of Jesus that he really had changed. The disciple Barnabas, who believed Saul, took him to the twelve disciples. He told them what had happened on the road to Damascus, and Jesus's followers decided to accept Saul's amazing turnaround.

As an outward sign of his new inner life, Saul changed his name to Paul. He put even more energy and dedication into preaching the gospel of Jesus Christ than he had previously spent in the persecution of Jesus's followers. He was a highly educated Pharisee with extensive knowledge of the Scriptures, and won arguments against the most learned Jewish elders in Jerusalem. The former favourite of the Sanhedrin soon became the most hated. As soon as the disciples heard that the elders wanted to kill Paul, they sent him off to Tarsus, far to the north, to teach far away from the people who had become his bitter enemies.

V ERY FEW PEOPLE EXPERIENCE SUCH A SUDDEN CONVERSION AS THIS. OCCASIONALLY SOME DRAMATIC EVENT HELPS PEOPLE PUT THEIR FAITH IN JESUS. MOST PEOPLE GROW INTO FAITH SLOWLY. ✒

Paul's journey to Damascus
Damascus is in Syria, the country to the north of Judea. In the first century, it was part of the same Roman province as Judea. It was about 240km north of Jerusalem and would have taken Saul several days to travel there and back.

Tarsus
This was Saul's home in south-east Asia Minor (modern Turkey). Tarsus was an important city in Roman times and may have housed up to half a million people. It was sited on important trade routes. These trade routes and its port made the city rich.

Aeneas and Tabitha

THE followers who had run away from Saul's persecution spread Jesus's teachings throughout Judea and Samaria, and into Jesus's home of Galilee. At the same time, the disciples were busy travelling from synagogue to synagogue, preaching the gospel of Jesus to large congregations of Jews and winning many believers by the miracles they worked in Jesus's name.

In a town called Lydda in the north-east of Judea, Peter was told about a man named Aeneas. All the locals respected him as a good and kind man. Aeneas had been very ill for over eight years and had become paralysed and confined to bed. His life had become a misery, with his healthy mind trapped inside a useless body.

"You must go and visit Aeneas," the people of Lydda

begged Peter. "The poor man has been terribly ill for so long. You are famous for the amazing healing miracles that you do in the name of Jesus Christ. We are sure you can cure Aeneas, too. Please help him!"

Peter went at once to Aeneas's house, and when he saw the faithful, God-fearing man lying in pain, he took pity on him straight away.

"Aeneas, Jesus Christ heals you," Peter said gently, taking his hand. "Get up now, and make your bed."

In front of all his neighbours, Aeneas swung his legs over the edge of the bed and stood up. Tears sparkled in his eyes. He flung his arms around Peter.

"I can walk!" he wept. "Praise be to God and all glory to His Son, Jesus Christ!"

A good example
Tabitha was a Christian who used her skills to help others. She was not known as a preacher, but she was known by her generosity.

Joppa
Tabitha lived in Joppa, which today is known as Jaffa and is part of the city of Tel Aviv. It is on the Mediterranean coast of Israel. It had been an important port since about 1600BC, although tradition suggests it was built earlier by Noah's son Japheth.

The celebrations at Lydda went on well into the night, but right in the middle of it all, two followers came hurrying from the nearby town of Joppa to find Peter.

"We've been sent to ask if you'll come to Joppa straight away," they begged Peter. "The people there are desperate for your help."

> **Aeneas, Jesus Christ heals you; rise and make your bed.**

Immediately, Peter set off to the little town and arrived to find the sound of wailing filling the streets. A woman called Tabitha had just died and the whole of Joppa was in mourning. Everyone had loved Tabitha. She had always put others first, never thinking about herself. Tabitha was always on the lookout for kind, generous things she could do for other people. Almost everyone in Joppa had benefited from her kindness, especially the needy.

Tabitha had been a skilled seamstress, and she had spent her own money and time in making clothes for many of the poor. Now she was gone, her dead body laid out in the upstairs room of her house, and everyone was deeply sad. The people of Joppa had heard that Peter was near and believed that, working through Peter, the power of Jesus Christ could help.

Peter looked around at the weeping faces of Tabitha's friends and relations and called for silence. He knelt down beside the dead woman and prayed for a long time. Apart from Jesus Himself, only the great prophets Elijah and Elisha had ever been granted the grace to bring someone back from the dead.

Eventually, Peter opened his eyes.

"Tabitha, get up," he said firmly.

The people in the crowded room stood anxiously, scanning Tabitha's body for any signs of life. There was a gasp as her eyelids flickered a few times and then opened. Tabitha turned her head and looked straight at Peter. He stretched out his hand and beckoned, and Tabitha placed her hand in Peter's and allowed him to help her up.

The faith of the people of Joppa had been rewarded. Peter had brought Tabitha back to life, in the name of Jesus Christ.

Spinning and weaving
In biblical times, many people made their own clothes. Wool was spun into threads on a spindle (which is what the woman on the left is doing) before being woven into a garment or a piece of cloth on a wooden-framed loom. Some people specialized in this trade and sold the cloth to others.

A devout woman
This statue shows a woman worshipping God. Tabitha always worshipped God faithfully.

❖ ABOUT THE STORY ❖

This story raises questions about God's attitude to suffering. Both Aeneas and Tabitha were well known as good people. Were they any more worthy of healing than other good people? The Bible suggests that people are not healed just because they are good or well known, but because God has a special purpose in healing them. In both these cases the publicity which followed the healing helped more people come to faith in Jesus.

Peter and Cornelius

It wasn't only Jews who were turning to follow Jesus Christ. Many non-Jews, or Gentiles, were showing a keen interest in Jesus's promise of salvation too. For a long time, the disciples knew that Jesus wanted them to spread the gospel to Jews through the whole world, but were not sure what to do about Gentiles. In the end, the Lord showed them.

After Peter had brought Tabitha back to life, he stayed in Joppa at the house of Simon, a tanner. One day, when Peter went up on the flat roof to pray, he saw the heavens open and a sheet being let down, spread like a picnic with all kinds of animals and birds.

"Kill something and eat it," said God into his mind.

Peter was horrified. He remembered all the Jewish laws about which animals and birds were considered clean to eat, the prayer rituals that should be said before killing them and the rules about how they should be cooked.

"No, Lord!" cried Peter in horror. "I could never eat anything unclean or not prepared properly."

"You must not consider unclean anything that God has cleansed," replied the voice, sternly.

The command was repeated twice, and Peter replied the same, before the sheet finally returned to heaven.

Peter was sure that God was trying to teach him something, but what? Peter's thoughts were interrupted by a voice speaking once again into his mind.

"Three men have arrived, looking for you," said God. "Go with them, for I have sent them."

It is very easy to look down on people who are different to us. This story tells us that God regards all people equally, and so should we. ∾

"Gentiles – keep out!"
Gentiles were only allowed into the first of three courts surrounding the temple in Jerusalem. It was here that the traders sold animals for sacrifices, and where the money changers had their stalls. There were notices up all round the temple – this is one of them – telling the Gentiles not to go any further.

The bemused Peter obediently went downstairs.

"I'm Peter," he said. "How can I help you?"

"Our master, Cornelius, has sent us to find you," the three men began. "He's a Gentile, a Roman centurion. He's always been a God-fearing man. He prays regularly and insists that his whole household does the same. He gives lots of money to charity and all the Jews in the neighbourhood think very highly of him." The servants looked at each other nervously. "An angel appeared to Cornelius while he was praying and told him to send for you."

"Well, in that case, I'd better come with you," Peter said, and the three men smiled with relief.

The next day, the three servants took Peter and his companions to Cornelius's house. The centurion had gathered a welcome party of his family and friends. When Peter walked through the door, Cornelius fell on his knees before him. At that very moment, Peter understood what his vision of the picnic blanket had meant.

"Don't kneel before me," Peter said, helping Cornelius to his feet. "You're a man just like I am."

> " *God has shown me that I should not call any man common or unclean.* "

Cornelius was startled. He knew that it was unlawful for Jews to have Gentile friends and that special cleansing rituals were necessary if a Jew ever went into a Gentile house. Peter didn't seem bothered.

"I understand now that God has no favourites," Peter said. "He will welcome anyone who does what is right – no matter who they are or where they're from, whether they're Jew or Gentile, man or woman."

While Peter was speaking, everyone in Cornelius's house felt a strange glow in their hearts. They had been filled with the Holy Spirit, and they began praising God.

The Jews who had come with Peter were astonished. Yet Peter now understood.

"See?" he said. "Who can possibly say that Gentiles shouldn't be allowed to follow Christ?"

Cornelius and his household were the first Gentiles anywhere to be baptized.

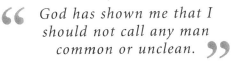

❀ CLEAN AND UNCLEAN ANIMALS ❀

Jewish people live by a series of dietary laws, called *kashrut* or *kosher*. These laws set down not only which foods can be eaten, but also which foods Jews can eat with which.

LAND ANIMALS
The Jews were allowed to eat any animal that had a completely split hoof and also chewed the cud. This included cows and sheep. They were not allowed to eat camels, rabbits or pigs.

WATER CREATURES
All fish which had fins and scales were considered clean. They could not eat any sea mammals such as dolphins, or shellfish.

INSECTS
Only one kind of insect was clean: the hoppers (grasshoppers, locusts etc). All other insects could not be eaten.

BIRDS
Poultry and similar birds were allowed (the Israelites ate quails in the desert after they left Egypt). Most other birds were banned as unclean, including hunting birds such as eagles, gulls and owls.

Tanning animal skins
This shows Egyptians tanning the skins of animals, as Simon in the story did. Tanning made the skin into soft leather.

Peter in Prison

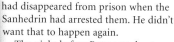

KING Herod Agrippa hated the growth of the church of Jesus Christ almost as much as Paul had done at first. The king knew that the followers drew great strength from their faith in God and the promises Jesus had made them. He feared them because of this. He was deeply worried by the way that the disciples had stood up to the Sanhedrin, saying that they obeyed only God, not men. Herod saw this as outright defiance of all human rulers and kings.

Herod determined to wipe out the followers of Jesus Christ once and for all. He ordered his guards to arrest Jesus's followers whenever possible. The king didn't stop at imprisonment. He had James, the brother of John, put to death. When he saw how this pleased the Jewish elders, and how he gained popularity among many traditional Jews because of it, he had Peter arrested and thrown into the dungeons too.

The only thing that stopped King Herod from executing Peter straight away was his concern not to be seen as a murderer. He had to be seen to give the disciple a trial first, even if it was on false charges and with bribed, corrupt witnesses. In the meantime, Herod kept Peter chained up to two soldiers – even while he slept – with a 24-hour guard outside his cell door. He knew how important Peter was to the disciples and he felt sure that the followers would try to come and rescue him. The king had also heard the strange stories of how Peter and John had disappeared from prison when the Sanhedrin had arrested them. He didn't want that to happen again.

The night before Peter was due to stand trial and face execution, he dreamt that a strange light blazed into his dingy cell and that an angel was stirring him awake.

"Quickly, get up!" the angel commanded him.

Peter dreamt that the chains and shackles fell from his feet and he was no longer bound up to the snoring soldiers on either side.

"Dress yourself," came the angel's urgent voice. "Put on your sandals."

In his hurry, Peter tripped and nearly fell over himself. The pain felt real, but Peter was sure he was dreaming.

"Wrap your cloak around you and follow me," came the final instruction.

Peter followed after the gliding angel, right through the dungeon door and past the sentries who were all fast asleep at their posts, up the prison steps to the great iron gate. It swung open on its own, and the angel and Peter stepped out into the moonlit street. At once, the angel vanished and Peter felt a chilly breeze brush his skin. It hadn't been a dream after all! He was really free!

"The Lord has rescued me!" Peter realized.

He hurried through the deserted city to the house belonging to Mark's mother, Mary. Peter had to get to a safe hiding place before the sun came up and Herod's guards realized that he was missing.

At last Peter arrived in front of the little door. Knock, knock, knock, he rapped softly. No answer.

Well, it is the middle of the night, he supposed. Everyone is probably asleep.

Thump, thump, thump. Peter knocked a little louder.

Please wake up, Peter thought. Hurry up and let me in before one of Herod's watchmen strolls past and sees me.

No one came to answer.

> ## And the chains fell off his hands.

Bang, bang, bang! The desperate Peter hit the door even harder, and to his great relief he at last heard footsteps. The door swung open a little way and an anxious pair of eyes peered nervously out at him. The eyes widened in surprise and then a mouth gasped, and the door was slammed shut in Peter's face.

Peter stood shivering on the doorstep while he heard the sound of arguing voices inside. A few moments later, the door opened a crack once more and a whole host of faces peered expectantly out.

"I told you it was!" yelled a voice.

"It is!" someone else cried.

Then the door was flung wide open and Peter was ushered in. Everyone was talking at once and slapping him on the back, asking how he had got out of prison.

When everyone finally quietened down, Peter began to tell of his miraculous escape. By dawn, he was going over his story for the thousandth time. Peter's joyful friends wanted to hear every last detail over and over again.

Meanwhile, Herod's soldiers woke up to find Peter's cell empty. Shaking with fear, they went to tell the king – who was, of course, furious. Herod exploded with rage and ordered that every guard under his command to immediately go and search high and low for Peter. It was no good. Peter was well and truly gone. The evil king ordered that every soldier who was on guard that night would be put to death in his place.

Wrist chains
Prisoners in ancient times were often chained to the wall, the floor or to each other. It was as much to shame them as restrain them.

Roman magistrate
This carving dates from about AD500 but the magistrates who Paul appeared before would have looked similar. He holds a sceptre as a sign of justice, and a money bag as a sign of mercy.

> ### ❧ ABOUT THE STORY ❧
> *This story tells of a miracle. It was not the first or last time that disciples were released from prison in some amazing way. What matters is not how it happened, but why. This was a great sign to all the Christians that God did not intend to let His message of new life in Christ be chained up by non-religious authorities. He would find a way of letting it loose. This is saying that God is greater than any human ruler.*

Paul's First Missionary Journey

In Jerusalem, the disciples heard that the followers who had fled Saul's persecution had spread the word of Jesus as far as Phoenicia, and the Greek states of Cyprus and Antioch. They decided to send Barnabas to guide them.

Barnabas went to Antioch first. He was met by so many eager followers that he went to Tarsus to fetch Paul to help him. For a whole year, Barnabas and Paul preached to the people of Antioch and baptized them. It was in Antioch that the disciples of Jesus were called Christians for the first time.

Paul was soon called by the Holy Spirit to sail to even more distant Gentile shores. Without questioning or hesitating, the disciple took Barnabas and John and several other followers to help him.

Paul's first port of call was the island of Cyprus. As usual, he and his companions began their preaching in the local synagogues. They worked their way across the island until they came to the town of Paphos, the home of the Roman governor, Sergius Paulus. He had heard about Jesus of Nazareth. The Roman governor summoned Paul and Barnabas to see him, so he could hear for himself.

When the disciples were ushered into the Roman governor's house, they noticed a pompous-looking local man sitting smugly next to him. Straight away the Holy Spirit told Paul who he was. His name was Elymas, an evil

man who had set himself up to be a prophet. He had completely taken in the Roman governor by his magic tricks.

Paul and Barnabas tried to ignore Elymas and began preaching to Sergius Paulus, but the evil magician argued with everything they said, doing his very best to keep the Roman governor from believing in Jesus. Eventually, Paul lost his temper.

"You son of the devil!" Paul cried, in a fury. "Stop trying to waylay those who want to follow the Lord!"

Paul flung out his hand in Elymas's direction, and the magician cowered away in fear.

"Feel the true power of Jesus Christ!" Paul cried at the cringing man. "You will be blind for a time, unable to see the light of the sun!"

Immediately, Elymas's eyes grew dark, and he whimpered at the governor's feet in terror. Sergius Paulus looked in astonishment at Paul and Barnabas. From that moment on, he believed wholeheartedly in all they had told him about Jesus of Nazareth.

From Paphos, Paul and Barnabas and their helpers set sail once again. After calling at Pergia, they returned to Antioch, to see how the church they had set up was doing.

Paul and Barnabas were pleased with what they found. On the first sabbath that they preached, the synagogue was packed with Jews who had come to hear them speak of Jesus Christ and forgiveness for all. Even when they had

---

❧ About the Story ❧

From the beginning, Christianity was a religion to be spread across the world. Jesus had told the disciples to take His message to "Jerusalem, Samaria and the ends of the earth". So far, the gospel had been preached mostly as people travelled because of persecution. Now the disciples travelled specifically in order to plant new churches. Their reason was simple. If Jesus was the Son of God, then everyone needed to know.

The first missionary journey of Paul
Paul did not make a circular journey. All the places he visited on the outward leg he visited again on the return journey, except for Cyprus. This took place about AD46–48. Paul never returned to Cyprus, but Barnabas went there with Mark.

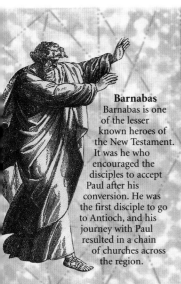

finished preaching, the congregation followed them out into the sun, urging them to carry on.

All week, the Jews of Antioch spoke so excitedly about the good news preached by Paul and Barnabas that the Gentiles of the city heard of it too. On the following sabbath, the disciples found that almost the entire population of Antioch had turned out to hear them speak.

When the Jews saw the masses of interested Gentiles, they were extremely jealous of them.

> ❝ *In Antioch the followers were for the first time called Christians.* ❞

"You can't preach to them too!" they yelled, quickly working themselves up into an angry mob. "We're God's chosen people! No one can be saved unless they're Jewish!"

Paul and Barnabas stood firm.

"Don't forget that we brought God's message to you first," they reminded the Jews. "The Lord Himself has commanded us to 'be a light for the Gentiles, to bring salvation to the uttermost ends of the earth.'"

When the anxious Gentiles heard this, they were filled with gladness. They beamed with delight and gave thanks to God, and many of them were baptized straight away.

Yet the Jews weren't at all satisfied. They argued and scowled and grumbled. As the days went on, they grew angrier and angrier with every Gentile whom Paul and Barnabas welcomed as a Christian. All the wealthy men and women who had been very strictly brought up in the Jewish faith were particularly outraged. Eventually they demanded that the Jewish elders should drive the two followers out of the city.

Paul and Barnabas weren't downhearted. They had sown the seeds of faith among the Gentiles of Antioch, and they sailed on their way with great joy in their hearts.

Barnabas
Barnabas is one of the lesser known heroes of the New Testament. It was he who encouraged the disciples to accept Paul after his conversion. He was the first disciple to go to Antioch, and his journey with Paul resulted in a chain of churches across the region.

Cyprus
Barnabas came originally from Cyprus, as did several of the other disciples, so he was on familiar ground when he went back there with Paul. This Belgian tapestry, which is now in Mantua in Italy, shows Paul and Barnabas striking Elymas blind.

Faith for the Gentiles

PAUL and Barnabas being chased from Antioch was only the start of their troubles. In Iconium, Paul and Barnabas found that things were just as bad. They managed to win over lots people to Christ, but the traditional Jews felt outraged that Gentiles were being baptized. Paul and Barnabas were determined not to give up, but the situation grew increasingly difficult for them. People shouted them down in the synagogue and jeered at them. Eventually, the city was split into two sides who hated each other – those who supported the Jews and those who followed the disciples. When an attempt was made to stone Paul and Barnabas, they decided it was time to move on.

While many Jews were finding it difficult to accept Jesus as the fulfilment of ancient prophecies, many Gentiles

were finding it hard to give up the beliefs they had held all their lives. People had shrines to other gods in their houses and massive stone temples to Greek gods such as Zeus dominated the towns. It was hard for them to grasp the idea of believing in just one God and His Son, Jesus Christ.

When Paul was preaching in Lystra, he saw a man who had been a cripple from birth. Paul knew that he had the faith in God to be made well, and he suddenly broke off from his preaching and shouted: "On your feet!"

The man obeyed at once. "I can walk!" he cried aloud.

The gasping crowd stared at Paul and Barnabas.

"The gods have come down to us in the form of men!" they yelled, falling on their knees before the disciples.

"All hail to Zeus, the great father of the gods!" they cried at Barnabas, bowing down.

"All hail to Hermes, his swift, silver-tongued messenger!" they worshipped Paul.

Paul is stoned
Stoning was the traditional way in which the Jews executed someone for blasphemy, speaking against God. This ivory from the 900s is a representation of Paul's stoning. He was very lucky to escape – the stones could fracture a victim's skull.

The birth of Athena
Athena was the patron goddess of the Greek city of Athens. She was one of many gods worshipped across the Roman Empire. She was said to have been born from the head of the great god Zeus.

The two disciples were horrified. The men and women of Iconium hadn't taken in what they had been telling them about Jesus Christ and had interpreted the miracle as the work of their own pagan gods! A priest from the temple of Zeus came with oxen to sacrifice to them.

> **66** *...through many tribulations we must enter the kingdom of God.* **99**

"No! No! No!" Paul and Barnabas cried. "Why are you doing this?" The disciples stopped the priests and their followers just before they had time to slaughter the oxen. "We are not gods! We are humans, just like you! We are just the bringers of the good news that there is only one, true God, who made everything."

There were other problems. The angry, non-believing Jews from Antioch and Iconium turned up.

"Don't listen to these strangers!" they told the people of Lystra. "They're filling your heads with an evil load of rubbish! Don't listen to them!"

The Jews stirred up the citizens into such a frenzy of hate that a mob even went after Paul and stoned him, leaving him for dead outside the city. Yet as soon as Paul recovered, he and Barnabas continued with their work undeterred. They travelled far and wide, strengthening the faith of those who did believe. They also explained that Jesus had warned that those who wanted to enter the kingdom of God would have to face a great many difficulties and dangers.

Still, it was with relief that Paul and Barnabas eventually returned to their faithful following in Antioch, and rested there for a while.

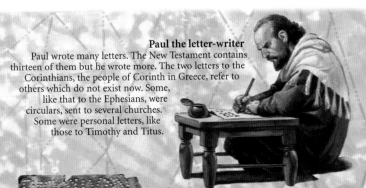

Paul the letter-writer
Paul wrote many letters. The New Testament contains thirteen of them but he wrote more. The two letters to the Corinthians, the people of Corinth in Greece, refer to others which do not exist now. Some, like that to the Ephesians, were circulars, sent to several churches. Some were personal letters, like those to Timothy and Titus.

Roman household shrine
People in the Roman Empire often had a shrine like this in their home where they would offer incense to their family god. The disciples had to explain that there was only one true God.

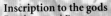

Inscription to the gods
People around Europe worshipped many gods at this time. This inscription was made by a coppersmith in Colchester, England. He put it in a temple to remind the god of his 'faith'.

The Disciples Hold a Council

WHILE Paul and Barnabas were staying in Antioch, some followers arrived from Judea and began teaching the Gentiles that they had to adopt Jewish customs as well as be baptized if they wanted to be Christians. The two disciples argued with the followers, but the stubborn men refused to back down. In the end, Paul and Barnabas went to Jerusalem to tell the other disciples about the trouble, and to find some way to stop it.

Paul and Barnabas called the top Christians in Jerusalem together to a council in order to discuss recruiting Gentiles. When Paul told the council of the uproar they had caused by recruiting Gentiles as well as Jews into the church, the other disciples looked worried.

At once, some Pharisees who had been baptized as Christians agreed with the traditional Jewish view.

"It's true," they said. "It is the law of Moses. Only Jews can be saved. We are God's chosen people."

That was the start of a very long, heated debate. After all, it was an important issue that was in danger of dividing the church. Everyone felt strongly about his or her particular opinion. Finally, Peter stood up and called for quiet. Many people thought of him as the leader of the apostles, and he commanded a great deal of respect.

"Remember, friends," Peter began, "that God Himself told me to take the word of Jesus Christ to the Gentiles, so that they can believe in Him. I have seen with my own eyes that the Holy Spirit blesses Gentiles who are baptized, just as He does Jews. Why do you insist that only Jews can be saved?"

✦ ABOUT THE STORY ✦

The problem facing the church was whether Christianity was just a development of Judaism, or something completely new. The disciples decided that it was both. Jesus had fulfilled the Jewish law through His death. So the church was something new, not a sect of Judaism. The old ceremonies could not make a person right with God. People needed only to believe in God and in Jesus.

Jewish faith today
Some practices have changed little among Jews since Bible times. One of them is ceremonial cleansing. Jews wash their hands in a special way before they eat or pray. The person who lights a candle for worship may hold out his or her hands for cleansing.

Don't get drunk
A drunken man is supported by his friends. Paul advised the people of Ephesus that they did not have to abstain from alcohol, but they did have to use it carefully.

No one dared argue with the great disciple. Everyone kept quiet as Barnabas and Paul told about all the amazing miracles God had done through them among the Gentiles. Then James stood up and reminded everyone about the words of the ancient prophets: "'I will return, and I will rebuild the dwelling of David, which has fallen .... that the rest of people may seek the Lord, and all the Gentiles who are called by my name.'

66 *Unless you are circumcised according to the custom of Moses, you cannot be saved.* 99

"So may I suggest," continued James, "that we stop troubling Gentiles who want to join us. It is God's will that they do not have to convert to the Jewish faith before being baptized in Christ. However, I'd like to propose that we give them some guidelines, so their fellow Jewish followers will not be offended. For instance, we should instruct the Gentiles not to have anything to do with pagan religions, to be faithful to their husband or wife and to prepare certain foods carefully."

Fortunately, this solution seemed to satisfy everyone present at the council. The disciples at once composed and copied a letter of instructions for all the Gentiles everywhere who wanted to follow the teachings of Christ. When Paul and Barnabas returned with it to the church in Antioch, the Gentiles rejoiced. They were finally officially accepted into the faith.

Marriage contract
James was anxious that the Jewish attitude to marriage should be followed by the Gentiles. This is because God had shown it to be His will for all people.

THIS STORY SHOWS HOW CHRISTIANS WHO DISAGREE CAN SORT OUT THEIR DIFFERENCES. THE DISCIPLES MET, HEARD THE EVIDENCE AND ARGUMENTS, AND PRAYED. THEN EVERYONE STOOD BY WHAT THE LEADERS SAID. THAT IS A GOOD MODEL TO FOLLOW TODAY.

Church council
This painting from Bulgaria shows the Second Ecumenical Council of the Christian church in AD381. Over the years since the meeting of the disciples there have been many important councils. As the world and people change, the church sometimes has to change to keep up.

Paul's Second Missionary Journey

PAUL and Barnabas remained in Antioch for some time, strengthening the faith of the church they had established there. Then the two men decided they should split up and revisit every place in which they had they proclaimed the word of the Lord so far, to see how the new Christian communities were getting on. Barnabas picked Mark to be his assistant and sailed away to Cyprus, while Paul chose Silas as his helper, and set off through Syria and Cilicia. In every town and city the missionaries passed through, they

showed the churches the letter from the Christian council in Jerusalem regarding the baptism of Gentiles. Every day, the number of believers in Jesus Christ grew and grew.

Throughout his travels, Paul never planned his route himself. He always trusted God to show him where he should go. The Holy Spirit gave Paul signs in many different ways. One night, in Troas, he had a vision as he slept. He dreamt that a stranger stole into his room and crept silently up to his bedside. The man stood over Paul and stretched out his hands in earnest.

> **" The Lord opened her heart to give heed to what was said by Paul. "**

"Come to Macedonia and help us," he asked.
Then the man's sad face faded away.
Next morning, Paul knew exactly where God wanted him to go. He and Silas gathered his companions and set off straight away to the Roman colony in the north of Greece.

Paul directed his little company of followers to Philippi, Macedonia's leading city. They found themselves in the midst of hustling, bustling streets, noisy market places, and buzzing shops and houses – but they knew no one. However, God made sure that He soon provided them with friends. The first sabbath that Paul and Silas were in Philippi, they went out of the city to a Jewish place of prayer beside a river. Many women were gathered there, and as Paul preached the good news of Jesus Christ, they listened eagerly. One woman in particular felt the joy of

❧ ABOUT THE STORY ❧

From now on, the story in the book of Acts includes many first-person accounts. It is believed that Luke, the author, was travelling with Paul for much of the time. This story also marks the parting of ways for Paul and Barnabas, and we hear no more of Barnabas again. The mission work increased, a sign that God was blessing it. Meanwhile, Paul's ministry was as powerful as ever.

Slave auction
This shows the harsh reality of the Roman slave system. The slaves had no rights of their own and could be bought and sold like cattle in a market. Many of these slaves were foreigners who had been brought to Rome as prisoners of war. A runaway slave could be executed if he or she was caught.

people to have their fortunes told. The two disciples weren't pleased at all. The slave girl followed them for days, crying out wildly after them wherever they went. Finally, Paul lost his patience. Without any warning, he turned and faced the slave girl, his face like thunder. Paul flung his hand out towards her and cried, "Spirit! I charge you in the name of Jesus Christ to come out of her!"

At once, the slave girl was quietened. She found she could no longer sense the strange unexplained things she had seen before. Her ability to see into the unknown had left her.

the Holy Spirit flood into her heart – a seller of fine cloths, called Lydia. Lydia begged that she and all her household should be baptized straight away, and she insisted that Paul and his companions come to stay with her during their stay in Philippi.

After that, Paul and Silas often returned to the river to pray and preach. One day, as they made their way there, they suddenly heard shouting behind them.

"These men are true servants of God!" came the shrill, excited voice. "They have come to tell everyone the way to salvation!"

Paul and Silas spun round to see a young slave girl hot on their heels, yelling as loud as she could and beckoning the startled passers-by to come and follow them.

The slave girl had a strange gift of prophecy, and her Roman owners were delighted with it. For years, they had made lots of money out of the slave girl by charging

Paul's second missionary journey
Much of Paul's journey was overland from Antioch and through Asia Minor. Paul told the Corinthians that he faced many dangers including bandits and fast-flowing rivers. He probably walked rather than rode animals.

Kindly slave owners
Many of the first Christians were slaves. Not all slaves were kept in chains and badly treated. Some slaves were like trusted colleagues. Slave owners could, if they chose to, free their slaves (they then became known as freedmen) and some even continued to support them as patrons. This tomb was set up by two former slaves in honour of their Roman masters.

Paul and Silas in Prison

WHEN the slave girl's Roman owners found out that her fortune-telling skills were gone, they were furious. They dragged Paul and Silas to the local courtroom to make an official complaint against them.

"These foreigners are making trouble in our city!" they yelled, stirring up an angry mob.

The Roman magistrates didn't give Paul and Silas a chance to explain.

"Arrest them for disturbing the peace!" they ordered, waving forward guards to take Paul and Silas away. "Strip them, beat them and throw them into prison!"

Several hours later, Paul and Silas were locked by the feet into wooden stocks. Their skin bled from the Roman soldiers' whips and their faces were black with bruises where the guards had punched them.

Paul and Silas didn't let their plight make them downhearted. Instead, they trusted in the Lord and sang hymns to God. The other prisoners were stunned. Their God must truly be wonderful to inspire such faith, they marvelled. Some of them even joined in.

At midnight, the singing was suddenly drowned out by a mighty rumbling under the earth. The prison floor shook and the walls crumbled. The floor heaved, throwing the prisoners from side to side, breaking their chains and bursting open the prison doors.

When the earthquake had stopped, the terrified jailer ran in, expecting to find his prisoners escaped. All the torches had gone out, and he could see no one. The jailer drew his sword, ready to kill himself rather than face punishment for having allowed all the prisoners to escape.

Paul and Silas were horrified when they realized what the ashamed jailer was about to do.

> **❝** *Let them come themselves and take us out.* **❞**

"No! Don't! We are all here!" Paul cried.

The jailer couldn't believe his ears.

"Torches!" he cried, as guards ran in.

The jailer was amazed at the two followers of Jesus Christ. They had worked a strange miracle on a slave girl. They had been unaffected by being whipped and thrown into prison. They were unafraid of an earthquake. They made sure all the prisoners stayed in jail when they had had a chance to escape! The jailer made up his mind.

Rumbling under the earth
An earthquake happens when the pressure on two sections of the earth's crust causes the earth to split open.

Lock and key
Most doors were locked with bolts which slid across them, but the Romans also used locks and keys not unlike those we use today. This bronze lock would have been used for a small box.

Certificate of citizenship
The only way to prove you were a Roman citizen was to have an official document. This document is etched into bronze. It says that a Spanish soldier is a citizen, which meant he had the full rights of someone who had been born into a Roman family.

washed Paul and Silas's wounds, and brought them food and clothes. Then he insisted that he and all his household be baptized at once, and they celebrated for hours.

The next morning Paul and Silas returned to the town's courtroom, where the magistrates smirked to themselves.

"Those strangers will have spent a horrible night in the cells," they said, gloating over their power. "They'll have learned their lesson. Let them go."

Paul and Silas weren't happy at all. They hadn't done anything wrong! They didn't want to creep away.

"We are freeborn Roman citizens," they reminded the jailer. "We want a public apology!"

The magistrates were worried when the jailer told them that they had ordered Roman citizens to be flogged without a trial. They hurried to apologize to Paul and Silas in front of the citizens, before they got in serious trouble. Then the magistrates begged them to leave Philippi. So Paul and Silas went back to Lydia's house in peace, to say goodbye to their friends before continuing on their mission.

Other people might say that Paul and Silas were phoney, but he thought differently. He believed that the two men were truly filled with the power of God.

The jailer gave the order for the other prisoners to be chained up again immediately, but to Paul and Silas's astonishment, he led them out of the prison and back to his own house. In front of his whole household, he fell on his knees before Paul and Silas.

"Tell me what I must do to be saved," the jailer begged.

"Just believe in the Lord Jesus Christ," Paul and Silas replied, "and you will be forgiven for your sins."

The two men told the jailer, his family and servants all about Jesus. When the jailer heard how Jesus wanted His followers to treat everyone with love and kindness, he

Paul arguing
This enamel plaque shows Paul arguing with both Jews and Greeks. Wherever he went, Paul got into debates. He taught that Jesus Christ was the Messiah, the person that God sent to save the people from their sins, and that He had risen from the dead. Many Greeks thought this was a crazy idea, and many Jews found it repugnant. Others believed it and became Christians.

Woman at worship
Many of the first Christians were women. Christianity liberated them, because they were considered by Jesus to be equal to men before God. Women covered their heads when they went into Church. This was an important custom, because at the time only prostitutes had bare heads.

❧ ABOUT THE STORY ❧
This is one of many instances in the Bible when something natural – an earthquake in this case – happens at just the right time to help God's servants. It is a miracle of God's timing. God did not stop His servants from being locked up – which was unlawful, without a proper trial – but He did rescue them and at the same time so impressed others with His power that they believed in Him too.

Paul's Travels and Miracles

PAUL and Silas pressed on to the city of Thessalonika. For three weeks Paul preached in the synagogue to argue that Jesus was the Saviour. Although a large number of people believed, many Jews were outraged. They gathered together a violent mob and went to speak to the city authorities.

"Paul and his companions are trying to turn the world upside down!" they protested. "They're against the Roman emperor, because they say there is another king – Jesus!"

That night, before the Romans took any action, the followers smuggled Paul and Silas out of the city.

> **66** *And God did extraordinary miracles by the hands of Paul...* **99**

Paul travelled south to Athens, the main city of Greece. The city was scattered with idols of pagan gods. The streets were full of worshippers taking offerings and sacrifices to and from the pagan temples. Paul strode into the busy market place and preached to passers-by. He also met with philosophers, men who tried to puzzle out the meaning of life and the universe for themselves.

The people of Athens loved nothing more than to hear different beliefs. While many Athenians didn't know what to make of Paul's preaching, others were keen to hear more. They took him to speak on a hill near the vast Acropolis. By the time Paul left Athens, some people had become Christians.

Corinthian capital
A capital is the top of a column that supports a building. The Greeks and Romans loved to build tall columns. They often had rows of them called colonnades. This capital is decorated with a face mask used in the theatre and stylized acanthus leaves under the arms. This design is called corinthian because it came from Corinth.

Helmet
This is a Greek helmet which has lots of protection for the neck, and a central strip to protect the soldier's nose.

Mirror
In biblical times mirrors like this were not made of glass, but of bronze which could be polished so that it gave a good but not perfect reflection. Paul in his letter to the Corinthians says that we see God's truth only dimly, or partially, as in a mirror. When we go to heaven, we shall see God 'face to face'.

Paul's next port of call was Corinth. He stayed with a Jewish couple called Aquila and Priscilla who had fled Rome when the Emperor Claudius had ordered all Jews to leave. Paul preached in the synagogue, and Crispus, the ruler of the synagogue, asked to be baptized. Even so, most of the Jews refused to listen to Paul.

"Your blood be upon your own heads!" Paul cried in the end. "I have done my best with you, and now I will take the message of Jesus Christ to the Gentiles instead."

Paul found that the Gentiles were much more ready to believe in Jesus Christ. Many began asking to be baptized. Then one night, the Lord appeared to Paul in a vision.

"Don't be afraid to speak out in this city, for I am with you," God said. "I will make sure that no harm comes to you, for there are many people here who will turn to me."

Inspired with new faith and courage, Paul stayed for a year and six months in Corinth, and established a strong Christian community there before travelling on to Ephesus, where he stayed for two years.

Everyone who witnessed Paul's miraculous deeds were amazed. In Ephesus, seven sons of a Jewish high priest were so envious that they decided to try it for themselves. They summoned a man who they knew was possessed by an evil spirit, and they tried to cast it out, as they had seen Paul do.

The unearthly voice of the evil spirit wailed, "I know Jesus and I know Paul, but who are you?"

With a howl, the man leapt onto the seven men and they ran from the house.

After that many people who had practised pagan rituals and black magic believed in Jesus.

The third missionary journey of Paul
Paul's third journey was very similar to his second. Once again he revisited the churches of Asia Minor. Paul was a carer as well as an evangelist. He wanted to make sure the Christians were going on with their faith.

❧ ABOUT THE STORY ❧

This story shows how adaptable and flexible Paul was. He did not just take one approach and organize every visit in the same way. He started in the Jewish synagogue if there was one. When he was thrown out of one building he went and hired another. This also shows that his teaching and miracles went side by side. He always began by teaching, but the miracles often helped people believe that Jesus was for real.

Demetrius and the Riot

IN Ephesus, a silversmith called Demetrius made shrines used in the worship of the Greek goddess Artemis. He was unhappy that Paul was turning people away from Artemis, to a religion where they wouldn't need the idols he made. Demetrius called together all the other workmen.

"The numbers of people who worship Artemis are diminishing," Demetrius warned his fellow tradesmen. "It's all due to that Paul. We may lose our livelihoods, and the worship of our great goddess might die out altogether!"

The workmen were outraged at the thought. They set off through the town, shouting, "Artemis of the Ephesians is great!" Soon, people were rushing to the amphitheatre for an emergency public meeting. There was utter confusion. Some people were screaming, "Artemis!", others were yelling, "Praise be to God and His Son, Jesus Christ!", while most people had no idea why they were there.

Paul's followers wouldn't let him enter the amphitheatre for his own safety, and it was several hours before the town clerk managed to quieten everyone down.

"Everyone knows that Ephesus is Artemis's special city!" he yelled. "So why are you getting so worked up over the strangers who have come here? They have said nothing against our goddess. If Demetrius and the craftsmen have a complaint, let them go through the proper legal system. We would be fools to start a riot that would bring the wrath of the Romans down upon us all. Now go home!"

The situation was too fragile for Paul to remain, so he left for Macedonia.

> " *Great is Artemis of the Ephesians!* "

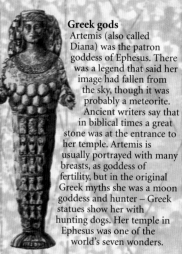

❧ ABOUT THE STORY ❧

Many of the clashes between Paul and others started because the Jewish leaders regarded him as a heretic who was stirring up trouble. This story shows that there was a head-on clash between the Christian faith and other religions too. Jesus Himself had said that He was the only way to God. The disciples taught that other religions could not bring people to know God fully and that only Jesus, God's Son, could forgive sins.

Greek gods
Artemis (also called Diana) was the patron goddess of Ephesus. There was a legend that said her image had fallen from the sky, though it was probably a meteorite. Ancient writers say that in biblical times a great stone was at the entrance to her temple. Artemis is usually portrayed with many breasts, as goddess of fertility, but in the original Greek myths she was a moon goddess and hunter – Greek statues show her with hunting dogs. Her temple in Ephesus was one of the world's seven wonders.

Ephesus
In Paul's day Ephesus was a magnificent city. It housed at least 250,000 people and had an arena that could hold 25,000. A long road flanked with pillars led to the harbour. Paul spent two years here.

Paul in Troas

PAUL decided to return to Jerusalem. He stayed in the city of Troas for a week, encouraging the followers to remain strong and faithful when he had gone. On the night before Paul was due to leave, he spoke well into the evening. No one stirred; everyone hung on his every word. They didn't know how long it would be before the great disciple passed that way again.

On and on spoke Paul. A young man named Eutychus found himself desperately trying to stay awake and listen. Eutychus tried propping himself up in a sitting position in the deep windowsill, opening the window to let in the chill night air, sitting on his hands to make himself uncomfortable, but it was no good. His eyelids began to droop. His head nodded. Finally, he fell fast asleep, lulled by Paul's voice.

> 66 *He sank into a deep sleep as Paul talked still longer.* 99

Everyone was concentrating far too hard on what Paul was saying to notice Eutychus drifting off. In fact, the first they knew of it was when Eutychus fell out of the window and landed with a sickening thud on the ground below. There were horrified gasps as everyone dashed to the window and peered out. Eutychus was lying in a lifeless heap on the floor below.

Paul was the first to race down the stairs and reach the young man. He took Eutychus in his arms.

"Don't worry, his life has now returned to him," Paul reassured everyone.

Amazingly, through the saving grace of the great disciple, Eutychus recovered almost at once. Rejoicing, all the friends made their way back into the house, where Paul continued preaching until daybreak. They didn't stop giving thanks to God even when Paul's ship had sailed into the distance and out of sight.

THE PEOPLE OF TROAS HAD A HUNGER TO LEARN ABOUT GOD. TODAY, SOME PEOPLE TAKE FAITH LESS SERIOUSLY, IT IS A HOBBY RATHER THAN A WAY OF LIFE. CHRISTIANS IN TROAS WOULD BE DISMAYED.

Paul
Like other disciples, Paul was canonized, made a saint, so is depicted with a halo as in this mural from the 1100s from Cyprus. He was a man of great vision and energy. He cared deeply for people but could be a stern critic of those who did not live up to his own strict standards.

⊹ ABOUT THE STORY ⊹
Paul had a lot of friends with him by the time he reached Troas. Among them were Timothy, who was later to lead the church in Ephesus, and Tychicus, who was like a messenger who went round the churches carrying news from place to place. Luke and several others were with him too. Paul valued the help and support of his friends, although they are not mentioned often in Acts. He did not work alone.

Paul in Jerusalem

PAUL was in a hurry to reach Jerusalem in time for the feast of Pentecost. Yet there were several sad farewells for him to make on the way.

"You won't see me again," Paul told the followers of the Ephesian church. "The Holy Spirit has warned me that suffering and imprisonment awaits me there. I'm not sad. The only reason I consider my life precious is because I can do the work the Lord Jesus Christ has asked me to do. Look after the church when I am gone, for many people will try to destroy your faith and lead you astray. Be alert, and God will give you His help."

At Caesarea, a prophet called Agabus took Paul's girdle and tied up his own hands and feet with it.

"The Holy Spirit has told me that the Jews of Jerusalem will bind you just like this and deliver you into the hands of the Gentiles," warned the prophet, sternly.

Paul's friends protested desperately against Paul continuing on his way. Yet the disciple stood firm.

> " *What are you doing, weeping and breaking my heart?* "

"Don't weep," he begged them. "For I'm ready not only to go to prison for the Lord Jesus Christ – I'm ready to die for Him too."

The moment Paul arrived in Jerusalem, Jesus's brother, James, warned him of trouble. "There are rumours about you," James explained. "We know they're untrue, but others don't. People say that you're encouraging Jews who have converted to Christianity to give up the law of Moses and live like Gentiles!"

Paul did his best to show that the stories weren't true. He began a special week-long Jewish purification ritual, going to the temple every day to pray. Just before the seven days were completed, Paul ran headlong into a group of Jews in the temple who came from a town the disciple had visited on his travels.

"Help, everyone! Help!" they cried. "This is Paul – the man who is leading Jews everywhere astray!"

To make things worse, earlier on in the day, the same group of Jews had glimpsed Paul in the streets with his Ephesian friend, Trophimus, and wrongly assumed Paul had brought the non-Jew inside the temple.

"Paul has defiled our holy building by smuggling in a Gentile!" the Jews yelled at the tops of their voices.

"Get him!" the men and women shouted, chasing Paul through the temple courtyards and out into the road. The furious people fell on him, punching and kicking him to the ground. Just in time, a Roman tribune burst onto the scene with his soldiers.

"Who is this man?" the tribune asked the crowd, as his soldiers put Paul in chains.

"He has defiled the temple!" some people yelled.

"He has done nothing! Let him go!" screamed others.

"He has broken the law of Moses!" voices roared.

"Rubbish! He's a faithful Jew!" argued still others.

The tribune ordered Paul to be taken back to his barracks. The mob followed, shouting, "Kill him!" When Paul tried to speak to them to explain, they refused to listen to him.

Paul was flung into the cells for the night, and the following morning he found himself hauled out for questioning in front of the Sanhedrin. The disciple held the burning eyes of the Jewish officials in his steady gaze.

"Brothers, I have always lived before God with a good conscience..." he began.

All at once, Paul realized something. The council was made up of half Pharisees, half Sadducees, a Jewish sect who didn't believe in life after death. Paul suddenly saw a way to split the council's opinion and win the Pharisees over to his side.

"Of course," he said, "I myself am a Pharisee. This trial is really about the resurrection of the dead."

The annoyed Sadducees leapt up and began to argue with the Pharisees. Of course, as they were under attack, the Pharisees began to stick up for Paul.

"This man is innocent," some of them began to shout. "We can't find that he's done anything wrong."

At that, the infuriated Sadducees flung themselves on the defiant Pharisees, and the despairing Roman tribune left them to it. He ordered Paul to be taken away again, before the arguing Jews ripped him apart.

Later on, back in the dungeons, Paul heard a voice. It was the Lord calling him.

"Take courage," said God. "For just as you have testified for me here at Jerusalem, so you must also bear witness for me in Rome."

Paul's rescue
This engraving shows the chaos of the Jerusalem riot. Paul was lucky to escape alive.

Caesarea
This city was one of Herod the Great's finest achievements. He built it in honour of the Roman emperor.

❖ ABOUT THE STORY ❖

Paul was getting quite old by now. It would have been quite natural for him to have listened to Agabus and his friends. What was the point of walking into a trap? Paul knew that the path of obedience lay along the way of suffering. In order to achieve all he could for Jesus, and to reach Rome, he had to accept more danger. He had Jesus as his model, who went willingly to the cross. Paul was practising what he preached.

Paul Stands Trial

PAUL was in grave danger. More than forty Jews had sworn not to eat or drink until they had killed the disciple. They hurried off with their plan to the Sanhedrin.

"Ask the tribune to bring Paul down to you again, as if you want to question him further," they suggested. "We'll ambush the soldiers and kill Paul. He'll be off our hands and it won't be your responsibility, either."

The Sanhedrin were pleased with the idea, but Paul's nephew heard the plan and hurried to the barracks to tell the Roman tribune. The tribune was grateful and decided to send the disciple to safety. He wrote a letter to the provincial governor, Felix, explaining that the Jews were after Paul's blood but that he himself couldn't find the disciple guilty of anything deserving death or even imprisonment. That night, Paul was escorted out of the barracks and away by a large number of soldiers.

The Sanhedrin didn't give up. The high priest, Ananias, soon arrived with a spokesman, Tertulus, to put their case before the Roman governor. Tertulus began by trying to persuade Felix with flattery.

"It's thanks to you that we enjoy peace in our province," he said. "This man threatens our stability. He is a ringleader of the sect of Jesus of Nazareth. Now he has broken our law and desecrated our temple!"

Felix brought Paul back to give his side of the story.

"I was only in Jerusalem for twelve days," the disciple began calmly, "and these people didn't find me arguing with anyone or stirring up a riot anywhere in the city. They can't prove any of their accusations except that yes, I worship God according to the way of Jesus Christ. I still believe everything laid down by Jewish law and I was actually purifying myself in the temple, not desecrating it!"

> ❝ *I appeal to Caesar.* ❞

Now Felix was interested in Christianity and he treated Paul kindly. He put off the Jews' demand for a judgement, saying that he wouldn't decide without further investigation, and he put Paul under house arrest, so that the disciple's friends could come and see him. Felix held Paul in this way for two years, during which time he often called the disciple to come and preach to him and his wife, Drusilla, who was a Jew. Finally, Felix was replaced by another governor, Festus, and representatives from the Sanhedrin arrived once again.

❖ ABOUT THE STORY ❖

The Roman governors were unsure what to do about Paul. They were fair, however, and gave him good protection. Paul used his citizen's right to a trial before the emperor more as a way of getting to Rome than anything else. Paul benefited from the Roman system. God's plan had ensured the free and swift spread of Christianity across a wide area in the short space of thirty years.

Synagogue
Paul often began his ministry in synagogues, where people would know of the promised Messiah. Synagogues are Jewish centres for worship, like this one, which is the Great Jerusalem synagogue. They have separate galleries or seating areas for women. The service consisted of prayers, readings and sermons.

Roman census
The Romans organized their empire very efficiently. A group of people called Censors counted all the men who owned property. This shows them at work.

"I have done nothing against the temple, the law of the Jews or against the emperor," Paul insisted. "I ask you not to hand me back to be tried among my enemies. Instead, I claim my right as a Roman citizen to be tried before the emperor himself."

"Then to Caesar you shall go," replied Festus.

Before he could send Paul off, King Agrippa and his wife Bernice arrived. Festus organized a royal audience, so Agrippa could question Paul too.

Paul was grateful for the chance to explain. He told how he had been a strict Pharisee who had persecuted Christians; how Jesus Christ had spoken to him on the road to Damascus and totally changed his life; and how he had preached to both Gentiles as well as Jews, which was the real reason why so many Jews were seeking his death. Finally, Paul reminded the king of the prophets who foretold that Christ would suffer and rise from the dead, and that He would bring salvation to all the world.

"Paul, all your research into the Scriptures has turned you mad!" scoffed Festus in a loud voice.

"I am not mad," replied Paul, calmly. "The king knows about these things and I'm sure that he believes in the words of the prophets. Don't you, King Agrippa?"

"Hmm," said Agrippa, thoughtfully. "I think that you're trying to turn me into a Christian in a very short time!"

"Whether now or later, I wish that everyone would become what I am," Paul said with a sad smile, "except for these chains, of course."

Later on, in private, Festus, Agrippa and Bernice went over everything again and again. They all agreed that Paul had done nothing wrong. They sighed. If the disciple hadn't appealed to be tried in Rome, he could have been freed straight away.

Christians fighting the lions
There is a story in the Old Testament of Daniel surviving a night in a lion's cage. Sadly, many Christians in the first two centuries AD did not survive their ordeals with lions. They were thrown to the hungry beasts as 'entertainment' for the crowds.

The Colosseum
This superb theatre in Rome still stands. In Paul's time it held 50,000 people. It was used for gladiator displays.

The Voyage to Rome

PAUL and several other prisoners sailed for Rome, under the protection of a centurion called Julius. Julius treated Paul with great kindness, and when the ship called at Sidon, he let the disciple visit his old friends. Then it was back to the boat for several days' hard sailing to Cyprus, for the wind was against them. Paul wasn't surprised that it was slow-going. He was an experienced sailor and knew that the stormy season was near. On the way to Crete, the ship was beginning to struggle against the gusts and the waves, and they only just made it to a harbour. Paul advised Julius that they should winter there, but the captain and shipowner just scoffed. They assured the centurion that it would be better to winter in a harbour on the other side of the island. As soon as a gentle south wind blew up, they set sail once again, cautiously keeping close to the shore.

The warm breeze didn't last long. A wild north-easterly gale came from behind the mountains, sweeping down over the sea and whipping up the waters, so that the ship was tossed and turned and driven far offshore. As the howling storm went on into the night, the terrified crew slid about the slippery decks trying to lash together the heaving, straining boards of the ship with ropes. Next day, as the waves crashed over the boat, they threw furniture and cargo overboard in an effort to keep afloat. On the third day, as the waves grew yet higher, the desperate crew hurled even spare sails and rigging into the deeps to lighten the load. Day after day, the storm continued to rage round them, showing no sign of ever blowing over. The sailors couldn't remember when they had last glimpsed the sun or the stars. They couldn't tell where the blackness of the sky ended and the blackness of the water began. It felt like the end of the world.

Everyone huddled together in deep despair, certain that they would meet a watery death.

"Take heart," Paul reassured them. "Last night, an angel of God told me that we will eventually run aground and that the ship will go down, but none of us will die."

Finally, during the fourteenth night of the storm, the crew realized the ship was running into shallower water. There was a sudden scramble as they raced to let down anchors, before the boat was tossed onto the rocks that surely lurked in the darkness. At last, there was a glimmer of hope! Everyone wept with relief when the rays of dawn began to light up

the horizon. They had been sure they would never feel the warmth of the sun again. To their joy, they could see land only a little way off. They cast off the anchors and hoisted the foresail and began to make for a bay. As they tried to run ashore, the bow stuck fast in a sandbank. To everyone's horror, the stern of the ship began to break up fast in the crashing surf. There was no other choice but to abandon themselves to the mercy of the sea and jumped overboard before the ship went down.

Incredibly, just as Paul had said, all 276 people made it safely to shore. Some swam. Others floated on broken bits of the ship. The soaked, shivering survivors were welcomed to the island of Malta by the local people, who made a bonfire to warm them up.

> **❝** *I now bid you take heart; for there will be no loss of life among you, but only of the ship.* **❞**

The locals soon realized that there was something unusual about Paul. An angry viper came slithering out of the fire, trying to escape from the heat, and sank its fangs into his hand. The Maltese people knew that a viper bite was fatal, and they fully expected Paul to die swiftly from the poison. They waited anxiously but nothing happened.

"He must be a god!" they whispered to each other.

The Roman governor of Malta, Publius, was just as generous as his people, and he gave the survivors lodgings in his own quarters. When Paul found out that Publius's father was terribly ill, he healed him to repay the governor's kindness. The news soon got out that the strange man who hadn't died from the snakebite had miraculous healing powers. Maltese from all over the island brought their sick to be cured by Paul. After three months it was time to set sail once again. Paul had won the greatest respect from the people of Malta, and they loaded down the ship with all sorts of provisions and gifts.

Finally, they reached Rome. The other prisoners were handed over to the captain of the guard and imprisoned. Paul, though, was given special treatment. He was allowed to live under house arrest. He awaited trial for two years, and during that time many people came to hear him preach about Jesus Christ and the kingdom of God. Paul also regularly wrote letters to all the friends he had made on his travels, urging them to keep the faith. He continued to do this right up to the very last days of his life, when he knew that he was going to be put to death for the sake of his belief in his master and teacher, Jesus Christ.

Paul's journey to Rome
This took place in the winter of AD59–60. It was not Paul's first experience of shipwreck. Before this journey he had told the Corinthians he had been shipwrecked three times, but did not say where.

❖ ABOUT THE STORY ❖
Sea travel in Paul's day was hazardous. The ships were relatively small, powered only by oars and sails. Navigation was by the stars. Most ships hugged the coast so that they would know where they were. No one sailed in winter, which was where the captain's gamble about the weather failed. Luke, the writer of the story, wants us to see that God would not let His servant die before his work was complete.

The Revelation to John

THE disciple John was in prison on the Greek island of Patmos, praying one sabbath, when he heard a voice filling his mind.

"Write down what I am about to show you and send it to the churches," it instructed.

John spun round to see Jesus Christ behind him, blazing with light brighter than the sun.

"Don't be afraid," Jesus said. "I am the first and the last. I died but I shall live for ever. I hold the keys of death."

John saw a door opening into heaven.

"Come here and I will show you the future of the world," thundered the voice. Suddenly John found himself standing before the very throne of God, surrounded by countless angels singing, "Blessings and honour and glory and might for ever and ever, amen!"

The Lord showed John the mighty battle between good and evil that was being played out on the earth. John saw the happiness of men and women who believe in the salvation of Christ, and the misery and fear of those who do not repent. He saw angels of destruction sweep over the earth to kill wicked men and women with plagues, as warnings to all those left to repent before it was too late. John heard the souls of those who had been killed for their Christian beliefs cry out to God, "O Lord, avenge us and wipe out the world and all its wickedness." God comforted them and told them it was not time.

There were others to come who would win their place in heaven by being martyred in Jesus's name.

John saw a woman representing the people of God giving birth to the Messiah. She stood with the moon under her feet and crowned with twelve stars. Then war broke out in heaven itself. The archangel Michael led God's angels against Satan and his wicked angels, and flung them down from heaven to earth. John watched as the furious Satan and his army went off to tempt all those who follow Jesus's teachings. Great evils rose up, and many people abandoned God to follow Satan. God sent angels over the earth, reminding people that they should fear His judgement and turn again to the Lord while there was still time.

Then John witnessed the end of the world. Jesus, the Lamb of God, was triumphant. There was rejoicing in heaven as Satan was flung into a lake of fire. God then passed judgement on everyone who had ever lived. If their name was not in His book of life, they were destroyed along with Satan.

Finally, John saw a new heaven and a new earth, that looked like the holy city of Jerusalem. The city shone and sparkled as though it was made from diamonds and gold, and decorated with precious jewels in every colour of the rainbow. Through the middle of the city flowed the river of life, as clear as crystal. On either side of the river grew groves of the healing tree of life. The gates of the city stood open, welcoming everything that was good. The city was lit with the glory of God, and there was no temple – because God Himself was there.

"Behold, God is living with all His people in His

> **I am the Alpha and the Omega, the beginning and the end.**

kingdom on earth," John heard a voice proclaim. "Pain and sorrow and death are no more."

John heard Jesus Christ speaking to him one last time. "Let all who are thirsty come and drink from the waters of life. I will be coming soon to judge the living and the dead, and the good will be blessed for ever. I am the first and the last, the beginning and the end."

"Amen," whispered John. "Amen!"

A glimpse of heaven
Artists have tried to portray John's vision of heaven with God surrounded by a sea of glass. However, it is really beyond words and imagining.

❧ ABOUT THE STORY ❧

The Book of Revelation is something of a mystery to people today, but in the 1st century AD it was a source of great encouragement. It is largely written in picture language which the Christians of the time would have understood clearly. It is really a series of sketches of the battle between good and evil, which takes place all through human history. It shows that God and His church always triumph in the end.

The Church Since the Apostles

CHRISTIANITY continues to grow around the world. In places, Christianity is growing at an amazing rate. In Russia, and China, for example, Christianity is growing very fast. But the church today is very different. This is how it developed.

Expansion and argument (AD100–700)

After the death of the apostles, Paul's prophecy that false teachers would attack the church came true. There were cults such as the gnostics, the forerunners of today's 'new age' movements. These people who did not believe in Jesus were called heretics. They denied important teachings, for example Marcion (d.160) rejected the Jewish elements in the New Testament.

These attacks were countered by writings built on the apostles' teaching. Justin Martyr (*c*.100–165) defended Christianity against Roman philosophers. The African Tertullian (*c*.160–225) showed how Jesus could be God and man. In 325 the Council of Nicea defined the basic truths of Christianity (although controversy continued for some time). Despite the arguments and continued persecution, the church grew. In 395 the Roman Emperor Constantine saw a vision of Christ and declared Christianity to be the official religion of the Empire. By 404 the Bible had been translated into Latin, and Augustine of Hippo (354–430) had produced the basis of Christian belief as it is today. Christianity spread across Europe. Columba went to Iona (north-east England) and Saint David converted Wales.

Aurelius Augustinus
Also called Augustine of Hippo, he was baptized by St Ambrose in AD386. He was a great writer, and wrote *Confessions* in AD400, about his own life.

Division and darkness (700–1400)

Then came a period that many Christians today are ashamed of. There were the Crusades, in which western kings tried to force Christianity on countries of the east. There were corrupt popes and clergy who were more interested in worldly wealth than spiritual truth. And in 1054 there was a major split which still exists to this day. The churches of the east (now called the Orthodox Churches) divided from the churches of the west over an important but obscure teaching about the relationship of the Holy Spirit to Jesus Christ.

Crusades
These are the sort of soldiers and knights that fought in the Crusades.

St Thomas Aquinas
He became a monk in 1244, and quickly became a great teacher. His teachings and writings largely represent the teachings of the Catholic Church.

However, there were good points. Thomas Aquinas (1225–74) was an important religious writer whose work is still influential, especially in the Roman Catholic Church. The great cathedrals of Europe were built, including Rheims, Cologne, Salisbury and York. Groups of travelling preachers called for reform and spread the gospel like the first Christians had. Among them was John Wycliffe (1330–84), who was influential in the church going back to believing closely in the detail of the Bible.

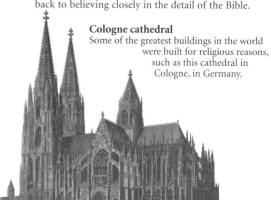

Cologne cathedral
Some of the greatest buildings in the world were built for religious reasons, such as this cathedral in Cologne, in Germany.

Reformation and renewal (1400–1800)

The most famous controversy came when a German monk, Martin Luther (1483–1546) nailed his 95 theses (statements for discussion) on the door of Wittenberg Church in 1517. He criticized many practices and beliefs which, he said, departed from the teaching of the Bible. From then on, other 'Protestants' (protesters) added their voices to his, among them Huldreich Zwingli in Zurich, and John Calvin in Geneva. This period, when the beliefs, or doctrines, of the Church changed, was called the 'Reformation'.

Martin Luther
Luther's reforms began after a trip to Rome. He disagreed with the sale of indulgences, that is, people buying forgiveness.

The Roman Catholic Church continued under the Pope, but other churches began: Lutherans on the continent, Presbyterians in Scotland, and Anglicans (Church of England) in England. The Reformation in England was a mixture of political and spiritual forces. Henry VIII was glad of an excuse to rid himself of the authority of the Pope so that he could get divorced.

Roman Catholicism continued much the same but Protestantism divided further as groups rediscovered old truths which they emphasised. These divisions were signs of life and vitality. The Baptist churches stressed the need for personal commitment in the rite of baptism. John Wesley (1703–91) founded Methodism when the Church of England disagreed with his open-air preaching and emphasis on spreading the word of Christ.

John Calvin
In 1559 Calvin founded a religious academy in the city of Geneva, Switzerland, which later became a university.

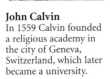

Henry VIII
When the Pope refused to declare that Henry's marriage to his first wife, Catherine of Aragon, was illegal, Henry made himself head of the church, and allowed his own second marriage.

Change and decay (1800–present)

Over the last 200 years there have been enormous social and cultural changes. 'Enlightenment' thinking (which emphasised the importance of human reason) and the growth of science challenged many Christian beliefs. Only late in the 1900s did western society begin to recognise a 'spiritual' dimension to life.

The Roman Catholic Church made major changes at the Second Vatican Council (1962–5), including allowing mass to be celebrated in local languages and not Latin. The Protestant churches began to talk and work together (and in some cases re-unite), and the World Council of Churches was formed in 1948.

The charismatic (or Pentecostal) movement and the work of evangelists such as Billy Graham have brought thousands of (often young) people into the churches. But it is overseas where the stories of growth which parallel those of the Acts of the Apostles are to be heard today. The missionary movement of the 1800s saw people from the west spread the gospel in Africa, India, China and South America. In the year 2000 there were more Christians (580 million) in Latin America than in Europe (420 million). In Africa, the growth was from 230 million in 1985 to 400 million in 2000. The Holy Spirit is still at work.

Television evangelist
Billy Graham claims to have converted millions of people to Christianity.

Modern cathedrals
This modern cathedral in Brazil in South America, shows that the Church has a modern and developing outlook. It is an energetic and exciting force in many parts of the world.

Faith, Love and Charity

THE Acts of the Apostles tells of people who risked everything for Jesus Christ. Their example has inspired thousands of Christians in every century since. Others have preached the message of Jesus in new places believing that it is the most important message anyone could ever hear. And still others, inspired by the love of Jesus, have sacrificed all to care for the sick and poor. Some, like the apostles, have even been killed by jealous opponents. Here are a few of their stories.

St Francis of Assisi (c.1181–1226)
The son of a wealthy Italian cloth merchant, Francis lived a worldly life until he had a vision of Jesus. Then, he gave up everything to teach the gospel. Others joined him in his mission and the Franciscan order of monks was born. He wrote a simple rule of life for their communities, which still exists today. He had a simple faith and a great love of nature.

Mother Julian of Norwich (c.1342–1420)
We do not know anything about Mother Julian's background. She became a hermit devoted to prayer at St Julian's Church in Norwich, in eastern England. She received fifteen visions from God, which she wrote in a famous book *Revelations of Divine Love*. She showed how sinful people could become united with a caring God in a mystical experience of spiritual love.

Elizabeth Fry (1780–1845)
The daughter of a banker in Norwich, she married a merchant. They were Quakers (the Christian group also known as The Society of Friends). She came from a wealthy background, and she was upset by the conditions of women in prison. She began to teach them the Bible, provide them with clothes, and help them to improve themselves. She also campaigned for many prison reforms.

William Booth (1829–1912)
A Methodist from Nottingham, he moved to London but left the church because people did not like his fiery open-air preaching. He was even sent to prison for it. His own mission in the east end of London helped the poor and preached the gospel. In 1878 he formed the Salvation Army, which fought social evils like child labour. The Salvation Army is famous for its social work across the world.

TIMELINE

• Jesus is crucified in Jerusalem by the Roman authorities.

• Matthias is chosen to replace Judas Iscariot as the twelfth apostle.

AD33

DISCIPLES VISITED BY THE HOLY SPIRIT AT PENTECOST

EARLY CHRISTIAN BAPTISM STONE

PENTECOSTAL ALTAR

• Peter heals the beggar by the Beautiful Gate.

• Philip baptizes the Ethiopian minister.

• Saul sees a vision of Jesus on the road to Damascus. He is converted to Christianity, and changes his name to Paul.

PETER HEALS AENEAS

Gladys Aylward (1902–1970)

This famous Christian missionary spent all her money on a one-way ticket to China in 1930. In 1938 she helped many children to safety from the China-Japan war. She later ran an orphanage in Taiwan.

Helda Camara (born 1909)

A Roman Catholic priest in Brazil, he became a bishop in 1952 and an archbishop in 1964. He spoken against the bad conditions of the poor, criticising the government and rich landowners whose policies caused the poverty and oppression. He was opposed by some even in his own church.

Mother Teresa of Calcutta (1910–1998)

Born in Macedonia in eastern Europe, she was a Roman Catholic nun who worked among the poor children of India. She founded the Sisters of Charity and became a world-renowned figure, always seen dressed in her blue robe. A woman of deep but simple faith, she impressed even the sceptics who came to see her, and was awarded the Nobel Peace Prize in 1979.

This is a nun of the Sisters of Charity helping deprived children.

Trevor Huddleston (1913–1998)

He went to South Africa, where he worked in Soweto. He became Bishop of Stepney in east London, before being made Archbishop of the Anglican Province of the Indian Ocean. He campaigned actively against apartheid, a system in South Africa of keeping different races apart.

Martin Luther King Junior (1929–1968)

He followed in his father's footsteps to become a Baptist pastor in Montgomery, Alabama, USA. He soon became involved in the struggle for civil rights among his fellow black people. He resigned from his church in 1959 to give all his time to black rights. He spoke for non-violent action and reconciliation between black and white people. This means that he wanted black and white people to get along peacefully. He was murdered by a white man in Memphis, Tennessee in the USA. in 1968. The third Monday in January is celebrated in the USA as Martin Luther King day.

Desmond Tutu (born 1931)

Tutu was made Anglican Archbishop of Cape Town in 1986. He was a passionate campaigner against apartheid, and successfully called on the west to impose economic sanctions (refusing to buy goods) on South Africa. He took a non-violent approach to his protest, and after apartheid fell became Chair of the Truth and Reconciliation Commission, set up to try and overcome the hate and distrust that resulted from apartheid.

PAUL AND BARNABAS
WORSHIPPED IN LYSTRA

• The disciples hold a council, and decide to allow Gentiles into the Christian Church.

JERUSALEM

• Paul leaves on his second missionary journey.

• Paul arrested in Philippi

• Riots in Ephesus.

• Paul leaves the city of Troas to return to Jerusalem.

PAUL WRITING HIS LETTERS

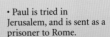

EGYPTIAN
STATUE
OF A
PRISONER

• Paul is tried in Jerusalem, and is sent as a prisoner to Rome.

• Paul is martyred in Rome for his belief in Jesus Christ.

AD60

REFERENCE

BIBLE TIMES
OF DAVID'S LINE
THE SPREAD OF CHRISTIANITY
OTHER RELIGIONS
PEOPLE AND PLACES

Bible Times

THE events in the Bible happened over about 4,000 years. Many of the early stories, such as the Tower of Babel, describe a time when the first human cities and civilizations were taking shape in Mesopotamia and ancient Egypt. We do not know exactly when these far-off happenings took place because dates were not written down. However, later events such as the Exodus and the destruction of Jerusalem were recorded by other people such as the kings of Egypt or Babylon. The Romans dated events from the foundation of Rome in 753BC. From them, we have an idea of the sequence of events. The dates we work from today – and those on which this timechart is based – are centred on the traditional date for the birth of Jesus, AD1.

1800–1500BC
1800BC Abraham treks from Ur to Canaan
1700BC Joseph invites his family and other Israelites to settle in Egypt
1600BC Israelites become slaves of the Egyptians

1499–900BC
1280BC Exodus of Israelites from Egypt under Moses
1200–1025BC Judges lead the Israelites
1025BC Saul is first Israelite king
1000BC David is anointed king
962BC Solomon begins building of first Temple
924BC The kingdom is divided into Israel in the north and Judah in the south

899–500BC
865BC Elijah preaches
854BC Assyrians fight Ahab of Isra
842BC Jehu becomes king of Israel
825BC Preaching of Elisha
753BC Founding of city of Rome
722BC Destruction of city of Samaria by Assyrians and fall of northern kingdom of Israel.
586BC Nebuchadnezzar captures Jerusalem and deports Jews to Babylon
539BC Persians defeat Babylon and Jews are allowed to return home

The Israelites are guided by God, and their leader, Moses, along a path of dry land through the Red Sea, while the pursuing Egyptians are drowned. The Israelite people had suffered over 400 years of slavery in Egypt. Their departure was a turning point in their history, as they set off on the long journey north to the land of Canaan. This was the land that God had promised Abram.

Gilgamesh was a heroic king from Mesopotamia who lived around 2700BC. Among stories of his great deeds was a description of a great flood like the one in the Bible. The stories were written on clay tablets.

John the Baptist christened Jesus on the banks of the River Jordan, around AD27. The act was accompanied by the voice of God, and heralded the start of Jesus's teaching.

God sent visions to the prophet Ezekiel of the rebuilding of the Promised Land and a new temple. The visions happened during the time that the Jews were in exile in Babylon, over 500 years before the birth of Jesus Christ. The Jews were allowed to return home in 539BC.

499–1BC
332BC Alexander the Great conquers Syria and Israel
322BC Rule of Egyptian kings in Israel begins
200BC Greek kings of Syria conquer Israel
166BC Start of Maccabean revolt against Antiochus
63BC Israel becomes part of the Roman Empire
37BC Herod the Great's rule over Israel begins
25BC Herod starts rebuilding of Temple in Jerusalem
6BC Probable birth of Christ and flight of Holy Family into Egypt

AD1–313
26 Pontius Pilate becomes Roman governor of Judea
27 Probable start of Christ's Ministry
30 Crucifixion and Resurrection
35 Conversion of Paul in Damascus
45 Paul and Barnabas start their missionary journeys
48 Grand Council of first Christians in Jerusalem
50/51 Paul preaches in Corinth, Greece
60 Paul travels to Rome and is shipwrecked on Malta
64 Peter and Paul are martyred by the Roman emperor Nero in the Persecution
68 Jewish revolt against Rome
69 Probable writing of the Book of Revelation by St John of Patmos
70 Destruction of the Temple by Roman general Titus
313 Emperor Constantine recognizes Christianity

The crucifixion of Jesus Christ – the central crisis in the New Testament story – probably happened around AD30.

Of David's Line

THIS family tree illustrates the Bible's record of Jesus's ancestors. The golden fruits on this pomegranate tree highlight all the key figures according to the New Testament. Abraham was the man who God made the father of the Jewish race, promising that his descendants would become a great people. Jesus was said to be 'of David's line', meaning that He was descended from David, the shepherd boy who became a great king of Israel. David was promised by God that he would begin a dynasty that would last forever. Jesus fulfilled this promise with His message of everlasting life.

ADAM
The Bible's first man. God created him from the Earth and gave him the breath of life. Adam named all living things in the Garden of Eden.

ABRAHAM
The first leader of the Jewish people. Abram (Abraham) was guided by God from his home in Mesopotamia to the Promised Land of Canaan. God told Abram that his descendants would become a great people, and that the land of Canaan would belong to them. This land became Israel.

Adam
Methuselah
Enoch
Jared
Lamech
Noah
Sh
Jacob
Isaac
Abraham
Terah
Judah
Perez
Hezron
Ram
Jotham
Uzziah
Joram
Aminada
Ahaz
Jehoshaphat
Hezekiah
Manasseh
Amos
Josiah
Jesus
Joseph
Jacob
Matthan

KING DAVID

David was chosen by God to be the second king of Israel. He was the son of a Bethlehem farmer who was looking after a flock of sheep when the prophet Samuel came to look for him. When Samuel saw David, he heard the voice of God saying "Bless him, for this is the one I have chosen to be Israel's new king."

Seth

Enos

Mahaleel

Cainan

Cainan

Shelah

Eber

Arphaxad

Peleg

Reu

Nahor

Serug

Obed

Boaz

Jesse

Nahshon

Salmon

David

Asa

Abijah

Rehoboam

Solomon

Abiud

Eliakim

Zerubbabel

Jechoniah

Shealtiel

Azor

Zadoc

Eleazar

Eliud

Achim

JESUS CHRIST

In the Gospel of St Luke, an angel tells Mary that the son that she is to have will be 'of the house and lineage of David.' The Gospel of St Matthew says that there are 28 generations between David and Jesus. Jesus was born in Bethlehem, the same town as David.

The Spread of Christianity

SINCE the time of Jesus's death and the preaching of the twelve apostles, Christianity has spread throughout the world. Over the years, people have had different beliefs about what Jesus and the apostles said and what their words meant. Different denominations have formed according to these opinions and there have been bloody battles between different peoples, who each believed their way was the right one.

However, the faith that Jesus brought to his apostles has also spread, to help bring comfort and security to people all over the world.

GREENLAND

NORTH AMERICA

⑧

Atlantic Ocea.

⑦

SOUTH AMERICA

KEY EVENTS IN THE CHRISTIAN FAITH

The Conversion of Constantine
The Roman Emperor Constantine's victory in AD312 convinced him that Christ had helped him. He officially accepted Christianity in the Edict of Milan. For the first time emperors were helping, rather than opposing Christianity, and within a century most people in the Roman Empire had become Christian.

The Great Schism
In 1054, Pope Leo IX, head of the Catholic Church, officially broke off relations with the Orthodox Church in Byzantium (Istanbul), and the Church in the East, called Greek or Russian Orthodox, went its own way. Many matters were disputed but the most important was the authority of the Pope, which the Greeks and Russians never accepted.

Luther and the Protestant Reformation
In 1521, Martin Luther, a German Catholic monk, broke away from the Church in Rome and began the Reformation. Within 50 years, most of northern and central Europe was Protestant, rejecting the power of the Pope and Catholic beliefs, such as the rule forbidding priests to marry. This split still divides the Christian world.

Second Vatican Council
In 1962, Pope John XXIII summoned a great Council of the Catholic Church to the Vatican in Rome to discuss church reforms. Among these were having services in the local language, like Protestants, rather than in Latin. This meant that people could understand better and it encouraged them to take more part in church services. The Council also looked on other Christian churches, and even on Jews, Hindus and Muslims, far more favourably.

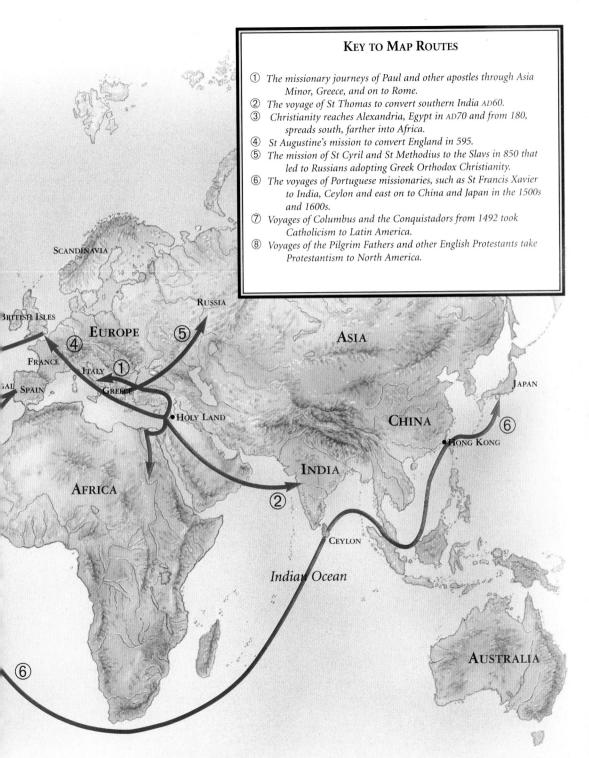

KEY TO MAP ROUTES

① *The missionary journeys of Paul and other apostles through Asia Minor, Greece, and on to Rome.*
② *The voyage of St Thomas to convert southern India AD60.*
③ *Christianity reaches Alexandria, Egypt in AD70 and from 180, spreads south, farther into Africa.*
④ *St Augustine's mission to convert England in 595.*
⑤ *The mission of St Cyril and St Methodius to the Slavs in 850 that led to Russians adopting Greek Orthodox Christianity.*
⑥ *The voyages of Portuguese missionaries, such as St Francis Xavier to India, Ceylon and east on to China and Japan in the 1500s and 1600s.*
⑦ *Voyages of Columbus and the Conquistadors from 1492 took Catholicism to Latin America.*
⑧ *Voyages of the Pilgrim Fathers and other English Protestants take Protestantism to North America.*

SCANDINAVIA

BRITISH ISLES

RUSSIA

EUROPE ⑤

FRANCE ④

ITALY ①

GAL SPAIN GREECE

ASIA

JAPAN

HOLY LAND

CHINA

⑥

HONG KONG

INDIA

②

AFRICA

CEYLON

Indian Ocean

AUSTRALIA

⑥

Other Religions

JUST like Christianity, most religions have now spread around the world. More than 1,000 years ago, Islam spread from Arabia, its first home, west to Morocco and east to India and finally Indonesia. Even earlier, Buddhism spread from its Indian homeland over much of eastern Asia as far as Japan, and has also found converts in the West. So, too, has Taoism, while Sikhs, Hindus and Jews have taken their religions with them wherever they settle. Only Shinto, the native religion of Japan, has remained limited to its homeland.

Jain monk

ANCIENT HINDUISM
The Hindu religion developed in the ancient civilization of the Indus Valley in northern India. Hindus believe in one supreme god called Brahman. Other major gods are Shiva (pictured), who is often called Natarajah, Lord of the Dance, and Vishnu who preserves life.

Shiva

PEACEFUL JAINISM
The Jains are famous for their total non-violence and believe in never taking life of any sort. To avoid harming even insects, Jains often wear face masks so that they will not swallow them and carry brooms with which they clear away any in their way. Most Jains still live in India.

BUDDHIST ENLIGHTENMENT
The Buddhist religion was developed in northeastern India by Prince Siddhartha Gautama. He later became known as Buddha, which means enlightened one. Buddhists believe that by following eight steps, a person can become enlightened. The path of enlightenment then takes them to a state of nirvana (supreme happiness and bliss).

Buddha

Star Gods of Taoism

LONG LIFE, WEALTH AND HAPPINESS
Taoism is one of the two religions of old China beginning more than 2,000 years ago. Taoists believe in three star gods who stand for long life, wealth and happiness. It is perhaps the most mysterious great religion, for its founder Lao-Tzu (Chinese for 'old gentleman') may never have really existed. But his poetic sayings, collected in the little book Tao te Ching (the Way and its Power), stress the need to live in harmony with nature.

ISLAM

The crescent and star is the symbol of the Islamic faith, and called 'hilal'. Devout Muslims must pray five times a day, prostrating themselves towards Mecca, the holiest city of Islam. The muezzin (priest) calls the faithful to prayers from the minaret, the tower beside each Muslim mosque. Along with making the 'haj' (pilgrimage to Mecca) once in a lifetime and giving to the poor, Muslims must sincerely proclaim 'There is no God but Allah (God) and Mohammed is his only prophet'.

Hilal

Guru Ram Das

SIKH EQUALITY

The Golden Temple at Amritsar, northern India, is the holiest Sikh shrine. It contains the remains of Guru Ram Das, who became the fourth guru (spiritual teacher) in 1574 and founded the city of Amritsar. Sikhism was founded by Guru Nanak in 1469. Sikhs believe that there is only one God and that all people are created equal.

The Sun Goddess

SHINTO RITUALS

According to the beliefs of the native Japanese religion of Shinto, Amaterasu, the Sun Goddess, is the ancestress of all Japanese emperors. Most Japanese worship in both Shinto and Buddhist temples because Shinto is mostly concerned with the rituals of worship, whereas Buddhism satisfies a need to know about how to live or life after death. Shinto used to be the Japanese state religion.

Menorah

JUDAISM

The Jewish religion goes back 4,000 years, when it was founded in Mesopotamia (modern Iraq) by Abraham. The symbol of Judaism is the menorah, a seven-branched candlestick which stood in King Solomon's temple in Jerusalem. For Jews, the Old Testament and the Talmud, a book of Jewish laws, are the basis for their faith.

People and Places

Aaron Older half-brother of Moses who was famous for his persuasive speeches. His rod turned into a serpent.

Abel Second son of Adam. He was killed by his brother Cain, who was jealous because God preferred Abel's sacrifice to his own.

Abigail The beautiful wife of the landowner Nabal (who angered David by his rudeness). After God killed Nabal, she became David's wife.

Abner Captain of King Saul's army who remained loyal to the king.

Abram First patriarch of the Israelites, whose name was changed by God to Abraham. He was born in Ur, Mesopotamia, and moved, with wife Sarah and nephew Lot, to Canaan, the land that God promised to his descendants. Father of Isaac.

Absalom King David's favourite son, who led a revolt against his father, and was killed by Joab.

Adam The first human created by God, who lived with Eve in the Garden of Eden until they were both expelled for disobeying God.

Aeneas Worthy man of Lydda, in Galilee, who was paralysed and restored to health by the apostle, Peter.

Ahab King of Israel (north kingdom) 869–850BC who worshipped the pagan god, Baal.

Amnon David's eldest son, who raped his half-sister Tamar, and was later killed by Absalom in revenge.

Amos One of the first prophets, who warned Israel of impending doom.

Ananias Wealthy early follower of the apostles, husband of Sapphira, who claimed to have sold all his goods to give the money to the poor but kept some back and was struck dead for lying.

Ananias Jewish follower of Christ in Damascus who laid hands on the blinded apostle Paul and so restored his sight.

Andrew First apostle to be called by Jesus, brother of Simon Peter.

Annas Former High Priest, father-in-law of Caiaphas, who interrogated Jesus.

Antioch Capital of Roman province of Syria

where Christians were first so-called. Paul escaped from it once in a basket.

Ararat A mountain in eastern Turkey where Noah's Ark landed.

Archelaus Son of Herod the Great, ruler of Judea, who was avoided by Joseph and Mary on their return from Egypt with the infant Jesus. Archelaus was soon replaced by Roman governors.

Assyria Powerful kingdom of northern Mesopotamia in what is now northern Iraq. The Assyrians destroyed the northern kingdom of Israel.

Augustus Roman Emperor at the time of Jesus's birth who ordered a census of all tax-payers. This forced Joseph and Mary to travel to Bethlehem when Mary was about to give birth.

Baal Canaanite god that was proved powerless by Elijah.

Babel Legendary tower in Babylonia, which was raised so high that God destroyed it.

Babylon Great city on the River Euphrates in what is now Iraq. It was the centre of an empire which destroyed Jerusalem. The Jews were taken into captivity in the city.

Balaam A prophet who was sent by the Moabites to curse Israel. His ass (donkey) refused to pass an angel until he agreed not to harm the Israelites.

Barabbas Robber whose release the Jerusalem mob demanded instead of Jesus's when Pilate offered them the choice.

Barnabas Companion of Paul on his first missionary journey.

Bartholomew One of the apostles.

Bartimaeus Blind beggar of Jericho whose sight Christ restored.

Bathsheba Wife of Uriah until David fell in love with her and had her husband killed. She bore David a son, Solomon, who succeeded him.

Beersheba Town in Judah (Palestine) where Abraham and Jacob lived.

Belshazzar Last king of Babylon, who was feasting when the Persians conquered the city.

Benjamin Youngest son of Jacob by Rachel. He was kept behind by Jacob when his brothers went to Egypt, but called for by Joseph. His descendants formed the tribe of Benjaminites.

Bethany Village 5km east of Jerusalem where Mary, Martha and Lazarus lived and where Christ raised Lazarus from the dead.

Bethel Town near the River Jordan where Jacob had his dream.

Bethlehem City in Judea where both David and Jesus were born.

Caesarea Ancient city on the coast of Israel built by Herod the Great, named after Augustus Caesar.

Caiaphas Head Priest, leader of the Sanhedrin, who plotted against Jesus and interrogated Him.

Cain Elder son of Adam and Eve. When he killed his brother Abel, God put a mark on his brow and Cain became an outcast.

Cana Town in Galilee where Jesus performed His first miracle, turning water into wine.

Canaan The Promised Land of the Israelites, in the eastern Mediterranean where the Israelites settled, in what is modern Israel and Palestine.

Capernaum Town on the west shore of the Sea of Galilee. The home of Peter and other disciples, where Jesus began His mission, preaching in the synagogue after being baptized by John.

Carmel Mountain range in northwest Israel.

Cleopas One of the disciples whom the risen Christ encountered on the road to Emmaus and who did not recognize Him.

Cornelius Roman centurion whom Peter baptized as the first non-Jewish Christian..

Damascus Capital of Syria, traditionally in Solomon's kingdom.

Daniel Captive in Babylon, who won King Belshazzar's favour by deciphering writing on the wall. He was later thrown to lions, but survived unharmed thanks to God.

David King of Israel, ancestor of Joseph.

Deborah Israel's only female prophet.

Delilah Samson's wife, who cut her husband's hair while he slept, so taking his strength away and handing him over to the Philistines.

Demetrius Silversmith of Ephesus who stirred up a riot against Paul because he feared that Christianity would damage his statue-making.

Eden Legendary garden in Mesopotamia where Adam and Eve lived.

Edomites Descendants of Edom, the Israelites' neighbours and nearest kin.

Egypt Strongest and richest power in the Near East that enslaved nearby peoples, including the Israelites, to increase its wealth.

Eli Prophet and priest at the holy city of Shiloh whose descendants sinned and so did not become prophets.

Elijah Prophet and opponent of evil King Ahab, who was swept up to heaven in a chariot of fire.

Elisha Prophet and Elijah's chosen successor who anointed Hazael and Jehu as kings.

Elizabeth Wife of Zechariah and mother of John the Baptist, whom she bore in old age.

Emmaus Village where Jesus appeared after the Crucifixion to the apostles.

Endor, Witch of A clairvoyant, who, against God's laws, was consulted by Saul when in despair.

Ephesus City in western Asia Minor (Turkey) where there was a riot against Paul.

Esau Isaac's elder son who was supplanted by his brother Jacob.

Esther Daughter of Mordecai who became wife of the Persian king Xerxes (Ahasuerus) and saved the Jews of the Persian empire from a plot.

Euphrates River in Mesopotamia (present-day Iraq) on which Babylon was sited, by whose waters the Israelites sat down and wept.

Eutychus Young man of Troas who was overcome by sleep during a long sermon by Paul and fell from a window.

Eve First woman and mother of all humanity, created by God from Adam's spare rib.

Ezekiel Israelite prophet during the Babylonian captivity.

Gabriel Archangel sent to announce the coming births of John to Elizabeth and of Jesus to Mary.

Galilee Region and lake of northern Israel/Palestine where Jesus grew up and began His ministry.

Gallo Roman governor of Corinth who was not interested in Jewish complaints against Paul preaching to Gentiles (non-Jews).

Gath One of the five Philistine cities, home of Goliath.

Gaza Philistine city on the coast where Samson was blinded.

Gethsemane Garden on the Mount of Olives outside Jerusalem where Jesus went to pray on the night before the Crucifixion and where He was arrested by the soldiers of the Sanhedrin, led by Judas.

Gideon Judge who delivered Israel from the Midianites' attack on Israelite homes.

Gilead Region east of the River Jordan.

Golgotha Place of execution (literally, hill of the skull) outside Jerusalem where Jesus was crucified.

Goliath Philistine giant warrior whom no Israelite dared face until David challenged and killed him.

Ham Son of Noah who was cursed for seeing his father drunk and naked. His descendants became the Hamites of North Africa.

Hannah Mother of the prophet Samuel.

Hebron Highest town in Palestine, 30km southwest of Jerusalem, where Abraham, Sarah and Jacob were buried.

Herod The Great Ruler of Judea and bloodthirsty tyrant. He learned of the birth of the Messiah from the Three Wise Men and ordered the massacre of all male children under two in Bethlehem.

Herod Antipas Son of Herod the Great, tetrarch (ruler) of Galilee. He married his niece and sister-in-law Herodias, for which he was condemned by John the Baptist. When Salome, Herodias's daughter, demanded John's head in return for dancing, Herod Antipas gave it to her.

Herodias The niece, sister-in-law, and wife of Herod Antipas, mother of Salome and enemy of John the Baptist.

Hezekiah King of Judah who turned to the prophet Isaiah for help against the Assyrians when they besieged Jerusalem.

Hiram King of Phoenician city of Tyre who supplied the cedar wood for the building of the Jerusalem temple.

Iconium City in Asia Minor (Turkey) where Paul and Barnabas were hailed as Greek gods for healing a crippled man.

Isaac Son born to Sarah and Abraham in their old age. Husband of Rebekah and father of Esau and Jacob. His grandsons were the twelve patriarchs of Israel.

Isaiah Prophet, and counsellor to the kings of Judah, who foresaw the destruction of Jerusalem and the coming of a Messiah.

Israel The Promised Land that was divided between the twelve Hebrew tribes. When the kingdom was divided after Solomon's death, Israel became the northern kingdom, while Judah was the southern one.

Jacob Favourite son of Rebekah, who helped him trick his father Isaac into blessing him. He had a dream of a ladder to heaven peopled with angels. God renamed Jacob Israel.

James An apostle and son of Alphaeus.

James Son of Zebedee and a fisherman by trade. Called James the Great Apostle who, with his brother John and Peter, formed the inner ring of apostles. Proposed a compromise over the admittance of Gentiles.

James the Less Traditionally recognized as the brother of Jesus, of whom little is known.

Jehu King of Israel, former general of Ahab, who restored the worship of God and founded a short-lived dynasty.

Jeremiah Prophet in the kingdom of Judah who foretold the Babylonian captivity of the Israelites.

Jericho Ancient city east of Jerusalem, the scene of the Israelites' first major conquest when they reached the Promised Land.

Jeroboam Servant of Solomon who formed the separate, northern state of Israel with ten of the twelve tribes when the kingdom was divided.

Jerusalem The Israelite capital and holy city in the Promised Land. David brought the Ark of the Covenant there and it was the site of Solomon's temple. Jesus's mission ended in Jerusalem in His trial and Crucifixion, but the apostles regarded it as their base for many years.

Jezebel Wife of Ahab, daughter of king of Sidon, who introduced the worship of the god Baal into Israel. After Ahab's death, she was thrown from a window at Jehu's orders and eaten by dogs.

Joab King David's nephew and the most successful military commander.

Job A virtuous man who became the object of a bet between God and Satan. He was burdened with sufferings, but refused to curse God.

John Son of Zebedee, apostle, fisherman and brother of James.

John the Baptist Cousin of Jesus, six months older, son of Elizabeth and Zechariah. He became a preacher and introduced baptism as the first step on the road to salvation. He was imprisoned and then beheaded by Herod Antipas for attacking the king's marriage.

John the Evangelist Writer of the fourth Gospel.

Jordan River in which John the Baptist baptized Jesus.

Joseph Elder son of Jacob who was betrayed by his brothers into slavery in Egypt. However, he rose to prominence there, and eventually his family joined him in Egypt.

Joseph Descendant of King David and husband of Mary, mother of Jesus.

Joseph of Arimathea Wealthy follower of Jesus who asked Pilate permission to take Jesus's corpse and bury it.

Joshua Moses's successor, who led the people of Israel into the Promised Land of Canaan and divided it between the twelve tribes.

Josiah King of Judah who tried to reverse the country's religious and political decline by adopting the book of Law.

Judaeus One of the apostles, also called Thaddeus.

Judah One of Jacob's sons and head of one of the twelve Hebrew tribes, who settled around Jerusalem after the move to the Promised Land. After the kingdom was divided, the southern area was called Judah, and the northern one Israel.

Judas Iscariot Apostle who betrayed Jesus for 30 pieces of silver.

Judea Area around Jerusalem where the purest Jews lived.

Laban Brother of Rebekah, who employed his nephew Jacob for 20 years and tried to cheat him out of marrying his daughter.

Lazarus A beggar who sat outside the gates of a rich man's home and begged for scraps. When they both died, Lazarus went to heaven, the rich man to hell.

Lazarus Brother of Martha and Mary, who died and was brought back to life by Jesus.

Levi The third son of Jacob who founded a priestly caste called the Levites.

Lot Nephew of Abraham who settled in the Jordan valley. His wife was turned into a pillar of salt because she looked back at the city of Sodom.

Luke Evangelist, writer of the third Gospel.

Lystra City in Asia Minor (Turkey) where Paul was stoned for preaching.

Manasseh Grandson of Jacob, elder son of Joseph, and ancestor of one of the twelve tribes of Israel.

Mark Evangelist, and writer of the second Gospel. He may also have been an apostle.

Martha of Bethany Sister of Mary and Lazarus, who worked hard when Jesus came to stay.

Mary Mother of Jesus.

Mary Magdalene Woman with a sinful past who was cured by Jesus of her demons and became a devoted follower.

Mary of Bethany Sister of Martha and Lazarus who, when Christ visited them, spent her time listening to Him rather than serving food. She was one of the women who went to the tomb where Christ's body had been put and found it empty.

Matthew Apostle and former tax collector. Once believed to be the writer of the first Gospel.

Matthew Writer of the first Gospel, probably a Greek-speaking Jew from Syria.

Matthias Apostle chosen to replace Judas.

Midianites People descended from Abraham's marriage to Keturah who raided and pillaged the Israelites' homes. Camel-riding semi-nomads, southern neighbours of the Edomites.

Miriam Sister of Aaron, half-sister of Moses, who led the Israelites in dancing and music-making when they were celebrating their escape from the Egyptians.

Moab Son of Lot, ancestor of the Moabites who lived east of the River Jordan.

Moses Israelite leader who, after being discovered in the bulrushes by the Pharaoh's daughter, grew up to lead the Israelites out of slavery. He received the Ten Commandments from God, and led the Israelites to within sight of the Promised Land.

Nabal Wealthy shepherd in Carmel, married to Abigail. Insulted David but saved from him by Abigail. Later killed by God.

Naboth Owner of a vineyard which he refused to hand over to King Ahab. He was falsely accused of blasphemy by Jezebel and then stoned to death.

Nazareth Town in Galilee, home of Joseph and Mary and where Jesus grew up.

Nazirites People who were dedicated to the service of God by special vows. Nazirites were not

allowed to drink alcohol, or to eat raisins or vinegar. They were forbidden to cut their hair, and had to avoid going near dead bodies.

Nebuchadnezzar King of Babylon who captured Jerusalem in 587BC and took the Israelites into captivity.

Nicodemus Wealthy Pharisee who came to Jesus for secret teaching and who provided the spices for His burial.

Nineveh Capital of Assyria on the River Tigris (modern Iraq).

Noah Righteous man favoured by God who built an ark so that his family, animals and plants could survive the Great Flood.

Paphos Capital of Cyprus where Paul converted the governor Sergius Paulus.

Paul Native of Tarsus. Originally called Saul and a keen persecutor of Christians as a devout Jew. He was blinded on the road to Damascus by God, and converted to become a great missionary, and writer of many Epistles.

Persia Empire (modern Iran) which overthrew Babylon and let Jewish captives return to Jerusalem.

Peter, Simon Chief of the apostles, called the Rock (*petros*) by Jesus and chosen by Him as the founder of the Church in Rome. The first apostle to recognize Jesus as the Messiah.

Pharisees A select group of people in Judea who were famous for being learned and pious. Their name means 'separated ones'. They were rivals of the Sadducees and much criticized by Jesus.

Philip One of the apostles who preached very successfully in Samaria.

Philippi City in Macedonia (northern Greece) where Paul and Silas preached.

Philistines Confederacy of pagan peoples who settled on the southwest coast of Palestine (and gave the country its name). They were often at war with the Israelites.

Phoenicians Canaanite people who settled on the coast of modern Lebanon, and were great seafarers and merchants.

Pontius Pilate Roman Procurator (governor) of the Roman province of Judea at the time of Jesus's trial.

Rabbah Ammonite city besieged by King David, modern Amman (Jordan).

Rachel The younger, prettier daughter of Laban, who, with her sister Leah, was married to Jacob. She died giving birth to Benjamin, her second son.

Rahab A prostitute in Jericho who helped Joshua's spies, and so helped to prevent a general massacre in the city.

Rebekah Cousin and wife of Isaac, mother of Esau and Jacob.

Red Sea Sea between Egypt and Arabian Peninsula which Moses parted when he led the Israelites out of slavery in Egypt.

Rehoboam Son and successor of Solomon, whose hard policies drove ten of the twelve tribes to break

away and form the northern kingdom of Israel.

Reuben Eldest son of Jacob, who opposed his brother's plot to kill Joseph.

Ruth Moabite ancestress of King David, who was devoted to her first mother-in-law Naomi, and later married Boaz, an older cousin.

Sadducees Elite social group of people in Judea who were devoted to the letter of the Mosaic Law, and did not believe in immortality. They were rivals of the Pharisees and equally attacked by Jesus, whom they plotted to kill.

Salome The daughter of Herodias, whose dancing bewitched her stepfather Herod Antipas. She demanded the head of John the Baptist as a reward for her performance.

Samaria City and region of north Palestine. The Samaritans, its Jewish inhabitants, were considered impure by Judean Jews because they intermarried with non-Jews and did not observe all the Laws of Moses.

Samson Judge who was renowned for his great strength. His wife Delilah cut off his hair and so took away his strength.

Sanhedrin Supreme Council of the Jews in Jerusalem before which Jesus was tried.

Sapphira Wife of Ananias who, together with her husband, was struck dead because she lied that she had given away all her money when she had not.

Saul Chosen by Samson as the first king of Israel.

Sheba, Queen of Fabulously wealthy queen from what is now the Red Sea area, who visited King Solomon.

Shem Eldest son of Noah from whom the Semite people are descended.

Shiloh Chief holy place of Israel until King David captured Jerusalem.

Sidon Phoenician city (now in Lebanon).

Silas One of Paul's chief companions on his missionary journeys.

Simon of Cyrene The strong man in the crowd who was made to carry Jesus's cross.

Simon the Magus Sorcerer from Samaria who tried to buy Peter's magic with money.

Simon the Zealot An apostle.

Sinai Peninsula dominated by a mountain on which Moses received the Ten Commandments.

Solomon King, and son of David and Bathsheba who built the first Temple at Jerusalem, and to whom God gave great wisdom and wealth.

Stephen The first Christian martyr, who was stoned to death for blasphemy on the orders of the Sanhedrin.

Tabitha Woman of Joppa who was raised from the dead by Peter.

Tarsus City in Cilicia (southern Turkey), with the privilege of Roman citizenships for all its inhabitants, including Paul, who was born there.

Thomas The apostle who doubted Jesus's resurrection until he touched His wounds.

Tiberias Town and lake (also called Sea of Galilee) in northern Israel.

Tyre Wealthy Phoenician city (now in Lebanon) from which cedar and fir wood were sent to Jerusalem for building the temple.

Ur City in Mesopotamia where Abraham was born.

Zacchaeus Tax collector of Jericho who climbed a tree to see Jesus and jumped down, offering to give half of what he had to the poor.

Zebedee Father of the apostles James and John.

Zechariah Prophet who urged Jews to return from Babylonian captivity and rebuild the Temple.

Zechariah Husband of Elizabeth and father of John the Baptist.

Glossary

altar
A holy table or platform where people make offerings or sacrifices to God.

altar of witness
A replica of the altar in the tabernacle in the holy city of Shiloh. It was built by the Hebrew tribes of Reuben, Gad and Manasseh to bear witness to future generations that even though they were separated from the rest of the tribes of Israel by the River Jordan, they all worshipped the same God.

angel
A messenger from God.

anoint
The ritual of marking with oil or ointment a person who has been chosen for holy service, such as a priest. In the New Testament, Jesus is referred to as 'the anointed one' because He was chosen by God to spread His word on earth.

apostles
The original group of twelve men picked by Jesus from His disciples (followers). They were closer to Him than anyone else, and learned from Him how to carry on His teachings after His death. The apostles were Peter, James and John, Andrew, Thomas, Bartholomew, Philip, Matthew, James the Less, Thaddeus, Simon the Zealot and Judas Iscariot (who, after his betrayal, was replaced by Matthias). Saul, who converted to Christianity after Jesus's death, and became Paul, was also considered an apostle.

archangel
An angel of the highest level. Gabriel and Michael were archangels.

Ark of the Covenant
A box built to hold the stone tablets of the Ten Commandments. It was the symbol of God's presence among His people.

Asherah
A Canaanite goddess, worshipped at the time that the Israelites invaded Canaan. She was worshipped as an Asherah pole, a figure carved from wood.

Baal
The main god of the Canaanites. He was a fertility god, and the people believed that he made the crops grow. He was also a thunder god, and he is often pictured holding or throwing a bolt of lightning.

banquet
A large feast, often in celebration of a person or event.

baptism
The ritual of becoming a Christian, also known as christening. It is marked by sprinkling water on the head, or by immersing a person in water. Jesus commanded that His followers be baptized to show they had made the decision to be Christians. The water represents cleansing.

birthright
A father's blessing to his firstborn son. It gave the son leadership over his younger brothers, but also the responsibility to take care of the family after his father's death.

bless
To make something or someone holy, or to give them holy protection.

census
An official way of counting how many people live in a region, country or town.

centurion
A soldier in the Roman army who was in charge of 100 men (*cent* means 100).

chariot
A two- or four-wheeled vehicle that is pulled by horses. In ancient times, chariots were used in wars and races.

Christian
The name given to people who follow the teachings of Jesus Christ.

citizen
A person who lives in a particular town or country.

cleansed
In a religious context, the action or state of being free of evil, sins and guilt. When people are baptized, their souls are said to be cleansed, so that they can start their new life afresh.

commandments
Orders or laws given by God. God gave the Ten Commandments to Moses on Mount Sinai. They were the terms of the covenant between God and His people and were produced on two stone tablets. There were probably two copies. At this time, when a covenant or agreement was made between two people or countries, they took a copy each so they both knew what they had to do.

conscience
Having a sense of what is right and wrong.

constellations
Groups of stars that form patterns in the sky. Through their studies of star constellations and their meanings, the three wise men found their way to the baby Jesus.

contract
A firm and binding agreement between two or more people that is written or spoken.

covenant
A promise in which God enters into a special relationship with His people. For example, He promised His protection and the land of Canaan to Abraham and his descendants as long as they were faithful to Him.

crucifixion
A means of execution by tying or nailing a person to a wooden cross. It was used by the Romans as a punishment for major crimes such as robbery or murder. However, Jesus was crucified for high treason, which Caiaphas, the high priest, charged Him with.

Dagon
The main god of the Philistines. He has often been represented as a fish god, but it is more likely that he was a corn god.

debt
Money or goods owed by one person to another.

defile
To make unclean, or to take away the holiness, goodness or purity of something.

demon
An evil spirit, or the devil. In Bible times, people who were insane were often described as being possessed by demons.

denarii
The currency (money) that was used in Jerusalem at the time of Jesus Christ.

disciples
People who believed in and followed the teachings of Jesus Christ. The first disciples were those who heard Jesus preaching as He travelled around Galilee. The twelve apostles were chosen from the many disciples.

divine
Belonging to or to do with God.

diviner
Someone who believes that they can tell the future by looking at different everyday objects.

dowry
A gift given by a man to his future father-in-law before his marriage, to compensate the father for the loss of his daughter.

empire
A group of countries or states that is ruled by one person who is called the emperor, king or queen.

epistle
A long letter recording important events and instructions. The letters, or Epistles, that make up a third of the New Testament, explain the teachings of the Gospels and give guidelines on how to behave. They include Paul's letters to the Ephesians which were written when he was in prison, and to the Corinthians.

eternal
Describes something that is forever, with no beginning or end. God is said to be eternal. Eternal life, or eternity, is the life

promised by God that continues after death.

Exile
The period that the Israelites spent under the domination of foreign kings after Judah and Israel were conquered.

Exodus
The name given to the journey that the Israelites made from Egypt to the Promised Land of Canaan. Exodus itself means 'going out', as in the Israelites' moving out of Egypt.

faith
A complete trust and unquestioning belief in something or someone. Followers of God are

devoted in such a way that they will do anything that is asked of them, believing that if God has requested something, then it must be right.

Fall of Man
Humans' first disobedience to God. Adam and Eve lived in Paradise with God, with no sin to spoil their lives. God forbade them to eat the fruit from the Tree of Knowledge of Good and Evil. However, they listened to the serpent instead of God, and ate the fruit. They were banished from God's protection.

frankincense
Resin of trees found in east Africa and Arabia that is burned to produce a sweet scent. It was used during religious ceremonies. One of the wise men who visited the baby Jesus was said to have brought a gift of frankincense as a symbol of God.

Gentile
A word that originally meant belonging to the same people. In the Bible, it refers to peoples who were not of the Jewish race. Jesus, although of the Jewish race, was determined that His message was for Gentiles as well as Jews.

gladiator
A swordsman trained to fight with other men or animals in a large arena. Unarmed early Christians were pitted against armed Roman soldiers with the taunt that if their God was so great He would protect them.

Gospels
Written records of Jesus's life and teachings. The word itself means 'good news'. The Gospels form part of the New Testament.

govern
To control the affairs of a country or state.

grace of God
The fact that God loves all the men and women He created even though no one on earth is completely without sin.

halo
A ring of light that is sometimes pictured around the heads of saints or angels in paintings to show that they are holy.

healer
A person who has the ability to heal others, without the aid of medicine, but through faith in God, for example. God gave Jesus the gift of healing and Jesus gave it to His apostles.

holy

Describes a person, a place, or an object that is sacred, or has a special relationship to God. Jesus, His apostles, and saints are said to be holy and Jerusalem is described as a holy city.

Holy of Holies

The very centre of the tabernacle, where the Ark of the Covenant is kept.

Holy Spirit

An invisible, life-giving, divine force which is one of the ways God chose to make His presence known to people on earth. The most vivid example is when He visited the apostles in the form of the Holy Spirit, following Jesus's death.

hypocrite

A person who pretends to have feelings or beliefs about something or someone but who really feels or believes the opposite.

idol

A statue of a person, god or animal. Idolatry is the act of worshipping such statues. This was forbidden by God and forms one of the Ten Commandments. The Israelites often ignored this commandment, and were reminded not to worship idols by prophets from God.

Israel

The nation that descended from Jacob, who was renamed Israel after wrestling with an angel by the river Jabbok. The new name, which means 'he who has wrestled with the Lord', was a sign that God was still with him.

Jews

The name given to the Israelites while they were in Exile in Babylon. It was originally used to mean people from Judah, but after the Exile it came to mean people of the Jewish faith.

Judah

The southern part of the divided kingdom. To punish King Solomon for disobeying Him, God split the Promised Land, Solomon's kingdom into two. Solomon's son, Rehoboam, ruled over the southern part, called Judah, while Jeroboam ruled the northern part which kept the name Israel.

Judges

Leaders of the Israelite nation for almost 200 years between the death of Joshua and the time of Samuel. They were people such as Samson and Ehud who kept the Israelite nation free from the domination of neighbouring tribes and rulers.

kingdom of God

A spiritual place that Jesus described as within reach of everyone who follows His teachings, and tries to live their life in a Christian way.

leper

A person with an illness called leprosy that caused paralysis and deformity. Because of this, and because people in Bible times believed the disease to be catching, lepers were avoided, and made to live together in isolated places called leper colonies.

manna

The main food of the Israelites for the 40 years when they were wandering in the desert. The Bible describes how after the dew had gone in the morning, a small round thing, whitish, like coriander seed was found on the

ground. It had a honey-like flavour. It was miraculously provided by God.

martyr
A person who chooses to suffer greatly or be put to death rather than give up his or her religious beliefs.

Messiah
One chosen by God, a Saviour, or anointed one, usually referring to Christ.

ministry
The work of teaching about God and how Christians should live their lives. It refers to the work carried out by priests, and by Jesus in His three years of travelling and preaching around Judea.

miracle
An amazing or supernatural act or event, or a mighty work, that is performed through the power of God. Jesus's many miracles during His ministry in Galilee included healing the sick, raising the dead to life, and making five loaves and two fishes stretch to feed a crowd of 5,000 people.

mission
A special purpose or reason for acting. Jesus's mission, given to Him by God, was to spread His word and teachings.

myrrh
Oil from African and Asian plants used in medicine and perfumes. It was one of the symbolic gifts given to the baby Jesus by the three wise men.

oasis
A place in the desert where water is found and plants can grow.

parable
A story which draws from real life to make a teaching point. Jesus used people and situations His audience would be familiar with to teach them about the kingdom of God. This made the point of His stories easy for people to remember and to understand.

Passover
The annual commemoration of the night that God killed all the firstborn children of Egypt to make Pharaoh release the Israelites. He 'passed over' the homes of the Israelites, leaving them unharmed. The event is remembered by an annual festival and a meal of lamb and bread made without yeast.

Patriarch
The four Patriarchs in the Old Testament are Abraham, Isaac, Jacob and Joseph. They are the male heads of the family, with whom God made or renewed His covenant.

persecution
The hunting down, tormenting and ill-treatment of people, particularly because of their religious beliefs. The early Christians in the Roman Empire were persecuted, by being imprisoned, tortured, and even put to death.

pilgrimage
A journey taken by believers to visit a religious

shrine or a town or city that is considered holy. It can also mean the journey through life towards the hope of eternal life.

prefect
A Roman official who ruled over a region, as in Judea during the time of Jesus.

priest
A person whose job is to perform religious duties, and to advise on the teachings of God.

Promised Land
Abraham, the ancestor of all the Israelites, was promised a large area at the eastern end of the Mediterranean Sea, then called the Great Sea. Here his descendants would live in freedom. When Moses led the Exodus from Egypt, he was leading the Israelites to this Promised Land. It was first known as Canaan and today is an area covered by Israel and Palestine.

prophesy
To be able to tell what will happen in the future. The coming of the Messiah was prophesied in the Old Testament, and Christians believe that Jesus fulfilled that prophecy.

prophets
Men or women called by God to speak for Him and to communicate His will to the people. The prophets first emerged as a group in the time of Samuel. They offered guidance to the Israelites and warned them of troubles ahead.

purify
To make pure and clean. In the religious sense, this means when a person is freed of sin, by praying or by being blessed by God or a priest.

religion
The belief in and worshipping of God or other gods, or a particular way of practising a faith, such as Christianity or Judaism.

repentance
The feeling of being truly sorry for wrong thoughts or deeds, coupled with the determination to try to do better in the future.

resurrection
Being restored to life after death. Jesus's resurrection, three days after He died on the cross, is the central point of the New Testament, and of Christian faith.

rhabdomancy
A way in which people believed that they could tell the future by throwing arrow heads into the air, and then trying to read the future from the way the arrows landed. The word comes from *rhabdos*, the Greek word for a rod or wand.

ritual
Set words and actions that make up a religious ceremony.

sacrifices
The offering of dead animals or people for the worship of a god.

Saviour

A person that saves somebody from danger. Jesus is described as a Saviour because He saved us from sin by showing us the Christian way of life.

scribes

Writers and learned people who, because of their skills, became important in matters of government.

Scriptures

The writings contained in the Bible that are accepted by the various faiths as the word of God, or people directly inspired by God. For the Jewish people, the Scriptures are the 39 books of the Old Testament. For Christians, the Scriptures also include the New Testament.

sermon

A speech designed to teach listeners about particular aspects of faith or religion, and how they should behave.

sin

A rebellion against God or act that is against God's laws. In the Old Testament a sin is described as not doing what God wants us to do.

soul

A person's inner self or spirit, the part of a living creature that Christians believe will live forever. Heaven is described as the kingdom of souls.

spiritual

Belonging or relating to the soul.

symbol

An easily recognizable visual aid that helps people understand something that is hard to describe or show, such as an emotion or feeling. The dove is used as a symbol of innocence in the Bible, although it has also become a symbol of peace.

synagogue

The building where Jewish people worship God. In Jesus's time, the synagogue had separate seating for men and women and also served as the school for Jewish children.

tabernacle

The tent of meeting which was the focus for the Israelites' worship of God while they were in the desert. The Ark was put into the central room of the tabernacle, and a cloud descended. A bright light shone from the tent, showing that God had taken up residence among His people.

temptation

Thoughts and ideas that make people feel they want to sin. Christians are told to always be on their guard against temptation, but they are also told that God will help them and that temptation need never become too great to bear.

treason

An act of betrayal or disloyalty against the government or ruler of a country.

tribute

Something that is done or said that gives thanks to a god or a person.

vision

A supernatural image seen by someone. The Bible tells of many visions that were sent by God which enabled people to foretell or forewarn of future events.

zealot

An extreme and determined supporter of a particular faith or religion. The Zealots were a group of militant Jewish people who fought against Roman rule in the decades following Jesus's death.

Index

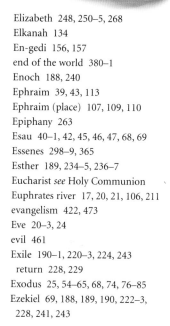

This edition is published by Hermes House

Hermes House is an imprint of Anness Publishing Ltd
Hermes House, 88–89 Blackfriars Road, London SE1 8HA
tel. 020 7401 2077; fax 020 7633 9499; info@anness.com

A CIP catalogue record for this book is
available from the British Library

Publisher: Joanna Lorenz
Managing Editor, Children's Books:
  Gilly Cameron Cooper
Editor: Jennifer Davidson
Designer: Roger McWilliam
Production Controller: Ben Worley

10 9 8 7 6 5 4 3 2 1

Previously published in eight separate volumes. These
single volumes were produced by Miles Kelly Limited.

PHOTOGRAPHIC ACKNOWLEDGEMENTS
Panos Pictures; 15, (BL), Hutchison Library; 20, (BR), Hutchison Library; 29,
(BL), The Stock Market; 37, (BL), The Stock Market; 39, (BL), The Stock Market;
44, (BL), Jeremy A Horner, Hutchison Library; 48, (BR), Hutchison Library; 49,
(BR), Hutchison Library; 72 (B/L) Erich Lessing/ AKG London; 95 (B/L) The
Stock Market; 96 (B/L) Erich Lessing/ AKG London; 98 (B/L) Jean-Léo Dugast/
AKG London; 107 (B/C) Erich Lessing/ AKG London; 108 (B/C) Erich Lessing/
AKG London; 113 (B/R) Erich Lessing/ AKG London; 114 (B/R) Erich Lessing/
AKG London; 130 (B/L) Sonia Halliday Photographs; 135 (B/R) Richard T.
Nowitz/ CORBIS; 156 (B/R) Erich Lessing/ AKG London; 164 (B/R) H Fenn/
Mary Evans Picture Library; 168 (B/L) John Spaull/ Panos Pictures; 188, (BL),
Bryan Knox, Sonia Halliday Pictures; 236 (BL), The Stock Market.Page 246 (BL)
Sonia Halliday Photographs; 252 (BL) Guy Mansfield, Panos Pictures; 266 (BR)
Penny Tweedie, Panos Pictures; 286 (BL) The Stock Market; 304 (BL) Sonia
Halliday Photographs; 318 (BC) The Stock Market; 332 (BR) Frank Spooner
Pictures; 339 (BR) The Stock Market; 362 (BL) J. C. Tordai/The Hutchison
Library; 369 (BL) Gianni Dagli Orti/CORBIS; 381 (BR) Richard T.
Nowitz/CORBIS; 387 (BR) AFP/CORBIS; 395 (BL) Richard T. Nowitz/CORBIS;
499 (BC) Dave Bartruff/CORBIS; 404 (BL) Richard T. Nowitz/CORBIS; 406 (BR)
Richard Hamilton Smith/CORBIS; 407 (BL) Richard T. Nowitz/CORBIS; 413
(BC) Arte & Immagini/CORBIS; 414 (BL) John Hatt/The Hutchison Library;
(BR) J. C. Tordai/The Hutchison Library; 415 (TL) The Hutchison Library; (BL)
The Hutchison Library; (BR) Dorig/The Hutchison Library; 420 (BL) John
Hatt/The Hutchison Library; 424 (BR) Sonia Halliday Photographs; 428 (BL)
Michael Nicholson/CORBIS; 434 (BL) Sonia Halliday Photographs; 437 (BC)
Sonia Halliday Photographs; 438 (BR) Hanan Isachar/CORBIS; 440 (BC) Jayne
Taylor/Sonia Halliday Photographs; 443 (BR) F. H. C. Birch/Sonia Halliday
Photographs; 444 (BR) Neil Beer/CORBIS; 451 (BR) Arte & Immagini/CORBIS;
455 (BC) Sonia Halliday Photographs; 465 (BC) Sonia Halliday Photographs; 471
(BL) Historical Picture Archive/CORBIS; 472 (BL) Bettmann/CORBIS; (CR) Arte
& Immagini/CORBIS; 473 (C) Archivo Iconografico, S.A./CORBIS; (C) The
Salvation Army International Heritage Centre; 475(BR) Paul Velasco/CORBIS. All
other images are from the Miles Kelly Archive.

Every effort has been made to trace the copyright holders of all images that
appear within this book. Anness Publishing Ltd apologizes for any unintentional
omissions and, if notified, would be happy to add an acknowledgement in
future editions